Python and Algorithmic Thinking fnner

Learn to Think Like a Programmer

Revised Second Edition

By
Aristides S. Bouras

Python and Algorithmic Thinking for the Complete Beginner
Revised Second Edition

Copyright © by Aristides S. Bouras
https://www.bouraspage.com

Cover illustration and design: Philippos Papanikolaou

ISBN-13: 978-1099184871

ISBN-10: 1099184878

Python and PyCon are trademarks or registered trademarks of the Python Software Foundation.

Eclipse™ is a trademark of the Eclipse Foundation, Inc.

All crossword puzzles were created with EclipseCrossword software powered by Green Eclipse

PyDev is a trademark of Appcelerator.

Oracle and Java are registered trademarks of Oracle and/or its affiliates.

PHP is a copyright of the PHP Group.

The following are either registered trademarks or trademarks of Microsoft Corporation in the United States and/or other countries: Microsoft, Windows, IntelliSense, SQL Server, VBA, Visual Basic, and Visual C#.

Mazda and Mazda 6 are trademarks of the Mazda Motor Corporation or its affiliated companies.

Ford and Ford Focus are trademarks of the Ford Motor Company.

Other names may be trademarks of their respective owners.

Warning and Disclaimer

This book is designed to provide information about learning "Algorithmic Thinking", mainly through the use of Python programming language. Every effort has been taken to make this book compatible with all releases of Python 3.x, and it is almost certain to be compatible with any future releases of Python.

The information is provided on an "as is" basis. The authors shall have neither liability nor responsibility to any person or entity with respect to any loss or damages arising from the information contained in this book or from the use of the files that may accompany it.

Contents at a Glance

Table of Contents

Preface

About the Author

Aristides[1] S. Bouras was born in 1973. During his early childhood, he discovered a love of computer programming. He got his first computer at the age of 12, a Commodore 64, which incorporated a ROM-based version of the BASIC programming language and 64 kilobytes of RAM!!!

He holds a degree in Computer Engineering from the Technological Educational Institute of Piraeus, and a Dipl. Eng. degree in Electrical and Computer Engineering from the Democritus University of Thrace.

He worked as a software developer at a company that specialized in industrial data flow and labelling of products. His main job was to develop software applications for data terminals, as well as PC software applications for collecting and storing data on a Microsoft SQL Server®.

He has developed many applications such as warehouse managing systems and websites for companies and other organizations. Nowadays, he works as a high school teacher. He mainly teaches courses in computer networks, programming tools for the Internet/intranets, and databases.

He has written a number of books, mainly about algorithmic and computational thinking through the use of Python, C#, Java, C++, PHP, and Visual Basic programming languages.

He is married and he has two children.

---

[1] Aristides (530 BC–468 BC) was an ancient Athenian statesman and general. The ancient historian Herodotus cited him as "the best and most honorable man in Athens". He was so fair in all that he did that he was often referred to as "Aristides the Just". He flourished in the early quarter of Athens's Classical period and helped Athenians defeat the Persians at the battles of Salamis and Plataea.

Acknowledgments

I would like to thank, with particular gratefulness, my friend and senior editor Victoria (Vicki) Austin for her assistance in copy editing. Without her, this book might not have reached its full potential. With her patient guidance and valuable and constructive suggestions, she helped me bring this book up to a higher level!

How This Book is Organized

The book you hold in your hands follows the spiral curriculum teaching approach, a method proposed in 1960 by Jerome Bruner, an American psychologist. According to this method, as a subject is being taught, basic ideas are revisited at intervals—at a more sophisticated level each time—until the reader achieves a complete understanding of the subject. First, the reader learns the basic elements without worrying about the details. Later, more details are taught and basic elements are mentioned again and again, eventually being stored in the brain's long term memory.

According to Jerome Bruner, learning requires the student's active participation, experimentation, exploration, and discovery. This book contains many examples, most of which can be practically performed. This gives the reader the opportunity to get his or her hands on Python® and become capable of creating his or her own programs.

Who Should Buy This Book?

Thoroughly revised for the latest version of Python, this book explains basic concepts in a clear and explicit way that takes very seriously one thing for granted—that the reader knows nothing about computer programming.

Addressed to anyone who has no prior programming knowledge or experience, but a desire to learn programming with Python, it teaches the first thing that every novice programmer needs to learn, which is *Algorithmic Thinking*. Algorithmic Thinking involves more than just learning code. It is a problem-solving process that involves learning *how to* code.

This edition contains all the popular features of the previous edition and adds a significant number of exercises, as well as extensive revisions and updates. Apart from Python's lists, it now also covers dictionaries, while a brand new section provides an effective introduction to the next field that a programmer needs to work with, which is Object Oriented Programming (OOP).

This book has a class course structure with questions and exercises at the end of each chapter so you can test what you have learned right away and improve your comprehension. With 250 solved and 450 unsolved exercises, 475 true/false, about 150 multiple choice, and 200 review questions and crosswords (the solutions and the answers to which can be found on the Internet), this book is ideal for

- ▶ novices or average programmers, for self-study
- ▶ high school students
- ▶ first-year college or university students
- ▶ teachers
- ▶ professors
- ▶ anyone who wants to start learning or teaching computer programming using the proper conventions and techniques

Conventions Used in This Book

Following are some explanations on the conventions used in this book. "Conventions" refer to the standard ways in which certain parts of the text are displayed.

Python Statements

This book uses plenty of examples written in Python language. Python statements are shown in a typeface that looks like this.

```
This is a Python statement
```

Keywords, Variables, Functions, and Arguments Within the Text of a Paragraph

Keywords, variables, functions, and arguments are sometimes shown within the text of a paragraph. When they are, the special text is shown in a typeface different from that of the rest of the paragraph. For instance, `first_name = 5` is an example of a Python statement within the paragraph text.

Words in Italics

You may notice that some of the special text is also displayed in italics. In this book, italicized words are general types that must be replaced with the specific name appropriate for your data. For example, the general form of a Python statement may be presented as

```
def name(arg1, arg2):
```

In order to complete the statement, the keywords *name*, *arg1*, and *arg2* must be replaced with something meaningful. When you use this statement in your program, you might use it in the following form.

```
def display_rectangle(width, height):
```

Three dots (...): an Ellipsis

In the general form of a statement you may also notice three dots (...), also known as an "ellipsis", following a list in an example. They are not part of the statement. An ellipsis indicates that you can have as many items in the list as you want. For example, the ellipsis in the general form of the statement

```
display_messages(arg1, arg2, … )
```

indicates that the list may contain more than two arguments. When you use this statement in your program, your statement might be something like this.

```
display_messages(message1, "Hello", message2, "Hi!")
```

Square Brackets

The general form of some statements or functions may contain "square brackets" [ ], which indicate that the enclosed section is optional. For example, the general form of the statement

```
range(initial_value, final_value [, step ] )
```

indicates that the section `[, step ]` can be omitted.

The following two statements produce different results but they are both syntactically correct.

```
range(0, 10)
range(0, 10, 2)
```

The Dark Header

Most of this book's examples are shown in a typeface that looks like this.

```
☐ file_29_2_3
a = 2
b = 3

c = a + b
print(c)
```

The header `file_29_2_3` on top indicates the filename that you must open to test the program. All the examples that contain this header can be found free of charge on my website.

Notices

Very often this book uses notices to help you better understand the meaning of a concept. Notices look like this.

This typeface designates a note.

Something Already Known or Something to Remember

Very often this book can help you recall something you have already learned (probably in a previous chapter). Other times, it will draw your attention to something you should memorize. Reminders look like this.

This typeface designates something to recall or something that you should memorize.

How to Report Errata

Although I have taken great care to ensure the accuracy of the content of this book, mistakes do occur. If you find a mistake in this book, either in the text or the code, I encourage you to report it to me. By doing so, you can save other readers from frustration and, of course, help me to improve the next release of this book. If you find any errata, please feel free to report them by visiting the following address:

https://www.bouraspage.com/report-errata

Once your errata are verified, your submission will be accepted and the errata will be uploaded to my website, and added to any existing list of errata.

Where to Download Material About this Book

Material about this book, such as:

▶ a list of verified errata (if any);

▶ the answers to all of the review questions, as well as the solutions to all review exercises; and

▶ all of this book's examples that have a header like this `file_29_2_3` on top

can be downloaded free of charge from the following address:

https://bit.ly/2HSFs9T

Section 1

Introductory Knowledge

Chapter 1
How a Computer Works

1.1 Introduction

In today's society, almost every task requires the use of a computer. In schools, students use computers to search the Internet and to send emails. At work, people use them to make presentations, to analyze data, and to communicate with customers. At home, people use computers to play games, to connect to social networks and to chat with other people all over the world. Of course, don't forget smartphones such as iPhones. They are computers as well!

Computers can perform so many different tasks because of their ability to be programmed. In other words, a computer can perform any job that a program tells it to. A *program* is a set of *statements* (often called *instructions* or *commands*) that a computer follows in order to perform a specific task.

Programs are essential to a computer, because without them a computer is a dummy machine that can do nothing at all. It is the program that actually tells the computer what to do and when to do it. On the other hand, the *programmer* or the *software developer* is the person who designs, creates, and often tests computer programs.

This book introduces you to the basic concepts of computer programming using the Python language.

1.2 What is Hardware?

The term *hardware* refers to all devices or components that make up a computer. If you have ever opened the case of a computer or a laptop you have probably seen many of its components, such as the microprocessor (CPU), the memory, and the hard disk. A computer is not a device but a system of devices that all work together. The basic components of a typical computer system are discussed here.

▶ **The Central Processing Unit (CPU)**

This is the part of a computer that actually performs all the tasks defined in a program (basic arithmetic, logical, and input/output operations).

▶ **Main Memory (RAM – Random Access Memory)**

This is the area where the computer holds the program (while it is being executed/run) as well as the data that the program is working with. All programs and data stored in this type of memory are lost when you shut down your computer or you unplug it from the wall outlet.

▶ **Main Memory (ROM – Read Only Memory)**

ROM or Read Only Memory is a special type of memory which can only be *read* by the computer (but cannot be changed). All programs and data stored in this type of memory are **not** lost when the computer is switched off. ROM usually contains manufacturer's instructions as well as a program called the *bootstrap loader* whose function is to start the operation of computer system once the power is turned on.

▶ **Secondary Storage Devices**

This is usually the hard disk or the SSD (Solid State Drive), and sometimes (but more rarely) the CD/DVD drive. In contrast to main memory, this type of memory can hold data for a longer period of time, even if there is no power to the computer. However, programs stored in this memory cannot be directly executed. They must be transferred to a much faster memory; that is, the main memory.

▶ **Input Devices**

Input devices are all those devices that collect data from the outside world and enter them into the computer for further processing. Keyboards, mice, and microphones are all input devices.

▶ **Output Devices**

Output devices are all those devices that output data to the outside world. Monitors (screens) and printers are output devices.

1.3   What is Software?

Everything that a computer does is controlled by software. There are two categories of software: system software and application software.

▶ *System software* is the program that controls and manages the basic operations of a computer. For example, system software controls the computer's internal operations. It manages all devices that are connected to it, and it saves data, loads data, and allows other programs to be executed. The three main types of system software are:

   ▶ the *operating system*. Windows, Linux, MacOS, Android, and iOS are all examples of operating systems.

   ▶ the *utility software*. This type of software is usually installed with the operating system. It is used to make the computer run as efficiently as possible. Antivirus utilities and backup utilities are considered utility software.

   ▶ the *device driver software*. A device driver controls a device that is attached to your computer, such as a mouse or a graphic card. A device driver is a program that acts like a translator. It translates the instructions of the operating system to instructions that a device can actually understand.

▶ *Application software* refers to all the other programs that you use for your everyday tasks, such as browsers, word processors, notepads, games, and many more.

1.4   How a Computer Executes (Runs) a Program

When you turn on your computer, the main memory (RAM) is completely empty. The first thing the computer needs to do is to transfer the operating system from the hard disk to the main memory.

After the operating system is loaded to main memory, you can execute (run) any program (application software) you like. This is usually done by clicking, double clicking, or tapping the program's corresponding icon. For example, let's say you click on the icon of your favorite word processor. This action orders your computer to copy (or load) the word processing program from your hard disk to the main memory (RAM) so the CPU can execute it.

📇 *Programs are stored on secondary storage devices such as hard disks. When you install a program on your computer, the program is copied to your hard disk. Then, when you execute a program, the program is copied (loaded) from your hard disk to the main memory (RAM), and that copy of the program is executed.*

✎ *The terms "run" and "execute" are synonymous.*

1.5   Compilers and Interpreters

Computers can execute programs that are written in a strictly defined computer language. You cannot write a program using a natural language such as English or Greek, because your computer won't understand you!

But what does a computer actually understand? A computer can understand a specific low-level language called the *machine language*. In a machine language all statements (or commands) are made up of zeros and ones. The following is an example of a program written in a machine language, that calculates the sum of two numbers.

```
0010 0001 0000 0100
0001 0001 0000 0101
0011 0001 0000 0110
0111 0000 0000 0001
```

Shocked? Don't worry, you are not going to write programs this way. Hopefully, no one writes computer programs this way anymore. Nowadays, all programmers write their programs in a high-level language and then they use a special program to translate them into a machine language.

✎ *A high-level language is one that is not limited to a particular type of computer.*

There are two types of programs that programmers use to perform translation: compilers and interpreters.

A *compiler* is a program that translates statements written in a high-level language into a separate machine language program. You can then execute the machine language program any time you wish. After the translation, there is no need to run the compiler again unless you make changes in the high-level language program.

An *interpreter* is a program that simultaneously translates and executes the statements written in a high-level language. As the interpreter reads each individual statement in the high-level language program, it translates it into a machine language code and then directly executes it. This process is repeated for every statement in the program.

1.6   What is Source Code?

The statements (often called instructions or commands) that the programmer writes in a high-level language are called *source code* or simply *code*. The programmer first types the source code into a program known as a *code editor*, and then uses either a compiler to translate it into a machine language program, or an interpreter to translate and execute it at the same time.

Eclipse is an example of an Integrated Development Environment (IDE) that enables programmers to both write and execute their source code. You will learn more about Eclipse in Chapter 3.

✎ *Python programs can even be written in a simple text editor!*

1.7   Review Questions: True/False

Choose **true** or **false** for each of the following statements.

1. Modern computers can perform so many different tasks because they have many gigabytes of RAM.
2. A computer can operate without a program.
3. A hard disk is an example of hardware.
4. Data can be stored in main memory (RAM) for a long period of time, even if there is no power to the computer.
5. Data is stored in main memory (RAM), but programs are not.
6. Speakers are an example of an output device.
7. Windows and Linux are examples of software.
8. A media player is an example of system software.
9. When you turn on your computer, the main memory (RAM) already contains the operating system.
10. When you open your word processing application, it is actually copied from a secondary storage device to the main memory (RAM).
11. In a machine language, all statements (commands) are a sequence of zeros and ones.
12. Nowadays, a computer cannot understand zeros and ones.
13. Nowadays, software is written in a language composed of ones and zeros.
14. Software refers to the physical components of a computer.
15. The compiler and the interpreter are software.
16. The compiler translates source code to an executable file.

17. The interpreter creates a machine language program.

18. After the translation, the interpreter is not required anymore.

19. Source code can be written using a simple text editor.

20. Source code can be executed by a computer without compilation or interpretation.

21. A program written in machine language requires compilation (translation).

22. A compiler translates a program written in a high-level language.

1.8   Review Questions: Multiple Choice

Select the correct answer for each of the following statements.

1. Which of the following is **not** computer hardware?
   a. a hard disk
   b. a DVD disc
   c. a sound card
   d. the main memory (RAM)

2. Which of the following is **not** a secondary storage device?
   a. a DVD reader/writer device
   b. a Solid State Drive (SSD)
   c. a USB flash drive
   d. RAM

3. Which one of the following operations can**not** be performed by the CPU?
   a. Transfer data to the main memory (RAM).
   b. Display data to the user.
   c. Transfer data from the main memory (RAM).
   d. Perform arithmetic operations.

4. A touch screen is
   a. an input device.
   b. an output device.
   c. both of the above

5. Which of the following is **not** software?
   a. Windows
   b. Linux
   c. iOS
   d. a video game
   e. a web browser
   f. All of the above are software.

6. Which of the following statements is correct?
   a. Programs are stored on the hard disk.
   b. Programs are stored on DVD discs.
   c. Programs are stored in main memory (RAM).
   d. All of the above are correct.

7. Which of the following statements is correct?

    a. Programs can be executed directly from the hard disk.

    b. Programs can be executed directly from a DVD disc.

    c. Programs can be executed directly from the main memory (RAM).

    d. All of the above are correct.

    e. None of the above is correct.

8. Programmers can**not** write computer programs in

    a. machine language.

    b. natural language such as English, Greek, and so on.

    c. Python.

9. A compiler translates

    a. a program written in machine language into a high-level language program.

    b. a program written in a natural language (English, Greek, etc.) into a machine language program.

    c. a program written in high-level computer language into a machine language program.

    d. none of the above

    e. all of the above

10. Machine language is

    a. a language that machines use to communicate with each other.

    b. a language made up of numerical instructions that is used directly by a computer.

    c. a language that uses English words for operations.

11. In a program written in high-level computer language, if two identical statements are one after the other, the interpreter

    a. translates the first one and executes it, then it translates the second one and executes it.

    b. translates the first one, then translates the second one, and then executes them both.

    c. translates only the first one (since they are identical) and then executes it two times.

Chapter 2
Python

2.1　What is Python?

Python is a widely used general-purpose, high-level computer programming language that allows programmers to create applications, web pages, and many other types of software.

Python is often referred to as a *scripting* language despite the fact that the official website says that it's a *programming* language. The truth, of course, is somewhere in the middle. Python can be used either as a scripting language, or a programming language!

2.2　What is the Difference Between a Script and a Program?

Technically speaking, a script is *interpreted* whereas a program is *compiled*, but this is actually not their major difference. There is another more important difference between them!

The main purpose of a script written in a scripting language such as JavaScript, or VBA (Visual Basic for Applications) is to control another application. So you can say that, in some ways JavaScript controls the web browser, and VBA controls a Microsoft® Office application such as MS Word or MS Excel.

On the other hand, a program written in a programming language such as C++, or C# executes independently of any other application. A program is compiled into a separate set of machine language instructions that can then be executed as stand-alone any time the user wishes.

✎ *Macros of Microsoft Office are scripts written in VBA. Their purpose is to automate certain functions within Microsoft Office.*

▢ *A script cannot be executed as stand-alone. It requires a hosting application in order to execute.*

2.3　Why You Should Learn Python

Python is what is known as a "high-level" computer language. Python is a very flexible yet powerful language, suitable for developing medium-scale applications or dynamic web pages. It is the perfect language for teaching programming, especially at the introductory level, and it is widely used in scientific and numerical computing. Its coding style is very easy to understand and very efficient.

One of Python's capabilities is the ability to interact with the file system of a computer. Python can create files, write into files, or read the contents from files. It can also create directories, copy files, delete files, rename files, or even change file attributes. Python can perform almost any task related to the file system, making it suitable even for system administration tasks. For example, you can write a Python program to back up your files or a program that processes text files by reformatting their contents.

Moreover, Python can execute system commands or any other program installed on your system. Thus, programs written and compiled in C, C++, Java, or any other computer language can be executed from Python and Python can make use of their output. This enables you to add functionality to your Python programs without spending time rewriting your old ones.

There are millions—probably even billions—of lines of code already written in Python and your possibilities for code reuse are huge! This is why many people prefer using Python to any other programming language. This is also a very good reason why you should actually learn Python!

2.4   How Python Works

Computers do not understand natural languages such as English or Greek, so you need a computer language such as Python to communicate with them. Python is a very powerful high-level computer language. The Python interpreter (or, actually, a combination of a compiler and an interpreter) converts Python language to a language that computers can actually understand, and that is known as the "machine language".

In the past, computer languages made use of either an interpreter or a compiler. Nowadays however, many computer languages including Python use both a compiler and an interpreter. The Python compiler translates Python statements into *bytecode* statements and saves them in a .pyc file. Later, when a user wants to execute the file, the interpreter (often called *Python Virtual Machine* or *Python VM*) converts the bytecode into low-level machine language code for direct execution on the hardware.

✎ *Python bytecode is a machine language executed by the Python Virtual Machine.*

✎ *Instead of a compiler and an interpreter, some languages use two compilers. In C#, for example, the first compiler translates C# statements into an intermediate language called Common Intermediate Language (CIL). The CIL code is stored on disk in an executable file called an assembly, typically with an extension of .exe. Later, when a user wants to execute the file, the .NET Framework performs a Just In Time (JIT) compilation to convert the CIL code into low-level machine language code for direct execution on the hardware.*

In **Figure 2–1** you can see how statements written in Python are compiled into bytecode and how bytecode is then executed using interpretation.

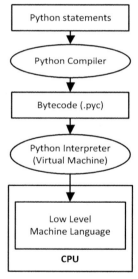

Figure 2–1 Executing Python statements using the Python Virtual Machine

Now come some reasonable questions: *Why all this trouble? Why does Python and other languages (such as C#) translate twice? Why are Python statements not directly translated into low-level machine language code?* The answer lies in the fact that Python is designed to be a platform-independent programming language. This means that a program is written once but it can be executed on any device, regardless of its operating system or its architecture, as long as the appropriate version of Python is installed on it. In the past, programs had to be recompiled, or even rewritten, for each computer platform. One of the biggest advantages of Python is that you only have to write and compile a program once! In **Figure 2–2** you can see how statements written in Python are compiled into bytecode and how bytecode can then be executed on any platform that has the appropriate version of Python installed on it.

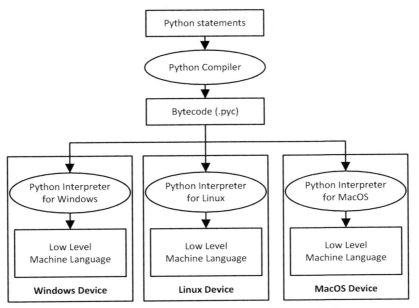

Figure 2–2 Executing Python statements on different platforms

Efficiency is another reason why Python statements are not directly translated into low-level machine language code because:

1. Small optimizations can be performed on the intermediate code (bytecode).

2. If a .pyc file with the same name as the .py file you invoke is present, Python automatically executes it. This means that if a .pyc file is present and you haven't made any changes in the source code, Python can save some time by not having to re-compile the source code.

Today few, if any, interpreters really interpret code directly, line by line. Almost all interpreters now use some type of intermediate representation.

Chapter 3
Software Packages to Install

3.1 How to Set Up Python

In order to install Python, you must download it free of charge from the following address:

https://www.python.org/downloads/

Choose and download the latest version that is suitable for your platform. This book shows the process of installing Python on a Windows platform. When the download completes, run the setup. The first screen of the Python installer (as shown in **Figure 3–1**) prompts you to select "Install Now" to install Python with default settings, or choose "Customize installation" to enable or disable features. Check the field "Add Python 3.7 to PATH" and click on the "Install Now" option.

Figure 3–1 The Python installer

When the installation process is complete, click on the "Close" button.

3.2 Eclipse

Eclipse is an Integrated Development Environment (IDE) that provides a great set of tools for many programming languages such as Java, C, C++, and PHP, and lets you easily create applications, as well as websites, web applications and web services. Via plugins installed separately, Eclipse can support Python, or even other languages such as Perl, Lisp, or Ruby.

Eclipse is much more than a text editor. It can indent lines, match words and brackets, and highlight source code that is written incorrectly. It also provides automatic code, which means that as you type, it displays a list of possible completions. The IDE also provides hints to help you analyze your code and find any potential problems. It even suggests some simple solutions to fix those problems.

The Eclipse IDE can be installed on all operating systems that support Java, from Windows to Linux to MacOS systems. Eclipse is free of charge and open source, and it has a large community of users and developers all around the world.

✎ *You can use Eclipse not only to write but also to execute your programs directly from the IDE.*

3.3   How to Set Up Eclipse

In order to install Eclipse, you can download it free of charge from the following address

https://www.eclipse.org/downloads/

When the download completes, run the setup. The first screen of the Eclipse installer (as shown in **Figure 3–2**) prompts you to select a "Package Solution". Select the one called "Eclipse IDE for Java Developers". Don't worry, you are not going to learn Java!

Figure 3–2 Selecting the "Package Solution"

✎ *Eclipse is written mostly in Java. During installation, you may receive the following message. This means that the Java Virtual Machine (JVM) was not found on your system.*

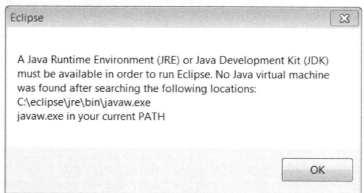

✎ *You can download Java Virtual Machine (JVM) free of charge from the following address:*

https://java.com/en/download/

When you are prompted to select the installation folder, it is advisable to leave the proposed one as shown in **Figure 3–3**.

Figure 3–3 Selecting the installation folder

Click on the "Install" button. When the Eclipse Foundation Software User Agreement pops up (**Figure 3–4**), you must read and accept its terms.

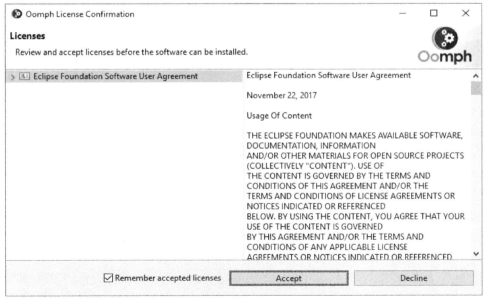

Figure 3–4 The Eclipse Foundation Software User Agreement

Click on the "Accept" button. When the Certificates window pops up (**Figure 3–5**), you must check the corresponding checkboxes and click on the "Accept selected" button.

Figure 3–5 The Eclipse Certificates window

When the installation process is complete, click on the "Launch" button.

The first screen of Eclipse (Eclipse IDE Launcher) prompts you to select the workspace folder. You can leave the proposed folder that appears there and check the field "Use this as the default and do not ask again", as shown in **Figure 3–6**.

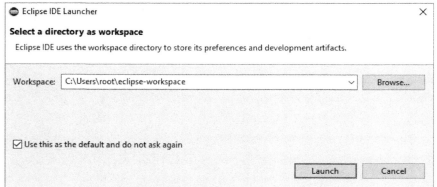

Figure 3–6 Selecting the workspace folder

✎ *The folder proposed on your computer may differ from that in **Figure 3–6** depending on the versions of the Eclipse or Windows that you have.*

When the Eclipse environment opens, it should appear as shown in **Figure 3–7**.

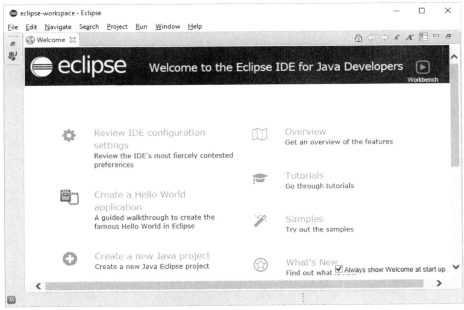

Figure 3–7 The Eclipse IDE

Now it's time to configure Eclipse so it will support Python. From the main menu, select "Help→Eclipse Marketplace". In the popup window that appears, search for the keyword "PyDev" as shown in **Figure 3–8**. Locate the plugin "PyDev – Python IDE for Eclipse" and click on the "Install" button.

Figure 3–8 The Eclipse Marketplace

In the next screen (**Figure 3–9**), keep all the proposed features and click on the "Confirm" button.

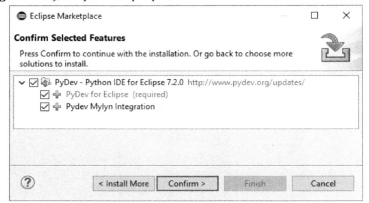

Figure 3–9 Confirming selected features

When the license agreements pop up (**Figure 3–10**), you must read and accept their terms. Click on the "Finish" button.

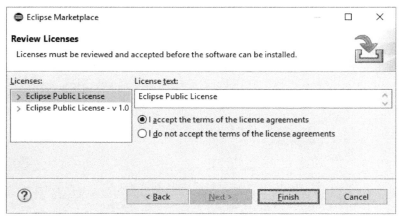

Figure 3–10 The License agreements

When the installation process finally completes, you will be prompted to restart Eclipse in order for the changes to take effect. Click on the "Restart Now" button.

Eclipse has been configured properly! Now it's time to conquer the world of Python! In the upcoming chapters you will learn all about how to write Python programs, how to execute them, and so many tips and tricks useful in your first steps as a budding programmer!

Review in "Introductory Knowledge"

Review Crossword Puzzles

1. Solve the following crossword puzzle.

Across

1. Statements or commands.
3. Windows is such a system.
4. A computer component.
6. A category of software.
8. An input device.
11. It's the person who designs computer programs.
14. An output device.
15. Antivirus is such a software.
16. In today's society, almost every task requires the use of this device.
17. A computer component.
18. All these devices make up a computer.

Down

2. These devices are also computers.
5. Computers can perform so many different tasks because of their ability to be _____.
7. Special memory that can only be read.
9. A secondary storage device.

     10.   A browser is this type of software.

     12.   An input device.

     13.   An operating system.

2.   Solve the following crossword puzzle.

Across

     3.   A category of programming language.

     4.   In a machine language all statements are made up of zeros and _____.

     8.   Widely used general-purpose, high-level computer programming language.

     9.   The statements that a programmer writes to solve a problem.

     12.   The CPU performs one of these basic operations.

     13.   All data stored in this type of memory are lost when you shut down your computer.

     14.   Python _____ Machine converts the bytecode into low-level machine language code.

     16.   A low-level language.

Down

     1.   A program that simultaneously translates and executes the statements written in a high-level language.

     2.   Python _____ is a machine language executed by the Python Virtual Machine.

     5.   A scripting language.

     6.   A set of statements.

     7.   Run a program.

     10.   This software controls a device that is attached to your computer.

     11.   A program that translates statements written in a high-level language into a separate machine language program.

     15.   Eclipse is such a software.

3. Solve the following crossword puzzle.

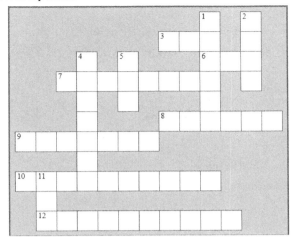

Across

3. A scripting language that can control Microsoft Word.

6. An intermediate language that C# uses.

7. A program that translates statements written in a high-level computer language into a separate machine language program.

8. Python can execute _____ commands .

9. A script requires a _____ application in order to execute.

10. An input device.

12. One reason why Python statements are not directly translated into low-level machine language code.

Down

1. Scripts written in VBA.

2. One of Python's capabilities is the ability to interact with the _____ system of a computer.

4. It displays data to the user.

5. It performs logical operations.

11. Eclipse is such a software

Review Questions

Answer the following questions.

1. What is hardware?

2. List the five basic components of a typical computer system.

3. Which part of the computer actually executes the programs?

4. Which part of the computer holds the program and its data while the program is running?

5. Which part of the computer holds data for a long period of time, even when there is no power to the computer?

6. How do you call the device that collects data from the outside world and enters them into the computer?

7. List some examples of input devices.

8. How do you call the device that outputs data from the computer to the outside world?

9. List some examples of output devices.
10. What is software?
11. How many software categories are there, and what are their names?
12. A word processing program belongs to what category of software?
13. What is a compiler?
14. What is an interpreter?
15. What is meant by the term "machine language"?
16. What is source code?
17. What is Python?
18. What is the difference between a script and a program?
19. What are some of the possible uses of Python?
20. What is Eclipse?

Section 2

Getting Started with Python

Chapter 4
Introduction to Basic Algorithmic Concepts

4.1 What is an Algorithm?

In technical terms, an *algorithm*[1] is a strictly defined finite sequence of well-defined statements (often called instructions or commands) that provides the solution to a problem or to a specific class of problems for any acceptable set of input values (if there are any inputs). In other words, an algorithm is a step-by-step procedure to solve a given problem. The term *finite* means that the algorithm must reach an end point and cannot run forever.

You can find algorithms everywhere in your real life, not just in computer science. For example, the process for preparing toast or a cup of tea can be expressed as an algorithm. Certain steps, in a certain order, must be followed in order to achieve your goal.

4.2 The Algorithm for Making a Cup of Tea

The following is an algorithm for making a cup of tea.

1. Put the teabag in a cup.
2. Fill the kettle with water.
3. Boil the water in the kettle.
4. Pour some of the boiled water into the cup.
5. Add milk to the cup.
6. Add sugar to the cup.
7. Stir the tea.
8. Drink the tea.

As you can see, certain steps must be followed. These steps are in a specific order, even though some of the steps could be rearranged. For example, steps 5 and 6 can be reversed. You could add the sugar first, and the milk afterwards.

✎ *Keep in mind that the order of some steps can probably be changed but you can't move them far away from where they should be. For example, you can't move step 3 ("Boil the water in the kettle.") to the end of the algorithm, because you will end up drinking a cup of iced tea (and not a warm one) which is totally different from your initial goal!*

4.3 Properties of an Algorithm

An algorithm must satisfy the following properties:

▶ **Input**: The algorithm must have input values from a specified set.

▶ **Output**: The algorithm must produce the output values from a specified set of input values. The output values are the solution to a problem.

---

[1] The word "algorithm" derives from the word "algorism" and the Greek word "arithmos" .The word "algorism" comes from the Latinization of the name of Al-Khwārizmī[2] whereas the Greek word "arithmos" means "number".

[2] Muḥammad ibn Al-Khwārizmī (780~850) was a Persian mathematician, astronomer, and geographer. He is considered one of the fathers of algebra.

▶ **Finiteness**: For any input, the algorithm must terminate after a finite number of steps.

▶ **Definiteness**: All steps of the algorithm must be precisely defined.

▶ **Effectiveness**: It must be possible to perform each step of the algorithm correctly and in a finite amount of time. That is, its steps must be basic enough so that, for example, someone using a pencil and a paper could carry them out exactly, and in a finite amount of time. It is not enough that each step is definite (or precisely defined), but it must also be feasible.

4.4   Okay About Algorithms. But What is a Computer Program Anyway?

A *computer program* is nothing more than an algorithm that is written in a language that computers can understand, like Python, Java, C++, or C#.

A computer program cannot actually *make* you a cup of tea or cook your dinner, although an algorithm can guide you through the steps to do it yourself. However, programs can (for example) be used to calculate the average value of a set of numbers, or to find the maximum value among them. Artificial intelligence programs can even play chess or solve logic puzzles.

4.5   The Three Parties!

There are always three parties involved in an algorithm—the one that writes the algorithm, the one that executes it, and the one that uses or enjoys it.

Let's take an algorithm for preparing a meal, for example. Someone writes the algorithm (the author of the recipe book), someone executes it (probably your mother, who prepared the meal following the steps from the recipe book), and someone uses it (probably you, who enjoys the meal).

Now consider a real computer program. Let's take a video game, for example. Someone writes the algorithm in a computer language (the programmer), someone or something executes it (usually a laptop or a computer), and someone else uses it or plays with it (the user).

Be careful however, because sometimes the terms "programmer" and "user" can be confusing. When you *write* a computer program, for that period of time you are "the programmer" but when you *use* your own program, you are "the user".

4.6   The Three Main Stages Involved in Creating an Algorithm

An algorithm should consist of three stages: *data input*, *data processing*, and *results output*. This order is specific and cannot be changed.

Consider a computer program that finds the average value of three numbers. First, the program must prompt (ask) the user to enter the numbers (the data input stage). Next, the program must calculate the average value of the numbers (the data processing stage). Finally, the program must display the result on the computer's screen (the results output stage).

Let's take a look at these stages in more detail.

First stage – Data input

1. Prompt the user to enter a number.
2. Prompt the user to enter a second number.
3. Prompt the user to enter a third number.

Second stage – Data processing

4. Calculate the sum of the three numbers.
5. Divide the sum by 3.

Third stage – Results output

6. Display the result on the screen.

In some rare situations, the input stage may be absent and the computer program may consist of only two stages. For example, consider a computer program that is written to calculate the following sum.

$$1 + 2 + 3 + 4 + 5$$

In this example, the user must enter no values at all because the computer program knows exactly what to do. It must calculate the sum of the numbers 1 to 5 and then display the value of 15 on the user's screen. The two required stages (data processing and results output) are shown here.

First stage – Data input

> Nothing to do

Second stage - Data processing

> 1. Calculate the sum of $1 + 2 + 3 + 4 + 5$.

Third stage – Results output

> 2. Display the result on the screen.

However, what if you want to let the user decide the upper limit of that sum? What if you want to let the user decide whether to sum the numbers 1 to 5 or the numbers 1 to 20? In that case, the program must include an input stage at the beginning of the program to let the user enter that upper limit. Once the user enters that upper limit, the computer can calculate the result. The three required stages are shown here.

First stage – Data input

> 1. Prompt the user to enter a number.

Second stage – Data processing

> 2. Calculate the sum $1 + 2 + \ldots$ (up to and including the upper limit the user entered).

Third stage – Results output

> 3. Display the results on the screen.

For example, if the user enters the number 6 as the upper limit, the computer would find the result of $1 + 2 + 3 + 4 + 5 + 6$.

4.7   Flowcharts

A flowchart is a graphical method of presenting an algorithm, usually on paper. It is the visual representation of the algorithm's flow of execution. In other words, it visually represents how the flow of execution proceeds from one statement to the next until the end of the algorithm is reached. The basic symbols that flowcharts use are shown in **Table 4-1**.

Flowchart Symbols	Description
	Start/End: Represents the beginning or the end of an algorithm. The Start symbol has one exit and the End symbol has one entrance.
	Arrow: Shows the flow of execution. An arrow coming from one symbol and ending at another symbol shows that control passes to the symbol that the arrow is pointing to. Arrows are always drawn as straight lines going up and down or sideways (never at an angle).

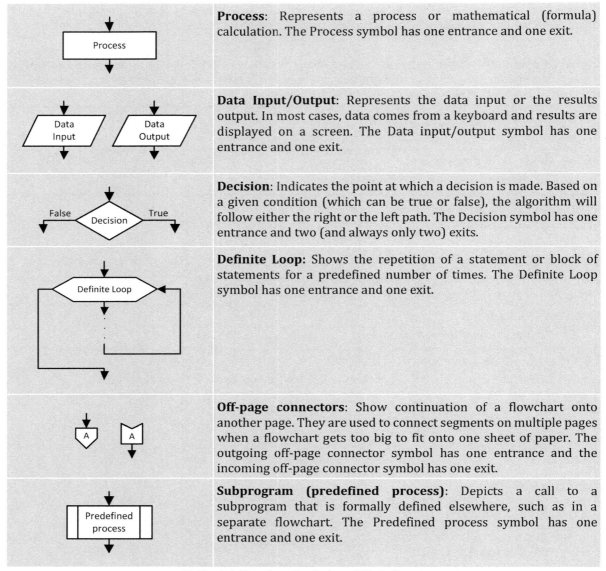

Process	**Process**: Represents a process or mathematical (formula) calculation. The Process symbol has one entrance and one exit.
Data Input / Data Output	**Data Input/Output**: Represents the data input or the results output. In most cases, data comes from a keyboard and results are displayed on a screen. The Data input/output symbol has one entrance and one exit.
False / Decision / True	**Decision**: Indicates the point at which a decision is made. Based on a given condition (which can be true or false), the algorithm will follow either the right or the left path. The Decision symbol has one entrance and two (and always only two) exits.
Definite Loop	**Definite Loop:** Shows the repetition of a statement or block of statements for a predefined number of times. The Definite Loop symbol has one entrance and one exit.
A A	**Off-page connectors**: Show continuation of a flowchart onto another page. They are used to connect segments on multiple pages when a flowchart gets too big to fit onto one sheet of paper. The outgoing off-page connector symbol has one entrance and the incoming off-page connector symbol has one exit.
Predefined process	**Subprogram (predefined process)**: Depicts a call to a subprogram that is formally defined elsewhere, such as in a separate flowchart. The Predefined process symbol has one entrance and one exit.

Table 4-1 Flowchart Symbols and Their Functions

An example of a flowchart is shown in **Figure 4–1.** The algorithm prompts the user to enter three numbers and then calculates their average value and displays it on the computer screen.

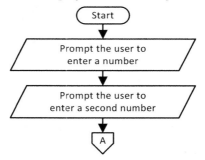

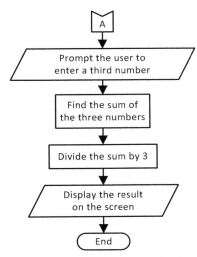

Figure 4–1 Flowchart for an algorithm that calculates and displays the average of three numbers

---

A flowchart always begins and ends with a Start/End symbol!

Exercise 4.7-1　　*Finding the Average Value of Three Numbers*

Design an algorithm that calculates the average value of three numbers. Whenever the average value is below 10, a message "Fail!" must be displayed. Otherwise, if the average value is 10 or above, a message "Pass!" must be displayed.

Solution

In this problem, two different messages must be displayed, but only one can appear each time the algorithm is executed; the wording of the message depends on the average value. The flowchart for the algorithm is presented here.

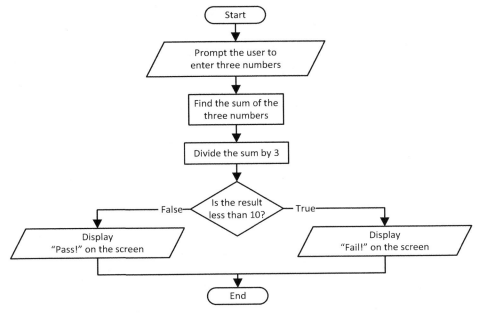

✎ *To save paper, you can prompt the user to enter all three numbers using one single oblique parallelogram.*

▢ *A Decision symbol always has one entrance and two exit paths!*

Of course it is very soon for you to start creating your own algorithms. This particular exercise is quite simple and is presented in this chapter as an exception, just for demonstration purposes. You need to learn more before you start creating your own algorithms or even Python programs. Just be patient! In a few chapters the big moment will come!

4.8   What are "Reserved Words"?

In a computer language, a *reserved word* (or *keyword*) is a word that has a strictly predefined meaning—it is reserved for special use and cannot be used for any other purpose. For example, the words Start, End, Read, and Write in flowcharts have a predefined meaning. They are used to represent the beginning, the end, the data input, and the results output, respectively.

Reserved words exist in all high-level computer languages as well. In Python, there are many reserved words such as if, while, else, and for. Their meanings are predefined, so these words cannot be used for any other purposes.

✎ *Reserved words exist in all high-level computer languages. However, each language has its own reserved words. For example, the reserved words* else if *in C# are written as* elif *in Python.*

4.9   What is the Difference Between a Statement and a Command?

There is a big discussion on the Internet about whether there is, or is not, any difference between a statement and a command. Some people prefer to use the term "statement", and some others the term "command". For a novice programmer, there is no difference; both are instructions to the computer!

4.10   What is Structured Programming?

Structured programming is a software development method that uses modularization and structured design. Large programs are broken down into smaller modules and each individual module uses structured code, which means that the statements are organized in a specific manner that minimizes errors and misinterpretation. As its name suggests, structured programming is done in a structured programming language and Python is one such language.

The structured programming concept was formalized in 1966 by Corrado Böhm[3] and Giuseppe Jacopini[4]. They demonstrated theoretical computer program design using sequences, decisions, and iterations.

4.11   The Three Fundamental Control Structures

There are three fundamental control structures in structured programming.

▶ **Sequence Control Structure**: This refers to the line-by-line execution, in which statements are executed sequentially, in the same order in which they appear in the program, without skipping any of them. It is also known as a *sequential control structure*.

▶ **Decision Control Structure**: Depending on whether a condition is true or false, the decision control structure may skip the execution of an entire block of statements or even execute one block of statements instead of another. It is also known as a *selection control structure*.

---

[3] Corrado Böhm (1923–2017) was a computer scientist known especially for his contribution to the theory of structured programming, and for the implementation of functional programming languages.

[4] Giuseppe Jacopini (1936–2001) was a computer scientist. His most influential contribution is the theorem about structured programming, published along with Corrado Böhm in 1966, under the title *Flow Diagrams, Turing Machines, and Languages with Only Two Formation Rules*

► **Loop Control Structure**: This is a control structure that allows the execution of a block of statements multiple times until a specified condition is met. It is also known as an *iteration control structure* or a *repetition control structure*.

✎ *Every computer program around the world is written in terms of only these three control structures!*

If you didn't quite understand the deeper meaning of these three control structures, don't worry, because upcoming chapters will analyze them very thoroughly. Patience is a virtue. All you have to do for now is wait!

Exercise 4.11-1　　*Understanding Control Structures Using Flowcharts*

Using flowcharts, give an example for each type of control structure.

Solution

Example of a Sequence Control Structure

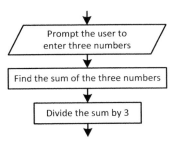

Example of a Decision Control Structure

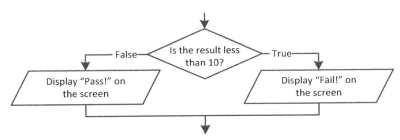

Example of a Loop Control Structure

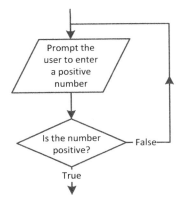

4.12   Your First Python Program

Converting a flowchart to a computer language such as Python results in a Python program. A Python program is nothing more than a text file including Python statements. Python programs can even be written in your text editor application! Keep in mind, though, that using Eclipse to write Python programs is a much better solution due to all of its included features that can make your life easier.

> 💾 *A Python source code is saved on your hard disk with the default .py file extension.*

Here is a very simple algorithm that displays three messages on the screen.

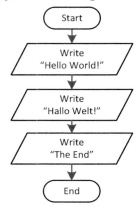

This algorithm can also be written as a Python program as follows.

```python
print("Hello World!")
print("Hallo Welt!")
print("The End")
```

4.13   What is the Difference Between a Syntax Error, a Logic Error, and a Runtime Error?

When programmers write code in a high-level language there are three types of errors that might happen: syntax errors, logic errors, and runtime errors.

A *syntax error* is a mistake such as a misspelled keyword, a missing punctuation character, or a missing closing bracket. The syntax errors are detected by the compiler or the interpreter. If you try to execute a Python program that contains a syntax error, you will get an error message on your screen and the program won't execute. You must correct any errors and then try to execute the program again.

> ✎ *Some IDEs, such as Eclipse, detect these errors as you type and underline the erroneous statements with a wavy red line.*

A *logic error* is an error that prevents your program from doing what you expected it to do. With logic errors you get no warning at all. Your code compiles and runs but the result is not the expected one. Logic errors are hard to detect. You must review your program thoroughly to find out where your error is. For example, consider a Python program that prompts the user to enter three numbers, and then calculates and displays their average value. In this program, however, the programmer made a typographical error (a "typo"); one of his or her statements divides the sum of the three numbers by 5, and not by 3 as it should. Of course the Python program executes as normal, without any error messages, prompting the user to enter three numbers and displaying a result, but obviously not the correct one! It is the programmer who has to find and correct the erroneously written Python statement, not the computer or the interpreter! Computers are not that smart after all!

A *runtime error* is an error that occurs during the execution of a program. A runtime error can cause a program to end abruptly or even cause system shut-down. Such errors are the most difficult errors to detect. There is no way to be sure, before executing the program, whether this error is going to happen, or not. You can suspect that it may happen though! For example, running out of memory or a division by zero causes a runtime error.

✎ *A logic error can be the cause of a runtime error!*

✎ *Logic errors and runtime errors are commonly referred to as "bugs", and are often found before the software is released. When errors are found after a software has been released to the public, programmers often release patches, or small updates, to fix the errors.*

4.14 Commenting Your Code

When you write a small and easy program, anyone can understand how it works just by reading it line-by-line. However, long programs are difficult to understand, sometimes even by the same person who wrote them.

Comments are extra information that can be included in a program to make it easier to read and understand. You can add explanations and other pieces of information, including:

- ▶ who wrote the program
- ▶ when the program was created or last modified
- ▶ what the program does
- ▶ how the program works

✎ *Comments are for human readers. Compilers and interpreters ignore any comments you may add to your programs.*

However, you should not over-comment. There is no need to explain every line of your program. Add comments only when a particular portion of your program is hard to follow.

In Python, you can add comments using the hash character (#) as shown here.

```
#Created By Aristides S. Bouras
#Date created: 12/25/2003
#Date modified: 04/03/2008
#Description: This program displays some messages on the screen

print("Hello Zeus!")   #It displays a message on the screen

#Display a second message on the screen
print("Hello Hera!")

#This is a comment        print("The End")
```

As you can see in the preceding program, you can add comments above a statement or at the end of it, but not in front of it. Look at the last statement, which is supposed to display the message "The End". This statement is never executed because it is considered part of the comment.

✎ *Comments are not visible to the user of a program while the program runs.*

4.15 User-Friendly Programs

What is a *user-friendly* program? It's one the user considers a friend instead of an enemy, one that is easy for a novice user.

If you want to write user-friendly programs you have to put yourself in the shoes of the user. Users want the computer to do their job their way, with a minimum of effort. Hidden menus, unclear labels and directions, and misleading error messages can all make a program user-unfriendly!

The law that best defines user-friendly designs is the *Law of Least Astonishment*: "*The program should act in a way that least astonishes the user*". This law is also commonly referred to as the *Principle of Least Astonishment* (*POLA*).

4.16   Review Questions: True/False

Choose **true** or **false** for each of the following statements.

1. The process for preparing a meal is actually an algorithm.
2. Algorithms are used only in computer science.
3. An algorithm can run forever.
4. In an algorithm, you can relocate a step in any position you wish.
5. An algorithm must produce the correct output values for at least one set of input values.
6. Computers can play chess.
7. An algorithm can always become a computer program.
8. Programming is the process of creating a computer program.
9. There are always three parties involved in a computer program: the programmer, the computer, and the user.
10. The programmer and the user can sometimes be the same person.
11. It is possible for a computer program to output no results.
12. A flowchart is a computer program.
13. A flowchart is composed of a set of geometric shapes.
14. A flowchart is a method used to represent an algorithm.
15. To represent an algorithm, you can design a flowchart without using any Start/End symbols.
16. You can design a flowchart without using any Process symbols.
17. You can design a flowchart without using any Data input/output symbols.
18. A flowchart must always include at least one Decision symbol.
19. In a flowchart, a Decision symbol can have one, two, or three exit paths, depending on the given problem.
20. Reserved words are all those words that have a strictly predefined meaning.
21. Structured programming includes structured design.
22. Python is a structured computer language.
23. The basic principle of structured programming is that it includes only four fundamental control structures.
24. One statement, written ten times, is considered a loop control structure.
25. Decision control structure refers to the line-by-line execution.
26. A misspelled keyword is considered a logic error.
27. A Python program can be executed even though it contains logic errors.
28. If you leave an exclamation mark at the end of a Python statement, it is considered a syntax error.
29. If you leave an exclamation mark at the end of a Python statement, it cannot prevent the whole Python program from being executed.

30. One of the advantages of structured programming is that no errors are made while writing a computer program.

31. Logic errors are caught during compilation.

32. Runtime errors are caught during compilation

33. Syntax errors are the most difficult errors to detect.

34. A program that calculates the area of a triangle but outputs the wrong results contains logic errors.

35. When a program includes no output statements, it contains syntax errors.

36. A program must always contain comments.

37. If you add comments to a program, the computer can more easily understand it.

38. You cannot add comments above a statement.

39. Comments are not visible to the users of a program.

40. A program is called user-friendly if it can be used easily by a novice user.

41. The acronym POLA stands for "Principle of Least Amusement".

4.17   Review Questions: Multiple Choice

Select the correct answer for each of the following statements.

1. An algorithm is a strictly defined finite sequence of well-defined statements that provides the solution to
   a. a problem.
   b. a specific class of problems.
   c. both of the above

2. Which of the following is **not** a property that an algorithm must satisfy?
   a. effectiveness
   b. fittingness
   c. definiteness
   d. input

3. A computer program is
   a. an algorithm.
   b. a sequence of instructions.
   c. both of the above
   d. none of the above

4. When someone prepares a meal, he or she is the
   a. "programmer"
   b. "user"
   c. none of the above

5. Which of the following does **not** belong in the three main stages involved in creating an algorithm?
   a. data protection
   b. data input
   c. results output
   d. data processing

6. A flowchart can be

    a. presented on a piece of paper.

    b. entered directly into a computer as is.

    c. both of the above

7. A rectangle in a flowchart represents

    a. an input/output operation.

    b. a processing operation.

    c. a decision.

    d. none of the above

8. Which of the following is/are control structures?

    a. a decision

    b. a sequence

    c. a loop

    d. All of the above are control structures.

9. Which of the following Python statements contains a syntax error?

    a. `print(Hello Poseidon)`

    b. `print("It's me! I contain a syntax error!!!")`

    c. `print("Hello Athena")`

    d. none of the above

10. Which of the following `print` statements is actually executed?

    a. `print("Hello Apollo)`

    b. `#print("Hello Artemis")`

    c. `#This will be executed  print("Hello Ares")`

    d. `print("Hello Aphrodite") #This will be executed`

    e. none of the above

Chapter 5
Variables and Constants

5.1   What is a Variable?

In computer science, a *variable* is a location in the computer's main memory (RAM) where a program can store a value and change it as the program executes.

Picture a variable as a transparent box in which you can insert and hold one thing at a time. Because the box is transparent, you can also see what it contains. Also, if you have two or more boxes you can give each box a unique name. For example, you could have three boxes, each containing a different number, and you could name the boxes numberA, numberB, and numberC.

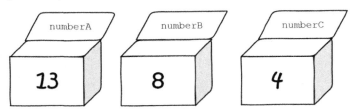

The boxes named numberA, numberB and numberC in the example contain the numbers 13, 8, and 4, respectively. Of course, you can examine or even alter the contained value of each one of these boxes at any time.

Now, let's say that someone asks you to find the sum of the values of the first two boxes and then store the result in the last box. The steps you must follow are:

1.   Look at the first two boxes and examine the values they contain.

2.   Use your CPU (this is your brain) to calculate the sum (the result).

3.   Insert the result in the last box. However, since each box can contain only one single value at a time, the value 4 is actually replaced by the number 21.

The boxes now look like this.

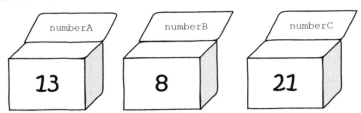

In a flowchart, the action of storing a value in a variable is represented by a left arrow

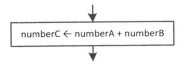

This action is usually expressed as "Assign a value, or the result of an expression, to a variable". The left arrow is called the *value assignment operator*.

✎ *Note that this arrow always points to the left. You are not allowed to use right arrows. Also, on the left side of the arrow only one single variable must exist.*

In real computer science, the three boxes are actually three individual regions in main memory (RAM), named numberA, numberB and numberC.

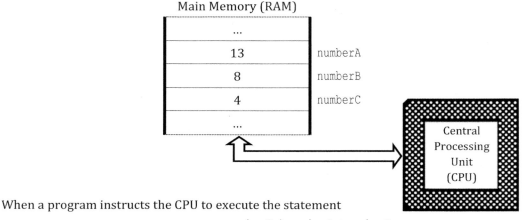

When a program instructs the CPU to execute the statement

$$numberC \leftarrow numberA + numberB$$

it follows the same three-step process as in the previous example.

1. The numbers 13 and 8 are transferred from the RAM's regions named numberA and numberB to the CPU.

    (This is the first step, in which you examined the values contained in the first two boxes).

2. The CPU calculates the sum of 13 + 8.

    (This is the second step, in which you used your brain to calculate the sum, or result).

3. The result, 21, is transferred from the CPU to the RAM's region named numberC, replacing the existing number 4.

    (This is the third step, in which you inserted the result in the last box).

After execution, the RAM looks like this.

Main Memory (RAM)

...	
13	numberA
8	numberB
21	numberC
...	

📖 *While a Python program is running, a variable can hold various values, but only one value at a time. When you assign a value to a variable, this value remains stored until you assign a new value replacing the old one.*

✎ *The content of a variable can change to different values, but its name will always be the same because the name is just an identifier of a location in memory.*

A variable is one of the most important elements in computer science because it helps you interact with data stored in the main memory (RAM). Soon, you will learn all about how to use variables in Python.

5.2   What is a Constant?

Sometimes you may need to use a value that cannot change while the program is running. Such a value is called a *constant*. In simple terms, you could say that a constant is a locked variable. This means that when a program begins to run and a value is assigned to the constant, nothing can change the value of the constant while the program is running. For example, in a financial program an interest rate can be declared as a constant.

A descriptive name for a constant can also improve the readability of your program and help you avoid some errors. For example, let's say that you are using the value 3.14159265 (but not as a constant) at many points throughout your program. If you make a typographic error when typing the number, this will produce the wrong results. But, if this value is given a name, any typographical error in the name is detected by the compiler, and you are notified with an error message.

✎ *Unfortunately, Python does **not** support constants. So, variables are all you have. You can use a variable in place of a constant, but take care not to accidentally change its initial value each time you use this variable in your program.*

In a flowchart, you can represent the action of setting a constant equal to a value with the equals (=) sign.

✎ *This book uses uppercase characters to distinguish a constant from a variable.*

Consider an algorithm that lets the user enter the prices of three different products and then calculates and displays the 20% Value Added Tax (known as VAT) for each product. The flowchart in **Figure 5-1** shows this process when no constant is used.

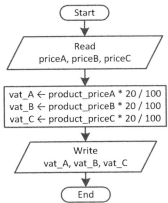

Figure 5-1 Calculating the 20% VAT for three products without the use of a constant

Even though this algorithm is absolutely correct, the problem is that the author used the 20% VAT (20/100) three times. If this were an actual computer program, the CPU would be forced to calculate the result of the division (20/100) three individual times.

✎ *Generally speaking, division and multiplication are CPU-time consuming operations that must be avoided when possible.*

A much better solution would be to use a variable, as shown in **Figure 5-2**. This reduces the number of division and multiplication operations and also decreases the potential for typographical errors.

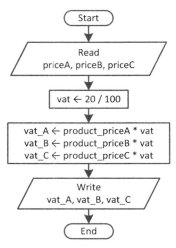

Figure 5-2 Calculating the 20% VAT for three products using a variable, vat

This time the division (20/100) is calculated only once, and then its result is used to calculate the VAT of each product.

But even now, the algorithm (which might later become a computer program) isn't perfect; vat is a variable and any programmer could accidentally change its value below in the program.

The ideal solution would be to change the variable vat to a constant VAT, as shown in **Figure 5-3**.

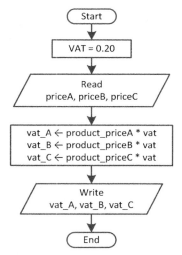

Figure 5-3 Calculating the 20% VAT for three products using a constant, VAT

✎ *Note that when a constant is declared in a flowchart, the equals (=) sign is used instead of the left arrow.*

This last solution is the best choice for many reasons.

▶ No one, including the programmer, can change the value of constant VAT just by accidentally writing a statement such as VAT ← 0.60 in any position of the program.

▶ The potential for typographical errors is minimized.

▶ The number of multiplication and division operations is kept as low as possible.

▶ If one day the finance minister decides to increase the Value Added Tax from 20% to 22%, the programmer needs to change just one line of code!

5.3 How Many Types of Variables and Constants Exist?

Many different types of variables and constants exist in most computer languages. The reason for this diversity is the different types of data each variable or constant can hold. Most of the time, variables and constants hold the following types of data.

▶ **Integers**: An *integer* value is a positive or negative number without any fractional part, such as 5, 100, 135, −25, and −5123.

▶ **Reals**: A *real* value is a positive or negative number that includes a fractional part, such as 5.1, 7.23, 5.0, 3.14, and −23.78976. Real values are also known as *floats*.

▶ **Booleans**[1]: A *Boolean* variable (or constant) can hold only one of two values: `True` or `False`.

▶ **Characters**: A *character* is an *alphanumeric* value (a letter, a symbol, or a number), and it is usually enclosed in single or double quotes, such as "a", "c", or "@". In computer science, a sequence of characters is known as a *string*!!! Probably the word "string" makes you visualize something wearable, but unfortunately it's not. Please keep your dirty precious mind focused on computer science! Examples of strings are "Hello Zeus", "I am 25 years old", or "Peter Loves Jane For Ever".

📖 *Python does **not** support constants.*

✎ *In Python, strings can be enclosed either in single or double quotes.*

5.4 Rules for Naming Variables and Constants in Python

Certain rules must be followed when you choose a name for your variable or constant.

▶ The name of a variable or constant can contain only Latin characters (English uppercase or lowercase characters), numbers, and the underscore character (_). Examples of variable names are `firstName`, `last_name1`, and `age`.

▶ Variable and constant names are case sensitive, which means there is a distinct difference between uppercase and lowercase characters. For example, `myVAR`, `myvar`, `MYVAR`, and `MyVar` are actually four different names.

▶ No space characters are allowed. If a variable or constant is described by more than one word, you can use the underscore character (_) between the words. For example, the variable name `student age` is wrong. Instead, you might use `student_age`, or even `studentAge`.

▶ A valid variable or constant name can start with a letter, or an underscore. Numbers are allowed, but they cannot be used at the beginning of the name. For example the variable name `1student_name` is not properly written. Instead, you might use something like `student_name1` or `student1_name`.

▶ A variable or constant name is usually chosen in a way that describes the meaning and the role of the data it contains. For example, a variable that holds a temperature value might be named `temperature`, `temp`, or even `t`.

✎ *Regarding constants, even though lowercase letters are permitted, it is advisable to use only uppercase letters. This helps you to visually distinguish constants from variables. Examples of constant names are VAT and COMPUTER_NAME.*

---

[1] George Boole (1815–1864) was an English mathematician, philosopher, and logician. He is best known as the architect of what is now called Boolean logic (Boolean algebra), the basis of the modern digital computer.

📖 *Unfortunately, Python does not support constants as do other computer languages (such as C#, or C++). You can use a variable instead, but take care not to accidentally change its initial value each time you use this variable in your program.*

5.5   What Does the Phrase "Declare a Variable" Mean?

Declaration is the process of reserving a portion in main memory (RAM) for storing the contents of a variable. In many high-level computer languages, the programmer must write a specific statement to reserve that portion in the RAM before the variable can be used. In most cases, they even need to specify the variable type so that the compiler or the interpreter knows exactly how much space to reserve.

Here are some examples showing how to declare a variable in different high-level computer languages.

Declaration Statement	High-level Computer Language
Dim sum As Integer	Visual Basic
int sum;	C#, C++, Java, and many more
sum: Integer;	Pascal, Delphi
var sum;	Javascript

5.6   How to Declare Variables in Python

In Python, there is no need to declare variables as you would in C# or C++. Variables are declared when first used. For example, the statement

```
number1 = 0
```

declares the variable `number1` and initializes it to 0.

✎ *In Python, you can represent the action of assigning a value to a variable by using the equals (=) sign. This is equivalent to the left arrow in flowcharts.*

5.7   How to Declare Constants in Python

You must accept it! You cannot declare constants in Python, there is no such option! However, you can still use variables (preferably in uppercase) instead and take care not to alter their initial values each time you use these variables in your program.

The following example shows how to declare variables (used as constants) in Python.

```
VAT = 0.22
NUMBER_OF_PLAYERS = 25
FAVORITE_SONG = "We are the world"
FAVORITE_CHARACTER = "w"
```

📖 *In computer programming, once a constant is defined, its value cannot be changed while the program is running. Unfortunately, this is not true for Python. Since you use a variable in place of a constant, you must be careful not to accidentally alter their initial values below in your programs.*

5.8   Review Questions: True/False

Choose **true** or **false** for each of the following statements.

1. A variable is a location in the computer's secondary storage device.
2. For a value assignment operator in a flowchart, you can use either a left or a right arrow.
3. The content of a variable can change while the program executes.

4. In general, the content of a constant can change while the program executes.

5. The value 10.0 is an integer.

6. A Boolean variable can hold only one of two values.

7. The value "10.0" enclosed in double quotes is a real value.

8. In computer science, a string is something that you can wear!

9. The name of a variable can contain numbers.

10. A variable can change its name while the program executes.

11. The name of a variable cannot be a number.

12. The name of a constant must always be a descriptive one.

13. The name `student name` is not a valid variable name.

14. The name `STUDENT_NAME` is a valid constant name.

15. In Python, the name of a variable can contain uppercase and lowercase letters.

16. In Python, there is no need to declare a variable.

17. In a Python program, you must always use at least one variable.

5.9   Review Questions: Multiple Choice

Select the correct answer for each of the following statements.

1. A variable is a place in

    a. a hard disk.

    b. a DVD disc.

    c. a USB flash drive.

    d. all of the above

    e. none of the above

2. A variable can hold

    a. one value at a time.

    b. many values at a time.

    c. all of the above

    d. none of the above

3. In general, using constants in a program

    a. helps programmers to completely avoid typographical errors.

    b. helps programmers to avoid using division and multiplication.

    c. all of the above

    d. none of the above

4. Which of the following is an integer?

    a. 5.0

    b. −5

    c. "5"

    d. none of the above is an integer.

5. A Boolean variable can hold the value

    a. one.

    b. "True".

     c. True.

     d. none of the above

6. In Python, strings can be

     a. enclosed in single quotes.

     b. enclosed in double quotes.

     c. both of the above

7. Which of the following is **not** a valid Python variable?

     a. `city_name`

     b. `cityName`

     c. `cityname`

     d. `city-name`

5.10 Review Exercises

Complete the following exercises.

1. Match each element from the first column with one element from the second column.

Value		Data Type
1. "True"		a. Boolean
2. 123		b. Real
3. False		c. String
4. 10.0		d. Integer

2. Match each element from the first column with one element from the second column.

Value		Data Type
1. The name of a person		a. Boolean
2. The age of a person		b. Real
3. The result of the division 5.0/2.0		c. Integer
4. Is it black or is it white?		d. String

3. Complete the following table

Value	Data Type	Declaration and Initialization
The name of my friend	String	`name = "Mark"`
My address		`address = "254 Lookout Rd. Wilson, NY 27893"`
The average daily temperature		
A telephone number		`phone_number = "1-891-764-2410"`
My Social Security Number (SSN)		
The speed of a car		
The number of children in a family		

Chapter 6
Handling Input and Output

6.1 Which Statement Outputs Messages and Results on a User's Screen?

A flowchart uses the oblique parallelogram and the reserved word "Write" to display a message or the final results to the user's screen.

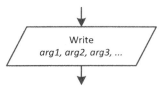

where *arg1*, *arg2*, and *arg3* can be variables, expressions, constant values, or even strings enclosed in double quotes.

The oblique parallelogram that you have just seen is equivalent to

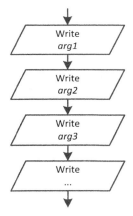

In Python, you can achieve the same result by using the print statement. Its general form is

```
print(arg1, arg2, arg3, …  [, sep = " "] [, end = "\n"])
```

where

► arg1, arg2, arg3, … are the arguments (values) to be printed. They can be variables, expressions, constant values, or strings enclosed in single or double quotes.

► sep is the string inserted between arguments. It is optional and its default value is one space character.

► end is the string appended after the last argument. It is optional and its default value is one "line break".

The following two statements:

```
a = 5 + 6
print("The sum of 5 and 6 is", a)
```

display the message shown in **Figure 6‑1**.

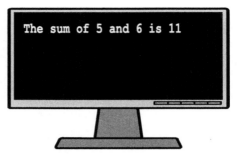

Figure 6–1 A string and an integer displayed on the screen

> 📱 *In Python, if you want to display a string on the screen, the string must be enclosed in single or double quotes.*
>
> ✎ *Note the space inserted automatically between the first string and the value of variable* a *(just after the word "is").*

You can also calculate the result of a mathematical expression directly in a `print` statement. The following statement:

```
print("The sum of 5 and 6 is", 5 + 6)
```

displays exactly the same message as in **Figure 6–1**.

6.2   How to Alter the Default Behavior of a `print` Statement

As already stated, Python automatically outputs a space between arguments. The following example

```
print("Morning", "Evening", "Night")
```

displays

Figure 6–2 The output result displays a space between arguments

Also keep in mind that the following three statements produce the same output result no matter how many space characters exist after the comma (,) delimiter:

```
print("Morning","Evening","Night")
print("Morning", "Evening", "Night")
print("Morning",    "Evening",    "Night")
```

as shown in **Figure 6–3**.

Figure 6-3 The output result always displays one space between arguments

If you wish to customize the separator character, you need to use a value for argument sep as shown here:

```
print("Morning", "Evening", "Night", sep = "#")
```

and the output result now becomes as shown in **Figure 6–4**.

Figure 6–4 The output result with a customized separator

Now, look carefully at the following example.

```
a = "Ares"
print("Hello", a)
print("Halo", a)
print("Salut", a)
```

The print statement in Python automatically appends a "line break" after the last argument (variable a); thus, these three messages are displayed one under the other as shown in **Figure 6–5**.

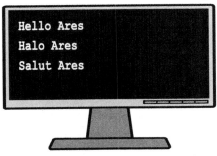

Figure 6–5 The output result displays on three lines

You can customize the value of the end argument as shown here:

```
a = "Ares"
print("Hello", a, end = " - ")
print("Halo", a, end = " - ")
```

```python
print("Salut", a)
```

The output result now becomes as shown in **Figure 6-6**.

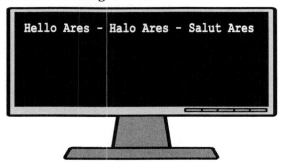

Figure 6-6 The output result displays on one line

You can also output a "line break" by putting the special sequence of characters \n after every argument as shown here:

```python
a = "Ares"
print("Hello ", a, "\nHalo ", a, "\nSalut ", a, sep = "")
```

and the output result is shown in **Figure 6-7**.

Figure 6-7 The output result displays on three lines

Another interesting sequence of characters is the \t which can be used to output a "tab stop". The tab character is useful for aligning output.

```python
print("John\tGeorge")
print("Sofia\tMary")
```

The output result now appears in **Figure 6-8**.

Figure 6-8 The output result now displays tabs

Of course, the same result can be accomplished with one single statement.

```python
print("John\tGeorge\nSofia\tMary")
```

6.3   Which Statement Prompts the User to Enter Data or Lets the User Enter Data?

Do you recall the three main stages involved in creating an algorithm or a computer program? The first stage was the "data input" stage, in which the computer lets the user enter data such as numbers, their name, their address, or their year of birth.

A flowchart uses the oblique parallelogram and the reserved word "Read" to let a user enter his or her data.

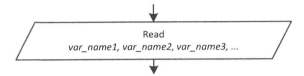

where *var_name1*, *var_name2*, and *var_name3* must be variables only.

The oblique parallelogram that you have just seen is equivalent to

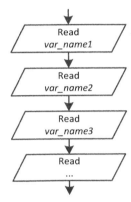

✎ *When a* Read *statement is executed, the flow of execution is interrupted until the user has entered all the data. When data entry is complete, the flow of execution continues to the next statement. Usually data are entered from a keyboard.*

In Python, data input is accomplished using one of the following statements:

```python
#Read a string from the keyboard
var_name_str = input([prompt])

#Read an integer from the keyboard
var_name_int = int(input([prompt]))

#Read a real from the keyboard
var_name_float = float(input([prompt]))
```

where

► *prompt* is the prompt message to be displayed. It can be either a variable or a string enclosed in single or double quotes. The argument *prompt* is optional.

► *var_name_str* can be any variable of type string.

► *var_name_int* can be any variable of type integer.

► *var_name_float* can be any variable of type float (real).

✎ *Functions* int() *and* float() *are discussed later in this book.*

Let's study the input() statement using the following example.

```python
name = input("What is your name? ")
print("Hello", name)
```

When the input() statement executes, the message "What is your name?" (without the double quotes) is displayed and the flow of execution stops, waiting for the user to enter his or her name. The print() statement is not yet executed! As long as the user doesn't enter anything, the computer just waits, as shown in **Figure 6-9**.

Figure 6-9 When an input() statement executes, the computer waits for data input.

When the user finally enters his or her name and hits the "Enter ↵" key, the flow of execution then continues to the next print() statement as shown in **Figure 6-10.**

Figure 6-10 The flow of execution continues when the user hits the "Enter ↵" key.

The following code fragment prompts the user to enter a string and a float, that is, a number that contains a fractional part.

```python
product_name = input("Enter product name: ")
product_price = float(input("Enter product price: "))
```

The following program prompts the user to enter a string and an integer, that is, a number without a fractional part and then displays a message.

```python
name = input("What is your name? ")
age = int(input("What is your age? "))
print("Wow, you are already", age, "years old,", name, "!")
```

In Python (even though it is not frequently used), you can read two or more values using just one line of code, as shown here.

```python
name, age = input("What is your name? "), int(input("What is your age? "))
print("Wow, you are already", age, "years old,", name, "!")
```

The corresponding flowchart fragment, however, must look like this

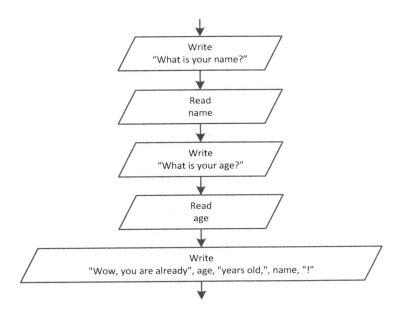

In Python, it is recommended to display the prompt messages using the input() statement. The following example is correct, but it is not frequently used.

```python
print("What is your name? ", end = "")
name = input()

print("What is your age? ", end = "")
age = int(input())

print("Wow, you are already", age, "years old,", name, "!")
```

In this book there is a slight difference between the words "prompts" and "lets". When an exercise says "Write a Python program that **prompts** the user to enter..." this means that you *must* include a prompt message. However, when the exercise says "Write a Python program that **lets** the user enter..." this means that you are not actually required to include a prompt message; that is, it is not wrong to include one but you don't have to! The following example lets the user enter his or her name and age (but does not prompt them to).

```python
name = input()
age = int(input())
```

What happens here (when the program is executed) is that the computer displays a text cursor without any prompt message and waits for the user to enter two values – one for name and one for age. The user, though, must be a prophet and guess what to enter! Does he have to enter his name first and then his age, or is it the opposite? So, obviously a prompt message is pretty much required, because it makes your program more user-friendly.

6.4 Review Questions: True/False

Choose **true** or **false** for each of the following statements.

1. In Python, the word print is a reserved word.
2. The print() statement can be used to display a message or the content of a variable.
3. When the input() statement is executed, the flow of execution is interrupted until the user has entered a value.

4. One single `input()` statement can be used to enter multiple data values.

5. Before data input, a prompt message must always be displayed.

6.5 Review Questions: Multiple Choice

Select the correct answer for each of the following statements.

1. The statement `print("Hello")` displays

   a. the word `Hello` (without the double quotes).

   b. the word `"Hello"` (including the double quotes).

   c. the content of the variable `Hello`.

   d. none of the above

2. The statement `print(Hello)` displays

   a. the word `Hello` (without the double quotes).

   b. the word `"Hello"` (including the double quotes).

   c. the content of the variable `Hello`.

   d. none of the above

3. The statement `print("Hello\nHermes")` displays

   a. the message `Hello Hermes`.

   b. the word `Hello` in one line and the word `Hermes` in the next one.

   c. the message `HelloHermes`.

   d. the message `Hello\nHermes`.

   e. none of the above

4. The statement `data1_data2 = input()`

   a. lets the user enter a value and assigns it to variable `data1`. Variable `data2` remains empty.

   b. lets the user enter a value and assigns it to variable `data1_data2`.

   c. lets the user enter two values and assigns them to variables `data1` and `data2`.

   d. none of the above

Chapter 7
Operators

7.1 The Value Assignment Operator

The most commonly used operator in Python is the value assignment operator (=). For example, the Python statement

```
x = 5
```

assigns a value of 5 to variable x.

As you read in Chapter 5, this is equivalent to the left arrow used in flowcharts.

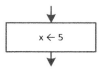

Probably the left arrow used in a flowchart is more convenient and clearer than the (=) sign because it shows in a more graphical way that the value or the result of an expression on the right is assigned to a variable on the left.

Be careful! The (=) sign is not equivalent to the one used in mathematics. In mathematics, the expression x = 5 is read as "x *is equal to 5*". However, in Python the expression x = 5 is read as "*assign the value 5 to* x" or "*set x equal to 5*". They look the same but they act differently!

For example, in mathematics, the following two lines are equivalent. The first one can be read as "x *is equal to the sum of* y *and* z" and the second one as "*the sum of* y *and* z *is equal to* x".

```
x = y + z
y + z = x
```

On the other hand, in Python, these two statements are definitely **not** equivalent. The first statement seems quite correct. It can be read as "*Set* x *equal to the sum of* y *and* z" or "*Assign the sum of* y *and* z *to* x". But what about the second one? Think! Is it possible to assign the value of x to y + z? The answer is obviously a big "NO!"

📇 *In Python, the variable on the left side of the (=) sign represents a region in main memory (RAM) where a value can be stored.*

📇 *On the left side of the (=) sign only variables can exist, whereas on the right side there can be a number, a variable, a string, or even a complex mathematical expression.*

In **Table 7-1** you can find some examples of value assignments.

Examples	Description
a = 9	Assign a value of 9 to variable a.
b = c	Assign the content of variable c to variable b.
d = "Hello Zeus"	Assign the string *Hello Zeus* to variable d.

d = a + b	Calculate the sum of the contents of variables a and b and assign the result to variable d.
b = a + 1	Calculate the sum of the content of variable a and 1 and assign the result to variable b. Please note that the content of variable a is not altered.
a = a + 1	Calculate the sum of the content of variable a and 1 and assign the result back to variable a. In other words, increase variable a by one.

Table 7-1 Examples of Value Assignments

Confused about the last one? Are you thinking about your math teacher right now? What would he/she say if you had written a = a + 1 on the blackboard? Can you personally think of a number that is equal to the number itself plus one? Are you nuts? This means that 5 is equal to 6 and 10 is equal to 11!

Obviously, things are different in computer science. The statement a = a + 1 is absolutely acceptable! It instructs the CPU to retrieve the value of variable a from main memory (RAM), to add 1 to that value, and to assign the result back to variable a. The old value of variable a is replaced by the new one.

Still don't get it? Let's take a look at how the CPU and main memory (RAM) cooperate with each other in order to execute the statement A ← A + 1 (this is the same as the statement a = a + 1 in Python).

Let's say that there is a region in memory, named A and it contains the number 13.

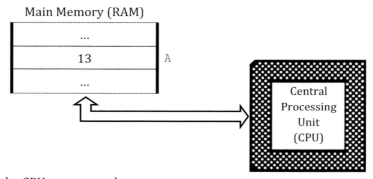

When a program instructs the CPU to execute the statement

$$A \leftarrow A + 1$$

the following procedure is executed:

► the number 13 is transferred from the RAM's region named A to the CPU;

► the CPU calculates the sum of 13 and 1; and

► the result, 14, is transferred from the CPU to the RAM's region named A replacing the existing number, 13.

After execution, the RAM looks like this.

Main Memory (RAM)

...
14
...

A

Now that you understand everything, let's see something more. In Python, you can assign a single value to multiple variables with one single statement. The following statement:

```
a = b = c = 4
```

assigns the value of 4 to all three variables a, b, and c.

In Python, you can also assign multiple values to multiple variables with one single statement. This is called *simultaneous assignment*. The following statement:

```
a, b, c = 2, 10, 3
```

assigns the value of 2 to variable a, the value of 10 to variable b, and the value of 3 to variable c.

7.2   Arithmetic Operators

Just like every high-level programming language, Python supports almost all types of *arithmetic operators*.

Arithmetic Operator	Description
+	Addition
–	Subtraction
*	Multiplication
/	Division
//	Quotient after integer division
%	Remainder after integer division (Modulus)
**	Exponentiation

The first two operators are straightforward and need no further explanation.

If you need to multiply two numbers or the content of two variables you have to use the asterisk (*) symbol. For example, if you want to multiply 2 times y, you must write 2 * y. Likewise, to perform a division, you must use the slash (/) symbol. For example, if you want to divide 10 by 2, you must write 10 / 2.

✎ *In mathematics it is legal to skip the multiplication operator and write* 3x, *meaning "3 times x". In Python, however, you must always use an asterisk anywhere a multiplication operation exists. This is one of the most common mistakes novice programmers make when they write mathematical expressions in Python.*

The integer division operator (//) returns the quotient of an integer division, which means that

```
a = 13 // 3
```

assigns a value of 4 to variable a.

The (//) operator can be used with floating-point numbers as well. For example, the operation

```
b = 14.4 // 3
```

assigns a value of 4 to variable b.

Correspondingly, the modulus operator (%) returns the remainder of an integer division, which means that

```
c = 13 % 3
```

assigns a value of 1 to variable c.

The modulus operator (%) can be used with floating-point numbers as well, but the result is a real (float). For example, the operation

```
d = 14.4 % 3
```

assigns a value of 2.4 (and not 2, as you may mistakenly expect) to variable d.

✎ *Keep in mind that flowcharts are a loose method used to represent an algorithm. Although the use of the integer quotient (//) and the integer remainder (%) operators is allowed in flowcharts, this book uses the commonly accepted DIV and MOD operators instead! For example, the Python statements* x = 13 // 3 *and* y = 13 % 3 *are represented in a flowchart as*

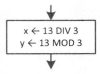

The exponentiation operator (**) raises the number on the left of the operator to the power of the number on the right. For example, the operation

```
f = 2 ** 3
```

calculates 2 to the power of 3 (2^3) and assigns a value of 8 to variable f.

✎ *The exponentiation operator (**) can be used to calculate the square root of a number as well. It is known from mathematics that $\sqrt[z]{X} = X^{\frac{1}{z}}$. So, you can write* y = x ** (1 / 2) *to calculate the square root of* x *or you can even write* y = x ** (1 / 3) *to calculate the cube root of* x, *and so on!*

In mathematics, as you may already know, you are allowed to use parentheses (round brackets) as well as braces (curly brackets) and square brackets.

$$y = \frac{5}{2}\left\{3 + 2\left[4 + 7\left(7 - \frac{4}{3}\right)\right]\right\}$$

However, in Python there is no such thing as braces and brackets. Parentheses are all you have; therefore, the same expression must be written using parentheses instead of braces or brackets.

```
y = 5 / 2 * (3 + 2 * (4 + 7 * (7 - 4 / 3)))
```

7.3   What is the Precedence of Arithmetic Operators?

Arithmetic operators follow the same precedence rules as in mathematics, and these are: exponentiation is performed first, multiplication and division are performed next, and addition and subtraction are performed last.

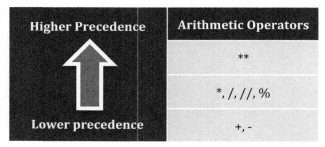

When multiplication and division exist in the same expression, and since both are of the same precedence, they are performed left to right (the same way as you read), which means that the expression

```
y = 6 / 3 * 2
```

is equivalent to $y = \frac{6}{3} \cdot 2$, and assigns a value of 4 to variable y, (division is performed before multiplication).

If you want, however, the multiplication to be performed before the division, you can use parentheses to change the precedence. This means that

```
y = 6 / (3 * 2)
```

is equivalent to $y = \frac{6}{3 \cdot 2}$, and assigns a value of 1 to variable y (multiplication is performed before division).

✎ *Python programs can be written using your computer's text editor application, but keep in mind that it is not possible to write fractions in the form of* $\frac{6}{3}$ *or* $\frac{4x+5}{6}$. *Forget it! There is no equation editor in a text editor! All fractions must be written on one single line. For example,* $\frac{6}{3}$ *must be written as* 6 / 3, *and* $\frac{4x+5}{6}$ *must be written as* (4 * x + 5) / 6.

The order of operations can be summarized as follows:

1. Any operations enclosed in parentheses are performed first.
2. Any exponentiations are performed next.
3. Then, any multiplication and division operations are performed from left to right.
4. In the end, any addition and subtraction operations are performed from left to right.

So, in statement `y = (20 + 3) + 12 + 2 ** 3 / 4 * 3`

the operations are performed as follows:

1. 20 is added to 3, yielding a result of 23.
2. 2 is raised to the power of 3, yielding a result of 8.
3. 8 is divided by 4, yielding a result of 2. This result is then multiplied by 3, yielding a result of 6.
4. 23 is added to 12, yielding a result of 35. This result is then added to 6, yielding a final result of 41.

Next is the same sequence of operations presented in a more graphical way.

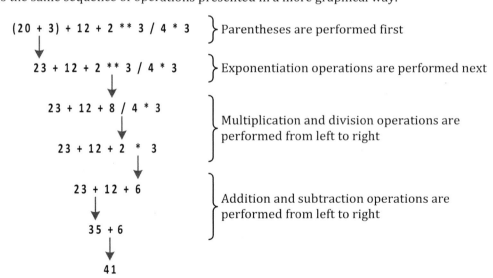

7.4   Compound Assignment Operators

Python offers a special set of operators known as *compound assignment operators*, which can help you write code faster.

Operator	Description	Example	Equivalent to
+=	Addition assignment	a += b	a = a + b
-=	Subtraction assignment	a -= b	a = a - b
*=	Multiplication assignment	a *= b	a = a * b
/=	Division assignment	a /= b	a = a / b
//=	Integer division assignment	a //= b	a = a // b
%=	Modulus assignment	a %= b	a = a % b
**=	Exponentiation assignment	a **= b	a = a ** b

Looking at the *"Equivalent to"* column, it becomes clear that same result can be achieved by just using the classic assignment (=) operator. So the question that arises here is *why do these operators exist?*

The answer is simple: It's a matter of convenience. Once you start using them, your life finds a different meaning!

✎ *Keep in mind that flowcharts are a loose method to represent an algorithm. Although the use of compound assignment operators is allowed in flowcharts, this book uses only the commonly accepted operators shown in the "Equivalent to" column. For example, the Python statement* a += b *is represented in a flowchart as*

Exercise 7.4-1   *Which Python Statements are Syntactically Correct?*

Which of the following Python assignment statements are syntactically correct?

i.	a = -10	*v.*	a = COWS	*ix.*	a = True
ii.	10 = b	*vi.*	a + b = 40	*x.*	a //= 2
iii.	a_b = a_b + 1	*vii.*	a = 3 b	*xi.*	a += 1
iv.	a = "COWS"	*viii.*	a = "True"	*xii.*	a =* 2

Solution

i.   **Correct**. It assigns the integer value −10 to variable a.

ii. **Wrong**. On the left side of the value assignment operator, only variables can exist.

iii. **Correct**. It increases variable a_b by one.

iv. **Correct**. It assigns the string (the text) COWS to variable a.

v.   **Correct**. It assigns the content of variable COWS to variable a.

vi. **Wrong**. On the left side of the value assignment operator, only variables (not expressions) can exist.

vii. **Wrong**. It should have been written as a = 3 * b.

viii. **Correct**. It assigns the string True to variable a.

ix. **Correct**. It assigns the value True to variable a.

x.   **Correct**. This is equivalent to a = a // 2.

xi. **Correct**. This is equivalent to a = a + 1

xii. **Wrong**. It should have been written as a *= 2 (which is equivalent to a = a * 2)

Exercise 7.4-2   *Finding Variable Types*

What is the type of each of the following variables?

i.	a = 15	iii.	b = "15"	v.	b = True
ii.	width = "10 meters"	iv.	temp = 13.5	vi.	b = "True"

Solution

i. The value 15 belongs to the set of integers, thus the variable a is an integer.

ii. The "*10 meters*" is text, thus the width variable is a string.

iii. The "15" is text string, thus the b variable is a string.

iv. The value 13.5 belongs to the set of real numbers, thus the variable temp is real.

v. The value True is Boolean, thus variable b is a Boolean.

vi. The value True is a text, thus variable b is a string.

7.5   String Operators

Joining two separate strings into a single one is called *concatenation*. There are two operators that you can use to concatenate (join) strings as shown in the table that follows.

Operator	Description	Example	Equivalent to
+	Concatenation	a = "Hi" + " there"	
+=	Concatenation assignment	a += "Hello"	a = a + "Hello"

The following example displays "What's up, dude?"

```
a = "What's "
b = "up, "
c = a + b
c += "dude?"

print(c)
```

Last but not least, there are two more string operators that can be used for string repetition, as shown in the following table.

Operator	Description	Example	Equivalent to
*	Repetition	a = "Hi" * 3	a = "HiHiHi"
*=	Repetition assignment	a *= 5	a = a * 5

The following example displays "catcat" and then "catcatcatcat".

```
a = "cat" * 2
print(a)    #It displays: catcat
a *= 2
print(a)    #It displays: catcatcatcat
```

Exercise 7.5-1   Concatenating Names

Write a Python program that prompts the user to enter his or her first and last name (assigned to two different variables) and then joins them together in a single string (concatenation).

Solution

The Python program is shown here.

```python
first_name = input("Enter first name: ")
last_name = input("Enter last name: ")


full_name = first_name + " " + last_name
print(full_name)
```

✎ *Note the extra space character added between the first and last name.*

7.6   Review Questions: True/False

Choose **true** or **false** for each of the following statements.

1. The statement x = 5 can be read as *"Variable x is equal to 5"*.

2. The value assignment operator assigns the result of an expression to a variable.

3. A string can be assigned to a variable only by using the input() statement.

4. The statement 5 = y assigns value 5 to variable y.

5. On the right side of a value assignment operator an arithmetic operator must always exist.

6. In Python, on the right side of a value assignment operator only variables can exist.

7. You cannot use the same variable on both sides of a value assignment operator.

8. The statement a = a + 1 decrements variable a by one.

9. The statement a = a + (-1) decrements variable a by one.

10. In Python, the word MOD is a reserved word.

11. The statement x = 0 % 5 assigns a value of 5 to variable x.

12. The operation 5 % 0 is not possible.

13. Addition and subtraction have the higher precedence among the arithmetic operators.

14. When division and multiplication operators co-exist in an expression, multiplication operations are performed before division.

15. The expression 8 / 4 * 2 is equal to 1.

16. The expression 4 + 6 / 6 + 4 is equal to 9.

17. The expression a + b + c / 3 calculates the average value of three numbers.

18. The statement a += 1 is equivalent to a = a + 1

19. The statement a = "True" assigns a Boolean value to variable a.

20. The statement a = 2·a doubles the content of variable a.

21. The statements a += 2 and a = a - (-2) are not equivalent.

22. The statement a -= a + 1 always assigns a value of -1 to variable a.

23. The statement a = "George" + " Malkovich" assigns value GeorgeMalkovich to variable a.

24. The following Python program satisfies the property of definiteness.

```
a = int(input())
b = int(input())
x = a / (b - 7)
print(x)
```

7.7   Review Questions: Multiple Choice

Select the correct answer for each of the following statements.

1. Which of the following Python statements assigns a value of 10.0 to variable a?

   a.   `10.0 = a`

   b.   `a ← 10.0`

   c.   `a = 100 / 10`

   d.   none of the above

2. The statement `a = b` can be read as

   a.   assign the content of variable `a` to variable `b`.

   b.   variable `b` is equal to variable `a`.

   c.   assign the content of variable `b` to variable `a`.

   d.   none of the above

3. The expression `0 % 10 + 2` is equal to

   a.   7.

   b.   2.

   c.   12.

   d.   none of the above

4. Which of the following Python statements is syntactically correct?

   a.   `a = 4 * 2y - 8 / (4 * q)`

   b.   `a = 4 * 2 * y - 8 / 4 * q)`

   c.   `a = 4 * 2 * y - 8 / (4 */ q)`

   d.   none of the above

5. Which of the following Python statements is syntactically correct?

   a.   `a ** 5 = b`

   b.   `b = a ** 5`

   c.   `a =** 5`

6. Which of the following Python statements assigns value `George Malkovich` to variable a?

   a.   `a = "George" + " " + "Malkovich"`

   b.   `a = "George" + " Malkovich"`

   c.   `a = "George " + "Malkovich"`

   d.   all of the above

7. The following code fragment

   ```
   x = 2
   x += 1
   ```

   does **not** satisfy the property of

   a.   finiteness.

    b.　definiteness.

    c.　effectiveness.

    d.　none of the above

8.　The following code fragment

```
a = int(input())
x = 1 / a
```

does **not** satisfy the property of

    a.　finiteness.

    b.　input.

    c.　definiteness.

    d.　none of the above

7.8　Review Exercises

Complete the following exercises.

1.　Which of the following Python assignment statements are syntactically correct?

i.	`a ← a + 1`	vi.	`a = 40"`
ii.	`a += b`	vii.	`a = b · 5`
iii.	`a b = a b + 1`	viii.	`a =+ "True"`
iv.	`a = a + 1`	ix.	`fdadstwsdgfgw = 1`
v.	`a = hello`	x.	`a = a ** 5`

2.　What is the type of each of the following variables?

i.	`a = "False"`	iii.	`b = "15 meters"`	v.	`b = 13.0`
ii.	`w = False`	iv.	`weight = "40"`	vi.	`b = 13`

3.　Match each element from the first column with one element from the second column.

Operation		Result	
i.	1 / 2	a.	100
ii.	1 / 2 * 2	b.	0.25
iii.	0 % 10 * 10	c.	0
iv.	10 % 2 + 7	d.	0.5
		e.	7
		f.	1

4.　What displays on the screen after executing each of the following code fragments?

i.
```
a = 5
b = a * a + 1
print(b + 1)
```

ii.
```
a = 9
b = a / 3 * a
print(b + 1)
```

5.　What displays on the screen after executing each of the following code fragments?

i.
```
a = 5
a += a - 5
print(a)
```

ii.
```
a = 5
a = a + 1
print(a)
```

6. What is the result of each of the following operations?

    i.   21 % 5   iv. 10 % 6 % 3

    ii. 10 % 2   v.   0 % 3

    iii. 11 % 2   vi. 100 / 10 % 3

7. What displays on screen after executing each of the following code fragments?

i.
```
a = 5
b = 2
c = a % (b + 1)
d = (b + 1) % (a + b)
print(c, "*", d)
```

ii.
```
a = 0.4
b = 8
a += 0.1
c = a * b % b
print(c)
```

8. Calculate the result of the expression a % b for the following cases.

    i.   a = 20, b = 3   iv.   a = 0, b = 3

    ii. a = 15, b = 3   v.   a = 3, b = 1

    iii. a = 22, b = 3   vi. a = 2, b = 2

9. Calculate the result of the expression

$$b * (a \% b) + a / b$$

for each of the following cases.

    i.   a = 10, b = 5   ii.   a = 10, b = 4

10. What displays on the screen after executing the following code fragment?
```
a = "My name is"
a += " "
a = a + "George Malkovich"
print(a)
```

11. Fill in the gaps in each of the following code fragments so that they display a value of 5.

i.
```
a = 2
a = a - ......
print(a)
```

ii.
```
a = 4
b = a * 0.5
b += a
a = b - ......
print(a)
```

12. What displays on the screen after executing the following code fragment?
```
city = "California"
California = city
print(city, California)
```

Chapter 8
Trace Tables

8.1 What is a Trace Table?

A *trace table* is a technique used to test algorithms or computer programs for logic errors that occur while the algorithm or program executes.

The trace table simulates the flow of execution. Statements are executed step by step, and the values of variables change as an assignment statement is executed.

Trace tables are typically used by novice programmers to help them visualize how a particular algorithm or program works. Trace tables can also help advanced programmers detect logic errors.

A typical trace table is shown here.

Step	Statement	Notes	variable1	variable2	variable3
1					
2					
...					

Let's see a trace table in action! For the following Python program, a trace table is created to determine the values of the variables in each step.

```python
x = 10
y = 15
z = x * y
z += 1
print(z)
```

The trace table for this program is shown below. Notes are optional, but they help the reader to better understand what is really happening.

Step	Statement	Notes	x	y	z
1	x = 10	The value 10 is assigned to variable x.	**10**	?	?
2	y = 15	The value 15 is assigned to variable y.	10	**15**	?
3	z = x * y	The result of the product x * y is assigned to z.	10	15	**150**
4	z += 1	Variable z is incremented by one.	10	15	**151**
5	print(z)	It displays: 151			

Exercise 8.1-1   Creating a Trace Table

What result is displayed when the following program is executed?

```python
Ugly = "Beautiful"
Beautiful = "Ugly"
Handsome = Ugly
```

```
print("Beautiful")
print(Ugly)
print(Handsome)
```

Solution

Let's create a trace table to find the output result.

Step	Statement	Notes	Ugly	Beautiful	Handsome
1	Ugly = "Beautiful"	The string "Beautiful" is assigned to the variable Ugly.	**Beautiful**	?	?
2	Beautiful = "Ugly"	The string "Ugly" is assigned to the variable Beautiful.	Beautiful	**Ugly**	?
3	Handsome = Ugly	The value of variable Ugly is assigned to the variable Handsome.	Beautiful	Ugly	**Beautiful**
4	print("Beautiful")	It displays: Beautiful			
5	print(Ugly)	It displays: Beautiful			
6	print(Handsome)	It displays: Beautiful			

Exercise 8.1-2   *Swapping Values of Variables*

Write a Python program that lets the user enter two values, in variables a and b. At the end of the program, the two variables must swap their values. For example, if variables a and b contain the values 5 and 7 respectively, after swapping their values, variable a must contain the value 7 and variable b must contain the value 5!

Solution

The following program, even though it may seem correct, is erroneous and doesn't really swap the values of variables a and b!

```
a = int(input())
b = int(input())

a = b
b = a

print(a)
print(b)
```

Let's see why! Suppose the user enters two values, 5 and 7. The trace table is shown here.

Step	Statement	Notes	a	b
1	a = int(input())	User enters the value 5	5	?
2	b = int(input())	User enters the value 7	5	7

3	a = b	The value of variable b is assigned to variable a. Value 5 is lost!	7	7
4	b = a	The value of variable a is assigned to variable b	7	7
5	print(a)	It displays: 7		
6	print(b)	It displays: 7		

Oops! Where is the value 5?

The solution wasn't so obvious after all! So, how do you really swap values anyway?

Consider two glasses: a glass of orange juice (called glass A), and a glass of lemon juice (called glass B). If you want to swap their content, all you must do is find and use one extra empty glass (called glass C).

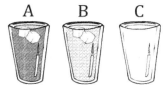

The steps that must be followed are:

1. Empty the contents of glass A (orange juice) into glass C.

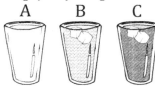

2. Empty the contents of glass B (lemon juice) into glass A.

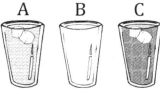

3. Empty the contents of glass C (orange juice) into glass B.

Swapping completed successfully!

You can follow the same steps to swap the contents of two variables in Python.

```python
a = int(input())
b = int(input())

c = a       #Empty the contents of glass A (orange juice) into glass C
a = b       #Empty the contents of glass B (lemon juice) into glass A
b = c       #Empty the contents of glass C (orange juice) into glass B
```

```
print(a)
print(b)
```

✎ *Note the hash characters (#) after each of the three assignment statements. The text after hash characters is considered a comment and is never executed.*

Last but not least, in Python you can also swap the contents of two variables like this:
```
a = int(input())
b = int(input())

a, b = b, a

print(a)
print(b)
```

Exercise 8.1-3   *Swapping Values of Variables – An Alternative Approach*

Write a Python program that lets the user enter two integer values, in variables a *and* b. *In the end, the two variables must swap their values.*

Solution

Since the variables contain only numeric values, you can use the following Python program (as an alternative approach).
```
a = int(input())
b = int(input())

a = a + b
b = a - b
a = a - b

print(a)
print(b)
```

✎ *The disadvantage of this method is that it cannot swap the contents of alphanumeric variables (strings).*

Exercise 8.1-4   *Creating a Trace Table*

Create a trace table to determine the values of the variables in each step of the Python program for three different executions.

The input values for the three executions are: (i) 0.3, (ii) 4.5, and (iii) 10.
```
b = float(input())
c = 3
c = c * b
a = 10 * c % 10

print(a)
```

Solution

    i.   For the input value of 0.3, the trace table looks like this.

Step	Statement	Notes	a	b	c
1	b = float(input())	User enters value 0.3	?	**0.3**	?
2	c = 3		?	0.3	**3**
3	c = c * b		?	0.3	**0.9**
4	a = 10 * c % 10		**9**	0.3	0.9
5	print(a)	It displays: 9			

    ii.   For the input value of 4.5, the trace table looks like this.

Step	Statement	Notes	a	b	c
1	b = float(input())	User enters value 4.5	?	**4.5**	?
2	c = 3		?	4.5	**3**
3	c = c * b		?	4.5	**13.5**
4	a = 10 * c % 10		**5**	4.5	13.5
5	print(a)	It displays: 5			

    iii.   For the input value of 10, the trace table looks like this.

Step	Statement	Notes	a	b	c
1	b = float(input())	User enters value 10	?	**10**	?
2	c = 3		?	10	**3**
3	c = c * b		?	10	**30**
4	a = 10 * c % 10		**0**	10	30
5	print(a)	It displays: 0			

Exercise 8.1-5   Creating a Trace Table

Create a trace table to determine the values of the variables in each step when a value of 3 is entered.

```
a = float(input())

b = a + 10
a = b * (a - 3)
c = 3 * b / 6
d = c * c
d -= 1

print(d)
```

Solution

For the input value of 3, the trace table looks like this.

Step	Statement	Notes	a	b	c	d
1	`a = float(input())`	User enters value 3	**3**	?	?	?
2	`b = a + 10`		3	**13**	?	?
3	`a = b * (a - 3)`		**0**	13	?	?
4	`c = 3 * b / 6`		0	13	**6.5**	?
5	`d = c * c`		0	13	6.5	**42.25**
6	`d -= 1`		0	13	6.5	**41.25**
7	`print(d)`	It displays: 41.25				

8.2   Review Questions: True/False

Choose **true** or **false** for each of the following statements.

1.   A trace table is a technique for testing a computer.

2.   Trace tables help a programmer find errors in a computer program.

3.   You cannot execute a computer program without first creating its corresponding trace table.

4.   In order to swap the values of two integer variables, you always need an extra variable.

8.3   Review Exercises

Complete the following exercises.

1.   Create a trace table to determine the values of the variables in each step of the Python program for three different executions.

The input values for the three executions are: (i) 3, (ii) 4, and (iii) 1.

```python
a = int(input())

a = (a + 1) * (a + 1) + 6 / 3 * 2 + 20
b = a % 13
c = b % 7
d = a * b * c
print(a, ",", b, ",", c, ",", d)
```

2.   Create a trace table to determine the values of the variables in each step of the Python program for two different executions.

The input values for the two executions are: (i) 8, 4; and (ii) 4, 4

```python
a = float(input())
b = float(input())

c = a + b
d = 1 + a / b * c + 2
e = c + d
c += d + e
e -= 1
d -= c + d % c
print(c, ",", d, ",", e)
```

Chapter 9
Using Eclipse

9.1   Creating a New Python Project

So far you have learned some really good basics about Python programs. Now it's time to learn how to enter programs into the computer, execute them, see how they perform, and see how they display the results.

The first thing you must do is create a new Python project. Eclipse provides a wizard to help you do that. Start Eclipse, and from its main menu select "File→New→PyDev Project" as shown in **Figure 9–1**.

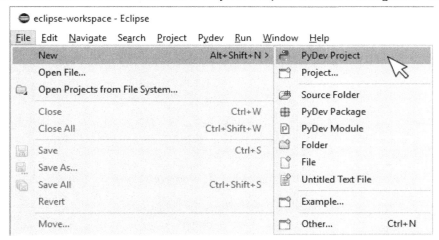

Figure 9–1 Starting a new Python project from Eclipse

If there isn't any such option in your Eclipse, you can alternatively select "File→New→Other" and in the popup window that appears, select the "PyDev Project" wizard as shown in **Figure 9–2**. Then, click on the "Next" button.

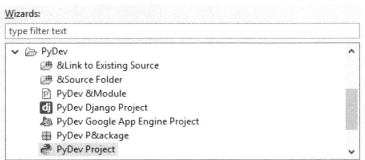

Figure 9–2 Selecting the "PyDev Project" wizard

The "PyDev Project" dialog box appears, allowing you to create a new PyDev Project. In the "Project name" field, type "testingProject" as shown in **Figure 9–3**.

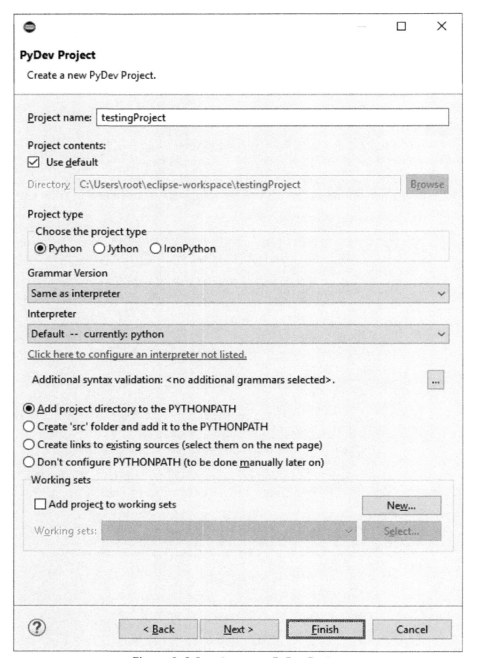

Figure 9–3 Creating a new PyDev Project

✎ *If the error message "Project interpreter not specified" is displayed in the "PyDev Project" dialog box, you must click on the link "Please configure an interpreter before proceeding". Then, in the popup window that appears click on the "Quick Auto-Config" button. If there is no such button, try to click on the "Config first in PATH".*

Click on the "Finish" button. If the popup window of **Figure 9–4** appears, check the field "Remember my decision" and click on the "Open Perspective" button.

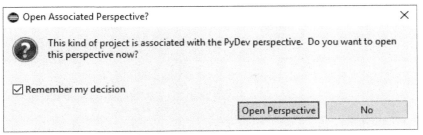

Figure 9–4 Opening Associated Perspective

The project is created in your Eclipse environment. If the "PyDev Package Explorer" window is minimized, click on the "Restore" button (shown in **Figure 9–5**) to restore it.

Figure 9–5 Restoring the "PyDev Package Explorer" window

In the "PyDev Package Explorer" window, select the "testingProject" that you just created and from the main menu select "File→New→PyDev Module". If there is no such option in your Eclipse, you can alternatively select "File→New→Other" and in the popup window that appears, select the "PyDev Module" wizard. Then, click on the "Next" button.

In the popup window that appears (shown in **Figure 9–6**), make sure that the "Source Folder" field contains the value "/testingProject". In the "Name" field, type "test" and click on the "Finish" button.

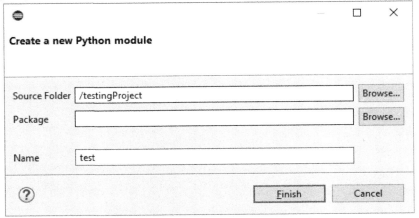

Figure 9–6 Creating a new PyDev module

If the popup window of **Figure 9–7** appears, leave all fields checked and click on the "OK" button.

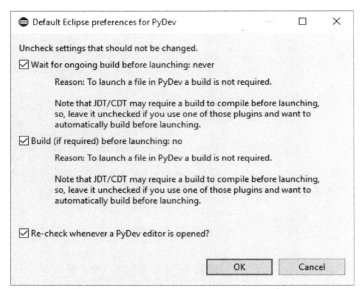

Figure 9–7 Selecting the default Eclipse preferences for PyDev

The next window that appears prompts you to select a template. Since you need no template you can just click on the "Cancel" button.

You should now see the following components (see **Figure 9–8**):

▶ the "PyDev Package Explorer" window, which contains a tree view of the components of the projects, including source files, libraries that your code may depend on, and so on.

▶ the "Source Editor" window with the file called "test.py" open. In this file you can write your Python code. Of course, one single project can contain many such files.

▶ the "Console" window in which Eclipse displays the output results of your Python programs, as well as messages useful for the programmer.

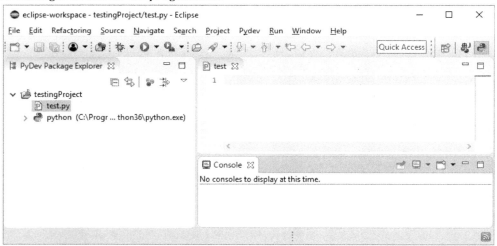

Figure 9–8 Viewing the "Package Explorer", "Source Editor", and "Console" windows in Eclipse

✎ *If the "Console" window is not open, you can open it by selecting "Window→Show View→Console" from the main menu.*

9.2   Writing and Executing a Python Program

You have just seen how to create a new Python project. Now let's write the following (terrifying, and quite horrifying!) Python program and try to execute it.

```python
print("Hello World")
```

In window "test" type only the first letter from the print statement by hitting the "p" key on your keyboard. Automatically, a popup window appears, as shown in **Figure 9–9**. This window contains some of the available Python statements, variables, functions, and other items that begin with the letter "p". Furthermore, by hitting the CTRL + Space key combination, you can get even more options!

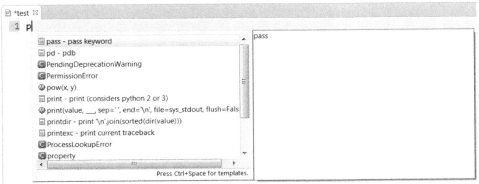

Figure 9–9 The popup screen in the Source Editor window

You can highlight a selection by using the up and down arrow keys on your keyboard. Notice that each time you change a selection, a yellow window displays a small Help document about the item selected.

Type the second character, "r", from the print statement. Now the options have become fewer, as shown here.

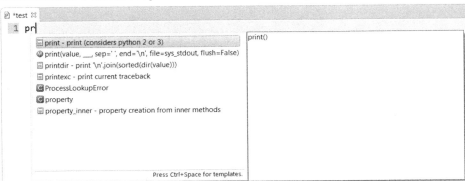

Select the "print – print (considers python 2 or 3)" option and hit the "Enter ↵" key. The statement is automatically entered into your program, as shown in the figure that follows!

Complete the statement by typing "Hello World" inside double quotes. Your Eclipse environment should look like this.

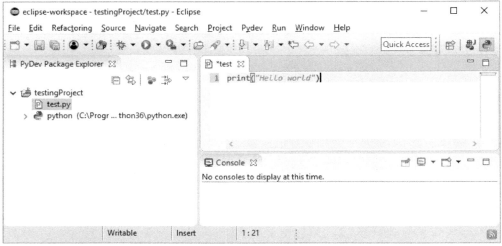

Figure 9–10 Entering a Python program in the "test.py" file

Now let's try to execute the program! From the toolbar, click on the "Run As" ⬤ icon. Alternatively, from the main menu, you can select "Run→Run" or even hit the CTRL + F11 key combination. The Python program executes and the output is displayed in the "Console" window as shown in **Figure 9–11**.

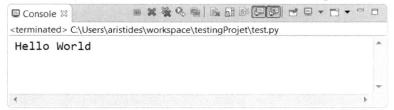

Figure 9–11 Viewing the results of the executed program in the Console window

✎ *If, while you are trying to execute your first program, a popup window asks you to select a way to run 'test.py,' select the "Python Run" option and click on the "OK" button.*

Congratulations! You have just written and executed your first Python program!

Now let's write another Python program, one that prompts the user to enter his or her name. Type the following Python statements into Eclipse and hit CTRL + F11 to execute the file.

📄 **file_9_2**

```
name = input("Enter your name: ")
print("Hello", name)
print("Have a nice day!")
```

🗔 *You can execute a program by clicking on the "Run As" ⬤ toolbar icon, or by selecting "Run→Run" from the main menu, or even by hitting the CTRL + F11 key combination.*

Once you execute the program, the message "Enter your name: " is displayed in the "Console" window. The program waits for you to enter your name, as shown in **Figure 9–12**.

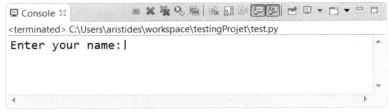

Figure 9–12 Viewing a prompt in the Console window

To enter your name, however, you must place the cursor inside the "Console" window. Then you can type your name and hit the "Enter ↵" key. Once you do that, your computer continues executing the rest of the statements. When execution finishes, the final output is as shown in **Figure 9–13**.

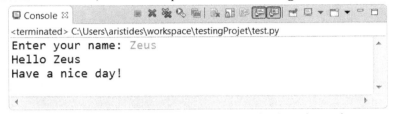

Figure 9–13 Responding to the prompt in the Console window

9.3   What "Debugging" Means

Debugging is the process of finding and reducing the number of defects (bugs) in a computer program, in order to make it perform as expected.

There is a myth about the origin of the term "debugging". In 1940, while Grace Hopper[1] was working on a Mark II Computer at Harvard University, her associates discovered a bug (a moth) stuck in a relay (an electrically operated switch). This bug was blocking the proper operation of the Mark II computer. So, while her associates where trying to remove the bug, Grace Hopper remarked that they were "debugging" the system!

9.4   Debugging Python Programs with Eclipse

As you already know, when someone writes code in a high-level language there are two types of errors that he or she might make—syntax errors and logic errors. Eclipse provides all the necessary tools to help you debug your programs and find the errors.

Debugging syntax errors

Fortunately, Eclipse detects syntax errors while you are typing (or when you are trying to run the project) and underlines them with a wavy red line as shown in **Figure 9–14**.

Figure 9–14 In Eclipse, syntax errors are underlined with a wavy red line

---

[1] Grace Murray Hopper (1906–1992) was an American computer scientist and US Navy admiral. She was one of the first programmers of the Harvard Mark I computer, and developed the first compiler for a computer programming language known as A–0 and later a second one, known as B–0 or FLOW-MATIC.

All you have to do is correct the corresponding error and the red line will disappear at once. However, if you are not certain about what is wrong with your code, you can just place your mouse cursor on the erroneous line. Eclipse will try to help you by showing a popup window with a brief explanation of the error, as shown in **Figure 9–15**.

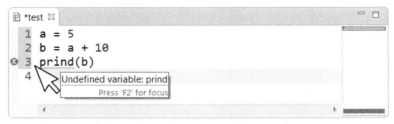

Figure 9–15 The Eclipse shows an explanation of a syntax error

Debugging logic errors by executing programs step by step

Compared to syntax errors, logic errors are more difficult to find. Since the Eclipse cannot spot and underline logic errors, you are all alone! Let's look at the following Python program, for example. It prompts the user to enter two numbers and calculates and displays their sum. However, it contains a logic error!

```
                                    📁 file_9_4a
S = 0
a = float(input("Enter 1st value: "))
b = float(input("Enter 2nd value: "))
s = a + b
print("The sum is:", S)
```

If you type this program into Eclipse, you will notice that there is not even one wavy red line indicating any error. If you run the program, however, and enter two values, 5 and 3, you can see for yourself that even though the sum of 5 and 3 is 8, Eclipse insists that it is zero, as shown in **Figure 9–16**.

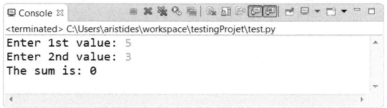

Figure 9–16 Viewing the result of a logic error in the Output window

What the heck is going on? Of course for an expert programmer, correcting this error would be a piece of cake. But for you, a novice one, even though you are trying hard you find nothing wrong. So, where is the error?

Sometimes human eyes get so tired that they cannot see the obvious. So, let's try to use some magic! Let's try to execute the program step by step using the debugger. This gives you the opportunity to observe the flow of execution and take a closer look at the current values of variables in each step.

To open the debugger, you need to open the "Debug" perspective. You can do this by selecting "Window→Perspective→Open Perspective→Other…" from the main menu. In the popup window that appears, select "Debug" and click on the "OK" button. Now, the Eclipse environment changes a little and looks like the one shown in **Figure 9–17**.

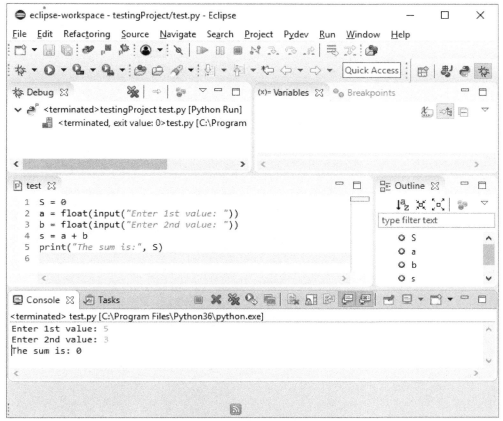
Figure 9–17 The "Debug" Perspective

Place the cursor at the line where the statement S = 0 exists and hit the SHIFT+CTRL+B key combination. A green icon appears in the gray margin as shown in **Figure 9–18**.

```
P test ⊠
● 1 S = 0|
  2 a = float(input("Enter 1st value: "))
  3 b = float(input("Enter 2nd value: "))
  4 s = a + b
  5 print("The sum is:", S)
  6
```
Figure 9–18 Adding a breakpoint in Eclipse

Start the debugger by selecting "Run→Debug" from the main menu or by hitting the F11 key. By doing this, you enable the debugger and more icons are enabled on the toolbar.

The program counter (the blue arrow ⇨ icon in the gray margin) has stopped at the first line of the program as shown in **Figure 9–19**.

```
test ⊠
⚑ 1  S = 0
   2  a = float(input("Enter 1st value: "))
   3  b = float(input("Enter 2nd value: "))
   4  s = a + b
   5  print("The sum is:", S)
   6
```

Figure 9–19 Using the debugger in the Eclipse

✎ *The program counter shows you, at any time, which statement is the next to be executed.*

In this step, the statement S = 0 is not yet executed. Click on the "Step Over" ⟳ toolbar icon or hit the F6 key. Now the statement S = 0 is executed, and the program counter moves to the subsequent Python statement, which is the next to be executed.

In the "Variables" window, you can watch all the variables declared in main memory (RAM) and the value they contain during each step of execution as shown in **Figure 9–20**.

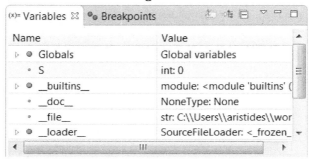

Figure 9–20 Variables and their values are displayed in the Variables window of the debugger

Click on the "Step Over" ⟳ toolbar icon again. The second statement is executed. You can see the output result in the "Console" window (see **Figure 9–21**).

```
Console ⊠   Tasks
test.py
pydev debugger: starting (pid: 4304)
Enter 1st value:



>>>
```

Figure 9–21 Viewing a prompt in the Output window

In this step, the program waits for you to enter a value. Place the cursor inside the "Console" window, type the value 5, and hit the "Enter ↵" key.

The program counter moves to the third Python statement. Click on the "Step Over" ⟳ toolbar icon again. This action executes the third Python statement. Place the cursor inside the "Console" window, type the value 3, and hit the "Enter ↵" key.

The program counter moves to the fourth Python statement. Click on the "Step Over" ⟳ toolbar icon once again. The statement s = a + b is executed. What you expected here was the sum of 5.0 and 3.0, which is 8.0, to be assigned to variable S with a capital S. Instead of this, the value 8.0 is assigned to the variable s, as shown in **Figure 9–22.**

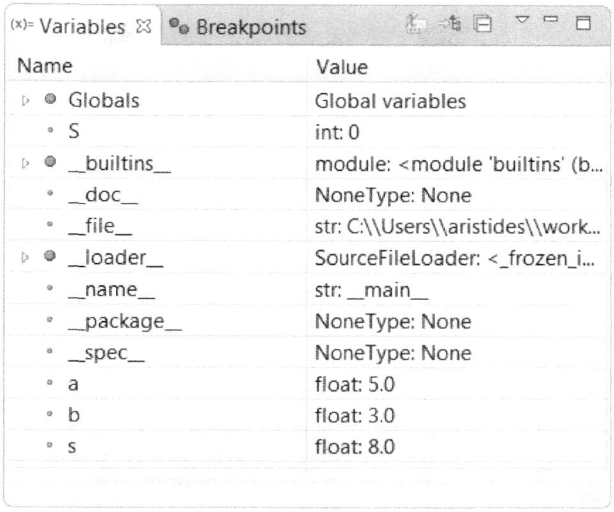

Figure 9–22 All declared variables are displayed in the Locals window of the debugger

Now it becomes more obvious to you! You mistakenly declared two variables in the main memory (RAM), the variable s and the variable S with a capital S. So, when the flow of execution goes to the last statement, print("The sum is:", S) the value 0 instead of the value 8 is displayed.

Congratulations! You have just found the error! Click on the "Terminate" ■ toolbar icon to cancel execution, correct the error by changing variable S to s, and you are ready! You just performed your first debugging! Re-execute the program and you will now see that it calculates and displays the sum correctly.

Debugging logic errors by adding breakpoints

Debugging step by step has a big disadvantage. You have to click on the "Step Over" ☜ toolbar icon again and again until you reach the position where the error might be. Can you imagine yourself doing this in a large program?

For large programs there is another approach. If you suspect that the error is somewhere at the end of the program there is no need to debug all of it right from the beginning. You can add a marker (called a "breakpoint") where you think that the error might be, execute the program and when flow of execution reaches that breakpoint, the flow of execution will pause automatically. You can then take a closer look at the current values of the variables at the position where the program was paused.

✎ *When the program pauses, you have two options for resuming the execution: you can add a second breakpoint somewhere below in the program, click on the "Resume" ▐▶ toolbar icon, and allow the program to continue execution until that new breakpoint; or, you can just use the "Step Over" ☜ toolbar icon and execute the program step by step thereafter.*

The next Python program prompts the user to enter two values and then it calculates their sum, their difference, and their average value.

However, the program contains a logic error. When the user enters the values 10 and 12, the value 16, instead of 11, is displayed as the average.

```
📁 file_9_4b
a = float(input("Enter 1st value: "))
b = float(input("Enter 2nd value: "))
s = a + b
d = a - b
```

```
average = a + b / 2
print("Sum:", s)
print("Difference:", d)
print("Average:", average)
```

You suspect that the problem is somewhere at the end of the program. However, you do not want to debug the entire program, but just the portion in which the error might be. So, let's try to add a breakpoint at the d = a - b statement (see **Figure 9–23**). There are two ways to do this: you can double click in the left gray margin on the corresponding line, or you can place the cursor at the line of interest and hit the SHIFT+CTRL+B key combination.

```
📄 *test ⊠                                              ▭ ◻
  1 a = float(input("Enter 1st value: "))          ┌────────┐
  2 b = float(input("Enter 2nd value: "))          └────────┘
  3 s = a + b
🔎 4 d = a - b|
  5 average = a + b / 2
  6 print("Sum:", s)
  7 print("Difference:", d)
  8 print("Average:", average)
  ◀                                              ▶
```

Figure 9–23 Adding a breakpoint to a program

🖊 *You know that a breakpoint has been set when the green icon 🔎 appears in the gray margin on the corresponding line.*

Make sure that the "Debug" perspective is open and hit F11 to start the debugger. Enter the values 10 and 12 when requested in the output window. You will notice that just after you enter the second number and hit the "Enter ↲" key, the flow of execution pauses at the breakpoint (the corresponding line has green background highlighting it).

📖 *You can debug a program by selecting "Run→Debug" from the main menu or by hitting the F11 key.*

Now you can take a closer look at the current values of the variables. Variables a, b, and s contain the values 10.0, 12.0, and 22 respectively, as they should, so there is nothing wrong so far, as shown in **Figure 9–24**.

```
(x)= Variables ⊠  ⦿ Breakpoints          ⮌ ⬓ ▤   ▽ ▭ ◻

Name                          Value
▷ ⦿ Globals                   Global variables
▷ ⦿ __builtins__              module: <module 'builtins' (b...
  • __doc__                   NoneType: None
  • __file__                  str: C:\\Users\\aristides\\work...
▷ ⦿ __loader__                SourceFileLoader: <_frozen_i...
  • __name__                  str: __main__
  • __package__               NoneType: None
  • __spec__                  NoneType: None
  • a                         float: 10.0
  • b                         float: 12.0
  • s                         float: 22.0
```

Figure 9–24 Viewing the current values of the variables in the Variables window

Click on the "Step Over" ⟳ toolbar icon once. The statement d = a - b executes and variables a, b, s and d contain the values 10.0, 12.0, 22.0, and −2.0 respectively, as they should, so there is still nothing wrong so far, as shown in **Figure 9–25.**

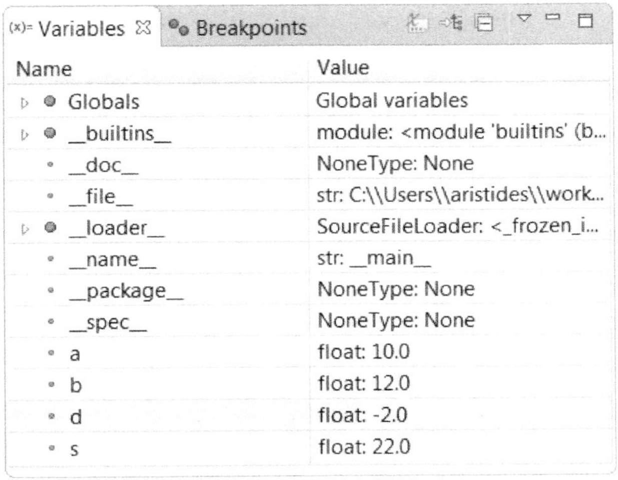

Figure 9–25 Viewing the current values of the variables in the Variables window

Click on the "Step Over" ⟳ toolbar icon once again. The statement average = a + b / 2 executes and variables a, b, s, d, and average contain the values 10.0, 12.0, 22, −2, and 16 respectively, as shown in **Figure 9–26.**

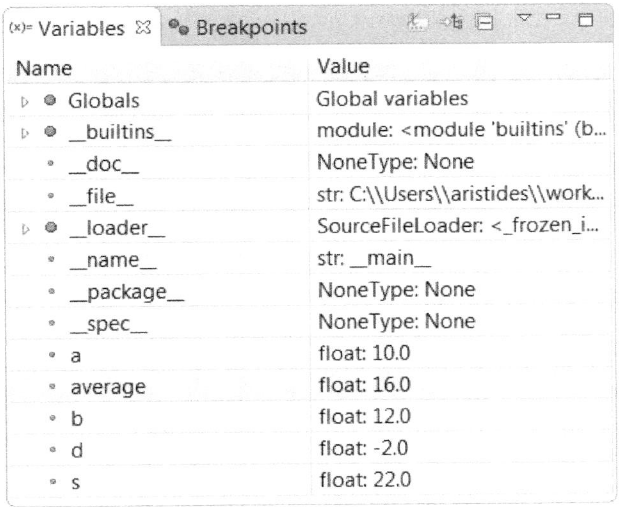

Figure 9–26 Viewing the current values of the variables in the Variables window

There it is! You just found the statement that erroneously assigns a value of 16.0, instead of 11.0, to the variable average! And now comes the difficult part; you should consider why this happens!

After two full days of thinking, it becomes obvious! You had just forgotten to enclose a + b inside parentheses; thus, only the variable b was divided by 2. Click on the "Terminate" ■ toolbar icon, remove all breakpoints, correct the error by enclosing a + b inside parentheses and you are ready! Re-execute the program and see now that it calculates and displays the average value correctly.

✎ *You can remove a breakpoint the same way you added it: double click in the left gray margin on the corresponding line number, or place the cursor at the line that contains a breakpoint and hit the SHIFT+CTRL+B key combination.*

9.5   Review Exercises

Complete the following exercises.

1. Type the following Python program into Eclipse and execute it step by step. Determine why it doesn't calculate correctly the sum of 1 + 3 + 5.

```
SS = 0
S1 = 1
S3 = 3
S5 = 5
S = S1 + S3 + SS
print(S)
```

2. Create a trace table to determine the values of the variables in each step of the Python program for two different executions. Then, type the program in the Eclipse, execute it step by step, and confirm the results.

    The input values for the two executions are: (i) 5, 5; and (ii) 4, 8.

```
a = float(input())
b = float(input())
c = a + b
d = 5 + a / b * c + 2
e = c - d
c += d + c
e -= 1
d += c + a / b
print(c, ",", d, ",", e)
```

3. Create a trace table to determine the values of the variables in each step of the Python program for three different executions. Then, type the program in the Eclipse, execute it step by step, and confirm the results.

    The input values for the three executions are: (i) 0.50, (ii) 3, and (iii) 15.

```
b = float(input())
c = 5
c = c * b
a = 10 * c / 2
print(a)
```

Review in "Getting Started with Python"

Review Crossword Puzzles

1. Solve the following crossword puzzle.

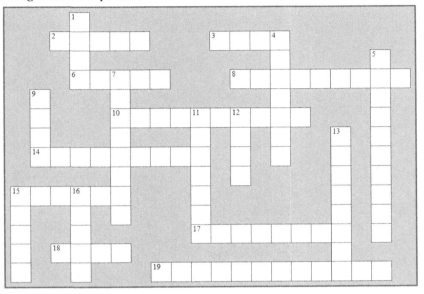

Across

2. These errors are hard to detect.
3. A control structure.
6. It shows the flow of execution in a flowchart.
8. A graphical method of presenting an algorithm.
10. _____ programming is a software development method that uses modularization and structured design.
14. Strictly defined finite sequence of well-defined statements that provides the solution to a problem.
15. The term _____ means that the algorithm must reach an end point and cannot run forever.
17. This flowchart symbol has one entrance and two exits.
18. Logic errors and runtime errors are commonly referred to as _____.
19. It must be possible to perform each step of the algorithm correctly and in a finite amount of time. This is one of the properties an algorithm must satisfy, and it is known as _____.

Down

1. The principle that best defines user-friendly designs.
4. This represents a mathematical (formula) calculation in a flowchart.
5. Data _____ is one of the three main stages involved in creating an algorithm.
7. A word that has a strictly predefined meaning in a computer language.
9. A programming language.
11. Statement.
12. He or she uses a program.

13. A control structure.

15. Real.

16. One of the properties an algorithm must satisfy.

2. Solve the following crossword puzzle.

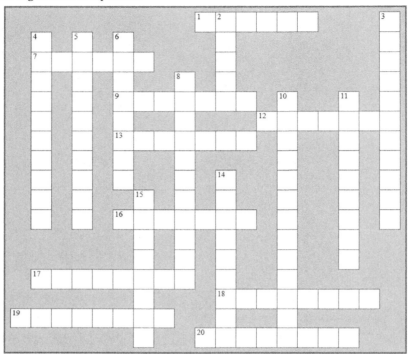

Across

1. An alphanumeric value.

7. A misspelled keyword is a _____ error.

9. A positive or negative number without any fractional part.

12. Extra information that can be included in a program to make it easier to read and understand.

13. It can hold only one of two values.

16. An error that occurs during the execution of a program.

17. This control structure is also known as a selection control structure.

18. This is a CPU-time consuming arithmetic operation.

19. A value that cannot change while the program is running.

20. A user-_____ program is one that is easy for a novice user.

Down

2. A _____ table is a technique used to test algorithms or computer programs for logic errors that occur while the algorithm or program executes.

3. Any arithmetic operations enclosed in _____ are performed first.

4. The left arrow in flowcharts is called the value _____ operator.

5. The only symbol character permitted in a variable name.

6. It represents a location in the computer's main memory (RAM) where a program can store a value.

8. The process of reserving a portion in main memory (RAM) for storing the contents of a variable.

10. Joining two separate strings into a single one.

11. The process of finding and reducing the number of logic errors in a computer program.

14. The modulus operator returns the _____ of an integer division.

15. The operator (//) returns the _____ of an integer division.

Review Questions

Answer the following questions.

1. What is an algorithm?

2. Give the algorithm for making a cup of coffee.

3. What are the five properties of algorithms?

4. Can an algorithm execute forever?

5. What is a computer program?

6. What are the three parties involved in an algorithm?

7. What are the three stages that make up a computer program?

8. Can a computer program be made up of two stages?

9. What is a flowchart?

10. What are the basic symbols that flowcharts use?

11. What is meant by the term "reserved words"?

12. What is structured programming?

13. What are the three fundamental control structures of structured programming?

14. Give an example of each control structure using flowcharts.

15. Can a programmer write Python programs in a text editor?

16. What is a syntax error? Give one example.

17. What is a logic error? Give one example.

18. What is a runtime error? Give one example.

19. What type of error is caused by a misspelled keyword?

20. Why should a programmer add comments in his or her code?

21. Why should a programmer write user-friendly programs?

22. What does the acronym POLA stand for?

23. What is a variable?

24. How many variables can exist on the left side of the left arrow in flowcharts?

25. In which part of a computer are the values of the variables stored?

26. What is a constant?

27. How can constants be used to help programmers?

28. Why should a programmer avoid division and multiplication operations whenever possible?

29. What are the four fundamental types of variables in Python?

30. What does the phrase "declare a variable" mean?

31. How do you declare a variable in Python? Give an example.

32. What symbol is used in flowcharts to display a message?

33. What special sequence of characters is used in Python to output a "line break"?

34. Which symbol is used in flowcharts to let the user enter data?

35. Which symbol is used in Python as a value assignment operator, and how is it represented in a flowchart?

36. Which arithmetic operators does Python support?

37. What is a modulus operator?

38. Summarize the rules for the precedence of arithmetic operators.

39. What compound assignment operators does Python support?

40. What string operators does Python support?

41. What is a trace table?

42. What are the benefits of using a trace table?

43. Describe the steps involved in swapping the contents (either numeric or alphanumeric) of two variables.

44. Three methods for swapping the values of two variables have been proposed in this book. Which one is better, and why?

45. What does the term "debugging" mean?

46. Describe the way in which Eclipse helps you find syntax errors.

47. Describe the ways in which Eclipse helps you find logic errors.

Section 3
Sequence Control Structures

Chapter 10
Introduction to Sequence Control Structures

10.1 What is the Sequence Control Structure?

Sequence control structure refers to the line-by-line execution by which statements are executed sequentially, in the same order in which they appear in the program, without skipping any of them. They might, for example, carry out a series of read or write operations, arithmetic operations, or assignments to variables.

The following program shows an example of Python statements that are executed sequentially.

```
                               📁 file_10_1
#Prompt the user to enter value for num
num = int(input("Enter a number: "))

#Calculate the square of num
result = num ** 2

#Display the result on user's screen
print("The square of", num, "is", result)
```

✎ *The sequence control structure is the simplest of the three fundamental control structures that you learned about in paragraph 4.11. The other two structures are "decision structure" and "loop structure". All problems in computer programming can be solved using only these three structures!*

⌨ *In Python, you can add comments using the hash character (#). Comments are for human readers. Compilers and interpreters ignore them.*

Exercise 10.1-1   Calculating the Area of a Rectangle

Write a Python program that prompts the user to enter the length of the base and the height of a rectangle, and then calculates and displays its area.

Solution

You probably know from school that you can calculate the area of a rectangle using the following formula:

$$Area = Base \times Height$$

In paragraph 4.6, you learned about the three main stages involved in creating an algorithm: data input, data processing, and results output.

In this exercise, these three main stages are as follows:

▶ **Data input** - the user must enter values for *Base* and *Height*

▶ **Data processing** - the program must calculate the area of the rectangle

▶ **Results output** – the program must display the area of the rectangle calculated in previous stage

The solution to this problem is shown here.

```
                               📁 file_10_1_1
#Data input - Prompt the user to enter values for base and height
base = float(input("Enter the length of Base: "))
```

```
height = float(input("Enter the length of Height: "))


#Data processing - Calculate the area of the rectangle
area = base * height


#Results output - Display the result on user's screen
print("The area of the rectangle is", area)
```

Exercise 10.1-2   *Calculating the Area of a Circle*

Write a Python program that calculates and displays the area of a circle.

Solution

You can calculate the area of a circle using the following formula:

$$Area = \pi \cdot Radius^2$$

The value of π is a known quantity, which is 3.14159. Therefore, the only value the user must enter is the value for *Radius*.

In this exercise, the three main stages that you learned in paragraph 4.6 are as follows:

▶   **Data input** - the user must enter a value for *Radius*

▶   **Data processing** - the program must calculate the area of the circle

▶   **Results output** – the program must display the area of the circle calculated in previous stage.

The solution to this problem is shown here.

```
                          📁 file_10_1_2a
#Data input - Prompt the user to enter a value for radius
radius = float(input("Enter the length of Radius: "))


#Data processing - Calculate the area of the circle
area = 3.14159 * radius ** 2


#Results output - Display the result on user's screen
print("The area of the circle is", area)
```

A much better approach would be with to use a constant, PI.

```
                          📁 file_10_1_2b
PI = 3.14159


#Data input - Prompt the user to enter a value for radius
radius = float(input("Enter the length of Radius: "))


#Data processing - Calculate the area of the circle
area = PI * radius ** 2


#Results output - Display the result on user's screen
print("The area of the circle is", area)
```

💬 *The exponentiation operation has a higher precedence and is performed before the multiplication operation.*

Exercise 10.1-3   *Calculating Fuel Economy*

In the United States, a car's fuel economy is measured in miles per gallon, or MPG. A car's MPG can be calculated using the following formula:

$$MPG = \frac{miles\ driven}{gallons\ of\ gas\ used}$$

Write a Python program that prompts the user to enter the total number of miles he or she has driven and the gallons of gas used. Then the program must calculate and display the car's MPG.

Solution

This is quite a simple case. The user enters the total number of miles he or she has driven and the gallons of gas used, and then the program must calculate and display the car's MPG.

```
                         📁 file_10_1_3
miles_driven = float(input("Enter miles driven: "))
gallons = float(input("Enter gallons of gas used: "))


mpg = miles_driven / gallons


print("Your car's MPG is:", mpg)
```

Exercise 10.1-4   *Where is the Car? Calculating Distance Traveled*

A car starts from rest and moves with a constant acceleration along a straight horizontal road for a given time. Write a Python program that prompts the user to enter the acceleration and the time the car traveled, and then calculates and displays the distance traveled. The required formula is

$$S = u_o + \frac{1}{2}at^2$$

where

- ▶   *S* is the distance the car traveled, in meters (m)
- ▶ u_o is the initial velocity (speed) of the car, in meters per second (m/sec)
- ▶   *t* is the time the car traveled, in seconds (sec)
- ▶   *a* is the acceleration, in meters per second² (m/sec²)

Solution

Since the car starts from rest, the initial velocity (speed) u_0 is zero. Thus, the formula becomes

$$S = \frac{1}{2}at^2$$

and the Python program is

```
                         📁 file_10_1_4
a = float(input("Enter acceleration: "))
t = float(input("Enter time traveled: "))


S = 0.5 * a * t ** 2


print("Your car traveled", S, "meters")
```

> 📖 *The exponentiation operation has a higher precedence and is performed before the multiplication operations.*

Exercise 10.1-5   Kelvin to Fahrenheit

Write a Python program that converts a temperature value from degrees Fahrenheit[1] to its degrees Kelvin[2] equivalent. The required formula is

$$1.8 \times Kelvin = Fahrenheit + 459.67$$

Solution

The formula given cannot be used in your program as is. In a computer language such as Python, it is **not** permitted to write

```
1.8 * kelvin = fahrenheit + 459.67
```

> 📖 *In the position on the left side of the (=) sign, only a variable may exist. This variable is actually a region in RAM where a value can be stored.*

The program converts degrees Fahrenheit to degrees Kelvin. The value for degrees Fahrenheit is a known value and it is given by the user, whereas the value for degrees Kelvin is what the Python program must calculate. So, you need to solve for Kelvin. After a bit of work, the formula becomes

$$Kelvin = \frac{Fahrenheit + 459.67}{1.8}$$

and the Python program is shown here.

```
📄 file_10_1_5
fahrenheit = float(input("Enter a temperature in Fahrenheit: "))

kelvin = (fahrenheit + 459.67) / 1.8

print("The temperature in Kelvin is", kelvin)
```

Exercise 10.1-6   Calculating Sales Tax

An employee needs a program to enter the before-tax price of a product and calculate its final price. Assume a value added tax (VAT) of 19%.

Solution

The sales tax can be easily calculated. You must multiply the before-tax price of the product by the sales tax rate. Be careful—the sales tax is not the final price, but only the tax amount.

The after-tax price can be calculated by adding the initial before-tax price and the sales tax that you calculated beforehand.

---

[1] Daniel Gabriel Fahrenheit (1686–1736) was a German physicist, engineer, and glass blower who is best known for inventing both the alcohol and the mercury thermometers, and for developing the temperature scale now named after him.

[2] William Thomson, 1st Baron Kelvin (1824–1907), was an Irish-born British mathematical physicist and engineer. He is widely known for developing the basis of absolute zero (the Kelvin temperature scale), and for this reason a unit of temperature measure is named after him. He discovered the Thomson effect in thermoelectricity and helped develop the second law of thermodynamics.

In this program you can use a constant named VAT for the sales tax rate.

```
□ file_10_1_6
VAT = 0.19

price_before_tax = float(input("Enter the before-tax price: "))

sales_tax = price_before_tax * VAT
price_after_tax = price_before_tax + sales_tax

print("The after-tax price is:", price_after_tax)
```

Exercise 10.1-7   Calculating a Sales Discount

Write a Python program that prompts the user to enter the price of an item and the discount offered as a percentage (on a scale of 0 to 100). The program must then calculate and display the new price.

Solution

The discount amount can be easily calculated. You must multiply the before-discount price of the product by the discount value and then divide it by 100. The division is necessary since the user enters a value for the discount on a scale of 0 to 100. Be careful—the result is not the final price but only the discount amount.

The final after-discount price can be calculated by subtracting the discount amount that you calculated beforehand from the initial before-discount price.

```
□ file_10_1_7
price_before_discount = float(input("Enter the price of a product: "))

discount = int(input("Enter the discount offered (0 - 100): "))

discount_amount = price_before_discount * discount / 100
price_after_discount = price_before_discount - discount_amount

print("The price after discount is:", price_after_discount)
```

Exercise 10.1-8   Calculating the Sales Tax Rate and Discount

Write a Python program that prompts the user to enter the before-tax price of an item and the discount offered as a percentage (on a scale of 0 to 100). The program must then calculate and display the new price. Assume a sales tax rate of 19%.

Solution

This exercise is just a combination of the previous two exercises!

```
□ file_10_1_8
VAT = 0.19

price_before_discount = float(input("Enter the price of a product: "))
discount = int(input("Enter the discount offered (0 - 100): "))

discount_amount = price_before_discount * discount / 100
```

```
price_after_discount = price_before_discount - discount_amount

sales_tax = price_after_discount * VAT
price_after_tax = price_after_discount + sales_tax

print("The discounted after-tax price is:", price_after_tax)
```

10.2   Review Exercises

Complete the following exercises.

1. Write a Python program that prompts the user to enter values for base and height, and then calculates and displays the area of a triangle.

2. Write a Python program that prompts the user to enter two angles of a triangle, and then calculates and displays the third angle.

   Hint: The sum of the measures of the interior angles of any triangle is 180 degrees

3. Write a Python program that lets a student enter his or her grades from four tests, and then calculates and displays the average grade.

4. Write a Python program that prompts the user to enter a value for radius, and then calculates and displays the perimeter of a circle. The required formula is

   $$Perimeter = 2\pi R$$

5. Write a Python program that prompts the user to enter a value for diameter in meters, and then calculates and displays the volume of a sphere. The required formula is

   $$V = \frac{4}{3}\pi R^3$$

   where R is the radius of the sphere.

6. Regarding the previous exercise, which of the following results output statements are correct? Which one would you choose to display the volume of the sphere on the user's screen, and why?

   a. `print V`

   b. `print V cubic meters`

   c. `print V, cubic meters`

   d. `print "The volume of the sphere is:" V`

   e. `print "The volume of the sphere is:", V`

   f. `print "The volume of the sphere is:", V, cubic meters`

   g. `print "The volume of the sphere is:", V, "cubic meters"`

7. Write a Python program that prompts the user to enter a value for diameter, and then calculates and displays the radius, the perimeter, and the area of a circle. For the same diameter, it must also display the volume of a sphere.

8. Write a Python program that prompts the user to enter the charge for a meal in a restaurant, and then calculates and displays the amount of a 10% tip, 7% sales tax, and the total of all three amounts.

9. A car starts from rest and moves with a constant acceleration along a straight horizontal road for a given time in seconds. Write a Python program that prompts the user to enter the acceleration (in m/sec^2) and the time traveled (in sec) and then calculates the distance traveled. The required formula is

   $$S = u_o + \frac{1}{2}at^2$$

10. Write a Python program that prompts the user to enter a temperature in degrees Fahrenheit, and then converts it into its degrees Celsius[3] equivalent. The required formula is
$$\frac{C}{5} = \frac{F - 32}{9}$$

11. The Body Mass Index (BMI) is often used to determine whether a person is overweight or underweight for his or her height. The formula used to calculate the BMI is
$$BMI = \frac{weight \cdot 703}{height^2}$$
Write a Python program that prompts the user to enter his or her weight (in pounds) and height (in inches), and then calculates and displays the user's BMI.

12. Write a Python program that prompts the user to enter the subtotal and gratuity rate (on a scale of 0 to 100) and then calculates the tip and total. For example if the user enters 30 and 10, the Python program must display "Tip is $3.00 and Total is $33.00".

13. An employee needs a program to enter the before-tax price of three products and then calculate the final after-tax price of each product, as well as their average value. Assume a value added tax (VAT) of 20%.

14. An employee needs a program to enter the after-tax price of a product, and then calculate its before-tax price. Assume a value added tax (VAT) of 20%.

15. Write a Python program that prompts the user to enter the initial price of an item and the discount offered as a percentage (on a scale of 0 to 100), and then calculates and displays the final price and the amount of money saved.

16. Write a Python program that prompts the user to enter the electric meter reading in kilowatt-hours (kWh) at the beginning and end of a month. The program must calculate and display the amount of kWh consumed and the amount of money that must be paid given a cost of each kWh of $0.06 and a value added tax (VAT) of 20%.

17. Write a Python program that prompts the user to enter two numbers, which correspond to current month and current day of the month, and then calculates the number of days until the end of the year. Assume that each month has 30 days.

---

[3] Anders Celsius (1701–1744) was a Swedish astronomer, physicist, and mathematician. He founded the Uppsala Astronomical Observatory in Sweden and proposed the Celsius temperature scale, which takes his name.

Chapter 11
Manipulating Numbers

11.1 Introduction

Just like every high-level programming language, Python provides many ready-to-use functions and methods (called *subprograms*) that you can use whenever and wherever you wish.

> ✎ A "subprogram" is simply a group of statements packaged as a single unit. Each subprogram has a descriptive name and performs a specific task.

To better understand functions and methods, let's take Heron's[1] iterative formula that calculates the square root of a positive number.

$$x_{n+1} = \frac{\left(x_n + \frac{y}{x_n}\right)}{2}$$

where

- ► *y* is the number for which you want to find the square root
- ► x_n is the *n*-th iteration value of the square root of *y*

Hey, don't get disappointed! No one at the present time calculates the square root of a number this way. Fortunately, Python includes a method for that purpose! This method, which is actually a small subprogram, has been given the name sqrt and the only thing you have to do is call it by its name and it will do the job for you. Method sqrt probably uses Heron's iterative formula, or perhaps a formula of another ancient or modern mathematician. The truth is that you don't really care! What really matters is that sqrt gives you the right result! An example is shown here.

```python
import math

x = float(input())
y = math.sqrt(x)
print(y)
```

> ✎ The method sqrt() is not accessible directly in Python, so you need to import math module.

> ✎ A "module" in Python is nothing more than a file that contains many ready-to-use functions (or methods). Python incorporates quite a lot such modules, but, if you wish to use a function or a method included in one of those modules, you need to import that module into your program.

Even though Python supports many mathematical functions (and methods), this chapter covers only those absolutely necessary for this book's purpose. However, if you need even more information you can visit

https://docs.python.org/3.7/library/math.html

---

[1] Heron of Alexandria (c. 10–c. 70 AD) was an ancient Greek mathematician, physicist, astronomer, and engineer. He is considered the greatest experimenter of ancient times. He described the first recorded steam turbine engine, called an "aeolipile" (sometimes called a "Hero engine"). Heron also described a method of iteratively calculating the square root of a positive number. Today, though, he is known best for the proof of "Heron's Formula" which finds the area of a triangle from its side lengths.

✎ *Mathematical functions are used whenever you need to calculate a square root, the sine, the cosine, an absolute value, and so on.*

11.2 Useful Mathematical Functions (Subprograms), and More

Absolute value

```
abs(number)
```

This function returns the absolute value of *number*.

Example

file_11_2a

```
a = -5
b = abs(a)

print(abs(a))          #It displays: 5
print(b)               #It displays: 5
print(abs(-5.2))       #It displays: 5.2
print(abs(5.2))        #It displays: 5.2
```

Pi

```
math.pi
```

This returns the value of π.

Example

file_11_2b

```
import math

print(math.pi)     #It displays: 3.141592653589793
```

✎ *Note that* pi *is neither a function nor a method. Therefore, you must not put parentheses at the end.*

✎ pi *is defined in module* math. *It is not accessible directly in Python, so you need to import the* math *module.*

Sine

```
math.sin(number)
```

This method returns the sine of *number*. The value of *number* must be expressed in radians. You can multiply by math.pi/180 to convert degrees to radians.

Example

file_11_2c

```
import math

a = math.sin(3 * math.pi / 2)        #Sine of 3π/2 radians
b = math.sin(270 * math.pi / 180)    #Sine of 270 degrees

print(a, b)                          #It displays: -1.0  -1.0
```

✎ *The method* sin() *is defined in module* math. *It is not accessible directly in Python, so you need to import the* math *module.*

Cosine

```
math.cos(number)
```

This method returns the cosine of *number*. The value of *number* must be expressed in radians. You can multiply by math.pi/180 to convert degrees to radians.

Example

> **📁 file_11_2d**

```
import math

a = math.cos(2 * math.pi)         #Cosine of 2π radians
b = math.cos(360 * math.pi / 180) #Cosine of 360 degrees

print(a, b)                       #It displays: 1.0  1.0
```

✎ *The method* cos() *is defined in module* math. *It is not accessible directly in Python, so you need to import the* math *module.*

Tangent

```
math.tan(number)
```

This method returns the tangent of *number*. The value of *number* must be expressed in radians. You can multiply by math.pi/180 to convert degrees to radians.

Example

> **📁 file_11_2e**

```
import math

a = math.tan(10 * math.pi / 180) #Tangent of 10 degrees
print(a)                         #It displays: 0.176326980708
```

✎ *The method* tan() *is defined in module* math. *It is not accessible directly in Python, so you need to import the* math *module.*

Quotient and remainder of integer division

```
divmod(number1, number2)
```

This function returns two values, and these are:

▶ the quotient of the integer division of *number1* and *number2*; and

▶ the remainder of the integer division of *number1* and *number2*

Example

> **📁 file_11_2f**

```
c, d = divmod(13, 4)

print(c, d, sep = ", ")    #It displays: 3, 1
```

✎ *It is possible in Python for a function or a method to return two or more values.*

Integer value

```
int(value)
```

This function returns the integer portion of *value*. It can also be used to convert a string representation of an integer to its numeric equivalent.

Example

```
                                        📁 file_11_2g
a = 5.4

print(int(a))              #It displays: 5
print(int(34))             #It displays: 34
print(int(34.9))           #It displays: 34
print(int(-34.999))        #It displays: -34


b = "15"
c = "3"
print(b + c)               #It displays: 153
print(int(b) + int(c))     #It displays: 18
```

Real value

> **float**(*value*)

This function converts a string representation of a real to its numeric equivalent. It can also be used to convert an integer to a real (float).

Example

```
                                        📁 file_11_2h
a = "5.2"
b = "2.4"

print(a + b)                      #It displays: 5.22.4
print(float(a) + float(b))        #It displays: 7.6

print(float(7))                   #It displays: 7.0
```

Maximum value

> **max**(*sequence*)
> **max**(*value1, value2, value3, … *)

This function returns the largest value of *sequence*, or the largest of two or more arguments.

Example

```
                                        📁 file_11_2i
print(max(5, 3, 2, 6, 7, 1, 5))     #It displays: 7

a = 5
b = 6
c = 3
d = 4
y = max(a, b, c, d)
print(y)                            #It displays: 6

seq = [2, 8, 4, 6, 2]               #This is a sequence of integers
```

```
print(max(seq))                         #It displays: 8
```

Minimum value

```
min(sequence)
min(value1, value2, value3, … )
```

This function returns the smallest value of *sequence,* or the smallest of two or more arguments.

Example

```
                        📁 file_11_2j
print(min(5, 3, 2, 6, 7, 1, 5))    #It displays: 1


a = 5
b = 6
c = 3
d = 4
y = min(a, b, c, d)
print(y)                           #It displays: 3

seq = [2, 8, 4, 6, 2]              #This is a sequence of integers
print(min(seq))                    #It displays: 2
```

Range

```
range( [initial_value,] final_value [, step] )
```

This function returns a sequence of integers between *initial_value* and *final_value* - *1.* The argument *initial_value* is optional. If omitted, its default value is 0. The argument *step* is the difference between each number in the sequence. This argument is also optional. This argument is also optional. If omitted, its default value is 1.

✎ *Note that* initial_value, final_value, *and* step *must be integers. Negative values are also permitted!*

Example

```
                        📁 file_11_2k
#Assign sequence [1, 2, 3, 4, 5] to x
x = range(1, 6)

#Assign sequence [0, 1, 2, 3, 4, 5] to y
y = range(6)

#Assign sequence [0, 10, 20, 30, 40] to w
w = range(0, 50, 10)

#Assign sequence [100, 95, 90, 85] to z
z = range(100, 80, -5)
```

Random

```
random.randrange( [minimum_value,] maximum_value [, step] )
```

This function returns a random integer from a given range. The parameters of randrange() follow the same logic as those of function range().

Example

```
📁 file_11_21
import random

#Display a random integer between 10 and 100
print(random.randrange(10, 101))

#Assign a random integer between 0 and 10 to variable y and display it
y = random.randrange(11)
print(y)

#Display a random integer between -20 and 20
print(random.randrange(-20, 21))

#Display a random odd integer between 1 and 99
print(random.randrange(1, 99, 2))

#Display a random even integer between 0 and 100
print(random.randrange(0, 100, 2))
```

✎ *Random numbers are widely used in computer games. For example, an "enemy" may show up at a random time or move in random directions. Also, random numbers are used in simulation programs, in statistical programs, in computer security to encrypt data, and so on.*

✎ *The method* randrange() *is defined in module* random. *It is not accessible directly in Python, so you need to import the* random *module.*

Round

| round(*number*)

This function returns the closest integer of *number*.

Example

```
📁 file_11_2m
a = 5.9
print(round(a))               #It displays: 6
print(round(5.4))             #It displays: 5
```

If you need the rounded value of *number* to a specified *precision*, you can use the following formula:

$$round(number * 10 ** precision) / 10 ** precision$$

Example

```
📁 file_11_2n
a = 5.312
y = round(a * 10 ** 2) / 10 ** 2
print(y)                      #It displays: 5.31

a = 5.315
y = round(a * 10 ** 2) / 10 ** 2
```

```
print(y)                              #It displays: 5.32

print(round(2.3447 * 1000) / 1000)   #It displays: 2.345
```

Square root

```
math.sqrt(number)
```

This method returns the square root of *number*.

Example

```
                          file_11_2o
import math

print(math.sqrt(9))             #It displays: 3.0
print(math.sqrt(2))             #It displays: 1.4142135623730951
```

✎ *The method* sqrt() *is defined in module* math. *It is not accessible directly in Python, so you need to import the* math *module.*

Sum

```
math.fsum(sequence)
```

This method returns the sum of the elements of *sequence*.

Example

```
                          file_11_2p
import math

seq = [5.5, 6.3, 2]            #Assign a sequence of numbers to seq
print(math.fsum(seq))          #It displays: 13.8
```

✎ *The method* fsum() *is defined in module* math. *It is not accessible directly in Python, so you need to import the* math *module.*

Exercise 11.2-1   *Calculating the Distance Between Two Points*

Write a Python program that prompts the user to enter the coordinates (x, y) of two points and then calculates the straight line distance between them. The required formula is

$$d = \sqrt{(x_1 - x_2)^2 + (y_1 - y_2)^2}$$

Solution

In this exercise, you need to use the method sqrt(), which returns the square root of a number.

To simplify things, the terms $(x_1 - x_2)^2$ and $(y_1 - y_2)^2$ are calculated individually and the results are assigned to two temporary variables.

The Python program is shown here.

```
                          file_11_2_1a
import math

print("Enter coordinates for point A: ")
```

```
x1, y1 = float(input()), float(input())

print("Enter coordinates for point B: ")
x2, y2 = float(input()), float(input())

x_temp = (x1 - x2) ** 2
y_temp = (y1 - y2) ** 2

d = math.sqrt(x_temp + y_temp)

print("Distance between points:", d)
```

Now let's see another approach.

You should realize that it is actually possible to perform an operation within a function (or a method) call. Doing that, the result of the operation is used as an argument for the function or the method. This is a writing style that most programmers prefer to follow because it can save a lot of code lines.

The Python program is shown here.

📁 **file_11_2_1b**

```
import math

print("Enter coordinates for point A: ")
x1, y1 = float(input()), float(input())

print("Enter coordinates for point B: ")
x2, y2 = float(input()), float(input())

d = math.sqrt((x1 - x2) ** 2 + (y1 - y2) ** 2)

print("Distance between points:", d)
```

Exercise 11.2-2   How Far Did the Car Travel?

A car starts from rest and moves with a constant acceleration along a straight horizontal road for a given distance. Write a Python program that prompts the user to enter the acceleration and the distance the car traveled and then calculates the time traveled. The required formula is

$$S = u_o + \frac{1}{2}at^2$$

where

- ▶ ***S*** *is the distance the car traveled, in meters (m)*
- ▶ ***u_o*** *is the initial velocity (speed) of the car, in meters per second (m/sec)*
- ▶ ***t*** *is the time the car traveled, in seconds (sec)*
- ▶ ***a*** *is the acceleration, in meters per second^2 (m/sec^2)*

Solution

Since the car starts from rest, the initial velocity (speed) u_0 is zero. Thus, the formula becomes

$$S = \frac{1}{2}at^2$$

Now, if you solve for time, the final formula becomes

$$t = \sqrt{\frac{2S}{a}}$$

In Python, you can use the `sqrt()` method, which returns the square root of a number.

```
📁 file_11_2_2
import math

a = float(input("Enter acceleration: "))
S = float(input("Enter distance traveled: "))

t = math.sqrt(2 * S / a)

print("Your car traveled for", t, "seconds")
```

11.3 Review Questions: True/False

Choose **true** or **false** for each of the following statements.

1. In general, functions are small subprograms that solve small problems.

2. Every programmer must use Heron's iterative formula to calculate the square root of a positive number.

3. The `abs()` function returns the absolute position of an item.

4. The statement `int(3.59)` returns a result of 3.6.

5. The `math.pi` constant is equal to 3.14.

6. The statement `2 ** 3` returns a result of 9.

7. The `randrange()` method can return negative random numbers.

8. There is a 50% possibility that the statement `y = random.randrange(0, 2)` will assign a value of 1 to variable `y`.

9. The statement `round(3.59)` returns a result of 4.

10. To calculate the sine of 90 degrees, you have to write `y = math.sin(math.pi / 2)`

11. The statement `y = math.sqrt(-2)` is valid.

12. The following code fragment satisfies the property of definiteness.

```
import math

a, b = float(input()), float(input())
x = a * math.sqrt(b)
print(x)
```

11.4 Review Questions: Multiple Choice

Select the correct answer for each of the following statements.

1. Which of the following calculates the result of the variable `a` raised to the power of 2?

    a. `y = a * a`

    b. `y = a ** 2`

    c. `y = a * a / a * a`

d. all of the above

2. What is the value of the variable y when the statement y = abs(+5.2) is executed?

   a. −5.2

   b. −5

   c. 0.2

   d. 5.2

   e. none of the above

3. Which of the following calculates the sine of 180 degrees?

   a. `math.sin(180)`

   b. `math.sin(math.pi)`

   c. all of the above

   d. none of the above

4. What is the value of the variable y when the statement y = int(5 / 2) is executed?

   a. 2.5

   b. 3

   c. 2

   d. 0.5

5. What is the value of the variable y when the statement y = math.sqrt(4) ** 2 is executed?

   a. 4

   b. 2

   c. 8

   d. 16

6. What is the value of the variable y when the statement y = round(5.2) / 2 is executed?

   a. 2

   b. 2.5

   c. 2.6

   d. none of the above

11.5 Review Exercises

Complete the following exercises.

1. Create a trace table to determine the values of the variables in each step of the Python program for two different executions.

   The input values for the two executions are: (i) 9, and (ii) 4.

```python
import math

a = float(input())

a += 6 / math.sqrt(a) * 2 + 20
b = round(a) % 4
c = b % 3

print(a, ",", b, ",", c)
```

2. Create a trace table to determine the values of the variables in each step of the Python program for two different executions.

The input values for the two executions are: (i) −2, and (ii) −3

```python
a = int(input())


b = abs(a) % 4 + a ** 4
c = b % 5


print(b, ",", c)
```

3. Write a Python that prompts the user to enter an angle θ in radians and then calculates and displays the angle in degrees. It is given that $2\pi = 360°$.

4. Write a Python program that prompts the user to enter the two right angle sides A and B of a right-angled triangle and then calculates its hypotenuse. It is known from the Pythagorean[2] theorem that

$$hypotenuse = \sqrt{A^2 + B^2}$$

5. Write a Python program that prompts the user to enter the angle θ (in degrees) of a right-angled triangle and the length of its adjacent side, and then calculates the length of the opposite side. It is known that

$$\tan(\theta) = \frac{Opposite}{Adjacent}$$

---

[2] Pythagoras of Samos (c. 571–c. 497 BC) was a famous Greek mathematician, philosopher, and astronomer. He is best known for the proof of the important Pythagorean theorem. He was an influence for Plato. His theories are still used in mathematics today.

Chapter 12
Complex Mathematical Expressions

12.1 Writing Complex Mathematical Expressions

In paragraph 7.2 you learned all about arithmetic operators but little about how to use them and how to write your own complex mathematical expressions. In this chapter, you are going to learn how easy is to convert mathematical expressions to Python statements.

📑 *Arithmetic operators follow the same precedence rules as in mathematics, which means that exponentiation is performed first, multiplication and division are performed next, and addition and subtraction are performed last. Moreover, when multiplication and division co-exist in the same expression, and since both are of the same precedence, these operations are performed left to right.*

Exercise 12.1-1   Representing Mathematical Expressions in Python

Which of the following Python statements correctly represent the following mathematical expression?

$$x = \frac{1}{10 + z} 27$$

i.	`x = 1 * 27 / 10 + z`	*v.*	`x = (1 / 10 + z) * 27`
ii.	`x = 1 · 27 / (10 + z)`	*vi.*	`x = 1 / ((10 + z) * 27)`
iii.	`x = 27 / 10 + z`	*vii.*	`x = 1 / (10 + z) * 27`
iv.	`x = 27 / (10 + z)`	*viii.*	`x = 1 / (10 + z) / 27`

Solution

i. **Wrong.** Since the multiplication and the division are performed before the addition, this is equivalent to $x = \frac{1 \cdot 27}{10} + z$.

ii. **Wrong.** An asterisk must have been used for multiplication.

iii. **Wrong.** Since the division is performed before the addition, this is equivalent to $x = \frac{27}{10} + z$.

iv. **Correct.** This is equivalent to $x = \frac{27}{10 + z}$.

v. **Wrong.** Inside parentheses, the division is performed before the addition. This is equivalent to $x = \left(\frac{1}{10} + z\right) 27$.

vi. **Wrong.** Parentheses are executed first and this is equivalent to $x = \frac{1}{(10+z)27}$

vii. **Correct.** Division is performed before multiplication (left to right). The term $\frac{1}{10+z}$ is calculated first and then, the result is multiplied by 27.

viii. **Wrong.** This is equivalent to $x = \frac{\frac{1}{10+z}}{27}$

Exercise 12.1-2   *Writing a Mathematical Expression in Python*

Write a Python program that calculates the mathematical expression

$$y = 10\,x - \frac{10 - z}{4}$$

Solution

First, you must distinguish between the data input and the output result. Obviously, the output result is assigned to y and the user must enter values for x and z. The solution for this exercise is shown here.

```
                                    📄 file_12_1_2
x = float(input("Enter value for x: "))
z = float(input("Enter value for z: "))


y = 10 * x - (10 - z) / 4


print("The result is:", y)
```

Exercise 12.1-3   *Writing a Complex Mathematical Expression in Python*

Write a Python program that calculates the mathematical expression

$$y = \frac{5\dfrac{3x^2 + 5x + 2}{7w - \dfrac{1}{z}} - z}{4\dfrac{3 + x}{7}}$$

Solution

Oops! Now the expression is more complex! In fact, it is much more complex! So, let's take a look at a quite different approach. The main idea is to break the complex expression into smaller, simpler expressions and assign each sub-result to temporary variables. In the end, you can build the original expression out of all these temporary variables! This approach is presented next.

```
                                    📄 file_12_1_3a
x = float(input("Enter value for x: "))
w = float(input("Enter value for w: "))
z = float(input("Enter value for z: "))


temp1 = 3 * x ** 2 + 5 * x + 2
temp2 = 7 * w - 1 / z
temp3 = (3 + x) / 7
nominator = 5 * temp1 / temp2 - z
denominator = 4 * temp3


y = nominator / denominator
print("The result is:", y)
```

You may say, "*Okay, but I wasted so many variables and as everybody knows, each variable is a portion of main memory. How can I write the original expression in one single line and waste less memory?*"

This job may be a piece of cake for an advanced programmer, but what about you? What about a novice programmer?

The next method will help you write even the most complex mathematical expressions without any syntax or logic errors! The rule is very simple. *"After breaking the complex expression into smaller, simpler expressions and assigning each sub-result to temporary variables, start backwards and replace each variable with its assigned expression. Be careful though! When you replace a variable with an expression, you must always enclose the expression in parentheses!"*

Confused? Don't be! It's easier in action. Let's try to rewrite the previous Python program. Starting backwards, replace variables `nominator` and `denominator` with their assigned expressions. The result is

```
y = (5 * temp1 / temp2 - z) / (4 * temp3)
        └──────────┬──────────┘   └────┬────┘
             nominator            denominator
```

✎ *Note the extra parentheses added.*

Now you must replace variables `temp1`, `temp2`, and `temp3` with their assigned expressions, and the one-line expression is complete!

```
y = (5 * (3 * x ** 2 + 5 * x + 2) / (7 * w - 1 / z) - z) / (4 * ((3 + x) / 7))
         └──────────┬──────────┘    └──────┬──────┘           └──────┬──────┘
               temp1                     temp2                     temp3
```

It may look scary at the end but it wasn't that difficult, was it?

The Python program can now be rewritten

```
📄 file_12_1_3b
```

```python
x = float(input("Enter value for x: "))
w = float(input("Enter value for w: "))
z = float(input("Enter value for z: "))

y = (5 * (3 * x ** 2 + 5 * x + 2) / (7 * w - 1 / z) - z) / (4 * ((3 + x) / 7))

print("The result is:", y)
```

12.2 Review Exercises

Complete the following exercises.

1. Match each element from the first table with one **or more** elements from the second table.

Expression		Expression	
i.	`5 / x ** 2 * y + x ** 3`	a.	`5 * y / x ** 2 + x ** 3`
ii.	`5 / (x ** 3 * y) + x ** 2`	b.	`5 * y / x * x + x ** 3`
		c.	`5 / (x * x * x * y) + x * x`
		d.	`5 / (x * x * x) * y + x * x`
		e.	`5 * y / (x * x) + x * x * x`
		f.	`1 / (x * x * x * y) * 5 + x * x`
		g.	`y / (x * x) * 5 + x ** 3`
		h.	`1 / (x * x) * 5 * y + x / 1 * x * x`

2. Write the following mathematical expressions in Python using one line of code for each.

    i. $y = \dfrac{(x+3)^{5w}}{7(x-4)}$

    ii. $y = \sqrt[5]{\left(3x^2 - \dfrac{1}{4}x^3\right)}$

    iii. $y = \dfrac{\sqrt{x^4 - 2x^3 - 7x^2 + x}}{\sqrt[3]{4\left(7x^4 - \frac{3}{4}x^3\right)(7x^2 + x)}}$

    iv. $y = \dfrac{x}{x-3(x-1)} + \left(x\sqrt[5]{x} - 1\right)\dfrac{1}{(x^3-2)(x-1)^3}$

    v. $y = \left(\sin\left(\dfrac{\pi}{3}\right) - \cos\left(\dfrac{\pi}{2}w\right)\right)^2$

    vi. $y = \dfrac{\left(\sin\left(\frac{\pi}{2}x\right) + \cos\left(\frac{3\pi}{2}w\right)\right)^3}{\left(\tan\left(\frac{2\pi}{3}w\right) - \sin\left(\frac{\pi}{2}x\right)\right)^{\frac{1}{2}}} + 6$

3. Write a Python program that prompts the user to enter a value for x and then calculates and displays the result of the following mathematical expression.

    $$y = \sqrt{x}(x^3 + x^2)$$

4. Write a Python program that prompts the user to enter a value for x and then calculates and displays the result of the following mathematical expression.

    $$y = \dfrac{7x}{2x + 4(x^2 + 4)}$$

    Suggestion: Try to write the expression in one line of code.

5. Write a Python program that prompts the user to enter a value for x and w and then calculates and displays the result of the following mathematical expression.

    $$y = \dfrac{x^{x+1}}{\left(\tan\left(\frac{2w}{3} + 5\right) - \tan\left(\frac{x}{2} + 1\right)\right)^3}$$

    Suggestion: Try to write the expression in one line of code

6. Write a Python program that prompts the user to enter a value for x and w and then calculates and displays the result of the following mathematical expression.

    $$y = \dfrac{3 + w}{6x - 7(x + 4)} + \left(x\sqrt[5]{3w + 1}\right)\dfrac{5x + 4}{(x^3 + 3)(x - 1)^7}$$

    Suggestion: Try to write the expression in one line of code.

7. Write a Python program that prompts the user to enter a value for x and w and then calculates and displays the result of the following mathematical expression.

    $$y = \dfrac{x^x}{\left(\sin\left(\frac{2w}{3} + 5\right) - x\right)^2} + \dfrac{(\sin(3x) + w)^{x+1}}{\left(\sqrt{7w}\right)^{\frac{3}{2}}}$$

    Suggestion: Try to write the expression in one line of code

8. Write a Python program that prompts the user to enter the lengths of all three sides A, B, and C, of a triangle and then calculates and displays the area of the triangle. You can use Heron's formula, which has been known for nearly 2,000 years!

    $$Area = \sqrt{S(S - A)(S - B)(S - C)}$$

    where S is the semi-perimeter $S = \dfrac{A+B+C}{2}$

Chapter 13
Exercises With a Quotient and a Remainder

13.1 Introduction

What types of problems might require the use of the quotient and the remainder of an integer division? There is no simple answer to that question! However, quotients and remainders can be used to:

- ▶ split a number into individual digits
- ▶ examine if a number is odd or even
- ▶ convert an elapsed time (in seconds) to hours, minutes, and seconds
- ▶ convert an amount of money (in USD) to a number of $100 notes, $50 notes, $20 notes, and such
- ▶ calculate the greatest common divisor
- ▶ determine if a number is a palindrome
- ▶ count the number of digits within a number
- ▶ determine how many times a specific digit occurs within a number

Of course, these are some of the uses and certainly you can find so many others. Next you will see some exercises that make use of the quotient and the remainder of integer division.

Exercise 13.1-1   Calculating the Quotient and Remainder of Integer Division

Write a Python program that prompts the user to enter two integers and then calculates the quotient and the remainder of the integer division.

Solution

You can use the (//) and the (%) operators of Python. The former performs an integer division and returns the integer quotient whereas the latter performs an integer division and returns the integer remainder. The solution is presented here.

```
📁 file_13_1_1a
number1 = int(input("Enter first number: "))
number2 = int(input("Enter second number: "))


q = number1 // number2
r = number1 % number2


print("Integer Quotient:", q, "\nInteger Remainder:", r)
```

✎ *In flowcharts, in order to calculate the quotient and the remainder of an integer division, you can use the popular* DIV *and* MOD *operators. An example is shown here.*

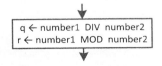

q ← number1 DIV number2
r ← number1 MOD number2

A more "Pythonic" way is to use the divmod() function as shown here.

```
file_13_1_1b
number1 = int(input("Enter first number: "))
number2 = int(input("Enter second number: "))

q, r = divmod(number1, number2)

print("Integer Quotient:", q, "\nInteger Remainder:", r)
```

Exercise 13.1-2   *Finding the Sum of Digits*

Write a Python program that prompts the user to enter a four-digit integer and then calculates the sum of its digits.

Solution

What you should keep in mind here is that statements like this one

```
number = int(input("Enter a four-digit integer: "))
```

assign the given four-digit integer to one single variable, number, and not to four individual variables. So, after the user enters the four-digit integer, the program must split the integer into its four digits and assign each digit to a separate variable. Then it can calculate the sum of these four variables and get the required result. There are two approaches available.

First Approach

Let's try to understand the first approach using an arithmetic example. Take the number 6753, for example.

First digit = 6	The first digit can be isolated if you divide the given number by 1000 using the (//) operator to get the integer quotient `digit1 = 6753 // 1000`
Remaining digits = 753	The remaining digits can be isolated if you divide the given number by 1000 again, this time using the (%) operator to get the integer remainder `r = 6753 % 1000`
Second digit = 7	The second digit can be isolated if you divide the remaining digits by 100 using the (//) operator to get the integer quotient `digit2 = 753 // 100`
Remaining digits = 53	The remaining digits are now `r = 753 % 100`
Third digit = 5	The third digit can be isolated if you divide the remaining digits by 10 using the (//) operator to get the integer quotient `digit3 = 53 // 10`
Fourth digit = 3	The last remaining digit, which happens to be the fourth digit, is `digit4 = 53 % 10`

The Python program that solves this algorithm is shown here.

```
file_13_1_2a
number = int(input("Enter a four-digit integer: "))
```

```
digit1 = number // 1000
r = number % 1000

digit2 = r // 100
r = r % 100

digit3 = r // 10
digit4 = r % 10

total = digit1 + digit2 + digit3 + digit4
print(total)
```

The trace table for the program that you have just seen is shown here.

Step	Statement	Notes	number	digit1	digit2	digit3	digit4	r	total
1	number = int(input("Enter …	User enters 6753	**6753**	?	?	?	?	?	?
2	digit1 = number // 1000		6753	**6**	?	?	?	?	?
3	r = number % 1000		6753	6	?	?	?	**753**	?
4	digit2 = r // 100		6753	6	**7**	?	?	753	?
5	r = r % 100		6753	6	7	?	?	**53**	?
6	digit3 = r // 10		6753	6	7	**5**	?	53	?
7	digit4 = r % 10		6753	6	7	5	**3**	53	?
8	total = digit1 + digit2 + digit3 + digit4		6753	6	7	5	3	53	**21**
9	print(total)	It displays: 21							

To further help you, there is also a general purpose Python program that can be used to split any given integer. Since the length of your program depends on the number of digits, N, all you have to do is write N-1 pairs of statements.

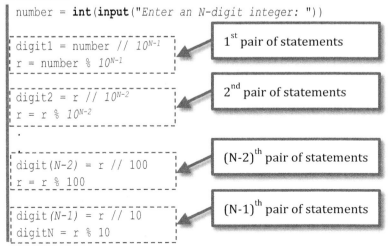

```
number = int(input("Enter an N-digit integer: "))

digit1 = number // 10^{N-1}       1st pair of statements
r = number % 10^{N-1}

digit2 = r // 10^{N-2}            2nd pair of statements
r = r % 10^{N-2}
        .

digit(N-2) = r // 100            (N-2)th pair of statements
r = r % 100

digit(N-1) = r // 10             (N-1)th pair of statements
digitN = r % 10
```

For example, if you want to split a six-digit integer, you need to write five pairs of statements as shown in the program that follows.

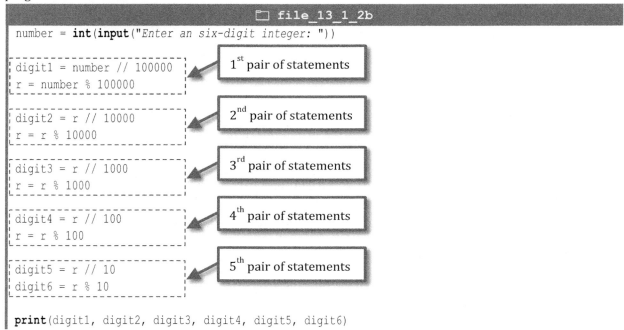

```
                              📁 file_13_1_2b
number = int(input("Enter an six-digit integer: "))

digit1 = number // 100000        1st pair of statements
r = number % 100000

digit2 = r // 10000              2nd pair of statements
r = r % 10000

digit3 = r // 1000              3rd pair of statements
r = r % 1000

digit4 = r // 100               4th pair of statements
r = r % 100

digit5 = r // 10                5th pair of statements
digit6 = r % 10

print(digit1, digit2, digit3, digit4, digit5, digit6)
```

This approach, however, can be refined a little using the divmod() function.

```
                              📁 file_13_1_2c
number = int(input("Enter an six-digit integer: "))

digit1, r = divmod(number, 100000)
digit2, r = divmod(r, 10000)
digit3, r = divmod(r, 1000)
digit4, r = divmod(r, 100)
digit5, digit6 = divmod(r, 10)
print(digit1, digit2, digit3, digit4, digit5, digit6)
```

Second Approach

Once more, let's try to understand the second approach using an arithmetic example. Take the same number, 6753, for example.

Fourth digit = 3	The fourth digit can be isolated if you divide the given number by 10 using the (%) operator to get the integer remainder digit4 = 6753 % 10
Remaining digits = 675	The remaining digits can be isolated if you divide the given number by 10 again, this time using the (//) operator to get the integer quotient r = 6753 // 10
Third digit = 5	The third digit can be isolated if you divide the remaining digits by 10 using the (%) operator to get the integer remainder digit3 = 675 % 10

Remaining digits = 67	The remaining digits are now r = 675 // 10
Second digit = 7	The second digit can be isolated if you divide the remaining digits by 10 using the (%) operator to get the integer remainder digit2 = 67 % 10
First digit = 6	The last remaining digit, which happens to be the first digit, is digit1 = 67 // 10

The Python program for this algorithm is shown here.

```
📁 file_13_1_2d
number = int(input("Enter a four-digit integer: "))

digit4 = number % 10
r = number // 10

digit3 = r % 10
r = r // 10

digit2 = r % 10
digit1 = r // 10

total = digit1 + digit2 + digit3 + digit4
print(total)
```

To further help you, there is also a general purpose Python program that can be used to split any given integer. This program uses the second approach. Once again, since the length of your program depends on the number of the digits, N, all you have to do is write N-1 pairs of statements.

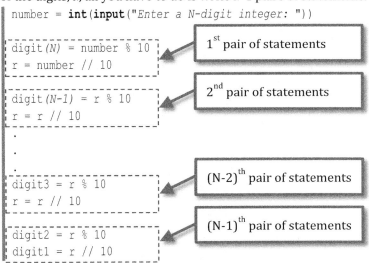

```
number = int(input("Enter a N-digit integer: "))

digit(N) = number % 10      1ˢᵗ pair of statements
r = number // 10

digit(N-1) = r % 10         2ⁿᵈ pair of statements
r = r // 10
        .
        .
        .
digit3 = r % 10             (N-2)ᵗʰ pair of statements
r = r // 10

digit2 = r % 10             (N-1)ᵗʰ pair of statements
digit1 = r // 10
```

For example, if you want to split a five-digit integer, you must use four pairs of statements as shown in the program that follows.

```
📁 file_13_1_2e
number = int(input("Enter a five-digit integer: "))
```

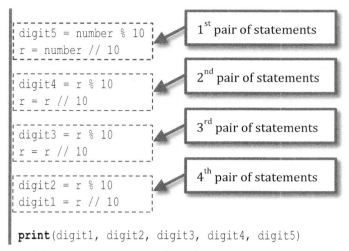

```
print(digit1, digit2, digit3, digit4, digit5)
```

As with the previous example, this approach can be refined a little, using the divmod() function.

```
□ file_13_1_2f
number = int(input("Enter an five-digit integer: "))

r, digit5 = divmod(number, 10)
r, digit4 = divmod(r, 10)
r, digit3 = divmod(r, 10)
digit1, digit2 = divmod(r, 10)

print(digit1, digit2, digit3, digit4, digit5)
```

Exercise 13.1-3   *Displaying an Elapsed Time*

Write a Python program that prompts the user to enter an integer that represents an elapsed time in seconds and then displays it in the format "DD days HH hours MM minutes and SS seconds". For example if the user enters the number 700005, the message "8 days 2 hours 26 minutes and 45 seconds" must be displayed.

Solution

Let's try to analyze the number 700005 using the first approach that you learned in the previous exercise.

As you may already know, there are 60 seconds in a minute, 3600 seconds in an hour (60 × 60), and 86400 seconds in a day (3600 × 24).

Days = 8	The number of days can be isolated if you divide the given integer by 86400 using the (//) operator to get the integer quotient days = 700005 // 86400
Remaining seconds = 8805	The remaining seconds can be isolated if you divide the given integer by 86400 again, this time using the (%) operator to get the integer remainder r = 700005 % 86400
Hours = 2	The number of hours can be isolated if you divide the remaining seconds by 3600 using the (//) operator to get the integer quotient hours = 8805 // 3600

Remaining seconds = 1605	The remaining seconds are now $$r = 8805 \% 3600$$
Minutes = 26	The number of minutes can be isolated if you divide the remaining seconds by 60 using the (//) operator to get the integer quotient $$minutes = 1605 // 60$$
Seconds = 45	The last remainder, which happens to be the number of seconds left, is $$seconds = 1605 \% 60$$

The Python program for this algorithm is as follows.

```
file_13_1_3a
number = int(input("Enter a period of time in seconds: "))

days, r = divmod(number, 86400)    # 60 * 60 * 24 = 86400
hours, r = divmod(r, 3600)         # 60 * 60 = 3600
minutes, seconds = divmod(r, 60)

print(days, "days", hours, "hours ")
print(minutes, "minutes and", seconds, "seconds")
```

You can also solve this exercise using the second approach from the previous exercises. All you have to do is first divide by 60, then divide again by 60, and finally divide by 24, as shown here.

```
file_13_1_3b
number = int(input("Enter a period of time in seconds: "))

r, seconds = divmod(number, 60)
r, minutes = divmod(r, 60)
days, hours = divmod(r, 24)

print(days, "days", hours, "hours ")
print(minutes, "minutes and", seconds, "seconds")
```

Exercise 13.1-4   Reversing a Number

Write a Python program that prompts the user to enter a three-digit integer and then reverses it. For example, if the user enters the number 375, the number 573 must be displayed.

Solution

To isolate the three digits of the given number, you can use either first or second approach. Afterward, the only difficulty in this exercise is to build the reversed number. Take the number 375, for example. The three digits, after isolation, are

```
digit1 = 3
digit2 = 7
digit3 = 5
```

You can build the reversed number by simply calculating the sum of the products:

$$digit3 \times 100 + digit2 \times 10 + digit1 \times 1$$

For a change, you can split the given number using the second approach. The Python program will look like this.

```
📄 file_13_1_4
number = int(input("Enter a three-digit integer: "))

digit3 = number % 10     #This is the rightmost digit
r = number // 10

digit2 = r % 10          #This is the digit in the middle
digit1 = r // 10         #This is the leftmost digit


reversed_number = digit3 * 100 + digit2 * 10 + digit1
print(reversed_number)
```

13.2 Review Exercises

Complete the following exercises.

1. Write a Python program that prompts the user to enter any integer and then multiplies its last digit by 8 and displays the result.

   Hint: It is not necessary to know the exact number of digits. You can isolate the last digit of any integer using a modulus 10 operation.

2. Write a Python program that prompts the user to enter a five-digit integer and then reverses it. For example, if the user enters the number 32675, the number 57623 must be displayed.

3. Write a Python program that prompts the user to enter an integer and then it displays 1 when the number is odd; otherwise, it displays 0. Try not to use any decision control structures since you haven't learned anything about them yet!

4. Write a Python program that prompts the user to enter an integer and then it displays 1 when the number is even; otherwise, it displays 0. Try not to use any decision control structures since you haven't learned anything about them yet!

5. Write a Python program that prompts the user to enter an integer representing an elapsed time in seconds and then displays it in the format "WW weeks DD days HH hours MM minutes and SS seconds". For example, if the user enters the number 2000000, the message "3 week(s) 2 day(s) 3 hour(s) 33 minute(s) and 20 second(s)" must be displayed.

6. Inside an ATM bank machine there are notes of $20, $10, $5, and $1. Write a Python program that prompts the user to enter the amount of money he or she wants to withdraw (using an integer value) and then displays the least number of notes the ATM must give. For example, if the user enters an amount of $76, the program must display the message "3 note(s) of $20, 1 note(s) of $10, 1 note(s) of $5, and 1 note(s) of $1".

7. A robot arrives on the moon in order to perform some experiments. Each of the robot's steps is 25 inches long. Write a Python program that prompts the user to enter the number of steps the robot made and then calculates and displays the distance traveled in miles, feet, yards, and inches. For example, if the distance traveled is 100000 inches, the program must display the message "1 mile, 1017 yards, 2 feet, and 4 inches".

   It is given that

   ▶ 1 mile = 63360 inches
   ▶ 1 yard = 36 inches
   ▶ 1 foot = 12 inches

Chapter 14
Manipulating Strings

14.1 Introduction

Generally speaking, a string is anything that you can type using the keyboard, including letters, symbols (such as &, *, and @), and digits. Sometimes a program deals with data that comes in the form of strings (text). In Python, a string is always enclosed in single or double quotes.

Each statement in the next example outputs a string.

```
a = "Everything enclosed in double quotes is a string, even the numbers:"
b = "3, 54, 731"
print(a, b)
print("You can even mix letters, symbols and digits like this:")
print("The result of 3 + 4 equals to 4")
```

Many times programs deal with data that comes in the form of strings. Strings are everywhere—from word processors, to web browsers, to text messaging programs. Many exercises in this book actually make extensive use of strings. Even though Python supports many useful functions and methods for manipulating strings, this chapter covers only those functions and methods that are necessary for this book's purpose. However, if you need even more information you can visit

https://docs.python.org/3.7/library/stdtypes.html#string-methods

✎ *Python string functions and methods can be used when there is a need, for example, to isolate a number of characters from a string, to remove spaces that might exist at the beginning of it, or to convert all of its characters to uppercase.*

▯ *Functions and methods are nothing more than small subprograms that solve small problems.*

14.2 The Position of a Character in a String

Let's use the text «Hello World» in the following example. The string consists of 11 characters (including the space character between the two words). The position of each character is shown here.

0	1	2	3	4	5	6	7	8	9	10
H	e	l	l	o		W	o	r	l	d

Python numerates characters assuming that the first one is at position 0, the second one is at position 1, and so on.

▯ *A space is a character just like any other character. Just because nobody can see it, it doesn't mean it doesn't exist!*

14.3 Useful String Functions (Subprograms), and More

Trimming

Trimming is the process of removing whitespace characters from the beginning or the end of a string.

Some of the whitespace characters that are removed with the trimming process are:

▶ an ordinary space

▶ a tab

▶　a new line (line feed)

▶　a carriage return

For example, you can trim any spaces that the user mistakenly entered at the end or at the beginning of a string.

The method that you can use to trim a string is

```
subject.strip()
```

This method returns a copy of *subject* in which any whitespace characters are removed from both the beginning and the end of the *subject* string.

Example

```
                                    file_14_3a
a = "       Hello       "
b = a.strip()

print(b, "Poseidon!")     #It displays: Hello Poseidon!
print(a, "Poseidon!")     #It displays:       Hello       Poseidon!
```

✎ *Note that the content of variable* a *is not altered. If you do need to alter its content, you can use the statement*
a = a.strip()

String replacement

```
subject.replace(search, replace)
```

This method searches in *subject* and returns a copy of it in which all occurrences of the *search* string are replaced with the *replace* string.

Example

```
                                    file_14_3b
a = "I am newbie in Java. Java rocks!"
b = a.replace("Java", "Python")

print(b)              #It displays: I am newbie in Python. Python rocks
print(a)              #It displays: I am newbie in Java. Java rocks
```

✎ *Note that the content of variable* a *is not altered. If you do need to alter its content, you can use the statement*
a = a.replace("Java", "Python")

Counting the number of characters

```
len(subject)
```

This function returns the length of *subject* or, in other words, the number of characters *subject* consists of (including space characters, symbols, numbers, and so on).

Example

```
                                    file_14_3c
a = "Hello Olympians!"
print(len(a))             #It displays: 16

b = "I am newbie in Python"
k = len(b)
```

```
print(k)                #It displays: 21
```

Finding string position

```
subject.find(search)
```

This method finds the numerical position of the first occurrence of *search* in *subject*.

Example

```
                            📁 file_14_3d
a = "I am newbie in Python. Python rocks!"

i = a.find("newbie")

print(i)                #It displays: 5
print(a.find("Python")) #It displays: 15
print(a.find("Java"))   #It displays: -1
```

💾 *The first character is at position 0.*

Converting to lowercase

```
subject.lower()
```

This method returns a copy of *subject* in which all the letters of the string *subject* are converted to lowercase.

Example

```
                            📁 file_14_3e
a = "My NaMe is JohN"
b = a.lower()

print(b)                #It displays: my name is john
print(a)                #It displays: My NaMe is JohN
```

✎ *Note that the content of variable* a *is not altered. If you do need to alter its content, you can use the statement*
```
a = a.lower()
```

Converting to uppercase

```
subject.upper()
```

This method returns a copy of *subject* in which all the letters of the string *subject* are converted to uppercase.

Example

```
                            📁 file_14_3f
a = "My NaMe is JohN"
b = a.upper()

print(b)                #It displays: MY NAME IS JOHN
print(a)                #It displays: My NaMe is JohN
```

✎ *Note that the content of variable* a *is not altered. If you do need to alter its content, you can use the statement*
```
a = a.upper()
```

Example

```
□ file_14_3g

a = "I am newbie in Java. Java rocks!"
b = a.replace("Java", "Python").upper()

print(b)              #It displays: I AM NEWBIE IN PYTHON. PYTHON ROCKS
```

✎ *Note how the method* replace() *is chained to the method* upper(). *The result of the first method is used as a subject for the second method. This is a writing style that most programmers prefer to follow because it helps to save a lot of code lines. Of course you can chain as many methods as you wish, but if you chain too many of them, no one will be able to understand your code.*

Retrieving an individual character from a string

| subject[index]

This returns the character located at *subject*'s specified *index*. As already mentioned, the string indexes start from zero. You can use index 0 to access the first character, index 1 to access the second character, and so on. The index of the last character is 1 less than the length of the string.

✎ *The notation* subject[index] *is called "substring notation". The substring notation lets you refer to individual characters within a string.*

Example

```
□ file_14_3h

a = "Hello World"

print(a[0])          #It displays: H (the first letter)
print(a[6])          #It displays: W
print(a[10])         #It displays: d (the last letter)
```

✎ *Note that the space between the words "Hello" and "World" is considered a character as well. So, the letter W exists in position 6 and not in position 5.*

If you want to start counting from the end of the string (instead of the beginning) you can use negative indexes. For example, an index of −1 refers to the right-most character.

In the text «Hello World», the position (using negative indexes) of each character is shown here.

−11	−10	−9	−8	−7	−6	−5	−4	−3	−2	−1
H	e	l	l	o		W	o	r	l	d

An example is shown here.

```
□ file_14_3i

a = "Hello World"

print(a[-1])         #It displays: d (the last letter)
print(a[-3])         #It displays: r
print(a[-11])        #It displays: H (the first letter)
```

If you attempt to use an invalid index such as an index greater than the length of the string, Python throws an error message as shown in **Figure 14–1**.

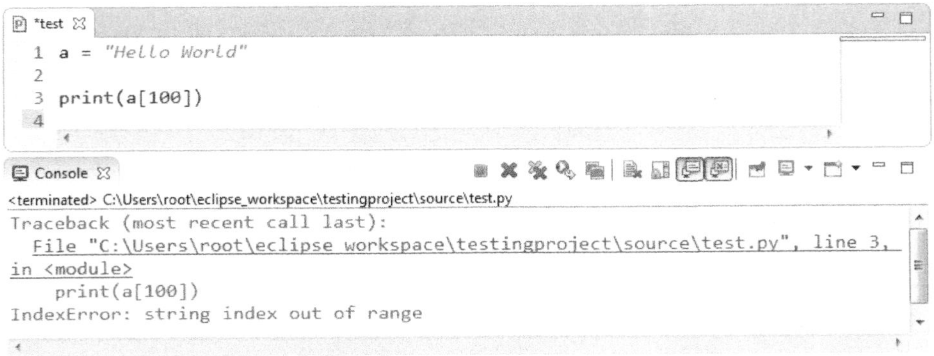

Figure 14–1 An error message indicating an invalid index

Another way of extracting single characters from strings in Python is to unpack them into individual variables.

Example

```
                            📁 file_14_3j
name = "Zeus"


a, b, c, d = name


print(a)      #It displays: Z
print(b)      #It displays: e
print(c)      #It displays: u
print(d)      #It displays: s
```

✎ *This last method requires you to know in advance how many characters are in the string. If the number of variables you supply does not match the number of characters in the string, Python displays an error.*

Getting part of a string (Slice Notation)

```
subject[ [beginIndex] : [endIndex] [: step]]
```

This notation returns a portion of subject. Specifically, it returns the substring starting from position *beginIndex* and running up to, but not including, position *endIndex*. Both arguments *beginIndex* and *endIndex* are optional. If *beginIndex* is omitted, the substring starting from position 0 and running up to, but not including, position *endIndex* is returned. If *endIndex* is omitted, the substring starting from position *beginIndex* until the end of *subject* is returned.

The last argument *step* is optional as well. If omitted, its default value is 1. If supplied, it defines the number of characters you want to move forward after each character is retrieved from the original string.

✎ *"Slicing" in Python is a mechanism to select a range of elements (here characters) from a sequence (here a string).*

Example

```
                            📁 file_14_3k
a = "Hello World"


print(a[7:9])        #It displays: or
print(a[4:10:2])     #Step is set to 2. It displays: oWr
```

```
print(a[7:])          #It displays: orld
print(a[:3])          #It displays: Hel
```

If you want to start counting from the end of the string (instead of the beginning) use negative indexes.

Example

```
                              📁 file_14_3l
a = "Hello World"

print(a[3:-2])        #It displays: lo Wor
print(a[-4:-2])       #It displays: or
print(a[-3:])         #It displays: rld
print(a[:-3])         #It displays: Hello Wo
```

Converting a number to string

```
str(number)
```

This function returns a string version of *number* or, in other words, it converts a number (real or integer) into a string.

Example

```
                              📁 file_14_3m
age = int(input("Enter your age: "))

new_age = age + 10
message = "You 'll be " + str(new_age) + " years old in 10 years from now!"

print(message)
```

Retrieving the English Alphabet in Lowercase

```
string.ascii_lowercase
```

This contains the English alphabet in lowercase.

Example

```
                              📁 file_14_3n
import string

print(string.ascii_lowercase)     #It displays: abcdefghijklmnopqrstuvwxyz
```

✎ ascii_lowercase *is defined in module* string. *It is not accessible directly in Python, so you need to import the* string *module.*

✎ *Note that* ascii_lowercase *is neither a function nor a method. Therefore, you must not put parentheses at the end.*

Retrieving the English Alphabet in Uppercase

```
string.ascii_uppercase
```

This contains the English alphabet in uppercase.

Example

```
                              📁 file_14_3o
import string
```

```
print(string.ascii_uppercase)    #It displays: ABCDEFGHIJKLMNOPQRSTUVWXYZ
```

✎ ascii_uppercase *is defined in module* string. *It is not accessible directly in Python, so you need to import the* string *module.*

▢ *A module is nothing more than a file that contains many ready-to-use functions (or methods). Python incorporates quite a lot such modules, but, if you wish to use a function or a method included in one of those modules, you need to import that module into your program.*

✎ *Note that* ascii_uppercase *is neither a function nor a method. This is why there are no parentheses at the end.*

✎ *If you need even more information about Python's string constants, you can visit*

https://docs.python.org/3.7/library/string.html#string-constants

Exercise 14.3-1   *Displaying a String Backwards*

Write a Python program that prompts the user to enter any string with four letters and then displays its contents backwards. For example, if the string entered is "Zeus", the program must display "sueZ".

Solution

Below, three approaches are presented.

First Approach

Let's say that user's input is assigned to variable s. You can access the fourth letter using s[3], the third letter using s[2], and so on. The Python program is shown here.

```
📁 file_14_3_1a
s = input("Enter a word with four letters: ")

s_reversed = s[3] + s[2] + s[1] + s[0]

print(s_reversed)
```

Second Approach

This approach unpacks the four letters given into four individual variables, as shown here.

```
📁 file_14_3_1b
s = input("Enter a word with four letters: ")

letter1, letter2, letter3, letter4 = s
s_reversed = letter4 + letter3 + letter2 + letter1

print(s_reversed)
```

Third Approach

This approach uses the slice notation and the negative value of −1 for argument *step*.

```
📁 file_14_3_1c
s = input("Enter a word with four letters: ")
```

```
s_reversed = s[::-1]

print(s_reversed)
```

✎ *The advantage of this approach is that the user is allowed to enter any string, no matter how short or long!*

Exercise 14.3-2   *Switching the Order of Names*

Write a Python program that prompts the user to enter in one single string both first and last name. In the end, the program must change the order of the two names.

Solution

This exercise is not the same as the one that you learned in Exercises 8.1-2 and 8.1-3, which swapped the numeric values of two variables. In this exercise both the first and last names are entered in one single string, so the first thing that the program must do is split the string and assign each name to a different variable. If you manage to do so, then you can just rejoin them in a different order.

Let's try to understand this exercise using an example. The string that you must split and the position of its individual character is shown here.

0	1	2	3	4	5	6	7	8
T	o	m		S	m	i	t	h

The character that visually separates the first name from the last name is the space character between them. The problem is that this character is not always at position 3. Someone can have a short first name like "Tom" and someone else can have a longer one like "Robert". Thus, you need something that actually finds the position of the space character regardless of the content of the string.

Method find() is what you are looking for! If you use it to find the position of the space character in the string "Tom Smith", it returns the value 3. But if you use it to find the space character in another string, such as "Angelina Brown", it returns the value 8 instead.

✎ *The value 3 is not just the position where the space character exists. It also represents the number of characters that the word "Tom" contains! The same applies to the value 8 that is returned for the string "Angelina Brown". It represents both the position where the space character exists and the number of characters that the word "Angelina" contains!*

The Python program for this algorithm is shown here.

```
                         📋 file_14_3_2
full_name = input("Enter your full name: ")

#Find the position of space character. This is also the number
#of characters first name contains
space_pos = full_name.find(" ")

#Get space_pos number of characters starting from position 0
name1 = full_name[:space_pos]

#Get the rest of the characters starting from position space_pos + 1
name2 = full_name[space_pos + 1:]
```

```
full_name = name2 + " " + name1
print(full_name)
```

✎ *Note that this program cannot be applied to a Spanish name such as "Maria Teresa García Ramírez de Arroyo". The reason is obvious!*

Exercise 14.3-3   *Creating a Login ID*

Write a Python program that prompts the user to enter his or her last name and then creates a login ID from the first four letters of the name (in lowercase) and a three-digit random integer.

Solution

To create a random integer you can use the `randrange()` method. Since you need a random integer of three digits, the range must be between 100 and 999.

The Python program for this algorithm is shown here.

```
                          📁 file_14_3_3

import random

last_name = input("Enter last name: ")

#Get random integer between 100 and 999
random_int = random.randrange(100, 1000)

print(last_name[:4].lower() + str(random_int))
```

Exercise 14.3-4   *Creating a Random Word*

Write a Python program that displays a random word consisting of five letters.

Solution

To create a random word you need the constant `ascii_lowercase` which contains all 26 letters of the English alphabet. This constant is defined in the `string` module, so, all you have to do is import the `string` module. Then you can use the `randrange()` method to choose a random letter between position 0 and 25.

The Python program for this algorithm is shown here.

```
                          📁 file_14_3_4a

import random
import string

alphabet = string.ascii_lowercase

random_word = alphabet[random.randrange(26)] +    \
              alphabet[random.randrange(26)] +    \
              alphabet[random.randrange(26)] +    \
              alphabet[random.randrange(26)] +    \
              alphabet[random.randrange(26)]
```

```
print(random_word)
```

✎ *Note that the method* `randrange(26)` *is called five times and each time it may return a different random integer between 0 and 25.*

✎ *In Python, you can break up a long line amongst multiple lines using the backslash (\ ) character at the end of each line (except the last one).*

You can also use the `len()` function to get the length of string `alphabet` as shown here.

▭ **file_14_3_4b**

```
import random
import string

alphabet = string.ascii_lowercase

random_word = alphabet[random.randrange(len(alphabet))] +    \
              alphabet[random.randrange(len(alphabet))] +    \
              alphabet[random.randrange(len(alphabet))] +    \
              alphabet[random.randrange(len(alphabet))] +    \
              alphabet[random.randrange(len(alphabet))]

print(random_word)
```

✎ *Note how the function* `len()` *is nested within the method* `randrange()`. *The result of the inner (nested) function is used as an argument for the outer method. This is a writing style that most programmers prefer to follow because it helps to save a lot of code lines. Of course, if you nest too many functions (or methods), no one will be able to understand your code. A nesting of up to four levels is quite acceptable.*

Exercise 14.3-5   Finding the Sum of Digits

Write a Python program that prompts the user to enter a three-digit integer and then calculates the sum of its digits. Solve this exercise without using the integer quotient (//) and the integer remainder (%) operators.

Solution

Now you may wonder why this exercise is placed in this chapter, where the whole discussion is about how to manipulate strings. You may also say that you already know how to split a three-digit integer into its three digits and assign each digit to a separate variable as you did learn a method in Chapter 13 using the integer quotient (//) and the integer remainder (%) operators. So, why is this exercise written here again?

The reason is that Python is a very powerful language and you can use its magic forces to solve this exercise in a totally different way. The main idea is to convert the given integer to type string.

First Approach

In this approach each digit (each character) is assigned to individual variables.

▭ **file_14_3_5a**

```
number = int(input("Enter an three-digit integer: "))

s_number = str(number)
```

```
digit1 = s_number[0]
digit2 = s_number[1]
digit3 = s_number[2]

total = int(digit1) + int(digit2) + int(digit3)
print(total)
```

Second Approach

In this approach each digit (each character) is <u>unpacked</u> into individual variables.

📄 **file_14_3_5b**

```
number = int(input("Enter an three-digit integer: "))

digit1, digit2, digit3 = str(number)

total = int(digit1) + int(digit2) + int(digit3)
print(total)
```

14.4 Review Questions: True/False

Choose **true** or **false** for each of the following statements.

1. A string is anything that you can type using the keyboard.
2. Strings must be enclosed in parentheses.
3. The phrase "Hi there!" contains 8 characters.
4. In the phrase "Hi there!" the letter "t" is at position 3.
5. The statement y = a[1] assigns the second character of the string contained in variable a to variable y.
6. The following code fragment
   ```
   a = "Hello"
   y = a[50]
   ```
   satisfies the property of definiteness.
7. Trimming is the process of removing whitespace characters from the beginning or the end of a string.
8. The statement y = "Hello   Aphrodite".strip() assigns the value "HelloAphrodite" to variable y.
9. The statement print("Hi there!".replace("Hi", "Hello")) displays the message "Hello there!".
10. The following code fragment
    ```
    a = "Hi there"
    index = a.find("the")
    ```
    assigns the value 4 to the variable index.
11. The statement print("hello there!".upper()) displays the message "Hello There".
12. The following code fragment
    ```
    a = "Hello there!"
    print(a[:])
    ```
    displays the message "Hello there!".
13. The statement print(a[:len(a)]) displays some letters of the variable a.
14. The statement print(a) is equivalent to the statement print(a[:len(a):]).

15. The following code fragment

```
y = "hello there!"
print(y[:5].upper())
```

displays the word "HELLO".

16. The statement `print(a[len(a) - 1])` is equivalent to the statement `print(a[-1])`.

14.5 Review Questions: Multiple Choice

Select the correct answer for each of the following statements.

1. Which of the following is **not** a string?
   a. "Hello there!"
   b. "13"
   c. "13.5"
   d. All of the above are strings.

2. In which position does the space character in the string "Hello Zeus!", exist?
   a. 6
   b. 5
   c. Space is not a character.
   d. none of the above

3. The statement `print(a[len(a) - 1])` displays
   a. the last character of variable a.
   b. the second to last character of variable a.
   c. The statement is not valid.

4. The statement

```
a.strip().replace("a", "b").replace("w", "y")
```

is equivalent to the statement
   a. `a.replace("a", "b").replace("w", "y").strip()`
   b. `a.replace("a", "b").strip().replace("w", "y")`
   c. `a.strip().replace("w", "y").replace("a", "b")`
   d. all of the above

5. The statement `a.replace(" ", "")`
   a. adds a space between each letter in the variable a.
   b. removes all space characters from the variable a.
   c. empties the variable a.

6. The statement `" Hello ".replace(" ", "")` is equivalent to the statement
   a. `" Hello ".replace("", " ")`.
   b. `" Hello ".strip()`.
   c. all of the above
   d. none of the above

7. The following code fragment

```
a = ""
print(len(a))
```

displays

    a. nothing.

    b. 1.

    c. 0.

    d. The statement is invalid.

    e. none of the above

8. Which value assigns the following code fragment

```
to_be_or_not_to_be = "2b Or Not 2b"
Shakespeare = to_be_or_not_to_be.find("b")
```

to the variable Shakespeare?

    a. 1

    b. 2

    c. 6

    d. none of the above

9. What does the following code fragment?

```
a = "Hi there"
b = a[a.find(" ") + 1:]
```

    a. It assigns the word "Hi" to the variable b.

    b. It assigns a space character to the variable b.

    c. It assigns the word "there" to the variable b.

    d. none of the above

14.6   Review Exercises

Complete the following exercises.

1. Write a Python program that prompts the user to enter his or her first name, middle name, last name, and his or her preferred title (Mr., Mrs., Ms., Dr., and so on) and displays them formatted in all the following ways.

    Title FirstName MiddleName LastName

    FirstName MiddleName LastName

    LastName, FirstName

    LastName, FirstName MiddleName

    LastName, FirstName MiddleName, Title

    FirstName LastName

For example, assume that the user enters the following:

    First name: Aphrodite

    Middle name: Maria

    Last name: Boura

    Title: Ms.

The program must display the user's name formatted in all the following ways:

    Ms. Aphrodite Maria Boura

    Aphrodite Maria Boura

    Boura, Aphrodite

Boura, Aphrodite Maria

Boura, Aphrodite Maria, Ms.

Aphrodite Boura

2. Write a Python program that creates and displays a random word consisting of five letters. The first letter must be a capital letter.

3. Write a Python program that prompts the user to enter his or her name and then creates a secret password consisting of three letters (in lowercase) randomly picked up from his or her name, and a random four-digit number. For example, if the user enters "Vassilis Bouras" a secret password can probably be one of "sar1359" or "vbs7281" or "bor1459".

4. Write a Python program that prompts the user to enter an integer and then reverses it. For example, if the user enters the number 375, the number 573 must be displayed. Solve this exercise without using the integer quotient (//) and the integer remainder (%) operators.

Review in "Sequence Control Structures"

Review Crossword Puzzle

1. Solve the following crossword puzzle.

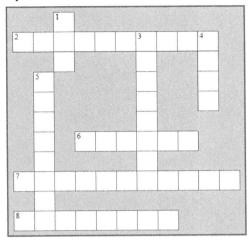

Across

2. The `len()` function returns the number of _____ in a string.
6. Anything that you can type using the keyboard.
7. Python provides many ready-to-use _____.
8. This control structure refers to the line-by-line execution by which statements are executed sequentially.

Down

1. A whitespace character.
3. The process of removing whitespace characters from the beginning or the end of a string.
4. The `math.sin()` method returns the _____ of a number.
5. The `abs()` function returns the _____ value of a number.

Review Questions

Answer the following questions.

1. What is a sequence control structure?
2. What operations can a sequence control structure perform?
3. Give some examples of how you can use the quotient and the remainder of an integer division.
4. What is a function or a method?
5. What does the term "chain a method" mean?
6. What does the term "nest a function" mean?
7. What is "slicing" in Python?

Section 4

Decision Control Structures

Chapter 15
Making Questions

15.1 Introduction

All you have learned so far is the sequence control structure, where statements are executed sequentially, in the same order in which they appear in the program. However, in serious Python programming, rarely do you want the statements to be executed sequentially. Many times you want a block of statements to be executed in one situation and an entirely different block of statements to be executed in another situation.

15.2 What is a Boolean Expression?

Let's say that variable x contains a value of 5. This means that if you ask the question "*is x greater than 2?*" the answer is obviously "*Yes*". For a computer, these questions are called *Boolean expressions*. For example, if you write $x > 2$, this is a Boolean expression, and the computer must check whether or not the expression $x > 2$ is True or False.

✎ *A Boolean expression is an expression that results in a Boolean value, that is, either* True *or* False.

✎ *Boolean expressions are questions and they should be read as "Is something equal to/greater than/less than something else?" and the answer is just a "Yes" or a "No"* (True *or* False).

⌨ *A decision control structure can evaluate a Boolean expression or a set of Boolean expressions and then decide which block of statements to execute.*

15.3 How to Write Simple Boolean Expressions

A simple Boolean expression is written as

$$Operand1 \quad \textbf{Comparison\_Operator} \quad Operand2$$

where

▶ *Operand1* and *Operand2* can be values, variables or mathematical expressions

▶ *Comparison_Operator* can be one of those shown in **Table 15-1**.

Comparison Operator	Description
==	Equal (not assignment)
!=	Not equal
>	Greater than
<	Less than
>=	Greater than or equal to
<=	Less than or equal to

Table 15-1 Comparison Operators in Python

Here are some examples of Boolean expressions:

▶ $x > y$. This Boolean expression is a question to the computer and can be read as "*is x greater than y?*"

▶ $x <= y$. This Boolean expression is also a question to the computer and can be read as "*is x less than or equal to y?*"

▶   x != 3 * y + 4. This can be read as "*is x not equal to the result of the expression* 3 * y + 4?"

▶   s == "Hello". This can be read as "*is s equal to the word 'Hello'?*" In other words, this question can be read as "*does s contain the word 'Hello'?*"

▶   x == 5. This can be read as "*is x equal to 5?*"

> ✎ *A very common mistake that novice programmers make when writing Python programs is to confuse the value assignment operator with the equal operator. They frequently make the mistake of writing* x = 5 *when they actually want to say* x == 5.

Exercise 15.3-1   *Filling in the Table*

Fill in the following table with the words "True" or "False" according to the values of the variables a, b, and c.

a	b	c	a == 10	b <= a	c > 3 * a - b
3	−5	7			
10	10	21			
−4	−2	−9			

Solution

The first two Boolean expressions are straightforward and need no further explanation.

Regarding the Boolean expression c > 3 * a - b, be very careful with the cases where b is negative. For example, in the first line, a is equal to 3 and b is equal to −5. The result of the expression 3 * a - b is 3 * 3 - (-5) = 3 * 3 + 5 = 14. Since the content of variable c (in the first line) is not greater than 14, the result of the Boolean expression c > 3 * a - b is False.

After a little work , the table becomes

a	b	c	a == 10	b <= a	c > 3 * a - b
3	−5	7	False	True	False
10	10	21	True	True	True
−4	−2	−9	False	False	True

15.4   Logical Operators and Complex Boolean Expressions

A more complex Boolean expression can be built of simpler Boolean expressions and can be written as

$$BE1 \ \textbf{\textit{Logical\_Operator}} \ BE2$$

where

▶   *BE1* and *BE2* can be any Boolean expression.

▶   *Logical_Operator* can be one of those shown in **Table 15-2**.

Logical Operator	Description
and	Also known as logical conjunction
or	Also known as logical disjunction
not	Also known as negation or logical complement

Table 15-2 Logical Operators in Python

✎ *When you combine simple Boolean expressions with logical operators, the whole Boolean expression is called a "complex Boolean expression". For example, the expression* x == 3 and y > 5 *is a complex Boolean expression.*

The and operator

When you use the and operator between two Boolean expressions (*BE1* and *BE2*), it means that the result of the whole complex Boolean expression is True only when both (*BE1* **and** *BE2*) Boolean expressions are True.

You can organize this information in something known as a *truth table*. A truth table shows the result of a logical operation between two or more Boolean expressions for all their possible combinations of values. The truth table for the and operator is shown here.

BE1 (Boolean Expression 1)	BE2 (Boolean Expression 2)	BE1 and BE2
False	False	False
False	True	False
True	False	False
True	True	True

Are you still confused? You shouldn't be! It is quite simple! Let's see an example. The complex Boolean expression

name == "John" and age > 5

is True only when the variable name contains the word "John" (without the double quotes) **and** variable age contains a value greater than 5. Both Boolean expressions must be True. If at least one of them is False, for example, the variable age contains a value of 3, then the whole complex Boolean expression is False.

The or operator

When you use the or operator between two Boolean expressions (*BE1* or *BE2*) , it means the result of the whole complex Boolean expression is True when either the first (*BE1*) **or** the second (*BE2*) Boolean expression is True (at least one).

The truth table for the or operator is shown here.

BE1 (Boolean Expression 1)	BE2 (Boolean Expression 2)	BE1 or BE2
False	False	False
False	True	True
True	False	True
True	True	True

Let's see an example. The complex Boolean expression

name == "John" or name == "George"

is True when the variable name contains the word "John" **or** the word "George" (without the double quotes). At least one Boolean expression must be True. If both Boolean expressions are False, for example, the variable name contains the word "Maria", then the whole complex Boolean expression is False.

The not operator

When you use the not operator in front of a Boolean expression (*BE*), it means that the whole complex Boolean expression is True when the Boolean expression *BE* is False and vice versa.

The truth table for the not operator is shown here.

BE (Boolean Expression)	not BE
False	True
True	False

For example, the complex Boolean expression

$$not\ age > 5$$

is True when the variable age contains a value less than <u>or equal to</u> 5. If, for example, the variable age contains a value of 6, then the whole complex Boolean expression is False.

✎ *The logical operator* not *reverses the result of a Boolean expression.*

15.5 Python's Membership Operators

In Python, a *membership operator* evaluates whether or not an operand exists in a specified sequence. There are two membership operators, as shown in **Table 15-3**.

Membership Operator	Description
in	It evaluates to True if it finds a value in the specified sequence; it evaluates to False otherwise.
not in	It evaluates to True if it does **not** find a value in the specified sequence; it evaluates to False otherwise.

Table 15-3 Membership Operators in Python

Next are some examples of Boolean expressions that use membership operators.

▶ x in [3, 5, 9]. This can be read as *"is x equal to 3, or equal to 5, or equal to 9?"*

It can also be written as

$$x == 3\ or\ x == 5\ or\ x == 9$$

▶ 3 in [x, y, z]. This can be read as *"is 3 equal to x, or equal to y, or equal to z?"*

It can also be written as

$$3 == x\ or\ 3 == y\ or\ 3 == z$$

▶ s in "ace". This can be read as *'does the content of variable s appear in the word "ace"'* or in other words, *'is s equal to letter "a", or equal to letter "c", or equal to letter "e", or equal to word "ac", or equal to word "ce", or equal to word "ace"?'*

It can be written equivalently as

$$s == "a"\ or\ s == "c"\ or\ s == "e"\ or\ s == "ac"\ or\ s == "ce"\ or\ s == "ace"$$

✎ *Note that the Boolean expression* s in "ace" *does not check whether or not s is equal to* "ae". *It only checks for the presence of the content of variable s within the specified sequence of letters in the word* "ace".

▶ s in ["a", "c", "e"]. This can be read as *'is s equal to letter "a", or equal to letter "c", or equal to letter "e"?'*

It can also be written as

$$s == "a"\ or\ s == "c"\ or\ s == "e"$$

► `s not in ["a", "c", "e"]`. This can be read as '*is s **not** equal to letter "a", nor equal to letter "c", nor equal to letter "e"?*'

It can also be written as

$$\text{not}(s == "a" \text{ or } s == "c" \text{ or } s == "e")$$

or as

$$s \mathrel{!=} "a" \text{ and } s \mathrel{!=} "c" \text{ and } s \mathrel{!=} "e"$$

15.6 Assigning the Result of a Boolean Expression to a Variable

Given that a Boolean expression actually returns a value (`True` or `False`), this value can be directly assigned to a variable. For example, the expression

```
a = x > y
```

assigns a value of `True` or `False` to Boolean variable a. It can be read as "*If the content of variable x is greater than the content of variable y, assign the value* `True` *to variable a; otherwise, assign the value* `False`". This next example displays the value `True` on the screen.

```
x, y = 8, 5
a = x > y
print(a)
```

15.7 What is the Order of Precedence of Logical Operators?

A more complex Boolean expression may use several logical operators like the expression shown here

$$\text{name} == "Peter" \textbf{ or } \text{age} > 10 \textbf{ and not } \text{name} == "Maria"$$

So, a reasonable question is "which logical operation is performed first?"

Logical operators follow the same precedence rules that apply to the majority of programming languages. The order of precedence is: logical complements (`not`) are performed first, logical conjunctions (`and`) are performed next, and logical disjunctions (`or`) are performed at the end.

Higher Precedence	Logical Operator
⬆	not
	and
Lower Precedence	or

Table 15-4 The Order of Precedence of Logical Operators

✎ *You can always use parentheses to change the default precedence.*

15.8 What is the Order of Precedence of Arithmetic, Comparison, and Logical Operators?

In many cases, an expression may contain different type of operators, such as the one shown here.

$$a * b + 2 > 21 \text{ or not}(c == b / 2) \text{ and } c > 13$$

In such cases, arithmetic operations are performed first, comparison operations are performed next, and logical operations are performed at the end, as shown in the following table.

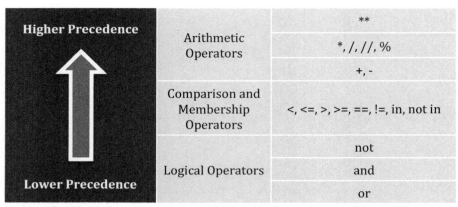

Table 15-5 The Order of Precedence of Arithmetic, Comparison, and Logical Operators

Exercise 15.8-1   Filling in the Truth Table

Fill in the following table with the words "True" or "False" according to the values of the variables a, b *and* c.

a	b	c	a > 2 or c > b and c > 2	not(a > 2 or c > b and c > 2)
1	-5	7		
10	10	3		
-4	-2	-9		

Solution

To calculate the result of complex Boolean expressions you can use the following graphical method.

For a = 1, b = -5, c = 7,

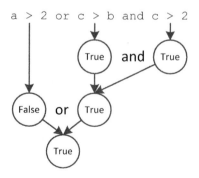

the final result is True.

📟 *The* and *operation has a higher precedence and is performed before the* or *operation.*

For a = 10, b = 10, c = 3,

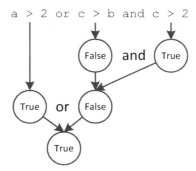

the final result is True.

For a = -4, b = -2, c = -9,

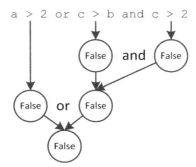

the final result is False.

The values in the table's fifth column can be calculated very easily because the Boolean expression in its column heading is almost identical to the one in the fourth column. The only difference is the not operator in front of the expression. So, the values in the fifth column can be calculated by simply negating the results in the fourth column!

The final truth table is shown here.

a	b	c	a > 2 or c > b and c > 2	not(a > 2 or c > b and c > 2)
1	-5	7	True	False
10	10	3	True	False
-4	-2	-9	False	True

Exercise 15.8-2   Calculating the Results of Complex Boolean Expressions

Calculate the results of the following complex Boolean expressions when variables a, b, c, and d contain the values 5, 2, 7, and –3 respectively.

     i.   (3 * a + b / 47 - c * b / a > 23) and (b != 2)

     ii.   (a * b - c / 2 + 21 * c / 3) or (a >= 5)

Solution

Don't be scared! The results can be found very easily. All you need is to recall what applies to and and or operators.

i.   The result of an and operator is True when both Boolean expressions are True. If you take a closer look, the result of the Boolean expression on the right (b != 2) is False. So, you don't have to waste your time calculating the result of the Boolean expression on the left. The final result is definitely False.

ii. The result of an or operator is True when at least one Boolean expression is True. If you take a closer look, the result of the Boolean expression on the right (a >= 5) is actually True. So, don't bother calculating the result of the Boolean expression on the left. The final result is definitely True.

Exercise 15.8-3   *Converting English Sentences to Boolean Expressions*

A head teacher asks the students to raise their hands according to their age. He wants to find the students who are

i.   *between the ages of 9 and 12.*

ii. *under the age of 8 and over the age of 11.*

iii. *8, 10, and 12 years old.*

iv. *between the ages of 6 and 8, and between the ages of 10 and 12.*

v.   *neither 10 nor 12 years old.*

Solution

To compose the required Boolean expressions, a variable age is used.

i.   The sentence "*between the ages of 9 and 12*" can be graphically represented as shown here.

Be careful though! It is valid to write 9 ≤ age ≤ 12 in mathematics, as well as in Python where you can write it as

$$9 <= age <= 12$$

In most computer languages, however, this is not a valid Boolean expression. What you can do is to split the expression into two parts, as shown here

$$age >= 9 \ and \ age <= 12$$

This last expression is valid in most computer languages, including Python!

> ✎ *For your confirmation, you can test this Boolean expression for several values inside and outside of the "region of interest" (the range of data that you have specified). For example, the result of the expression is* False *for the age values 7, 8, 13, and 17. On the contrary, for the age values 9, 10, 11, and 12, the result is* True.

ii. The sentence "*under the age of 8 and over the age of 11*" can be graphically represented as shown here.

> ✎ *Note the absence of the two circles that you saw in solution (i). This means the values 8 and 11 are* **not** *included within the two regions of interest.*

Be careful with the sentence "Under the age of 8 **and** over the age of 11". It's a trap! Don't make the mistake of writing

age < 8 and age > 11

There is no person on the planet Earth that can be under the age of 8 **and** over the age of 11 concurrently!

The trap is in the word "**and**". Try to rephrase the sentence and make it *"Children! Please raise your hand if you are under the age of 8 **or** over the age of 11."* Now it's better and the correct Boolean expression becomes

age < 8 or age > 11

✎ *For your confirmation, you can test this expression for several values inside and outside of the regions of interest. For example, the result of the expression is* False *for the age values 8, 9, 10 and 11. On the contrary, for the age values 6, 7, 12, and 15, the result is* True.

In Python, however, don't make the mistake of writing

8 > age > 11

because, if you split the expression into two parts, it is equivalent to

age < 8 and age > 11

which, as already mentioned, is incorrect!

iii. Oops! Another trap in the sentence "*8, 10, and 12 years old*" with the "**and**" word again! Obviously, the next Boolean expression is wrong.

age == 8 and age == 10 and age == 12

As before, there isn't any student who is 8 **and** 10 **and** 12 years old concurrently! Once again, the correct Boolean expression must use the or operator.

age == 8 or age == 10 or age == 12

✎ *For your confirmation, you can test this expression for several values inside and outside of the regions of interest. For example, the result of the expression is* False *for the age values 7, 9, 11, and 13. For the age values 8, 10, and 12, the result is* True.

In Python, this complex Boolean expression can also be written as

age in [8, 10, 12]

iv. The sentence "*between the ages of 6 and 8, and between the ages of 10 and 12*" can be graphically represented as shown here.

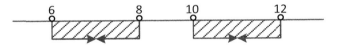

and the Boolean expression is

age >= 6 and age <= 8 or age >= 10 and age <= 12

✎ *For your confirmation, the result of the expression is* False *for the age values 5, 9, 13, and 16. For the age values 6, 7, 8, 10, 11, and 12, the result is* True.

In Python, this complex Boolean expression can also be written as

6 <= age <= 8 or 10 <= age <= 12

v.   The Boolean expression for the sentence "*neither 10 nor 12 years old*" can be written as

```
age != 10 and age != 12
```

or as

```
not(age == 10 or age == 12)
```

In Python, this complex Boolean expression can also be written as

```
age not in [10, 12]
```

✎ *When the arrows of the region of interest are pointing toward each other, a logical operator* and *must be used; otherwise, a logical operator* or *must be used.*

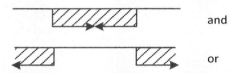

15.9 How to Negate Boolean Expressions

Negation is the process of reversing the meaning of a Boolean expression. There are two approaches used to negate a Boolean expression.

First Approach

The first approach is the easiest one. Just use a not operator in front of the original Boolean expression and your negated Boolean expression is ready! For example, if the original Boolean expression is

```
x > 5 and y == 3
```

the negated Boolean expression becomes

```
not(x > 5 and y == 3)
```

✎ *Note that the entire expression must be enclosed in parentheses. It would be completely incorrect if you had written the expression without parentheses, as* not x > 5 and y == 3. *In this case the* not *operator would negate only the first Boolean expression,* x > 5.

Second Approach

The second approach is a little bit more complex but not difficult to learn. All you must do is negate every operator according to the following table.

Original Operator	Negated Operator
==	!=
!=	==
>	<=
<	>=
<=	>
>=	<
in	not in
not in	in

and	or
or	and
not	not

✎ *Note that the* not *operator remains intact.*

For example, if the original Boolean expression is

$$x > 5 \text{ and } y == 3$$

the negated Boolean expression becomes

$$x <= 5 \text{ or } y \text{ != } 3$$

Exercise 15.9-1   *Negating Boolean Expressions*

Negate the following Boolean expressions using both approaches.

i.   `b != 4`

ii.   `a * 3 + 2 > 0`

iii.   `not(a == 5 and b >= 7)`

iv.   `a == True`

v.   `b > 7 and not(x > 4)`

vi.   `a == 4 or b != 2`

Solution

First Approach

i.   `not(b != 4)`

ii.   `not(a * 3 + 2 > 0)`

iii.   `not(not(a == 5 and b >= 7))`, or the equivalent `a == 5 and b >= 7`

✎ *Two negations result in an affirmative. That is, two* not *operators in a row negate each other.*

---

iv.   `not(a == True)`

v.   `not(b > 7 and not(x > 4))`

vi.   `not(a == 4 or b != 2)`

Second Approach

i.   `b == 4`

ii.   `a * 3 + 2 <= 0`

✎ *Note that arithmetic operators are **not** "negated". Don't you ever dare replace the plus (+) with a minus (−) operator!*

---

iii.   `not(a != 5 or b < 7)`

✎ *Note that the* not *operator remains intact.*

---

iv.   `a != True`

v.   `b <= 7 or not(x <= 4)`

vi.   `a != 4 and b == 2`

15.10 Review Questions: True/False

Choose **true** or **false** for each of the following statements.

1. A Boolean expression is an expression that always results in one of two values.
2. A Boolean expression includes at least one logical operator.
3. In Python, the expression x = 5 tests if the variable x is equal to 5.
4. The statement a = b == c is not a valid Python statement.
5. The Boolean expression b < 5 tests if the variable b is 5 or less.
6. The and operator is also known as a logical disjunction operator.
7. The or operator is also known as a logical complement operator.
8. The result of a logical conjunction of two Boolean expressions equals the result of the logical disjunction of them, given that both Boolean expressions are True.
9. The result of a logical disjunction of two Boolean expressions is definitely True, given that the Boolean expressions have different values.
10. The expression c == 3 and d > 7 is considered a complex Boolean expression.
11. The result of the logical operator or is True when both operands (Boolean expressions) are True.
12. The result of the Boolean expression not(x == 5) is True when the variable x contains any value except 5.
13. The not operator has the highest precedence among logical operators.
14. The or operator has the lowest precedence among logical operators.
15. In the Boolean expression x > y or x == 5 and x <= z, the and operation is performed before the or operation.
16. In the Boolean expression a * b + c > 21 or c == b / 2, the program first tests if c is greater than 21.
17. When a teacher wants to find the students who are under the age of 8 and over the age of 11, the corresponding Boolean expression is 8 > a > 11.
18. The Boolean expression x < 0 and x > 100 is, for any value of x, always False.
19. The Boolean expression x > 0 or x < 100 is, for any value of x, always True.
20. The Boolean expression x > 5 is equivalent to not(x < 5).
21. The Boolean expression not(x > 5 and y == 5) is not equivalent to not(x > 5) and y == 5.
22. In William Shakespeare[1]'s *Hamlet* (Act 3, Scene 1), the main character says "To be, or not to be: that is the question:...." If you write this down as a Boolean expression to_be or not to_be, the result of this "Shakesboolean" expression is True for the following code fragment.

    ```
    to_be = 1 > 0
    that_is_the_question = to_be or not to_be
    ```

23. The Boolean expression not(not(x > 5)) is equivalent to x > 5.

---

[1] William Shakespeare (1564–1616) was an English poet, playwright, and actor. He is often referred to as England's national poet. He wrote about 40 plays and several long narrative poems. His works are counted among the best representations of world literature. His plays have been translated into every major living language and are still performed today.

15.11 Review Questions: Multiple Choice

Select the correct answer for each of the following statements.

1. Which of the following is **not** a comparison operator?

    a. >=

    b. =

    c. <

    d. All of the above are comparison operators.

2. Which of the following is not a Python logical operator?

    a. nor

    b. not

    c. All of the above are logical operators.

    d. None of the above is a logical operator.

3. If variable x contains a value of 5, what value does the statement y = x % 2 == 1 assign to variable y?

    a. True

    b. False

    c. none of the above

4. If variable x contains a value of 5, what value does the statement y = x % 2 == 0 or int(x / 2) == 2 assign to variable y?

    a. True

    b. False

    c. none of the above

5. The temperature in a laboratory room must be between 50 and 80 degrees Fahrenheit. Which of the following Boolean expressions tests for this condition?

    a. t >= 50 or t <= 80

    b. 50 < t < 80

    c. t >= 50 and t <= 80

    d. t > 50 or t < 80

    e. none of the above

6. Which of the following is equivalent to the Boolean expression t == 3 or t > 30?

    a. t == 3 and not(t <= 30)

    b. t == 3 and not(t < 30)

    c. not(t != 3) or not(t < 30)

    d. not(t != 3 and t <= 30)

    e. none of the above

15.12 Review Exercises

Complete the following exercises.

1. Match each element from the first column with one or more elements from the second column.

Operator		Sign	
i.	Logical operator	a.	%
ii.	Arithmetic operator	b.	+=
iii.	Comparison operator	c.	and
iv.	Assignment operator (in general)	d.	==
		e.	or
		f.	>=
		g.	not
		h.	=
		i.	*=
		j.	/

2. Fill in the following table with the words "True" or "False" according to the values of variables a, b, and c.

a	b	c	a != 1	b > a	c / 2 > 2 * a
3	-5	8			
1	10	20			
-4	-2	-9			

3. Fill in the following table with the words "True" or "False" according to the values of the Boolean expressions BE1 and BE2.

Boolean Expression1 (BE1)	Boolean Expression2 (BE2)	BE1 or BE2	BE1 and BE2	not(BE2)
False	False			
False	True			
True	False			
True	True			

4. Fill in the following table with the words "True" or "False" according to the values of variables a, b, and c.

a	b	c	a > 3 or c > b and c > 1	a > 3 and c > b or c > 1
4	-6	2		
-3	2	-4		
2	5	5		

5. For x = 4, y = -2 and flag = True, fill in the following table with the corresponding values.

Expression	Value
(x + y) ** 3	
(x + y) / (x ** 2 - 14)	
(x - 1) == y + 5	
x > 2 and y == 1	
x == 1 or y == -2 and not(flag == False)	
not(x >= 3) and (x % 2 > 1)	

6. Calculate the result of each the following complex Boolean expressions when variables a, b, c, and d contain the values 6, −3, 4, and 7 respectively.

    i.   (3 * a + b / 5 - c * b / a > 4) and (b != -3)

    ii.   (a * b - c / 2 + 21 * c / 3 != 8) or (a >= 5)

7. A head teacher asks the students to raise their hands according to their age. He wants to find the students who are:

    i.   under the age of 12, but not those who are 8 years old.

    ii.   between the ages of 6 and 9, and also those who are 11 years old.

    iii. over the age of 7, but not those who are 10 or 12 years old.

    iv. 6, 9, and 11 years old.

    v.   between the ages of 6 and 12, but not those who are 8 years old.

    vi. neither 7 nor 10 years old.

To compose the required Boolean expressions, use a variable age.

8. Negate the following Boolean expressions without using the not operator.

    i.   x == 4 and y != 3   iv. x != False

    ii.   x + 4 <= 0   v.   not(x >= 4 or z > 4)

    iii. not(x > 5) or y == 4   vi. x != 2 and x >= -5

9. As you already know, two negations result in an affirmative. Write the equivalent of the following Boolean expressions by negating them twice (applying both methods).

    i.   x >= 4 and y != 10   iv. x != False or y == 3

    ii.   x - 2 >= 9   v.   not(x >= 2 and y >= 2)

    iii. not(x >= 2) or y != 4   vi. x != -2 and x <= 2

Chapter 16
The Single-Alternative Decision Structure

16.1   The Single-Alternative Decision Structure

This is the simplest decision control structure. It includes a statement or block of statements on the "True" path only.

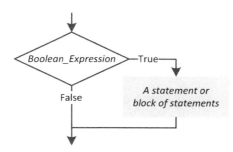

If *Boolean_Expression* evaluates to True, the statement, or block of statements, of the structure is executed; otherwise, the statements are skipped.

The general form of the Python statement is

```
if Boolean_Expression:

    A statement or block of statements
```

✎ *Note that the statement or block of statements is indented by 4 spaces.*

In the next example, the message "You are underage!" displays only when the user enters a value less than 18. Nothing is displayed when the user enters a value that is greater than <u>or equal to</u> 18.

```
                            📄 file_16_1a
age = int(input("Enter your age: "))

if age < 18:
    print("You are underage!")
```

✎ *Note that the* print() *statement is indented by 4 spaces.*

In the next example, the message "You are underage!" and the message "You have to wait for a few more years" are displayed only when the user enters a value less than 18. Same as previously, no messages are displayed when the user enters a value that is greater than or equal to 18.

```
                            📄 file_16_1b
age = int(input("Enter your age: "))

if age < 18:
    print("You are underage!")
    print("You have to wait for a few more years.")
```

✎ *Note that both* `print()` *statements are indented by 4 spaces.*

✎ *Python was one of the first programming languages to enforce indentation. Python specifies that several statements are part of a group by indenting them. The indented group is called a "block of statements" or "code block". Indentation is considered good practice in other languages, but in Python indentation is mandatory. Code that is part of a block must be indented. For example, all statements that appear inside an* if *statement must be indented to the right by the same number of spaces; otherwise they are not considered part of the* if *statement and you probably get an error message. There are two simple rules to remember about code blocks' syntax:*

▶ *The statement on the first line of a code block always ends with a colon (:) character.*

▶ *The code underneath the first line must be indented.*

✎ *Python's official website recommends the use of 4 spaces per indentation level. If you need more information you can visit*

https://www.python.org/dev/peps/pep-0008

✎ *In order to indent the text cursor, instead of typing space characters, you can hit the "Tab ⇆" key once!*

✎ *In order to indent an existing statement or a block of statements, select it and hit the "Tab ⇆" key!*

✎ *In order to unindent a statement or a block of statements, select it and hit the "Shift ↑ + Tab ⇆" key combination!*

✎ *In computer languages other than Python, such as C, C++, C#, Java, or Visual Basic, indentation is not obligatory but it is quite necessary in order to make code easier to read. It also helps programmers to more easily study and understand code written by others.*

In the next example, the message "You are the King of the Gods!" is displayed only when the user enters the name "Zeus". The message "You live on Mount Olympus", however, is always displayed, no matter what name the user enters.

```
📄 file_16_1c
```
```
name = input("Enter the name of an Olympian: ")

if name == "Zeus":
    print("You are the King of the Gods!")

print("You live on Mount Olympus.")
```

✎ *Note that the last* `print()` *statement is **not** indented, and so it does **not** belong to the block of statements of the single-alternative decision structure.*

✎ *A very common mistake that novice programmers make when writing Python programs is to confuse the value assignment operator with the "equal" operator. They frequently make the mistake of writing* `if name = "Zeus"` *when they actually want to say* `if name == "Zeus"`.

When only one single statement is used in the `if` statement, you can write it on one single line, like this:
```
if Boolean_Expression: One_Single_Statement
```

Exercise 16.1-1   Trace Tables and Single-Alternative Decision Structures

Design the corresponding flowchart and create a trace table to determine the values of the variables in each step of the next Python program for two different executions.

The input values for the two executions are (i) 10, and (ii) 51.

```
☐ file_16_1_1
a = int(input())


y = 5
if a * 2 > 100:
    a = a * 3
    y = a * 4

print(a, y)
```

Solution

The flowchart is shown here.

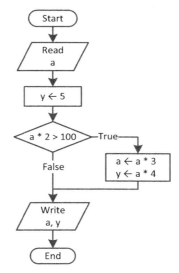

The trace tables for each input are shown here.

i. For the input value of 10, the trace table looks like this.

Step	Statement	Notes	a	y
1	a = int(input())	User enters the value 10	**10**	?
2	y = 5		10	**5**
3	if a * 2 > 100:	This evaluates to False		
4	print(a, y)	It displays: 10 5		

ii. For the input value of 51, the trace table looks like this.

Step	Statement	Notes	a	y
1	a = int(input())	User enters the value 51	**51**	?

2	`y = 5`		51	**5**
3	`if a * 2 > 100:`	This evaluates to True		
4	`a = a * 3`		**153**	5
5	`y = a * 4`		153	**612**
6	`print(a, y)`	It displays: 153 612		

Exercise 16.1-2   *The Absolute Value of a Number*

Design a flowchart and write the corresponding Python program that lets the user enter a number and then displays its absolute value.

Solution

Actually, there are two approaches. The first approach uses a single-alternative decision structure, whereas the second one uses the built-in abs() function.

First Approach – Using a single-alternative decision structure

The approach is simple. If the user enters a negative value, for example −5, this value is changed and displayed as +5. A positive number or zero, however, must remain as is. The solution is shown in the flowchart that follows.

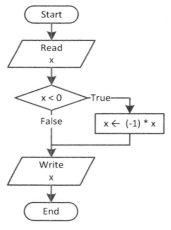

The corresponding Python program is as follows.

```
                          📄 file_16_1_2a
x = float(input())

if x < 0:
    x = (-1) * x

print(x)
```

Second Approach – Using the abs() function

In this case, you need just two lines of code without any decision control structure!

```
                          📄 file_16_1_2b
x = float(input())
```

```
print(abs(x))
```

16.2   Review Questions: True/False

Choose **true** or **false** for each of the following statements.

1. The single-alternative decision structure is used when a sequence of statements must be executed.
2. You use a single-alternative decision structure to allow other programmers to more easily understand your program.
3. It is a possible that none of the statements enclosed in a single-alternative decision structure will be executed.
4. In a flowchart, the Decision symbol represents the beginning and the end of an algorithm.
5. The following code

    ```
    if = 5
    x = if + 5
    print(x)
    ```

    is syntactically correct.
6. The single-alternative decision structure uses the reserved keyword else.
7. The following code fragment satisfies the property of definiteness.

    ```
    if b != 3:
        x = a / (b - 3)
    ```

8. The following Python program satisfies the property of definiteness.

    ```
    a = float(input())
    b = float(input())

    if b != 3:
        x = a / (b - 3)

    print(x)
    ```

9. Python programs that include decision control structures and written without code indentation cannot be executed by a computer.

16.3   Review Questions: Multiple Choice

Select the correct answer for each of the following statements.

1. The single-alternative decision structure is used when
    a. statements are executed one after another.
    b. a decision must be made before executing some statements.
    c. none of the above
    d. all of the above
2. The single-alternative decision structure includes a statement or block of statements on
    a. the false path only.
    b. both paths.
    c. the true path only.
3. In the following code fragment,

    ```
    if x == 3:
        x = 5
    ```

```
y += 1
```

the statement `y += 1` is executed

    a.   only when variable x contains a value of 3.

    b.   only when variable x contains a value of 5.

    c.   only when variable x contains a value other than 3.

    d.   either way.

4.   In the following code fragment,

```
if x % 2 == 0: y += 1
```

the statement `y += 1` is executed when

    a.   variable x is exactly divisible by 2.

    b.   variable x contains an even number.

    c.   variable x does not contain an odd number.

    d.   all of the above

    e.   none of the above

5.   In the following code fragment,

```
x = 3 * y
if x > y: y += 1
```

the statement `y += 1` is

    a.   always executed.

    b.   never executed.

    c.   executed either way.

    d.   executed only when variable y contains positive values.

    e.   none of the above

6.   The following program

```
x = int(input())
if x < 0:
x = (-1) * x
print(x)
```

cannot be executed by a computer because

    a.   it does not use code indentation.

    b.   it includes logic errors.

    c.   none of the above

16.4   Review Exercises

Complete the following exercises.

1.   Identify the syntax errors in the following Python program:

```
x = float(input())

y ← - 5
if x * y / 2 > 20
    y =* 1
    x += 4 * x²
```

```
print(x   y)
```

2. Create a trace table to determine the values of the variables in each step of the following Python program for two different executions. Then, design the corresponding flowchart.

   The input values for the two executions are (i) 10, and (ii) –10.

```
x = float(input())

y = - 5
if x * y / 2 > 20:
    y -= 1
    x -= 4

if x > 0:
    y += 30
    x = x ** 2

print(x, ",", y)
```

3. Create a trace table to determine the values of the variables in each step of the following Python program for two different executions. Then, design the corresponding flowchart.

   The input values for the two executions are (i) –11, and (ii) 11.

```
x = int(input())

y = 8
if abs(x) > 10:
    y += x
    x -= 1

if abs(x) > 10:
    y *= 3

print(x, ",", y)
```

4. Create a trace table to determine the values of the variables in each step of the following Python program for two different executions. Then, design the corresponding flowchart.

   The input values for the two executions are (i) 1, 2, 3; and (ii) 4, 2, 1.

```
x = int(input())
y = int(input())
z = int(input())

if x + y > z: x = y + z
if x > y + z: y = x + z
if x > y - z: z = x - z % 2

print(x, ",", y, ",", z)
```

5. Write a Python program that prompts the user to enter a number, and then displays the message "Positive" when the given number is positive.

6. Write a Python program that prompts the user to enter two numbers, and then displays the message "Positive" when both given numbers are positives.

7. Write a Python program that prompts the user to enter his or her age and then displays the message *"You can drive a car in Kansas (USA)"* when the given age is greater than 14.

8. Write a Python program that prompts the user to enter a string, and then displays the message "Uppercase" when the given string contains only uppercase characters.

    Hint: Use the upper() method.

9. Write a Python program that prompts the user to enter a string, and then displays the message "Many characters" when the given string contains more than 20 characters.

    Hint: Use the len() function.

10. Write a Python program that prompts the user to enter four numbers and, if one of them is negative, it displays the message "Among the given numbers, there is a negative one!"

11. Write a Python program that prompts the user to enter two numbers. If the first number given is greater than the second one, the program must swap their values. In the end, the program must display the numbers, always in ascending order.

12. Write a Python program that prompts the user to enter three temperature values measured at three different points in New York, and then displays the message "Heat Wave" if the average value is greater than 60 degrees Fahrenheit.

Chapter 17
The Dual-Alternative Decision Structure

17.1 The Dual-Alternative Decision Structure

In contrast to the single-alternative decision structure, this type of decision control structure includes a statement or block of statements on both paths.

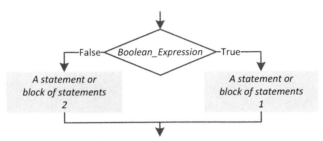

If *Boolean_Expression* evaluates to `True`, the statement or block of statements 1 is executed; otherwise, the statement or block of statements 2 is executed.

The general form of the Python statement is

```
if Boolean_Expression:
        A statement or block of statements 1
else:
        A statement or block of statements 2
```

In the next example, the message "You are an adult" is displayed when the user enters a value greater than or equal to 18. The message "You are underage!" is displayed otherwise.

□ file_17_1

```
age = int(input("Enter your age: "))
if age >= 18:
    print("You are an adult!")
else:
    print("You are underage!")
```

Exercise 17.1-1   Finding the Output Message

For the following flowchart, determine the output message for three different executions.

The input values for the three executions are (i) 3, (ii) −3, and (iii) 0.

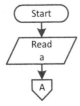

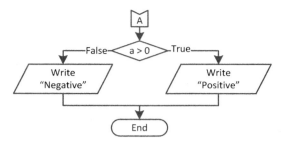

Solution

i.   When the user enters the value 3, the Boolean expression evaluates to `True`. The flow of execution follows the right path and the message "Positive" is displayed.

ii.   When the user enters the value −3, the Boolean expression evaluates to `False`. The flow of execution follows the left path and the message "Negative" is displayed.

iii.   Can you predict what happens when the user enters the value 0? If you believe that none of the messages will be displayed, you are wrong! The dual-alternative decision structure must always follow a path, either the right or the left! It cannot skip the execution of both of its blocks of statements. At least one statement or block of statements must be executed. So, when the user enters the value 0, the Boolean expression evaluates to `False`, the flow of execution follows the left path, and the message "Negative" is displayed!

Obviously, something is not quite right with this flowchart! As you already know, zero is not a negative value! And it is not a positive value either. Later in this book (in Exercise 19.1-2), you will learn how to display three messages, depending on whether the given value is greater than, less than, or equal to zero.

A Decision symbol has one entrance and two exit paths! You cannot have a third exit!

Exercise 17.1-2   Trace Tables and Dual-Alternative Decision Structures

Create a trace table to determine the values of the variables in each step of the next Python program for two different executions.

The input values for the two executions are (i) 5, and (ii) 10.

```
file_17_1_2

a = float(input())

z = a * 10
w = (z - 4) * (a - 3) / 7 + 36

if a < z >= w:
    y = 2 * a
else:
    y = 4 * a

print(y)
```

Solution

i.   For the input value of 5, the trace table looks like this.

Step	Statement	Notes	a	z	w	y
1	`a = float(input())`	User enters the value 5	**5**	?	?	?
2	`z = a * 10`		5	**50**	?	?
3	`w = (z - 4) * (a - 3) / 7 + 36`		5	50	**49.142**	?
4	`if a < z >= w:`	This evaluates to True				
5	`y = 2 * a`		5	50	49.142	**10**
6	`print(y)`	It displays: 10				

ii.   For the input value of 10, the trace table looks like this.

Step	Statement	Notes	a	z	w	y
1	`a = float(input())`	User enters the value 10	**10**	?	?	?
2	`z = a * 10`		10	**100**	?	?
3	`w = (z - 4) * (a - 3) / 7 + 36`		10	100	**132**	?
4	`if a < z >= w:`	This evaluates to False				
5	`y = 4 * a`		10	100	132	**40**
6	`print(y)`	It displays: 40				

Exercise 17.1-3   *Who is the Greatest?*

Design a flowchart and write the corresponding Python program that lets the user enter two numbers A and B and then determines and displays the greater of the two numbers.

Solution

This exercise can be solved using either the single- or dual-alternative decision structure. Moreover, a third approach shows you how to do this in a more Pythonic way!

First Approach – Using a dual-alternative decision structure

This approach tests if the value of number B is greater than that of number A. If so, number B is the greatest; otherwise, number A is the greatest.

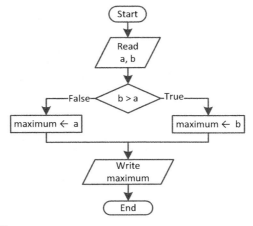

and the Python program is as follows.

```
                          📁 file_17_1_3a
a = float(input())
b = float(input())

if b > a:
    maximum = b
else:
    maximum = a

print("Greatest value:", maximum)
```

✎ *Note that this exercise is trying to determine the greatest value and not which variable this value is actually assigned to (to variable A or to variable B).*

Second Approach – Using a single-alternative decision structure

This approach initially assumes that number A is probably the greatest value (this is why it assigns the value of variable a to variable maximum). However, if it turns out that number B is actually greater than number A, then the greatest value is updated, that is, variable maximum is assigned a new value, the value of variable b. Thus, whatever happens, in the end, variable maximum always contains the greatest value!

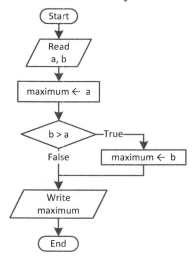

The Python program is shown here.

```
                          📁 file_17_1_3b
a = float(input())
b = float(input())

maximum = a
if b > a:
    maximum = b

print("Greatest value:", maximum)
```

Third Approach – The Pythonic way

This approach is the most simple, without any decision control structure. It just uses the max() function of Python as shown here.

```
📁 file_17_1_3c
```
```
a = float(input())
b = float(input())

maximum = max(a, b)
print("Greatest value:", maximum)
```

or you can do it in a more compact way, as shown here.

```
📁 file_17_1_3d
```
```
a = float(input())
b = float(input())

print("Greatest value:", max(a, b))
```

Exercise 17.1-4   Finding Odd and Even Numbers

Design a flowchart and write the corresponding Python program that prompts the user to enter a positive integer, and then displays a message indicating whether this number is even; it must display "Odd" otherwise.

Solution

Next you can find various odd and even numbers:
- ▶ Odd numbers: 1, 3, 5, 7, 9, 11, …
- ▶ Even numbers: 0, 2, 4, 6, 8, 10, 12, ….

 Note that zero is considered an even number.

In this exercise, you need to find a way to determine whether a number is odd or even. You need to find a common attribute between all even numbers, or between all odd numbers. And actually there is one! All even numbers are exactly divisible by 2. So, when the result of the operation x MOD 2 equals 0, x is even; otherwise, x is odd.

The flowchart is shown here.

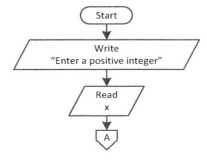

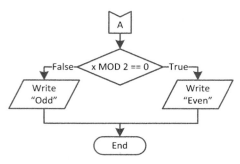

and the Python program is as follows.

```
📁 file_17_1_4
x = int(input("Enter a positive integer: "))

if x % 2 == 0:
    print("Even")
else:
    print("Odd")
```

Exercise 17.1-5   Weekly Wages

Gross pay depends on the pay rate and the total number of hours worked per week. However, if someone works more than 40 hours, he or she gets paid time-and-a-half for all hours worked over 40. Design a flowchart and write the corresponding Python program that lets the user enter a pay rate and the hours worked and then calculates and displays the gross pay.

Solution

This exercise can be solved using the dual-alternative decision structure. When the hours worked are over 40, the gross pay is calculated as follows:

$$gross\ pay = (pay\ rate) \times 40 + 1.5 \times (pay\ rate) \times (all\ hours\ worked\ over\ 40)$$

The flowchart that solves this problem is shown here.

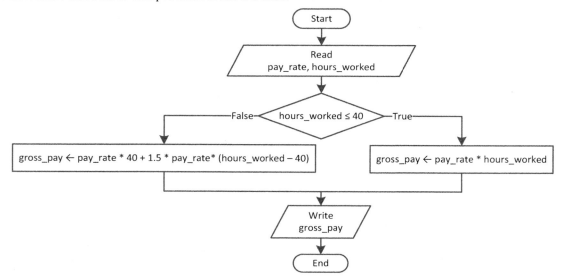

and the Python program is shown here.

```
🗅 file_17_1_5
pay_rate = float(input())
hours_worked = int(input())

if hours_worked <= 40:
    gross_pay = pay_rate * hours_worked
else:
    gross_pay = pay_rate * 40 + 1.5 * pay_rate * (hours_worked - 40)

print("Gross Pay:", gross_pay)
```

17.2   Review Questions: True/False

Choose **true** or **false** for each of the following statements.

1. It is a possible that none of the statements enclosed in a dual-alternative decision structure will be executed.

2. The dual-alternative decision structure must include at least two statements.

3. The dual-alternative decision structure uses the reserved keyword `else`.

4. The statement

    ```
    else = 5
    ```

    is syntactically correct.

5. In a dual-alternative decision structure, the evaluated Boolean expression can return more than two values.

6. The following code fragment satisfies the property of effectiveness.

    ```
    x = int(input())
    y = int(input())
    z = int(input())

    if x > y and x > z:
        print("Value", x, "is the greatest one")
    else:
        print("Value", y, "is the greatest one")
    ```

17.3   Review Questions: Multiple Choice

Select the correct answer for each of the following statements.

1. The dual-alternative decision structure includes a statement or block of statements on

    a. the false path only.

    b. both paths.

    c. the true path only.

2. In the following code fragment,

    ```
    if x % 2 == 0:
        x = 0
    else:
        y += 1
    ```

the statement `y += 1` is executed when

    a.   variable x is exactly divisible by 2.

    b.   variable x contains an even number.

    c.   variable x contains an odd number.

    d.   none of the above

3.   In the following code fragment,

```python
if x == 3:
    x = 5
else:
    x = 7
y += 1
```

the statement `y += 1` is executed

    a.   when variable x contains a value of 3.

    b.   when variable x contains a value other than 3.

    c.   both of the above

17.4 Review Exercises

Complete the following exercises.

1.   Create a trace table to determine the values of the variables in each step of the next Python program for two different executions. Then, design the corresponding flowchart.

The input values for the two executions are (i) 3, and (ii) 0.5.

```python
a = float(input())
z = a * 3 - 2
if z >= 1:
    y = 6 * a
else:
    z += 1
    y = 6 * a + z

print(z, ",", y)
```

2.   Create a trace table to determine the values of the variables in each step of the next Python program. Then, design the corresponding flowchart.

```python
import math

x = 3
y = x ** 3 + 9
z = 2 * x + y - 4
if x > y:
    y = z % x
    z = math.sqrt(x)
else:
    x = z % y
    z = math.sqrt(y)
```

```
print(x, ",", y, ",", z)
```

3. Write the Python program that corresponds to the following flowchart and then create a trace table to determine the values of the variables in each step for two different executions.

The input values for the two executions are (i) 10, and (ii) 2.

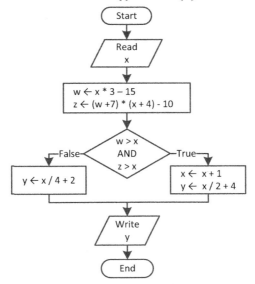

4. Two football teams play against each other in the UEFA Champions League. Write a Python program that prompts the user to enter the names of the two teams and the goals that each team scored, and then displays the name of the winner. Assume that the user enters valid values and there is no tie (draw).

5. Write a Python program that lets the user enter an integer, and then displays a message indicating whether the given number is a multiple of 6; it must display "NN is not a multiple of 6" otherwise (where NN is the given number). Assume that the user enters a non-negative[1] value.

6. Write a Python program that lets the user enter an integer, and then displays one of two possible messages. One message indicates if the given number is a multiple of 6 or a multiple of 7; the other message indicates if the given number is neither a multiple of 6 nor a multiple of 7. Assume that the user enters a non-negative value.

7. Write a Python program that lets the user enter an integer, and then displays a message indicating whether the given number is a multiple of 4; it must display "NN is not a multiple of 4" otherwise (where NN is the given number). Moreover, the Python program must display the structure of the given integer, including the given integer, the quotient, and any remainder. For example, if the given integer is 14, the message "14 = 3 x 4 + 2" must be displayed. Assume that the user enters a non-negative value.

8. Write a Python program that lets the user enter an integer, and then displays a message indicating whether the given integer is a four-digit integer; it must display "NN is not a four-digit integer" otherwise (where NN is the given number). Assume that the user enters a non-negative value.

Hint: Four-digit integers are between 1000 and 9999.

9. Design a flowchart and write the corresponding Python program that lets the user enter two values, and then determines and displays the smaller of the two values. Assume that the user enters two different values.

---

[1] A quantity that is either zero or positive.

10. Write a Python program that lets the user enter three numbers, and then displays a message indicating whether the given numbers can be lengths of the three sides of a triangle; it must display "Given numbers cannot be lengths of the three sides of a triangle" otherwise. Assume that the user enters valid values.

    Hint: In any triangle, the length of each side is less than the sum of the lengths of the other two sides.

11. Write a Python program that lets the user enter three numbers, and then displays a message indicating whether the given numbers can be lengths of the three sides of a right triangle (or right-angled triangle); it must display "Given numbers cannot be lengths of the three sides of a right triangle" otherwise. Assume that the user enters valid values.

    Hint 1: Use the Pythagorean theorem.

    Hint 2: You can use lengths of 3, 4 and 5 (which can be lengths of the three sides of a right triangle) to test your program.

12. Athletes in the long jump at the Olympic Games in Athens in 2004 participated in three different qualifying jumps. An athlete, in order to qualify, has to achieve an average jump distance of at least 8 meters. Write a Python program that prompts the user to enter the three performances, and then displays the message "Qualified" when the average value is greater than or equal to 8 meters; it displays "Disqualified" otherwise. Assume that the user enters valid values.

13. Gross pay depends on the pay rate and the total number of hours worked per week. However, if someone works more than 40 hours, he or she gets paid double for all hours worked over 40. Design a flowchart and write the corresponding Python program that lets the user enter the pay rate and hours worked and then calculates and displays net pay. Net pay is the amount of pay that is actually paid to the employee after any deductions. Deductions include taxes, health insurance, retirement plans, on so on. Assume a total deduction of 30% and that the user enters valid values.

14. Regular servicing will keep your vehicle more reliable, reducing the chance of breakdowns, inconvenience and unnecessary expenses. In general, there are two types of service you need to perform:

    a. a minor service every 6000 miles

    b. a major service every 12000 miles

    Write a Python program that prompts the user to enter the miles traveled, and then calculates and displays how many miles are left until the next service, as well as the type of the next service. Assume that the user enters a valid value.

15. Two cars start from rest and move with a constant acceleration along a straight horizontal road for a given time. Write a Python program that prompts the user to enter the time the two cars traveled (same for both cars) and the acceleration for each one of them, and then calculates and displays the distance between them as well as a message "Car A is first" or "Car B is first" depending on which car is leading the race. The required formula is

$$S = u_o + \frac{1}{2}at^2$$

    Assume that the user enters valid values.

Chapter 18
The Multiple-Alternative Decision Structure

18.1 The Multiple-Alternative Decision Structure

The multiple-alternative decision structure is used to expand the number of alternatives, as shown in the following flowchart fragment.

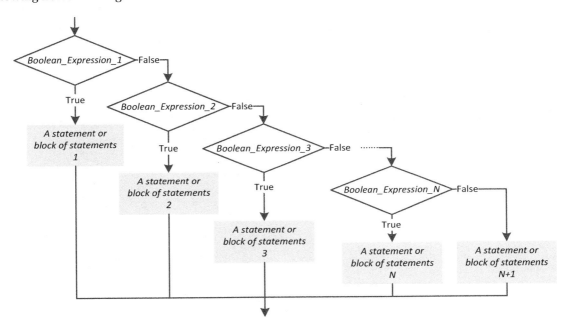

When a multiple-alternative decision structure is executed, *Boolean_Expression_1* is evaluated. If *Boolean_Expression_1* evaluates to True, the corresponding statement or block of statements that immediately follows it is executed; then the rest of the structure is skipped, continuing to any remaining statements that may exist **after** the multiple-alternative decision structure. However, if *Boolean_Expression_1* evaluates to False, the flow of execution evaluates *Boolean_Expression_2*. If it evaluates to True, the corresponding statement or block of statements that immediately follows it is executed and the rest of the structure is skipped. This process continues until one Boolean expression evaluates to True or until no more Boolean expressions are left.

The last statement or block of statements N+1 is executed when none of the previous Boolean expressions has evaluated to True. Moreover, this last statement or block of statements N+1 is optional and can be omitted. It depends on the algorithm you are trying to solve.

The general form of the Python statement is

```python
if Boolean_Expression_1:
    A statement or block of statements 1
elif Boolean_Expression_2:
    A statement or block of statements 2
```

```
elif Boolean_Expression_3:
    A statement or block of statements 3
    .
    .
    .
elif Boolean_Expression_N:
    A statement or block of statements N
else:
    A statement or block of statements N + 1
```

✎ *The keyword* elif *is an abbreviation for "else if".*

A simple example is shown here.

📁 file_18_1

```
name = input("What is your name? ")

if name == "John":
    print("You are my cousin!")
elif name == "Aphrodite":
    print("You are my sister!")
elif name == "Loukia":
    print("You are my mom!")
else:
    print("Sorry, I don't know you.")
```

Exercise 18.1-1   *Trace Tables and Multiple-Alternative Decision Structures*

Create a trace table to determine the values of the variables in each step for three different executions of the next Python program.

The input values for the three executions are (i) 5, 8; (ii) –13, 0; and (iii) 1, –1.

📁 file_18_1_1

```
a = int(input())
b = int(input())

if a > 3:
    print("Message #1")
elif a > 4 and b <= 10:
    print("Message #2")
    print("Message #3")
elif a * 2 == -26:
    print("Message #4")
    print("Message #5")
    b += 1
elif b == 1:
```

```
        print("Message #6")
else:
    print("Message #7")
    print("Message #8")

print("The end!")
```

Solution

i. For the input values of 5 and 8, the trace table looks like this.

Step	Statement	Notes	a	b
1	a = int(input())	User enters the value 5	**5**	?
2	b = int(input())	User enters the value 8	5	**8**
3	if a > 3:	This evaluates to True		
4	print("Message #1")	It displays: Message #1		
5	print("The end!")	It displays: The end!		

✎ *Note that even though the second Boolean expression* (a > 4 and b <= 10) *could also have evaluated to* True, *it was never checked.*

ii. For the input values of −13 and 0, the trace table looks like this.

Step	Statement	Notes	a	b
1	a = int(input())	User enters the value −13	**−13**	?
2	b = int(input())	User enters the value 0	−13	**0**
3	if a > 3:	This evaluates to False		
4	elif a > 4 and b <= 10:	This evaluates to False		
5	elif a * 2 == -26:	This evaluates to True		
6	print("Message #4")	It displays: Message #4		
7	print("Message #5")	It displays: Message #5		
8	b += 1		−13	**1**
9	print("The end!")	It displays: The end!		

✎ *Note that after step 8 the fourth Boolean expression* (b == 1) *could also have evaluated to* True, *but it was never checked.*

iii. For the input values of 1 and −1, the trace table looks like this.

Step	Statement	Notes	a	b
1	a = int(input())	User enters the value 1	**1**	?
2	b = int(input())	User enters the value −1	1	**−1**
3	if a > 3:	This evaluates to False		

4	`elif a > 4 and b <= 10:`	This evaluates to `False`
5	`elif a * 2 == -26:`	This evaluates to `False`
6	`elif b == 1:`	This evaluates to `False`
7	`print("Message #7")`	It displays: Message #7
8	`print("Message #8")`	It displays: Message #8
9	`print("The end!")`	It displays: The end!

Exercise 18.1-2   The Days of the Week

Design a flowchart and write the corresponding Python program that prompts the user to enter an integer between 1 and 5, and then displays the corresponding work day (Monday, Tuesday, Wednesday, Thursday, or Friday). If the value entered is invalid, an error message must be displayed.

Solution

The flowchart is shown here.

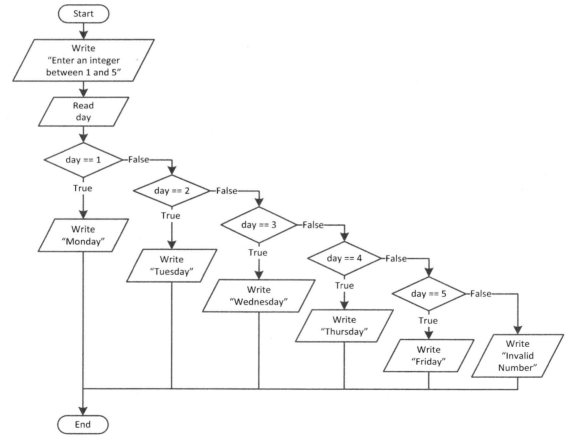

and the corresponding Python program is shown here.

```
                              📁 file_18_1_2
day = int(input("Enter an integer between 1 and 5: "))
```

```
if day == 1:
    print("Monday")
elif day == 2:
    print("Tuesday")
elif day == 3:
    print("Wednesday")
elif day == 4:
    print("Thursday")
elif day == 5:
    print("Friday")
else:
    print("Invalid Number")
```

Exercise 18.1-3   Counting the Digits

Write a Python program that prompts the user to enter an integer between 0 and 999 and then counts its total number of digits. In the end, a message "You entered a N-digit number" must be displayed, where N is the total number of digits. Assume that the user enters a valid integer between 0 and 999.

Solution

You may be trying to figure out how to solve this exercise using DIV operations. You are probably thinking of dividing the given integer by 10 and checking whether the integer quotient is 0. If it is, this means that the given integer is a one-digit integer. And you can divide it by 100, or by 1000 to check for two-digit and three-digit integers correspondingly. Your thinking is partly true!

The following multiple-alternative decision structure depicts your thoughts.

```
if x // 10 == 0:
    digits = 1
elif x // 100 == 0:
    digits = 2
elif x // 1000 == 0:
    digits = 3
```

If the given integer (in variable x) has one digit, the first Boolean expression evaluates to True and the rest of the Boolean expressions are never checked! If the given integer has two digits, the first Boolean expression evaluates to False, the second one evaluates to True, and the last one is never checked! And finally, if the given integer has three digits, the first two Boolean expressions evaluate to False and the last one evaluates to True!

So, you may now wonder where the problem is.

What if the wording of the exercise was *"Write a Python program that prompts the user to enter an integer and displays a message when the given integer has two digits"*. Probably you would do something such as the following:

```
x = int(input("Enter an integer: "))
if x // 100 == 0:
    print("A 2-digit integer entered")
```

The Boolean expression x // 100 == 0 works perfectly well for all given integers that have two digits or more. If the given integer has two digits, it evaluates to True and if the given integer has three digits or more, it evaluates to False. *"Problem solved!"* you may say. But is it really? What about a one-digit integer? Does this Boolean expression evaluate to False? Unfortunately not!

The solution is much easier that you would probably believe! What is the smallest two-digit integer that you can think of? It is 10, right? And what is the greatest one that you can think of? It is 99, right? So, the proper solution is as follows.

```python
x = int(input("Enter an integer: "))
if 10 <= x <= 99:
    print("A 2-digit integer entered")
```

And the complete solution to the exercise is as follows!

```
                            📁 file_18_1_3a
x = int(input("Enter an integer (0 - 999): "))

if 0 <= x <= 9:
    digits = 1
elif 10 <= x <= 99:
    digits = 2
else:
    digits = 3

print("A ", digits, "-digit integer entered", sep = "")
```

Since the wording of this exercise assumes that the user enters a valid integer between 0 and 999, the program should not include checking the validity of data input. However, if you wish to make your program even better and display an error message to the user when he or she enters a value that is not between 0 and 999, you can do something like this:

```
                            📁 file_18_1_3b
x = int(input("Enter an integer (0 - 999): "))

if 0 <= x <= 9:
    print("A 1-digit integer entered")
elif 10 <= x <= 99:
    print("A 2-digit integer entered")
elif 100 <= x <= 999:
    print("A 3-digit integer entered")
else:
    print("Wrong number!")
```

18.2   Review Questions: True/False

Choose **true** or **false** for each of the following statements.

1.   The multiple-alternative decision structure is used to expand the number of alternatives.

2.   The multiple-alternative decision structure can have at most three alternatives.

3.   In a multiple-alternative decision structure, once a Boolean expression evaluates to True, the next Boolean expression is also evaluated.

4.   In a multiple-alternative decision structure, the last statement or block of statements N+1 (appearing below the else Python keyword) is always executed.

5.   In a multiple-alternative decision structure, the last statement or block of statements N+1 (appearing below the else Python keyword) is executed when at least one of the previous Boolean expressions has evaluated to True.

6. In a multiple-alternative decision structure, the last statement or block of statements N+1, and by extension the `else` Python keyword, can be omitted.

7. In the following code fragment, the statement `y += 1` is executed only when variable `a` contains a value other than 1, 2, or 3.

```python
if a == 1:
    x += 5
elif a == 2:
    x -= 2
elif a == 3:
    x -= 9
else:
    x += 3
y += 1
```

8. In the code fragment of the previous exercise, the statement `x += 3` is executed only when variable `a` contains a value other than 1, 2, or 3.

18.3 Review Exercises

Complete the following exercises.

1. Create a trace table to determine the values of the variables in each step for four different executions of the next Python program.

   The input values for the four executions are (i) 5, (ii) 150, (iii) 250, and (iv) −1.

```python
q = int(input())
if 0 < q <= 50:
    b = 1
elif 50 < q <= 100:
    b = 2
elif 100 < q <= 200:
    b = 3
else:
    b = 4
print(b)
```

2. Create a trace table to determine the values of the variables in each step for three different executions of the next Python program.

   The input values for the three executions are (i) 5, (ii) 150, and (iii) −1.

```python
amount = float(input())
discount = 0
if amount < 20:
    discount = 0
elif 20 <= amount < 60:
    discount = 5
elif 60 <= amount < 100:
    discount = 10
elif amount >= 100:
    discount = 15
payment = amount - amount * discount / 100
print(discount, ",", payment)
```

3. Create a trace table to determine the values of the variables in each step of the next Python program for three different executions. Then, design the corresponding flowchart.

    The input values for the three executions are (i) 1, (ii) 3, and (iii) 250.

    ```python
    a = int(input())
    x = 0
    y = 0
    if a == 1:
        x = x + 5
        y = y + 5
    elif a == 2:
        x = x - 2
        y -= 1
    elif a == 3:
        x = x - 9
        y = y + 3
    else:
        x = x + 3
        y += 1
    print(x, ",", y)
    ```

4. Create a trace table to determine the values of the variables in each step of the next Python program for three different executions. Then, design the corresponding flowchart.

    The input values for the three executions are (i) 10, 2, 5; (ii) 5, 2, 3; and (iii) 4, 6, 2.

    ```python
    a = int(input())
    x = int(input())
    y = float(input())
    if a == 10:
        x = x % 2
        y = y ** 2
    elif a == 3:
        x = x * 2
        y -= 1
    elif a == 5:
        x = x + 4
        y += 7
    else:
        x -= 3
        y += 1
    print(x, ",", y)
    ```

5. Write the following Python program using correct indentation.

    ```python
    a = float(input())
    if a < 1:
    y = 5 + a
    print(y)
    elif a < 5:
    y = 23 / a
    print(y)
    ```

```
elif a < 10:
y = 5 * a
print(y)
else:
print("Error!")
```

6. Two football teams play against each other in the UEFA Champions League. Write a Python program that prompts the user to enter the names of the two teams and the goals each team scored and then displays the name of the winner or the message "It's a tie!" when both teams score equal number of goals. Assume that the user enters valid values.

7. Design a flowchart and write the corresponding Python program that lets the user enter an integer between –9999 and 9999, and then counts its total number of digits. In the end, a message "You entered a N-digit number" is displayed, where N is the total number of digits. Assume that the user enters a valid integer between –9999 and 9999.

8. Rewrite the Python program of the previous exercise to validate the data input. An error message must be displayed when the user enters an invalid value.

9. Write a Python program that displays the following menu:

    1. Convert USD to Euro (EUR)

    2. Convert USD to British Pound Sterling (GBP)

    3. Convert USD to Japanese Yen (JPY)

    4. Convert USD to Canadian Dollar (CAD)

    It then prompts the user to enter a choice (of 1, 2, 3, or 4) and an amount in US dollars and calculates and displays the required value. Assume that the user enters valid values. It is given that

    ▶ $1 = 0.87 EUR (€)

    ▶ $1 = 0.78 GBP (£)

    ▶ $1 = ¥ 108.55 JPY

    ▶ $1 = 1.33 CAD ($)

10. Write a Python program that prompts the user to enter the number of a month between 1 and 12, and then displays the corresponding season. Assume that the user enters a valid value. It is given that

    ▶ Winter includes months 12, 1, and 2

    ▶ Spring includes months 3, 4, and 5

    ▶ Summer includes months 6, 7, and 8

    ▶ Fall (Autumn) includes months 9, 10, and 11

11. Rewrite the Python program of the previous exercise to validate the data input. An error message must be displayed when the user enters an invalid value.

12. Write a Python program that prompts the user to enter the name of a month, and then displays the corresponding number (1 for January, 2 for February, and so on). If the value entered is invalid, an error message must be displayed.

13. Write a Python program that prompts the user to enter a number between 1.0 and 4.9, and then displays the number as English text. For example, for the number 2.3, it must display "Two point three". Assume that the user enters a valid value. Try not to check each real number individually (1.0, 1.1, 1.2, … 4.9). Find a more clever way!

14. The most popular and commonly used grading system in the United States uses discrete evaluation in the form of letter grades. Design a flowchart and write the corresponding Python program that prompts the user to enter a letter between A and F, and then displays the corresponding percentage according to the following table.

Grade	Percentage
A	90 – 100
B	80 – 89
C	70 – 79
D	60 – 69
E / F	0 – 59

Assume that the user enters a valid value.

15. Design a flowchart and write the corresponding Python program that displays the following menu:

1. Convert Miles to Yards

2. Convert Miles to Feet

3. Convert Miles to Inches

It then prompts the user to enter a choice (of 1, 2, or 3) and a distance in miles. Then, it calculates and displays the required value. Assume that the user enters a valid value for the distance. However, if the choice entered is invalid, an error message must be displayed. It is given that

► 1 mile = 1760 yards

► 1 mile = 5280 feet

► 1 mile = 63360 inches

16. Roman numerals are shown in the following table.

Number	Roman Numeral
1	I
2	II
3	III
4	IV
5	V
6	VI
7	VII
8	VIII
9	IX
10	X

Write a Python program that prompts the user to enter a Roman numeral between I and X, and then displays the corresponding number. However, if the choice entered is invalid, an error message must be displayed.

17. An online CD shop awards points to its customers based on the total number of audio CDs purchased each month. The points are awarded as follows:

► If the customer purchases 1 CD, he or she is awarded 3 points.

► If the customer purchases 2 CDs, he or she is awarded 10 points.

► If the customer purchases 3 CDs, he or she is awarded 20 points.

► If the customer purchases 4 CDs or more, he or she is awarded 45 points.

Write a Python program that prompts the user to enter the total number of CDs that he or she has purchased in a month, and then displays the number of points awarded. Assume that the user enters a valid value.

18. Write a Python program that prompts the user to enter his or her name, and then displays "Good morning NN" or "Good evening NN" or "Good night NN", where NN is the name of the user. The message to be displayed must be chosen randomly.

19. Write a Python program that lets the user enter a word such as "zero", "one" or "two", and then converts it into the corresponding digit, such as 0, 1, or 2. This must be done for the numbers 0 to 9. Display "I don't know this number!" when the user enters an unknown.

20. The Beaufort[1] scale is an empirical measure that relates wind speed to observed conditions on land or at sea. Write a Python program that prompts the user to enter the Beaufort number, and then displays the corresponding description from the following table. However, if the number entered is invalid, an error message must be displayed.

Beaufort Number	Description
0	Calm
1	Light air
2	Light breeze
3	Gentle breeze
4	Moderate breeze
5	Fresh breeze
6	Strong breeze
7	Moderate gale
8	Gale
9	Strong gale
10	Storm
11	Violent storm
12	Hurricane force

---

[1] Francis Beaufort (1774–1857) was an Irish hydrographer and officer in Britain's Royal Navy. He is the inventor of the Beaufort wind force scale.

Chapter 19
Nested Decision Control Structures

19.1   What are Nested Decision Control Structures?

Nested decision control structures are decision control structures that are "nested" (enclosed) within another decision control structure. This means that one decision control structure can nest (enclose) another decision control structure (which then becomes the "nested" decision control structure). In turn, that nested decision control structure can enclose another decision structure, and so on.

An example of a nested decision control structure is shown here.

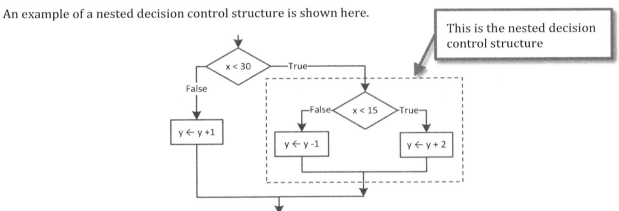

This can be rearranged to become

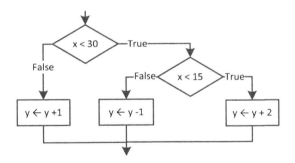

and the Python program is shown here.

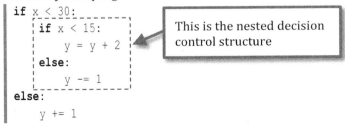

There are no practical limitations to how deep this nesting can go. As long as the syntax rules are not violated, you can nest as many decision control structures as you wish. For practical reasons however, as you move to three or four levels of nesting, the entire structure becomes very complex and difficult to understand.

✎ *Complex code may lead to invalid results! Try to keep your code as simple as possible by breaking large nested decision control structures into multiple smaller ones, or by using other types of decision control structures.*

Obviously, you can nest **any** decision control structure inside **any other** decision control structure as long as you keep them syntactically and logically correct. In the next example, a multiple-alternative decision structure is nested within a dual-alternative decision structure.

📁 **file_19_1**

```python
x = int(input("Enter a choice: "))

if x < 1 or x > 4:
    print("Invalid choice")
else:
    print("Valid choice")

    if x == 1:
        print("1st choice selected")
    elif x == 2:
        print("2nd choice selected")
    elif x == 3:
        print("3rd choice selected")
    else:
        print("4th choice selected")
```

> This is a nested multiple-alternative decision structure.

✎ *Note that keyword* else *is missing from the multiple-alternative decision structure.*

Exercise 19.1-1   Trace Tables and Nested Decision Control Structures

Create a trace table to determine the values of the variables in each step of the next Python program for three different executions.

The input values for the three executions are (i) 13, (ii) 18, and (iii) 30.

📁 **file_19_1_1**

```python
x = int(input())
y = 10

if x < 30:
    if x < 15:
        y = y + 2
    else:
        y -= 1
else:
    y += 1

print(y)
```

Solution

i.   For the input value of 13, the trace table looks like this.

Step	Statement	Notes	x	y
1	x = int(input())	User enters the value 13	13	?
2	y = 10		13	10
3	if x < 30:	This evaluates to True		
4	if x < 15:	This evaluates to True		
5	y = y + 2		13	12
6	print(y)	It displays: 12		

ii.   For the input value of 18, the trace table looks like this.

Step	Statement	Notes	x	y
1	x = int(input())	User enters the value 18	18	?
2	y = 10		18	10
3	if x < 30:	This evaluates to True		
4	if x < 15:	This evaluates to False		
5	y -= 1		18	9
6	print(y)	It displays: 9		

iii.   For the input value of 30, the trace table looks like this.

Step	Statement	Notes	x	y
1	x = int(input())	User enters the value 30	30	?
2	y = 10		30	10
3	if x < 30:	This evaluates to False		
4	y += 1		30	11
5	print(y)	It displays: 11		

Exercise 19.1-2   Positive, Negative or Zero?

Design a flowchart and write the corresponding Python program that lets the user enter a number from the keyboard and then displays the messages "Positive", "Negative", or "Zero" depending on whether the given value is greater than, less than, or equal to zero.

Solution

The flowchart is shown here.

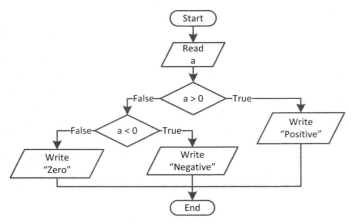

This Python program can be written using either a nested decision control structure or a multiple-alternative decision structure. Let's try them both!

First approach – Using a nested decision control structure

```
                              📁 file_19_1_2a
a = float(input())

if a > 0:
    print("Positive")
else:
    if a < 0:
        print("Negative")
    else:
        print("Zero")
```

Second approach – Using a multiple-alternative decision structure

```
                              📁 file_19_1_2b
a = float(input())

if a > 0:
    print("Positive")
elif a < 0:
    print("Negative")
else:
    print("Zero")
```

19.2   A Mistake That You Will Probably Make!

In flowcharts, a very common mistake that novice programmers make is to leave some paths unconnected, as shown in the flowchart that follows.

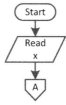

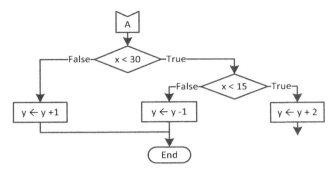

Please keep in mind that every path tries to reach the end of the algorithm, thus you cannot leave any of them unconnected.

On the other hand, try to avoid flowcharts that use many End symbols, as shown below, since these algorithms are difficult to read and understand.

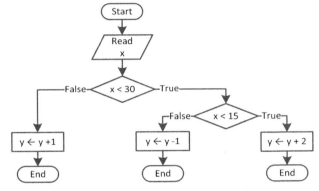

Let's say that you are in the middle of designing a flowchart (see the flowchart that follows), and you want to start closing all of its decision control structures.

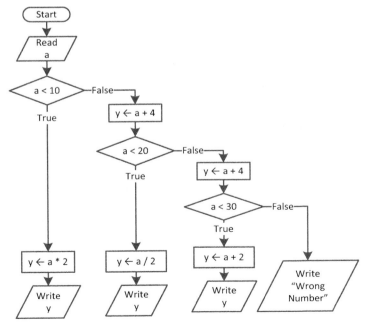

Just remember that the decision control structure that opens last must be the first one to close! In this example, the last decision control structure is the one that evaluates the expression a < 30. This is the first one that you need to close, as shown here.

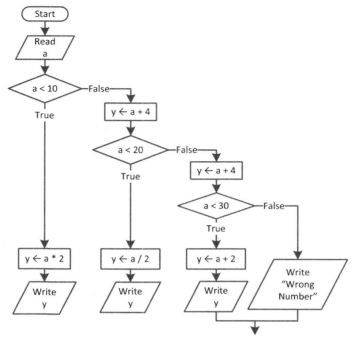

Next, you need to close the second to last decision control structure as shown here.

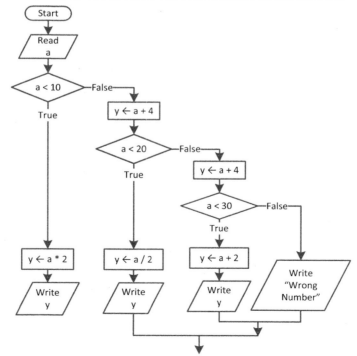

And finally, you need to close the third to last decision control structure as shown here.

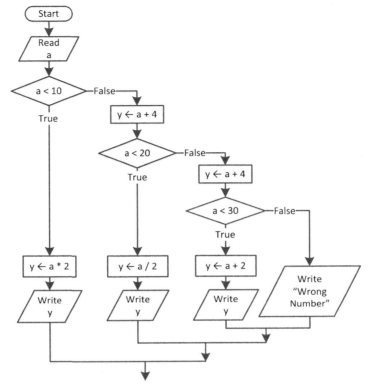

The last flowchart can be rearranged to become like the one shown here.

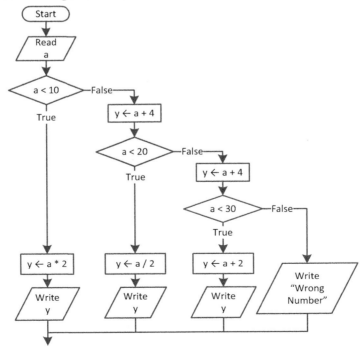

19.3   Review Questions: True/False

Choose **true** or **false** for each of the following statements.

1. Nesting of decision control structures describes a situation in which one or more than one path of a decision control structure enclose other decision control structures.

2. Nesting level can go as deep as the programmer wishes.

3. When a problem can be solved using either a multiple-alternative decision structure or nested decision control structures, the second option is better because the program becomes more readable.

4. It is possible to nest a multiple-alternative decision structure within a simple-alternative decision structure, but not the opposite.

5. When designing flowcharts with nested decision control structures, the decision control structure that opens first must be the last one to close.

19.4   Review Exercises

Complete the following exercises.

1. Create a trace table to determine the values of the variables in each step of the next Python program for four different executions.

    The input values for the four executions are (i) 20, 1; (ii) 20, 3; (iii) 12, 8; and (iv) 50, 0.

    ```python
    x = int(input())
    y = int(input())

    if x < 30:
        if y == 1:
            x = x % 3
            y = 5
        elif y == 2:
            x = x * 2
            y = 2
        elif y == 3:
            x = x + 5
            y += 3
        else:
            x -= 2
            y += 1
    else:
        y += 1

    print(x, ",", y)
    ```

2. Create a trace table to determine the values of the variables in each step of the next Python program for four different executions.

    The input values for the four executions are (i) 60, 25; (ii) 50, 8; (iii) 20, 15; and (iv) 10, 30.

    ```python
    x = int(input())
    y = int(input())

    if (x + y) / 2 <= 20:
        if y < 10:
    ```

```
        x = x % 3
        y += 2
    elif y < 20:
        x = x * 5
        y += 2
    else:
        x = x - 2
        y += 3
else:
    if y < 15:
        x = x % 4
        y = 2
    elif y < 23:
        x = x % 2
        y -= 2
    else:
        x = 2 * x + 5
        y += 1

print(x, ",", y)
```

3. Write the following Python program using correct indentation.

```
a = int(input())
if a > 1000:
print("Big Positive")
else:
if a > 0:
print("Positive")
else:
if a < -1000:
print("Big Negative")
else:
if a < 0:
print("Negative")
else:
print("Zero")
```

4. Write a Python program that prompts the user to enter the lengths of three sides of a triangle, and then determines whether or not the given numbers can be lengths of the three sides of a triangle. If the lengths are not valid, a corresponding message must be displayed; otherwise the program must further determine whether the triangle is

   a. equilateral

      Hint: In an equilateral triangle, all sides are equal.

   b. right (or right-angled)

      Hint: Use the Pythagorean Theorem.

   c. not special

   Hint: In any triangle, the length of each side is less than the sum of the lengths of the other two sides.

5. Inside an automated teller machine (ATM) there are notes of $10, $5, and $1. Write a Python program to emulate the way this ATM works. At the beginning, the machine prompts the user to enter the four-digit PIN and then checks for PIN validity (assume "1234" as the valid PIN). If given PIN is correct, the program must prompt the user to enter the amount of money (an integer value) that he or she wants to withdraw and finally it displays the least number of notes the ATM must dispense. For example, if the user enters an amount of $36, the program must display "3 note(s) of $10, 1 note(s) of $5, and 1 note(s) of $1". Moreover, if the user enters a wrong PIN, the machine will allow him or her two retries. If the user enters an incorrect PIN all three times, the message "PIN locked" must be displayed and the program must end. Assume that the user enters a valid value for the amount.

6. Write a Python program that prompts the user to enter two values, one for temperature and one for wind speed. If the temperature is above 75 degrees Fahrenheit, the day is considered hot, otherwise it is cold. If the wind speed is above 12 miles per hour, the day is considered windy, otherwise it is not windy. The program must display one single message, depending on values given. For example, if a user enters 60 for temperature and 10 for wind speed, the program must display "The day is cold and not windy". Assume that the user enters valid values.

Chapter 20
More about Flowcharts with Decision Control Structures

20.1 Introduction

By working through the previous chapters, you've become familiar with all the decision control structures. Since flowcharts are an ideal way to learn "Algorithmic Thinking" and to help you better understand specific control structures, this chapter is dedicated to teaching you how to convert a Python program to a flowchart, or a flowchart to a Python program.

20.2 Converting Python Programs to Flowcharts

To convert a Python program to its corresponding flowchart, you need to recall all the decision control structures and their corresponding flowchart fragments. They are all summarized here.

The single-alternative decision structure

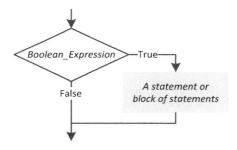

The dual-alternative decision structure

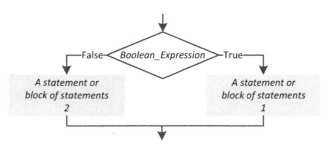

The multiple-alternative decision structure

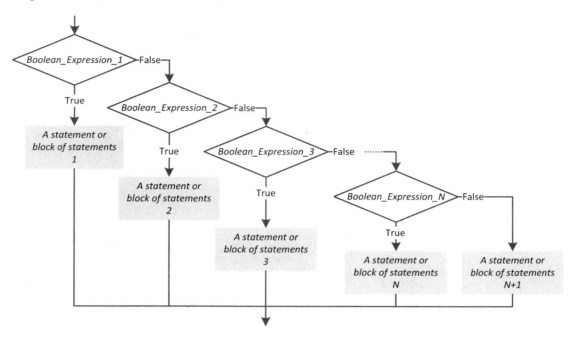

Exercise 20.2-1   Designing the Flowchart

Design the flowchart that corresponds to the following Python program.

```python
x = float(input())

z = x ** 3
w = (z - 4) * (x - 3) / 7 + 36

if z >= w and x < z:
    y = 2 * x
    if y > 0:       #This is a nested single-
        y += 1      #alternative decision structure
else:
    y = 4 * x
    a += 1

print(y)
```

Solution

In this Python program there is a single-alternative decision structure nested within a dual-alternative decision structure. Its corresponding flowchart is as follows.

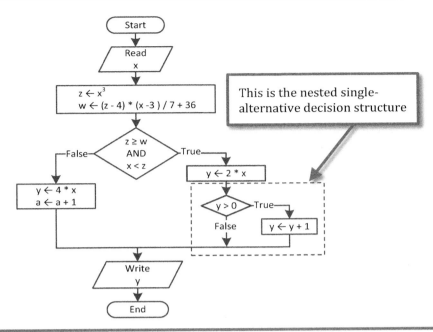

📖 *A flowchart is a very loose method of representing an algorithm. Thus, it is quite permissible to write x³ or even to use the Python operator (**). Do whatever you wish; everything is permitted, on condition that anyone familiar with flowcharts can clearly understand what you are trying to say!*

Exercise 20.2-2   Designing the Flowchart

Design the flowchart that corresponds to the following code fragment given in general form.

```
if Boolean_Expression_A:

    Block of statements A1

    if Boolean_Expression_B:

        Block of statements B1

    Block of statements A2

else:

    Block of statements A3

    if Boolean_Expression_C:

        Block of statements C1

    else:

        Block of statements C2
```

Solution

For better observation, the initial code fragment is presented again with all the nested decision control structures enclosed in rectangles.

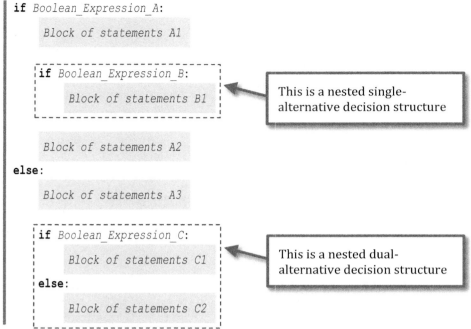

and the flowchart fragment in general form is shown here.

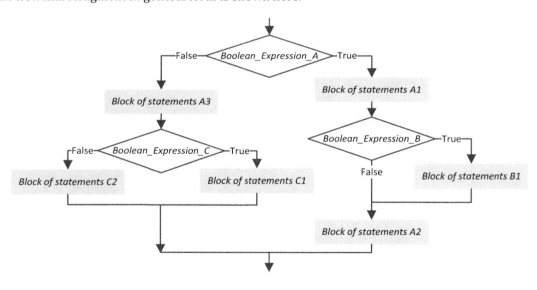

Exercise 20.2-3   Designing the Flowchart

Design the flowchart that corresponds to the following Python program.

```python
a = float(input())

if a < 0:
    y = a * 2
elif a < 10:
    y = a / 2
```

```
elif a < 100:
    y = a + 2
else:
    b = float(input())
    y = a * b
    if y > 0:        #This is a nested dual-alternative decision structure
        y -= 1
    else:
        y += 1

print(y)
```

Solution

In this Python program, a dual-alternative decision structure is nested within a multiple-alternative decision structure.

The flowchart is shown here.

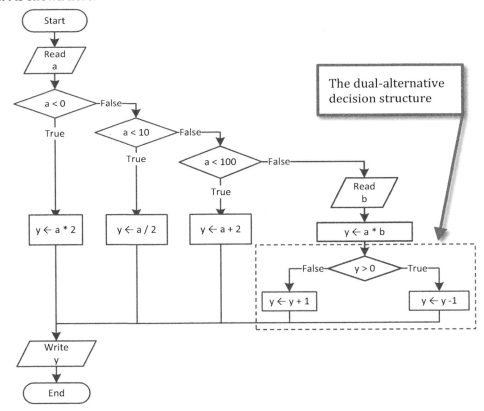

20.3 Converting Flowcharts to Python Programs

This conversion is not always an easy one. There are cases in which the flowchart designers follow no particular rules, so the initial flowchart may need some modifications before it can become a Python program. An example of one such case is as follows.

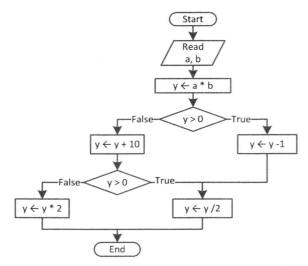

As you can see, the decision control structures included in this flowchart fragment match none of the structures that you have already learned, such as the single-alternative, the dual-alternative, and the multiple-alternative. Thus, you have only one choice and this is to modify the flowchart by adding extra statements or removing existing ones until known decision control structures start to appear. Following are some exercises in which the initial flowchart does need modification.

Exercise 20.3-1   *Writing the Python Program*

Write the Python program that corresponds to the following flowchart.

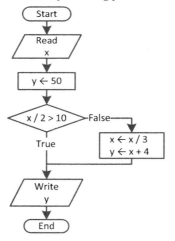

Solution

This is quite easy. The only obstacle you must overcome is that the true and false paths are not quite in the right positions. You need to use the true path, and not the false path, to actually include the statements in the single-alternative decision structure.

It is possible to switch the two paths, but you also need to negate the corresponding Boolean expression. The following two flowchart fragments are equivalent.

Thus, the flowchart can be modified and look like this.

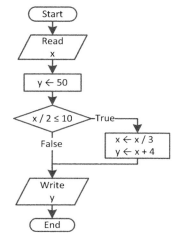

and the corresponding Python program is shown here.

```python
x = float(input())

y = 50
if x / 2 <= 10:
    x = x / 3
    y = x + 4

print(y)
```

Exercise 20.3-2   Writing the Python Program

Write the Python program that corresponds to the following flowchart.

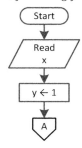

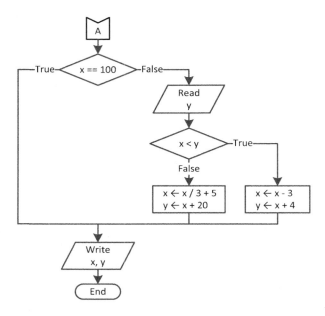

Solution

In this exercise there is a dual-alternative decision structure nested within a single-alternative one. You just need to negate the Boolean expression x == 100 and switch the true/false paths. The Python program is shown here.

```python
x = float(input())

y = 1

if x != 100:    #This is a single-alternative decision structure
    y = float(input())
    if x < y:       #This is a nested dual-alternative decision structure
        x = x - 3
        y = x + 4
    else:
        x = x / 3 + 5
        y = x + 20

print(x, y)
```

Exercise 20.3-3   Writing the Python Program

Write the Python program that corresponds to the following flowchart.

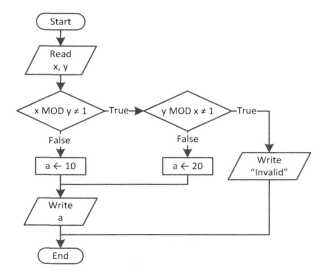

Solution

In this flowchart, the decision control structures match none of the decision control structures that you have already learned, such as the single-alternative, the dual-alternative, and the multiple-alternative. Thus, you must modify the flowchart by adding extra statements or removing existing ones until known decision control structures start to appear!

The obstacle you must overcome in this exercise is the decision control structure that evaluates the y MOD x ≠ 1 Boolean expression. Note that when flow of execution follows the false path, it executes the statement a ← 20 and then the statement Write a before it reaches the end of the algorithm. Thus, if you simply add a new statement, Write a, inside its false path you can keep the flow of execution intact. The following flowchart is equivalent to the initial one.

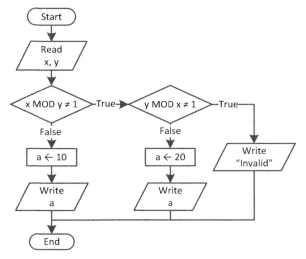

Now, the flowchart includes known decision control structures; that is, a dual-alternative decision structure nested within another dual-alternative one.

The corresponding Python program is as follows.

```python
x = int(input())
y = int(input())
```

```
if x % y != 1:
    if y % x != 1:
        print("Invalid")
    else:
        a = 20
        print(a)
else:
    a = 10
    print(a)
```

However, there is something better that you can do! If you negate all Boolean expressions and also switch their true/false paths, you can have a multiple-alternative decision structure, which is more convenient in Python than nested decision control structures. The modified flowchart is shown here.

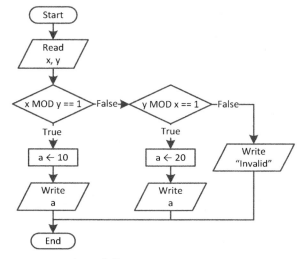

and the corresponding Python program is as follows.

```
x = int(input())
y = int(input())
if x % y == 1:
    a = 10
    print(a)
elif y % x == 1:
    a = 20
    print(a)
else:
    print("Invalid")
```

20.4   Review Exercises

Complete the following exercises.

1.   Design the flowchart that corresponds to the following Python program.

```
a = int(input())
if a % 10 == 0:
    a += 1
```

```python
    print("Message #1")
if a % 3 == 1:
    a += 5
    print("Message #2")
if a % 3 == 2:
    a += 10
    print("Message #3")
print(a)
```

2. Design the flowchart that corresponds to the following Python program.

```python
a = int(input())
if a % 10 == 0:
    a += 1
    print("Message #1")

if a % 3 == 1:
    a += 5
    print("Message #2")
else:
    a += 7

print(a)
```

3. Design the flowchart that corresponds to the following Python program.

```python
a = float(input())

if a < 0:
    y = a * 2
    if y > 0:
        y +=2
    elif y == 0:
        y *= 6
    else:
        y /= 7
elif a < 22:
    y = a / 3
elif a < 32:
    y = a - 7
else:
    b = float(input())
    y = a - b
print(y)
```

4. Design the flowchart that corresponds to the following code fragment given in general form.

```python
if Boolean_Expression_A:
    if Boolean_Expression_B:
        Block of statements B1
    else:
```

```
            Block of statements B2

        Block of statements A1
else:
        Block of statements A2
        if Boolean_Expression_C:
                Block of statements C1
        elif Boolean_Expression_D:
                Block of statements D1
        else:
                Block of statements E1

        Block of statements A3
```

5. Design the flowchart that corresponds to the following Python program.

```python
a = int(input())
y = 0

if a == 1:
    y = a * 2
elif a == 2:
    y = a - 3
elif a == 3:
    y = a + 3
    if y % 2 == 1:
        y += 2
    elif y == 0:
        y *= 6
    else:
        y /= 7
elif a == 4:
    b = float(input())
    y = a + b + 2
print(y)
```

6. Write the Python program that corresponds to the following flowchart.

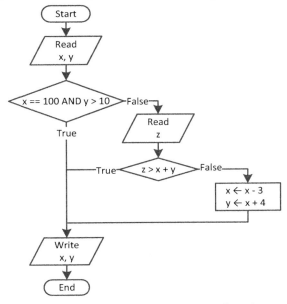

7. Write the Python program that corresponds to the following flowchart.

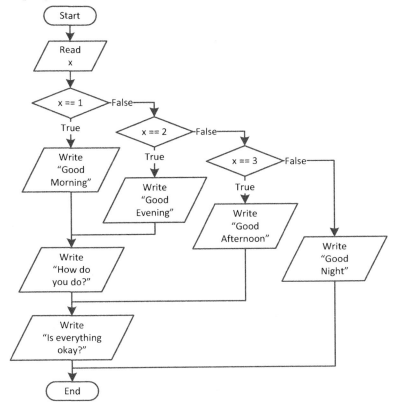

8. Write the Python program that corresponds to the following flowchart.

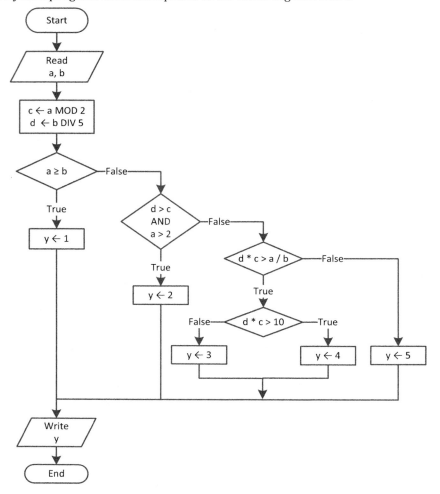

9. Write the Python program that corresponds to the following flowchart.

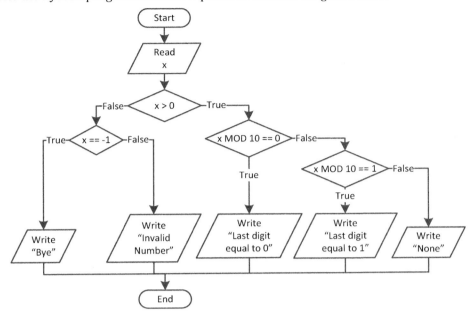

10. Write the Python program that corresponds to the following flowchart.

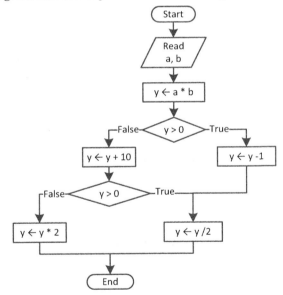

11. Write the Python program that corresponds to the following flowchart.

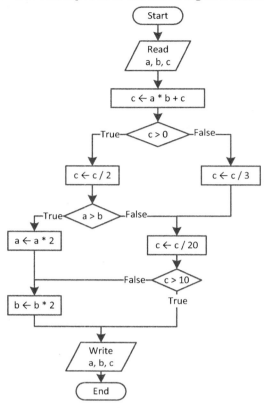

Chapter 21
Tips and Tricks with Decision Control Structures

21.1 Introduction

This chapter is dedicated to teaching you some useful tips and tricks that can help you write "better" code. You should always keep them in mind when you design your own algorithms, or even your own Python programs.

These tips and tricks can help you increase your code's readability and help make the code shorter or even faster. Of course there is no single perfect methodology because on one occasion the use of a specific tip or trick may help, but on another occasion the same tip or trick may have exactly the opposite result. Most of the time, code optimization is a matter of programming experience.

> *Smaller algorithms are not always the best solution to a given problem. In order to solve a specific problem, you might write a very short algorithm that unfortunately proves to consume a lot of CPU time. On the other hand, you may solve the same problem with another algorithm which, even though it seems longer, calculates the result much faster.*

21.2 Choosing a Decision Control Structure

The following diagram can help you decide which decision control structure is a better choice for a given problem depending on the number of variables checked.

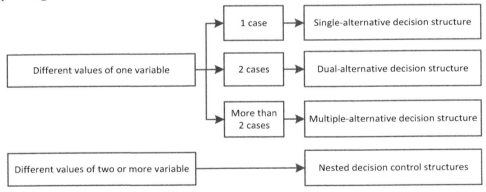

> *This diagram recommends the best option, not the only option. For example, when there are more than two cases for one variable, it is not wrong to use a nested decision control structure instead. The proposed multiple-alternative decision structure, though, is better since it is more convenient.*

21.3   Streamlining the Decision Control Structure

Look carefully at the following flowchart fragment given in general form.

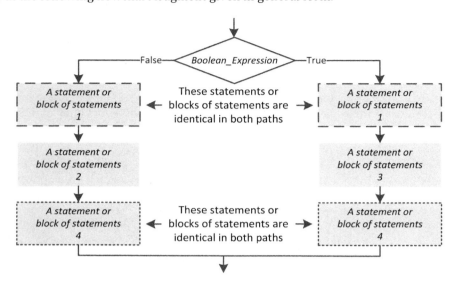

As you can see, two identical statements or blocks of statements exist at the beginning and two other identical statements or blocks of statements exist at the end of both paths of the dual-alternative decision structure. This means that, regardless of the result of *Boolean_Expression*, these statements are executed either way. Thus, you can simply move them outside and (respectively) right before and right after the dual-alternative decision structure, as shown in this equivalent structure.

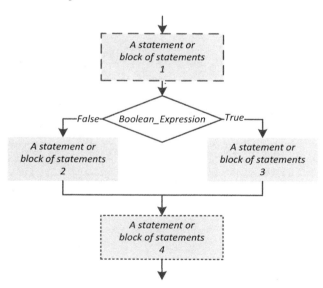

The same tip can be applied to any decision control structure, as long as an identical statement or block of statements exists in all paths. Of course, there are also cases where this tip cannot be applied.

Are you still confused? Next, you will find some exercises that can help you to understand better.

Exercise 21.3-1   "Shrinking" the Algorithm

Redesign the following flowchart using fewer statements.

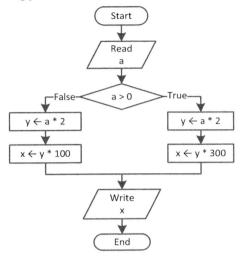

Solution

As you can see, the statement y ← a * 2 exists in both paths of the dual-alternative decision structure. This means that, regardless of the result of the Boolean expression, this statement is executed either way. Therefore, you can simply move the statement outside and right before the dual-alternative decision structure, as follows.

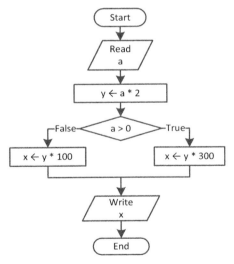

Exercise 21.3-2   "Shrinking" the Python Program

Rewrite the following Python program using fewer statements.

```python
a = int(input())

if a > 0:
    y = a * 4
```

```
    print(y)
else:
    y = a * 3
    print(y)
```

Solution

As you can see, the statement `print(y)` exists in both paths of the dual-alternative decision structure. This means that, regardless of the result of the Boolean expression, this statement is executed either way. Therefore, you can simply move the statement outside and right after the dual-alternative decision structure, as shown here.

```
a = int(input())

if a > 0:
    y = a * 4
else:
    y = a * 3

print(y)
```

Exercise 21.3-3   "Shrinking" the Algorithm

Redesign the following flowchart using fewer statements.

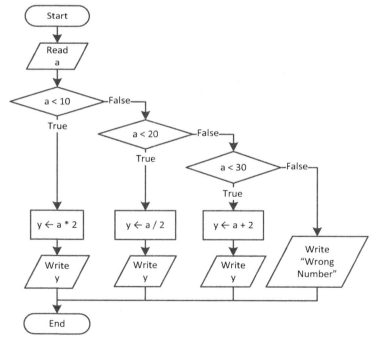

Solution

In this case, nothing special can be done. If you try to move the `Write y` statement outside of the multiple-alternative decision structure, the resulting flowchart that follows is definitely **not** equivalent to the initial one.

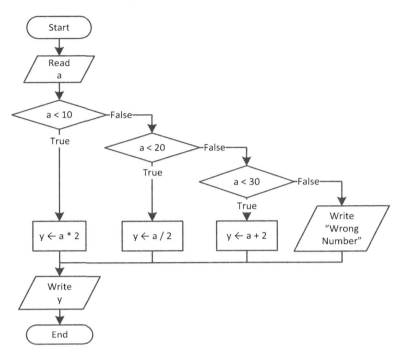

This is because of the last path on the right side which, in the initial flowchart, didn't include the `Write y` statement.

Examine both flowcharts to see whether they produce the same result. For example, suppose a user enters a wrong number. In both flowcharts, the flow of execution goes to the `Write "Wrong Number"` statement. After that, the initial flowchart executes no other statements but on the contrary, the second flowchart executes an extra `Write y` statement.

📖 *You cannot move a statement or block of statements outside of a decision control structure if it does not exist in all paths.*

You may now wonder whether there is any other way to move the `Write y` statement outside of the multiple-alternative decision structure. The answer is "yes", but you need to slightly rearrange the flowchart. You need to completely remove the last path on the right and use a brand new decision control structure in the beginning to check whether or not the given number is wrong. One possible solution is shown here.

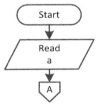

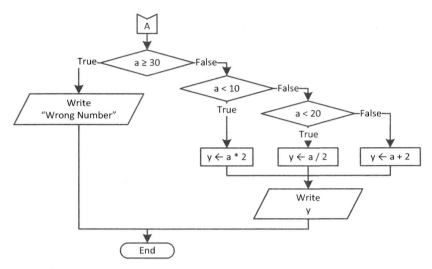

and the Python program is

```python
a = float(input())
if a >= 30:
    print("Wrong Number")
else:
    if a < 10:
        y = a * 2
    elif a < 20:
        y = a / 2
    else:
        y = a + 2

    print(y)
```

21.4 Logical Operators – to Use, or not to Use: That is the Question!

There are some cases in which you can use a logical operator instead of nested decision control structures, and this can lead to increased readability. Take a look at the following flowchart fragment given in general form.

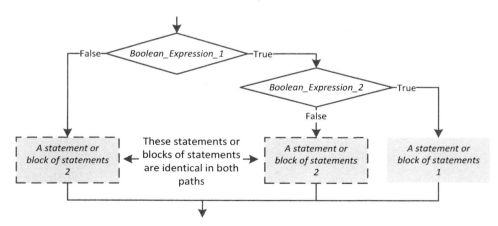

As you can see, the statement or block of statements 1 is executed only when **both** Boolean expressions evaluate to True. The statement or block of statements 2 is executed in all other cases. Therefore, this flowchart fragment can be redesigned using the AND logical operator.

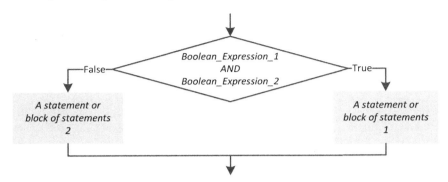

Now, let's take a look at another flowchart fragment given in general form.

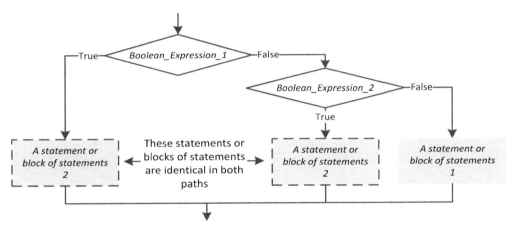

In this flowchart fragment, the statement or block of statements 2 is executed when **either** Boolean_Expression_1 evaluates to True **or** Boolean_Expression_2 evaluates to True. Therefore, you can redesign this flowchart fragment using the OR logical operator as shown here.

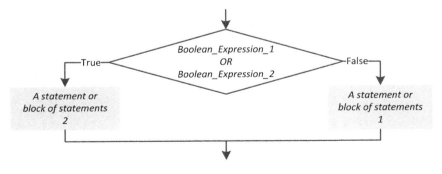

✎ *Obviously, these methodologies can be adapted to be used on nested decision control structures as well.*

Exercise 21.4-1   Rewriting the Code

Rewrite the following Python program using logical operators.

```python
today = input()
name = input()

if today == "February 16":
    if name == "Loukia":
        print("Happy Birthday!!!")
    else:
        print("No match!")
else:
    print("No match!")
```

Solution

The `print("Happy Birthday!!!")` statement is executed only when **both** Boolean expressions evaluate to True. The statement `print("No match!")` is executed in all other cases. Therefore, you can rewrite the Python program using the and logical operator.

```python
today = input()
name = input()

if today == "February 16" and name == "Loukia":
    print("Happy Birthday!!!")
else:
    print("No match!")
```

Exercise 21.4-2   Rewriting the Code

Rewrite the following Python program using logical operators.

```python
a = int(input())
b = int(input())

y = 0
if a > 10:
    y += 1
elif b > 20:
    y += 1
else:
    y -= 1

print(y)
```

Solution

The `y += 1` statement is executed when **either** variable a is greater than 10 **or** variable b is greater than 20. Therefore, you can rewrite the Python program using the or logical operator.

```python
a = int(input())
b = int(input())
```

```
y = 0
if a > 10 or b > 20:
    y += 1
else:
    y -= 1

print(y)
```

21.5 Merging Two or More Single-Alternative Decision Structures

Many times, an algorithm contains two or more single-alternative decision structures in a row which actually evaluate the same Boolean expression. An example is shown here.

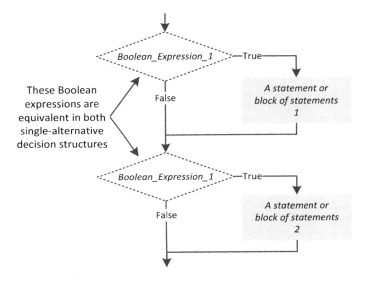

When a situation like this occurs, you can just merge all single-alternative decision structures to a single one, as follows.

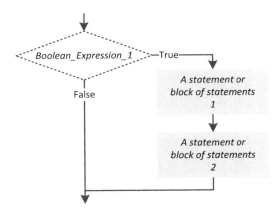

📖 *The single-alternative decision structures need to be adjacent to each other. If any statement exists between them, you can't merge them unless you are able to move this statement to somewhere else in your code.*

Exercise 21.5-1   Merging the Decision Control Structures

In the following Python program, merge the single-alternative decision structures.

```python
a = int(input())

if a > 0:
    print("Hello")

if a > 0:
    print("Hermes")
```

Solution

The first and second decision control structures are evaluating exactly the same Boolean expressions, so they can simply be merged into a single one.

The Python program becomes

```python
a = int(input())

if a > 0:
    print("Hello")
    print("Hermes")
```

Exercise 21.5-2   Merging the Decision Control Structures

In the following Python program, merge as many single-alternative decision structures as possible.

```python
a = int(input())

y = 0

if a > 0:
    y += a + 1

b = int(input())

if not(a <= 0):
    print("Hello Hera")

a += 1

if a > 0:
    print("Hallo Welt")

print(y)
```

This statement is not affected by the previous decision control structure and does not affect the next one.

The previous and next decision control structures are affected by this statement

Solution

If you take a closer look at the Python program, it becomes clear that the first and second decision control structures are actually evaluating exactly the same Boolean expression. Negation of a > 0 results in a <= 0, and a second negation of a <= 0 (using the not operator this time) results in not(a <= 0). Thus, a > 0 is in fact equivalent to not(a <= 0).

> 💾 *Two negations result in an affirmative.*

However, between the first and second decision control structures there is the statement b = int(input()), which prevents you from merging them into a single one. Fortunately, this statement can be moved to the beginning of the program since it doesn't really affect the rest flow of execution.

On the other hand, between the second and third decision control structures there is the statement a += 1, which also prevents you from merging; unfortunately, this statement cannot be moved anywhere else because it does affect the rest of the flow of execution (the second and third decision control structures are dependent upon this statement). Thus, the third decision control structure cannot be merged with the first and second ones!

The final Python program looks like this.

```python
a = int(input())
b = int(input())

y = 0

if a > 0:
    y += a + 1
    print("Hello Hera")

a += 1

if a > 0:
    print("Hallo Welt")

print(y)
```

21.6 Replacing Two Single-Alternative Decision Structures with a Dual-Alternative One

Take a look at the next example.

```python
if x > 40:
    #Do something

if x <= 40:
    #Do something else
```

The first decision control structure evaluates variable x to test if it is bigger than 40, and right after that, a second decision control structure evaluates the same variable again to test if it is less than or equal to 40!

This is a very common "mistake" that novice programmers make. They use two single-alternative decision structures even though one dual-alternative decision structure can accomplish the same thing.

The previous example can be rewritten using only one dual-alternative decision structure, as shown here.

```python
if x > 40:
    #Do something
else:
    #Do something else
```

Even though both examples are absolutely correct and work perfectly well, the second alternative is better. The CPU needs to evaluate only one Boolean expression, which results in faster execution time.

> ✎ *The two single-alternative decision structures must be adjacent to each other. If any statement exists between them, you can't "merge" them (that is, replace them with a dual-alternative decision structure) unless you are able to move this statement to somewhere else in your code.*

Exercise 21.6-1   "Merging" the Decision Control Structures

In the following Python program, "merge" as many single-alternative decision structures as possible.

```python
a = int(input())

y = 0

if a > 0:
    y += a

b = int(input())

if not(a > 0):
    print("Hello Zeus")

if y > 0:
    print(y + 5)

y += 1

if y <= 0:
    print(y + 12)
```

Solution

The first decision control structure evaluates variable a to test if it is greater than zero, and just right after that the second decision control structure evaluates variable a again to test if it is not greater than zero. Even though there is the statement b = int(input()) between them, this statement can be moved somewhere else because it doesn't really affect the rest of the flow of execution. Therefore, the first and second decision control structures can be merged!

On the other hand, between the third and fourth decision control structures there is the statement y += 1 which also prevents you from merging. Unfortunatelly, this statement cannot be moved anywhere else because it does affect the rest of the flow of execution (the third and fourth decision control structures are dependent upon this statement). Therefore, the third and fourth decision control structures cannot be merged!

The final Python program becomes

```python
a = int(input())
b = int(input())

y = 0
```

```
if a > 0:
    y += a
else:
    print("Hello Zeus")

if y > 0:
    print(y + 5)

y += 1

if y <= 0:
    print(y + 12)
```

21.7 Put the Boolean Expressions Most Likely to be True First

The multiple-alternative decision structure often needs to check several Boolean expressions before deciding which statement or block of statements to execute. In the next decision control structure,

```
if Boolean_Expression_1:

    A statement or block of statements 1

elif Boolean_Expression_2:

    A statement or block of statements 2

elif Boolean_Expression_3:

    A statement or block of statements 3
```

the program first tests if *Boolean_Expression_1* is True. If not, it tests if *Boolean_Expression_2* is True, and if not, it tests *Boolean_Expression_3*. However, what if *Boolean_Expression_1* is False most of the time and *Boolean_Expression_3* is True most of the time? This means that time is wasted testing *Boolean_Expression_1*, which is usually False, before testing *Boolean_Expression_3*, which is usually True.

To make your programs more efficient, you can put the Boolean expressions that are most likely to be True at the beginning, and the Boolean expressions that are most likely to be False at the end, as follows.

```
if Boolean_Expression_3:

    A statement or block of statements 3

elif Boolean_Expression_2:

    A statement or block of statements 2

elif Boolean_Expression_1:

    A statement or block of statements 1
```

Although this method may seem nonessential, every little bit of time that you save can add up to make your programs run faster and more efficiently.

Exercise 21.7-1   Rearranging the Boolean Expressions

According to an ultra-high top secret report, America's favorite pets are dogs, with cats at second place, guinea pigs next, and parrots coming in last. In the following Python program, rearrange the Boolean expressions to make the program run faster and more efficiently for most of the cases.

```python
kind = input("What is your favorite pet? ")


if kind == "Parrots":
    print("It screeches!")
elif kind == "Guinea pig":
    print("It squeaks")
elif kind == "Dog":
    print("It barks")
elif kind == "Cat":
    print("It meows")
```

Solution

For this top secret report, you can rearrange the Python program to make it run a little bit faster for most of the cases.

```python
kind = input("What is your favorite pet? ")


if kind == "Dog":
    print("It barks")
elif kind == "Cat":
    print("It meows")
elif kind == "Guinea pig":
    print("It squeaks")
elif kind == "Parrots":
    print("It screeches!")
```

21.8   Review Questions: True/False

Choose **true** or **false** for each of the following statements.

1.   Smaller algorithms are always the best solution to a given problem.

2.   You can move a statement outside, and right before, a dual-alternative decision structure as long as it exists at the beginning of both paths of the decision structure.

3.   You can always use a logical operator instead of nested decision control structures to increase readability.

4.   Two single-alternative decision structures can be merged into one single-alternative decision only when they are in a row and when they evaluate the same Boolean expression.

5.   Conversion from a dual-alternative decision structure to two single-alternative decision structures is always possible.

6.   Two single-alternative decision structures can be replaced by one dual-alternative decision only when they are in a row and only when they evaluate the same Boolean expression.

21.9   Review Questions: Multiple Choice

Select the correct answer for each of the following statements.

1.   The following two programs

```
a = int(input())           a = int(input())
if a > 40:                 print(a * 2)
    print(a * 2)           if a > 40:
    a += 1                     a += 1
else:                      else:
    print(a * 2)               a += 5
    a += 5
```

    a.   produce the same result.

    b.   do not produce the same result.

    c.   none of the above

2. The following two programs

```
a = int(input())           a = int(input())
if a > 40:                 if a > 40:
    print(a * 2)               print(a * 2)
if a > 40:                     print(a * 3)
    print(a * 3)
```

    a.   produce the same results, but the left program is faster.

    b.   produce the same results, but the right program is faster.

    c.   do not produce the same results.

    d.   none of the above

3. The following two programs

```
a = int(input())           a = int(input())

if a > 40:                 if a > 40:
    print(a * 2)               print(a * 2)
else:                      if a <= 40:
    print(a * 3)               print(a * 3)
```

    a.   produce the same result(s), but the left program is faster.

    b.   produce the same result(s), but the right program is faster.

    c.   do not produce the same result(s).

    d.   none of the above

21.10 Review Exercises

Complete the following exercises.

1. Rewrite the following Python program using fewer statements.

```
y = int(input())

if y > 0:
    x = int(input())
    a = x * 4 * y
    print(y)
    a += 1
else:
    x = int(input())
```

```
        a = x * 2 * y + 7
        print(y)
        a -= 1
    print(a)
```

2. Redesign the following flowchart using fewer statements.

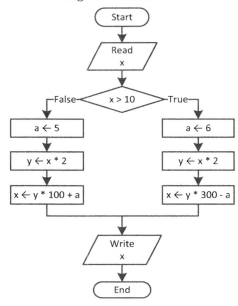

3. Rewrite the following Python program using fewer statements.

```
a = float(input())

if a < 1:
    y = 5 + a
    print(y)
elif a < 5:
    y = 23 / a
    print(y)
elif a < 10:
    y = 5 * a
    print(y)
else:
    print("Error!")
```

4. Rewrite the following Python program using logical operators.

```
day = int(input())
month = int(input())
name = input()

if day == 16:
    if month == 2:
        if name == "Loukia":
            print("Happy Birthday!!!")
```

```python
    else:
        print("No match!")
    else:
        print("No match!")
else:
    print("No match!")
```

5. A teacher asks her students to rewrite the following Python program without using logical operators.

```python
a = float(input())
b = float(input())
c = float(input())

if a > 10 and c < 2000:
    d = (a + b + c) / 12
    print("The result is:", d)
else:
    print("Error!")
```

One student wrote the following Python program:

```python
a = float(input())
b = float(input())
c = float(input())

if a > 10:
    if c < 2000:
        d = (a + b + c) / 12
        print("The result is:", d)
    else:
        print("Error!")
```

Determine if the program operates the same way for all possible paths as the one given by his teacher. If not, try to modify it and make it work the same way.

6. Rewrite the following Python program using only single-alternative decision structures.

```python
a = float(input())
b = float(input())
c = float(input())

if a > 10:
    if b < 2000:
        if c != 10:
            d = (a + b + c) / 12
            print("The result is:", d)
else:
    print("Error!")
```

7. In the following Python program, replace the two single-alternative decision structures by one dual-alternative decision structure.

```python
a = int(input())
```

```
y = 3
if a > 0:
    y = y * a
b = int(input())
if not(a <= 0):
    print("Hello Zeus")

print(y, b)
```

8. Rewrite the following Python program, using only one dual-alternative decision structure.

```
a = float(input())

y = 0
if a > 0:
    y = y + 7
b = float(input())
if not(a > 0):
    print("Hello Zeus")
if a <= 0:
    print(abs(a))
print(y)
```

9. According to research from 2013, the most popular operating system on tablet computers was iOS, with Android being in second place and Microsoft Windows in last place. In the following Python program, rearrange the Boolean expressions to make the program run more efficiently for most of the cases.

```
os = input("What is your tablet's OS? ")

if os == "Windows":
    print("Microsoft")
elif os == "iOS":
    print("Apple")
elif os == "android":
    print("Google")
```

Chapter 22
More Exercises with Decision Control Structures

22.1 Simple Exercises with Decision Control Structures

Exercise 22.1-1   Both Odds or Both Evens?

Write a Python program that prompts the user to enter two integers and then displays a message indicating whether both numbers are odd or both are even; otherwise the message "Nothing special" must be displayed.

Solution

The Python program is shown here.

```
file_22_1_1
n1 = int(input("Enter an integer: "))
n2 = int(input("Enter a second integer: "))

if n1 % 2 == 0 and n2 % 2 == 0:
    print("Both numbers are evens")
elif n1 % 2 != 0 and n2 % 2 != 0:
    print("Both numbers are odds")
else:
    print("Nothing special!")
```

Exercise 22.1-2   Is it an Integer?

Write a Python program that prompts the user to enter a number and then displays a message indicating whether the data type of this number is integer or real.

Solution

It is well known that a number is considered an integer when it contains no fractional part. In Python, you can use the int() function to get the integer portion of any real number. If the number given is equal to its integer portion, then the number is considered an integer.

For example, if the user enters the number 7, this number and its integer portion, int(7), are equal.

On the other hand, if the user enters the number 7.3, this number and its integer portion, int(7.3), are not equal.

The Python program is as follows.

```
file_22_1_2
x = float(input("Enter a number: "))

if x == int(x):
    print(x, "is integer")
else:
    print(x, "is real")
```

Exercise 22.1-3   Validating Data Input and Finding Odd and Even Numbers

Design a flowchart and write the corresponding Python program that prompts the user to enter an non-negative integer, and then displays a message indicating whether this number is even; it must display "Odd" otherwise. Moreover, if the user enters a negative value or a float, an error message must be displayed.

(This exercise gives you some practice in working with data validation).

Solution

Data validation is the process of restricting data input, forcing the user to enter only valid values.

In this exercise, you need to display an error message when the user enters either a negative value or a float. The flowchart that solves this exercise given in general form is as follows.

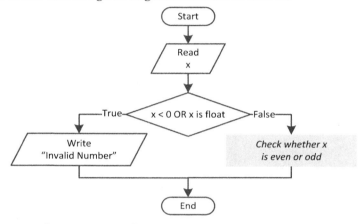

The following decision control structure is taken from Exercise 17.1-4. It tests whether variable x is even or odd.

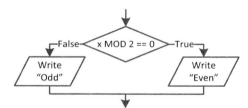

After combining both flowcharts, the final flowchart looks like this.

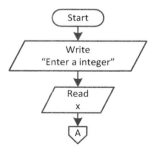

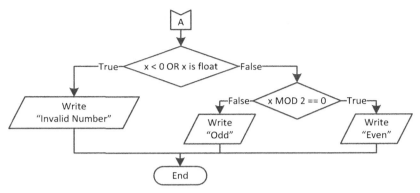

The Python program is shown here.

```
file_22_1_3
x = float(input("Enter an integer: "))

if x < 0 or x != int(x):
    print("Invalid Number")
else:
    if x % 2 == 0:
        print("Even")
    else:
        print("Odd")
```

✎ *Instead of the function* int(), *the function* float() *is used in the data input stage. This is necessary in order to allow the user to enter either an integer or a float.*

Exercise 22.1-4   *Converting Gallons to Liters, and Vice Versa*

Write a Python program that displays the following menu:

1. *Convert gallons to liters*
2. *Convert liters to gallons*

The program prompts the user to enter a choice (1 or 2) and a quantity. Then, it calculates and displays the required value. It is given that

$$1 \text{ gallon} = 3.785 \text{ liters}$$

Solution

The Python program is shown here.

```
file_22_1_4
COEFFICIENT = 3.785

print("1: Gallons to liters")
print("2: Liters to gallons")
choice = int(input("Enter choice: "))
quantity = float(input("Enter quantity: "))

if choice == 1:
```

```
    result = quantity * COEFFICIENT
    print(quantity, "gallons =", result, "liters")
else:
    result = quantity / COEFFICIENT
    print(quantity, "liters =", result, "gallons")
```

Exercise 22.1-5   *Converting Gallons to Liters, and Vice Versa (with Data Validation)*

Rewrite the Python program of the previous exercise to validate the data input. Individual error messages must be displayed when the user enters a choice other than 1 or 2, or a negative gas quantity.

Solution

The following Python program, given in general form, solves this exercise. It prompts the user to enter a choice. If the choice is invalid, it displays an error message; otherwise, it prompts the user to enter a quantity. However, if the quantity entered is invalid too, it displays another error message; otherwise it proceeds to data conversion, depending on the user's choice.

```
                              Main Code
COEFFICIENT = 3.785

print("1: Gallons to liters")
print("2: Liters to gallons")
choice = int(input("Enter choice: "))

if choice not in [1, 2]:
    print("Wrong choice!")
else:
    quantity = float(input("Enter quantity: "))
    if quantity < 0:
        print("Invalid quantity!")
    else:

        Code Fragment 1: Convert gallons to liters or
        liters to gallons depending on user's choice.
```

Code Fragment 1 shown below is taken from the previous exercise (Exercise 22.1-4). It converts gallons to liters, or liters to gallons, depending on the user's choice.

```
                          Code Fragment 1
if choice == 1:
    result = quantity * COEFFICIENT
    print(quantity, "gallons =", result, "liters")
else:
    result = quantity / COEFFICIENT
    print(quantity, "liters =", result, "gallons")
```

After embedding **Code Fragment 1** in **Main Code**, the final Python program becomes

```
                          🗀 file_22_1_5
COEFFICIENT = 3.785
```

```
print("1: Gallons to liters")
print("2: Liters to gallons")
choice = int(input("Enter choice: "))

if choice not in [1, 2]:
    print("Wrong choice!")
else:
    quantity = float(input("Enter quantity: "))
    if quantity < 0:
        print("Invalid quantity!")
    else:
        if choice == 1:
            result = quantity * COEFFICIENT
            print(quantity, "gallons =", result, "liters")
        else:
            result = quantity / COEFFICIENT
            print(quantity, "liters =", result, "gallons")
```

Exercise 22.1-6   Where is the Tollkeeper?

In a toll gate, there is an automatic system that recognizes whether the passing vehicle is a motorcycle, a car, or a truck. Write a Python program that lets the user enter the type of the vehicle (M for motorcycle, C for car, and T for truck) and then displays the corresponding amount of money the driver must pay according to the following table.

Vehicle Type	Amount to Pay
Motorcycle	$1
Car	$2
Track	$4

If the user enters a character other than M, C, or T, an error message must be displayed.

(Some more practice with data validation!)

Solution

The solution to this problem is quite simple. The only catch is that the user may enter the uppercase letters M, C, or T, or even the lowercase letters m, c, or t. The program needs to accept both. To handle this, you can convert the user's input to uppercase using the upper() method. Then you need to test only for the M, C, or T characters in uppercase.

The Python program is shown here.

```
                            📁 file_22_1_6
v = input().upper()

if v == "M":                #You need to test only for capital M
    print("You need to pay $1")
elif v == "C":              #You need to test only for capital C
    print("You need to pay $2")
```

```
elif v == "T":                    #You need to test only for capital T
    print("You need to pay $4")
else:
    print("Invalid vehicle")
```

✎ *Note how Python converts the user's input to uppercase.*

Exercise 22.1-7   The Most Scientific Calculator Ever!

Write a Python program that prompts the user to enter a number, the type of operation (+, -, *, /), and a second number. The program must execute the required operation and display the result.

Solution

The only thing that you need to take care of in this exercise is the possibility the user could enter zero for the divisor (the second number). As you know from mathematics, division by zero is not possible.

The following Python program uses the multiple-alternative decision structure to check the type of operation.

```
                            📁 file_22_1_7
a = float(input("Enter 1st number: "))
op = input("Enter type of operation: ")    #Variable op is of type string
b = float(input("Enter 2nd number: "))

if op == "+":
    print(a + b)
elif op == "-":
    print(a - b)
elif op == "*":
    print(a * b)
elif op == "/":
    if b == 0:
        print("Error: Division by zero")
    else:
        print(a / b)
```

22.2   Decision Control Structures in Solving Mathematical Problems

Exercise 22.2-1   Finding the Value of y

Design a flowchart and write the corresponding Python program that finds and displays the value of y (if possible) in the following formula.

$$Y = \frac{5 + x}{x} + \frac{x + 9}{x - 4}$$

Solution

In this exercise the user must not be allowed to enter values 0 or 4 because they make the denominator equal to zero. Therefore, the program needs to take these restrictions into consideration. The flowchart is shown here.

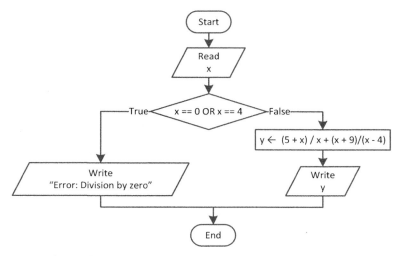

and the Python program is shown here.

```
file_22_2_1
```
```
x = float(input())

if x == 0 or x == 4:
    print("Error: Division by zero!")
else:
    y = (5 + x) / x + (x + 9) / (x - 4)
    print(y)
```

Exercise 22.2-2   Finding the Values of y

Design a flowchart and write the corresponding Python program that finds and displays the values of y (if possible) in the following formula.

$$y = \begin{cases} \dfrac{7 + x}{x - 3} + \dfrac{3 - x}{x}, & x \geq 0 \\ \dfrac{40x}{x - 5} + 3, & x < 0 \end{cases}$$

Solution

The formula has two different results.

1. When *x* is greater than or equal to zero, the value of *y* in $\frac{7+x}{x-3} + \frac{3x}{x}$ can be found following the method shown in the previous exercise.

2. However, for an *x* less than zero, a small detail can save you some lines of Python code. If you look carefully, you can see that there are no restrictions on the fraction $\frac{40x}{x-5}$ because *x* can never be +5. Why? Because in the given formula *x* is less than zero!

The flowchart is shown here.

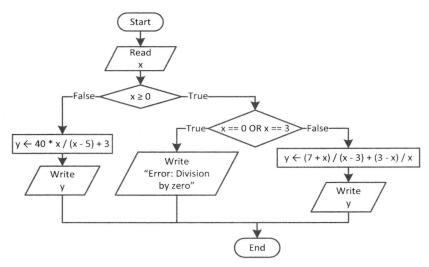

The Python program is shown here.

```
                    file_22_2_2
x = float(input())

if x >= 0:
    if x == 0 or x == 3:
        print("Error: Division by zero!")
    else:
        y = (7 + x) / (x - 3) + (3 - x) / x
        print(y)
else:
    y = 40 * x / (x - 5) + 3
    print(y)
```

Exercise 22.2-3   Solving the Linear Equation ax + b = 0

Design a flowchart and write the corresponding Python program that finds and displays the root of the linear equation

$$ax + b = 0$$

Solution

In the equation $ax + b = 0$, the coefficients a and b are known real numbers and x represents an unknown quantity to be found. Because x appears to the first power, this equation is called a *linear equation* or an *equation of the first degree*.

The *root of the equation* is the value of x, for which this equation is satisfied; that is, the left side of the equality $ax + b$ equals zero.

In this exercise, the user must enter values for coefficients a and b, and the program must find the value of x for which $ax + b$ equals zero.

The equation $ax + b = 0$, when solved for x, becomes $x = -b / a$. Depending on the user's entered data, three possible situations can arise:

i. The user might enter the value 0 for coefficient a and a non-zero value for coefficient b. In this situation, the result of x = $-b$ / a is undefined. The division by zero, as you already know from mathematics, cannot be performed.

ii. The user might enter the value 0 for both coefficients a and b. In this situation, the result of x = $-b$ / a has no defined value, and it is called an indeterminate form.

iii. The user might enter any other pair of values.

Therefore, these three situations result in three paths, respectively.

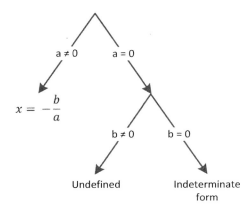

These three paths are represented in the flowchart that follows with the use of a multiple-alternative decision structure.

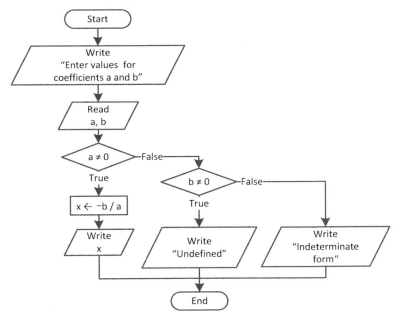

The Python program is shown here.

```
                        📁 file_22_2_3
print("Enter values for coefficients a and b")
a, b = float(input()), float(input())

if a != 0:
```

```
    x = -b / a
    print(x)
elif b != 0:
    print("Undefined")
else:
    print("Indeterminate form")
```

Exercise 22.2-4   Solving the Quadratic Equation $ax^2 + bx + c = 0$

Design a flowchart and write the corresponding Python program that finds and displays the roots of the quadratic equation

$$ax^2 + bx + c = 0$$

Solution

In the equation $ax^2 + bx + c = 0$, the coefficients a, b, and c are known real numbers and x represents an unknown quantity to be found. Because x appears to the second power, this equation is called a *quadratic equation* or an *equation of the second degree*.

The *roots of the equation* are the values of x, for which this equation is satisfied; that is, the left side of the equality $ax^2 + bx + c$ equals zero.

In this exercise, the user must enter values for coefficients a, b, and c, and the program must find the value(s) of x for which $ax^2 + bx + c$ equals zero.

This problem can be divided into two individual subproblems depending on the value of coefficient a.

    i.   If coefficient a is not equal to zero, the roots of the equation can be found using the discriminant D. Please note that this solution finds no complex roots when $D < 0$; this is beyond the scope of this book.

    ii.   If coefficient a is equal to zero, the equation becomes a linear equation, $bx + c = 0$, for which the solution was given in the previous exercise.

All necessary paths are shown here.

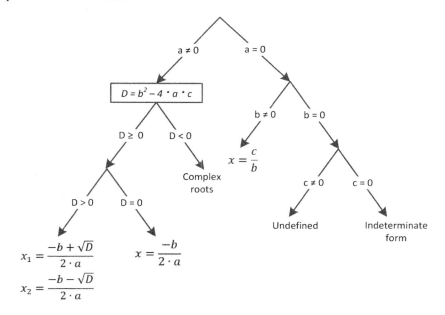

✎ *The path on the right* (a = 0) *is the solution to the linear equation* bx + c = 0, *which was shown in the previous exercise.*

Using this diagram you can design the following flowchart.

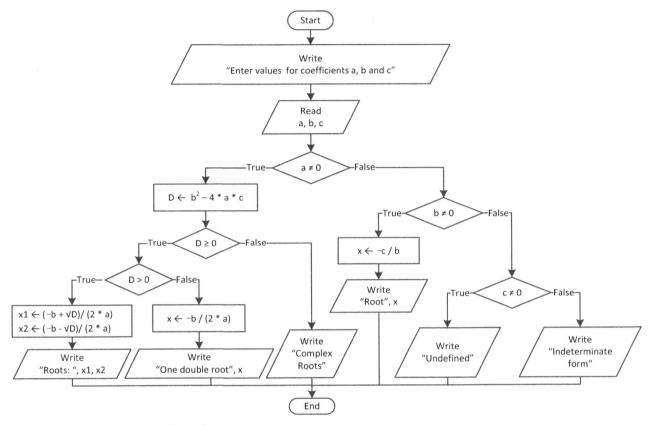

The Python program is shown here.

```
                          📁 file_22_2_4

import math

print("Enter values for coefficients a, b and c")
a, b, c = float(input()), float(input()), float(input())

if a != 0:
    D = b ** 2 - 4 * a * c
    if D >= 0:
        if D > 0:
            x1 = (-b + math.sqrt(D)) / (2 * a)
            x2 = (-b - math.sqrt(D)) / (2 * a)
            print("Roots:", x1, ",", x2)
        else:
            x = -b / (2 * a)
```

```
            print("One double root:", x)
        else:
            print("Complex Roots")
else:
    if b != 0:
        x = -c / b
        print("Root:", x)
    elif c != 0:
        print("Undefined")
    else:
        print("Indeterminate form")
```

22.3 Finding Minimum and Maximum Values with Decision Control Structures

Suppose there are some men and you want to find the lightest one. Let's say that each one of them comes by and tells you his weight. What you must do is, memorize the weight of the first person that has come by and for each new person, you have to compare his weight with the one that you keep memorized. If he is heavier, you ignore his weight. However, if he is lighter, you need to forget the previous weight and memorize the new one. The same procedure continues until all the people have come by.

Let's ask four men to come by at a random order. Assume that their weights, in order of appearance, are 165, 170, 160, and 180 pounds.

Procedure	Value of Variable minimum in Your Mind!
The first person comes by. He weighs 165 pounds. Keep his weight in your mind (imagine a variable in your mind named minimum).	minimum = 165
The second person comes by. He weighs 170 pounds. He does not weigh less than the weight you are keeping in variable minimum, so you must ignore his weight. Variable minimum in your mind still contains the value 165.	minimum = 165
The third person comes by. He weighs 160 pounds, which is less than the weight you are keeping in variable minimum, so you must forget the previous value and keep the value 160 in variable minimum.	minimum = 160
The fourth person comes by. He weighs 180 pounds. He does not weigh less than the weight you are keeping in variable minimum, so you must ignore his weight. Variable minimum still contains the value 160.	minimum = 160

When the procedure finishes, the variable minimum in your mind contains the weight of the lightest man!

Following are the flowchart and the corresponding Python program that prompts the user to enter the weight of four people and then finds and displays the lightest weight.

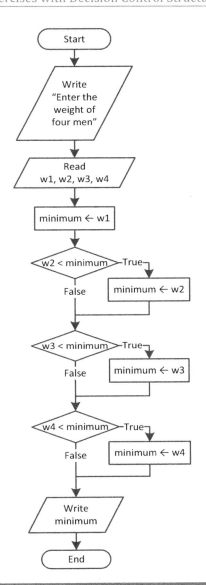

file_22_3a

```python
print("Enter the weight of four men:")

w1 = int(input())
w2 = int(input())
w3 = int(input())
w4 = int(input())

#Memorize the weight of the first person
minimum = w1

#If second one is lighter, forget
#everything and memorize this weight
if w2 < minimum:
    minimum = w2

#If third one is lighter, forget
#everything and memorize this weight
if w3 < minimum:
    minimum = w3

#If fourth one is lighter, forget
#everything and memorize this weight
if w4 < minimum:
    minimum = w4


print(minimum)
```

✎ *You can find the maximum instead of the minimum value by simply replacing the "less than" with a "greater than" operator in all Boolean expressions.*

A more Pythonic way, however, is to use the `min()` function as shown here.

file_22_3b

```python
print("Enter the weight of four men:")

w1 = int(input())
w2 = int(input())
w3 = int(input())
w4 = int(input())

print(min(w1, w2, w3, w4))
```

Exercise 22.3-1   *Finding the Name of the Heaviest Person*

Write a Python program that prompts the user to enter the weights and the names of three people and then displays the name and the weight of the heaviest person.

Solution

In this exercise, along with the maximum weight, you need to store in another variable the name of the person who actually has that weight. The Python program is shown here.

```
📁 file_22_3_1
w1 = int(input("Enter the weight of the 1st person: "))
n1 = input("Enter the name of the 1st person: ")

w2 = int(input("Enter the weight of the 2nd person: "))
n2 = input("Enter the name of the 2nd person: ")

w3 = int(input("Enter the weight of the 3rd person: "))
n3 = input("Enter the name of the 3rd person: ")

maximum = w1          #Memorize the weight of the first person.
m_name = n1           #Memorize his or her name.

if w2 > maximum:      #If second one is heavier,
    maximum = w2      #memorize his or her weight
    m_name = n2       #and his or her name.

if w3 > maximum:      #If third one is heavier,
    maximum = w3      #memorize his or her weight
    m_name = n3       #and his or her name.

print("The heaviest person is", m_name)
print("His or her weight is", maximum)
```

✎ *In case the two heaviest people happen to have the same weight, the name of the first one in order is found and displayed.*

✎ *You cannot use the function* max() *in this exercise! It would return the greatest weight, not the name of the person with that greatest weight!*

22.4   Exercises with Series of Consecutive Ranges of Values

As you have already seen, in many problems the value of a variable or the result of an expression can define which statement or block of statements must be executed. In the exercises that follow, you will learn how to test if a value or the result of an expression belongs within a specific range of values (from a series of consecutive ranges of values).

Suppose that you want to display a message indicating the types of clothes a woman might wear at different temperatures.

Outdoor Temperature (in degrees Fahrenheit)	Types of Clothes a Woman Might Wear
Temperature < 45	Sweater, coat, jeans, shirt, shoes
45 ≤ Temperature < 65	Sweater, jeans, jacket, shoes
65 ≤ Temperature < 75	Capris, shorts, t-shirt, tank top, flip flops, athletic shoes
75 ≤ Temperature	Shorts, t-shirt, tank top, skort, skirt, flip flops

At first glance you might be tempted to use single-alternative decision structures. It is not wrong actually but if you take a closer look, it becomes clear that each condition is interdependent, which means that when one of these evaluates to True, none of the others should be evaluated. You need to select just one alternative from a set of possibilities.

To solve this type of exercise, you can use a multiple-alternative decision structure or nested decision control structures. However, the former is the best choice. It is more convenient and increases readability, as you can see in the code fragment that follows.

```python
if temperature < 45:
    print("Sweater, coat, jeans, shirt, shoes")
elif temperature >= 45 and temperature < 65:
    print("Sweater, jeans, jacket, shoes")
elif temperature >= 65 and temperature < 75:
    print("Capris, shorts, t-shirt, tank top, flip flops, athletic shoes")
elif temperature >= 75:
    print("Shorts, t-shirt, tank top, skort, skirt, flip flops")
```

A closer examination, however, reveals that all the underlined Boolean expressions are not actually required. For example, if the first Boolean expression (temperature < 45) evaluates to False, the flow of execution continues to evaluate the second Boolean expression. In this step, however, variable temperature is definitely greater than or equal to 45 because of the first Boolean expression, which has already evaluated to False. Therefore, the Boolean expression temperature >= 45, when evaluated, is always True and thus can be omitted. The same logic applies to all cases; you can omit all the underlined Boolean expressions. The final code fragment is shown here, with all unnecessary evaluations removed.

```python
if temperature < 45:
    print("Sweater, coat, jeans, shirt, shoes")
elif temperature < 65:
    print("Sweater, jeans, jacket, shoes")
elif temperature < 75:
    print("Capris, shorts, t-shirt, tank top, flip flops, athletic shoes")
else:
    print("Shorts, t-shirt, tank top, skort, skirt, flip flops")
```

Exercise 22.4-1   Calculating the Discount

A customer receives a discount based on the total amount of his or her order. If the total amount ordered is less than $30, no discount is given. If the total amount is equal to or greater than $30 and less than $70, a discount of 5% is given. If the total amount is equal to or greater than $70 and less than $150, a discount of 10% is given. If the total amount is $150 or more, the customer receives a discount of 20%. Write a Python program that prompts the user to enter the total amount of his or her order and then calculates and displays the discount given as a *percentage (for example, 0%, 5%, and so on), the discount amount in dollars, and the final after-discount amount. Assume that the user enters a non-negative value for the amount.*

Solution

The following table summarizes the various discounts that are offered.

Range	Discount
amount < $30	0%
$30 ≤ amount < $70	5%
$70 ≤ amount < $150	10%
$150 ≤ amount	20%

The Python program is as follows.

```
                    file_22_4_1a
amount = float(input("Enter total amount: "))

if amount < 30:
    discount = 0
elif amount >= 30 and amount < 70:
    discount = 5
elif amount >= 70 and amount < 150:
    discount = 10
elif amount >= 150:
    discount = 20

discount_amount = amount * discount / 100
final_amount = amount - discount_amount

print("You got a discount of ", discount, "%", sep = "")
print("You saved $", discount_amount, sep = "")
print("You must pay $", final_amount, sep = "")
```

As previously, all the underlined Boolean expressions are not actually required. The final Python program is shown here, with all unnecessary evaluations removed.

```
                    file_22_4_1b
amount = float(input("Enter total amount: "))

if amount < 30:
    discount = 0
elif amount < 70:
    discount = 5
elif amount < 150:
    discount = 10
else:
    discount = 20
```

```
discount_amount = amount * discount / 100
final_amount = amount - discount_amount

print("You got a discount of ", discount, "%", sep = "")
print("You saved $", discount_amount, sep = "")
print("You must pay $", final_amount, sep = "")
```

Exercise 22.4-2   Validating Data Input and Calculating the Discount

Rewrite the Python program of the previous exercise to validate the data input. An error message must be displayed when the user enters a negative value.

Solution

The Python program that solves this exercise, given in general form, is as follows.

```
                              Main Code
amount = float(input("Enter total amount: "))

if amount < 0:
    print("Entered value is negative")
else:

    Code Fragment 1: Calculate and display the discount given,
    the discount amount and the final after-discount amount.
```

Code Fragment 1 that follows is taken from the previous exercise (Exercise 22.4-1). It calculates and displays the discount given as a percentage (for example, 0%, 5%, and so on), the discount amount in dollars, and the final after-discount amount.

```
                           Code Fragment 1
if amount < 30:
    discount = 0
elif amount < 70:
    discount = 5
elif amount < 150:
    discount = 10
else:
    discount = 20

discount_amount = amount * discount / 100
final_amount = amount - discount_amount

print("You got a discount of ", discount, "%", sep = "")
print("You saved $", discount_amount, sep = "")
print("You must pay $", final_amount, sep = "")
```

After embedding **Code Fragment 1** in **Main Code**, the final Python program becomes

```
                         📄 file_22_4_2
amount = float(input("Enter total amount: "))
```

```python
if amount < 0:
    print("Entered value is negative")
else:
    if amount < 30:
        discount = 0
    elif amount < 70:
        discount = 5
    elif amount < 150:
        discount = 10
    else:
        discount = 20

    discount_amount = amount * discount / 100
    final_amount = amount - discount_amount

    print("You got a discount of ", discount, "%", sep = "")
    print("You saved $", discount_amount, sep = "")
    print("You must pay $", final_amount, sep = "")
```

Exercise 22.4-3   Sending a Parcel

In a post office, the shipping cost for sending a medium parcel depends on its weight and whether its destination is inside or outside the country. Shipping costs are calculated according to the following table.

Parcel's Weight (in lb)	Destination Inside the Country (in USD per lb)	Destination Outside the Country (in USD)
weight ≤ 1	$0.010	$10
1 < weight ≤ 2	$0.013	$20
2 < weight ≤ 4	$0.015	$50
4 < weight	$0.020	$60

Design a flowchart and write the corresponding Python program that prompts the user to enter the weight of a parcel and its destination (I: inside the country, O: outside the country) and then calculates and displays the shipping cost.

Solution

The following flowchart, given in general form, solves this exercise.

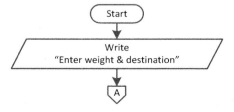

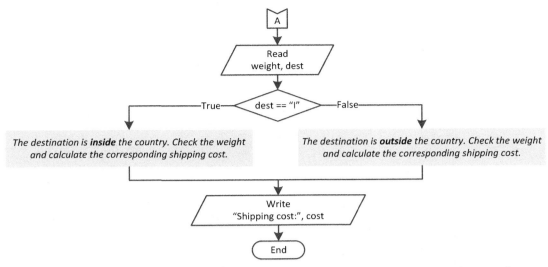

Now you need a multiple-alternative decision structure to calculate the shipping cost for parcels sent **inside** the country, as shown here.

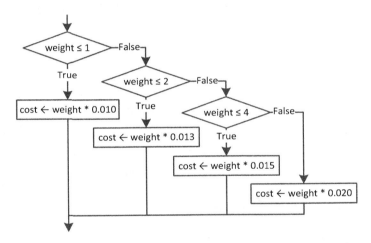

And you need another multiple-alternative decision structure to calculate the shipping cost for parcels sent **outside** the country, as shown here.

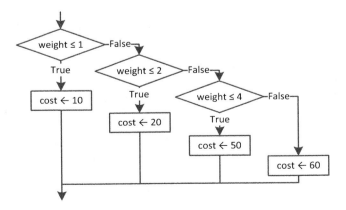

After combining all three flowcharts, the final flowchart becomes

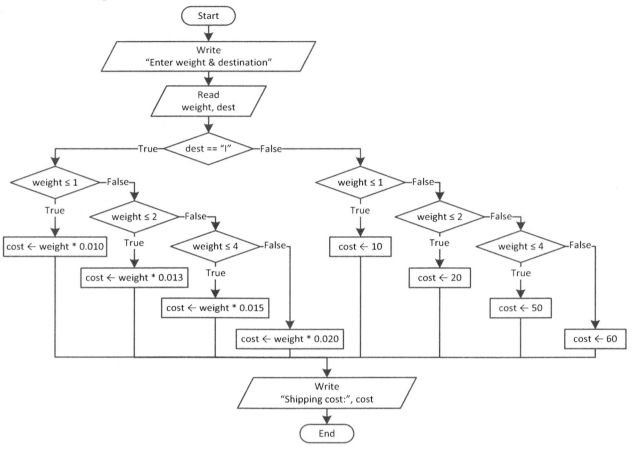

The corresponding Python program is shown here.

```
                              file_22_4_3
print("Enter weight & destination: ")
weight = float(input())
dest = input()

if dest.upper() == "I":
    if weight <= 1:
        cost = weight * 0.010
    elif weight <= 2:
        cost = weight * 0.013
    elif weight <= 4:
        cost = weight * 0.015
    else:
        cost = weight * 0.020
else:
    if weight <= 1:
        cost = 10
```

```
        elif weight <= 2:
            cost = 20
        elif weight <= 4:
            cost = 50
        else:
            cost = 60


print("Shipping cost:", cost)
```

✎ *A user may enter the letter I (for destination) in lowercase or uppercase. The method* `upper()` *ensures that the program executes properly for both cases.*

Exercise 22.4-4 Finding the Values of y

Design a flowchart and write the corresponding Python program that finds and displays the values of y (if possible) in the following formula

$$
y = \begin{cases} \dfrac{x}{x-3} + \dfrac{8+x}{x+1}, & -5 < x \le 0 \\[2mm] \dfrac{40x}{x-8}, & 0 < x \le 6 \\[2mm] \dfrac{3x}{x-9}, & 6 < x \le 20 \\[2mm] |x|, & for\ all\ other\ values\ of\ x \end{cases}
$$

Solution

In this exercise, there are two restrictions on the fractions:

1. In fraction $\dfrac{8+x}{x+1}$, the value of x cannot be −1.

2. In fraction $\dfrac{3x}{x-9}$, the value of x cannot be +9.

For all other fractions, it's impossible for the denominators to be set to zero because of the range in which x belongs.

The Python program is shown here.

```
                            📄 file_22_4_4a
x = float(input("Enter a value for x: "))


if x > -5 and x <= 0:
    if x != -1:
        y = x / (x - 3) + (8 + x) / (x + 1)        -5 < x ≤ 0
        print(y)
    else:
        print("Invalid value")
elif x > 0 and x <= 6:
    y = 40 * x / (x - 8)                           0 < x ≤ 6
    print(y)
elif x > 6 and x <= 20:
```

```
if x != 9:
    y = 3 * x / (x - 9)
    print(y)
else:
    print("Invalid value")
else:
    y = abs(x)
    print(y)
```

6 < x ≤ 20

All other values of x

If you are wondering whether you can remove all `print(y)` statements and write them as a single statement at the end of the program, the answer is "no". Since there are paths that do not include the `print(y)` statement, you must write this statement, again and again, in every path required.

One thing you should learn in computer programming, however, is that you must never give up! By modifying your code a little, checking for invalid values in the beginning, gives you the opportunity to remove the statement `print(y)` outside of all paths and move it at the end of them. The modified Python program is shown here.

```
📁 file_22_4_4b
```
```
x = float(input("Enter a value for x: "))

if x == -1 or x == 9:
    print("Invalid value")
else:
    if x > -5 and x <= 0:
        y = x / (x - 3) + (8 + x) / (x + 1)
    elif x > 0 and x <= 6:
        y = 40 * x / (x - 8)
    elif x > 6 and x <= 20:
        y = 3 * x / (x - 9)
    else:
        y = abs(x)

    print(y)
```

Now, if you are speculating about whether the underlined Boolean expressions are redundant, the answer is "no" again. Why? Suppose you do remove them and the user enters a value of −20 for x. The flow of execution then reaches the Boolean expression $x <= 0$, which evaluates to `True`. Then the fraction $\frac{x}{x-3} + \frac{8+x}{x+1}$, instead of the absolute value of x, is calculated.

Yet still there is hope! Next, you can find a proposed solution in which unnecessary Boolean expressions are actually removed. The trick here is that the case of the absolute value of x is examined first.

```
📁 file_22_4_4c
```
```
x = float(input("Enter a value for x: "))

if x == -1 or x == 9:
    print("Invalid value")
else:
    if x <= -5 or x > 20:
        y = abs(x)
```

```
    elif x <= 0:
        y = x / (x - 3) + (8 + x) / (x + 1)
    elif x <= 6:
        y = 40 * x / (x - 8)
    else:
        y = 3 * x / (x - 9)

    print(y)
```

✎ *It is obvious that one problem can have many solutions. It is up to you to find the optimal one!*

Exercise 22.4-5   *Progressive Rates and Electricity Consumption*

The LAV Electricity Company charges subscribers for their electricity consumption according to the following table (monthly rates for domestic accounts). Assume that all extra charges such as transmission service charges and distribution charges are all included.

Kilowatt-hours (kWh)	USD per kWh
kWh ≤ 500	$0.10
501 ≤ kWh ≤ 2000	$0.25
2001 ≤ kWh ≤ 4500	$0.40
4501 ≤ kWh	$0.60

Write a Python program that prompts the user to enter the total number of kWh consumed and then calculates and displays the total amount to pay.

Please note that the rates are progressive.

Solution

The term *progressive rates* means that when a customer consumes, for example, 2200 kWh, not all of the kilowatt-hours are charged at $0.40. The first 500 kWh are charged at $0.10, the next 1500 kWh are charged at $0.25 and only the last 200 kWh are charged at $0.40. Thus, the customer must pay

$$500 \times \$0.10 + 1500 \times \$0.25 + 200 \times \$0.40 = \$505$$

The same logic can be used to calculate the total amount to pay when the customer consumes, for example, 4800 kWh. The first 500 kWh are charged at $0.10, the next 1500 kWh are charged at $0.25, the next 2500 kWh are charged at 0.40, and only the last 300 kWh are charged at $0.60. Thus, the customer must pay

$$500 \times \$0.10 + 1500 \times \$0.25 + 2500 \times \$0.40 + 300 \times \$0.60 = \$1605$$

The following diagram can help you fully understand how to calculate the total amount to pay when the rates are progressive.

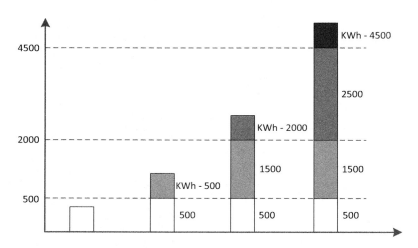

The Python program is shown here.

```
┌─ file_22_4_5
kwh = int(input("Enter number of Kilowatt-hours consumed: "))

if kwh <= 500:
    t = kwh * 0.10
elif kwh <= 2000:
    t = 500 * 0.10 + (kwh - 500) * 0.25
elif kwh <= 4500:
    t = 500 * 0.10 + 1500 * 0.25 + (kwh - 2000) * 0.40
else:
    t = 500 * 0.10 + 1500 * 0.25 + 2500 * 0.4 + (kwh - 4500) * 0.60

print("Total amount to pay:", t)
```

Exercise 22.4-6   *Progressive Rates and Text Messaging Services*

The LAV Cell Phone Company charges customers a basic rate of $8 per month to send text messages. Additional rates are charged based on the total number of text messages sent, as shown in the following table.

Number of Text Messages Sent	Additional Rates (in USD per text message)
Up to 50	Free of charge
51 – 150	$0.05
151 and above	$0.10

Federal, state, and local taxes add a total of 10% to each bill.

Write a Python program that prompts the user to enter the number of text messages sent and then calculates and displays the total amount to pay.

Please note that the rates are progressive.

Solution

The Python program is presented here.

```
                          📄 file_22_4_6
count = int(input("Enter number of text messages sent: "))

if count <= 50:
    extra = 0
elif count <= 150:
    extra = (count - 50) * 0.05
else:
    extra = 100 * 0.05 + (count - 150) * 0.10

total_without_taxes = 8 + extra          #Add basic rate of $8
taxes = total_without_taxes * 10 / 100   #Calculate the total taxes
total = total_without_taxes + taxes      #Calculate the total amount to pay

print("Total amount to pay:", total)
```

22.5 Exercises of a General Nature with Decision Control Structures

Exercise 22.5-1 Finding a Leap Year

Write a Python program that prompts the user to enter a year and then displays a message indicating whether it is a leap year; otherwise the message "Not a leap year" must be displayed. Moreover, if the user enters a year less than 1582, an error message must be displayed.

(Note that this involves data validation!)

Solution

According to the Gregorian calendar, which was first introduced in 1582, a year is a leap year when <u>at least one</u> of the following conditions is met:

   1st Condition: The year is exactly divisible by 4, and not by 100.

   2nd Condition: The year is exactly divisible by 400.

In the following table, some years are not leap years because neither of the two conditions evaluates to True.

Year	Conditions	Leap Year
1600	2nd Condition is True. It is exactly divisible by 400	*Yes*
1900	Both conditions are False.	*No*
1918	Both conditions are False.	*No*
2000	2nd Condition is True. It is exactly divisible by 400	*Yes*
2002	Both conditions are False.	*No*
2004	1st Condition is True. It is exactly divisible by 4, and not by 100	*Yes*
2020	1st Condition is True. It is exactly divisible by 4, and not by 100	*Yes*

The Python program is shown here.

```
📁 file_22_5_1
y = int(input("Enter a year: "))

if y < 1582:
    print("Error! The year cannot be less than 1582")
else:
    if y % 4 == 0 and y % 100 != 0 or y % 400 == 0:
        print("Leap year!")
    else:
        print("Not a leap year")
```

📖 *The* and *operator has a higher precedence than the* or *operator.*

Exercise 22.5-2   *Displaying the Days of the Month*

Write a Python program that prompts the user to enter a year and a month and then displays how many days are in that month. The program needs to take into consideration the leap years. In case of a leap year, February has 29 instead of 28 days. Moreover, if the user enters a year less than 1582, an error message must be displayed.

Solution

The following Python program, given in general form, solves this exercise.

```
Main Code
y = int(input("Enter a year: "))
if y < 1582:
    print("Error! The year cannot be less than 1582")
else:
    m = int(input("Enter month 1 - 12: "))
    if m == 2:

        Code Fragment 1: Check whether the year (in variable y)
        is a leap year and display how many days are in February.

    elif m in [4, 6, 9, 11]:
        print("This month has 30 days")
    else:
        print("This month has 31 days")
```

Code Fragment 1, shown here, checks whether the year (in variable y) is a leap year and displays how many days are in February.

```
Code Fragment 1
if y % 4 == 0 and y % 100 != 0 or y % 400 == 0:
    print("This month has 29 days")
else:
    print("This month has 28 days ")
```

After embedding **Code Fragment 1** in **Main Code**, the final Python program becomes

```
📁 file_22_5_2
```

```python
y = int(input("Enter a year: "))
if y < 1582:
    print("Error! The year cannot be less than 1582")
else:
    m = int(input("Enter month 1 - 12: "))
    if m == 2:
        if y % 4 == 0 and y % 100 != 0 or y % 400 == 0:
            print("This month has 29 days")
        else:
            print("This month has 28 days ")
    elif m in [4, 6, 9, 11]:
        print("This month has 30 days")
    else:
        print("This month has 31 days")
```

Exercise 22.5-3   Is the Number a Palindrome?

A palindrome is a number that remains the same after reversing its digits. For example, the number 13631 is a palindrome. Write a Python program that lets the user enter a five-digit integer and tests whether or not this number is a palindrome. Moreover, individual error messages must be displayed when the user enters a float, or any integer with either less than or more than five digits.

(Note that this involves data validation!)

Solution

There are two different approaches, actually! The first one splits the number's digits into five different variables while the second one handles the number as if it were a string. Let's analyze them both!

First Approach

To test if the user enters a palindrome number, you need to split its digits into five different variables as you learned in Chapter 13. Then, you can check whether the 1st digit is equal to the 5th digit and the 2nd digit is equal to the 4th digit. If this evaluates to True, the number is a palindrome.

To validate data input, you need to check whether the user has entered a five-digit number. Keep in mind that all five-digit numbers are in the range of 10000 to 99999. Therefore, you can just restrict the data input to within this range.

In order to display many different error messages, the best practice is to use a multiple-alternative decision structure which first checks data input validity for all cases, and then tries to solve the required problem. For example, if you need to check for various errors, you can do something like the following.

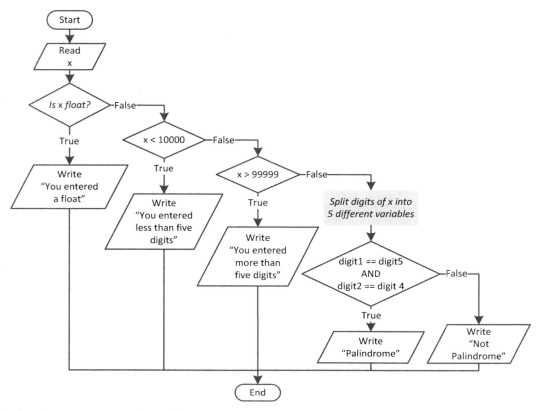

The final Python program is shown here.

```
file_22_5_3a
```

```python
x = float(input())

if x != int(x):
    print("You entered a float")
elif x < 10000:
    print("You entered less than five digits")
elif x > 99999:
    print("You entered more than five digits")
else:
    digit1, r = divmod(x, 10000)
    digit2, r = divmod(r, 1000)
    digit3, r = divmod(r, 100)
    digit4, digit5 = divmod(r, 10)

    if digit1 == digit5 and digit2 == digit4:
        print("Palindrome")
    else:
        print("Not palindrome")
```

Second Approach

This approach handles the number as if it were a string. It reverses it and compares the initial string to the reversed one. If they are equal, it means that the number is a palindrome. The Python program is shown here.

```
file_22_5_3b
```

```python
x = float(input())

if x != int(x):
    print("You entered a float")
elif x < 10000:
    print("You entered less than five digits")
elif x > 99999:
    print("You entered more than five digits")
else:
    x_str = str(int(x))
    x_reversed = x_str[::-1]

    if x_str == x_reversed:
        print("Palindrome")
    else:
        print("Not palindrome")
```

Exercise 22.5-4   Checking for Proper Capitalization and Punctuation

Write a Python program that prompts the user to enter a sentence and then checks it for proper capitalization and punctuation. The program must determine if the string begins with an uppercase letter and ends with a punctuation mark (check only for periods, question marks, and exclamation marks).

Solution

In this exercise you need to isolate the first and the last character of the string. As you already know, you can access any individual character of a string using substring notation. You can use index 0 to access the first character, index 1 to access the second character, and so on. On the other hand, you can use index −1 to access the last character, index −2 to access the last but one character and so on. Thus, you can isolate the first character of string sentence using the following Python statement

```python
first_char = sentence[0]
```

and the last character using the following Python statement.

```python
last_char = sentence[-1]
```

The Python program is shown here.

```
file_22_5_4a
```

```python
sentence = input("Enter a sentence: ")

#Get first character
first_char = sentence[0]

#Get last character
last_char = sentence[-1]
```

```
sentence_is_okay = True

if first_char != first_char.upper():
    sentence_is_okay = False
elif last_char not in [".", "?", "!"]:
    sentence_is_okay = False

if sentence_is_okay == True:
    print("Sentence is okay!")
```

In the beginning, the program assumes that the sentence is okay (sentence_is_okay = True). Then, it checks for proper capitalization and proper punctuation and if it finds something wrong, it assigns the value False to the variable sentence_is_okay.

Another more Pythonic way, however, is shown here.

file_22_5_4b

```
sentence = input("Enter a sentence: ")

if sentence[0] == sentence[0].upper() and sentence[-1] in [".", "?", "!"]:
    print("Sentence is okay!")
```

22.6 Review Exercises

Complete the following exercises.

1. Write a Python program that prompts the user to enter a numeric value and then calculates and displays its square root. Moreover, an error message must be displayed when the user enters a negative value.

2. Design a flowchart that lets the user enter an integer and, if its last digit is equal to 5, a message "Last digit equal to 5" is displayed; otherwise, a message "Nothing special" is displayed. Moreover, if the user enters a negative value, an error message must be displayed.

   Hint: You can isolate the last digit of any integer using a modulus 10 operation.

3. Design a flowchart and write the corresponding Python program that lets the user enter two integers and then displays a message indicating whether at least one integer is odd; otherwise, a message "Nothing special" is displayed. Moreover, if the user enters negative values, an error message must be displayed.

4. Design a flowchart and write the corresponding Python program that prompts the user to enter an integer, and then displays a message indicating whether this number is even; it must display "Odd" otherwise. Moreover, individual error messages must be displayed when the user enters a negative value or a float.

5. Design a flowchart and write the corresponding Python program that prompts the user to enter an integer and then displays a message indicating whether this number is exactly divisible 3 and by 4; otherwise the message "NN is not what you are looking for!" must be displayed (where NN is the given number). For example, 12 is exactly divisible by 3 and by 4. Moreover, an error message must be displayed when the user enters a negative value or a float.

6. Design a flowchart and write the corresponding Python program that lets the user enter two integers and then displays a message indicating whether they are both divisible exactly by 3 and by 4; otherwise the message "X and Y are not what you are looking for!" must be displayed (where X and Y are the given numbers). Moreover, individual error messages must be displayed when the user enters any negative values or any floats.

7. Write a Python program that displays the following menu:

   1. Convert Kelvin to Fahrenheit

   2. Convert Fahrenheit to Kelvin

   3. Convert Fahrenheit to Celsius

   4. Convert Celsius to Fahrenheit

   It then prompts the user to enter a choice (of 1 to 4) and a temperature value. It then calculates and displays the required value. Moreover, individual error messages must be displayed when the user enters a choice other than 1, 2, 3, or 4, or a temperature value lower than absolute zero[1].

   It is given that

   $$1.8 \times Kelvin = Fahrenheit + 459.67$$

   and

   $$\frac{Celsius}{5} = \frac{Fahrenheit - 32}{9}$$

8. Write a Python program that prompts the user to enter an integer, the type of operation (+, −, *, /, DIV, MOD, POWER), and a second integer. The program must execute the required operation and display the result.

9. Rewrite the Python program of the previous exercise to validate the data input. If the user enters an input other than +, −, *, /, DIV, MOD, POWER, an error message must be displayed.

10. Design a flowchart and write the corresponding Python program that finds and displays the value of y (if possible) in the following formula.

    $$y = \frac{5x + 3}{x - 5} + \frac{3x^2 + 2x + 2}{x + 1}$$

11. Design a flowchart and write the corresponding Python program that finds and displays the values of y (if possible) in the following formula.

    $$y = \begin{cases} \dfrac{x^2}{x + 1} + \dfrac{3 - \sqrt{x}}{x + 2}, & x \geq 10 \\ \dfrac{40x}{x - 9} + 3x, & x < 10 \end{cases}$$

12. Write a Python program that finds and displays the values of y (if possible) in the following formula.

    $$y = \begin{cases} \dfrac{x}{\sqrt{x + 30}} + \dfrac{(8 + x)^2}{x + 1}, & -15 < x \leq -10 \\ \dfrac{|40x|}{x - 8}, & -10 < x \leq 0 \\ \dfrac{3x}{\sqrt{x - 9}}, & 0 < x \leq 25 \\ x - 1, & \text{for all other values of x} \end{cases}$$

13. Write a Python program that prompts the user to enter the names and the ages of three people and then displays the names of the youngest person and the oldest person.

14. Write a Python program that prompts the user to enter the ages of three people and then finds and displays the age in the middle.

---

[1] The value of −459.67° (on the Fahrenheit scale) is the lowest temperature possible and it is called *absolute zero*.

15. Write a Python program that prompts the user to enter the names and the ages of three people and then displays the name of the youngest person or the oldest person, depending on which one is closer to the third age in the middle.

16. A positive integer is called an Armstrong number when the sum of the cubes of its digits is equal to the number itself. The number 371 is such a number, since $3^3 + 7^3 + 1^3 = 371$. Write a Python program that lets the user enter a three-digit integer and then displays a message indicating whether or not the given number is an Armstrong one. Moreover, individual error messages must be displayed when the user enters a float or any number other than a three-digit one.

17. Write a Python program that prompts the user to enter a day (1 – 31), a month (1 – 12), and a year and then finds and displays how many days are left until the end of that month. The program must take into consideration the leap years. In the case of a leap year, February has 29 instead of 28 days.

18. Write a Python program that lets the user enter a word of six letters and then displays a message indicating whether or not every second letter is capitalized. The word "AtHeNa" is such a word, but it can be also given as "aThEnA".

19. An online book store sells e-books for $10 each. Quantity discounts are given according to the following table.

Quantity	Discount
3 – 5	10%
6 – 9	15%
10 – 13	20%
14 – 19	27%
20 or more	30%

Write a Python program that prompts the user to enter the total number of e-books purchased and then displays the amount of discount (if any), and the total amount of the purchase after the discount.

20. In a supermarket, the discount that a customer receives based on the before-tax amount of their order is presented in the following table.

Range	Discount
amount < $50	0%
$50 ≤ amount < $100	1%
$100 ≤ amount < $200	2%
$250 ≤ amount	3%

Write a Python program that prompts the user to enter the before-tax amount of his or her order and then calculates and displays the discount amount that customers receive (if any). A VAT (Value Added Tax) of 19% must be added in the end. Moreover, an error message must be displayed when the user enters a negative value.

21. The Body Mass Index (BMI) is often used to determine whether an adult person is overweight or underweight for his or her height. The formula used to calculate the BMI of an adult person is

$$BMI = \frac{weight \cdot 703}{height^2}$$

Write a Python program that prompts the user to enter his or her age, weight (in pounds) and height (in inches) and then displays a description according to the following table.

Body Mass Index	Description
BMI < 15	Very severely underweight
15.0 ≤ BMI < 16.0	Severely underweight
16.0 ≤ BMI < 18.5	Underweight
18.5 ≤ BMI < 25	Normal
25.0 ≤ BMI < 30.0	Overweight
30.0 ≤ BMI < 35.0	Severely overweight
35.0 ≤ BMI	Very severely overweight

The message "Invalid age" must be displayed when the user enters an age less than 18.

22. The LAV Water Company charges for subscribers' water consumption according to the following table (monthly rates for domestic accounts).

Water Consumption (cubic feet)	USD per cubic foot
consumption ≤ 10	$3
11 ≤ consumption ≤ 20	$5
21 ≤ consumption ≤ 35	$7
36 ≤ consumption	$9

Write a Python program that prompts the user to enter the total amount of water consumed (in cubic feet) and then calculates and displays the total amount to pay. Please note that the rates are progressive. Federal, state, and local taxes add a total of 10% to each bill. Moreover, an error message must be displayed when the user enters a negative value.

23. Write a Python program that prompts the user to enter his or her taxable income and the number of his or her children and then calculates the total tax to pay according to the following table. However, total tax is reduced by 2% when the user has at least one child. Please note that the rates are progressive.

Taxable Income (USD)	Tax Rate
income ≤ 8000	10%
8000 < income ≤ 30000	15%
30000 < income ≤ 70000	25%
70000 < income	30%

24. The Beaufort scale is an empirical measure that relates wind speed to observed conditions on land or at sea. Write a Python program that prompts the user to enter the wind speed and then displays the corresponding Beaufort number and description according to the following table. An additional message "It's Fishing Day!!!" must be displayed when wind speed is 3 Beaufort or less. Moreover, an error message must be displayed when the user enters a negative value.

Wind Speed (miles per hour)	Beaufort Number	Description
wind speed < 1	0	Calm
1 ≤ wind speed < 4	1	Light air
4 ≤ wind speed < 8	2	Light breeze
8 ≤ wind speed < 13	3	Gentle breeze
13 ≤ wind speed < 18	4	Moderate breeze
18 ≤ wind speed < 25	5	Fresh breeze
25 ≤ wind speed < 31	6	Strong breeze
31 ≤ wind speed < 39	7	Moderate gale
39 ≤ wind speed < 47	8	Gale
47 ≤ wind speed < 55	9	Strong gale
55 ≤ wind speed < 64	10	Storm
64 ≤ wind speed < 74	11	Violent storm
74 ≤ wind speed	12	Hurricane force

Review in "Decision Control Structures"

Review Crossword Puzzle

1. Solve the following crossword puzzle.

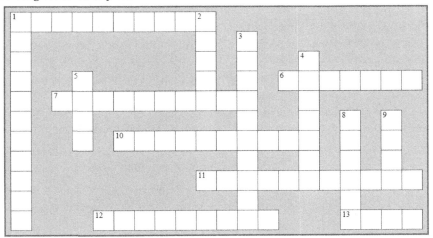

Across

1. The `not` operator is also known as a logical _____.
6. This Boolean expression can be built of simpler Boolean expressions.
7. This operator evaluates whether or not an operand exists in a specified sequence.
10. This number remains the same after reversing its digits.
11. The `or` operator is also known as a logical _____.
12. A positive integer where the sum of the cubes of its digits is equal to the number itself.
13. The _____–alternative decision structure includes a statement or block of statements on both paths.

Down

1. The `and` operator is also known as a logical _____.
2. This table shows the result of a logical operation between two or more Boolean expressions for all their possible combinations of values.
3. The (>) is a _____ operator.
4. This is an expression that results in a value that is either `True` or `False`.
5. This year is exactly divisible by 4 and not by 100, or it is exactly divisible by 400.
8. This control structure is a structure that is enclosed within another structure.
9. This number is considered an even number.

Review Questions

Answer the following questions.

1. What is a Boolean expression?
2. Which comparison operators does Python support?
3. Which logical operator performs a logical conjunction?

4. Which logical operator performs a logical disjunction?

5. When does the logical operator and return a result of True?

6. When does the logical operator or return a result of True?

7. State the order of precedence of logical operators.

8. State the order of precedence of arithmetic, comparison, membership, and logical operators.

9. What is code indentation?

10. Design the flowchart and write the corresponding Python statement (in general form) of a single-alternative decision structure. Describe how this decision structure operates.

11. Design the flowchart and write the corresponding Python statement (in general form) of a dual-alternative decision structure. Describe how this decision structure operates.

12. Design the flowchart and write the corresponding Python statement (in general form) of a multiple-alternative decision structure. Describe how this decision structure operates.

13. What does the term "nesting a decision structure" mean?

14. How deep can the nesting of decision control structures go? Is there any practical limit?

15. Create a diagram that shows all possible paths for solving a linear equation.

16. Create a diagram that shows all possible paths for solving a quadratic equation.

17. When is a year considered a leap year?

18. What is a palindrome number?

Section 5

Loop Control Structures

Chapter 23
Introduction to Loop Control Structures

23.1 What is a Loop Control Structure?

A loop control structure is a control structure that allows the execution of a statement or block of statements multiple times until a specified condition is met.

23.2 From Sequence Control to Loop Control Structures

The next example lets the user enter four numbers and it then calculates and displays their sum. As you can see, there is no loop control structure yet, just your familiar sequence control structure.

```
x = float(input())
y = float(input())
z = float(input())
w = float(input())

total = x + y + z + w

print(total)
```

This program is quite short. However, think of an analogous program that lets the user enter 1000 numbers instead of four! Can you imagine writing the statement float(input()) 1000 times? Wouldn't it be much easier if you could write this statement only once but "tell" the computer to execute it 1000 times? Of course it would be! But for this you need a loop control structure!

Let's try to solve a riddle first! Without using a loop structure yet, try to rewrite the previous program, but using only two variables, x and total. Yes, you heard that right! This program must calculate and display the sum of four given numbers, <u>but</u> it must do it with only two variables! Can you find a way?

Hmmm... it's obvious what you are thinking right now: "*The only thing that I can do with two variables is to read one single value in variable x and then assign that value to* total". Your thinking is quite correct, and it is presented here.

```
x = float(input())
total = x
```

which can equivalently be written as

```
total = 0

x = float(input())
total = total + x
```

And now what? Now, there are three things that you can actually do, and these are: think, think, and of course, think!

The first number has been stored in variable total, so variable x is now free for further use! Thus, you can reuse variable x to read a second value which will also be accumulated in variable total, as follows.

```
total = 0

x = float(input())
total = total + x
```

```
x = float(input())
total = total + x
```

✎ *Statement* `total = total + x` *accumulates the value of* x *to* `total`, *which means that it adds the value of* x *to* `total` *along with any previous value in* `total`. *For example, if variable* `total` *contains the value 5 and variable* x *contains the value 3, the statement* `total = total + x` *assigns the value 8 to variable* `total`.

Since the second number has been accumulated in variable `total`, variable x can be re-used! This process can go on again and again until all four numbers are read and accumulated in variable `total`. The final Python program is as follows. Please note that this program does not use any loop control structure yet!

```
total = 0

x = float(input())
total = total + x

x = float(input())
total = total + x

x = float(input())
total = total + x

x = float(input())
total = total + x

print(total)
```

✎ *This program and the initial one are considered equivalent. The main difference between them, however, is that this one has four identical pairs of statements.*

Of course, you can use this example to read and find the sum of more than four numbers. However, you can't write that pair of statements over and over again because soon you will realize how painful this is. Also, if you forget to write at least one pair of statements, it will eventually lead to incorrect results.

What you really need here is to keep only **one** pair of those statements but use a loop control structure that executes it four times (or even 1000 times, if you wish). You can use something like the following code fragment.

```
total = 0

execute_these_statements_4_times:
    x = float(input())
    total = total + x

print(total)
```

Obviously there isn't any *execute_these_statements_4_times* statement in Python. This is for demonstration purposes only but soon enough you will learn everything about all the loop control structures that Python supports!

23.3 Review Questions: True/False

Choose **true** or **false** for each of the following statements.

1. A loop control structure is a structure that allows the execution of a statement or block of statements multiple times until a specified condition is met.

2. It is possible to use a sequence control structure that prompts the user to enter 1000 numbers and then calculates their sum.

3. The following code fragment

```
total = 10
a = 0
total = total + a
```

accumulates the value 10 in variable `total`.

4. The following Python program (not code fragment)

```
a = 5
total = total + a
print(total)
```

satisfies the property of definiteness.

5. The following two code fragments are considered equivalent.

```
a = 5
total = a
```

```
total = 0
a = 5
total = total + a
```

Chapter 24
Pre-Test, Mid-Test and Post-Test Loop Structures

24.1   The Pre-Test Loop Structure

The pre-test loop structure is shown in the following flowchart.

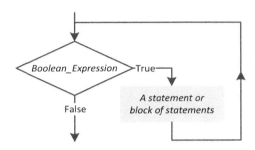

✎ *The Decision symbol (the diamond, or rhombus) is used both in decision control structures and in loop control structures. However, in loop control structures, one of the diamond's exits always has an upward direction.*

Let's see what happens when the flow of execution reaches a pre-test loop structure. If *Boolean_Expression* evaluates to True, the statement or block of statements of the structure is executed and the flow of execution goes back to check *Boolean_Expression* once more. If *Boolean_Expression* evaluates to True again, the process repeats. The iterations stop when *Boolean_Expression*, at some point, evaluates to False and the flow of execution exits the loop.

✎ *A "pre-test loop structure" is named this way because first the Boolean expression is evaluated, and afterwards the statement or block of statements of the structure is executed.*

✎ *Because the Boolean expression is evaluated before entering the loop, a pre-test loop may perform from zero to many iterations.*

✎ *Each time the statement or block of statements of a loop control structure is executed, the term used in computer science is "the loop is iterating" or "the loop performs an iteration".*

The general form of the Python statement is

```
while Boolean_Expression:
    A statement or block of statements
```

The following example displays the numbers 1 to 10.

📄 **file_24_1**

```
i = 1
while i <= 10:
    print(i)
    i += 1
```

✎ *Just as in decision control structures, the statements inside a loop control structure must be indented.*

In Python, while-loops can also be combined with an `else` keyword as shown here.

```
while Boolean_Expression:
    A statement or block of statements 1
else:
    A statement or block of statements 2
```

However, this unusual feature is rarely used in practice, so it will not be further discussed in this book.

Exercise 24.1-1   Designing the Flowchart and Counting the Total Number of Iterations

Design the corresponding flowchart for the following Python program. How many iterations does this Python program perform?

```
i = 4
while i > 0:
    i -= 1

print("The end")
```

Solution

The corresponding flowchart is as follows.

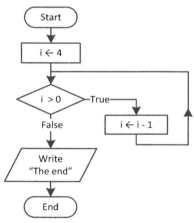

Next, a trace table can help you observe the flow of execution.

Step	Statement	Notes	i
1	i = 4		4
2	while i > 0:	This evaluates to True	
3	i = i - 1		3
4	while i > 0:	This evaluates to True	
5	i = i - 1		2
6	while i > 0:	This evaluates to True	
7	i = i - 1		1

1st Iteration (steps 2–3)
2nd Iteration (steps 4–5)
3rd Iteration (steps 6–7)

8	while i > 0:	This evaluates to True		4th Iteration
9	i = i - 1		0	
10	while i > 0:	This evaluates to False		
11	print("The end")	It displays: The end		

As you can see from the trace table, the total number of iterations is four.

Now, let's draw some conclusions!

► If you want to find the total number of iterations, you need to count the number of times the statement or block of statements of the structure is executed and not the number of times the Boolean expression is evaluated.

► In a pre-test loop structure, when the statement or block of statements of the structure is executed N times, the Boolean expression is evaluated N+1 times.

Exercise 24.1-2   Counting the Total Number of Iterations

How many iterations does this Python program perform?
```
i = 4
while i >= 0:
    i -= 1

print("The end")
```

Solution

This exercise is almost identical to the previous one. The only difference is that the Boolean expression here remains True, even for i = 0. Therefore, it performs an additional iteration, that is, five iterations.

Exercise 24.1-3   Designing the Flowchart and Counting the Total Number of Iterations

Design the corresponding flowchart for the following Python program. How many iterations does this Python program perform?
```
i = 1
while i != 6:
    i += 2

print("The end")
```

Solution

The corresponding flowchart is as follows.

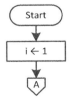

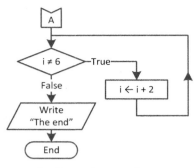

Now, let's create a trace table to observe the flow of execution.

Step	Statement	Notes	i
1	`i = 1`		**1**
2	`while i != 6:`	This evaluates to True	
3	`i += 2`		**3**
4	`while i != 6:`	This evaluates to True	
5	`i += 2`		**5**
6	`while i != 6:`	This evaluates to True	
7	`i += 2`		**7**
8	`while i != 6:`	This evaluates to True	
9	...	...	

1st Iteration — steps 2, 3
2nd Iteration — steps 4, 5
3rd Iteration — steps 6, 7

As you can see from the trace table, since the value 6 is never assigned to variable i, this program will iterate for an infinite number of times! Obviously, this program does not satisfy the property of finiteness.

Exercise 24.1-4   Counting the Total Number of Iterations

How many iterations does this Python program perform?

```python
i = -10
while i > 0:
    i -= 1
print("The end")
```

Solution

Initially, the value −10 is assigned to variable i. The Boolean expression directly evaluates to False and the flow of execution goes right to the print("The end") statement. Thus, this program performs zero iterations.

Exercise 24.1-5   Finding the Sum of Four Numbers

Using a pre-test loop structure, write a Python program that lets the user enter four numbers and then calculates and displays their sum.

Solution

Do you remember the example in paragraph 23.2 for calculating the sum of four numbers? At the end, after a little work, the proposed Python program became

```
total = 0
execute_these_statements_4_times:
    x = float(input())
    total = total + x

print(total)
```

Now, you need a way to "present" the statement *execute_these_statements_4_times* with real Python statements. The while statement is actually able to do this, but you need one extra variable to count the total number of iterations. Then, when the desired number of iterations has been performed, the flow of execution must exit the loop.

Following is a general purpose code fragment that iterates for the number of times specified by *total_number_of_iterations*,

```
i = 1
while i <= total_number_of_iterations:

    A statement or block of statements

    i += 1
```

where *total_number_of_iterations* can be a constant value or even a variable or an expression.

✎ *The name of the variable* i *is not binding. You can use any variable name you wish such as* counter, *count,* k, *and more.*

After combining this code fragment with the previous one, the final program becomes

📁 **file_24_1_5**

```
total = 0


i = 1
while i <= 4:
    x = float(input())
    total = total + x


    i += 1

print(total)
```

This pair of statements is executed 4 times forcing the user to enter 4 numbers.

Exercise 24.1-6   *Finding the Sum of Odd Numbers*

Design a flowchart and write the corresponding Python program that lets the user enter 20 integers, and then calculates and displays the sum of the odd numbers.

Solution

This is quite easy. What the program must do inside the loop is check whether or not a given number is odd and, if it is, that number must accumulate to variable total; even numbers must be ignored. The flowchart is as follows. It includes a single-alternative decision structure nested within a pre-test loop structure.

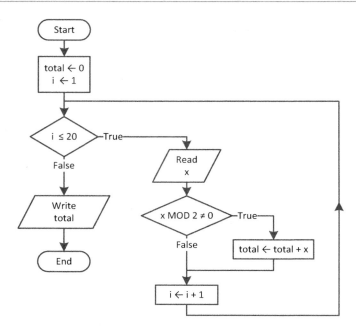

The corresponding Python program is as follows.

```
📄 file_24_1_6
total = 0

i = 1
while i <= 20:
    x = int(input())
    if x % 2 != 0:
        total += x       #This is equivalent to total = total + x
    i += 1

print(total)
```

✎ *You can nest **any** decision control structure inside **any** loop control structure as long as you keep them syntactically and logically correct.*

Exercise 24.1-7   Finding the Sum of N Numbers

Write a Python program that lets the user enter N numbers and then calculates and displays their sum. The value of N must be given by the user at the beginning of the program.

Solution

In this exercise, the total number of iterations depends on a value that the user must enter. Following is a general purpose code fragment that iterates for N times, where N is given by the user.

```
n = int(input())

i = 1
while i <= n:
```

```
    A statement or block of statements

    i += 1
```

According to what you have learned so far, the final program becomes

📁 **file_24_1_7**

```
total = 0

n = int(input())

i = 1
while i <= n:
    x = float(input())
    total += x
    i += 1

print(total)
```

Exercise 24.1-8   *Finding the Sum of an Unknown Quantity of Numbers*

Write a Python program that lets the user enter numeric values repeatedly until the value −1 is entered. When data input is completed, the sum of the numbers entered must be displayed. (The value of −1 must not be included in the final sum). Next, create a trace table to check if your program operates properly using 10, 20, 5, and −1 as input values.

Solution

In this exercise, the total number of iterations is unknown. If you were to use decision control structures, your program would look something like the code fragment that follows.

```
total = 0

x = float(input())
if x != -1:       #Check variable x
    total += x              #and execute this statement
    x = float(input())    #and this one
    if x != -1:       #Check variable x
        total += x              #and execute this statement
        x = float(input())    #and this one
        if x != -1:       #Check variable x
            total += x              #and execute this statement
            x = float(input())    #and this one
            ...

            ...
print(total)
```

> This is the part of the program that actually repeats.

Now let's rewrite this program using a loop control structure instead. The final program is presented next. If you try to follow the flow of execution, you will find that it operates equivalently to the previous one.

📁 **file_24_1_8**

```
total = 0
```

```
x = float(input())
while x != -1:        #Check variable x
    total += x                #and execute this statement
    x = float(input())    #and this one

print(total)
```

Now let's create a trace table to determine if this program operates properly using 10, 20, 5, and −1 as input values.

Step	Statement	Notes	x	total
1	total = 0		?	0
2	x = float(input())		10	0
3	while x != -1:	This evaluates to True		
4	total += x		10	10
5	x = float(input())		20	10
6	while x != -1:	This evaluates to True		
7	total += x		20	30
8	x = float(input())		5	30
9	while x != -1:	This evaluates to True		
10	total += x		5	35
11	x = float(input())		−1	35
12	while x != -1:	This evaluates to False		
13	print(total)	It displays: 35		

As you can see, in the end, variable total contains the value 35, which is, indeed, the sum of the values 10 + 20 + 5. Moreover, the final given value of −1 does not participate in the final sum.

✎ *When the number of iterations is known before the loop starts iterating the loop is often called "definite loop". In this exercise, however, the number of iterations is not known before the loop starts iterating, and it depends on a certain condition. This type of loop is often called "indefinite loop".*

Exercise 24.1-9   *Finding the Product of 20 Numbers*

Write a Python program that lets the user enter 20 numbers and then calculates and displays their product.

Solution

If you were to use a sequence control structure, it would be something like the next code fragment.

```
p = 1

x = float(input())
p = p * x
```

This must be written 20 times

```
x = float(input())
p = p * x

...

...
x = float(input())
p = p * x
```

✎ *Note that variable* p *is initialized to 1 instead of 0. This is necessary for the statement* p = p * x *to operate properly; the final product would be zero otherwise.*

Using knowledge from the previous exercises, the final program becomes

📁 **file_24_1_9**

```
p = 1

i = 1
while i <= 20:
    x = float(input())
    p = p * x

    i += 1

print(p)
```

24.2   The Post-Test Loop Structure

The post-test loop structure is shown in the following flowchart.

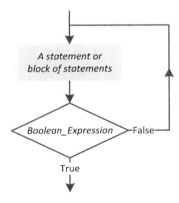

📝 *In loop control structures, one of the diamond's exits always has an upward direction.*

Let's see what happens when the flow of execution reaches a post-test loop structure. The statement or block of statements of the structure is directly executed and if *Boolean_Expression* evaluates to False, the flow of execution goes back to the point just above the statement or block of statements of the structure. The statement or block of statements is executed once more and if *Boolean_Expression* evaluates to False again, the process repeats. The iterations stop when *Boolean_Expression*, at some point, evaluates to True and the flow of execution exits the loop.

✎ *The post-test loop differs from the pre-test loop in that first the statement or block of statements of the structure is executed and afterwards the Boolean expression is evaluated. Consequently, the post-test loop performs at least one iteration!*

▣ *Each time the statement or block of statements of a loop control structure is executed, the term used in computer science is "the loop is iterating" or "the loop performs an iteration".*

Although the post-test loop structure is directly supported in most computer languages such as C, C++, C#, Java, PHP, and Visual Basic (to name a few), unfortunately this is not true for Python since there is no direct statement for this kind of structure. So now the question is: "*What can you do if you still want to use post-test loop structures in your Python programs?*"

In Python, you can still write post-test loops (indirectly, of course) using the while statement along with an if and a break statement. The main idea is to create an *endless loop* (also known as an *infinite loop*) and break out of it when the Boolean expression that exists at the end of the block of statements of the structure evaluates to True . The idea is shown in the following code fragment, given in general form.

```
while True:

    A statement or block of statements

    if Boolean_Expression: break
```

✎ *You can break out of a loop before it actually completes all of its iterations by using the* break *statement*

The following example displays the numbers 1 to 10.

```
                              📁 file_24_2
i = 1
while True:
    print(i)
    i += 1
    if i > 10: break
```

Exercise 24.2-1   Designing the Flowchart and Counting the Total Number of Iterations

Design the corresponding flowchart for the following Python program. How many iterations does this Python program perform?

```
i = 3
while True:
    i = i - 1
    if i <= 0: break

print("The end")
```

Solution

The corresponding flowchart is as follows.

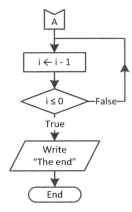

Now, let's create a trace table to observe the flow of execution.

Step	Statement	Notes	i
1	i = 3		3
2	i = i - 1		2
3	if i <= 0: break	This evaluates to False	
4	i = i - 1		1
5	if i <= 0: break	This evaluates to False	
6	i = i - 1		0
7	if i <= 0: break	This evaluates to True	
8	print("The end")	It displays: The end	

1st Iteration (steps 2–3)
2nd Iteration (steps 4–5)
3rd Iteration (steps 6–7)

As you can see from the trace table, the total number of iterations is three.

Now, let's draw some conclusions!

► If you have to find the total number of iterations, you can count the number of times the statement or block of statements of the structure is executed but also the number of times the Boolean expression is evaluated, since both numbers are equal.

► In a post-test loop structure, when the statement or block of statements of the structure is executed N times, the Boolean expression is evaluated N times as well.

Exercise 24.2-2   *Counting the Total Number of Iterations*

How many iterations does this Python program perform?

```python
i = 3
while True:
    i -= 1
    if i < 0: break

print("The end")
```

Solution

This exercise is almost identical to the previous one. The only difference is that the Boolean expression i < 0 here remains False even for i = 0. Therefore, it performs an additional iteration, that is, four iterations.

Exercise 24.2-3   Designing the Flowchart and Counting the Total Number of Iterations

Design the corresponding flowchart for the following Python program. How many iterations does this Python program perform? What happens if you switch the post-test loop with a pre-test loop structure?

```python
i = -1
while True:
    i -= 1
    print("Hello there!")
    if i <= 0: break
print("The end")
```

Solution

The corresponding flowchart is as follows.

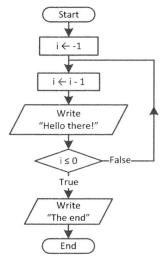

Initially the value −1 is assigned to variable i. Inside the loop, variable i is decremented by one (value −2 is assigned) and the message "Hello there!" is displayed. The Boolean expression i ≤ 0 evaluates to True and the flow of execution goes right to the Write ("The end") statement. Thus, this algorithm and the corresponding Python program perform one iteration!

Now, in the flowchart that follows, let's see what happens if you switch the post-test loop with a pre-test loop structure .

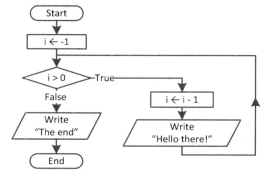

The value −1 is assigned to variable i. The Boolean expression i > 0 evaluates to False and the flow of execution goes directly to the Write ("The end") statement. Thus, this algorithm performs zero iterations!

✎ *The post-test loop structure iterates while its Boolean expression* (i ≤ 0) *is* False, *which means that it iterates until variable* i *becomes greater than zero. If you want to use a pre-test loop structure instead, you need to use the corresponding negated Boolean expression* i > 0. *This is because the pre-test loop structure iterates while its Boolean expression is* True.

✎ *A pre-test loop structure may perform zero iterations in contrast to the post-test loop structure which performs **at least** one iteration!*

Exercise 24.2-4   *Counting the Total Number of Iterations*

How many iterations does this Python program perform?

```python
i = 1
while True:
    i = i + 2
    if i == 4: break
print("The end")
```

Solution

Let's create a trace table to observe the flow of execution.

Step	Statement	Notes	i
1	i = 1		1
2	i = i + 2		3
3	if i == 4: break	This evaluates to False	
4	i = i + 2		5
5	if i == 4: break	This evaluates to False	
6	i = i + 2		7
7	if i == 4: break	This evaluates to False	
8	...	...	.
9	...	...	.

- Steps 2–3: 1st Iteration
- Steps 4–5: 2nd Iteration
- Steps 6–7: 3rd Iteration

As you can see from the trace table, since the value 4 is never assigned to variable i, this program will iterate for an infinite number of times! Obviously, this program does not satisfy the property of finiteness.

Exercise 24.2-5   *Finding the Product of N Numbers*

Write a Python program that lets the user enter N numbers and then calculates and displays their product. The value of N must be given by the user at the beginning of the program. What happens if you switch the post-test loop structure with a pre-test loop structure? Do both programs operate exactly the same way for all possible input values of N?

Solution

Both programs below let the user enter N numbers and then calculate and display their product. The left one, however, uses a pre-test while the right one uses a post-test loop structure. If you try to execute them and enter any value greater than zero for N, both programs operate exactly the same way!

```
┌ file_24_2_5a
n = int(input())

p = 1

i = 1
while i <= n:
    x = float(input())
    p = p * x

    i += 1


print(p)
```

```
┌ file_24_2_5b
n = int(input())

p = 1

i = 1
while True:
    x = float(input())
    p = p * x

    i += 1
    if i > n: break


print(p)
```

The two Python programs, however, operate in different ways when the user enters a non-positive[1] value for N. For example, if the value 0 is entered, the left program performs **zero** iterations whereas the right program performs **one** iteration!

📱 *A pre-test loop structure may perform zero iterations in contrast to the post-test loop structure, which performs **at least** one iteration!*

✎ *Obviously, the left program (the one that uses a pre-test loop structure) is the best choice to solve this exercise. Suppose the user executes the program but then decides not to enter any values. He or she can then enter value zero for N and the program won't ask for any other values!*

24.3   The Mid-Test Loop Structure

The mid-test loop structure is shown in the following flowchart.

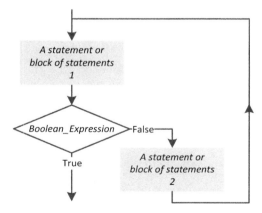

Let's see what happens when the flow of execution reaches a mid-test loop structure. The statement or block of statements 1 of the structure is directly executed and if *Boolean_Expression* evaluates to False, the statement or block of statements 2 is executed and the flow of execution goes back to the point just above the statement or block of statements 1 of the structure. The statement or block of statements 1 is executed once

---

[1] A quantity that is either zero or negative.

more and if *Boolean_Expression* evaluates to False again, the process repeats. The iterations stop when *Boolean_Expression*, at some point, evaluates to True and the flow of execution exits the loop.

Although this loop control structure is directly supported in some computer languages such as Ada, unfortunately this is not true for Python. However, you can still write mid-test loops using the while statement along with an if and a break statement. The main idea is to create an endless loop and break out of it when the Boolean expression that exists between the two statements (or block of statements) of the structure evaluates to True. The idea is shown in the code fragment given in general form that follows.

```python
while True:

    A statement or block of statements 1

    if Boolean_Expression: break

    A statement or block of statements 2
```

✎ *You can break out of a loop before it actually completes all of its iterations by using the* break *statement.*

The following example displays the numbers 1 to 10.

📁 **file_24_3**

```python
i = 1
while True:
    print(i)
    if i >= 10: break
    i += 1
```

Exercise 24.3-1   *Designing the Flowchart and Counting the Total Number of Iterations*

Design the corresponding flowchart for the following Python program and create a trace table to determine the values of variable i in each step.

```python
i = 10
while True:
    print(i)
    i += 5
    if i > 45: break
    print(i ** 2)
    i += 10

print("The end")
```

Solution

The corresponding flowchart is as follows.

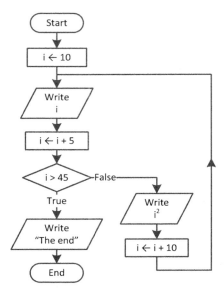

Now, let's create a trace table to observe the flow of execution.

Step	Statement	Notes	i
1	`i = 10`		**10**
2	`print(i)`	It displays: 10	
3	`i += 5`		**15**
4	`if i > 45: break`	This evaluates to False	
5	`print(i ** 2)`	It displays: 225	
6	`i += 10`		**25**
7	`print(i)`	It displays: 25	
8	`i += 5`		**30**
9	`if i > 45: break`	This evaluates to False	
10	`print(i ** 2)`	It displays: 900	
11	`i += 10`		**40**
12	`print(i)`	It displays: 40	
13	`i += 5`		**45**
14	`if i > 45: break`	This evaluates to False	
15	`print(i ** 2)`	It displays: 2025	
16	`i += 10`		**55**
17	`print(i)`	It displays: 55	
18	`i += 5`		**60**
19	`if i > 45: break`	This evaluates to True	
20	`print("The end")`	It displays: The end	

24.4 Review Questions: True/False

Choose **true** or **false** for each of the following statements.

1. A pre-test loop may perform zero iterations.

2. In flowcharts, both exits of the diamond symbol in a pre-test loop structure, have an upwards direction.

3. The statement or block of statements of a pre-test loop structure is executed at least one time.

4. A pre-test loop stops iterating when its Boolean expression evaluates to `True`

5. In a pre-test loop structure, when the statement or block of statements of the structure is executed N times, the Boolean expression is evaluated N - 1 times.

6. A post-test loop may perform zero iterations.

7. A post-test loop stops iterating when its Boolean expression evaluates to `True`.

8. In a post-test loop structure, when the statement or block of statements of the structure is executed N times, its Boolean expression is evaluated N times as well.

9. You cannot nest a decision control structure inside a post-test loop structure.

10. In the mid-test loop structure, the statement or block of statements 1 is executed the same number of times as the statement or block of statements 2.

11. In the following code fragment

    ```python
    i = 1
    while i <= 10:
        print("Hello")
    i += 1
    ```

    the word "Hello" is displayed 10 times

12. The following Python program

    ```python
    i = 1
    while i != 10:
        print("Hello")
        i += 2
    ```

    does **not** satisfy the property of finiteness

13. In the following code fragment

    ```python
    i = 1
    while True:
        print("Hello")
        if i < 10: break
    ```

    the word "Hello" is displayed an infinite number of times.

14. The following Python program (not code fragment)

    ```python
    while True:
        print("Hello")
        i += 1
        if i > 10: break
    ```

    satisfies the property of definiteness.

15. The following Python program

    ```python
    b = int(input())
    while True:
    ```

```
        a = 1 / (b - 1)
        b += 1
        if b > 10: break
```

does **not** satisfy the property of definiteness.

16. In the following code fragment

```
    i = 1
    while True:
        print("Zeus")
        if i > 10: break
        i += 1
```

the word "Zeus" is displayed 10 times.

24.5   Review Questions: Multiple Choice

Select the correct answer for each of the following statements.

1. In flowcharts, the diamond symbol is being used

    a.   in decision control structures.

    b.   in loop control structures.

    c.   all of the above

2. A post-test loop structure

    a.   performs one iteration more than the pre-test loop structure does.

    b.   performs the same number of iterations as the pre-test loop structure does.

    c.   none of the above

3. In a post-test loop structure, the statement or block of statements of the structure

    a.   are executed before the loop's Boolean expression is evaluated.

    b.   are executed after the loop's Boolean expression is evaluated.

    c.   none of the above

4. In the following code fragment

```
    i = 1
    while i < 10:
        print("Hello Hermes")
        i += 1
```

    the message "Hello Hermes" is displayed

    a.   10 times.

    b.   9 times.

    c.   1 time.

    d.   0 times.

    e.   none of the above

5. In the following code fragment

```
    i = 1
    while i < 10:
        print("Hi!")
    print("Hello Ares")
    i += 1
```

the message "Hello Ares" is displayed

    a.   10 times.

    b.   11 time.

    c.   1 times.

    d.   none of the above

6.   In the following code fragment

```python
i = 1
while i < 10:
    i += 1
print("Hi!")
print("Hello Aphrodite")
```

the message "Hello Aphrodite" is displayed

    a.   10 times.

    b.   1 time.

    c.   0 times.

    d.   none of the above

7.   In the following code fragment

```python
i = 1
while i >= 10:
    print("Hi!")
    print("Hello Apollo")
    i += 1
```

the message "Hello Apollo" is displayed

    a.   10 times.

    b.   1 time.

    c.   0 times.

    d.   none of the above

8.   The following Python program

```python
n = int(input())
s = 0
i = 1
while i < n:
    a = float(input())
    s = s + a
    i += 1
print(s)
```

calculates and displays the sum of

    a.   as many numbers as the value of variable n denotes.

    b.   as many numbers as the result of the expression n - 1 denotes.

    c.   as many numbers as the value of variable i denotes.

    d.   none of the above

9. In the following code fragment

```
i = 1
while True:
    print("Hello Poseidon")
    i += 1
    if i <= 5: break
```

the message "Hello Poseidon" is displayed

    a.   5 times.

    b.   1 time.

    c.   0 times.

    d.   none of the above

10. In the following code fragment

```
i = 1
while True:
    print("Hello Athena")
    i += 5
    if i == 50: break
```

the message "Hello Athena" is displayed

    a.   at least one time.

    b.   at least 10 times.

    c.   an infinite number of times.

    d.   all of the above

11. In the following code fragment

```
i = 0
while True:
    print("Hello Apollo")
    if i <= 10: break
```

the message "Hello Apollo" is displayed

    a.   at least one time.

    b.   an infinite number of times.

    c.   none of the above

12. In the following code fragment

```
i = 10
while True:
    i -= 1
    if i > 0: break
    print("Hello Aphrodite")
```

the message "Hello Aphrodite" is displayed

    a.   at least one time.

    b.   an infinite number of times.

    c.   ten times

    d.   none of the above

24.6 Review Exercises

Complete the following exercises.

1. Identify the error(s) in the following Python program. It must display the numbers 3, 2, 1 and the message "The end".

    ```python
    i = 3
    while True
        print(i)
        i -= 1
        if i < 0 break
    print(The end)
    ```

2. Create a trace table to determine the values of the variables in each step of the next Python program. How many iterations does this Python program perform?

    ```python
    i = 3
    x = 0
    while i >= 0:
        i -= 1
        x += i
    print(x)
    ```

3. Design the corresponding flowchart and create a trace table to determine the values of the variables in each step of the next Python program. How many iterations does this Python program perform?

    ```python
    i = -5
    while i < 10:
        i -= 1
    print(i)
    ```

4. Create a trace table to determine the values of the variables in each step of the next Python program. How many iterations does this Python program perform?

    ```python
    a = 2
    while a <= 10:
        b = a + 1
        c = b * 2
        d = c - b + 1
        if d == 4:
            print(b, ",", c)
        elif d == 5:
            print(c)
        elif d == 8:
            print(a, ",", b)
        else:
            print(a, ",", b, ",", d)
        a += 4
    ```

5. Create a trace table to determine the values of the variables in each step of the next Python program. How many iterations does this Python program perform?

    ```python
    a = 1
    b = 1
    c = 0
    ```

```
d = 0
while b < 2:
    x = a + b
    if x % 2 != 0:
        c = c + 1
    else:
        d = d + 1
    a = b
    b = c
    c = d
```

6. Fill in the gaps in the following code fragments so that all loops perform exactly four iterations.

i.
```
a = 3
while a > ...... :
    a -= 1
```

ii.
```
a = 5
while a < ...... :
    a += 1
```

iii.
```
a = 9
while a != 10:
    a = a + ......
```

iv.
```
a = 1
while a != ...... :
    a -= 2
```

v.
```
a = 2
while a < ...... :
    a = 2 * a
```

vi.
```
a = 1
while a < ...... :
    a = a + 0.1
```

7. Create a trace table to determine the values of the variables in each step of the next Python program. How many iterations does this Python program perform?

```
y = 5
x = 38
while True:
    y *= 2
    x += 1
    print(y)
    if y >= x: break
```

8. Create a trace table to determine the values of the variables in each step of the next Python program. How many iterations does this Python program perform?

```
x = 1
while True:
    if x % 2 == 0:
        x += 1
    else:
        x += 3
    print(x)
    if x >= 12: break
```

9. Create a trace table to determine the values of the variables in each step of the next Python program. How many iterations does this Python program perform?

```
y = 2
x = 0
while True:
    y = y ** 2
```

```
if x < 256:
    x = x + y
print(x, ",", y)
if y >= 65535: break
```

10. Create a trace table to determine the values of the variables in each step of the next Python program. How many iterations does this Python program perform?

```
a = 2
b = 4
c = 0
d = 0
while True:
    x = a + b
    if x % 2 != 0:
        c = c + 5
    elif d % 2 == 0:
        d = d + 5
    else:
        c = c + 3
    a = b
    b = d
    if c >= 11: break
```

11. Fill in the gaps in the following code fragments so that all loops perform exactly six iterations.

i.
```
a = 5
while True:
    a -= 1
    if a <= ...... : break
```

ii.
```
a = 12
while True:
    a += 1
    if a >= ...... : break
```

iii.
```
a = 20
while True:
    a = a + ......
    if a == 23: break
```

iv.
```
a = 100
while True:
    a -= 20
    if a == ...... : break
```

v.
```
a = 2
while True:
    a = 2 * a
    if a == ...... : break
```

vi.
```
a = 10
while True:
    a = a + 0.25
    if a > ...... : break
```

12. Fill in the gaps in the following code fragments so that all display the value 10 at the end.

i.
```
x = 0
y = 0
while True:
    x += 1
    y += 2
    if x > ...... : break
print(y)
```

ii.
```
x = 1
y = 20
while True:
    x -= 1
    y -= 2.5
    if x < ...... : break
print(y)
```

iii.
```
x = 3
y = 2.5
while True:
    x -= 1
    y *= 2
    if x < ...... : break
print(y)
```

iv.
```
x = 30
y = 101532
while True:
    x -= ......
    y = y // 10
    if x < 0: break
print(y)
```

13. Using a pre-test loop structure, write a Python program that lets the user enter N numbers and then calculates and displays their sum and their average. The value of N must be given by the user at the beginning of the program.

14. Using a pre-test loop structure, write a Python program that lets the user enter N integers and then calculates and displays the product of those that are even. The value of N must be given by the user at the beginning of the program.

15. Using a pre-test loop structure, write a Python program that lets the user enter 100 integers and then calculates and displays the sum of those with a last digit of 0. For example, the values 10, 2130, and 500 are such numbers.

    Hint: You can isolate the last digit of any integer using a modulus 10 operation.

16. Using a pre-test loop structure, write a Python program that lets the user enter 20 integers and then calculates and displays the sum of those that consist of three digits.

    Hint: All three-digit integers are between 100 and 999.

17. Using a pre-test loop structure, write a Python program that lets the user enter numeric values repeatedly until the value 0 is entered. When data input is completed, the product of the numbers entered must be displayed. (The last 0 entered must not be included in the final product). Next, create a trace table to check if your program operates properly using 3, 2, 9, and 0 as input values.

18. The population of a town is now at 30000 and is expanding at a rate of 3% per year. Using a pre-test loop structure, write a Python program to determine how many years it will take for the population to exceed 100000.

19. Using a post-test loop structure, design a flowchart and write the corresponding Python program that lets the user enter 50 integers and then calculates and displays the sum of those that are odd and the sum of those that are even.

20. Using a post-test loop structure, write a Python program that lets the user enter N integers and then calculates and displays the product of those that are negative. The value of N must be given by the user at the beginning of the program, and the final product must always be displayed as a positive value. Assume that the user enters a value greater than 0 for N.

21. Using a post-test loop structure, write a Python program that prompts the user to enter five integers and then calculates and displays the product of all three-digit integers with a first digit of 5. For example, the values 512, 555, and 593 are all such numbers

    Hint: All three-digit integers with a first digit of 5 are between 500 and 599.

22. The population of a beehive is now at 50000, but due to environmental reasons it is contracting at a rate of 10% per year. Using a post-test loop structure, write a Python program to determine how many years it will take for the population to be less than 20000.

Chapter 25
The `for` statement

25.1 The `for` statement

In Chapter 24, as you certainly noticed, the `while` statement was used to create both definite and indefinite loops. In other words, it was used to iterate for a known number of times but also for an unknown number of times. Since definite loops are so frequently used in computer programming, almost every computer language, including Python, incorporates a special statement that is much more readable and convenient than the `while` statement—and this is the `for` statement.

The general form of the `for` statement, is

```
for var in sequence:
    A statement or block of statements
```

where *var* is a variable that is assigned each successive value of *sequence*, and the statement or block of statements of the structure is executed once for each value.

The flowchart of the Python's `for` statement is shown here.

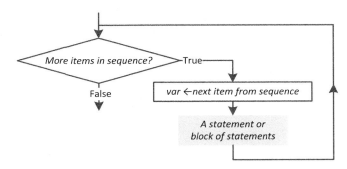

You will notice, however, that this book uses a more simplified flowchart, which is shown here.

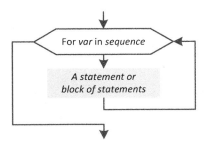

The following example displays the numbers 1, 2, 3, 4, and 5.

```
📄 file_25_1a
```

```
for i in [1, 2, 3, 4, 5]:
    print(i)
```

Its corresponding flowchart is shown here

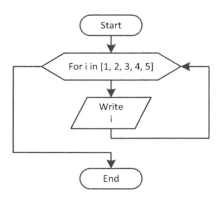

The following example displays the letters "H", "e", "l", "l", and "o" (all without the double quotes).

```
☐ file_25_1b
```

```python
for letter in "Hello":
    print(letter)
```

Its corresponding flowchart is shown here

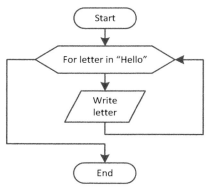

As you learned in paragraph 11.2, the Python's range() function can be used to create a sequence of integers. You can use this function along with the for statement, to expand the possibilities of the for statement as shown here

```python
for var in range([initial_value,] final_value [, step ]):

    A statement or block of statements
```

where

▶   *initial_value* is the starting value of the sequence. This argument is optional. If omitted, its default value is 0.

▶   the sequence is up to, but not including, *final_value*.

▶   *step* is the difference between each number in the sequence. This argument is optional. If omitted, its default value is 1.

The arguments initial_value, final_value, *and* step *must be integers. Negative values are also permitted.*

The following example displays the numbers 0 to 10.

```
☐ file_25_1c
```

```python
for i in range(0, 11, 1):
```

```
    print(i)
```

When step is 1, you can omit the third argument. The previous example can also be written as

📁 **file_25_1d**

```
for i in range(0, 11):
    print(i)
```

Moreover, when initial value is 0, you can omit the first argument. The previous example can also be written as

📁 **file_25_1e**

```
for i in range(11):
    print(i)
```

The next example displays the numbers 2, 4, 6, 8, and 10.

📁 **file_25_1f**

```
for i in range(2, 12, 2):
    print(i)
```

Last, but now least, if you wish a sequence of numbers in reverse order, you can use a negative value for *step*. The following example displays odd numbers from 11 to 1.

📁 **file_25_1g**

```
a = 11
b = 0
for i in range(a, b, -2):
    print(i)
```

> ✎ *Don't ever dare alter the value of* var *inside the loop! The same applies to* initial_value, final_value, *and* step *(in case they are variables and not constant values). This makes your code unreadable. If you insist, though, please use a* while *statement instead.*

In Python, as in the case of the while statement, the for statement can be combined with an else keyword as shown here.

```
for var in sequence:

        A statement or block of statements 1

else:

        A statement or block of statements 2
```

However, this unusual feature is rarely used in practice, so it will not be further discussed in this book.

Exercise 25.1-1   Creating the Trace Table

Create a trace table to determine the values of the variables in each step of the next Python program when the input value 1 is entered.

```
a = int(input())

for i in range(-3, 5, 2):
    a = a * 3
print(i, ",", a)
```

Solution

The `range()` function returns the sequence [−3, −1, 1, 3]. The for-loop assigns the values −3, −1, 1, and 3 to variable i, one value at each iteration. The corresponding trace table is shown here.

Step	Statement	Notes	a	i
1	`a = int(input())`		**1**	?
2	`i = -3`		1	**−3**
3	`a = a * 3`		**3**	−3
4	`i = -1`		3	**−1**
5	`a = a * 3`		**9**	−1
6	`i = 1`		9	**1**
7	`a = a * 3`		**27**	1
8	`i = 3`		27	**3**
9	`a = a * 3`		**81**	3
10	`print(i, ",", a)`	It displays: 3, 81		

- Steps 2–3: 1st Iteration
- Steps 4–5: 2nd Iteration
- Steps 6–7: 3rd Iteration
- Steps 8–9: 4th Iteration

Exercise 25.1-2   Creating the Trace Table

Create a trace table to determine the values of the variables in each step of the next Python program when the input value 4 is entered.

```python
a = int(input())

for i in range(6, a - 1, -1):
    print(i)
```

Solution

The `range()` function returns the sequence [6, 5, 4]. Following is the trace table used to determine the values of the variables in each step.

Step	Statement	Notes	a	i
1	`a = int(input())`		**4**	?
2	`i = 6`		4	**6**
3	`print(i)`	It displays: 6		
4	`i = 5`		4	**5**
5	`print(i)`	It displays: 5		
6	`i = 4`		4	**4**
7	`print(i)`	It displays: 4		

Exercise 25.1-3   Counting the Total Number of Iterations

Count the total number of iterations performed by the following code fragment for two different executions.

The input values for the two executions are: (i) 6, and (ii) 5.

```python
n = int(input())
for i in range(5, n + 1):
    print(i)
```

Solution

For the input value 6, the `range()` function returns a sequence that includes the numbers 5 and 6. Thus, the loop performs two iterations.

Correspondingly, for the input value 5 the loop obviously performs only one iteration.

Exercise 25.1-4   *Finding the Sum of Four Numbers*

Write a Python program that prompts the user enter four numbers and then calculates and displays their sum.

Solution

In Exercise 24.1-5, the solution proposed with a `while` statement was the following:

```python
total = 0

i = 1
while i <= 4:
    x = float(input())
    total = total + x

    i += 1

print(total)
```

It's now very easy to rewrite it using a `for` statement and have it display a prompt message before every data input.

```
                        📁 file_25_1_4
total = 0

for i in range(4):
    x = float(input("Enter a number: "))
    total = total + x

print(total)
```

Exercise 25.1-5   *Finding the Square Roots from 0 to N*

Write a Python program that prompts the user to enter an integer and then calculates and displays the square root of all integers from 0 to that given integer.

Solution

It's a piece of cake! The Python program is as follows.

```
                        📁 file_25_1_5
import math
```

```
n = int(input("Enter an integer: "))

for i in range(n + 1):
    print(math.sqrt(i))
```

Exercise 25.1-6   Finding the Sum of 1 + 2 + 3 + ... + 100

Write a Python program that calculates and displays the following sum:

$$S = 1 + 2 + 3 + ... + 100$$

Solution

If you were to use a sequence control structure to solve this exercise, it would be something like the next code fragment.

```
s = 0

i = 1
s = s + i

i = 2
s = s + i

i = 3
s = s + i
...

...
i = 100
s = s + i
```

Let's use a trace table to better understand it.

Step	Statement	Notes	i	s
1	s = 0	0	?	0
2	i = 1		1	0
3	s = s + i	0 + 1 = **1**	1	**1**
4	i = 2		2	1
5	s = s + i	0 + 1 + 2 = **3**	2	**3**
6	i = 3		3	3
7	s = s + i	0 +1 + 2 + 3 = **6**	3	**6**
8	i = 4		4	6
...	...		...	...
...	...		...	...
199	i = 99		**99**	4851
200	s = s + i		99	**4950**

201	i = 100			**100**	4950
202	s = s + i	0 + 1 + 2 + 3 + ...+ 99 + 100 = **5050**		100	**5050**

Now that everything has been cleared up, you can do the same using instead a for-loop which, in each iteration, assigns the values from 1 to 100 to variable i.

```
                            📁 file_25_1_6
s = 0
for i in range(1, 101):
    s = s + i
print(s)
```

Exercise 25.1-7   Finding the Product of 2 × 4 × 6 × 8 × 10

Write a Python program that calculates and displays the following product:

$$P = 2 \times 4 \times 6 \times 8 \times 10$$

Solution

As in the previous exercise, let's study this exercise using the following sequence control structure.

```
p = 1

i = 2
p = p * i

i = 4
p = p * i

i = 6
p = p * i

i = 8
p = p * i

i = 10
p = p * i
```

The corresponding trace table is shown here.

Step	Statement	Notes	i	p
1	p = 1	1	?	**1**
2	i = 2		**2**	1
3	p = p * i	1 × 2 = **2**	2	**2**
4	i = 4		**4**	2
5	p = p * i	2 × 4 = **8**	4	**8**
6	i = 6		**6**	8
7	p = p * i	2 × 4 × 6 = **48**	6	**48**

8	i = 8		8	48
9	p = p * i	$2 \times 4 \times 6 \times 8 = 384$	8	384
10	i = 10		10	384
11	p = p * i	$2 \times 4 \times 6 \times 8 \times 10 = 3840$	8	3840

Now that everything has been cleared up, you can do the same thing, this time using a for-loop which, in each iteration, assigns the values 2, 4, 6, 8, and 10 to variable i.

```
📁 file_25_1_7
p = 1
for i in range(2, 12, 2):
    p = p * i
print(p)
```

Exercise 25.1-8   Finding the Sum of $2^2 + 4^2 + 6^2 + ... (2N)^2$

Write a Python program that lets the user enter an integer N and then calculates and displays the following sum:
$$S = 2^2 + 4^2 + 6^2 + ... (2N)^2$$

Solution

In this exercise, in each iteration the for-loop must assign the values 2, 4, 6, ... 2N to variable i and each of these values must be raised to the second power before being accumulated in variable s. The final Python program is as follows.

```
📁 file_25_1_8
N = int(input())
s = 0
for i in range(2, 2 * N + 2, 2):
    s = s + i ** 2

print(s)
```

Exercise 25.1-9   Finding the Sum of $3^3 + 6^6 + 9^9 + ... (3N)^{3N}$

Write a Python program that lets the user enter an integer N and then calculates and displays the following sum:
$$S = 3^3 + 6^6 + 9^9 + ...+ (3N)^{3N}$$

Solution

This is pretty much the same as the previous exercise. The only difference is that variable i must be raised to the ith power before it is accumulated in variable s. Using the for-loop, the final Python program is as follows.

```
📁 file_25_1_9
N = int(input())
s = 0
for i in range(3, 3 * N + 3, 3):
    s = s + i ** i

print(s)
```

Exercise 25.1-10   Finding the Average Value of Positive Numbers

Write a Python program that lets the user enter 100 numbers and then calculates and displays the average value of the positive numbers. Add all necessary checks to make the program satisfy the property of definiteness.

Solution

Since you know the total number of iterations, you can use a for-loop. Inside the loop, however, a decision control structure must check whether or not the given number is positive; if so, it must accumulate the given number in variable s. The variable `count` counts the number of positive numbers given. When the flow of execution exits the loop, the average value can then be calculated. The Python program is as follows.

```
                          file_25_1_10
s = 0
count = 0
for i in range(100):
    x = float(input())
    if x > 0:
        s = s + x
        count += 1

if count != 0:
    print(s / count)
else:
    print("No numbers entered!")
```

✎ *The* if count != 0 *statement is necessary, because there is a possibility that the user may enter negative values only. By including this check, the program prevents any division-by-zero errors and thereby satisfies the property of definiteness.*

Exercise 25.1-11   Counting the Vowels

Write a Python program that prompts the user to enter a message and then counts and displays the number of vowels the message contains.

Solution

The following Python program counts the vowels in an English message.

```
                          file_25_1_11
message = input("Enter an English message: ")
vowels = "AEIOU"

count = 0

for character in message:
    if character.upper() in vowels:
        count += 1

print("Vowels:", count)
```

✎ *Note the two ways the operator* in *is used here. In the first case it is used to determine the number of iterations, whereas in the second case it is used to check whether a letter exists in the string* vowels (*see paragraph 15.5*).

25.2   Rules that Apply to For-Loops

There are certain rules you must always follow when writing programs with for-loops, since they can save you from undesirable side effects.

▶   **Rule 1**: The *var* variable can appear in a statement inside the for-loop but its value should never be altered. The same applies to *initial_value*, *final_value*, and *step* in case they are variables and not constant values.

▶   **Rule 2:** The *step* must never be zero. If it is set to zero, Python displays an error!

▶   **Rule 3:** If *initial_value* is smaller than *final_value* and the *step* is negative, the loop performs zero iterations. The following example prints **nothing** on the screen

```
for i in range(5, 9, -1):
    print(i)
```

▶   **Rule 4:** If *initial_value* is greater than *final_value* and the *step* is positive, the loop performs zero iterations. The following example also prints **nothing** on the screen

```
for i in range(10, 6):
    print(i)
```

Exercise 25.2-1   Finding the Sum of N Numbers

Write a Python program that prompts the user to enter N numbers and then calculates and displays their sum. The value of N must be given by the user at the beginning of the program.

Solution

The solution is presented here.

```
                            🗀 file_25_2_1
n = int(input("Enter quantity of numbers to enter: "))

total = 0
for i in range(n):
    a = float(input("Enter number No" + str(i + 1) + ": "))
    total += a    #This is equivalent to total = total + a

print("Sum:", total)
```

✎ *Even though it breaks the fourth rule of for-loops, in this particular exercise this situation is very useful. If the user enters a non-positive value for variable* n, *the* for *statement performs zero iterations.*

25.3   Review Questions: True/False

Choose **true** or **false** for each of the following statements.

1.   In a for statement, the variable *var* is automatically assigned each successive value of *sequence* at the beginning of each loop.

2.   A definite loop can be used when the number of iterations is known.

3.   In a definite loop, the statement or block of statements of the loop is executed at least one time.

4. In a range() function, the *initial_value* cannot be greater than the *final_value*.

5. When flow of execution exits a for-loop, the value of *var* is not equal to *final_value*.

6. In a range() function, the value of *initial_value*, *final_value* and *step* cannot be a float.

7. In Python, when *step* is set to zero the loop performs infinite number of iterations.

8. In a for statement, the *var* variable can appear in a statement inside the loop but its value should never be altered.

9. In a for statement, the *step* can be zero for certain situations.

10. In the following code fragment
```
for i in range(1, 10):
    print("Hello")
```
the word "Hello" is displayed 10 times.

11. The following code fragment
```
b = int(input())
for i in range(0, 9, b):
    print("Hello")
```
can always be executed.

12. The following code fragment
```
import math

b = int(input())
for i in range(10):
    a = math.sqrt(b) + i
    b *= 2
```
satisfies the property of definiteness.

25.4   Review Questions: Multiple Choice

Select the correct answer for each of the following statements.

1. A definite loop that uses the for statement
   a. executes one iteration more than the equivalent post-test loop structure (that uses the while statement).
   b. executes one iteration less than the equivalent post-test loop structure (that uses the while statement).
   c. none of the above

2. A for-loop can be used in a problem in which
   a. the user enters numbers repeatedly until the value −1 is entered.
   b. the user enters numbers repeatedly until the value entered is greater than *final_value*.
   c. all of the above
   d. none of the above

3. In a for-loop *initial_value*, *final_value*, and *step* can be
   a. a constant value.
   b. a variable.
   c. an expression.

    d.   all of the above

4.   In a for-loop, when *initial_value*, *final_value*, and *step* are variables, their values

    a.   cannot change inside the loop.

    b.   should not change inside the loop.

    c.   none of the above

5.   In a for-loop, when *var* increments, the *step* is

    a.   greater than zero.

    b.   equal to zero.

    c.   less than zero.

    d.   none of the above

6.   In a for-loop, the initial value of *var*

    a.   must be 0.

    b.   can be 0.

    c.   cannot be a negative one.

    d.   none of the above

7.   In a for-loop, variable *var* is automatically assigned each successive value of *sequence*

    a.   at the beginning of each iteration.

    b.   at the end of each iteration.

    c.   It is not assigned automatically.

    d.   none of the above

8.   In the following code fragment

```python
i = 1
for i in range(5, 6):
    print("Hello Hera")
```

the message "Hello Hera" is displayed

    a.   5 times.

    b.   1 time.

    c.   0 times.

    d.   none of the above

9.   In the following code fragment

```python
for i in range(5, 5):
    i = 1
    print("Hello Artemis")
```

the message "Hello Artemis" is displayed

    a.   1 time.

    b.   an infinite number of times.

    c.   0 times.

    d.   none of the above

10. In the following code fragment

```python
for i in range(5, 6):
    i = 6
```

```
print("Hello Ares")
```

the message "Hello Ares" is displayed

    a.   an infinite number of times.

    b.   1 time.

    c.   0 times.

    d.   none of the above

11. In the following code fragment

```
for i in range(2, 9):
    if i % 2 == 0:
        print("Hello Demeter")
```

the message "Hello Demeter" is displayed

    a.   8 times.

    b.   7 times.

    c.   5 times.

    d.   none of the above

12. In the following code fragment

```
for i in range(40, 51):
    print("Hello Dionysus")
```

the message "Hello Dionysus" is displayed

    a.   1 time.

    b.   2 times.

    c.   10 times.

    d.   11 times.

13. In the following code fragment

```
k = 0
for i in range(1, 7, 2):
    k = k + i
print(i)
```

the value displayed is

    a.   3.

    b.   6.

    c.   9.

    d.   none of the above

14. In the following code fragment

```
k = 0
for i in range(100, -105, -5):
    k = k + i
print(i)
```

the value displayed is

    a.   −95.

    b.   −105.

    c.   −100.

d.   none of the above

25.5   Review Exercises

Complete the following exercises.

1.   Create a trace table to determine the values of the variables in each step of the next Python program. How many iterations does this Python program perform?

```python
a = 0
b = 0
for j in range(0, 10, 2):
    if j < 5:
        b += 1
    else:
        a += j - 1
print(a, ",", b)
```

2.   Create a trace table to determine the values of the variables in each step of the next Python program for two different executions.

The input values for the two executions are: (i) 10, and (ii) 21.

```python
a = int(input())
b = a
for j in range(a - 5, a + 1, 2):
    if j % 2 != 0:
        b = a + j + 5
    else:
        b = a - j
print(b)
```

3.   Create a trace table to determine the values of the variables in each step of the next Python program for the input value 12.

```python
a = int(input())
for j in range(2, a, 3):
    x = j * 3 + 3
    y = j * 2 + 10
    if y - x > 0 or x > 30:
        y *= 2
    x += 4
    print(x, ",", y)
```

4.   Fill in the gaps in the following code fragments so that all loops perform exactly five iterations.

i.
```python
for a in range(5, ...... + 1):
    b += 1
```

ii.
```python
for a in range(0, ......, 4):
    b += 1
```

iii.
```python
for a in range(......, -17, -2):
    b += 1
```

iv.
```python
for a in range(-11, -16, ......):
    b += 1
```

5. Without using a trace table, can you find out what the next Python program displays?

```python
word = "Zeus"
i = 1
s = ""
for letter in word:
    s = s + i * letter
    i += 1
print(s)
```

6. Design a flowchart and write the corresponding Python program that prompts the user to enter 20 numbers and then calculates and displays their product and their average value.

7. Write a Python program that calculates and displays the sine of all numbers from 0 to 360°, using a step of 0.5. It is given that $2\pi = 360°$.

8. Write a Python program that prompts the user to enter a number in degrees and then calculates and displays the cosine of all numbers from 0 to that given number, using a step of 1. It is given that $2\pi = 360°$.

9. Write a Python program that calculates and displays the sum of the following:
$$S = 1 + 3 + 5 + \ldots + 99$$

10. Write a Python program that lets the user enter an integer N and then calculates and displays the product of the following:
$$P = 2^1 \times 4^3 \times 6^5 \times \ldots \times 2N^{(N-1)}$$

11. Write a Python program that calculates and displays the sum of the following:
$$S = 1 + 2 + 4 + 7 + 11 + 16 + 22 + 29 + 37 + \ldots + 191$$

12. Design a flowchart and write the corresponding Python program that lets a teacher enter the total number of students as well as their grades and then calculates and displays the average value of those who got an "A", that is 90 to 100. Add all necessary checks to make the program satisfy the property of definiteness.

13. Design a flowchart and write the corresponding Python program that prompts the user to enter 30 four-digit integers and then calculates and displays the sum of those with a first digit of 5 and a last digit of 3. For example, values 5003, 5923, and 5553 are all such integers.

14. Design a flowchart and write the corresponding Python program that prompts the user to enter N integers and then displays the total number of those that are even. The value of N must be given by the user at the beginning of the program. Moreover, if all integers given are odd, the message "You entered no even integers" must be displayed.

15. Design a flowchart and write the corresponding Python program that prompts the user to enter 50 integers and then calculates and displays the average value of those that are odd and the average value of those that are even.

16. Design a flowchart and write the corresponding Python program that prompts the user to enter two integers into variables start and finish and then displays all integers from start to finish. However, at the beginning the program must check if variable start is bigger than variable finish. If this happens, the program must swap their values so that they are always in the proper order.

17. Design a flowchart and write the corresponding Python program that prompts the user to enter two integers into variables start and finish and then displays all integers from start to finish that are multiples of five. However, at the beginning the program must check if variable start is bigger than variable finish. If this happens, the program must swap their values so that they are always in the proper order.

18. Write a Python program that prompts the user to enter a real and an integer and then displays the result of the first number raised to the power of the second number, without using the exponentiation operator (**).

19. Write a Python program that prompts the user to enter a message and then displays the number of words it contains. For example, if the string entered is "My name is Bill Bouras", the program must display "The message entered contains 5 words". Assume that the words are separated by a single space character.

    Hint: Use the len() function to get the number of characters that the given message contains.

20. Write a Python program that prompts the user to enter a message and then displays the average number of letters in each word. For example, if the message entered is "My name is Aphrodite Boura", the program must display "The average number of letters in each word is 4.4". Space characters must not be counted.

21. Write a Python program that prompts the user to enter a message and then counts and displays the number of consonants the message contains.

22. Write a Python program that prompts the user to enter a message and then counts and displays the number of vowels, the number of consonants, and the number of arithmetic characters the message contains.

Chapter 26
Nested Loop Control Structures

26.1 What is a Nested Loop?

A *nested loop* is a loop within another loop or, in other words, an inner loop within an outer one.

The outer loop controls the number of **complete** iterations of the inner loop. This means that the first iteration of the outer loop triggers the inner loop to start iterating until completion. Then the second iteration of the outer loop triggers the inner loop to start iterating until completion again. This process repeats until the outer loop has performed all of its iterations.

Take the following Python program, for example.

```
                              📁 file_26_1
for i in range(1, 3):
    for j in range(1, 4):        ⬅ Nested loop
        print(i, j)
```

The outer loop, the one that is controlled by variable i, controls the number of complete iterations that the inner loop performs. That is, when variable i contains the value 1, the inner loop performs three iterations (for j = 1, j = 2, and j = 3). The inner loop finishes but the outer loop needs to perform one more iteration (for i = 2). Therefore, the inner loop starts over and performs three new iterations again (for j = 1, j = 2 and j = 3).

The previous example is similar to the following one.

```
i = 1                      #Outer loop assigns value 1 to variable i
for j in range(1, 4):      #and inner loop performs three iterations
    print(i, j)


i = 2                      #Outer loop assigns value 2 to variable i
for j in range(1, 4):      #and inner loop starts over and
    print(i, j)            #performs three new iterations
```

The output result is as follows.

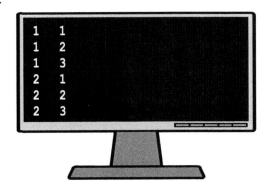

```
1   1
1   2
1   3
2   1
2   2
2   3
```

✎ *As long as the syntax rules are not violated, you can nest as many loop control structures as you wish. For practical reasons however, as you move to four or five levels of nesting, the entire loop structure becomes very complex and difficult to understand. However, experience shows that the maximum levels of nesting that you will do in your entire life as a programmer is probably three or four.*

✎ *The inner and outer loops do not need to be the same type. For example, a* for *statement may nest (enclose) a* while *statement, or vice versa.*

Exercise 26.1-1   Say "Hello Zeus". Counting the Total Number of Iterations.

Find the number of times message "Hello Zeus" is displayed.

```
                                    📄 file_26_1_1
for i in range(3):
    for j in range(4):
        print("Hello Zeus")
```

Solution

The values of variables i and j (in order of appearance) are as follows:

▶   For i = 0, the inner loop performs 4 iterations (for j = 0, j = 1, j = 2, and j = 3) and the message "Hello Zeus" is displayed 4 times.

▶   For i = 1, the inner loop performs 4 iterations (for j = 0, j = 1, j = 2, and j = 3) and the message "Hello Zeus" is displayed 4 times.

▶   For i = 2, the inner loop performs 4 iterations (for j = 0, j = 1, j = 2, and j = 3) and the message "Hello Zeus" is displayed 4 times.

Therefore, the message "Hello Zeus" is displayed a total of 3 × 4 = 12 times.

📖 *The outer loop controls the number of complete iterations of the inner one!*

Exercise 26.1-2   Creating the Trace Table

For the next code fragment, determine the value that variable a *contains at the end.*

```
a = 1
i = 5
while i < 7:
    for j in range(1, 5, 2):
        a = a * j + i
    i += 1
print(a)
```

Solution

The trace table is shown here.

Step	Statement	Notes	a	i	j
1	a = 1		**1**	?	?
2	i = 5		1	**5**	?
3	while i < 7	This evaluates to True			

4	j = 1		1	5	**1**
5	a = a * j + i		**6**	5	1
6	j = 3		6	5	**3**
7	a = a * j + i		**23**	5	3
8	i += 1		23	**6**	3
9	while i < 7	This evaluates to True			
10	j = 1		23	6	**1**
11	a = a * j + i		**29**	6	1
12	j = 3		29	6	**3**
13	a = a * j + i		**93**	6	3
14	i += 1		93	**7**	3
15	while i < 7	This evaluates to False			
16	print(a)	It displays: 93			

At the end of the program, variable a contains the value 93.

26.2 Rules that Apply to Nested Loops

Beyond the four rules that apply to for-loops, there are two extra rules that you should always follow when writing programs with nested loops, since they can save you from undesirable side effects.

► **Rule 1**: The inner loop must begin and end entirely within the outer loop, which means that the loops must not overlap.

► **Rule 2**: An outer loop and the inner (nested) loop must not use the same *var* variable.

Exercise 26.2-1   Breaking the First Rule

Design a flowchart fragment that breaks the first rule of nested loops, which states, "The inner loop must begin and end entirely within the outer loop".

Solution

The following flowchart fragment breaks the first rule of nested loops.

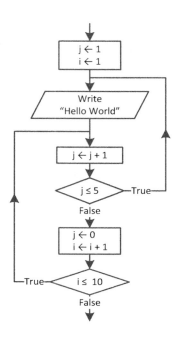

If you try to follow the flow of execution, you can see how smoothly it performs 5 × 10 = 50 iterations. No one can tell that this flowchart is wrong; on the contrary, it is absolutely correct. The problem, however, is that this flowchart is completely unreadable. No one can tell, at first glance, what this flowchart really does. Moreover, this structure matches none of the already known loop control structures that you have been taught, so it cannot become a Python program as is. Try to avoid this kind of nested loop!

Exercise 26.2-2   *Counting the Total Number of Iterations*

Find the number of times message "Hello" is displayed.

```python
i = 1
while i <= 3:
    for i in range(5, 0, -1):
        print("Hello")
    i += 1
```

Solution

At first glance, one would think that the word "Hello" is displayed 3 × 5 = 15 times. However, a closer second look reveals that things are not always as they seem. This program breaks the second rule of nested loops, which states, "*An outer loop and the inner (nested) loop must not use the same* var *variable*". Let's design the corresponding flowchart.

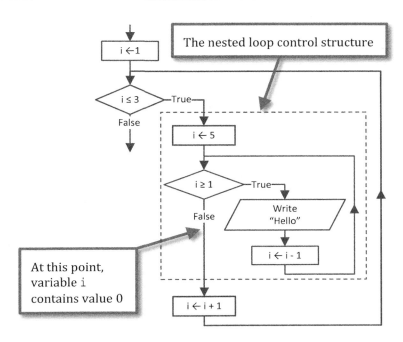

If you try to follow the flow of execution in this flowchart fragment, you can see that when the inner loop completes all of its five iterations, variable i contains the value 0. Then, variable i increments by 1 and the outer loop repeats again. This process can continue forever since variable i can never exceed the value 3 that the Boolean expression of the outer loop requires. Therefore, the message "Hello" is displayed an infinite number of times.

26.3 Review Questions: True/False

Choose **true** or **false** for each of the following statements.

1. A nested loop is an inner loop within an outer one.

2. It is possible to nest a mid-test loop structure within a pre-test loop structure.

3. The maximum number of levels of nesting in a loop control structure is four.

4. When two loop control structures are nested one within the other, the loop that starts last must complete first.

5. When two loop control structures are nested one within the other, they should not use the same variable as *var*.

6. In the following code fragment

```python
for i in range(1, 4):
    for j in range(1, 4):
        print("Hello")
```

the word "Hello" is displayed six times.

7. In the following code fragment

```python
for i in range(2):
    for j in range(1, 4):
        for k in range(1, 5, 2):
            print("Hello")
```

the word "Hello" is displayed 12 times.

8. In the following code fragment

```python
i = 1
while i <= 4:
    for i in range(3, 0, -1):
        print("Hello")
    i += 1
```

the word "Hello" is displayed an infinite number of times.

9. In the following code fragment

```python
for i in range(3):
    j = 1
    while True:
        print("Hello")
        j += 1
        if j >= 4: break
```

the word "Hello" is displayed nine times.

10. In the following program

```python
s = 0
while not False:
    while not False:
        a = int(input())
        if a >= -1: break
    if a == -1: break
    s += a
print(s)
```

there is at least one mid-test loop structure.

26.4 Review Questions: Multiple Choice

Select the correct answer for each of the following statements.

1. In the following code fragment

```python
for i in range(1, 3):
    for j in range(1, 3):
        print("Hello")
```

the values of variables i and j (in order of appearance) are

a. j = 1, i = 1, j = 1, i = 2, j = 2, i = 1, j = 2, i = 2

b. i = 1, j = 1, i = 1, j = 2, i = 2, j = 1, i = 2, j = 2

c. i = 1, j = 1, i = 2, j = 2

d. j = 1, i = 1, j = 2, i = 2

2. In the following code fragment

```python
x = 2
while x > -2:
    while True:
        x -= 1
        print("Hello Hestia")
        if x >= -2: break
```

the message "Hello Hestia" is displayed

    a. 4 times.

    b. an infinite number of times.

    c. 0 times.

    d. none of the above

3. In the following code fragment

```python
x = 1
while x != 500:
    for i in range(x, 4):
        print("Hello Artemis")
    x += 1
```

the message "Hello Artemis" is displayed

    a. an infinite number of times.

    b. 1500 times.

    c. 6 times.

    d. none of the above

4. The following code fragment

```python
for i in range(1, 4):
    for j in range(1, i + 1):
        print(i * j, ", ", sep = "", end = "")
print("The End!")
```

displays

    a. 1, 2, 4, 3, 6, 9, The End!

    b. 1, 2, 3, 4, 6, 9, The End!

    c. 1, 2, The End!, 4, 3, The End!, 6, 9, The End!

    d. none of the above

5. The following code fragment

```python
i = 1
while i <= 10:
    for i in range(10, 0, -1):
        print("Hello Dionysus")
    i += 1
```

does **not** satisfy the property of

    a. definiteness.

    b. finiteness.

    c. effectiveness.

    d. none of the above

26.5 Review Exercises

Complete the following exercises.

1. Fill in the gaps in the following code fragments so that all code fragments display the message "Hello Hephaestus" exactly 100 times.

i.
```python
for a in range(6, ……):
    for b in range(25):
        print("Hello Hephaestus")
```

ii.
```python
for a in range(0, …… , 5):
    for b in range(10, 20):
        print("Hello Hephaestus")
```

iii.
```python
for a in range(……, -17, -2):
    for b in range(150, 50, -5):
        print("Hello Hephaestus")
```

iv.
```python
for a in range(-11, -16, -1):
    for b in range(100, …… + 2, 2):
        print("Hello Hephaestus")
```

2. Design the corresponding flowchart and create a trace table to determine the values of the variables in each step of the next code fragment.
```python
a = 1
j = 1
while j <= 2:
    i = 10
    while i < 30:
        a = a + j + i
        i += 10
    j += 0.5
print(a)
```

3. Create a trace table to determine the values of the variables in each step of the next code fragment. How many times is the statement s = s + i * j executed?
```python
s = 0
for i in range(1, 5):
    for j in range(3, i - 1, -1):
        s = s + i * j
print(s)
```

4. Create a trace table to determine the values of the variables in each step of the next Python program for three different executions. How many iterations does this Python program perform?

The input values for the three executions are: (i) NO, (ii) YES, NO; and (iii) YES, YES, NO.
```python
s = 1
y = 25
while True:
    for i in range(1, 4):
        s = s + y
        y -= 5
    ans = input()
    if ans != "YES": break
print(s)
```

5. Write a Python program that displays an hours and minutes table in the following form.

```
0          0
0          1
0          2
0          3
...
0          59
1          0
1          1
1          2
1          3
...
23         59
```

Please note that the output is aligned with tabs.

6. Using nested loop control structures, write a Python program that displays the following output.

```
5 5 5 5 5
4 4 4 4
3 3 3
2 2
1
```

7. Using nested loop control structures, write a Python program that displays the following output.

```
0
0 1
0 1 2
0 1 2 3
0 1 2 3 4
0 1 2 3 4 5
```

8. Using nested loop control structures, write a Python program that displays the following rectangle.

```
*  *  *  *  *  *  *  *  *  *
*  *  *  *  *  *  *  *  *  *
*  *  *  *  *  *  *  *  *  *
*  *  *  *  *  *  *  *  *  *
```

Then, try to do the same without using any loop control structure!

9. Write a Python program that prompts the user to enter an integer N between 3 and 20 and then displays a square of size N on each side. For example, if the user enters 4 for N, the program must display the following square.

```
*  *  *  *
*  *  *  *
*  *  *  *
*  *  *  *
```

Then, try to do the same without using any loop control structure!

10. Write a Python program that prompts the user to enter an integer N between 3 and 20 and then displays a hollow square of size N on each side. For example, if the user enters 4 for N, the program must display the following hollow square.

```
*   *   *   *

*           *

*           *

*   *   *   *
```

Then, try to do the same without using any loop control structure!

11. Using nested loop control structures, write a Python program that displays the following triangle.

```
*

*   *

*   *   *

*   *   *   *

*   *   *   *   *

*   *   *   *

*   *   *

*   *

*
```

Then, try to do the same using just one for-loop (no nested loop control structures allowed!)

Chapter 27
Tips and Tricks with Loop Control Structures

27.1 Introduction

This chapter is dedicated to teaching you some useful tips and tricks that can help you write "better" code. You should always keep them in mind when you design your own algorithms, or even your own Python programs.

These tips and tricks can help you increase your code's readability, help you choose which loop control structure is better to use in each given problem, and help make the code shorter or even faster. Of course there is no single perfect method because on one occasion the use of a specific tip or trick may help, but on another occasion the same tip or trick may have exactly the opposite result. Most of the time, code optimization is a matter of programming experience.

Smaller algorithms are not always the best solution to a given problem. In order to solve a specific problem, you might write a short algorithm that unfortunately proves to consume a lot of CPU time. On the other hand, you might solve the same problem with another algorithm that seems longer but calculates the result much faster.

27.2 Choosing a Loop Control Structure

The following diagram can help you choose which loop control structure is better to use in each given problem, depending on the number of iterations.

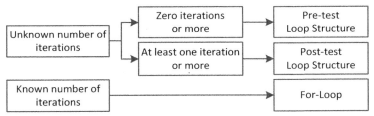

This diagram recommends the best option, not the only option. For example, when the number of iterations is known, it is not wrong to use a pre-test or a post-test loop structure instead. The proposed for-loop, though, is more convenient.

27.3 The "Ultimate" Rule

One question that often preys on programmers' minds when using pre-test or post-test loop structures, is how to determine which statements should be written inside, and which outside, the loop control structure and in which order.

There is one simple yet powerful rule—the *"Ultimate" rule*! Once you follow it, the potential for making a logic error is reduced to zero!

The "Ultimate" rule states:

▶ The variable or variables that participate in a loop's Boolean expression must be initialized before entering the loop.

▶ The value of the variable or variables that participate in a loop's Boolean expression must be updated (altered) within the loop. And more specifically, the statement that does this update/alteration must be one of the **last** statements of the loop.

For example, if variable x is the variable that participates in a loop's Boolean expression, a pre-test loop structure should always be in the following form,

```
Initialize x
while Boolean_Expression(x) :
        A statement or block of statements
        Update/alter x
```

and a post-test loop structure should always be in the following form,

```
Initialize x
while True:
        A statement or block of statements
        Update/alter x
    if Boolean_Expression(x) : break
```

where

▶ *Initialize* x is any statement that assigns an initial value to variable x. It can be either an input statement such as input("Enter a number: "), or an assignment statement using the value assignment operator (=). In a post-test loop structure though, this statement may sometimes be redundant and can be omitted since initialization of x can occur directly inside the loop.

▶ *Boolean_Expression(x)* can be any Boolean expression from a simple to a complex one, dependent on variable x.

▶ *Update/alter x* is any statement that alters the value of x such as an input statement, an assignment statement using the value assignment operator (=), or even compound assignment operators. This statement must be placed just before the point at which the loop's Boolean expression is evaluated. This is why it must be one of the **last** statements of the loop.

Following are some examples that use the "Ultimate" rule.

Example 1

```
a = int(input())          #Initialization of a
while a > 0:              #A Boolean expression dependent on a
    print(a)
    a = a - 1            #Update/alteration of a
```

Example 2

```
a = int(input())          #Initialization of a
b = int(input())          #Initialization of b
while a > b:              #A Boolean expression dependent on a and b
    print(a, b)
    a = int(input())     #Update/alteration of a
    b = int(input())     #Update/alteration of b
```

Example 3

```
s = 0                     #Initialization of s
while True:
    y = int(input())
```

```
        s = s + y              #Update/alteration of s
        if s >= 1000: break #A Boolean expression dependent on s
```

Example 4

```
y = 0                      #Initialization of y
while True:
    y = int(input())       #Update/alteration of y
    if y >= 0: break       #A Boolean expression dependent on y
```

In this example, though, initialization of variable y outside the loop is redundant and can be omitted since initialization is done inside the loop, as shown here.

```
while True:
    y = int(input())       #Initialization and update/alteration of y
    if y >= 0: break       #A Boolean expression dependent on y
```

Example 5

```
odd = 0                    #Initialization of odd
even = 0                   #Initialization of even
while odd + even < 5:      #A Boolean expression dependent on odd and even
    x = int(input())
    if x % 2 == 0:
        even += 1          #Update/alteration of even
    else:
        odd += 1           #Update/alteration of odd

print("Odds:", odd, "Evens:", even)
```

Now, you will realize why you should always follow the "Ultimate" rule"! Let's take a look at the following exercise:

Write a Python program that lets the user enter numbers repeatedly until the total number of positives given is three.

This exercise was given to a class, and a student gave the following Python program as an answer.

```
positives_given = 0

x = float(input())
while positives_given != 3:
    if x > 0:
        positives_given += 1
    x = float(input())

print("Three positives given!")
```

At first sight the program looks correct. It lets the user enter a number, it enters the loop and checks whether or not the given number is positive, then it lets the user enter a second number, and so on. However, this program contains a logic error—and unfortunately a difficult one. Can you spot it?

If you try to follow the flow of execution, you can confirm for yourself that the program runs smoothly—so smoothly that it makes you wonder if this book is reliable or if you must throw it away!

The problem becomes clear only when you try to enter all three of the expected positive values. The trace table that follows can help you determine where the problem lies. Assume that the user wants to enter the values 5, −10, −2, 4, and 20.

Step	Statement	Notes	positives_given	x
1	positives_given = 0		**0**	?
2	x = float(input())		0	**5**
3	while positives_given != 3	This evaluates to True		
4	if x > 0	This evaluates to True		
5	positives_given += 1		**1**	5
6	x = float(input())		1	**−10**
7	while positives_given != 3	This evaluates to True		
8	if x > 0	This evaluates to False		
9	x = float(input())		1	**−2**
10	while positives_given != 3	This evaluates to True		
11	if x > 0	This evaluates to False		
12	x = float(input())		1	**4**
13	while positives_given != 3	This evaluates to True		
14	if x > 0	This evaluates to True		
15	positives_given += 1		**2**	4
16	x = float(input())		2	**20**
17	while positives_given != 3	This evaluates to True		
18	if x > 0	This evaluates to True		
19	positives_given += 1		**3**	20
20	x = float(input())		3	**???**

And here is the logic error! At step 20, even though the total number of positives given is three, and you expect that the program will stop, unfortunately it asks the user to enter an additional number!

You needed a Python program that lets the user enter three numbers, not four!

This is why you should always go by the book! Let's see how this program should be written.

Since the Boolean expression of the while-loop is dependent on the variable positives_given, this is the variable that must be initialized outside of the loop. This variable must also be updated or altered within the loop. The statement that does this update or alteration must be the last statement within the loop, as shown in the code fragment (in general form) that follows.

```
positives_given = 0     #Initialization of positives_given
while positives_given != 3: #This is dependent on positives_given

    A statement or block of statements

    if x > 0:
        positives_given += 1    #Update/alteration of positives_given
```

Now you can add any necessary statements to complete the program. The only statements that are missing here are the statement that lets the user enter a number (this must be done within the loop), and the statement that displays the last message (this must be done when the loop finishes all of its iterations). So, the final program becomes

```python
positives_given = 0
while positives_given != 3:
    x = float(input("Enter a number: "))
    if x > 0:
        positives_given += 1

print("Three positives given!")
```

27.4 Breaking Out of a Loop

Loops can consume too much CPU time so you have to be very careful when you use them. There are times when you need to break out of, or end, a loop before it completes all of its iterations, usually when a specified condition is met.

Suppose there is a hidden password and you know that it is three characters long and it contains only digits. The following for-loop performs 900 iterations and tries to find that hidden password using a *brute-force attack*.

```python
found = False
for i in range(100, 1000):
    if i == hidden_password:
        password = i
        found = True

if found == True:
    print("Hidden password is:", password)
```

✎ *A brute-force attack is the simplest method to gain access to anything that is password protected. An attacker tries combinations of letters, numbers, and symbols with the hope of eventually guessing correctly.*

Now, suppose that the hidden password is 123. As you already know, the for-loop iterates a specified number of times, and in this case, it doesn't care whether the hidden password is actually found or not. Even though the password is found in the 24th iteration, the loop unfortunately continues to iterate until variable i reaches the value of 999, thus wasting CPU time.

Someone may say "*So what? 900 iterations is not a big deal!*" But it is a big deal, actually! In large scale data processing everything counts, so you should be very careful when using loop control structures, especially those that iterate too many times. What if the hidden password was ten characters long? This means that the for-loop would have to perform 9,000,000,000 iterations!

There are two approaches that can help you make programs like the previous one run faster. The main idea, in both of them, is to break out of the loop when a specified condition is met; in this case when the hidden password is found.

First Approach – Using the break statement

You can break out of a loop before it actually completes all of its iterations by using the break statement.

Look at the following Python program. When the hidden password is found, the flow of execution immediately exits (breaks out of) the for-loop.

```python
found = False
for i in range(100, 1000):
    if i == hidden_password:
```

```
            password = i
            found = True
            break

if found:
    print("Hidden password is:", password)
```

> ✎ *The statement* `if found` *is equivalent to the statement* `if found == True`

Second Approach – Using a flag

The `break` statement doesn't actually exist in all computer languages; and since this book's intent is to teach you "Algorithmic Thinking" (and not just special statements that only Python supports), let's look at an alternate approach.

In the following Python program, when the hidden password is found, the Boolean expression `found == False` forces the flow of execution to exit the loop.

```
found = False
i = 100
while i <= 999 and found == False:
    if i == hidden_password:
        password = i
        found = True
    i += 1

if found:
    print("Hidden password is:", password)
```

> ✎ *Imagine variable* `found` *as a flag. Initially, the flag is not "raised"* (`found = False`). *The flow of execution enters the loop, and the loop continues iterating as long as the flag is down* (`while ... found == False`). *When something (usually a condition) raises the flag (assigns value* `True` *to variable* `found`), *the flow of execution exits the loop.*

> ✎ *The* `while i <= 999   and found == False` *can alternatively be written as* `while i <= 999 and not found`.

27.5   Cleaning Out Your Loops

As already stated, loops can consume too much CPU time, so you must be very careful and use them sparingly. Although a large number of iterations is sometimes inevitable, there are always things that you can do to make your loops perform better.

The next code fragment calculates the average value of the numbers 1, 2, 3, 4, 5, ... 10000.

```
s = 0
i = 1
while True:
    count_of_numbers = 10000
    s = s + i
    i += 1
    if i > count_of_numbers : break

average = s / count_of_numbers
```

```
print(average)
```

What you should always keep in mind when using loops, especially those that perform many iterations, is to avoid putting any statement inside a loop that serves no purposes in that loop. In the previous example, the statement count_of_numbers = 10000 is such a statement. Unfortunately, as long as it exists inside the loop, the computer executes it 10000 times for no reason, which of course affects the computer's performance.

To resolve this problem, you can simply move this statement outside the loop, as follows.

```
count_of_numbers = 10000
s = 0
i = 1
while True:
    s = s + i
    i += 1
    if i > count_of_numbers: break

average = s / count_of_numbers
print(average)
```

Exercise 27.5-1   Cleaning Out the Loop

The following code fragment calculates the average value of numbers 1, 2, 3, 4, ... 10000. Try to move as many statements as possible outside the loop to make the program more efficient.

```
s = 0
for i in range(1, 10001):
    s = s + i
    average = s / 10000

print(average)
```

Solution

One very common mistake that novice programmers make when calculating average values is to put the statement that divides the total sum by how many numbers there are in the sum (here average = s / 10000) inside the loop. Think about it! Imagine that you want to calculate your average grade in school. Your first step would be to calculate the sum of the grades for all of the courses that you're taking. Then, when all your grades have been summed up, you would divide that sum by the number of courses that you're taking.

✎ *Calculating an average is a two-step process.*

Therefore, it is pointless to calculate the average value inside the loop. You can move this statement outside and right after the loop, and leave the loop just to sum up the numbers as follows.

```
s = 0
for i in range(1, 10001):
    s = s + i

average = s / 10000
print(average)
```

Exercise 27.5-2   Cleaning Out the Loop

The next formula

$$S = \frac{1}{1^1 + 2^2 + 3^3 + \cdots + N^N} + \frac{2}{1^1 + 2^2 + 3^3 + \cdots + N^N} + \cdots + \frac{N}{1^1 + 2^2 + 3^3 + \cdots + N^N}$$

is solved using the following Python program, where N is given by the user.

```python
n = int(input("Enter N: "))
s = 0
for i in range(1, n + 1):
    denom = 0
    for j in range(1, n + 1):
        denom += j ** j
    s += i / denom

print(s)
```

Try to move as many statements as possible outside the loop to make the program more efficient.

Solution

As you can see from the formula, the denominator is common for all fractions. Thus, it is pointless to calculate it again and again for every fraction. You can calculate the denominator just once and use the result many times, as follows.

```python
n = int(input("Enter N: "))

denom = 0
for j in range(1, n + 1):
    denom += j ** j

s = 0
for i in range(1, n + 1):
    s += i / denom

print(s)
```

This code fragment calculates the denominator.

27.6   Endless Loops and How to Avoid Them

All loop control structures must include a way to stop endless iterations from occurring within them. This means that there must be something inside the loop that eventually makes the flow of execution exit the loop.

The next example contains an endless loop. Unfortunately, the programmer forgot to increase variable i inside the loop; therefore, variable i can never reach the value 10.

```python
i = 1
while i != 10:
    print("Hello there!")
```

✎ *If a loop cannot stop iterating, it is called an endless loop or an infinite loop.*

An endless loop continues to iterate forever and the only way to stop it from iterating is to use magic forces! For example, when an application in a Windows operating system "hangs" (probably because the flow of execution entered an endless loop), the user must use the key combination ALT+CTRL+DEL to force the application to end. In Eclipse, on the other hand, when you accidentally write and execute an endless loop, you can just click on the "Terminate" ■ toolbar icon and the Python compiler immediately stops any action.

So, always remember to include at least one such statement that makes the flow of execution exit the loop. But still, this is not always enough! Take a look at the following code fragment.

```python
i = 1
while i != 10:
    print("Hello there!")
    i += 2
```

Even though this code fragment does contain a statement that increases variable i inside the loop (i += 2), unfortunately the flow of execution never exits the loop because the value 10 is never assigned to the variable i.

One thing that you can do to avoid this type of mistake is to never check the counter variable (here, variable i) using == and != comparison operators, especially in cases in which the counter variable increments or decrements by a value other than 1. You can use <, <=, >, and >= comparison operators instead; they guarantee that the flow of execution exits the loop when the counter variable exceeds the termination value. The previous example can be fixed by replacing the != with a <, or even a <= comparison operator.

```python
i = 1
while i < 10:
    print("Hello there!")
    i += 2
```

27.7 The "From Inner to Outer" Method

From inner to outer is a method proposed by this book to help you learn "Algorithmic Thinking" from the inside out. This method first manipulates and designs the inner (nested) control structures and then, as the algorithm (or the program) is developed, more and more control structures are added, nesting the previous ones. This method can be used in large and complicated control structures as it helps you design error-free flowcharts or even Python programs. This book uses this method wherever and whenever it seems necessary.

Let's try the following example.

Write a Python program that displays the following multiplication table as it is shown below.

1x1=1	1x2=2	1x3=3	1x4=4	1x5=5	1x6=6	1x7=7	1x8=8	1x9=9
2x1=2	2x2=4	2x3=6	2x4=8	2x5=10	2x6=12	2x7=14	2x8=16	2x9=18
3x1=3	3x2=6	3x3=9	3x4=12	3x5=15	3x6=18	3x7=21	3x8=24	3x9=27
4x1=4	4x2=8	4x3=12	4x4=16	4x5=20	4x6=24	4x7=28	4x8=32	4x9=36
5x1=5	5x2=10	5x3=15	5x4=20	5x5=25	5x6=30	5x7=35	5x8=40	5x9=45
6x1=6	6x2=12	6x3=18	6x4=24	6x5=30	6x6=36	6x7=42	6x8=48	6x9=54
7x1=7	7x2=14	7x3=21	7x4=28	7x5=35	7x6=42	7x7=49	7x8=56	7x9=63
8x1=8	8x2=16	8x3=24	8x4=32	8x5=40	8x6=48	8x7=56	8x8=64	8x9=72
9x1=9	9x2=18	9x3=27	9x4=36	9x5=45	9x6=54	9x7=63	9x8=72	9x9=81

According to the "from inner to outer" method, you start by writing the inner control structure and then, when everything is tested and operates fine, you can add the outer control structures.

So, let's try to display only the first line of the multiplication table. If you examine this line it reveals that, in each multiplication, the multiplicand is always 1. Imagine a variable i that contains the value 1. The loop control structure that displays only the first line of the multiplication table is as follows.

Code Fragment 1

```python
for j in range(1, 10):
```

```
print(i, "x", j, "=", i * j, end = "\t")
```

If you execute this code fragment, the result is

1x1=1   1x2=2   1x3=3   1x4=4   1x5=5   1x6=6   1x7=7   1x8=8   1x9=9

> 📖 *The special sequence of characters \t "displays" a tab character after each iteration. This ensures that everything is aligned properly.*

The inner (nested) loop control structure is ready. What you need now is a way to execute this control structure nine times, but each time variable i must contain a different value, from 1 to 9. This code fragment is as follows.

Code Fragment 2

```
for i in range(1, 10):

    Code Fragment 1: Display one single line
    of the multiplication table

    print()
```

> ✎ *The* print() *statement is used to "display" a line break between lines.*

Now, you can combine both code fragments, nesting the first into the second one. The final Python program becomes

📂 file_27_7

```
for i in range(1, 10):
    for j in range(1, 10):
        print(i, "x", j, "=", i * j, end = "\t")
    print()
```

27.8   Review Questions: True/False

Choose **true** or **false** for each of the following statements.

1. When the number of iterations is unknown, you can use a definite loop.

2. When the number of iterations is known, you cannot use a post-test loop structure.

3. According to the "Ultimate" rule, in a pre-test loop structure, the initialization of the variable that participates in the loop's Boolean expression must be done inside the loop.

4. According to the "Ultimate" rule, in a pre-test loop structure, the statement that updates/alters the value of the variable that participates in the loop's Boolean expression must be the last statement within the loop.

5. According to the "Ultimate" rule, in a post-test loop structure, the initialization of the variable that participates in the loop's Boolean expression can sometimes be done inside the loop.

6. According to the "Ultimate" rule, in a post-test loop structure, the update/alteration of the variable that participates in the loop's Boolean expression must be the first statement within the loop.

7. In Python, you can break out of a loop before it completes all iterations using the `break_loop` statement.

8. A statement that assigns a constant value to a variable is better placed inside a loop control structure.

9. In the following code fragment:

    ```
    for i in range(30):
        a = "Hello"
    ```

```
    print(a)
```

there is at least one statement that can be moved outside the for-loop.

10. In the following code fragment:

```
s = 0
count = 1
while count < 100:
    a = int(input())
    s += a
    average = s / count
    count += 1
print(average)
```

there is at least one statement that can be moved outside the while-loop.

11. In the following code fragment:

```
s = 0
y = int(input())
while y != -99:
    s = s + y
    y = int(input())
```

there is at least one statement that can be moved outside the while-loop.

12. The following code fragment:

```
i = 1
while i != 100:
    print("Hello there!")
    i += 5
```

satisfies the property of finiteness.

13. When the not equal (!=) comparison operator is used in the Boolean expression of a pre-test loop structure, the loop always iterates endlessly.

14. The following code fragment:

```
i = 0
while True:
    print("Hello there!")
    i += 5
    if i >= 100: break
```

satisfies the property of finiteness.

27.9 Review Questions: Multiple Choice

Select the correct answer for each of the following statements.

1. When the number of iterations is unknown, you can use

    a. the pre-test loop structure.

    b. the post-test loop structure.

    c. all of the above

2. When the number of iterations is known, you can use

    a. the pre-test loop structure.

    b. the post-test loop structure.

     c.   a for-loop.

     d.   all of the above

3.   According to the "Ultimate" rule, in a pre-test loop structure, the initialization of the variable that participates in the loop's Boolean expression must be done

     a.   inside the loop.

     b.   outside the loop.

     c.   all of the above

4.   According to the "Ultimate" rule, in a pre-test loop structure, the update/alteration of the variable that participates in the loop's Boolean expression must be done

     a.   inside the loop.

     b.   outside the loop.

     c.   all of the above

5.   According to the "Ultimate" rule, in a post-test loop structure, the update/alteration of the variable that participates in the loop's Boolean expression must be done

     a.   inside the loop.

     b.   outside the loop.

     c.   all of the above

6.   In the following code fragment

```python
s = 0
for i in range(100):
    s = s + i
    x = 100
    average = s / 100
```

the number of statements that can be moved outside of the for-loop is

     a.   0.

     b.   1.

     c.   2.

     d.   3.

7.   When this comparison operator is used in the Boolean expression of a post-test loop structure, the loop iterates forever.

     a.   ==

     b.   !=

     c.   it depends

27.10 Review Exercises

Complete the following exercises.

1.   The following program is supposed to prompt the user to enter names repeatedly until the word "STOP" (used as a name) is entered. At the end, the program must display the total number of names entered as well as how many of these names were not "John".

```python
count_not_johns = 0
count_names = 0
name = ""
while name != "STOP":
```

```
name = input("Enter a name: ")
count_names += 1
if name != "John":
    count_not_johns += 1

print("Names other than John entered", count_not_johns, "times")
print(count_names, "names entered")
```

However, the program displays wrong results! Using the "Ultimate" Rule, try to modify the program so that it displays the correct results.

2. Write a Python program that prompts the user to enter some text. The text can be either a single word or a whole sentence. Then, the program must display a message stating whether the given text is one single word or a complete sentence.

    Hint: Search for a space character! If a space character is found, it means that the user entered a sentence. The program must stop searching further when it finds at least one space character.

3. Write a Python program that prompts the user to enter a sentence. The program then displays the message "The sentence contains a number" if the sentence contains at least one number. The program must stop searching further when it finds at least one digit.

4. Correct the following code fragment so that it does not iterate endlessly.

    ```
    print("Printing all integers from 1 to 100")
    i = 1
    while i < 101:
        print(i)
    ```

5. Correct the Boolean expression of the following loop control structure so that it does not iterate endlessly.

    ```
    print("Printing odd integers from 1 to 99")
    i = 1
    while not(i == 100):
        print(i)
        i += 2
    ```

6. The following code fragment calculates the average value of 100 numbers entered by the user. Try to move as many statements as possible outside the loop to make it more efficient.

    ```
    s = 0
    for i in range(100):
        number = float(input())
        s = s + number
        average = s / 100
    print(average)
    ```

7. The following formula

    $$S = \frac{1}{1 \cdot 2 \cdot 3 \cdot \ldots \cdot 100} + \frac{2}{1 \cdot 2 \cdot 3 \cdot \ldots \cdot 100} + \cdots + \frac{100}{1 \cdot 2 \cdot 3 \cdot \ldots \cdot 100}$$

    is solved using the following Python program.

    ```
    s = 0
    for i in range(1, 101):
        denom = 1
        for j in range(1, 101):
    ```

```
        denom *= j
    s += i / denom
print(s)
```

Try to move as many statements as possible outside the loop to make it more efficient.

8. Write a Python program that displays every combination of two integers as well as their resulting product, for pairs of integers between 1 and 4. The output must display as follows.

```
1 x 1 = 1
1 x 2 = 2
1 x 3 = 3
1 x 4 = 4
2 x 1 = 2
2 x 2 = 4
2 x 3 = 6
2 x 4 = 8
...

...
4 x 1 = 4
4 x 2 = 8
4 x 3 = 12
4 x 4 = 16
```

9. Write a Python program that displays the multiplication table for pairs of integers between 1 and 12, as shown next. Please note that the output is aligned with tabs.

```
     |  1   2   3   4   5   6   7   8   9   10  11  12
----------------------------------------------------
 1   |  1   2   3   4   5   6   7   8   9   10  11  12
 2   |  2   4   6   8   10  12  14  16  18  20  22  24
 3   |  3   6   9   12  15  18  21  24  27  30  33  36
...  |  ... ... ... ... ... ... ... ... ... ... ... ...
11   |  11  22  33  44  55  66  77  88  99  110 121 132
12   |  12  24  36  48  60  72  84  96  108 120 132 144
```

10. Write a Python program that prompts the user to enter an integer and then displays the multiplication table for pairs of integers between 1 and that integer. For example, if the user enters the value 5, the output must be as shown next. Please note that the output is aligned with tabs.

```
     |  1   2   3   4   5
------------------------
 1   |  1   2   3   4   5
 2   |  2   4   6   8   10
 3   |  3   6   9   12  15
 4   |  4   8   12  16  20
 5   |  5   10  15  20  25
```

Chapter 28
Flowcharts with Loop Control Structures

28.1 Introduction

By working through the previous chapters, you've become familiar with all the loop control structures, how to use them, and which to use in every case. You've learned about the "Ultimate" rule, how to break out of a loop, how to convert from one loop control structure to another, and much more. Since flowcharts are an ideal way to learn "Algorithmic Thinking" and to help you better understand specific control structures, this chapter will teach you how to convert a Python program to a flowchart and vice versa, that is, a flowchart to a Python program.

28.2 Converting Python Programs to Flowcharts

To convert a Python program to a flowchart, you need to recall all loop control structures and their corresponding flowcharts. Following you will find them all summarized.

The Pre-Test Loop Structure

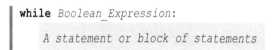

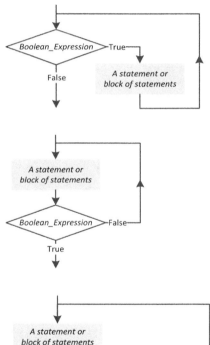

The Post-Test Loop Structure

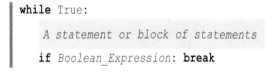

The Mid-Test Loop Structure

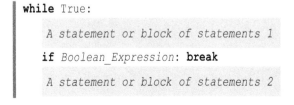

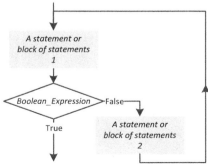

The For-Loop

```
for var in sequence

    A statement or block of statements
```

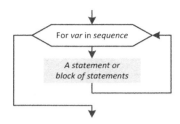

Next, you will find many exercises that can clarify things that you might still need help understanding.

Exercise 28.2-1   Designing the Flowchart

Design the flowchart that corresponds to the following Python program.

```
i = 50
while i > 10:
    if i % 2 == 1:
        print(i)
    i -= 5
```

Solution

This Python program contains a pre-test loop structure which nests a single-alternative decision structure. The corresponding flowchart that follows includes what you have been taught so far.

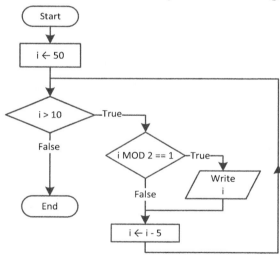

Exercise 28.2-2   Designing the Flowchart

Design the flowchart that corresponds to the following Python program.

```
i = 30
while True:
    if i % 8 == 0:
        print(i, "is a multiple of 8")
    if i % 4 == 0:
```

```
        print(i, "is a multiple of 4")
    if i % 2 == 0:
        print(i, "is a multiple of 2")
    i -= 2
    if i <= 0: break
```

Solution

This Python program contains a post-test loop structure that nests three single-alternative decision structures. The corresponding flowchart is as follows.

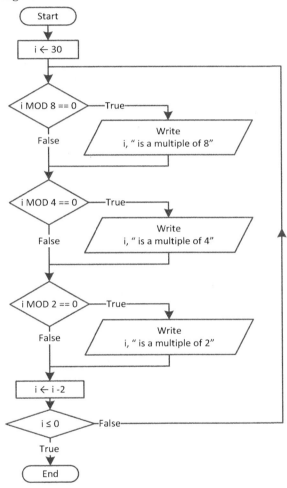

Exercise 28.2-3 Designing the Flowchart

Design the flowchart that corresponds to the following Python program.

```
for hour in range(1, 25):
    print("Hour is", hour, ":00.")
    if hour >= 4 and hour < 12:
        print("Good Morning")
    elif hour >= 12 and hour < 20:
```

```
        print("Good Afternoon")
    elif hour >= 20 and hour < 24:
        print("Good Evening")
    else:
        print("Good Night")
```

Solution

This Python program contains a for-loop that nests a multiple-alternative decision structure. The corresponding flowchart is as follows.

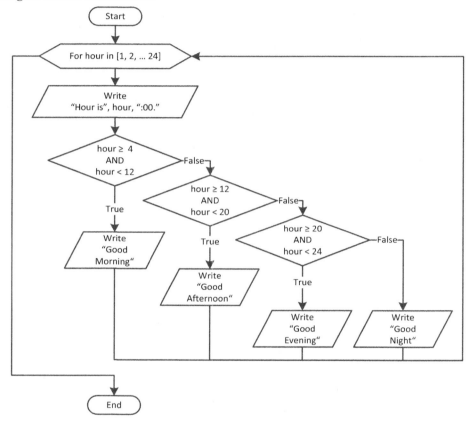

Exercise 28.2-4   Designing the Flowchart

Design the flowchart that corresponds to the following Python program.

```
a = int(input())

if a == 1:
    for i in range(1, 11, 2):
        print(i)
elif a == 2:
    for i in range(9, -1, -2):
        print(i)
else:
```

```
    print("nothing to do!")

print("The End!")
```

Solution

This Python program contains a multiple-alternative decision structure that nests two for-loops. The corresponding flowchart is as follows.

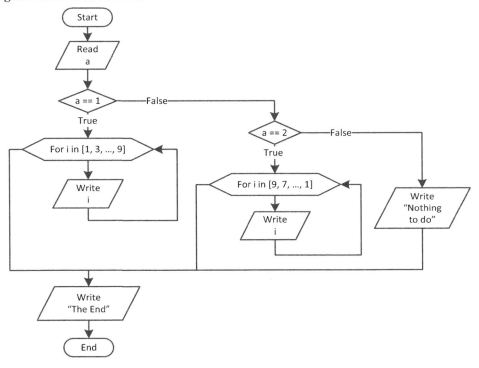

Exercise 28.2-5   Designing the Flowchart

Design the flowchart that corresponds to the following Python program.

```python
n = int(input())
m = int(input())

total = 0
for i in range(n):
    for j in range(m):
        total += i * j + j
print(total)
```

Solution

This Python program contains nested loop control structures; a for-loop nested within another for-loop. The corresponding flowchart is as follows.

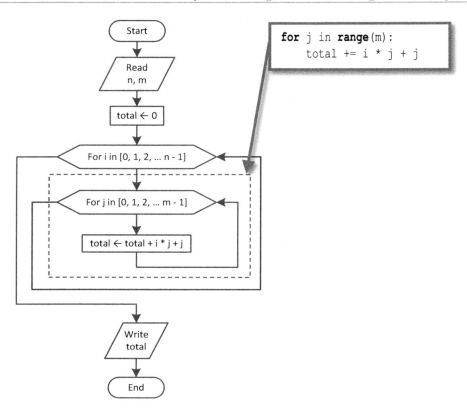

Exercise 28.2-6   Designing the Flowchart

Design the flowchart that corresponds to the following code fragment.

```python
s = 0
for i in range(100):
    n = float(input())
    while n < 0:
        print("Error")
        n = float(input())
    s += math.sqrt(n)
print(s)
```

Solution

This Python program contains nested loop control structures; a pre-test loop structure nested within a for-loop. The corresponding flowchart is as follows.

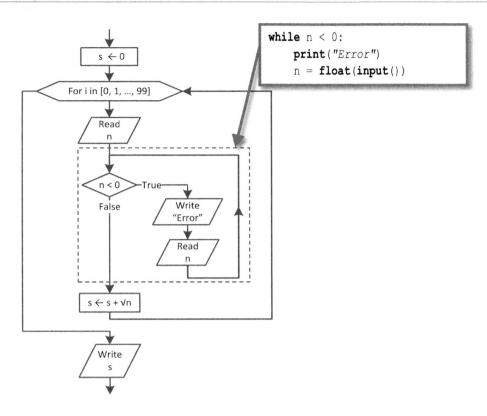

28.3 Converting Flowcharts to Python Programs

This conversion is not always an easy one. There are cases in which the flowchart designers follow no particular rules, so the initial flowchart may need some modifications before it can become a Python program. The following is an example of one such case.

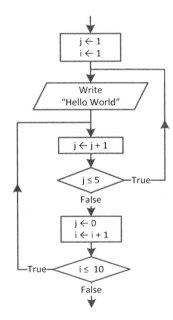

As you can see, the loop control structures included in this flowchart fragment match none of the structures that you have already learned, such the pre-test, the post-test, the mid-test, or even the for-loop control structure. Thus, you have only one choice and this is to modify the flowchart by adding extra statements or removing existing ones until known loop control structures start to appear. Following are some exercises in which the initial flowchart does need modification.

Exercise 28.3-1   Writing the Python Program

Write the Python program that corresponds to the following flowchart fragment.

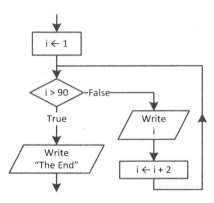

Solution

This is an easy one. The only obstacle you have to overcome is that the true and false paths are not quite in the right position. You need the true and not the false path to actually iterate. As you already know, it is possible to switch the two paths but you need to negate the Boolean expression as well. Thus, the code fragment becomes

```python
i = 1
while i <= 90:
    print(i)
    i = i + 2

print("The End")
```

Exercise 28.3-2   Writing the Python Program

Write the Python program that corresponds to the following flowchart.

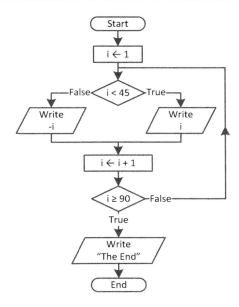

Solution

This flowchart contains a post-test loop structure that nests a dual-alternative decision structure. The Python program is as follows.

```python
i = 1
while True:
    if i < 45:
        print(i)
    else:
        print(-i)
    i += 1
    if i >= 90: break

print("The End")
```

This is the dual-alternative decision structure

Exercise 28.3-3   Writing the Python Program

Write the Python program that corresponds to the following flowchart.

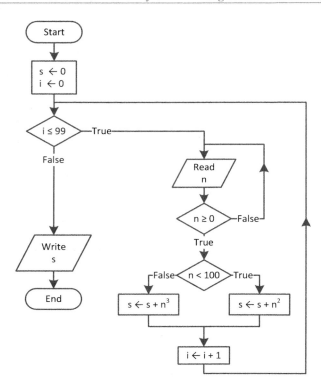

Solution

Oops! What a mess! So many diamonds here! Be careful though, because one of them is actually a decision control structure! Can you spot it?

You should be quite familiar with loop control structures so far. As you already know, in loop control structures, one of the diamond's (rhombus's) exits always has an upward direction. Thus, the following flowchart fragment, extracted from the initial one, is obviously the decision control structure that you are looking for.

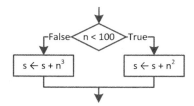

And of course, it's a dual-alternative decision structure!

Now, let's identify the rest of the structures. Right before the dual-alternative decision structure, there is a post-test loop structure. Its flowchart fragment is as follows.

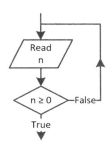

And finally, both the dual-alternative decision structure and the post-test loop structure, mentioned before, are nested within the next flowchart fragment,

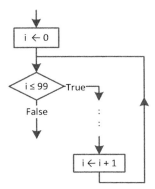

which happens to be a pre-test loop structure. The corresponding Python program is as follows.

```python
s = 0
i = 0
while i <= 99:
    while True:
        n = float(input())
        if n >= 0: break

    if n < 100:
        s = s + n ** 2
    else:
        s = s + n ** 3

    i += 1
print(s)
```

This is the post-test loop structure

This is the dual-alternative decision structure

Wasn't so difficult after all, was it?

Exercise 28.3-4   *Writing the Python Program*

Write the Python program that corresponds to the following flowchart.

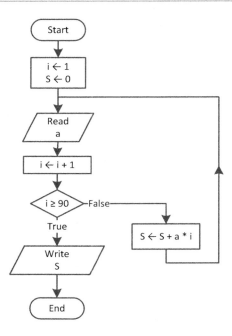

Solution

This is a mid-test loop structure. Since there is no direct Python statement for this structure, you can use the break statement—or you can even convert the flowchart to something more familiar as shown in the next two approaches

First Approach – Using the break statement

The main idea is to create an endless loop (while True) and break out of it when the Boolean expression that exists between the two statements or blocks of statements evaluates to True.

According to this approach, the initial flowchart can be written in Python as follows.

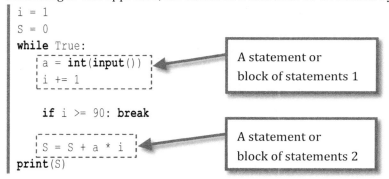

Keep in mind that even though the break statement can sometimes be useful, it may also lead you to write code that is difficult to read and understand, especially when you make extensive use of it. So, please use it cautiously and sparingly!

Second Approach – Converting the flowchart

The mid-test loop structure and its equivalent, using a pre-test loop structure, are as follows.

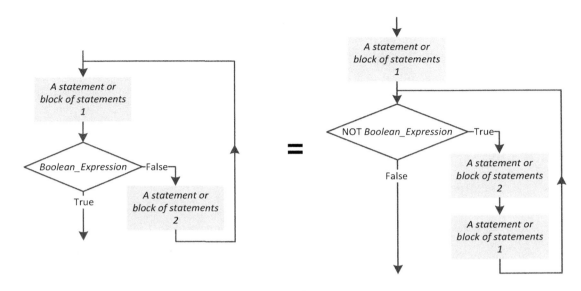

Accordingly, the initial flowchart becomes

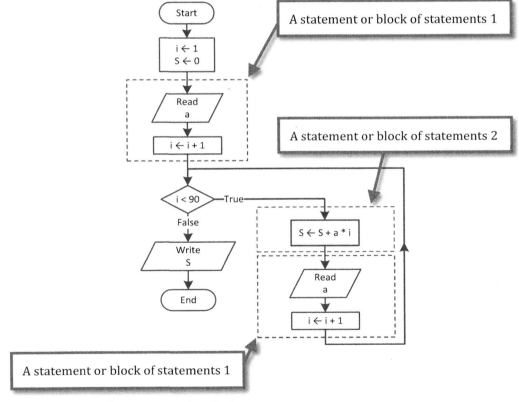

Now, it's easy to write the corresponding Python program.

```
i = 1
S = 0
```

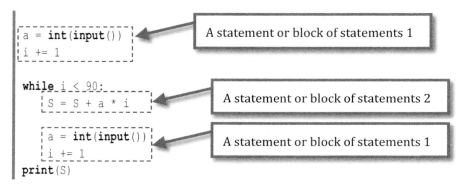

28.4 Review Exercises

Complete the following exercises.

1. Design the flowchart that corresponds to the following Python program.

```python
i = 100
while i > 0:
    print(i)
    i -= 5
```

2. Design the flowchart that corresponds to the following Python program.

```python
i = -100
while i <= 100:
    print(i)
    i += 1
```

3. Design the flowchart that corresponds to the following Python program.

```python
i = int(input())
while True:
    print(i)
    i += 1
    if i > 100: break
```

4. Design the flowchart that corresponds to the following Python program.

```python
a = int(input())
b = int(input())
for i in range(a, b + 1):
    print(i)
```

5. Design the flowchart that corresponds to the following Python program.

```python
i = 35
while i > -35:
    if i % 2 == 0:
        print(2 * i)
    else:
        print(3 * i)
    i -= 1
```

6. Design the flowchart that corresponds to the following Python program.

```python
i = -20
while True:
```

```
    x = int(input())
    if x == 0:
        print("Zero")
    elif x % 2 == 0:
        print(2 * i)
    else:
        print(3 * i)
    i += 1
    if i > 20: break
```

7. Design the flowchart that corresponds to the following Python program.

```
a = int(input())
if a > 0:
    i = 0
    while i <= a:
        print(i)
        i += 5
else:
    print("Non-Positive Entered!")
```

8. Design the flowchart that corresponds to the following Python program.

```
a = int(input())
if a > 0:
    i = 0
    while i <= a:
        print(3 * i + i / 2)
        i += 1
else:
    i = 10
    while True:
        print(2 * i - i / 3)
        i -= 3
        if i < a: break
```

9. Design the flowchart that corresponds to the following Python program.

```
a = int(input())
if a > 0:
    for i in range(a + 1):
        print(3 * i + i / 2)
elif a == 0:
    b = int(input())
    while b > 0:
        b = int(input())
    print(2 * a + b)
else:
    b = int(input())
    while b < 0:
        b = int(input())
```

```python
    for i in range(a, b + 1):
        print(i)
```

10. Design the flowchart that corresponds to the following Python program.

```python
a = int(input())
b = int(input())
c = int(input())
d = int(input())

total = 0
for i in range(a, b):
    for j in range(c, d + 1, 2):
        total += i + j
print(total)
```

11. Design the flowchart that corresponds to the following Python program.

```python
import math

s = 0
for i in range(1, 51):
    while True:
        n = int(input())
        if n >= 0: break
    s += math.sqrt(n)
print(s)
```

12. Design the flowchart that corresponds to the following Python program.

```python
while True:
    while True:
        a = int(input())
        if a >= 0: break
    while True:
        b = int(input())
        if b >= 0: break
    print(abs(a - b))
    if abs(a - b) <= 100: break
```

13. Design the flowchart that corresponds to the following Python program.

```python
while True:
    while True:
        a = int(input())
        b = int(input())
        if a >= 0 and b >= 0: break

    if a > b:
        print(a - b)
    else:
        print(a * b)
    if abs(a - b) <= 100: break
```

14. Write the code fragment in Python that corresponds to the following flowchart fragment.

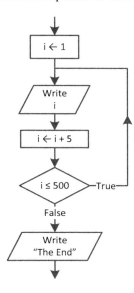

15. Write the Python program that corresponds to the following flowchart.

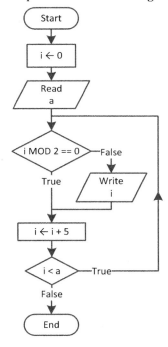

16. Write the Python program that corresponds to the following flowchart.

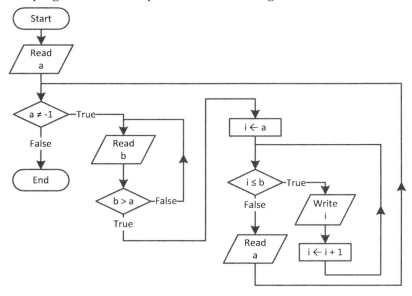

17. Write the Python program that corresponds to the following flowchart.

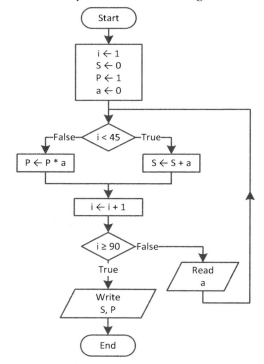

Chapter 29
More Exercises with Loop Control Structures

29.1 Simple Exercises with Loop Control Structures

Exercise 29.1-1 Counting the Numbers According to Which is Greater

Write a Python program that prompts the user to enter 10 pairs of numbers and then counts and displays the number of times that the first number given was greater than the second one and the number of times that the second one was greater than the first one.

Solution

The Python program is as follows. It uses variable count_a to count the number of times that the first number given was greater than the second one and variable count_b to count the number of times that the second one was greater than the first one.

```
                            📄 file_29_1_1
count_a = 0
count_b = 0

for i in range(10):
    a = int(input("Enter number A: "))
    b = int(input("Enter number B: "))

    if a > b:
        count_a += 1
    elif b > a:
        count_b += 1

print(count_a, count_b)
```

A reasonable question that someone may ask is "*Why is a multiple-decision control structure being used? Why not use a dual-alternative decision structure instead?*"

Suppose that a dual-alternative decision structure, such as the following, is used.

```
if a > b:
    count_a += 1
else:
    count_b += 1
```

In this decision control structure, the variable count_b increments when variable b is greater than variable a (this is desirable) but also when variable b is <u>equal to</u> variable a (this is undesirable). Using a multiple-decision control structure instead ensures that variable count_b increments only when variable b is greater than (and not when it is equal to) variable a.

Exercise 29.1-2   Counting the Numbers According to Their Digits

Write a Python program that prompts the user to enter 20 integers and then counts and displays the total number of one-digit, two-digit, and three-digit integers. Assume that the user enters values between 1 and 999.

Solution

Using knowledge from Exercise 18.1-3, the Python program is as follows.

```
                            📁 file_29_1_2
count1 = count2 = count3 = 0

for i in range(20):
    a = int(input("Enter a number: "))

    if a <= 9:
        count1 += 1
    elif a <= 99:
        count2 += 1
    else:
        count3 += 1

print(count1, count2, count3)
```

Exercise 29.1-3   How Many Numbers Fit in a Sum

Write a Python program that lets the user enter numeric values repeatedly until the sum of them exceeds 1000. At the end, the program must display the total quantity of numbers entered.

Solution

In this case, you don't know the exact number of iterations, so you cannot use a for-loop. Let's use a while-loop instead, but, in order to make your program free of logic errors you should follow the "Ultimate" rule discussed in paragraph 27.3. According to this rule, a pre-test loop structure should always be as follows, given in general form.

```
Initialize total
while total <= 1000 :

    A statement or block of statements

    Update/alter total
```

✎ *Since loop's Boolean expression depends on variable* total, *this is the variable that must be initialized before the loop starts and also updated (altered) within the loop. And more specifically, the statement that updates/alters variable* total *must be the **last** statement of the loop.*

Following this, the Python program becomes

```
                            📁 file_29_1_3
count = 0
```

```
total = 0                #Initialization of total
while total <= 1000:     #A Boolean expression dependent on total
    x = float(input())
    count += 1

    total += x           #Update/alteration of total

print(count)
```

Exercise 29.1-4   Finding the Total Number of Positive Integers

Write a Python program that prompts the user to enter integer values repeatedly until a real one is entered. At the end, the program must display the total number of positive integers entered.

Solution

Once again, you don't know the exact number of iterations, so you cannot use a for-loop.

According to the "Ultimate" rule, the pre-test loop structure should always be as follows, given in general form.

```
x = float(input("Enter a number: "))        #Initialization of x
while int(x) == x:    #A Boolean expression dependent on x

    A statement or block of statements

    x = float(input("Enter a number: "))    #Update/alteration of x
```

The final Python program is as follows.

```
📁 file_29_1_4
count = 0

x = float(input("Enter a number: "))
while int(x) == x:
    if x > 0:
        count += 1
    x = float(input("Enter a number: "))

print(count)
```

✎ Note that the program operates properly even if the first number given is real. The pre-test loop structure ensures that the flow of execution never enters the loop!

Exercise 29.1-5   Iterating as Many Times as the User Wishes

Write a Python program that prompts the user to enter two numbers and then calculates and displays the first number raised to the power of the second one. The program must iterate as many times as the user wishes. At the end of each calculation, the program must ask the user if he or she wishes to calculate again. If the answer is "yes" the program must repeat; it must end otherwise. Make your program accept the answer in all possible forms such as "yes", "YES", "Yes", or even "YeS".

Solution

According to the "Ultimate" rule, the post-test loop structure should be as follows, given in general form.

```
answer = "yes"    #Redundant initialization of answer.
while True:

      Prompt the user to enter two numbers and
      then calculate and display the first number
      raised to the power of the second one.


      #Update/alteration of answer
      answer = input("Would you like to repeat? ")
      #The loop's Boolean expression depends on variable answer
      if answer.upper() != "YES": break
```

✎ *The* upper() *method ensures that the program operates properly for any given answer: "yes", "YES", "Yes", or even "YeS" or "yEs"!*

The solution to this exercise becomes

> 🗀 **file_29_1_5**

```
while True:
    print("Enter two numbers: ")
    a = int(input())
    b = int(input())

    result = a ** b
    print("The result is:", result)

    answer = input("Would you like to repeat? ")
    if answer.upper() != "YES": break
```

Exercise 29.1-6   *Finding the Sum of the Digits*

Write a Python program that lets the user enter an integer and then calculates the sum of its digits.

Solution

In Exercise 13.1-2, you learned how to split the digits of an integer when its total number of digits was known. In this exercise however, the user is allowed to enter any value, no matter how small or large; thus, the total number of the digits can be unknown.

To solve this exercise, a loop control structure could be used. However, there are two approaches that you can use.

First Approach

In this approach, the main idea is to isolate one digit at each iteration. But what you don't really know is the total number of iterations that must be performed because this number depends on the given integer. So, is this a dead end? Of course not!

Inside the loop, the given integer can be getting "smaller" and "smaller" in every iteration until eventually it becomes zero. The value of zero can serve to stop the loop control structure from iterating. For example, if the given number is 4753, it can become 475 in the first iteration, then 47, then 4, and finally 0. When it becomes 0, the iterations can stop.

Let's try to comprehend the proposed solution using the following flowchart. Some statements are written in general form.

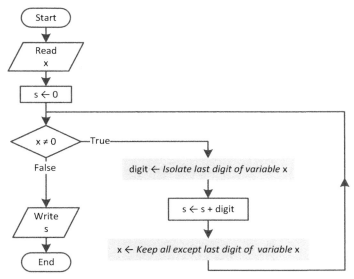

The statement

$$\text{digit} \leftarrow \textit{Isolate last digit of variable x.}$$

can be written using the well-known MOD 10 operation as shown here.

$$\text{digit} \leftarrow \text{x MOD 10}$$

The whole concept, however, relies on the statement

$$x \leftarrow \textit{Keep all except last digit of variable x.}$$

This is the statement that eventually zeros the value of variable x, and the flow of execution then exits the loop. To write this statement you can use a DIV 10 operation as shown here.

$$x \leftarrow \text{x DIV 10}$$

Accordingly, the Python program becomes

```
                          📁 file_29_1_6a
x = int(input())
s = 0


while x != 0:
    digit = x % 10      #This is the x MOD 10 operation
    s = s + digit
    x = x // 10         #This is the x DIV 10 operation


print(s)
```

Let's create a trace table for the input value 4753 to better understand what is really happening.

Step	Statement	Notes	x	digit	s
1	x = int(input())	User enters the value 4753	**4753**	?	?
2	s = 0		4753	?	**0**

3	`while x != 0:`	This validates to True			
4	`digit = x % 10`		4753	3	0
5	`s = s + digit`		4753	3	3
6	`x = x // 10`		475	3	3
7	`while x != 0:`	This validates to True			
8	`digit = x % 10`		475	5	3
9	`s = s + digit`		475	5	8
10	`x = x // 10`		47	5	8
11	`while x != 0:`	This validates to True			
12	`digit = x % 10`		47	7	8
13	`s = s + digit`		47	7	15
14	`x = x // 10`		4	7	15
15	`while x != 0:`	This validates to True			
16	`digit = x % 10`		4	4	15
17	`s = s + digit`		4	4	19
18	`x = x // 10`		0	4	19
19	`while x != 0:`	This validates to False			
20	`print(s)`	It displays: 19			

Second Approach

In this approach, the main idea is to convert the given integer to a string and then use a for-loop to iterate for all its characters (digits). In the for-loop, however, you need to convert each digit from type string back to type integer before it is accumulated in variable s. The Python program is as follows.

```
📁 file_29_1_6b
x = int(input())
s = 0

for digit in str(x):
    s += int(digit)

print(s)
```

29.2   Exercises with Nested Loop Control Structures

Exercise 29.2-1   Displaying all Three-Digit Integers that Contain a Given Digit

Write a Python program that prompts the user to enter a digit (0 to 9) and then displays all three-digit integers that contain that given digit at least once. For example, for the given value 7, the values 357, 771, and 700 are such integers.

Solution

There are three different approaches! The first one uses just one for-loop, the second one uses three for-loops, nested one within the other, and the last one uses Python's magic forces. Let's analyze them all!

First Approach – Using a for-loop and a decision control structure

The main idea is to use a for-loop where the value of variable *counter* goes from 100 to 999. Inside the loop, the *counter* variable is split into its individual digits ($digit_3$, $digit_2$, $digit_1$) and a decision control structure is used to check if at least one of its digits is equal to the given one. The Python program is as follows.

```
📁 file_29_2_1a
x = int(input("Enter a digit 0 - 9: "))

for i in range(100, 1000):
    digit3 = i // 100
    r = i % 100
    digit2 = r // 10
    digit1 = r % 10

    if digit3 == x or digit2 == x or digit1 == x:
        print(i)
```

Of course, after a little refinement, the same program can become

```
📁 file_29_2_1b
x = int(input("Enter a digit 0 - 9: "))

for i in range(100, 1000):
    digit3, r = divmod(i, 100)
    digit2, digit1 = divmod(r, 10)

    if x in [digit1, digit2, digit3]:
        print(i)
```

Second Approach – Using nested loop control structures and a decision control structure

The main idea here is to use three for-loops, nested one within the other. In this case, there are three *counter* variables and each one of them corresponds to one digit of the three-digit integer. The Python program is as follows.

```
📁 file_29_2_1c
x = int(input("Enter a digit 0 - 9: "))

for digit3 in range(1, 10):
    for digit2 in range(10):
        for digit1 in range(10):
            if x in [digit1, digit2, digit3]:
                print(digit3 * 100 + digit2 * 10 + digit1)
```

If you follow the flow of execution, the value 100 is the first "integer" evaluated (digit3 = 1, digit2 = 0, digit1 = 0). Then, the most-nested loop control structure increments variable digit1 by one and the next value evaluated is "integer" 101. This continues until digit1 reaches the value 9; that is, until the "integer" reaches the value 109. The flow of execution then exits the most-nested loop control structure, variable digit2 increments by one, and the most-nested loop control structure starts over again, thus the values evaluated are the "integers" 110, 111, 112, … 119. The process goes on until all integers up to the value 999 are evaluated.

 Note that variable digit3 *starts from 1, whereas variables* digit2 *and* digit1 *start from 0. This is necessary since the scale for three-digit numbers begins from 100 and not from 000.*

 Note how the print *statement composes the three-digit integer.*

Third Approach – The Pythonic way

In this approach, the *counter* variable of a for-loop is converted to string and unpacked into three individual variables as shown here.

```
📁 file_29_2_1d
x = input("Enter a digit 0 - 9: ")

for i in range(100, 1000):
    digit3, digit2, digit1 = str(i)
    if x in [digit3, digit2, digit1]:
        print(i)
```

 Note that variable x, *as well as variables* digit1, digit2, *and* digit3, *are of type string.*

Exercise 29.2-2   *Displaying all Instances of a Specified Condition*

Write a Python program that displays all three-digit integers in which the first digit is smaller than the second digit and the second digit is smaller than the third digit. For example, the values 357, 456, and 159 are such integers.

Solution

There are three different approaches, actually! Let's analyze them all!

First Approach – Using a for-loop and a decision control structure

The Python program is as follows.

```
📁 file_29_2_2a
for i in range(100, 1000):
    digit3, r = divmod(i, 100)
    digit2, digit1 = divmod(r, 10)

    if digit3 < digit2 and digit2 < digit1:
        print(i)
```

Second Approach – Using nested loop control structures and a decision control structure

The Python program is as follows.

```
📁 file_29_2_2b
for digit3 in range(1, 10):
    for digit2 in range(10):
        for digit1 in range(10):
            if digit3 < digit2 and digit2 < digit1:
                print(digit3 * 100 + digit2 * 10 + digit1)
```

Third Approach – Using nested loop control structures only

This approach is based on the previous one. The main difference between them is that in this case, variable digit1 always begins from a value greater than digit2, and variable digit2 always begins from a value greater than digit3. In that way, the first integer that will be displayed is 123.

> ✎ *There are no integers below the value 123 and above the value 789 that can validate the Boolean expression* digit3 < digit2 and digit2 < digit1 *to* True.

The Python program is as follows.

```
📁 file_29_2_2c
```
```python
for digit3 in range(1, 8):
    for digit2 in range(digit3 + 1, 9):
        for digit1 in range(digit2 + 1, 10):
            print(digit3 * 100 + digit2 * 10 + digit1)
```

> ✎ *This solution is the most efficient since it doesn't use any decision control structure and, moreover, the number of iterations is kept to a minimum!*

> 🖰 *As you can see, one problem can have many solutions. It is up to you to find the optimal one!*

29.3 Data Validation with Loop Control Structures

As you already know, data validation is the process of restricting data input, which forces the user to enter only valid values. You have already encountered one method of data validation using decision control structures. Let's see an example.

```python
import math
x = float(input("Enter a non-negative number: "))

if x < 0:
    print("Error: Negative number entered!")
else:
    print(math.sqrt(x))
```

This approach, however, is not the most appropriate because if the user does enter an invalid number, the program displays the error message and the flow of execution inevitably reaches the end. The user must then execute the program again in order to re-enter a valid number.

Next, you will see three approaches given in general form that validate data input using loop control structures. If the user persistently enters an invalid value, the main idea is to prompt him or her repeatedly, until he or she gets bored and finally enters a valid one. Of course, if the user enters a valid value right from the beginning, the flow of execution simply continues to the next part of the program.

Which approach you use depends on whether or not you wish to display an error message and whether you wish to display an individual error message for each error or just a single error message for any kind of error.

First Approach – Validating data input without error messages

To validate data input without displaying any error messages, you can use the following code fragment given in general form.

```python
while True:
    input_data = input("Prompt message")
    if input_data test 1 succeeds and     \
        input_data test 2 succeeds and     \
```

```
        ...
    input_data test N succeeds: break
```

Second Approach – Validating data input with one error message

To validate data input and display an error message (that is, the same error message for any type of input error), you can use the following code fragment given in general form.

```
input_data = input("Prompt message")
while input_data test 1 fails or     \
      input_data test 2 fails or     \
      ...
      input_data test N fails:
    print("Error message")
    input_data = input("Prompt message")
```

Third Approach – Validating data input with individual error messages

To validate data input and display an error message (that is, individual error messages, one for each type of input error), you can use the following code fragment given in general form.

```
while True:
    input_data = input("Prompt message")
    failure = False
    if input_data test 1 fails:
        print("Error message 1")
        failure = True
    elif input_data test 2 fails:
        print("Error message 2")
        failure = True
    elif ...
        ...
    elif input_data test N fails:
        print("Error message N")
        failure = True

    if not failure: break
```

✎ *The statement* if not failure *is equivalent to the statement* if failure == False

---

Exercise 29.3-1   *Finding Odd and Even Numbers - Validation Without Error Messages*

Write a Python program that prompts the user to enter a non-negative integer, and then displays a message indicating whether this number is even; it must display "Odd" otherwise. Using a loop control structure, the program must also validate data input, allowing the user to enter only a non-negative integer. There is no need to display any error messages.

Solution

First, let's write the program without data validation.

```
x = float(input("Enter a non-negative integer: "))

if x % 2 == 0:
```

Data input stage without validation.

```
        print("Even")
    else:
        print("Odd")
```

To validate data input without displaying any error messages you can use the first approach. All you need to do is replace the statement marked with a dashed rectangle with the following code fragment.

```
    while True:
        x = float(input("Enter a non-negative integer: "))
        if x >=0 and int(x) == x: break
```

✎ *Instead of the function* int(), *the function* float() *is used in the data input stage. This is necessary in order to allow the user to enter either an integer or a float.*

The final Python program becomes

```
                          📁 file_29_3_1
    while True:
        x = float(input("Enter a non-negative integer: "))
        if x >= 0 and int(x) == x: break

    if x % 2 == 0:
        print("Even")
    else:
        print("Odd")
```

Data input validation without error messages.

Exercise 29.3-2   *Finding Odd and Even Numbers - Validation with One Error Message*

Write a Python program that prompts the user to enter a non-negative integer, and then displays a message indicating whether this number is even; it must display "Odd" otherwise. Using a loop control structure, the program must also validate data input and display an error message when the user enters a negative value or a float.

Solution

In the previous exercise, the statement marked with the dashed rectangle was replaced with a code fragment that validated data input without displaying any error message. The same method is followed here, except that the replacing code fragment is based on the second approach. The Python program is as follows.

```
                          📁 file_29_3_2
    x = float(input("Enter a non-negative integer: "))
    while x < 0 or x != int(x):
        print("Error! A negative value or a float entered.")
        x = float(input("Enter a non-negative integer: "))

    if x % 2 == 0:
        print("Even")
    else:
        print("Odd")
```

Data input validation with one single error message.

Exercise 29.3-3　　*Finding Odd and Even Numbers - Validation with Individual Error Messages*

Write a Python program that prompts the user to enter a non-negative integer, and then displays a message indicating whether this number is even; it must display "Odd" otherwise. Using a loop control structure, the program must also validate data input and display individual error messages when the user enters a negative value or a float.

Solution

This is the same as in the previous exercise, except that the replacing code fragment is now based on the third approach. The Python program is as follows.

```
☐ file_29_3_3

while True:
    x = float(input("Enter a non-negative integer: "))

    failure = False
    if x < 0:
        print("Error! You entered a negative value")
        failure = True
    elif x != int(x):
        print("Error! You entered a float")
        failure = True

    if not failure: break

if x % 2 == 0:
    print("Even")
else:
    print("Odd")
```

Data input validation with individual error messages, one for each type of error.

Exercise 29.3-4　　*Finding the Sum of Four Numbers*

Write a Python program that prompts the user to enter four positive numbers and then calculates and displays their sum. Using a loop control structure, the program must also validate data input and display an error message when the user enters any non-positive value.

Solution

This exercise was already discussed in Exercise 25.1-4. The only difference here is that this program must validate data input and display an error message when the user enters invalid values. For your convenience, the solution proposed in that exercise is reproduced next.

```
total = 0

for i in range(4):
    x = float(input("Enter a number: "))
    total = total + x

print(total)
```

Data input stage without validation

Now, replace the statement marked with a dashed rectangle with the following code fragment

```
x = float(input("Enter a number: "))
while x <= 0:
    print("Please enter a positive value!")
    x = float(input("Enter a number: "))
```

and the final Python program becomes

```
┌──────────────────── file_29_3_4 ────────────────────┐
total = 0

for i in range(4):
    ┌ ─ ─ ─ ─ ─ ─ ─ ─ ─ ─ ─ ─ ─ ─ ─ ─ ─ ─ ─ ─ ─ ─ ┐
    │ x = float(input("Enter a number: ")) │
    │ while x <= 0: │
    │     print("Please enter a positive value!") │
    │     x = float(input("Enter a number: ")) │
    └ ─ ─ ─ ─ ─ ─ ─ ─ ─ ─ ─ ─ ─ ─ ─ ─ ─ ─ ─ ─ ─ ─ ┘

    total = total + x

print(total)
```

Data input validation with one single error message

✎ *The basic purpose of this exercise was to show you how to nest the loop control structure that validates data input into other already existing loop control structures.*

29.4 Using Loop Control Structures to Solve Mathematical Problems

Exercise 29.4-1 *Calculating the Area of as Many Triangles as the User Wishes*

Write a Python program that prompts the user to enter the lengths of all three sides A, B, and C of a triangle and then calculates and displays its area. You can use Heron's formula,

$$Area = \sqrt{S(S - A)(S - B)(S - C)}$$

where S is the semi-perimeter

$$S = \frac{A + B + C}{2}$$

The program must iterate as many times as the user wishes. At the end of each area calculation, the program must ask the user if he or she wishes to calculate the area of another triangle. If the answer is "yes" the program must repeat; it must end otherwise. Make your program accept the answer in all possible forms such as "yes", "YES", "Yes", or even "YeS".

Moreover, using a loop control structure, the program must validate data input and display an error message when the user enters any non-positive value.

Solution

According to the "Ultimate" rule, the while-loop must be as follows, given in general form.

```
answer = "yes"    #Redundant initialization of answer.
while True:

    Prompt the user to enter the lengths of all three sides A,
    B, C of a triangle and then calculate and display its area.


    #Update/alteration of answer
```

```
    answer = input("Would you like to repeat? ")
    if answer.upper() != "YES": break
```

> 📖 *The* upper() *method ensures that the programs operates properly for any given answer "Yes", "yes", "YES" or even "YeS" or "yEs"!*

The solution to this exercise is as follows.

📁 **file_29_4_1**

```python
import math

while True:
    a = float(input("Enter side A: "))
    while a <= 0:
        a = float(input("Invalid side. Enter side A: "))

    b = float(input("Enter side B: "))
    while b <= 0:
        b = float(input("Invalid side. Enter side B: "))

    c = float(input("Enter side C: "))
    while c <= 0:
        c = float(input("Invalid side. Enter side C: "))

    s = (a + b + c) / 2
    area = math.sqrt(s * (s - a) * (s - b) * (s - c))
    print("The area is:", area)

    answer = input("Would you like to repeat? ")
    if answer.upper() != "YES": break
```

Exercise 29.4-2   Finding x and y

Write a Python program that displays all possible integer values of x and y within the range –20 to +20 that validate the following formula:

$$3x^2 - 6y^2 = 6$$

Solution

If you just want to display **all** possible combinations of variables x and y, you can use the following Python program.

```python
for x in range(-20, 21):
    for y in range(-20, 21):
        print(x, y)
```

However, from all those combinations, you need only those that validate the expression $3x^2 - 6y^2 = 6$. A decision control structure is perfect for that purpose! The final Python program is as follows.

📁 **file_29_4_2**

```python
for x in range(-20, 21):
```

```python
    for y in range(-20, 21):
        if 3 * x ** 2 - 6 * y ** 2 == 6:
            print(x, y)
```

Exercise 29.4-3 The Russian Multiplication Algorithm

You can multiply two positive integers using the "Russian multiplication algorithm", which is presented in the following flowchart.

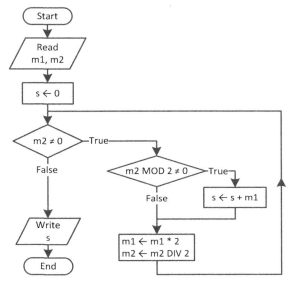

Write the corresponding Python program and create a trace table to determine the values of the variables in each step for the input values 5 and 13.

Solution

In the given flowchart, a single-alternative decision structure is nested within a pre-test loop structure. The corresponding Python program is as follows.

```
📁 file_29_4_3
```

```python
m1 = int(input())
m2 = int(input())

s = 0
while m2 != 0:
    if m2 % 2 != 0:
        s += m1

    m1 *= 2
    m2 //= 2

print(s)
```

For the input values of 5 and 13, the trace table looks like this.

Step	Statement	Notes	m1	m2	s
1	m1 = int(input())	User enters the value 5	**5**	?	?
2	m2 = int(input())	User enters the value 13	5	**13**	?
3	s = 0		5	13	**0**
4	while m2 != 0:	This evaluates to True			
5	if m2 % 2 != 0:	This evaluates to True			
6	s += m1		5	13	**5**
7	m1 *= 2		**10**	13	5
8	m2 //= 2		10	**6**	5
9	while m2 != 0:	This evaluates to True			
10	if m2 % 2 != 0:	This evaluates to False			
11	m1 *= 2		**20**	6	5
12	m2 //= 2		20	**3**	5
13	while m2 != 0:	This evaluates to True			
14	if m2 % 2 != 0:	This evaluates to True			
15	s += m1		20	3	**25**
16	m1 *= 2		**40**	3	25
17	m2 //= 2		40	**1**	25
18	while m2 != 0:	This evaluates to True			
19	if m2 % 2 != 0:	This evaluates to True			
20	s += m1		40	1	**65**
21	m1 *= 2		**80**	1	65
22	m2 //= 2		80	**0**	65
23	while m2 != 0:	This evaluates to False			
24	print(s)	The value 65 is displayed which is, of course, the result of the multiplication 5 × 13			

Exercise 29.4-4   Finding the Number of Divisors

Write a Python program that lets the user enter a positive integer and then displays the total number of its divisors.

Solution

Let's see some examples.

 ▶   The divisors of value 12 are numbers 1, 2, 3, 4, 6, 12.

 ▶   The divisors of value 15 are numbers 1, 3, 5, 15.

 ▶   The divisors of value 20 are numbers 1, 2, 4, 5, 10, 20.

▶ The divisors of value 50 are numbers 1, 2, 5, 10, 25, 50.

If variable x contains the given integer, all possible divisors of x are between 1 and x. Thus, all you need here is a for-loop where the value of variable *counter* goes from 1 to x and, in each iteration, a simple-alternative decision structure checks whether the value of *counter* is a divisor of x, The Python program is as follows.

□ file_29_4_4a

```
x = int(input())

number_of_divisors = 0
for i in range(1, x + 1):
    if x % i == 0:
        number_of_divisors += 1

print(number_of_divisors)
```

This program, for input value 20, performs 20 iterations. However, wouldn't it be even better if it could perform almost the half of the iterations and achieve the same result? Of course it would! So, let's make it more efficient!

As you probably know, for any integer given (in variable x)

▶ the value 1 is always a divisor.

▶ the integer given is always a divisor of itself.

▶ except for the integer given, there are no other divisors after the middle of the range 1 to x.

Accordingly, for any integer there are certainly 2 divisors, the value 1 and the given integer itself. Therefore, the program must check for other possible divisors starting from the value 2 until the middle of the range 1 to x. The improved Python program is as follows.

□ file_29_4_4b

```
x = int(input())

number_of_divisors = 2
for i in range(2, x // 2 + 1):
    if x % i == 0:
        number_of_divisors += 1

print(number_of_divisors)
```

This Python program performs less than half of the iterations that the previous program did! For example, for the input value 20, this Python program performs only (20 – 2) DIV 2 = 9 iterations!

Exercise 29.4-5 Is the Number a Prime?

Write a Python program that prompts the user to enter an integer greater than 1 and then displays a message indicating if this number is a prime. A prime number is any integer greater than 1 that has no divisors other than 1 and itself. The numbers 7, 11, and 13 are all such numbers.

Solution

This exercise is based on the previous one. It is very simple! If the given integer has only two divisors (1 and itself), the number is a prime. The Python program is as follows.

```
📁 file_29_4_5a
```

```python
x = int(input("Enter an integer greater than 1: "))

number_of_divisors = 2
for i in range(2, x // 2 + 1):
    if x % i == 0:
        number_of_divisors += 1

if number_of_divisors == 2:
    print("Number", x, "is prime")
```

Now let's make the program more efficient. The flow of execution can break out of the loop when a third divisor is found, because this means that the given integer is definitely not a prime. The Python program is as follows.

```
📁 file_29_4_5b
```

```python
x = int(input("Enter an integer greater than 1: "))

number_of_divisors = 2
for i in range(2, x // 2 + 1):
    if x % i == 0:
        number_of_divisors += 1
        break

if number_of_divisors == 2:
    print("Number", x, "is prime")
```

Exercise 29.4-6   *Finding all Prime Numbers from 1 to N*

Write a Python program that prompts the user to enter a positive integer and then displays all prime numbers from 1 to that given integer. Using a loop control structure, the program must also validate data input and display an error message when the user enters any values less than 1.

Solution

The following Python program, given in general form, solves this exercise.

```
Main Code
```

```python
N = int(input("Enter a positive integer: "))
while N < 1:
    N = int(input("Wrong number. Enter a positive integer: "))

for x in range(1, N + 1):

    Code Fragment 1: Check whether variable x contains a prime number
```

Code Fragment 1, shown below, is taken from the previous exercise (Exercise 29.4-5). It checks whether variable x contains a prime number.

```
Code Fragment 1
```

```python
number_of_divisors = 2
for i in range(2, x // 2 + 1):
```

```
        if x % i == 0:
            number_of_divisors += 1
            break


    if number_of_divisors == 2:
        print("Number", x, "is prime")
```

After embedding **Code Fragment 1** in **Main Code**, the final Python program becomes

```
                          📁 file_29_4_6
N = int(input("Enter a positive integer: "))
while N < 1:
    N = int(input("Wrong number. Enter a positive integer: "))

for x in range(1, N + 1):
    number_of_divisors = 2
    for i in range(2, x // 2 + 1):
        if x % i == 0:
            number_of_divisors += 1
            break

    if number_of_divisors == 2:
        print("Number", x, "is prime")
```

Exercise 29.4-7 Heron's Square Root

Write a Python program that prompts the user to enter a non-negative value and then calculates its square root using Heron's formula, as follows.

$$x_{n+1} = \frac{\left(x_n + \frac{y}{x_n}\right)}{2}$$

where

▶ *y is the number for which you want to find the square root*

▶ *x_n is the n-th iteration value of the square root of y*

Moreover, using a loop control structure, the program must validate data input and display an error message when the user enters any negative values.

Solution

It is almost certain that you are a little bit confused and you are scratching your head right now. Don't be scared by all this math stuff! You can try to understand Heron's formula through the following flowchart instead!

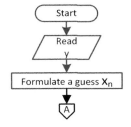

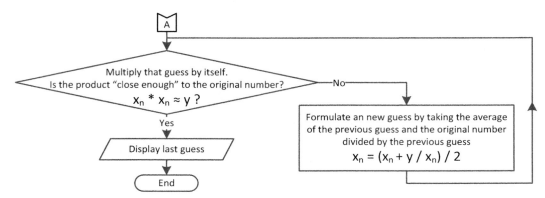

Still confused? Let's see an example. Let's find the square root of 25:

▶ Assume 8 as your first guess.

▶ The product of 8 × 8 is 64.

▶ Since 64 isn't "close enough" to 25, you can create a new guess by calculating the expression

$$\frac{\left(guess + \frac{number}{guess}\right)}{2} = \frac{\left(8 + \frac{25}{8}\right)}{2} \approx 5.56$$

▶ The product of 5.56 × 5.56 is about 30.91

▶ Since 30.91 isn't "close enough" to 25 you can create a new guess by calculating the expression

$$\frac{\left(guess + \frac{number}{guess}\right)}{2} = \frac{\left(5.56 + \frac{25}{5.56}\right)}{2} \approx 5.02$$

▶ The product of 5.02 × 5.02 is 25.2

▶ Now you can say that 25.2 is "close enough" to 25. Therefore, you can stop the whole process and say that the approximate square root of 25 is 5.02

Now, let's see the corresponding Python program.

```
🗀 file_29_4_7
import random
ACCURACY = 0.0000000000001

y = float(input("Enter a non-negative number: "))
while y < 0:
    y = float(input("Invalid value. Enter a non-negative number: "))

guess = random.randrange(1, y + 1)      #Make a random first guess between 1 and given value

while abs(guess * guess - y) > ACCURACY:      #Is it "close enough"?
    guess = (guess + y / guess) / 2           #No, create a new "guess"!

print(guess)
```

✎ *Note the way that "Is it close enough" is checked. When the absolute value of the difference | guess² − given_value | becomes less than 0.0000000000001, the flow of execution exits the loop.*

Exercise 29.4-8   Calculating π

Write a Python program that calculates π using the Madhava–Leibniz[1,2] series, which follows, with an accuracy of 0.00001.

$$\frac{\pi}{4} = 1 - \frac{1}{3} + \frac{1}{5} - \frac{1}{7} + \cdots$$

Solution

The Madhava–Leibniz series can be solved for π, and becomes

$$\pi = \frac{4}{1} - \frac{4}{3} + \frac{4}{5} - \frac{4}{7} + \cdots$$

The more fractions you have, the better the accuracy! Thus, to calculate this formula the program needs to perform many iterations so as to use as many fractions as possible. But, of course, it can't iterate forever! The loop must actually stop iterating when the current value of π and the one calculated in the previous iteration are "close enough", which means that the absolute value of their difference has become very small. The constant ACCURACY defines how small this difference must be. The Python program is shown here.

```
📁 file_29_4_8
ACCURACY = 0.00001

pi = 0

sign = 1          #This is the sign of the first fraction
denom = 1         #This is the denominator of the first fraction
while True:
    pi_previous = pi          #Keep previous pi
    pi += sign * 4 / denom    #Calculate new pi by adding an extra fraction
    sign = -sign              #Prepare sign for the next fraction
    denom += 2                #Prepare denominator for the next fraction
    if abs(pi - pi_previous) <= ACCURACY: break   #Is it "close enough"?

print("Pi ~=", pi)
```

✎ *Note the way in which variable* sign *toggles between the values –1 and +1 in each iteration.*

If you reduce the value of the constant ACCURACY, π will be calculated more and more accurately. Depending on how fast your computer is, you can calculate the first five digits of π fairly quickly. However, the time it takes to calculate each succeeding digit of π goes up exponentially. To calculate 40 digits of π on a modern computer using this method could take years!

---

[1] Madhava of Sangamagrama (c. 1340–c. 1425), was an Indian mathematician and astronomer from the town of Sangamagrama (present day Irinjalakuda) of India. He founded the Kerala School of Astronomy and Mathematics and was the first to use infinite series approximations for various trigonometric functions. He is often referred to as the "father of mathematical analysis".

[2] Gottfried Wilhelm von Leibniz (1646–1716) was a German mathematician and philosopher. He made important contributions to the fields of metaphysics, logic, and philosophy, as well as mathematics, physics, and history. In one of his works, *On the Art of Combination (Dissertatio de Arte Combinatoria)*, published in 1666, he formulated a model that is considered the theoretical ancestor of modern computers.

Exercise 29.4-9   *Approximating a Real with a Fraction*

Write a Python program that prompts the user to enter a real between 0 and 100 and then tries to find the fraction $\frac{N}{M}$ that better approximates it, where N is an integer between 0 and 100 and M is an integer between 1 and 100. Using a loop control structure, the program must also validate data input, allowing the user to enter only values between 0 and 100. There is no need to display any error messages.

Solution

The solution is simple. All you need to do is iterate through all possible combinations of variables n and m and check which one better approximates the real given.

To iterate through all possible combinations of variables n and m, you can use a nested loop control structure, that is, two for-loops, one nested within the other, as follows.

```python
for n in range(101):
    for m in range(1, 101):
        ...
```

✎ *The total number of iterations is 101 × 100 = 10100. Quite a big number but, for a modern computer, this is peanuts!*

✎ *Variable m represents the denominator of the fraction, and a denominator cannot be zero. This is why it starts from 1, and not from 0.*

The following criteria

$$minimum\ of\ \left(\left| \frac{N}{M} - real\ given \right| \right)$$

can evaluate how "good" an approximation is.

Confused? Let's try to approximate the value 0.333 with a fraction, iterating through all possible combinations of N and M.

- ▶ For N = 1, M = 1 the criteria equals to $\left| \frac{1}{1} - 0.333 \right| = 0.6670$

- ▶ For N = 1, M = 2 the criteria equals to $\left| \frac{1}{2} - 0.333 \right| = 0.1670$

- ▶ For N = 1, M = 3 the criteria equals to $\left| \frac{1}{3} - 0.333 \right| = 0.0003$

- ▶ For N = 1, M = 4 the criteria equals to $\left| \frac{1}{4} - 0.333 \right| = 0.0830$

- ▶ ...

- ▶ For N = 100, M = 99 the criteria equals to $\left| \frac{100}{99} - 0.333 \right| = 0.6771$

- ▶ For N = 100, M = 100 the criteria equals to $\left| \frac{100}{100} - 0.333 \right| = 0.6670$

It is obvious that the value 0.0003 is the minimum value among all possible results. Thus, the combination N = 1 and M = 3 (which corresponds to the fraction 1/3) is considered the best approximation for the value 0.333.

And now the Python program:

```python
                              📁 file_29_4_9
while True:
    x = float(input("Enter a real between 0 and 100: "))
    if 0 <= x <= 100: break
```

```
best_n = 1
best_m = 1
for n in range(101):
    for m in range(1, 101):
        if abs(n / m - x) < abs(best_n / best_m - x):
            best_n = n
            best_m = m

print("The fraction is:", best_n, "/", best_m)
```

29.5   Finding Minimum and Maximum Values with Loop Control Structures

In paragraph 22.3 you learned how to find the minimum and maximum values among four values using single-alternative decision structures. Now, the following code fragment does pretty much the same but uses only one variable w to hold all of the user's given values.

```
w = int(input())       #User enters 1st value
maximum = w


w = int(input())       #User enters 2nd value
if w > maximum:
    maximum = w


w = int(input())       #User enters 3rd value
if w > maximum:
    maximum = w


w = int(input())       #User enters 4th value
if w > maximum:
    maximum = w
```

Except for the first pair of statements, all other blocks of statements are identical; therefore, only one of those can be enclosed within a loop control structure and be executed three times, as follows.

```
w = int(input())       #User enters 1st value
maximum = w


for i in range(3):
    w = int(input()) #User enters 2nd, 3rd and 4th value
    if w > maximum:
        maximum = w
```

Of course, if you want to allow the user to enter more values, you can simply increase the *final_value* of the for-loop.

Accordingly, if you want a program that finds and displays the heaviest person among 10 people, the solution is presented next.

📁 **file_29_5a**

```
w = int(input("Enter a weight (in pounds): "))
maximum = w
```

```
for i in range(9):
    w = int(input("Enter a weight (in pounds): "))
    if w > maximum:
        maximum = w

print(maximum)
```

✎ *Note that the for-loop iterates one time less than the total number of values given.*

Even though this Python program operates perfectly well, let's do something different. Instead of prompting the user to enter one value before the loop and nine values inside the loop, let's prompt him or her to enter all values inside the loop.

The problem that arises here is that no matter what, before the loop starts iterating, an initial value must be assigned to variable maximum. However, you cannot assign any initial value. It depends on the given problem. An "almost arbitrary" initial value must be chosen carefully, since a wrong one may lead to incorrect results.

In this exercise, all given values have to do with people's weight. Since there is no chance of finding any person with a negative weight (at least not on planet Earth), you can safely assign the initial value −1 to variable maximum, as follows.

📄 **file_29_5b**

```
maximum = -1

for i in range(10):
    w = int(input("Enter a weight: "))
    if w > maximum:
        maximum = w

print(maximum)
```

As soon as the flow of execution enters the loop, the user enters the first value and the decision control structure validates to True. The value −1 in variable maximum is overwritten by that first given value and after that, flow of execution proceeds normally.

✎ *Note that this method cannot be used in every case. If an exercise needs to prompt the user to enter any number (not only a positive one) this method cannot be applied since the user could potentially enter only negative values. If this were to occur, the initial value −1 would never be overwritten by any of the given values. You can use this method to find the maximum value only when you know the lower limit of given values or to find the minimum value only when you know the upper limit of given values. For example, if the exercise needs to find the lightest person, you can assign the initial value +1500 to variable minimum, since there is no human on Earth that can be so heavy! For the record, Jon Brower Minnoch was an American who, at his peak weight, was the heaviest human being ever recorded, weighing approximately 1.400 lb!!!!!*

Exercise 29.5-1   *Validating and Finding the Minimum and the Maximum Value*

Write a Python program that prompts the user to enter the weight of 10 people and then finds the lightest and the heaviest weights. Using a loop control structure, the program must also validate data input and display an error message when the user enters any non-positive value, or any value greater than 1500.

Solution

Using the previous exercise as a guide, you should now be able to do this with your eyes closed!

To validate data input, all you have to do is replace the following line of code of the previous exercise,

```
w = int(input("Enter a weight: "))
```

with the following code fragment:

```
w = int(input("Enter a weight between 1 and 1500: "))
while w <= 0 or x > 1500:
    print("Invalid value!")
    w = int(input("Enter a weight between 1 and 1500: "))
```

Following is the final program that finds the lightest and the heaviest weights.

```
                              📁 file_29_5_1
minimum = 1500
maximum = 0


for i in range(10):
    w = int(input("Enter a weight between 1 and 1500: "))
    while w <= 0 or w > 1500:
        print("Invalid value!")
        w = int(input("Enter a weight between 1 and 1500: "))


    if w < minimum:
        minimum = w


    if w > maximum:
        maximum = w


print(minimum, maximum)
```

Exercise 29.5-2   Validating and Finding the Hottest Planet

Write a Python program that prompts the user to repeatedly enter the names and the average temperatures of planets from space, until the word "STOP" (used as a name) is entered. In the end, the program must display the name of the hottest planet. Moreover, since −459.67° (on the Fahrenheit scale) is the lowest temperature possible (it is called absolute zero), the program must also validate data input (using a loop control structure) and display an error message when the user enters temperature values lower than absolute zero.

Solution

First, let's write the Python program without using data validation. According to the "Ultimate" rule, the pre-test loop structure must be as follows, given in general form:

```
#Initialization of name
name = input("Enter the name of a planet: ")


while name.upper() != "STOP":

    A statement or block of statements


    #Update/alteration of name
    name = input("Enter the name of a planet: ")
```

Now, let's add the rest of the statements, still without data input validation. Keep in mind that, since value −459.67° is the lower limit of the temperature scale, you can use a value lower than this as the initial value of variable `maximum`.

```python
maximum = -460
m_name = ""

name = input("Enter the name of a planet: ")
while name.upper() != "STOP":
    t = float(input("Enter its average temperature: "))

    if t > maximum:
        maximum = t
        m_name = name

    name = input("Enter the name of a planet: ")

if maximum != -460:
    print("The hottest planet is:", m_name)
else:
    print("Nothing Entered!")
```

✎ *The* `if maximum != -460` *statement is required because there is a possibility that the user could enter the word "STOP" right from the beginning.*

To validate the data input, all you have to do is replace the following line of code:

```python
t = float(input("Enter its average temperature: "))
```

with the following code fragment:

```python
t = float(input("Enter its average temperature: "))
while t < -459.67:
    print("Invalid value!")
    t = float(input("Enter its average temperature: "))
```

The final program is as follows.

```
📁 file_29_5_2
```

```python
maximum = -460
m_name = ""

name = input("Enter the name of a planet: ")
while name.upper() != "STOP":
    t = float(input("Enter its average temperature: "))
    while t < -459.67:
        print("Invalid value!")
        t = float(input("Enter its average temperature: "))

    if t > maximum:
        maximum = t
        m_name = name
```

```
    name = input("Enter the name of a planet: ")

if maximum != -460:
    print("The hottest planet is:", m_name)
else:
    print("Nothing Entered!")
```

Exercise 29.5-3   "Making the Grade"

*In a classroom, there are 20 students. Write a Python program that prompts the teacher to enter the grades (0 –
100) that students received in a math test and then displays the highest grade as well as the number of students
that got an "A" (that is, 90 to 100). Moreover, the program must validate data input. Given values must be within
the range 0 to 100.*

Solution

Let's first write the program without data validation. Since the number of students is known, you can use a
for-loop. For an initial value of variable maximum, you can use value −1 as there is no grade lower than 0.

```
maximum = -1
count = 0

for i in range(20):
    grade = int(input("Grade for student No" + str(i + 1) + ": "))

    if grade > maximum:
        maximum = grade

    if grade >= 90:
        count += 1

print(maximum, count)
```

Now, you can deal with data validation. As the wording of the exercise implies, there is no need to display any
error messages. So, all you need to do is replace the following line of code:

```
grade = int(input("Grade for student No" + str(i + 1) + ": "))
```

with the following code fragment:

```
while True:
    grade = int(input("Grade for student No" + str(i + 1) + ": "))
    if 0 <= grade <= 100: break
```

and the final program becomes

📂 **file_29_5_3**

```
maximum = -1
count = 0

for i in range(20):
    while True:
        grade = int(input("Grade for student No" + str(i + 1) + ": "))
```

```
        if 0 <= grade <= 100: break

    if grade > maximum:
        maximum = grade

    if grade >= 90:
        count += 1

print(maximum, count)
```

29.6   Exercises of a General Nature with Loop Control Structures

Exercise 29.6-1   Fahrenheit to Kelvin, from 0 to 100

Write a Python program that displays all degrees Fahrenheit from 0 to 100 and their equivalent degrees Kelvin. Use an increment value of 0.5. It is given that

$$1.8 \cdot Kelvin = Fahrenheit + 459.67$$

Solution

The formula, solved for Kelvin becomes

$$Kelvin = \frac{Fahrenheit + 459.67}{1.8}$$

All you need here is a while-loop that increments the value of variable fahrenheit from 0 to 100 using an *step* of 0.5. The solution is presented next.

📁 **file_29_6_1a**

```
fahrenheit = 0
while fahrenheit <= 100:
    kelvin = (fahrenheit + 459.67) / 1.8
    print("Fahrenheit:", fahrenheit, "Kelvin:", kelvin)
    fahrenheit += 0.5
```

Of course, you may now wonder if this exercise can be solved using a for-loop. One could say "*No, this is impossible! The* step *in the* range() *function must be an integer!*" However, there is an easy trick that you can do to solve this exercise with a for-loop, as shown here.

📁 **file_29_6_1b**

```
for f in range(0, 1001, 5):
    fahrenheit = f / 10
    kelvin = (fahrenheit + 459.67) / 1.8
    print("Fahrenheit:", fahrenheit, "Kelvin:", kelvin)
```

✎ *Generally speaking, division and multiplication are CPU-time consuming operations. Though this second approach works well, it is not the best option. The statement* fahrenheit = f / 10 *included within the for-loop may look innocent, but actually it is not, because the division* f / 10 *is executed 1001 times! It is like having a sequence control structure of 1001 statements that perform 1001 divisions! Try to avoid division and multiplication operations within loops as much as possible!*

Exercise 29.6-2   *Rice on a Chessboard*

There is a myth about a poor man who invented chess. The King of India was so pleased with that new game that he offered to give the poor man anything he wished for. The poor but wise man told his King that he would like one grain of rice for the first square of the board, two grains for the second, four grains for the third and so on, doubled for each of the 64 squares of the game board. This seemed to the King to be a modest request, so he ordered his servants to bring the rice.

Write a Python program that calculates and displays how many grains of rice, and how many pounds of rice, will be on the chessboard in the end. Suppose that one pound of rice contains about 30,000 grains of rice.

Solution

Assume a chessboard of only 2 × 2 = 4 squares and a variable `grains` assigned the initial value 1 (this is the number of grains of the 1st square). A for-loop that iterates three times can double the value of variable `grains` in each iteration, as shown in the next code fragment.

```python
grains = 1
for i in range(3):
    grains = 2 * grains
```

The value of variable `grains` at the end of each iteration is shown in the next table.

Iteration	Value of grains
1st	2 × 1 = **2**
2nd	2 × 2 = **4**
3rd	2 × 4 = **8**

At the end of the 3rd iteration, variable `grains` contains the value 8. This value is not the total number of grains on the chessboard but only the number of grains on the 4th square. If you need to find the total number of grains on the chessboard you can sum up the grains on all squares, that is, 1 + 2 + 4 + 8 = 15.

In the real world a real chessboard contains 8 × 8 = 64 squares, thus you need to iterate for 63 times. The Python program is as follows.

```python
                            file_29_6_2
grains = 1
total = 1
for i in range(63):
    grains = 2 * grains
    total += grains   #This is equivalent to total = total + grains

weight = total / 30000
print(total, weight)
```

In case you are wondering how big these numbers are, here is your answer: On the chessboard there will be 18,446,744,073,709,551,615 grains of rice; that is, 614,891,469,123,651.8 pounds!

Exercise 29.6-3   *Just a Poll*

A public opinion polling company asks 1000 citizens if they eat breakfast in the morning. Write a Python program that prompts the citizens to enter their gender (M for Male, F for Female) and their answer to the question (Y for Yes, N for No, S for Sometimes), and then calculates and displays the number of citizens that gave "Yes" as an answer, as well as the percentage of women among the citizens that gave "No" as an answer. Using a loop control structure, the program must also validate data input and accept only values M or F for gender and Y, N, or S for answer.

Solution

The Python program is as follows.

```
📁 file_29_6_3a
CITIZENS = 1000

total_yes = 0
female_no = 0
for i in range(CITIZENS):
    while True:
        gender = input("Enter gender: ").lower()
        if gender == "m" or gender == "f": break

    while True:
        answer = input("Do you eat breakfast in the morning? ").lower()
        if answer == "y" or answer == "n" or answer == "s": break

    if answer == "y":
        total_yes += 1

    if gender == "f" and answer == "n":
        female_no += 1

print(total_yes, female_no * 100 / CITIZENS)
```

✎ *Note how Python converts the user's input to lowercase.*

Of course, after a little refinement, this program can become

```
📁 file_29_6_3b
CITIZENS = 1000

total_yes = 0
female_no = 0
for i in range(CITIZENS):
    while True:
        gender = input("Enter gender: ").lower()
        if gender in ["m", "f"]: break

    while True:
        answer = input("Do you eat breakfast in the morning? ").lower()
        if answer in ["y", "n", "s"]: break

    if answer == "y":
        total_yes += 1
```

```
        elif gender == "f":
            female_no += 1

    print(total_yes, female_no * 100 / CITIZENS)
```

Exercise 29.6-4   *Is the Message a Palindrome?*

A palindrome is a word or sentence that reads the same both backwards and forward. (You may recall from Exercise 22.5-3 that a number can also be a palindrome!) Write a Python program that prompts the user to enter a word or sentence and then displays a message stating whether or not the given word or sentence is a palindrome. Following are some palindrome messages.

► *Anna*

► *A nut for a jar of tuna.*

► *Dennis and Edna sinned.*

► *Murder for a jar of red rum.*

► *Borrow or rob?*

► *Are we not drawn onward, we few, drawn onward to new era?*

Solution

There are some things that you should keep in mind before you start comparing the letters one by one and checking whether the first letter is the same as the last one, the second letter is the same as the last but one, and so on.

► In a given sentence or word, some letters may be in uppercase and some in lowercase. For example, in the sentence "*A nut for a jar of tuna*", even though the first and last letters are the same, unfortunately they are not considered equal. Thus, the program must first change all the letters—for example, to lowercase—and then it can start comparing them.

► There are some characters such as spaces, periods, question marks, and commas that should be removed or else the program cannot actually compare the rest of the letters one by one. For example, in the sentence "*Borrow or rob?*" the Python program may mistakenly assume that the sentence is not a palindrome because it will compare the first letter "B" with the last question mark "?"

► Assume that the sentence "*Borrow or rob?*", after changing all letters to lowercase and after removing all unwanted spaces and the question mark, becomes "borroworrob". These letters and their corresponding position in the string are as follows.

0	*1*	*2*	*3*	*4*	*5*	*6*	*7*	*8*	*9*	*10*
b	o	r	r	o	w	o	r	r	o	b

What you should keep in mind here is that the for-loop should iterate for only half of the letters. Can you figure out why?

The program starts the iterations and compares the letter at position 0 with the letter at position 10. Then it compares the letter at position 1 with the letter at position 9, and so on. The last iteration should be the one that compares the letters at positions 4 and 6. It is meaningless to continue checking thereafter, since all letters have already been compared.

There are many solutions to this problem. Some of them are presented below. Comments written within the programs can help you fully understand the way they operate. However, if you still have doubts about how they operate you can still use Eclipse to execute them step by step and observe the values of the variables in each step.

First Approach

The solution is presented here.

```
📁 file_29_6_4a
message = input("Enter a message: ").lower()

#Create a new string which contains all except spaces, commas, periods, and question marks
message_clean = ""
for letter in message:
    if letter != " " and letter != "," and letter != "." and letter != "?":
        message_clean += letter

#This is the last position of message_clean
j = len(message_clean) - 1

#This is the middle position of message_clean
middle_pos = j // 2

#In the beginning, assume that sentence is palindrome
palindrome = True

#This for-loop compares letters one by one.
for i in range(middle_pos + 1):
    left_letter = message_clean[i]
    right_letter = message_clean[j]
    #If at least one pair of letters fails to validate set variable palindrome to False
    if left_letter != right_letter:
        palindrome = False
    j -= 1

#If variable palindrome is still True
if palindrome:
    print("The message is palindrome")
```

Second Approach

The previous approach works fine, but assume that the user enters a very large sentence that is not a palindrome. Let's say, for example, that the second letter is not the same as the last but one. Unfortunately, in the previous approach the last for-loop continues to iterate until the middle of the sentence despite the fact that variable palindrome has been set to False, even from the second iteration. So, let's try to make this program even better. As you already know, you can break out of a loop before it completes all of its iterations using the break statement.

Furthermore, you can improve the previous approach in two ways:

▶ You can remove spaces, commas, periods, and question marks from the variable message, using the not in membership operator.

▶ Instead of using the variable j to access the letters of variable message_clean on the right, you can use negative indexes.

The solution is shown here.

```
                              📁 file_29_6_4b
message = input("Enter a message: ").lower()

#Remove spaces, commas, periods and question marks using the "not in" membership operator
message_clean = ""
for letter in message:
    if letter not in " ,.?":
        message_clean += letter

middle_pos = (len(message_clean) - 1) // 2

palindrome = True

for i in range(middle_pos + 1):
    left_letter = message_clean[i]
    #Access letters on the right using negative indexes
    right_letter = message_clean[-i - 1]
    if left_letter != right_letter:
        palindrome = False
        break

if palindrome:
    print("The message is palindrome")
```

Fourth Approach

A more Pythonic and more sophisticated way is to remove spaces, commas, periods, and question marks using the replace() method, and then just compare message_clean to its reversed value.

The solution is shown here.

```
                              📁 file_29_6_4c
message = input("Enter a message: ").lower()

#Create a new string which contains letters except spaces, commas, periods or question marks
message_clean = message
for c in " ,.?":
    message_clean = message_clean.replace(c, "")

if message_clean == message_clean[::-1]:
    print("The message is palindrome")
```

Furthermore, since there are just four different characters that must be removed (spaces, commas, periods, and question marks) you can avoid the first loop if you just chain four replace() methods, as shown in the Python program that follows.

```
                              📁 file_29_6_4d
message = input("Enter a message: ").lower()

message_clean = message.replace(" ", "").replace(",", "").replace(".", "").replace("?", "")
```

```
if message_clean == message_clean[::-1]:
    print("The message is palindrome")
```

✎ *It is obvious that one problem can have many solutions. It is up to you to find the optimal one!*

29.7 Review Questions: True/False

Choose **true** or **false** for each of the following statements.

1. Data validation is the process of restricting data input, forcing the user to enter only valid values.

2. You can use a for-loop to validate data input.

3. You can use any loop control structure to validate data input.

4. To force a user to enter only positive numbers, without displaying any error messages, you can use the following code fragment.

```
while True:
    x = float(input("Enter a positive number: "))
    if x > 0: break
```

5. To force a user to enter numbers between 1 and 10, you can use the following code fragment.

```
x = float(input("Enter a number between 1 and 10: "))
while x >= 1 and x <= 10:
    print("Wrong number")
    x = float(input("Enter a number between 1 and 10: "))
```

6. When a Python program is used to find the maximum value among 10 given values, the loop control structure that is used must always iterate 9 times.

7. In order to find the lowest number among 10 numbers given, you can use the following code fragment.

```
minimum = 0
for i in range(10):
    w = float(input())
    if w < minimum: minimum = w
```

8. In order to find the highest number among 10 numbers given, you can use the following code fragment.

```
maximum = 0
for i in range(10):
    w = float(input())
    if w > maximum: maximum = w
```

9. In order to find the highest number among 10 <u>positive</u> numbers given, you can use the following code fragment.

```
maximum = 0
for i in range(10):
    w = float(input())
    if w > maximum: maximum = w
```

29.8 Review Exercises

Complete the following exercises.

1. Design a flowchart and write the corresponding Python program that prompts the user to repeatedly enter non-negative values until their average value exceeds 3000. At the end, the program must display the total number of zeros entered.

2. Write a Python program that prompts the user to enter an integer between 1 and 20 and then displays all four-digit integers for which the sum of their digits is less than the integer given. For example, if the user enters 15, the value 9301 is such a number, since

$$9 + 3 + 0 + 1 < 15$$

3. Write a Python program that displays all four-digit integers that satisfy all of the following conditions:

   ▶ the number's first digit is greater than its second digit
   ▶ the number's second digit is equal to its third digit
   ▶ the number's third digit is smaller than its fourth digit

   For example, the values 7559, 3112, and 9889 are such numbers.

4. Write a Python program that prompts the user to enter an integer and then displays the number of its digits.

5. A student wrote the following code fragment which is supposed to validate data input, forcing the user to enter only values 0 and 1. Identify any error(s) in the code fragment.

```python
while x != 1 or x != 0:
    print("Error")
    x = int(input())
```

6. Using a loop control structure, write the code fragment that validates data input, forcing the user to enter a valid gender (M for Male, F for Female). Moreover, it must validate correctly both for lowercase and uppercase letters.

7. Write a Python program that prompts the user to enter a non-negative number and then calculates its square root. Using a loop control structure, the program must also validate data input and display an error message when the user enters any negative values. Additionally, the user has a maximum number of two retries. If the user enters more than three negative values, a message "Dude, you are dumb!" must be displayed and the program execution must end.

8. The area of a circle can be calculated using the following formula:

$$Area = \pi \cdot Radius^2$$

Write a Python program that prompts the user to enter the length of the radius of a circle and then calculates and displays its area. The program must iterate as many times as the user wishes. At the end of each area calculation, the program must ask the user if he or she wishes to calculate the area of another circle. If the answer is "yes" the program must repeat; it must end otherwise. Make your program accept the answer in all possible forms such as "yes", "YES", "Yes", or even "YeS".

Moreover, using a loop control structure, the program must validate data input and display an error message when the user enters any non-positive value for *Radius*.

Hint: Use the `math.pi` constant to get the value of π.

9. Write a Python program that displays all possible integer values of *x* and *y* within the range −100 to +100 that validate the following formula:

$$5x + 3y^2 = 0$$

10. Write a Python program that displays all possible integer values of x, y, and z within the range -10 to $+10$ that validate the following formula:

$$\frac{x + y}{2} + \frac{3z^2}{x + 3y + 45} = \frac{x}{3}$$

11. Write a Python program that lets the user enter three positive integers and then finds their product using the Russian multiplication algorithm.

12. Rewrite the Python program of Exercise 29.4-4 to validate the data input using a loop control structure. If the user enters a non-positive integer, an error message must be displayed.

13. Rewrite the Python program of Exercise 29.4-5 to validate the data input using a loop control structure. If the user enters an integer less than or equal to 1, an error message must be displayed.

14. Write a Python program that prompts the user to enter two positive integers and then displays all prime integers between them. Using a loop control structure, the program must also validate data input and display an error message when the user enters a value less than $+2$.

    Hint: To make your Python program operate correctly, independent of which integer given is the lowest, you can swap their values (if necessary) so that they are always in the proper order.

15. Write a Python program that prompts the user to enter two positive four-digit integers and then displays all integers between them that are palindromes. Using a loop control structure, the program must also validate data input and display an error message when the user enters any numbers other than four-digit ones.

    Hint: To make your Python program operate correctly, independent of which integer given is the lowest, you can swap their values (if necessary) so that they are always in the proper order.

16. Write a Python program that displays all possible RAM sizes between 1 byte and 1GByte, such as 1, 2, 4, 8, 16, 32, 64, 128, and so on.

    Hint: 1GByte equals 2^{30} bytes, or 1073741824 bytes

17. Write a Python program that displays the following sequence of numbers:

    $$1, 11, 23, 37, 53, 71, 91, 113, 137, \ldots 401$$

18. Write a Python program that displays the following sequence of numbers:

    $$-1, 1, -2, 2, -3, 3, -4, 4, \ldots -100, 100$$

19. Write a Python program that displays the following sequence of numbers:

    $$1, 11, 111, 1111, 11111, \ldots 11111111$$

20. The Fibonacci[3] sequence is a series of numbers in the following sequence:

    $$1, 1, 2, 3, 5, 8, 13, 21, 34, 55, \ldots$$

    By definition, the first two numbers are 1 and 1 and each subsequent number is the sum of the previous two.

    Write a Python program that lets the user enter a positive integer and then displays as many Fibonacci numbers as that given integer.

21. Write a Python program that lets the user enter a positive integer and then displays all Fibonacci numbers that are less than that given integer.

---

[3] Leonardo Pisano Bigollo (c. 1170–c. 1250), also known as Fibonacci, was an Italian mathematician. In his book *Liber Abaci* (published in 1202), Fibonacci used a special sequence of numbers to try to determine the growth of a rabbit population. Today, that sequence of numbers is known as the Fibonacci sequence. He was also one of the first people to introduce the Arabic numeral system to Europe; this is the numeral system we use today, based on ten digits with a decimal point and a symbol for zero. Before then, the Roman numeral system was being used, making numerical calculations difficult.

22. Write a Python program that prompts the user to enter a positive integer N and then finds and displays the value of y in the following formula:

$$y = \frac{2 + 4 + 6 + \ldots + 2N}{1 \cdot 2 \cdot 3 \cdot 4 \cdot \ldots \cdot N}$$

Moreover, using a loop control structure, the program must validate data input and display an error message when the user enters a value less than 1.

23. Write a Python program that prompts the user to enter a positive integer N and then finds and displays the value of y in the following formula

$$y = \frac{1 - 3 + 5 - 7 + \ldots + (2N + 1)}{N}$$

Moreover, using a loop control structure, the program must validate data input and display an error message when the user enters a non-positive value.

24. Write a Python program that prompts the user to enter a positive integer N and then finds and displays the value of y in the following formula:

$$y = 1 - \frac{1}{2} + \frac{1}{3} - \frac{1}{5} + \ldots + \frac{1}{N}$$

Moreover, using a loop control structure, the program must validate data input and display an error message when the user enters a non-positive value.

25. Write a Python program that prompts the user to enter a positive integer N and then finds and displays the value of y in the following formula:

$$y = \frac{1}{1^N} + \frac{1}{2^{N-1}} + \frac{1}{3^{N-2}} + \ldots + \frac{1}{N^1}$$

Moreover, using a loop control structure, the program must validate data input and display an error message when the user enters a non-positive value.

26. In mathematics, the factorial of a non-negative integer N is the product of all positive integers less than or equal to N, and it is denoted by N! The factorial of 0 is, by definition, equal to 1. In mathematics, you can write

$$N! = \begin{cases} 1 \cdot 2 \cdot 3 \cdot \ldots N, & for\ N > 0 \\ 1, & for\ N = 0 \end{cases}$$

For example, the factorial of 5 is written as 5! and is equal to $1 \times 2 \times 3 \times 4 \times 5 = 120$.

Write a Python program that prompts the user to enter a non-negative integer N and then calculates its factorial.

27. Write a Python program that lets the user enter a value for x and then calculates and displays the exponential function e^x using the Taylor[4] series, shown next, with an accuracy of 0.00001.

$$e^x = 1 + \frac{x^1}{1!} + \frac{x^2}{2!} + \frac{x^3}{3!} + \cdots$$

Hint: Keep in mind that $\frac{x^0}{0!} = 1$.

---

[4] Brook Taylor (1685–1731) was an English mathematician who is best known for the Taylor series and his contributions to the theory of finite differences.

28. Write a Python program that lets the user enter a value for x and then calculates and displays the sine of x using the Taylor series, shown next, with an accuracy of 0.00001.

$$sinx = x - \frac{x^3}{3!} + \frac{x^5}{5!} - \frac{x^7}{7!} + \cdots$$

Hint: Keep in mind that x is in radians and $\frac{x^1}{1!} = x$.

29. Write a Python program that lets the user enter a value for x and then calculates and displays the cosine of x using the Taylor series, shown next, with an accuracy of 0.00001.

$$cosx = 1 - \frac{x^2}{2!} + \frac{x^4}{4!} - \frac{x^6}{6!} + \cdots$$

Hint: Keep in mind that x is in radians and $\frac{x^0}{0!} = 1$.

30. Write a Python program that prompts the user to enter the daily temperatures (in degrees Fahrenheit) recorded at the same hour each day in August and then calculates and displays the average as well as the highest temperature.

Since $-459.67°$ (on the Fahrenheit scale) is the lowest temperature possible (it is called absolute zero), using a loop control structure, the program must also validate data input and display an error message when the user enters a value lower than absolute zero.

31. A scientist needs a software application to record the level of the sea based on values recorded at specific times (HH:MM), in order to extract some useful information. Write a Python program that lets the scientist enter the level of the sea, the hour, and the minutes, repeatedly until the value of 9999 (used as a sea level) is entered. Then, the program must display the highest and the lowest sea levels as well as the hour and the minutes at which these levels were recorded.

32. Suppose that the letter A corresponds to the number 1, the letter B corresponds to the number 2, and so on. Write a Python program that prompts the user to enter two integers and then displays all alphabet letters that exist between them. For example, if the user enters 3 and 6, the program must display C, D, E, F. Using a loop control structure, the program must also validate data input and display individual error messages when the user enters any negative, or any value greater than 26.

Hint: To make your Python program operate correctly, independent of which integer given is the lowest, you can swap their values (if necessary) so that they are always in the proper order.

33. Write a Python program that assigns a random secret integer between 1 and 100 to a variable and then prompts the user to guess the number. If the integer given is less than the secret one, a message *"Your guess is smaller than my secret number. Try again."* must be displayed. If the integer given is greater than the secret one, a message *"Your guess is bigger than my secret number. Try again."* must be displayed. This process must repeat until the user finally finds the secret number. Then, a message *"You found it!"* must be displayed, as well as the total number of the user's attempts.

34. Expand the previous exercise/game by making it operate for two players. The player that wins is the one that finds the random secret number in fewer attempts.

35. The size of a TV screen always refers to its diagonal measurement. For example, a 40-inch TV screen is 40 inches diagonally, from one corner on top to the other corner on bottom. The old TV screens had a width-to-height aspect ratio of 4:3, which means that for every 3 inches in TV screen height, there were 4 inches in TV screen width. Today, most TV screens have a width-to-height aspect ratio of 16:9, which means that for every 9 inches in TV screen height there are 16 inches in TV screen width. Using these aspect ratios and the Pythagorean Theorem, you can easily determine that:

▶ **for all 4:3 TVs**

Width = Diagonal × 0.8

Height = Diagonal × 0.6

▶ **for all 16:9 TVs**

Width = Diagonal × 0.87

Height = Diagonal × 0.49

Write a Python program that displays the following menu:

1. 4/3 TV Screen

2. 16/9 TV Screen

3. Exit

and prompts the user to enter a choice as well as the diagonal screen size in inches. Then, the Python program must display the width and the height of the TV screen. This process must continue repeatedly, until the user selects choice 3 (Exit) from the menu.

36. Write a Python program that prompts a teacher to enter the total number of students, their grades, and their gender (M for Male, F for Female), and then calculates and displays all of the following:

   a. the average value of those who got an "A" (90 - 100)

   b. the average value of those who got a "B" (80 - 89)

   c. the average value of boys who got an "A" (90 - 100)

   d. the total number of girls that got less than "B"

   e. the highest and lowest grade

   f. the average grade of the whole class

   Add all necessary checks to make the program satisfy the property of definiteness. Moreover, using a loop control structure, the program must validate data input and display an error message when the teacher enters any of the following:

   ▶ non-positive values for total number of students

   ▶ negatives, or values greater than 100 for student grades

   ▶ values other than M or F for gender

37. Write a Python program that calculates and displays the discount that a customer receives based on the amount of his or her order, according to the following table.

Amount	Discount
$0 < amount < $20	0%
$20 ≤ amount < $50	3%
$50 ≤ amount < $100	5%
$100 ≤ amount	10%

At the end of each discount calculation, the program must ask the user if he or she wishes to calculate the discount of another amount. If the answer is "yes", the program must repeat; it must end otherwise. Make your program accept the answer in all possible forms such as "yes", "YES", "Yes", or even "YeS".

Moreover, using a loop control structure the program must validate data input and display an error message when the user enters any non-positive value for amount.

38. The LAV Electricity Company charges subscribers for their electricity consumption according to the following table (monthly rates for domestic accounts).

Kilowatt-hours (kWh)	USD per kWh
$0 \leq kWh \leq 400$	$0.11
$401 \leq kWh \leq 1500$	$0.22
$1501 \leq kWh \leq 3500$	$0.25
$3501 \leq kWh$	$0.50

Write a Python program that prompts the user to enter the total number of kWh consumed by a subscriber and then calculates and displays the total amount to pay. This process must repeat until the value −1 for kWh is entered.

Moreover, using a loop control structure, the program must validate data input and display an error message when the user enters any negative value for kWh. An exception for the value −1 must be made.

Transmission services and distribution charges, as well as federal, state, and local taxes, add a total of 25% to each bill.

Please note that the rates are progressive.

Review in "Loop Control Structures"

Review Crossword Puzzle

1. Solve the following crossword puzzle.

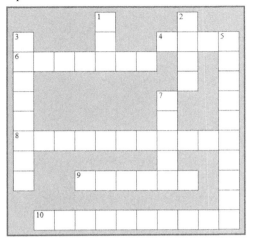

Across

4. This control structure allows the execution of a block of statements multiple times.
6. A loop that cannot stop iterating.
8. The "Ultimate" rule states that the variable that participates in a loop's Boolean expression must be _____ before entering the loop.
9. A loop within another loop.
10. In this loop structure, the number of iterations in not known before the loop starts iterating.

Down

1. In a _____–test loop structure, first the Boolean expression is evaluated, and afterward the statement or block of statements of the structure is executed.
2. The _____–test loop performs at least one iteration.
3. In this loop structure, the number of iterations is known before the loop starts iterating.
5. A word or sentence that reads the same both backward and forward.
7. Any integer greater than 1 that has no divisors other than 1 and itself.

Review Questions

Answer the following questions.

1. What is a loop control structure?
2. In a flowchart, how can you distinguish a decision control structure from a loop control structure?
3. Design the flowchart and write the Python statement (in general form) of a pre-test loop structure. Explain how this loop control structure operates.
4. Why is a pre-test loop structure named this way, and what is the fewest number of iterations it may perform?
5. If the statement or block of statements of a pre-test loop structure is executed N times, how many times is the Boolean expression of the structure evaluated?

6. Design the flowchart and write the corresponding Python statement (in general form) of a post-test loop structure. Explain how this loop control structure operates.

7. Why is a post-test loop structure named this way, and what is the fewest number of iterations it may perform?

8. If the statement or block of statements of a post-test loop structure is executed N times, how many times is the Boolean expression of the structure evaluated?

9. Design the flowchart and write the corresponding Python statement (in general form) of a mid-test loop structure. Explain how this loop control structure operates.

10. Design the flowchart and write the corresponding Python statement (in general form) of a for-loop. Explain how this loop control structure operates.

11. State the rules that apply to for-loops.

12. What are nested loops?

13. Write an example of a program with nested loop control structures and explain how they are executed.

14. State the rules that apply to nested loops.

15. Design a diagram that could help someone decide on the best loop control structure to choose.

16. Describe the "Ultimate" rule and give two examples, in general form, using a pre-test and a post-test loop structure.

17. Suppose that a Python program uses a loop control structure to search for a given word in an electronic dictionary. Why is it critical to break out of the loop when the given word is found?

18. Why is it critical to clean out your loops?

19. What is an infinite loop?

Section 6

Data Structures in Python

Chapter 30
One-Dimensional Lists and Dictionaries

30.1 Introduction

Variables are a good way to store values in memory but they have one limitation—they can hold only one value at a time. There are many cases, however, where a program needs to keep a large amount of data in memory, and variables are not the best choice.

For example, consider the following exercise.

Write a Python program that prompts the user to enter the names of five students. It then displays them in the exact reverse of the order in which they were given.

In the code fragment that follows

```python
for i in range(5):
    name = input("Enter a name: ")
```

when the loop finally finishes iterating, the variable name contains only that last name that was given. Unfortunately, all the previous four names have been lost! Using this code fragment, it is impossible to display them in the exact reverse of the order in which they were given.

One possible solution would be to use five individual variables, as follows.

```python
name1 = input("Enter a name: ")
name2 = input("Enter a name: ")
name3 = input("Enter a name: ")
name4 = input("Enter a name: ")
name5 = input("Enter a name: ")

print(name5)
print(name4)
print(name3)
print(name2)
print(name1)
```

Not a perfect solution, but it works! However, what if the wording of this exercise asked the user to enter 1,000 names instead of five? Think about it! Do you have the patience to write a similar Python program for each of those names? Of course not! Fortunately, there are *data structures*!

✎ *In computer science, a data structure is a collection of data organized so that you can perform operations on it in the most effective way.*

There are quite a few data structures available in Python, such as *lists, tuples, dictionaries, sets, frozensets,* and *strings*. Yes, you heard that right! Strings are data structures because a string is nothing more than a collection of alphanumeric characters!

Beyond strings (for which you have already learned enough), lists and dictionaries are the most commonly used data structures in Python. The following chapters will analyze both of them.

30.2 What is a List?

A *list* is a type of data structure that can hold multiple values under one common name. A list can be thought of as a collection of *elements* where each element is assigned a unique number known as an *index position*, or simply an *index*. Lists are *mutable* (changeable), which means that, once the list is created, the values of their elements can be changed, and new elements can be added to or removed from the list.

✎ *Lists in computer science resemble the matrices used in mathematics. A mathematical matrix is a collection of numbers or other mathematical objects, arranged in rows and columns.*

✎ *In many computer languages, such as Java, C++, and C# (to name a few), there are no lists. These languages support another kind of data structure that is called an "array". Lists, however, are more powerful than arrays.*

There are one-dimensional and multidimensional lists. A multidimensional list can be two-dimensional, three-dimensional, four-dimensional, and so on.

One-Dimensional Lists

The following example presents a one-dimensional list that holds the grades of six students. The name of the list is Grades. For your convenience, the corresponding index is written above each element. By default, in Python, index numbering always starts at zero.

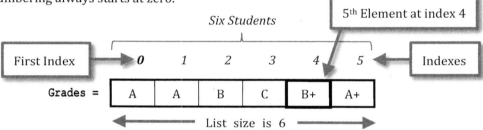

📟 *Since index numbering starts at zero, the index of the last element of a list is 1 less than the total number of elements in the list.*

You can think of a list as if it were six individual variables—Grades0, Grades1, Grades2, … Grades5—with each variable holding the grade of one student. The advantage of the list, however, is that it can hold multiple values under one common name.

Two-Dimensional Lists

In general, multidimensional lists are useful for working with multiple sets of data. For example, suppose you want to hold the daily high temperatures for California for the four weeks of April. One approach would be to use four one-dimensional lists, one for each week. Furthermore, each list would have seven elements, one for each day of the week, as follows.

Days

	0	1	2	3	4	5	6
Temperatures_week1 =	57	58	65	71	75	68	56

Temperatures_week2 =	64	71	74	63	61	64	57

Temperatures_week3 =	62	68	62	51	55	59	69

Temperatures_week4 =	73	60	67	54	59	62	64

However, this approach is a bit awkward because you would have to process each list separately. A better approach would be to use a two-dimensional list with four rows (one for each week) and seven columns (one for each day of the week), as follows.

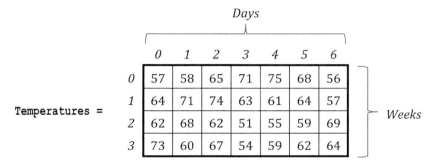

Three-Dimensional Lists

The next example shows a three-dimensional list that holds the daily high temperatures for California for the four weeks of April for the years 2013, 2014, and 2015.

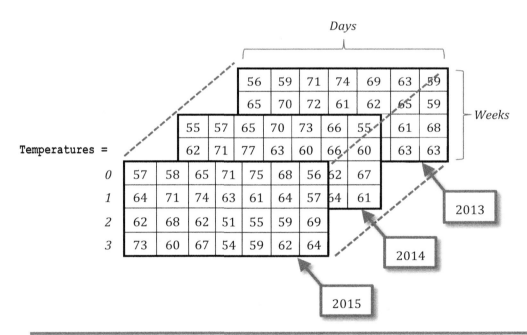

✎ *Note that four-dimensional, five-dimensional, or even one-hundred–dimensional lists can exist. However, experience shows that the maximum list dimension that you will need in your life as a programmer is probably two or three.*

Exercise 30.2-1   Designing a List

Design a list that can hold the ages of 8 people, and then add some typical values to the list.

Solution

This is an easy one. All you have to do is design a list with 8 elements (indexes 0 to 7). It can be a list with either one row or one column, as follows.

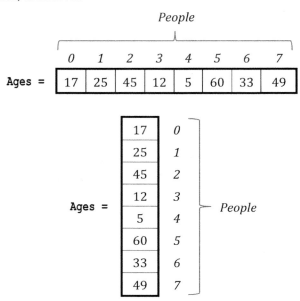

Keep in mind, however, that there are no lists with one row or one column in Python. These concepts may exist in mathematical matrices (or in your imagination!) but not in Python. The lists in Python are one-dimensional—end of story! If you want to visualize them having one row or one column, that is up to you.

Exercise 30.2-2   Designing Lists

Design the necessary lists to hold the names and the ages of seven people, and then add some typical values to the lists.

Solution

This exercise can be implemented with two lists. Let's design them with one column each.

	Names =		Ages =		
	John Thompson		17	0	
	Ava Brown		25	1	
	Ryan Miller		45	2	
	Alexander Lewis		33	4	⎱ People
	Samantha Clark		23	5	
	Andrew Scott		21	6	
	Chloe Parker		49	7	

Exercise 30.2-3   Designing Lists

Design the necessary lists to hold the names of ten people as well as the average weight (in pounds) of each person for January, February, and March. Then add some typical values to the lists.

Solution

In this exercise, you need a one-dimensional list for names, and a two-dimensional list for people's weights.

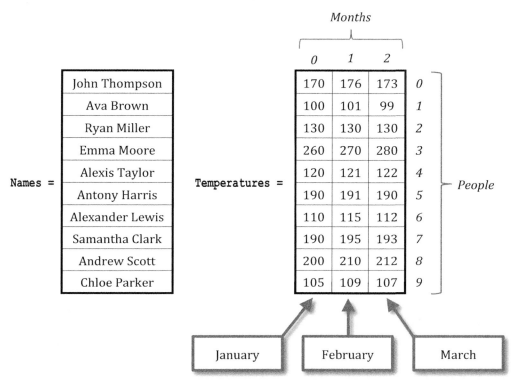

30.3   Creating One-Dimensional Lists in Python

Python has many ways to create a list and add elements (and values) to it. Depending on the given problem, it's up to you which one to use.

Let's try to create the following list using the most common approaches.

	0	1	2	3
ages =	12	25	9	11

First Approach

To create a list and directly assign values to its elements, you can use the next Python statement, given in general form.

```
list_name = [ value0, value1, value2, …, valueM ]
```

For this approach, you can create the list ages using the following statement:

```
ages = [12, 25, 9, 11]
```

In this approach, indexes are set automatically. The value 12 is assigned to the element at index position 0, value 25 is assigned to the element at index position 1, and so on. Index numbering always starts at zero by default.

Second Approach

You can create a list of *size* empty elements in Python using the following statement given in general form:

```
list_name = [None] * size
```

where *size* can be any positive integer value, or it can even be a variable that contains any positive integer value.

The next statement creates the list ages with 4 empty elements.

```
ages = [None] * 4
```

✎ *The statement* ages = [None] * 4 *reserves four locations in main memory (RAM).*

You can assign a value to a list element using the following statement, given in general form:

```
list_name[index] = value
```

where *index* is the index position of the element in the list.

The next code fragment creates the list ages (reserving four locations in main memory) and then assigns values to its elements.

```
ages = [None] * 4

ages[0] = 12
ages[1] = 25
ages[2] = 9
ages[3] = 11
```

✎ *The size of the list* ages *is 4.*

✎ *In paragraph 5.4 you learned about the rules that must be followed when assigning names to Python variables. Assigning names to lists follows exactly the same rules!*

Of course, instead of using constant values for *index*, you can also use variables or expressions, as follows.

```
ages = [None] * 4

k = 0

ages[k] = 12
ages[k + 1] = 25
ages[k + 2] = 9
ages[k + 3] = 11
```

Third Approach

In this approach, you can create a totally empty list (without elements) and then add elements (and values) to it using the append() method, as shown in the following Python statements, given in general form.

```
list_name = []

list_name.append(value0)
list_name.append(value1)
list_name.append(value2)
…
list_name.append(valueM)
```

Using this approach, you can create the list ages using the following code fragment:

```
ages = []
ages.append(12)
```

```
ages.append(25)
ages.append(9)
ages.append(11)
```

✎ *Note that in this approach as well,* index *numbering starts at zero by default.*

✎ *The statement* ages = [] *does not reserve any locations in main memory (RAM). It just states that the list* ages *is ready to accept new elements.*

30.4   How to Get Values from a One-Dimensional List

Getting values from a list is just a matter of pointing to a specific element. Each element of a list can be uniquely identified using an index. The following code fragment creates a list and displays "A+" (without the double quotes) on the screen.

```
grades = ["B+", "A+", "A", "C-"]
print(grades[1])
```

Of course, instead of using constant values for *index*, you can also use variables or expressions. The following example creates a list and displays "Aphrodite and Hera" (without the double quotes) on the screen.

```
gods = ["Zeus", "Ares", "Hera", "Aphrodite", "Hermes"]
k = 3
print(gods[k], "and", gods[k - 1])
```

A negative index accesses an element by starting to count from the end of the list. In the list grades, the position of each element (using negative indexes) is as follows.

	−4	−3	−2	−1
grades =	B+	A+	A	C−

The following example

```
grades = ["B+", "A+", "A", "C-"]
print(grades[-1] , "and", grades[-3])
```

displays C- and A+ on the screen.

If you wish to display all the elements of a list, you can do the following

```
grades = ["B+", "A+", "A", "C-"]

print(grades)         #It displays: ['B+', 'A+', 'A', 'C-']
```

🖳 *In Python, you can define a string using either single or double quotes.*

Just like in strings, you can get a subset of a list, called a "slice", as shown here.

```
grades = ["B+", "A+", "A", "C-"]

print(grades[1:3])        #It displays ["A+", "A"]
```

✎ *Slicing in Python is a mechanism to select a range of elements from a list (or from a sequence, in general).*

As you already know, the slicing mechanism can also have a third argument, called *step*, as shown here.

```
grades = ["B+", "A+", "A", "C-", "A-", "B-", "C", "B", "C+"]
print(grades[1:7:2])          #It displays: ['A+', 'C-', 'B-']
```

A negative *step* returns a list in reverse order

```python
gods = ["Ares", "Hera", "Aphrodite", "Hermes"]
print(gods[::-1])      #It displays: ('Hermes', 'Aphrodite', 'Hera', 'Ares')
```

Exercise 30.4-1   Creating the Trace Table

Create the trace table for the next code fragment.

```python
a = [None] * 4

a[3] = 9
x = 0
a[x] = a[3] + 4
a[x + 1] = a[x] * 3
x += 1
a[x + 2] = a[x - 1]
a[2] = a[1] + 5
a[3] = a[3] + 1
```

Solution

Don't forget that you can manipulate each element of a list as if it were a variable. Thus, when you create a trace table for a Python program that uses a list, you can have one column for each element as follows.

Step	Statement	Notes	x	a[0]	a[1]	a[2]	a[3]
1	a = [None] * 4	This creates list a with no values in it	?	?	?	?	?
2	a[3] = 9		?	?	?	?	**9**
3	x = 0		**0**	?	?	?	9
4	a[x] = a[3] + 4		0	**13**	?	?	9
5	a[x + 1] = a[x] * 3		0	13	**39**	?	9
6	x += 1		**1**	13	39	?	9
7	a[x + 2] = a[x - 1]		1	13	39	?	**13**
8	a[2] = a[1] + 5		1	13	39	**44**	13
9	a[3] = a[3] + 1		1	13	39	44	**14**

Exercise 30.4-2   Using a Non-Existing Index

Which properties of an algorithm are not satisfied by the following Python program?

```python
grades = ["B+", "A+", "A", "C-"]
print(grades[100])
```

Solution

Two properties are not satisfied by this Python program. The first one is obvious: there is no data input. The second one is the property of definiteness. You must never refer to a non-existing element of a list and, in this exercise, there is no element at index position 100.

30.5   How to Alter the Value of a List Element

To alter the value of an existing list element is a piece of cake. All you need to do is use the appropriate index and assign a new value to that element. The example that follows shows exactly this.

```python
#Create a list
indian_tribes = [ "Navajo", "Cherokee", "Sioux" ]
print(indian_tribes)     #It displays: ['Navajo', 'Cherokee', 'Sioux']

#Alter the value of an existing element
indian_tribes[1] = "Apache"
print(indian_tribes)     #It displays: ['Navajo', 'Apache', 'Sioux']
```

30.6   How to Iterate Through a One-Dimensional List

Now comes the interesting part. A program can iterate through the elements of a list using a loop structure (usually a for-loop). There are two approaches you can use to iterate through a one-dimensional list.

First Approach

This approach refers to each list element using its index. Following is a code fragment, written in general form

```python
for index in range(size):

    process structure_name[index]
```

in which *process* is any Python statement or block of statements that processes one element of the list *structure_name* at each iteration.

The following Python program displays all elements of the list gods, one at each iteration.

```python
gods = ["Zeus", "Ares", "Hera", "Aphrodite", "Hermes"]
for i in range(5):
    print(gods[i])
```

✎ *The name of the variable* i *is not binding. You can use any variable name you want, such as* index, ind, j, *and many more.*

✎ *Note that since the list* gods *contains five elements, the for-loop must iterate from 0 to 4 and not from 1 to 5. This is because the indexes of the four elements are 0, 1, 2, 3, and 4, correspondingly.*

Since lists are mutable, you can use a loop structure to alter all or some of its values. The following code fragment doubles the values of some elements of the list b.

```python
b = [80, 65, 60, 72, 30, 40]
for i in range(3):
    b[i] = b[i] * 2
```

Second Approach

This approach is very simple but not as flexible as the previous one. There are cases where it cannot be used, as you will see below. Following is a code fragment, written in general form

```python
for element in structure_name:

    process element
```

in which *process* is any Python statement or block of statements that processes one element of the list *structure_name* at each iteration.

The following Python program, displays all elements of the list grades, one at each iteration.

```
grades = ["B+", "A+", "A", "C-"]

for grade in grades:
    print(grade)
```

✎ *In the first iteration, the value of the first element is assigned to variable* grade. *In the second iteration, the value of the second element is assigned to variable* grade *and so on!*

The following Python program displays all elements of the list gods, one at each iteration, in reverse order.

```
gods = ["Hera", "Zeus", "Ares", "Aphrodite", "Hermes"]
for god in gods[::-1]:
    print(god)
```

Unfortunately, this approach cannot be used to alter the values of the elements of a list. For example, if you want to double the values of all elements of the list numbers, you can**not** do the following:

```
numbers = [5, 10, 3, 2]

for number in numbers:
    number *= 2
```

✎ number *is a simple variable where, at each iteration, each successive value of the list* numbers *is assigned to. However, the opposite never happens! The value of* number *is never assigned back to any element!*

✎ *If you want to alter the values of the elements of a list, you should use the first approach.*

Exercise 30.6-1   *Finding the Sum*

Write a Python program that creates a list with the following values

$$56, 12, 33, 8, 3, 2, 98$$

and then calculates and displays their sum.

Solution

You have learned two ways to iterate through the list elements. Let's use both ways and see the differences. You will find an extra third approach below, which is the Pythonic way to calculate the sum of the elements of a one-dimensional list.

First approach

The solution is as follows.

```
                          📁 file_30_6_1a
values = [56, 12, 33, 8, 3, 2, 98]

total = 0
for i in range(7):
    total += values[i]   #This is equivalent to total = total + values[i]

print(total)
```

Second approach

The solution is as follows.

```
📁 file_30_6_1b
```
```
values = [56, 12, 33, 8, 3, 2, 98]

total = 0
for value in values:
    total += value

print(total)
```

Third approach

This approach uses no loop structures. It just uses the fsum() function of the math module.

```
📁 file_30_6_1c
```
```
import math

values = [56, 12, 33, 8, 3, 2, 98]

total = math.fsum(values)

print(total)
```

✎ *If you don't remember anything about the* fsum() *function, refresh your memory by re-reading paragraph 11.2.*

30.7   How to Add User-Entered Values to a One-Dimensional List

There is nothing new here. Instead of reading a value from the keyboard and assigning that value to a variable, you can directly assign that value to a specific list element. The next code fragment prompts the user to enter the names of three people, and assigns them to the elements at index positions 0, 1, 2, and 3, of the list names.

```
names = [None] * 4     #Pre-reserve 4 locations in main memory (RAM)

names[0] = input("Enter name No 1: ")
names[1] = input("Enter name No 2: ")
names[2] = input("Enter name No 3: ")
names[3] = input("Enter name No 4: ")
```

Using a for-loop, this code fragment can equivalently be written as

```
ELEMENTS = 4

names = [None] * ELEMENTS   #Pre-reserve 4 locations in main memory (RAM)
for i in range(ELEMENTS):
    names[i] = input("Enter name No " + str(i + 1)  + ": ")
```

You can, of course, do the same, using the append() method instead, as shown in the code fragment that follows.

```
ELEMENTS = 4

names = []    #Create a totally empty list
```

```
for i in range(ELEMENTS):
    name = input("Enter name No " + str(i + 1)  + ": ")
    names.append(name)
```

📝 *When the* `append()` *method is used, elements are appended to a list (added at the end of the list).*

✎ *A very good tactic for dealing with list sizes is to use constants.*

Exercise 30.7-1   *Displaying Words in Reverse Order*

Write a Python program that lets the user enter 20 words. The program then displays them in the exact reverse of the order in which they were given.

Solution

Lists are perfect for problems like this one. The following is an appropriate solution.

```
                        🗀 file_30_7_1a
words = [None] * 20    #Pre-reserve 20 locations in main memory (RAM)
for i in range(20):
    words[i] = input()

for i in range(19, -1, -1):
    print(words[i])
```

📝 *Since index numbering starts at zero, the index of the last list element is 1 less than the total number of elements in the list.*

Keep in mind that in Python you can iterate in reverse order through the list elements using the slicing mechanism and a value of −1 for *step*. The following program creates a totally empty list and then uses the `append()` method to add elements to the list. Finally, the slicing mechanism is used to display them in the exact reverse of the order in which they were given.

```
                        🗀 file_30_7_1b
words = []    #Create a totally empty list
for i in range(20):
    words.append(input())

for word in words[::-1]:
    print(word)
```

✎ *Sometimes the wording of an exercise may say nothing about using a data structure. However, this doesn't mean that you can't use one. Use data structures (lists, tuples, dictionaries etc.) whenever you think they are necessary.*

✎ *A "tuple" is almost identical to a list. The main difference is that tuples are immutable (unchangeable).*

✎ *An "immutable" data structure is a structure in which the value of its elements cannot be changed once the data structure is created. Obviously, you cannot add new elements to an immutable data structure or remove existing elements from it.*

Exercise 30.7-2 Displaying Positive Numbers in Reverse Order

Write a Python program that lets the user enter 100 numbers and then displays only the positive ones in the exact reverse of the order in which they were given.

Solution

In this exercise, the program must accept all values from the user and store them in a list. However, within the for-loop that is responsible for displaying the list elements, a nested decision control structure must check for and display only the positive values. The solution is as follows.

```
                          📁 file_30_7_2
ELEMENTS = 100

values = [None] * ELEMENTS
for i in range(ELEMENTS):
    values[i] = float(input())

for value in values[::-1]:
    if value > 0:
        print(value)
```

📖 *Even though Python does not support constants as do other computer languages (such as C#, or C++), you can use a variable instead. However, it is advisable to use only uppercase letters. This helps you to visually distinguish those variables that are used as constants from the actual variables.*

Exercise 30.7-3 Finding the Average Value

Write a Python program that prompts the user to enter 20 numbers into a list. It then displays a message only when their average value is less than 10.

Solution

To find the average value of the given numbers the program must first find their sum and then divide that sum by 20. Once the average value is found, the program must check whether to display the corresponding message.

```
                          📁 file_30_7_3a
ELEMENTS = 20

values = [None] * ELEMENTS
for i in range(ELEMENTS):
    values[i] = float(input("Enter a value: "))

#Accumulate values in total
total = 0
for i in range(ELEMENTS):
    total += values[i]

average = total / ELEMENTS
```

```
if average < 10:
    print("Average value is less than 10")
```

If you are wondering whether or not this exercise could have been solved using just one for-loop, the answer is "yes". An alternative solution is presented next.

```
☐ file_30_7_3b
```

```
ELEMENTS = 20

total = 0

values = [None] * ELEMENTS
for i in range(ELEMENTS):
    values[i] = float(input("Enter a value: "))
    total += values[i]

average = total / ELEMENTS

if average < 10:
    print("Average value is less than 10")
```

But let's clarify something! Even though many processes can be performed inside just one for-loop, it is simpler to <u>carry out each individual process in a separate</u> for-loop. This is probably not so efficient but, since you are still a novice programmer, try to adopt this programming style just for now. Later, when you have the experience and become a Python guru, you will be able to "merge" many processes in just one for-loop!

Now, let's see a more Pythonic approach using the fsum() function.

```
☐ file_30_7_3c
```

```
import math
ELEMENTS = 20

values = []
for i in range(ELEMENTS):
    values.append(float(input("Enter a value: ")))

if math.fsum(values) / ELEMENTS < 10:
    print("Average value is less than 10")
```

Exercise 30.7-4   *Displaying Reals Only*

Write a Python program that prompts the user to enter 10 numeric values in a list. The program then displays the indexes of the elements that contain reals.

Solution

In Exercise 22.1-2 you learned how to check whether or not, a number is an integer. Accordingly, to check whether or not, a number is a real (float), you can use the Boolean expression

$$number \ != int(number)$$

The solution is as follows.

```
                            📄 file_30_7_4
ELEMENTS = 10

b = [None] * ELEMENTS
for i in range(ELEMENTS):
    b[i] = float(input("Enter a value for element " + str(i) + ": "))


for i in range(ELEMENTS):
    if b[i] != int(b[i]):
        print("A real found at index:", i)
```

Exercise 30.7-5   Displaying Elements with Odd-Numbered Indexes

Write a Python program that prompts the user to enter 8 numeric values in a list and then displays the elements with odd-numbered indexes (that is, indexes 1, 3, 5, and 7).

Solution

Following is one possible solution.

```
                            📄 file_30_7_5a
ELEMENTS = 8

values = [None] * ELEMENTS
for i in range(ELEMENTS):
    values[i] = float(input("Enter a value for element " + str(i) + ": "))


#Display the elements with odd-numbered indexes
for i in range(ELEMENTS):
    if i % 2 != 0:
        print(values[i])
```

However, you know that only the values in odd-numbered index positions must be displayed. Therefore, the for-loop that is responsible for displaying the elements of the list, instead of starting counting from 0 and using a *step* of +1, it can start counting from 1 and use a *step* of +2. This modification decreases the number of iterations by half. The modified Python program follows.

```
                            📄 file_30_7_5b
ELEMENTS = 8

values = [None] * ELEMENTS
for i in range(ELEMENTS):
    values[i] = float(input("Enter a value for element " + str(i) + ": "))


#Display the elements with odd-numbered indexes
for i in range(1, ELEMENTS, 2):              #Start from 1 and increment by 2
    print(values[i])
```

As already stated, in Python you can iterate through the list elements using the slicing mechanism. In the following program the slicing mechanism is used to display only the elements with odd-numbered indexes.

```
📁 file_30_7_5c
ELEMENTS = 8

values = [None] * ELEMENTS
for i in range(ELEMENTS):
    values[i] = float(input("Enter a value for element " + str(i) + ": "))


#Display the elements with odd-numbered indexes
for value in values[1::2]:       #Start from 1 and increment by 2
    print(value)
```

Exercise 30.7-6   *Displaying Even Numbers in Odd–Numbered Index Positions*

Write a Python program that lets the user enter 100 integers into a list and then displays any even values that are stored in odd–numbered index positions.

Solution

Following is one possible solution.

```
📁 file_30_7_6a
ELEMENTS = 100

values = [None] * ELEMENTS
for i in range(ELEMENTS):
    values[i] = int(input())

for i in range(1, ELEMENTS, 2):
    if values[i] % 2 == 0:
        print(values[i])
```

However, a more Pythonic way is to use the slicing mechanism as shown here.

```
📁 file_30_7_6b
ELEMENTS = 100

values = []
for i in range(ELEMENTS):
    values.append(int(input()))

for value in values[1::2]:
    if value % 2 == 0:
        print(value)
```

30.8   More about the Concatenation and Repetition Operators

In paragraph 7.5, you learned how to concatenate and how to repeat strings using the string operators (+) and (*) correspondingly. The same operators, as well as their corresponding assignment operators (+=) and (*=), can also be used in lists. To be more specific, the concatenation operator (+) and the concatenation assignment operator (+=) can be used to join two (or more) lists, whereas the repetition operator (*) and the repetition assignment operator (*=) can be used to repeat the same list multiple times. Let's see some examples.

The following code fragment creates list x, which, in the end, contains the values [1, 2, 3, 4, 5, 6].

```
a = [1, 2]
b = [3, 4]
x = a + b    #List x contains the values [1, 2, 3, 4]
x += [5, 6]  #List x contains the values [1, 2, 3, 4, 5, 6]
```

You have already used the repetition operator (*) in paragraph 30.3 to create a list with empty elements using the following statement given in general form:

```
list_name = [None] * size
```

What this statement actually did was to iterate a list of one empty element (this is the [None] list) *size* times. For example, the following code fragment iterates the list [None] 3 times.

```
x = [None] * 3    #List x contains the values [None, None, None]
```

The following code fragment creates list x, which, in the end, contains the values [5, 6, 5, 6, 5, 6, 5, 6, 5, 6, 5, 6].

```
x = [5, 6] * 2    #List x contains the values [5, 6, 5, 6]
x *= 3    #List x contains the values [5, 6, 5, 6, 5, 6, 5, 6, 5, 6, 5, 6]
```

30.9 What is a Dictionary?

The main difference between a *dictionary* and a list is that the dictionary elements can be uniquely identified using a key and not necessarily an integer value. Each key of a dictionary is associated (or mapped, if you prefer) to an element. The keys of a dictionary can be of type string, integer, float, or tuple.

The following example presents a dictionary that holds the names of a family. The name of the dictionary is family and the corresponding keys are written above each element.

	father	mother	son	daughter
family =	John	Maria	George	Helen

Keys

✎ *The keys of dictionary elements must be unique within the dictionary. This means that in the dictionary* family, *for example, you cannot have two keys named* father.

✎ *The values of dictionary elements can be of any type.*

30.10 Creating Dictionaries in Python

Let's try to create the following dictionary using the most common approaches.

	first_name	last_name	age	class
pupil =	Ann	Fox	8	2nd

First Approach

To create a dictionary and directly assign values to its elements, you can use the next Python statement, given in general form.

```
dict_name = {key0: value0, key1: value1, key2: value2, …, keyM: valueM }
```

Using this approach, the dictionary pupil can be created using the following statement:

```
pupil = {"first_name": "Ann", "last_name": "Fox", "age": 8, "class": "2nd"}
```

✎ *Each key is separated from its value by a colon (:), the elements are separated by commas, and everything is enclosed within curly brackets { }.*

Second Approach

In this approach, you can create a totally empty dictionary using the following statement, given in general form

```
dict_name = {}
```

and then add elements (key-value pairs), as shown in the following Python statements, given in general form.

```
dict_name[key0] = value0
dict_name[key1] = value1
dict_name[key2] = value2
...
dict_name[keyM] = valueM
```

Using this approach, the dictionary pupil can be created using the following code fragment:

```
pupil = {}

pupil["first_name"] = "Ann"
pupil["last_name"] = "Fox"
pupil["age"] = 8
pupil["class"] = "2nd"
```

30.11 How to Get a Value from a Dictionary

To get the value of a specific dictionary element, you must point to that element using its corresponding key. The following code fragment creates a dictionary, and then displays "Ares is the God of War", without the double quotes, on the screen.

```
olympians = {"Zeus": "King of the Gods",
             "Hera": "Goddess of Marriage",
             "Ares": "God of War",
             "Poseidon": "God of the Sea",
             "Demeter": "Goddess of the Harvest",
             "Artemis": "Goddess of the Hunt",
             "Apollo": "God of Music and Medicine",
             "Aphrodite": "Goddess of Love and Beauty",
             "Hermes": "Messenger of the Gods",
             "Athena": "Goddess of Wisdom",
             "Hephaistos": "God of Fire and the Forge",
             "Dionysus": "God of the Wine"
             }

print("Ares is the", olympians["Ares"])
```

✎ *Only keys can be used to access an element. This means that* olympians["Ares"] *correctly returns "God of War" but* olympians["God of War"] *cannot return "Ares".*

Exercise 30.11-1   Using a Non-Existing Key in Dictionaries

What is wrong in the following Python program?

```
family = { "Father": "John", "Mother": "Maria", "Son": "George"}
print(family["daughter"])
```

Solution

Similar to lists, you must never refer to a non-existing dictionary element. In this exercise, there is no key "daughter", therefore the second statement will throw an error!

30.12 How to Alter the Value of a Dictionary Element

To alter the value of an existing dictionary element you need to use the appropriate key and assign a new value to that element. The example that follows shows exactly this.

```python
#Create a dictionary
tribes = {"Indian": "Navajo", "African": "Zulu"}
print(tribes) #It displays: {'Indian': 'Navajo', 'African': 'Zulu'}


#Alter the value of an existing element
tribes["Indian"] = "Apache"
print(tribes) #It displays: {'Indian': 'Apache', 'African': 'Zulu'}
```

Exercise 30.12-1   Assigning a Value to a Non-Existing Key

Is there anything wrong in the following code fragment?

```python
indian_tribes = {0: "Navajo", 1: "Cherokee", 2: "Sioux"}
indian_tribes[3] = "Apache"
```

Solution

No, this time there is absolutely nothing wrong in this code fragment. At first glance, you might have thought that the second statement tries to alter the value of a non-existing key and it will throw an error. This is **not** true for Python's dictionaries, though. Since indian_tribes is a dictionary and key "3" does not exist, the second statement **adds** a brand new fourth element to the dictionary!

> 🗂 *The keys of a dictionary can be of type string, integer, float, or tuple.*

Keep in mind though, if indian_tribes were actually a list, the second statement would certainly throw an error. Take a look at the following code fragment

```python
indian_tribes_list = ["Navajo", "Cherokee", "Sioux"]
indian_tribes_list[3] = "Apache"
```

In this example, since indian_tribes is a list and index 3 does not exist, the second statement tries to **alter** the value of a non-existing element and obviously throws an error!

30.13 How to Iterate Through a Dictionary

To iterate through the elements of a dictionary you can use a for-loop. There are two approaches actually. Let's study them both!

First Approach

Following is a code fragment, written in general form

```python
for key in structure_name:

    process structure_name[key]
```

in which *process* is any Python statement or block of statements that processes one element of the dictionary *structure_name* at each iteration.

The following Python program displays the letters A, B, C, and D, and their corresponding Morse[1] code.

```python
morse_code = {"A": ".-", "B": "-...", "C": "-.-.", "D": "-.."}


for letter in morse_code:
    print(letter, morse_code[letter])
```

The next example gives a bonus of $2000 to each employee of a computer software company!

```python
salaries = { "Project Manager": 83000,
             "Software Engineer": 81000,
             "Network Engineer": 64000,
             "Systems Administrator": 61000,
             "Software Developer": 70000
           }


for title in salaries:
    salaries[title] += 2000
```

Second Approach

Following is a code fragment, written in general form

```python
for key, value in structure_name.items():
    process key, value
```

in which *process* is any Python statement or block of statements that processes one element of the dictionary *structure_name* at each iteration.

The following Python program displays all elements of the list grades, one at each iteration.

```python
grades = {"John": "B+", "George": "A+", "Maria": "A", "Helen": "A-"}


for name, grade in grades.items():
    print(name, "got", grade)
```

Unfortunately, this approach cannot be used to alter the values of the elements of a dictionary. For example, if you want to double the values of all elements of the dictionary salaries, you can**not** do the following:

```python
salaries = { "Project Manager": 83000,
             "Software Engineer": 81000,
             "Network Engineer": 64000,
             "Systems Administrator": 61000,
             "Software Developer": 70000
           }


for title, salary in salaries.items():
    salary += 2000
```

✎ salary *is a simple variable that, at each iteration, each successive value of the dictionary* salaries *is assigned to. However, the opposite never happens! The value of* salary *is never assigned back to any element!*

---

[1] Samuel Finley Breese Morse (1791–1872) was an American painter and inventor. Morse contributed to the invention of a single-wire telegraph system and he was a co-developer of the Morse code.

📟 *If you want to alter the values of the elements of a dictionary, you should use the first approach.*

30.14 More about the Membership Operators

In paragraph 15.5, you learned about Python's membership operators in and not in. You can, as well, use the same operators to evaluate whether or not an operand exists in a specified data structure. Let's see some examples.

The following example displays "It exists!"

```
x = [1, 2, 3, 4, 5, 6]
if 3 in x:
    print("It exists!")
```

The following example looks for "George" in list y.

```
y = ["John", "Maria", "Anna", "George", "Tes"]
if "George" in y:
    print("I found George!!!!")
```

✎ *Note that the in operator checks whether an operand exists in a data structure. It cannot find the index position where the operand is found!*

The following example prompts the user to enter a name and then checks whether it does **not** exist in the list y.

```
y = ["John", "Maria", "Anna", "George", "Tes"]
name = input("Enter a name to search: ")
if name not in y:
    print(name, "not found!!!!")
```

The following example checks whether key "Son" exists in dictionary family.

```
family = { "Father": "John", "Mother": "Maria", "Son": "George"}

if "Son" in family:
    print("Key 'Son' found!")
```

30.15 Review Questions: True/False

Choose **true** or **false** for each of the following statements.

1. Lists are structures that can hold multiple values.
2. List elements are located in main memory (RAM).
3. There can be only one-dimensional and two-dimensional lists.
4. There cannot be four-dimensional lists.
5. A list is called "multidimensional" because it can hold values of different types.
6. Each list element has a unique index.
7. There can be two identical keys within a dictionary.
8. In lists, index numbering always starts at zero by default.
9. The index of the last list element is equal to the total number of its elements.
10. A two-hundred–dimensional list can exist.
11. The next statement contains a syntax error.
    ```
    student names = [None] * 10
    ```

12. In a Python program, two lists cannot have the same name.

13. The next statement is syntactically correct.

```
student = {"first_name": "Ann" - "last_name": "Fox" - "age": 8}
```

14. In a Python program, two lists cannot have the same number of elements.

15. You cannot use a variable as an index in a list.

16. You can use a mathematical expression as an index in a list.

17. You cannot use a variable as a key in a dictionary.

18. The following code fragment throws no errors.

```
a = "a"
fruits = {"o": "Orange", "a": "Apple", "w": "Watermelon"}
print(fruits[a])
```

19. If you use a variable as an index in a list, this variable must contain an integer value.

20. In order to calculate the sum of 20 numeric values given by a user, you must use a list.

21. You can let the user enter a value into list b using the statement b[k] = input()

22. The following statement creates a one-dimensional list of two empty elements.

```
names = [None] * 3
```

23. The following code fragment assigns the value 10 to the element at index 7.

```
values[5] = 7
values[values[5]] = 10
```

24. The following code fragment assigns the value "Sally" without the double quotes to the element at index 3.

```
names = [None] * 3
names[2] = "John"
names[1] = "George"
names[0] = "Sally"
```

25. The following statement assigns the value "Sally" without the double quotes to the element at index 2.

```
names = ["John", "George", "Sally"]
```

26. The following code fragment displays "Sally", without the double quotes, on the screen.

```
names = [None] * 3
k = 0
names[k] = "John"
k += 1
names[k] = "George"
k += 1
names[k] = "Sally"
k -= 1
print(names[k])
```

27. The following code fragment is syntactically correct.

```
names = [None] * 3
names[0] = "John"
names[1] = "George"
names[2] = "Sally"
```

```
print(names[])
```

28. The following code fragment displays "Maria", without the double quotes, on the screen.
```
names = ["John", "George", "Sally", "Maria"]
print(names[int(math.pi)])
```

29. The following code fragment satisfies the property of definiteness.
```
grades = ["B+", "A+", "A"]
print(grades[3])
```

30. The following code fragment satisfies the property of definiteness.
```
v = [1, 3, 2, 9]
print(v[v[v[0]]])
```

31. The following code fragment displays the value of 1 on the screen.
```
v = [1, 3, 2, 0]
print(v[v[v[v[0]]]])
```

32. The following code fragment displays all the elements of the list names.
```
names = ["John", "George", "Sally", "Maria"]
for i in range(1, 5):
    print(names[i])
```

33. The following code fragment satisfies the property of definiteness.
```
names = ["John", "George", "Sally", "Maria"]
for i in range(2, 5):
    print(names[i])
```

34. The following code fragment lets the user enter 100 values to list b.
```
for i in range(100):
    b[i] = input()
```

35. If list b contains 30 elements, the following code fragment doubles the values of all of its elements.
```
for i in range(29, -1, -1):
    b[i] = b[i] * 2
```

36. It is possible to use a for-loop to double the values of some of the elements of a list.

37. If list b contains 30 elements, the following code fragment displays all of them.
```
for element in b[0:29]:
    print(element)
```

38. If b is a dictionary, the following code fragment displays all of its elements.
```
for key, element in b:
    print(element)
```

39. The following code fragment throws an error.
```
fruits = {"O": "Orange",
          "A": "Apple",
          "W": "Watermelon"
         }
print(fruits["Orange"])
```

30.16 Review Questions: Multiple Choice

Select the correct answer for each of the following statements.

1. The following statement
    ```
    last names = [None] * 5
    ```
    a. contains a logic error.
    b. contains a syntax error.
    c. contains two syntax errors.
    d. contains three syntax errors.

2. The following code fragment
    ```
    x = 5
    names[x / 2] = 10
    ```
    a. does not satisfy the property of definiteness.
    b. does not satisfy the property of finiteness.
    c. does not satisfy the property of effectiveness.
    d. none of the above

3. If variable x contains the value 4, the following statement
    ```
    names[x + 1] = 5
    ```
    a. assigns the value 4 to the element at index 5.
    b. assigns the value 5 to the element at index 4.
    c. assigns the value 5 to the element at index 5.
    d. none of the above

4. The following statement
    ```
    names = [5, 6, 9, 1, 1, 1]
    ```
    a. assigns the value 5 to the element at index 1.
    b. assigns the value 5 to the element at index 0.
    c. does not satisfy the property of definiteness.
    d. none of the above

5. The following code fragment
    ```
    values[0] = 1
    values[values[0]] = 2
    values[values[1]] = 3
    values[values[2]] = 4
    ```
    a. assigns the value 4 to the element at index 3.
    b. assigns the value 3 to the element at index 2.
    c. assigns the value 2 to the element at index 1.
    d. all of the above
    e. none of the above

6. If list values contains numeric values, the following statement
    ```
    print(values[values[1] - values[1 % 2]] - values[int(1/2)])
    ```
    a. does not satisfy the property of definiteness.
    b. always displays 0.

    c.   always displays 1.

    d.   none of the above

7.   You can iterate through a one-dimensional list with a for-loop that uses

    a.   variable i as a counter.

    b.   variable j as a counter.

    c.   variable k as a counter.

    d.   any variable as a counter.

8.   The following code fragment

```
names = ["George", "John", "Maria", "Sally"]
for i in range(3, 0, -1):
    print(names[i])
```

    a.   displays all names in ascending order.

    b.   displays some names in ascending order.

    c.   displays all names in descending order.

    d.   displays some names in descending order.

    e.   none of the above

9.   The following code fragment

```
fruits = ["apple", "orange", "onion", "watermelon"]
print(fruits[1])
```

    a.   displays "orange"

    b.   displays apple

    c.   displays orange

    d.   throws an error because onion is not a fruit!

    e.   none of the above

10. If list b contains 30 elements, the following code fragment

```
for i in range(29, 0, -1):
    b[i] = b[i] * 2
```

    a.   doubles the values of some of its elements.

    b.   doubles the values of all of its elements.

    c.   none of the above

11. The following code fragment

```
struct = {"first_name": "George", "last_name": "Miles", "age": 28}
for a, b in struct.items():
    print(b)
```

    a.   displays all the keys of the dictionary elements.

    b.   displays all the values of the dictionary elements.

    c.   displays all the key-value pairs of the dictionary elements.

    d.   none of the above

12. The following code fragment

```
struct = {"first_name": "George", "last_name": "Miles", "age": 28}
for x in struct:
```

```
print(x)
```

a. displays all the keys of the dictionary elements.

b. displays all the values of the dictionary elements.

c. displays all the key-value pairs of the dictionary elements.

d. none of the above

13. The following code fragment

```
indian_tribes = {0: "Navajo", 1: "Cherokee", 2: "Sioux", 3: "Apache"}

for i in range(4):
    print(indian_tribes[i])
```

a. displays all the keys of the dictionary elements.

b. displays all the values of the dictionary elements.

c. displays all the key-value pairs of the dictionary elements.

d. none of the above

14. The following code fragment

```
tribes = {"tribeA": "Navajo", "tribeB": "Cherokee", "tribeC": "Sioux"}
for x in tribes:
    tribes[x] = tribes[x].upper()
```

a. converts all the keys of the dictionary elements to uppercase.

b. converts all the values of the dictionary elements to uppercase.

c. convert all the key-value pairs of the dictionary elements to uppercase.

d. none of the above

30.17 Review Exercises

Complete the following exercises.

1. Design a data structure to hold the weights (in pounds) of five people, and then add some typical values to the structure.

2. Design the necessary data structures to hold the names and the weights (in pounds) of seven people, and then add some typical values to the structure.

3. Design the necessary data structures to hold the names of five lakes as well as the average area (in square miles) of each lake in June, July, and August. Then add some typical values to the structures.

4. Design a data structure to hold the three dimensions (width, height, and depth in inches) of 10 boxes. Then add some typical values to the structure.

5. Design the necessary data structures to hold the names of eight lakes as well as the average area (in square miles) and maximum depth (in feet) of each lake. Then add some typical values to the structures.

6. Design the necessary data structures to hold the names of four lakes as well as their average areas (in square miles) for the first week of June, the first week of July, and the first week of August.

7. Create the trace table for the following code fragment.

```
a = [None] * 3
a[2] = 1
x = 0
```

```
a[x + a[2]] = 4
a[x] = a[x + 1] * 4
```

8. Create the trace table for the following code fragment.

```
a = [None] * 5
a[1] = 5
x = 0
a[x] = 4
a[a[0]] = a[x + 1] % 3
a[a[0] / 2] = 10
x += 2
a[x + 1] = a[x] + 9
```

9. Create the trace table for the following code fragment for three different executions.

   The input values for the three executions are: (i) 3, (ii) 4, and (iii) 1.

```
a = [None] * 4
a[1] = int(input())

x = 0
a[x] = 3
a[a[0]] = a[x + 1] % 2
a[a[0] % 2] = 10
x += 1
a[x + 1] = a[x] + 9
```

10. Create the trace table for the following code fragment for three different executions.

    The input values for the three executions are: (i) 100, (ii) 108, and (iii) 1.

```
a = [None] * 4
a[1] = int(input())
x = 0
a[x] = 3
a[a[0]] = a[x + 1] % 10
if a[3] > 5:
    a[a[0] % 2] = 9
    x += 1
    a[x + 1] = a[x] + 9
else:
    a[2] = 3
```

11. Fill in the gaps in the following trace table. In steps 6 and 7, fill in the name of a variable; for all other cases, fill in constant values, arithmetic, or comparison operators.

Step	Statement	x	y	a[0]	a[1]	a[2]
1	a = [None] * 3	?	?	?	?	?
2	x = ...	4	?	?	?	?
3	y = x -	4	3	?	?	?

4, 5	`if x ...... y:`
	    `a[0] = ......`
	`else`
	    `a[0] = y`
		4	3	**1**	?	?

6	`a[1] = ...... + 3`	4	3	1	**7**	?
7	`y = ...... - 1`	4	**2**	1	7	?
8	`a[y] = (x + 5) ...... 2`	4	2	1	7	**1**

12. Create the trace table for the following code fragment.

```python
a = [17, 12, 45, 12, 12, 49]

for i in range(6):
    if a[i] == 12:
        a[i] -= 1
    else:
        a[i] += 1
```

13. Create the trace table for the following code fragment.

```python
a = [10, 15, 12, 23, 22, 19]

for i in range(1, 5):
    a[i] = a[i + 1] + a[i - 1]
```

14. Try, without using a trace table, to determine the values that are displayed when the following code fragment is executed.

```python
tribes = {"Indian-1": "Navajo", "Indian-2": "Cherokee",
          "Indian-3" : "Sioux", "African-1": "Zulu",
          "African-2": "Maasai", "African-3": "Yoruba"}

for x, y in tribes.items():
    if x[:6] == "Indian":
        print(y)
```

15. Write a Python program that lets the user enter 100 numbers in a list and then displays these values raised to the power of three.

16. Write a Python program that lets the user enter 80 numbers in a list. Then, the program must raise the list values to the power of two, and finally display them in the exact reverse of the order in which they were given.

17. Write a Python program that lets the user enter 90 integers in a list and then displays those that are exactly divisible by 5 in the exact reverse of the order in which they were given.

18. Write a Python program that lets the user enter 50 integers in a list and then displays those that are even or greater than 10.

19. Write a Python program that lets the user enter 30 numbers in a list and then calculates and displays the sum of those that are positive.

20. Write a Python program that lets the user enter 50 integers in a list and then calculates and displays the sum of those that have two digits.

Hint: All two-digit integers are between 10 and 99.

21. Write a Python program that lets the user enter 40 numbers in a list and then calculates and displays the sum of the positive numbers and the sum of the negative ones.

22. Write a Python program that lets the user enter 20 numbers in a list and then calculates and displays their average value.

23. Write a Python program that prompts the user to enter 50 integer values in a list. It then displays the indexes of the elements that contain values lower than 20.

24. Write a Python program that prompts the user to enter 60 numeric values in a list. It then displays the elements with even-numbered indexes (that is, indexes 0, 2, 4, 6, and so on).

25. Write a Python program that prompts the user to enter 20 numeric values in a list. It then calculates and displays the sum of the elements that have even indexes.

26. Write code fragment in Python that creates the following list of 100 elements.

$$a = \boxed{\begin{array}{c|c|c|c|c} 1 & 2 & 3 & \ldots & 100 \end{array}}$$

27. Write code fragment in Python that creates the following list of 100 elements.

$$a = \boxed{\begin{array}{c|c|c|c|c} 2 & 4 & 6 & \ldots & 200 \end{array}}$$

28. Write a Python program that prompts the user to enter an integer N and then creates and displays the following list of N elements. Assume that the user enters an integer greater than 1.

$$a = \boxed{\begin{array}{c|c|c|c|c} 1 & 4 & 9 & \ldots & N^2 \end{array}}$$

29. Write a Python program that prompts the user to enter 10 numeric values in a list and then displays the indexes of the elements that contain integers.

30. Write a Python program that prompts the user to enter 50 numeric values in a list and then counts and displays the total number of negative elements.

31. Write a Python program that prompts the user to enter 50 words in a list and then displays those that contain at least 10 characters.

    Hint: Use the `len()` function.

32. Write a Python program that lets the user enter 30 words in a list. It then displays those words that have less than 5 characters, then those that have less than 10 characters, and finally those that have less than 20 characters.

    Hint: Try to display the words using two for-loops nested one within the other.

33. Write a Python program that prompts the user to enter 40 words in a list and then displays those that contain the letter "w" at least twice.

Chapter 31
Two-Dimensional Lists

31.1 Creating Two-Dimensional Lists in Python

A list that can hold the grades of four lessons for three students is as follows.

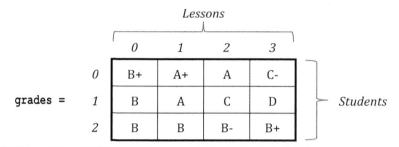

> ✎ *A two-dimensional list has rows and columns. In this particular example, list* grades *has 3 rows and 4 columns.*

Actually, Python supports only one-dimensional lists, but there is a trick that you can use to overcome this problem and create multidimensional lists. You can create a list of lists! Just imagine the list grades as a one-column list with three elements, each of which contains a whole new list of four elements, as follows.

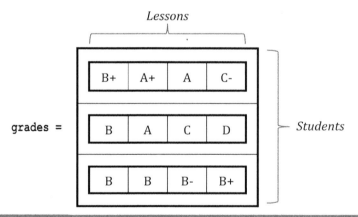

> *Notice! In Python, a two-dimensional list is a list of lists, a three-dimensional list is a list of lists of lists, and so on.*

As in one-dimensional lists, there are four approaches to creating and adding elements (and values) to a two-dimensional list. Let's try to create the list grades using each of these approaches.

First Approach

You can create a two-dimensional list in Python using the following statement, given in general form,

```
list_name = [None] * number_of_rows
```

where *number_of_rows* can be any positive integer and then you can assign a whole new list to one of its elements using the following statement, given in general form

```
list_name[index] = [value0, value1, value2, …, valueM]
```

where *index* is the index position of the element in the list.

The following code fragment creates the list grades and assigns three lists (and values) to its elements.

```
grades = [None] * 3
grades[0] = ["B+", "A+", "A", "C-"]
grades[1] = ["B", "A", "C", "D"]
grades[2] = ["B", "B", "B-", "B+"]
```

Second Approach

You can create a totally empty list and add new lists to it without using *index*, as shown in the following code fragment, given in general form.

```
list_name = []
list_name.append([value0-0, value0-1, value0-2, …, value0-M])
list_name.append([value1-0, value1-1, value1-2, …, value1-M])
list_name.append([value2-0, value2-1, value2-2, …, value2-M])

…

list_name.append([valueN-0, valueN-1, valueN-2, …, valueN-M])
```

The next code fragment creates the list grades and adds three lists (and values) to it.

```
grades = []
grades.append(["B+", "A+", "A", "C-"])
grades.append(["B", "A", "C", "D"])
grades.append(["B", "B", "B-", "B+"])
```

✎ *Note that in this approach,* index *numbering starts at zero by default.*

Third Approach

You can create a list and directly add values to it, as shown in the following Python statement, given in general form.

```
list_name = [ [value0-0, value0-1, value0-2, …, value0-M],
              [value1-0, value1-1, value1-2, …, value1-M],
              [value2-0, value2-1, value2-2, …, value2-M],

              …

              [valueN-0, valueN-1, valueN-2, …, valueN-M]
            ]
```

Thus, the list grades can be created using the following statement.

```
grades = [ ["B+", "A+", "A", "C-"],
           ["B", "A", "C", "D"],
           ["B", "B", "B-", "B+"]
         ]
```

which can also be written as

```
grades = [["B+", "A+", "A", "C-"], ["B", "A", "C", "D"], ["B", "B", "B-", "B+"]]
```

Fourth Approach

Last but not least, you can create a two-dimensional list in Python using the following statement, given in general form:

```
list_name = [ [None] * number_of_columns for i in range(number_of_rows) ]
```

where *number_of_rows* and *number_of_columns* can be any positive integer.

Then you can assign a value to a list element using the following statement, given in general form:

```
list_name[row_index][column_index] = value
```

where *row_index* and *column_index* are the row index and the column index positions, respectively, of the element in the list.

The following code fragment creates the list grades and assigns values to its elements.

```
grades = [ [None] * 4 for i in range(3) ]
grades[0][0] = "B+"
grades[0][1] = "A+"
grades[0][2] = "A"
grades[0][3] = "C-"
grades[1][0] = "B"
grades[1][1] = "A"
grades[1][2] = "C"
grades[1][3] = "D"
grades[2][0] = "B"
grades[2][1] = "B"
grades[2][2] = "B-"
grades[2][3] = "B+"
```

31.2 How to Get Values from Two-Dimensional Lists

A two-dimensional list consists of rows and columns. The following example shows a two-dimensional list with three rows and four columns.

	Column 0	Column 1	Column 2	Column 3
Row 0				
Row 1				
Row 2				

Each element of a two-dimensional list can be uniquely identified using a pair of indexes: a row index, and a column index, as shown next.

```
list_name[row_index][column_index]
```

The following Python program creates the two-dimensional list grades having three rows and four columns, and then displays some of its elements.

```
grades = [ ["B+", "A+", "A", "C-"],
           ["B", "A", "C", "D"],
           ["B", "B", "B-", "B+"]
         ]

print(grades[1][2])        #It displays: C
print(grades[2][2])        #It displays: B-
print(grades[0][0])        #It displays: B+
```

Exercise 31.2-1   Creating the Trace Table

Create the trace table for the next code fragment.

```
a = [ [0, 0],
      [0, 0],
      [0, 0]
    ]

a[1][0] = 9
a[0][1] = 1
a[0][0] = a[0][1] + 6
x = 2
a[x][1] = a[0][0] + 4
a[x - 1][1] = a[0][1] * 3
a[x][0] = a[x - 1][1] - 3
```

Solution

This code fragment uses a 3 × 2 list, that is, a list that has 3 rows and 2 columns. The trace table is as follows.

Step	Statement	Notes	x	a	
1	a = [[0, 0], [0, 0], [0, 0]]	This creates list a with zero values in it.	?	0 0 0	0 0 0
2	a[1][0] = 9		?	0 9 0	0 0 0
3	a[0][1] = 1		?	0 9 0	1 0 0
4	a[0][0] = a[0][1] + 6		?	7 9 0	1 0 0
5	x = 2		2	7 9 0	1 0 0
6	a[x][1] = a[0][0] + 4		2	7 9 0	1 0 11

7	`a[x - 1][1] = a[0][1] * 3`		2	

	7	1
	9	3
	0	11

8	`a[x][0] = a[x - 1][1] - 3`		2	

	7	1
	9	3
	0	11

31.3 How to Iterate Through a Two-Dimensional List

Since a two-dimensional list consists of rows and columns, a program can iterate either through rows or through columns.

Iterating through rows

Iterating through rows means that row 0 is processed first, row 1 is process next, row 2 afterwards, and so on. Next there is an example of a 3 × 4 list. The arrows show the "path" that is followed when iteration through rows is performed or in other words, they show the order in which the elements are processed.

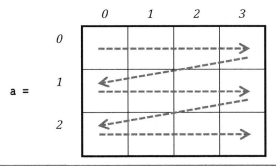

📖 *A 3 × 4 list is a two-dimensional list that has 3 rows and 4 columns. In the notation Y × X, the first number (Y) always represents the total number of rows and the second number (X) always represents the total number of columns.*

When iterating through rows, the elements of the list are processed as follows:

▶ the elements of row 0 are processed in the following order

`a[0][0]` → `a[0][1]` → `a[0][2]` → `a[0][3]`

▶ the elements of row 1 are processed in the following order

`a[1][0]` → `a[1][1]` → `a[1][2]` → `a[1][3]`

▶ the elements of row 2 are processed in the following order

`a[2][0]` → `a[2][1]` → `a[2][2]` → `a[2][3]`

Using Python statements, let's try to process all elements of a 3 × 4 list (3 rows × 4 columns) iterating through rows.

```
i = 0                  #Variable i refers to Row 0.
for j in range(4):     #This loop control structure processes all elements of Row 0

    process a[i][j]
```

```
i = 1                    #Variable i refers to Row 1.
for j in range(4):       #This loop control structure processes all elements of Row 1

    process a[i][j]


i = 2                    #Variable i refers to Row 2.
for j in range(4):       #This loop control structure processes all elements of Row 2

    process a[i][j]
```

Of course, the same results can be achieved using a nested loop control structure as shown next.

```
for i in range(3):
    for j in range(4):

        process a[i][j]
```

Let's see some examples. The following code fragment lets the user enter 10 × 10 = 100 values to list b.

```
for i in range(10):
    for j in range(10):
        b[i][j] = input()
```

The following code fragment decreases all values of list b by one.

```
for i in range(10):
    for j in range(10):
        b[i][j] -= 1
```

The following code fragment displays all elements of list b.

```
for i in range(10):
    for j in range(10):
        print(b[i][j], end = "\t")
    print()
```

✎ *The* print() *statement is used to "display" a line break between rows.*

There is also another approach that is very simple but not as flexible as the previous one. There are cases where it cannot be used, as you will see below. Following is a code fragment, written in general form

```
for row in list_name:
    for element in row:

        process element
```

in which *process* is any Python statement or block of statements that processes one element of the list at each iteration.

The following Python program, displays all elements of list b, one at each iteration.

```
for row in b:
    for element in row:
        print(element, end = "\t")
    print()
```

Unfortunately, this approach cannot be used to alter the values of the elements of a list. For example, if you wish to double the values of all elements of the list numbers, you can**not** do the following:

```
numbers = [ [5, 10, 3, 2],
            [2, 4, 1, 6]
          ]

for x in numbers:
    for number in x:
        number *= 2
```

Iterating Through Columns

Iterating through columns means that column 0 is processed first, column 1 is processed next, column 2 afterwards, and so on. Next there is an example of a 3 × 4 list. The arrows show the order in which the elements are processed.

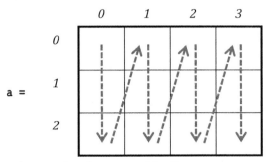

When iterating through columns, the elements of the list are processed as follows:

► the elements of column 0 are processed in the following order

$$a[0][0] \rightarrow a[1][0] \rightarrow a[2][0]$$

► the elements of column 1 are processed in the following order

$$a[0][1] \rightarrow a[1][1] \rightarrow a[2][1]$$

► the elements of column 2 are processed in the following order

$$a[0][2] \rightarrow a[1][2] \rightarrow a[2][2]$$

► the elements of column 3 are processed in the following order

$$a[0][3] \rightarrow a[1][3] \rightarrow a[2][3]$$

Using Python statements, let's try to process all elements of a 3 × 4 list (3 rows × 4 columns) by iterating through columns.

```
j = 0                   #Variable j refers to Column 0.
for i in range(3):      #This loop control structure processes all elements of Column 0

    process a[i][j]


j = 1                   #Variable j refers to Column 1.
for i in range(3):      #This loop control structure processes all elements of Column 1

    process a[i][j]


j = 2                   #Variable j refers to Column 2.
for i in range(3):      #This loop control structure processes all elements of Column 2

    process a[i][j]
```

```
j = 3                       #Variable j refers to Column 3.
for i in range(3):          #This loop control structure processes all elements of Column 3
    process a[i][j]
```

Of course, the same result can be achieved using a nested loop control structure as shown next.

```
for j in range(4):
    for i in range(3):
        process a[i][j]
```

As you can see, this code fragment differs on only one single point from the one that iterates through rows: the two for-loops have switched places. Be careful though. Don't try switching places of the two index variables i and j in the statement *process* a[i][j]. Take the following code fragment, for example. It tries to iterate through columns in a 3 × 4 list (3 rows × 4 columns) but it does not satisfy the property of definiteness. Can you find out why?

```
for j in range(4):
    for i in range(3):
        process a[j][i]
```

The trouble arises when variable j becomes equal to 3. The statement *process* a[j][i] tries to process the elements at **row** index 3 (this is the fourth row) which, of course, does not exist! Still confused? Don't be! There is no row index 3 in a 3 × 4 list! Why? Since row index numbering starts at 0, only rows 0, 1, and 2 actually exist!

31.4 How to Add User-Entered Values to a Two-Dimensional List

Just as in one-dimensional lists, instead of reading a value entered from the keyboard and assigning that value to a variable, you can directly assign that value to a specific list element. The next code fragment creates a two-dimensional list test, lets the user enter six values, and assigns those values to the elements of the list.

```
names = [ [None] * 2 for i in range(3) ]

names[0][0] = input("Name for Row 0, Column 0: ")
names[0][1] = input("Name for Row 0, Column 1: ")
names[1][0] = input("Name for Row 1, Column 0: ")
names[1][1] = input("Name for Row 1, Column 1: ")
names[2][0] = input("Name for Row 2, Column 0: ")
names[2][1] = input("Name for Row 2, Column 1: ")
```

Using nested for-loops, this code fragment can equivalently be written as

```
ROWS = 3
COLUMNS = 2

names = [ [None] * COLUMNS for i in range(ROWS) ]

for i in range(ROWS):
    for j in range(COLUMNS):
        names[i][j] = input("Name for Row " + str(i) + ", Column " + str(j)+": ")
```

You can, of course, do the same, using the `append()` method instead, as shown in the code fragment that follows.

```
ROWS = 3
COLUMNS = 2


names = []    #Create a totally empty list


for i in range(ROWS):
    names.append([])    #Append a totally empty list within list names
    for j in range(COLUMNS):
        name = input("Name for Row " + str(i) + ", Column " + str(j) + ": ")
        names[i].append(name)
```

Exercise 31.4-1   Displaying Reals Only

Write a Python program that prompts the user to enter numeric values in a 5 × 7 list and then displays the indexes of the elements that contain reals.

Solution

Iterating through rows is the most popular approach, so let's use it. The solution is as follows.

```
                            📁 file_31_4_1
ROWS = 5
COLUMNS = 7


a = [ [None] * COLUMNS for i in range(ROWS) ]
for i in range(ROWS):
    for j in range(COLUMNS):
        print("Enter a value for element", i, ",", j, ": ")
        a[i][j] = float(input())


for i in range(ROWS):
    for j in range(COLUMNS):
        if a[i][j] != int(a[i][j]):    #Check if it is real (float)
            print("A real found at position:", i , ",", j)
```

Exercise 31.4-2   Displaying Odd Columns Only

Write a Python program that prompts the user to enter numeric values in a 5 × 7 list and then displays the elements of the columns with odd-numbered indexes (that is, column indexes 1, 3, and 5).

Solution

The Python program is presented next. User-entered values are added to list b using the `append()` method.

```
                            📁 file_31_4_2
ROWS = 5
COLUMNS = 7


b = []
```

```
for i in range(ROWS):
    b.append([])
    for j in range(COLUMNS):
        print("Enter a value for element", i, ",", j, ": ", end = "")
        b[i].append(float(input()))

#Iterate through columns
for j in range(1, COLUMNS, 2):        #Start from 1 and increment by 2
    for i in range(ROWS):
        print(b[i][j])
```

✎ *This book tries to use, as often as possible, variable* i *as the row index and variable* j *as the column index. Of course, you can use other variable names as well, such as* row, r *for row index, or* column, c *for column index, but variables* i *and* j *are widely used by the majority of programmers. After using them for a while, your brain will relate* i *to rows and* j *to columns. Thus, every algorithm or program that uses these variable names as indexes in two-dimensional lists will be more readily understood.*

31.5   What's the Story on Variables i and j?

Many programmers believe that the name of variable i stands for "index" and j is used just because it is after i. Others believe that the name i stands for "integer". Probably the truth lies somewhere in the middle.

Mathematicians were using i, j, and k to designate integers in mathematics long before computers were around. Later, in FORTRAN, one of the first high-level computer languages, variables i, j, k, l, m, and n were integers by default. Thus, the first programmers picked up the habit of using variables i and j in their programs and it became a convention in most computer languages.

31.6   Square Matrices

In mathematics, a matrix that has the same number of rows and columns is called a *square matrix.* Following are some examples of square matrices.

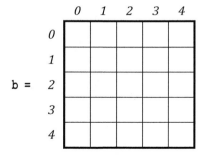

Exercise 31.6-1   *Finding the Sum of the Elements of the Main Diagonal*

Write a Python program that lets the user enter numeric values into a 10 × 10 list and then calculates the sum of the elements of its main diagonal.

Solution

In mathematics, the main diagonal of a square matrix is the collection of those elements that runs from the top left corner to the bottom right corner. Following are some examples of square matrices with their main diagonals highlighted by a dark background.

✎ *Note that the elements of the main diagonal have their row index equal to their column index.*

You can calculate the sum of the elements of the main diagonal using two different approaches. Let's study them both.

First Approach – Iterating through all elements

In this approach, the program iterates through rows and checks if the row index is equal to the column index. For square matrices (in this case, lists) represented as N × N, the number of rows and columns is equal, so you can define just one constant, N. The solution is as follows.

```
                            📄 file_31_6_1a
N = 10
a = [ [None] * N for i in range(N) ]
for i in range(N):
    for j in range(N):
        a[i][j] = float(input())

#Calculate total
total = 0
for i in range(N):
    for j in range(N):
        if i == j:
            total += a[i][j]

print("Sum =", total)
```

✎ *Note that the program iterates through rows and checks if the row index is equal to the column index. Alternatively, the same result can be achieved by iterating through columns.*

✎ *In this approach, the nested loop control structure that is responsible for calculating the sum performs 10 × 10 = 100 iterations.*

Second Approach – Iterating directly through the main diagonal

In this approach, one single loop control structure iterates directly through the main diagonal. The solution is as follows.

```
                            📄 file_31_6_1b
N = 10
a = []
for i in range(N):
```

```
        a.append([])
        for j in range(N):
            a[i].append(float(input()))


    #Calculate total
    total = 0
    for k in range(N):
        total += a[k][k]


    print("Sum =", total)
```

✎ *This approach is much more efficient than the first one since the total number of iterations performed by the for-loop that is responsible for calculating the sum is just 10.*

Exercise 31.6-2   *Finding the Sum of the Elements of the Antidiagonal*

Write a Python program that lets the user enter numeric values in a 5 × 5 list and then calculates the sum of the elements of its antidiagonal.

Solution

In mathematics, the antidiagonal of a square matrix is the collection of those elements that runs from the top right corner to the bottom left corner of the list. Next, you can find an example of a 5 × 5 square matrix with its antidiagonal highlighted by a dark background.

	0	1	2	3	4
0	-3	44	-12	25	**22**
1	10	-1	29	**12**	-9
2	5	-3	**16**	22	-8
3	11	**25**	12	25	-5
4	**12**	22	53	44	-15

a =

Any element of the antidiagonal of an N × N list satisfies the following equation:

$$i + j = N - 1$$

where variables i and j correspond to the row and column indexes of the element respectively.

If you solve for j, the equation becomes

$$j = N - i - 1$$

Using this formula, you can calculate, for any value of variable i, the corresponding value of variable j. For example, in the previous 5 × 5 square list in which N equals 5, when i is 0 the value of variable j is

$$j = N - i - 1 \Leftrightarrow j = 5 - 0 - 1 = \Leftrightarrow j = 4$$

Using all this knowledge, let's now write the corresponding Python program.

📁 **file_31_6_2**

```
N = 5
a = [ [None] * N for i in range(N) ]
for i in range(N):
```

```
        for j in range(N):
            a[i][j] = float(input())


    #Calculate total
    total = 0
    for i in range(N):
        j = N - i - 1
        total += a[i][j]


    print("Sum =", total)
```

✎ Note that the for-loop that is responsible for finding the sum of the elements of the antidiagonal iterates directly through the antidiagonal.

Exercise 31.6-3   Filling in the List

Write a Python program that creates and displays the following list.

	0	1	2	3	4
0	−1	20	20	20	20
1	10	−1	20	20	20
2	10	10	−1	20	20
3	10	10	10	−1	20
4	10	10	10	10	−1

a =

Solution

As you can see, in the main diagonal, there is the value of −1. You already know that the main diagonal of a square matrix is the collection of those elements that have their row index equal to their column index. Now, what you also need is to find a common characteristic between all elements that contain the value 10, and another such common characteristic between all elements that contain the value 20. And actually there are! The row index of any of the elements that contains the value 10 is always greater than its corresponding column index and, similarly, the row index of any of the elements that contains the value 20 is always less than its corresponding column index.

Accordingly, the Python program is as follows.

```
                        📄 file_31_6_3
N = 5
a = [ [None] * N for i in range(N) ]
for i in range(N):
    for j in range(N):
        if i == j:
            a[i][j] = -1
        elif i > j:
            a[i][j] = 10
        else:
            a[i][j] = 20
```

```
for i in range(N):
    for j in range(N):
        print(a[i][j], end = "\t")
    print()
```

31.7   Review Questions: True/False

Choose **true** or **false** for each of the following statements.

1.   All the elements of a two-dimensional list must contain different values.

2.   In order to refer to an element of a two-dimensional list you need two indexes.

3.   The two indexes of a two-dimensional list must be either both variables, or both constant values.

4.   A 5 × 6 list is a two-dimensional list that has five columns and six rows.

5.   To refer to an element of list b that exists at the second row and third column, you would write b[2][3].

6.   Iterating through rows means that first row of a two-dimensional list is processed first, the second row is process next, and so on.

7.   You cannot use variables other than i and j to iterate through a two-dimensional list.

8.   The following Python statement creates a two-dimensional list.
```
names = [ [None] * 2 for i in range(6) ]
```

9.   The following code fragment creates a two-dimensional list of four elements.
```
names = [ [None] * 2 for i in range(2) ]
names[0][0] = "John"
names[0][1] = "George"
names[1][0] = "Sally"
names[1][1] = "Angelina"
```

10. The following code fragment assigns the value 10 to an element that exists in the row with index 0.
```
values[0][0] = 7
values[0][values[0][0]] = 10
```

11. The following statement adds the name "Sally" to an element that exists in the row with index 1.
```
names = [ ["John", "George"], ["Sally", "Angelina"] ]
```

12. The following code fragment displays the name "Sally" on the screen.
```
names = [ [None] * 2 for i in range(2) ]
k = 0
names[0][k] = "John"
k += 1
names[0][k] = "George"
names[1][k] = "Sally"
k -= 1
names[1][k] = "Angelina"
print(names[1][1])
```

13. The following code fragment satisfies the property of definiteness.
```
grades = [ ["B+", "A+"], ["A", "C-"] ]
print(grades[2][2])
```

14. The following code fragment satisfies the property of definiteness.

```
values = [ [1, 0], [2, 0] ]
print(values[values[0][0]][values[0][1]])
```

15. The following code fragment displays the value 2 on the screen.

```
values = [ [0, 1], [2, 0] ]
print(values[values[0][1]][values[0][0]])
```

16. The following code fragment displays all the elements of a 3 × 4 list.

```
for k in range(12):
    i, j = divmod(k, 4)
    print(names[i][j])
```

17. The following code fragment lets the user enter 100 values to list b.

```
for i in range(10):
    for j in range(10):
        b[i][j] = input()
```

18. If list b contains 10 × 20 elements, the following code fragment doubles the values of all of its elements.

```
for i in range(9, -1, -1):
    for j in range(19, -1, -1):
        b[i][j] *= 2
```

19. If list b contains 10 × 20 elements, the following code fragment displays some of them.

```
for i in range(0, 10, 2):
    for j in range(20):
        print(b[i][j])
for i in range(1, 10, 2):
    for j in range(20):
        print(b[i][j])
```

20. The following code fragment displays only the columns with even-numbered indexes.

```
for j in range(0, 12, 2):
    for i in range(10):
        print(a[i][j])
```

21. A 5 × 5 list is a square list.

22. In the main diagonal of a N × N list, all elements have their row index equal to their column index.

23. In mathematics, the antidiagonal of a square matrix is the collection of those elements that runs from the top left corner to the bottom right corner of the list.

24. Any element of the antidiagonal of an N × N list satisfies the equation $i + j = N - 1$, where variables i and j correspond to the row and column indexes of the element respectively.

25. The following code fragment calculates the sum of the elements of the main diagonal of a N × N list.

```
total = 0
for k in range(N):
    total += a[k][k]
```

26. The following code fragment displays all the elements of the antidiagonal of an N × N list.

```
for i in range(N - 1, -1, -1):
    print(a[i][N - i - 1])
```

27. The column index of any element of a N × N list that is below the main diagonal is always greater than its corresponding row index.

31.8 Review Questions: Multiple Choice

Select the correct answer for each of the following statements.

1. The following statement

```
last_names = [None] * 5 for i in range(4)
```

   a. contains a logic error.

   b. contains a syntax error.

   c. none of the above

2. The following code fragment

```
values = [ [1, 0] [2, 0] ]
print(values[values[0][0], values[0][1]])
```

   a. contains logic error(s).

   b. contains syntax error(s).

   c. none of the above

3. The following code fragment

```
x = int(input())
y = int(input())
names[x][y] = 10
```

   a. does not satisfy the property of finiteness.

   b. does not satisfy the property of effectiveness.

   c. does not satisfy the property of definiteness.

   d. none of the above

4. If variable x contains the value 4, the following statement

```
names[x + 1][x] = 5
```

   a. assigns the value 5 to the element with row index 5 and column index 4.

   b. assigns the value 5 to the element with row index 4 and column index 5.

   c. assigns the value 5 to the element with row index 5 and column index 5.

   d. none of the above

5. The following statement

```
names = [ [3, 5, 2] ]
```

   a. assigns the value 5 to the element with row index 0 and column index 1.

   b. assigns the value 3 to the element with row index 0 and column index 0.

   c. assigns the value 2 to the element with row index 0 and column index 2.

   d. all of the above

   e. none of the above

6. The following statement

```
values = [ [None] * 2 ]
```

   a. creates a 1 × 2 list.

   b. creates a 2 × 1 list.

   c. creates a one-dimensional list.

d. none of the above

7. You can iterate through a two-dimensional list with two nested loop control structures that use

   a. variables i and j as counters.

   b. variables k and l as counters.

   c. variables m and n as counters.

   d. any variables as counters.

8. The following code fragment

```
names = [ ["John", "Sally"], ["George", "Maria"] ]
for j in range(2):
    for i in range(1, -1, -1):
        print(names[i][j])
```

   a. displays all names in descending order.

   b. displays some names in descending order.

   c. displays all names in ascending order.

   d. displays some names in ascending order.

   e. none of the above

9. If list b contains 30 × 40 elements, the following code fragment

```
for i in range(30, 0, -1):
    for j in range(40, 0, -1):
        b[i][j] *= 3
```

   a. triples the values of some of its elements.

   b. triples the values of all of its elements.

   c. none of the above

10. If list b contains 30 × 40 elements, the following code fragment

```
total = 0
for i in range(29, -1, -1):
    for j in range(39, -1, -1):
        total += b[i][j]
average = total / 120
```

   a. calculates the sum of all of its elements.

   b. calculates the average value of all of its elements.

   c. all of the above

11. The following two code fragments calculate the sum of the elements of the main diagonal of an N × N list,

```
total = 0                      total = 0
for i in range(N):             for k in range(N):
    for j in range(N):             total += a[k][k]
        if i == j:
            total += a[i][j]
```

   a. but the first one is more efficient.

   b. but the second one is more efficient.

   c. none of the above; both code fragments perform equivalently

31.9   Review Exercises

Complete the following exercises.

1. Create the trace table for the following code fragment.

```
a = [ [None] * 3 for i in range(2) ]
a[0][2] = 1
x = 0
a[0][x] = 9
a[0][x + a[0][2]] = 4
a[a[0][2]][2] = 19
a[a[0][2]][x + 1] = 13
a[a[0][2]][x] = 15
```

2. Create the trace table for the following code fragment.

```
a = [ [None] * 3 for i in range(2) ]
for i in range(2):
    for j in range(3):
        a[i][j] = (i + 1) * 5 + j
```

3. Create the trace table for the following code fragment.

```
a = [ [None] * 3 for i in range(3) ]
for j in range(3):
    for i in range(3):
        a[i][j] = (i + 1) * 2 + j * 4
```

4. Try, without using a trace table, to determine the values that the list will contain when the following code fragment is executed. Do this for three different executions. The corresponding input values are: (i) 5, (ii) 9, and (iii) 3.

```
a = [ [None] * 3 for i in range(2) ]
x = input()
for i in range(2):
    for j in range(3):
        a[i][j] = (x + i) * j
```

5. Try, without using a trace table, to determine the values that the list will contain when the following code fragment is executed. Do this for three different executions. The corresponding input values are: (i) 13, (ii) 10, and (iii) 8.

```
a = [ [None] * 3 for i in range(2) ]
x = input()
for i in range(2):
    for j in range(3):
        if j < x % 4:
            a[i][j] = (x + i) * j
        else:
            a[i][j] = (x + j) * i + 3
```

6. Try, without using a trace table, to determine the values that the list will contain when the following code fragment is executed.

```
a = [ [18, 10, 35], [32, 12, 19] ]
for j in range(3):
    for i in range(2):
```

```
        if a[i][j] < 13:
            a[i][j] /= 2
        elif a[i][j] < 20:
            a[i][j] += 1
        else:
            a[i][j] -= 4
```

7. Try, without using a trace table, to determine the values that the list will contain when the following code fragment is executed.

```
a = [ [11, 10], [15, 19], [22, 15] ]

for j in range(2):
    for i in range(3):
        if i == 2:
            a[i][j] += a[i - 1][j]
        else:
            a[i][j] += a[i + 1][j]
```

8. Assume that list a contains the following values.

	0	1	2	3
0	-1	15	22	3
1	25	12	16	14
2	7	9	1	45
3	40	17	11	13

a =

What displays on the screen after executing each of the following code fragments?

i)
```
for i in range(3):
    for j in range(3):
        print(a[i][j], end = " ")
```

ii)
```
for i in range(2, -1, -1):
    for j in range(3):
        print(a[i][j], end = " ")
```

iii)
```
for i in range(3):
    for j in range(2, -1, -1):
        print(a[i][j], end = " ")
```

iv)
```
for i in range(2, -1, -1):
    for j in range(2, -1, -1):
        print(a[i][j], end = " ")
```

v)
```
for j in range(3):
    for i in range(3):
        print(a[i][j], end = " ")
```

vi)
```
for j in range(3):
    for i in range(2, -1, -1):
        print(a[i][j], end = " ")
```

vii)
```
for j in range(2, -1, -1):
    for i in range(3):
        print(a[i][j], end = " ")
```

viii)
```
for j in range(2, -1, -1):
    for i in range(2, -1, -1):
        print(a[i][j], end = " ")
```

9. Write a Python program that lets the user enter integer values in a 10 × 15 list and then displays the indexes of the elements that contain odd numbers.

10. Write a Python program that lets the user enter numeric values in a 10 × 6 list and then displays the elements of the columns with even-numbered indexes (that is, column indexes 0, 2, and 4).

11. Write a Python program that lets the user enter numeric values in a 12 × 8 list and then calculates and displays the sum of the elements that have even column indexes and odd row indexes.

12. Write a Python program that lets the user enter numeric values in an 8 × 8 square list and then calculates the average value of the elements of its main diagonal and the average value of the elements of its antidiagonal. Try to calculate both average values within the same loop control structure.

13. Write a Python program that creates and displays the following list.

	0	1	2	3	4
0	11	11	11	11	5
1	11	11	11	5	88
2	11	11	5	88	88
3	11	5	88	88	88
4	5	88	88	88	88

a = (rows 0–4 above)

14. Write a Python program that creates and displays the following list.

	0	1	2	3	4
0	0	11	11	11	5
1	11	0	11	5	88
2	11	11	0	88	88
3	11	5	88	0	88
4	5	88	88	88	0

a = (rows 0–4 above)

15. Write a Python program that lets the user enter numeric values in a 5 × 4 list and then displays the row and column indexes of the elements that contain integers.

16. Write a Python program that lets the user enter numeric values in a 10 × 4 list and then counts and displays the total number of negative elements.

17. Write a Python program that lets the user enter words in a 3 × 4 list and then displays them with a space character between them.

18. Write a Python program that lets the user enter words in a 20 × 14 list and then displays those who have less than five characters.

    Hint: Use the len() function.

19. Write a Python program that lets the user enter words in a 20 × 14 list and displays those that have less than 5 characters, then those that have less than 10 characters, and finally those that have less than 20 characters. Assume that the user enters only words with less than 20 characters.

    Hint: Try to display the words using three for-loops nested one within the other.

Chapter 32
Tips and Tricks with Lists

32.1 Introduction

Since lists are handled with the same sequence, decisioñ, and loop control structures that you learned about in previous chapters, there is no need to repeat all of that information here. However, what you will discover in this chapter is how to process each row or column of a two-dimensional list individually, how to solve problems that require the use of more than one list, how to create a two-dimensional list from a one-dimensional list (and vice versa), and some useful built-in list functions and methods that Python supports.

32.2 Processing Each Row Individually

Processing each row individually means that every row is processed separately and the result of each row (which can be the sum, the average value, and so on) can be used individually for further processing.

Suppose you have the following 4 × 5 list.

	0	1	2	3	4
0	2	3	5	2	9
1	9	8	3	14	12
2	5	2	15	20	9
3	7	8	3	5	6

b =

Let's try to find the sum of each row individually. Each of the following four approaches iterates through rows.

First Approach – Creating an auxiliary list

In this approach, the program processes each row individually and creates an auxiliary list in which each element stores the sum of one row. This approach gives you much flexibility since you can use this new list later in your program for further processing. The auxiliary list total is shown on the right.

Now, let's write the corresponding code fragment. To more easily understand the process, the "from inner to outer" method is used. The following code fragment calculates the sum of the first row (row index 0) and stores the result in the element at position 0 of the auxiliary list total. Assume variable i contains the value 0.

```python
s = 0
for j in range(COLUMNS):
    s += b[i][j]
total[i] = s
```

This code fragment can equivalently be written as

```
    total[i] = 0
    for j in range(COLUMNS):
        total[i] += b[i][j]
```

Now, nesting this code fragment in a for-loop that iterates for all rows results in the following.

```
total = [None] * ROWS
for i in range(ROWS):
    total[i] = 0
    for j in range(COLUMNS):
        total[i] += b[i][j]
```

The same result, however, can be achived using the magic forces of Python! The code fragment is as follows.

```
total = []
for row in b:
    total.append(math.fsum(row))
```

Second Approach – Just find it and process it.

This approach uses no auxiliary list; it just calculates and directly processes the sum. The code fragment is as follows.

```
for i in range(ROWS):
    total = 0
    for j in range(COLUMNS):
        total += b[i][j]

    process total
```

What does *process* total mean? It depends on the given problem. It may just display the sum, it may calculate the average value of each individual row and display it, or it may use the sum for calculating even more complex mathematical expressions.

For instance, the following example calculates and displays the average value of each row of list b.

```
for i in range(ROWS):
    total = 0
    for j in range(COLUMNS):
        total += b[i][j]
    average = total / COLUMNS
    print(average)
```

The same result, however, can be achived using the magic forces of Python! The code fragment is as follows

```
for row in b:
    total = math.fsum(row)
    print(total / COLUMNS)
```

Exercise 32.2-1   *Finding the Average Value*

There are 20 students and each one of them has received his or her grades for 10 lessons. Write a Python program that prompts the user to enter the grades of each student for all lessons and then calculates and displays, for each student, all average values that are greater than 89.

Solution

Since you've learned four approaches for processing each row individually, let's use them all.

First Approach – Creating an auxiliary list

In this approach, the program processes each row individually and creates an auxiliary list in which each element stores the average value of one row. The two required lists are shown next.

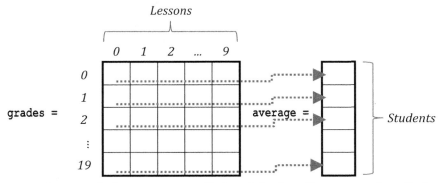

After the list average is created, the program can find and display all average values that are greater than 89. The Python program is as follows.

```
                        📁 file_32_2_1a
STUDENTS = 20
LESSONS = 10
grades = [ [None] * LESSONS for i in range(STUDENTS) ]
for i in range(STUDENTS):
    print("For student No.", (i + 1), "...")
    for j in range(LESSONS):
        grades[i][j] = int(input("enter grade for lesson No." + str(j + 1) + ": "))

#Create list average. Iterate through rows
average = [None] * STUDENTS
for i in range(STUDENTS):
    average[i] = 0
    for j in range(LESSONS):
        average[i] += grades[i][j]
    average[i] /= LESSONS

#Display all average values that are greater than 89
for i in range(STUDENTS):
    if average[i] > 89:
        print(average[i])
```

Using Python's magic forces the auxiliary list average can also be created as shown here.

```
                        📁 file_32_2_1b
import math
STUDENTS = 20
LESSONS = 10
grades = [ [None] * LESSONS for i in range(STUDENTS) ]
for i in range(STUDENTS):
    print("For student No.", (i + 1), "...")
```

```python
    for j in range(LESSONS):
        grades[i][j] = int(input("enter grade for lesson No." + str(j + 1) + ": "))

#Create list average. Iterate through rows
average = []
for row in grades:
    average.append(math.fsum(row) / LESSONS)

#Display all average values that are greater than 89
for i in range(STUDENTS):
    if average[i] > 89:
        print(average[i])
```

Second Approach – Just find it and display it!

This approach uses no auxiliary list; it just calculates and directly displays all average values that are greater than 89. The Python program is as follows.

📁 **file_32_2_1c**

```python
STUDENTS = 20
LESSONS = 10
grades = [ [None] * LESSONS for i in range(STUDENTS) ]
for i in range(STUDENTS):
    print("For student No.", (i + 1), "...")
    for j in range(LESSONS):
        grades[i][j] = int(input("enter grade for lesson No." + str(j + 1) + ": "))

#Calculate the average value of each row and directly display those who are greater than 89
for i in range(STUDENTS):
    average = 0
    for j in range(LESSONS):
        average += grades[i][j]
    average /= LESSONS
    if average > 89:
        print(average)
```

Once again, using Python's magic forces and no auxiliary list, the Python program is as follows.

📁 **file_32_2_1d**

```python
import math
STUDENTS = 20
LESSONS = 10
grades = []
for i in range(STUDENTS):
    grades.append([])
    print("For student No.", (i + 1), "...")
    for j in range(LESSONS):
        grades[i].append(int(input("enter grade for lesson No." + str(j + 1) + ": ")))

#Calculate the average value of each row using Python's magic forces!
```

```
for row in grades:
    average = math.fsum(row) / LESSONS
    if average > 89:
        print(average)
```

32.3 Processing Each Column Individually

Processing each column individually means that every column is processed separately and the result of each column (which can be the sum, the average value, and so on) can be used individually for further processing. Suppose you have the following 4 × 5 list.

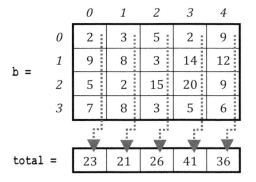

As before, let's try to find the sum of each column individually. Yet again, there are two approaches that you can use. Both of these approaches iterate through columns.

First Approach – Creating an auxiliary list

In this approach, the program processes each column individually and creates an auxiliary list in which each element stores the sum of one column. This approach gives you much flexibility since you can use this new list later in your program for further processing. The auxiliary list total is shown at the bottom.

Now, let's write the corresponding code fragment. To more easily understand the process, the "from inner to outer" method is used again. The following code fragment calculates the sum of the first column (column index 0) and stores the result in the element at position 0 of the auxiliary list total. Assume variable j contains the value 0.

```
s = 0
for i in range(ROWS):
    s += b[i][j]
total[j] = s
```

This program can equivalently be written as

```
total[j] = 0
for i in range(ROWS):
    total[j] += b[i][j]
```

Now, nesting this code fragment in a for-loop that iterates for all columns results in the following.

```
total = [None] * COLUMNS
for j in range(COLUMNS):
    total[j] = 0
    for i in range(ROWS):
        total[j] += a[i][j]
```

Second Approach – Just find it and process it.

This approach uses no auxiliary list; it just calculates and directly processes the sum. The code fragment is as follows.

```
for j in range(COLUMNS):
    total = 0
    for i in range(ROWS):
        total += a[i][j]

    process total
```

Accordingly, the following code fragment calculates and displays the average value of each column.

```
for j in range(COLUMNS):
    total = 0
    for i in range(ROWS):
        total += a[i][j]
    print(total / ROWS)
```

Exercise 32.3-1   Finding the Average Value

There are 10 students and each one of them has received his or her grades for five lessons. Write a Python program that prompts the user to enter the grades of each student for all lessons and then calculates and displays, for each lesson, all average values that are greater than 89.

Solution

Since you've learned two approaches for processing each column individually, let's use them both.

First Approach – Creating an auxiliary list

In this approach, the program processes each column individually and creates an auxiliary list in which each element stores the average value of one column. The two required lists are shown next.

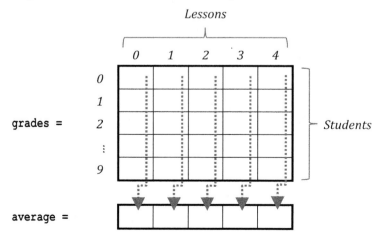

After the list average is created, the program can find and display all average values that are greater than 89. The Python program is as follows.

```
                          📁 file_32_3_1a
STUDENTS = 10
LESSONS = 5

grades = [ [None] * LESSONS for i in range(STUDENTS) ]
for i in range(STUDENTS):
    print("For student No.", (i + 1), "...")
    for j in range(LESSONS):
        grades[i][j] = int(input("enter grade for lesson No." + str(j + 1) + ": "))

#Create list average. Iterate through columns
average = [None] * LESSONS
for j in range(LESSONS):
    average[j] = 0
    for i in range(STUDENTS):
        average[j] += grades[i][j]
    average[j] /= STUDENTS

#Display all average values than are greater than 89
for j in range(LESSONS):
    if average[j] > 89:
        print(average[j])
```

Second Approach – Just find it and display it!

This approach uses no auxiliary list; it just calculates and directly displays all average values that are greater than 89. The Python program is as follows.

```
                          📁 file_32_3_1b
STUDENTS = 10
LESSONS = 5

grades = [ [None] * LESSONS for i in range(STUDENTS) ]

for i in range(STUDENTS):
    print("For student No.", (i + 1), "...")
    for j in range(LESSONS):
        grades[i][j] = int(input("enter grade for lesson No." + str(j + 1) + ": "))

#Calculate the average value of each column individually
#and directly display those who are greater than 89
for j in range(LESSONS):
    average = 0
    for i in range(STUDENTS):
        average += grades[i][j]
    average /= STUDENTS
```

```
if average > 89:
    print(average)
```

32.4   How to Use More Than One Data Structures in a Program

So far, every example or exercise has used just one list or one dictionary. But what if a problem requires you to use two lists, or one list and one dictionary, or one list and two dictionaries? Next you will find some exercises that show you how various data structures can be used together to solve a particular problem.

Exercise 32.4-1   *Finding the Average Value of Two Grades*

There are 20 students and each one of them has received his or her grades for two lessons. Write a Python program that prompts the user to enter the name and the grades of each student for all lessons. It then calculates and displays the names of all students who have an average grade greater than 89.

Solution

Following are the required lists containing some typical values.

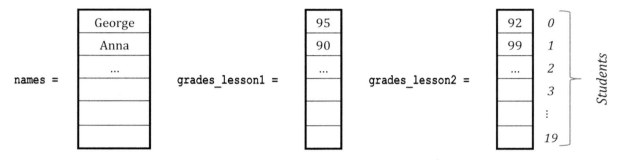

As you can see, there is a one-to-one match between the index positions of the elements of list names and those of lists grades_lesson1, and grades_lesson2. The first of the twenty students is George and the grades he received for the two lessons are 95 and 92. The name "George" is stored at index 0 of the list names, and exactly at the same index, in the lists grades_lesson1 and grades_lesson2, there are stored his grades for the two lessons. The next student (Anna) and her grades are stored at index 1 of the lists names, grades_lesson1, and grades_lesson2 correspondingly, and so on.

The Python program is as follows.

```
📁 file_32_4_1

STUDENTS = 20

names = [None] * STUDENTS
grades_lesson1 = [None] * STUDENTS
grades_lesson2 = [None] * STUDENTS

for i in range(STUDENTS):
    names[i] = input("Enter student name No" + str(i + 1) + ": ")
    grades_lesson1[i] = int(input("Enter grade for lesson 1: "))
    grades_lesson2[i] = int(input("Enter grade for lesson 2: "))

#Calculate the average grade for each student
#and display the names of those who are greater than 89
```

```
for i in range(STUDENTS):
    total = grades_lesson1[i] + grades_lesson2[i]
    average = total / 3.0
    if average > 89:
        print(names[i])
```

Exercise 32.4-2   *Finding the Average Value of More than Two Grades*

There are 10 students and each one of them has received his or her grades for five lessons. Write a Python program that prompts the user to enter the name of each student and the grades for all lessons and then calculates and displays the names of the students who have more than one grade greater than 89.

Solution

In this exercise, you can do what you did in the previous one. You can use a one-dimensional list to store the names of the students and five one-dimensional lists to store the grades for each student for each lesson. Not very convenient, but it can work. Obviously, when there are more than two grades, this is not the most suitable approach.

The best approach here is to use a one-dimensional list to store the names of the students and a two-dimensional list to store the grades for each student for each lesson.

There are actually two approaches. Which one to use depends clearly on you! If you decide that, in the two-dimensional list, the rows should refer to students and the columns should refer to lessons then you can use the first approach discussed below. If you decide that the rows should refer to lessons and the columns should refer to students then you can use the second approach.

First Approach – Rows for students, columns for lessons

In this approach, the two-dimensional list must have 10 rows, one for every student and 5 columns, one for every lesson. All other lists can be placed in relation to this two-dimensional list as follows.

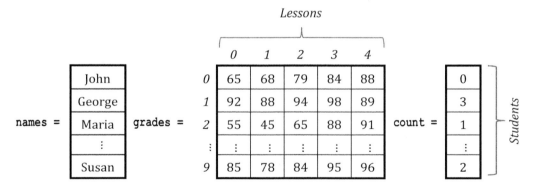

✎ *The auxiliary list* count *is created by the program and contains the number of grades for each student that are greater than 89.*

Now, let's see how to read values and store them in the lists names and grades. One simple solution would be to use one loop control structure for reading names, and another, independent, loop control structure for reading grades. However, it is not very practical for the user to first enter all names and later enter all grades. A more practical way would be to prompt the user to enter one student name and then all of his or her grades, then another student name and again all of his or her grades, and so on. The solution is as follows.

file_32_4_2a

```
STUDENTS = 10
LESSONS = 5

names = [None] * STUDENTS
grades = [ [None] * LESSONS for i in range(STUDENTS) ]

#Read names and grades all together. Iterate through rows in list grades
for i in range(STUDENTS):
    names[i] = input("Enter name for student No." + str(i + 1) + ": ")
    for j in range(LESSONS):
        grades[i][j] = int(input("Enter grade No." + str(j + 1) + " for " + names[i] + ": "))

#Create list count. Iterate through rows
count = [None] * STUDENTS
for i in range(STUDENTS):
    count[i] = 0
    for j in range(LESSONS):
        if grades[i][j] > 89:
            count[i] += 1

#Displays the names of the students who have
#more than one grade greater than 89
for i in range(STUDENTS):
    if count[i] > 1:
        print(names[i])
```

Second Approach – Rows for lessons, columns for students

In this approach, the two dimensional list must have 5 rows, one for every lesson and 10 columns, one for every student. All other lists can be placed in relation to this two-dimensional list, as shown next.

Students

names =	John	George	Maria	...	Susan

		0	*1*	*2*	...	*9*
grades =	*0*	65	92	55	...	85
	1	68	88	45	...	78
	2	79	94	65	...	84
	3	84	98	88	...	95
	4	88	89	91	...	96

Lessons

count =	0	3	1	...	2

✎ *The auxiliary list* count *is created by the program and contains the number of grades for each lesson that are greater than 89.*

The solution is as follows.

```
                            📄 file_32_4_2b
STUDENTS = 10
LESSONS = 5

#Read names and grades together. Iterate through columns in list grades
names = [None] * STUDENTS
grades = [ [None] * STUDENTS for i in range(LESSONS) ]
for j in range(STUDENTS):
    names[j] = input("Enter name for student No." + str(j + 1) + ": ")
    for i in range(LESSONS):
        grades[i][j] = int(input("Enter grade No." + str(i + 1) + " for " + names[j] + ": "))


#Create list count. Iterate through columns
count = [None] * STUDENTS
for j in range(STUDENTS):
    count[j] = 0
    for i in range(LESSONS):
        if grades[i][j] > 89:
            count[j] += 1


#Displays the names of the students who have more than one grade greater than 89
for j in range(STUDENTS):
    if count[j] > 1:
        print(names[j])
```

Exercise 32.4-3   *Using a List Along with a Dictionary*

There are 30 students and each one of them has received his or her grades for a test. Write a Python program that prompts the user to enter the grades (as a letter) for each student. It then displays, for each student, the grade as a percentage according to the following table.

Grade	Percentage
A	90 – 100
B	80 – 89
C	70 – 79
D	60 – 69
E / F	0 – 59

Solution

A dictionary that holds the given table can be used. The solution is as follows.

```
                              📁 file_32_4_3
STUDENTS = 30
grades_table = {"A": "90-100", "B": "80-89", "C": "70-79",
                "D": "60-69", "E": "0-59", "F": "0-59"}


names = [None] * STUDENTS
grades = [None] * STUDENTS


for i in range(STUDENTS):
    names[i] = input("Enter student name No" + str(i + 1) + ": ")
    grades[i] = input("Enter his or her grade: ")


for i in range(STUDENTS):
    grade = grades[i]
    grade_as_percentage = grades_table[grade]

    print(names[i], grade_as_percentage)
```

Now, if you fully understood how the last for-loop works, then take a look in the code fragment that follows. It is equivalent to that last for-loop, but it performs more efficiently, since it uses fewer variables!

```
for i in range(STUDENTS):
    print(names[i], grades_table[grades[i]])
```

32.5   Creating a One-Dimensional List from a Two-Dimensional List

To more easily understand how to create a one-dimensional list from a two-dimensional list, let's use an example.

Write a program that creates a one-dimensional list of 12 elements from an existing two-dimensional list of 3 × 4 (shown below), as follows: The elements of the first column of the two-dimensional list must be placed in the first three positions of the one-dimensional list, the elements of the second column must be placed in the next three positions, and so on.

The two-dimensional 3 × 4 list is as follows.

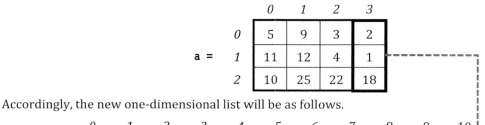

Accordingly, the new one-dimensional list will be as follows.

The Python program that follows creates the new one-dimensional list, iterating through columns, which is more convenient. It uses the existing list given in the example.

```
                              📁 file_32_5a
ROWS = 3
COLUMNS = 4
```

```
ELEMENTS = ROWS * COLUMNS

a = [ [5, 9, 3, 2],
      [11, 12, 4, 1],
      [10, 25, 22, 18]
    ]

b = [None] * ELEMENTS

k = 0   #This is the index of the new list b.
for j in range(COLUMNS):          #Iterate through columns
    for i in range(ROWS):
        b[k] = a[i][j]
        k += 1

for k in range(ELEMENTS):
    print(b[k], end = "\t")
```

Instead of using the index k for the new list, you can also use the append() method, as shown here.

```
┌  file_32_5b
ROWS = 3
COLUMNS = 4
ELEMENTS = ROWS * COLUMNS

a = [ [5, 9, 3, 2],
      [11, 12, 4, 1],
      [10, 25, 22, 18]
    ]

b = []   #Create a totally empty list
for j in range(COLUMNS):          #Iterate through columns
    for i in range(ROWS):
        b.append(a[i][j])

for k in range(ELEMENTS):
    print(b[k], end = "\t")
```

32.6   Creating a Two-Dimensional List from a One-Dimensional List

To more easily understand how to create a two-dimensional list from a one-dimensional list, let's use an example.

Write a Python program that creates a two-dimensional list of 3 × 4 from an existing one-dimensional list of 12 elements (shown below), as follows: The first three elements of the one-dimensional list must be placed in the first column of the two-dimensional list, the next three elements of the one-dimensional list must be placed in the next column of the two-dimensional list, and so on.

The one-dimensional list of 12 elements is as follows.

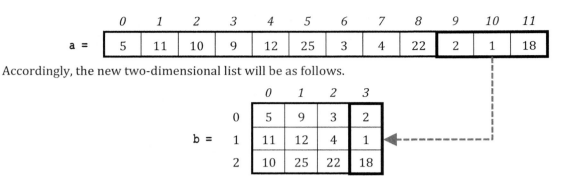

Accordingly, the new two-dimensional list will be as follows.

The Python program that follows creates the new two-dimensional list, iterating through columns, which is more convenient. It uses the existing list given in the example.

```
☐ file_32_6
ROWS = 3
COLUMNS = 4
ELEMENTS = ROWS * COLUMNS

a = [5, 11, 10, 9, 12, 25, 3, 4, 22, 2, 1, 18]
b = [ [None] * COLUMNS for i in range(ROWS) ]

k = 0     #This is the index of list a.
for j in range(COLUMNS):              #Iterate through columns
    for i in range(ROWS):
        b[i][j] = a[k]
        k += 1

for i in range(ROWS):                 #Iterate through rows
    for j in range(COLUMNS):
        print(b[i][j], end = "\t")
    print()
```

32.7   Useful List Functions and Methods

Counting the number of elements

❘ len(*structure_name*)

You already know this function from a previous chapter. In paragraph 14.3 you learned that the len() function returns the number of characters in a string. Now it's time to learn that the function len() returns the number of elements of any structure such as a list or a dictionary!

Example

```
☐ file_32_7a
a = [3, 6, 10, 12, 4, 2, 1]

print(len(a))                  #It displays: 7

length = len(a[2:4])
print(length)                  #It displays: 2
```

```
for i in range(len(a)):
    print (a[i], end = "  ")        #It displays: 3  6  10  12  4  2  1
```

Finding the maximum value

```
max(structure_name)
```

This function returns the greatest value of a list or tuple. In the case of a dictionary, it returns the greatest key.

Example

```
                                     📁 file_32_7b
a = [3, 6, 10, 2, 1, 12, 4]

print(max(a))                    #It displays: 12

maximum = max(a[1:4])
print(maximum)                   #It displays: 10

b = [ [4, 6, 8],
      [3, 11, 9],
      [2, 9, 1]
    ]

print(max(b[1]))                 #It displays: 11

c = ("Apollo", "Hermes", "Athena", "Aphrodite", "Dionysus")
print(max(c))                    #It displays: Hermes
```

Finding the minimum value

```
min(structure_name)
```

This function returns the smallest value of a list or a tuple. In the case of a dictionary, it returns the smallest key.

Example

```
                                     📁 file_32_7c
a = [3, 6, 10, 2, 1, 12, 4]

print(min(a))                    #It displays: 1

minimum = min(a[1:4])
print(minimum)                   #It displays: 2

b = [ [4, 6, 8],
      [3, 11, 9],
      [2, 9, 1]
    ]

print(min(b[0]))                 #It displays: 4
```

```
c = ("Apollo", "Hermes", "Athena", "Aphrodite", "Dionysus")
print(min(c))                   #It displays: Aphrodite
```

Sorting a list

Sorting is the process of putting the elements of a list in a certain order. Here you have two options: you can sort a list using the sort() method, or you can get a new sorted list from an initial list using the sorted() function, leaving the initial list intact.

Using the sort() method

```
list.sort([reverse = True])
```

This method sorts a list in ascending or in descending order.

Example

📁 **file_32_7d**

```
a = [3, 6, 10, 2, 1, 12, 4]
a.sort()
print(a)    #It displays: [1  2  3  4  6  10  12]

#Sort in reverse order
a.sort(reverse = True)
print(a)    #It displays: [12  10  6  4  3  2  1]

b = [ [4, 6, 8],
      [3, 11, 9],
      [2, 9, 1]
    ]

#Sort the last row
b[2].sort()

for row in b:
    for element in row:
        print(element, end = "\t")   #It displays: 4   6   8
                                     #             3   11  9
    print()                          #             1   2   9

c = ["Hermes", "Apollo", "Dionysus"]
c.sort()
print(c)    #It displays: ['Apollo', 'Dionysus', 'Hermes']
```

✎ *The* sort() *method cannot be used with immutable data types, such as tuples.*

Using the sorted() function

```
sorted(structure_name [, reverse = True])
```

This function returns a new sorted list or a tuple, either in ascending or in descending order, leaving the initial *list* intact.

Example

```
┌ file_32_7e
a = [3, 6, 10, 2, 1, 12, 4]
b = sorted(a)


print(a)    #It displays: [3, 6, 10, 2, 1, 12, 4]
print(b)    #It displays: [1  2  3  4  6  10  12]


c = ["Hermes", "Apollo", "Dionysus"]
for element in sorted(c, reverse = True):
    print(element, end = " ")    #It displays: Hermes  Dionysus  Apollo
```

32.8   Review Questions: True/False

Choose **true** or **false** for each of the following statements.

1. Processing each row individually means that every row is processed separately, and the result of each row can then be used individually for further processing.

2. The following code fragment displays the word "Okay" when the sum of the elements of each column is less than 100.
    ```
    for i in range(ROWS):
        total = 0
        for j in range(COLUMNS):
            total += a[i][j]
        if total < 100: print("Okay")
    ```

3. Processing each column individually means that every column is processed separately and the result of each column can be then used individually for further processing.

4. The following code fragment displays the sum of the elements of each column.
    ```
    total = 0
    for j in range(COLUMNS):
        for i in range(ROWS):
            total += a[i][j]
        print(total)
    ```

5. Suppose that there are 10 students and each one of them has received his or her grades for five lessons. Given this information, it is possible to design a list so that the rows refer to students and the columns refer to lessons, but not the other way around.

6. A one-dimensional list can be created from a two-dimensional list, but not the opposite.

7. A one-dimensional list can be created from a three-dimensional list.

8. The following two code fragments display the same value.
    ```
    a = [1, 6, 12, 2, 1]
    print(len(a))
    ```
    ```
    a = "Hello"
    print(len(a))
    ```

9. The following code fragment displays three values.
    ```
    a = [10, 20, 30, 40, 50]
    for i in range(3, len(a)):
        print(a[i])
    ```

10. The following code fragment displays the values of all elements of the list b.

```
b = [10, 20, 30, 40, 50]
for i in range(len(b)):
    print(i)
```

11. The following code fragment doubles the values of all elements of the list b.

```
for i in range(len(b)):
    b[i] *= 2
```

12. The following code fragment displays the value of 30 on the screen.

```
a = [20, 50, 10, 30, 15]
print(max(a[2:len(a)]))
```

13. The following code fragment displays the value of 50 on the screen.

```
a = [20, 50, 10, 30, 15]
b = [-1, -3, -2, -4, -1]
print(a[min(b)])
```

14. The following code fragment displays the smallest value of list b.

```
b = [3, 6, 10, 2, 1, 12, 4]
b.sort()
print(b[0])
```

15. The following code fragment displays the smallest value of list b.

```
b = [3, 1, 2, 10, 4, 12, 6]
print(sorted(a, reverse = True)[-1])
```

16. The following code fragment throws an error.

```
b = [3, 1, 2]
a = sort(b)
```

17. The following code fragment throws an error.

```
b = (3, 1, 2)
a = b.sorted()
```

32.9   Review Questions: Multiple Choice

Select the correct answer for each of the following statements.

1. The following code fragment

```
for i in range(ROWS):
    total[i] = 0
    for j in range(COLUMNS):
        total[i] += a[i][j]
    print(total[i])
```

    a. displays the sum of the elements of each row.

    b. displays the sum of the elements of each column.

    c. displays the sum of all the elements of the list.

    d. none of the above

2. The following code fragment

```
for j in range(COLUMNS):
    total = 0
    for i in range(ROWS):
```

```
        total += a[i][j]
    print(total)
```

    a.   displays the sum of the elements of each row.

    b.   displays the sum of the elements of each column.

    c.   displays the sum of all the elements of the list.

    d.   none of the above

3.   The following code fragment

```
b = [None] * (ROWS * COLUMNS)
k = 0
for i in range(ROWS, 0, -1):
    for j in range(COLUMNS, 0, -1):
        b[k] = a[i][j]
        k += 1
```

    a.   creates a one-dimensional list from a two-dimensional list.

    b.   creates a two-dimensional list from a one-dimensional list.

    c.   none of the above

4.   The following code fragment

```
b = [ [None] * COLUMNS for i in range(ROWS) ]
k = 0
for i in range(ROWS):
    for j in range(COLUMNS - 1, -1, -1):
        b[i][j] = a[k]
        k += 1
```

    a.   creates a one-dimensional list from a two-dimensional list.

    b.   creates a two-dimensional list from a one-dimensional list.

    c.   none of the above

5.   The following two code fragments

```
a = [3, 6, 10, 2, 4, 12, 1]        a = [3, 6, 10, 2, 4, 12, 1]
for i in range(7):                 for i in range(len(a)):
    print(a[i])                        print(a[i])
```

    a.   produce the same results, but the left program is faster.

    b.   produce the same results, but the right program is faster.

    c.   do not produce the same results.

    d.   none of the above

6.   The following two code fragments

```
for i in range(len(a)):            for element in a:
    print(a[i])                        print(element)
```

    a.   produce the same results.

    b.   do not produce the same results.

    c.   none of the above

7.   The statement `min(b[1:len(b)])`

    a.   returns the lowest value of a portion of list b.

b. returns the lowest value of list b.

c. none of the above

8. The following code fragment

```
a = [3, 6, 10, 1, 4, 12, 2]
print(a[-min(a)])
```

a. displays the value of 1 on the screen.

b. displays the value of 6 on the screen.

c. displays the value of 2 on the screen.

d. none of the above

9. The following two code fragments

```
for i in range(len(a)):
    print(sorted(a)[i])
```

```
for element in sorted(a):
    print(element)
```

a. produce the same results, but the left program is faster.

b. produce the same results, but the right program is faster.

c. do not produce the same results.

d. none of the above

10. The following three code fragments

```
b.sort(reverse = True)
print(b[0])
```

```
print(sorted(b)[-1])
```

```
print(max(b))
```

a. display the greatest value of the list b on the screen.

b. display the smallest value of the list b on the screen.

c. none of the above

32.10 Review Exercises

Complete the following exercises.

1. There are 15 students and each one of them has received his or her grades for five tests. Write a Python program that lets the user enter the grades (as a percentage) for each student for all tests. It then calculates and displays, for each student, the average grade as a letter grade according to the following table.

Grade	Percentage
A	90 – 100
B	80 – 89
C	70 – 79
D	60 – 69
E / F	0 – 59

2. On Earth, a free-falling object has an acceleration of 9.81 m/s² downward. This value is denoted by g. A student wants to calculate that value using an experiment. She allows five different objects to fall downward from a known height and measures the time they need to reach the floor. She does this 10 times for each object. Then, using a formula she calculates g for each object, for each fall. But since her chronometer is not so accurate, she needs a Python program that lets her enter all calculated values of g in a 5 × 10 list and then, it calculates and displays

     a.   for each object, the average value of g (per fall)

     b.   for each fall, the average value of g (per object)

     c.   the overall average value of g

3. A basketball team with 15 players plays 12 matches. Write a Python program that lets the user enter, for each player, the number of points scored in each match. The program must then display

     a.   for each player, the total number of points scored

     b.   for each match, the total number of points scored

4. Write a Python program that lets the user enter the hourly measured temperatures of 20 cities for a period of one day, and then displays the hours in which the average temperature of all the cities was below 10 degrees Fahrenheit.

5. In a football tournament, a football team with 24 players plays 10 matches. Write a Python program that lets the user enter, for each player, a name as well as the number of goals scored in each match. The program must then display

     a.   for each player, a name and the average number of goals scored

     b.   for each match, the index number of the match (1, 2, 3, and so on) and the total number of goals scored

6. There are 12 students and each one of them has received his or her grades for six lessons. Write a Python program that lets the user enter the name of the student as well as his or her grades in all lessons and then displays

     a.   for each student, his or her name and average grade

     b.   for each lesson, the average grade

     c.   the names of the students who have an average grade less than 60

     d.   the names of the students who have an average grade greater than 89, and the message "Bravo!" next to it

Assume that the user enters values between 0 and 100.

7. In a song contest, each artist sings a song of his or her choice. There are five judges and 15 artists, each of whom is scored for his or her performance. Write a Python program that prompts the user to enter the names of the judges, the names of the artists, the title of the song that each artist sings, and the score they get from each judge. The program must then display

     a.   for each artist, his or her name, the title of the song, and his or her total score

     b.   for each judge, his or her name and the average value of the score he or she gave (per artist)

8. The Body Mass Index (BMI) is often used to determine whether a person is overweight or underweight for his or her height. The formula used to calculate BMI is

$$BMI = \frac{weight \cdot 703}{height^2}$$

Write a Python program that lets the user enter into two lists the weight (in pounds) and height (in inches) of 30 people, measured on a monthly basis, for a period of one year (January to December). The program must then calculate and display

     a.   for each person, his or her average weight, average height, and average BMI

     b.   for each person, his or her BMI in May and in August

Please note that all people are adults but some of them are between the ages of 18 and 25. This means they may still grow taller, thus their height might be different each month!

9. Write a Python program that lets the user enter the electric meter reading in kilowatt-hours (kWh) at the beginning and at the end of a month for 1000 consumers. The program must calculate and display

    a.   for each consumer, the amount of kWh consumed and the amount of money that must be paid given a cost of each kWh of $0.07 and a value added tax (VAT) of 19%

    b.   the total consumption and the total amount of money that must be paid.

10. Write a Python program that prompts the user to enter an amount in US dollars and calculates and displays the corresponding currency value in Euros, British Pounds Sterling, Australian Dollars, and Canadian Dollars. The tables below contain the exchange rates for each currency for a one-week period. The program must calculate the average value of each currency and do the conversions based on that average value.

currency =		rate =				
British Pound Sterling		1.320	1.321	1.332	1.331	1.341
Euro		1.143	1.156	1.138	1.122	1.129
Canadian Dollar		0.757	0.764	0.760	0.750	0.749
Australian Dollar		0.720	0.725	0.729	0.736	0.739

11. Gross pay depends on the pay rate and the total number of hours worked per week. However, if someone works more than 40 hours, he or she gets paid time-and-a-half for all hours worked over 40. Write a Python program that lets the user enter a pay rate as well as the names of 10 employees and the number of hours that they worked each day (Monday to Friday). The program must then calculate and display

    a.   the names of the employees who worked overtime

    b.   for each employee, his or her name and the average gross pay (per day)

    c.   for each employee, his or her name, the name of the day he or she worked overtime (more than 8 hours), and the message "Overtime!"

    d.   for each day, the name of the day and the total gross pay

12. Write a Python program to create a one-dimensional list of 12 elements from the two-dimensional list shown below, as follows: the first row of the two-dimensional list must be placed in the first four positions of the one-dimensional list, the second row of the two-dimensional list must be placed in the next four positions of the one-dimensional list, and the last row of the two-dimensional list must be placed in the last four positions of the one-dimensional list.

a =			
9	9	2	6
4	1	10	11
12	15	7	3

13. Write a Python program to create a 3 × 3 list from the one-dimensional list shown below, as follows: the first three elements of the one-dimensional list must be placed in the last row of the two-dimensional list, the next three elements of the one-dimensional list must be placed in the second row of the two-dimensional list, and the last three elements of the one-dimensional list must be placed in the first row of the two-dimensional list.

a =	16	12	3	5	6	9	18	19	20

Chapter 33
More Exercises with Lists

33.1 Simple Exercises with Lists

Exercise 33.1-1   *Creating a List that Contains the Average Values of its Neighboring Elements*

Write a Python program that lets the user enter 100 positive numerical values into a list. Then, the program must create a new list of 98 elements. This new list must contain, in each position the average value of the three elements that exist in the current and the next two positions of the given list.

Solution

Let's try to understand this exercise through an example using 10 elements.

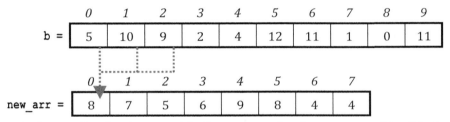

List `new_arr` is the new list that is created. In list `new_arr`, the element at position 0 is the average value of the elements in the current and the next two positions of list b; that is, (5 + 10 + 9) / 3 = 8. The element at position 1 is the average value of the elements in the current and the next two positions of list b; that is, (10 + 9 + 2) / 3 = 7, and so on.

The Python program is as follows.

```
                        📁 file_33_1_1a
ELEMENTS_OF_A = 100
ELEMENTS_OF_NEW = ELEMENTS_OF_A - 2

a = [None] * ELEMENTS_OF_A
for i in range(ELEMENTS_OF_A):
    a[i] = float(input())

new_arr = [None] * ELEMENTS_OF_NEW
for i in range(ELEMENTS_OF_NEW):
    new_arr[i] = (a[i] + a[i + 1] + a[i + 2]) / 3

for i in range(ELEMENTS_OF_NEW):
    print(new_arr[i])
```

If you prefer a more Pythonic way, though, the solution is shown here.

```
                        📁 file_33_1_1b
import math
ELEMENTS_OF_A = 100
```

```
a = []
for i in range(ELEMENTS_OF_A):
    a.append(float(input()))

new_arr = []
for i in range(ELEMENTS_OF_A - 2):
    new_arr.append(math.fsum(a[i:i + 3]) / 3)

for element in new_arr:
    print(element)
```

Exercise 33.1-2   *Creating a List with the Greatest Values*

Write a Python program that lets the user enter numerical values into lists a and b of 20 elements each. Then the program, must create a new list new_arr of 20 elements. The new list must contain in each position the greatest value of lists a and b of the corresponding position.

Solution

Nothing new here! You need two for-loops to read the values for lists a and b, one for creating the list new_arr, and one to display list new_arr on the screen.

The Python program is shown here.

```
📁 file_33_1_2
```
```
ELEMENTS = 20

#Read lists a and b
a = [None] * ELEMENTS
b = [None] * ELEMENTS
for i in range(ELEMENTS):
    a[i] = float(input())
for i in range(ELEMENTS):
    b[i] = float(input())

#Create list new_arr
new_arr = [None] * ELEMENTS
for i in range(ELEMENTS):
    if a[i] > b[i]:
        new_arr[i] = a[i]
    else:
        new_arr[i] = b[i]

#Display list new_arr
for i in range(ELEMENTS):
    print(new_arr[i])
```

Exercise 33.1-3   *Merging One-Dimensional Lists*

Write a Python program that, for two given lists a and b of 10 and 15 elements, respectively, creates a new list new_arr of 25 elements. This new list must contain in the first 10 positions the elements of list a, and in the next 15 positions the elements of list b.

Solution

Since not all computer languages are so powerful in the field of lists (or in arrays, if you prefer) as Python, let's study three approaches here. The first one can be applied to most computer languages, whereas the second and the third ones are more Pythonic!.

First Approach

As you can see in the example presented next, there is a one-to-one match between the index positions of the elements of list a and those of list new_arr. The element from position 0 of list a is stored in position 0 of list new_arr, the element from position 1 of list a is stored in position 1 of list new_arr, and so on. However, there is no one-to-one match between the index positions of the elements of list b and those of list new_arr. The element from position 0 of list b must be stored in position 10 of list new_arr, the element from position 1 of list b must be stored in position 11 of list new_arr, and so on.

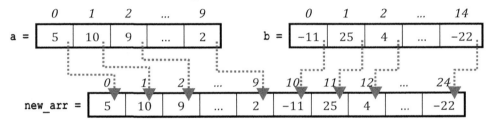

In order to assign the values of list a to list new_arr you can use the following code fragment.

```python
for i in range(len(a)):
    new_arr[i] = a[i]
```

However, to assign the values of list b to list new_arr your code fragment should be quite different as shown here.

```python
for i in range(len(b)):
    new_arr[len(a) + i] = b[i]
```

The final Python program is as follows.

□ file_33_1_3a

```python
#Create lists a and b
a = [5, 10, 9, 6, 7, -6, 13, 12, 11, 2]
b = [-11, 25, 4, 45, 67, 87, 34, 23, 33, 55, 13, 15, -4, -2, -22]

#Create list new_arr .
new_arr = [None] * (len(a) + len(b))
for i in range(len(a)):
    new_arr[i] = a[i]
for i in range(len(b)):
    new_arr[len(a) + i] = b[i]
```

```
#Display list new_arr
for i in range(len(new_arr)):
    print(new_arr[i], end = "\t")
```

Second Approach

This approach uses the append() method of Python.

```
                            📁 file_33_1_3b
#Create lists a and b
a = [5, 10, 9, 6, 7, -6, 13, 12, 11, 2]
b = [-11, 25, 4, 45, 67, 87, 34, 23, 33, 55, 13, 15, -4, -2, -22]

#Create list new_arr
new_arr = []
for element in a:
    new_arr.append(element)
for element in b:
    new_arr.append(element)

#Display list new_arr
for i in range(len(new_arr)):
    print(new_arr[i], end = "\t")
```

Third Approach

This approach uses the magic forces of Python. In order to merge two lists in Python, you can simply use the concatenation operator (+). Python will do the rest for you!

```
                            📁 file_33_1_3c
#Create lists a and b
a = [5, 10, 9, 6, 7, -6, 13, 12, 11, 2]
b = [-11, 25, 4, 45, 67, 87, 34, 23, 33, 55, 13, 15, -4, -2, -22]

#Create list new_arr
new_arr = a + b

#Display list new_arr
for i in range(len(new_arr)):
    print(new_arr[i], end = "\t")
```

Exercise 33.1-4   *Merging Two-Dimensional Lists*

Write a Python program that for two given lists a *and* b *of 3 × 4 and 5 × 4 elements respectively it creates a new list* new_arr *of 8 × 4 elements. In this new list, the first 3 rows must contain the elements of list* a *and the next 5 rows must contain the elements of list* b.

Solution

Using knowledge from the previous exercise, the proposed three solutions are as follows. In the beginning, the two given lists a and b are created with randomly chosen values.

First Approach

```
                              📁 file_33_1_4a
COLUMNS = 4
ROWS_OF_A = 3
ROWS_OF_B = 5
ROWS_OF_NEW = ROWS_OF_A + ROWS_OF_B

#Create lists a and b
a = [ [10, 11, 12, 85], [3, 1, 5, 10], [-1, 2, -5, -10] ]

b = [ [10, 11, 16, 33], [11, 13, 5, 55], [-1, -2, -4, 44],
      [55, 33, 77, 12], [-110, 120, 132, 43]
    ]

#Create list new_arr
new_arr = [ [None] * COLUMNS for i in range(ROWS_OF_NEW) ]
for i in range(ROWS_OF_A):
    for j in range(COLUMNS):
        new_arr[i][j] = a[i][j]
for i in range(ROWS_OF_B):
    for j in range(COLUMNS):
        new_arr[ROWS_OF_A + i][j] = b[i][j]

#Display list new_arr
for i in range(ROWS_OF_NEW):
    for j in range(COLUMNS):
        print(new_arr[i][j], end = "\t")
    print()
```

Second Approach

```
                              📁 file_33_1_4b
COLUMNS = 4
ROWS_OF_A = 3
ROWS_OF_B = 5
ROWS_OF_NEW = ROWS_OF_A + ROWS_OF_B

#Create lists a and b
a = [ [10, 11, 12, 85], [3, 1, 5, 10], [-1, 2, -5, -10] ]

b = [ [10, 11, 16, 33], [11, 13, 5, 55], [-1, -2, -4, 44],
      [55, 33, 77, 12], [-110, 120, 132, 43]
    ]

#Create list new_arr
new_arr = []
for row in a:
```

```
        new_arr.append(row)
    for row in b:
        new_arr.append(row)

    #Display list new_arr
    for i in range(ROWS_OF_NEW):
        for j in range(COLUMNS):
            print(new_arr[i][j], end = "\t")
        print()
```

Third Approach

```
                        🗂 file_33_1_4c
COLUMNS = 4
ROWS_OF_A = 3
ROWS_OF_B = 5
ROWS_OF_NEW = ROWS_OF_A + ROWS_OF_B

#Create lists a and b
a = [ [10, 11, 12, 85], [3, 1, 5, 10], [-1, 2, -5, -10] ]

b = [ [10, 11, 16, 33], [11, 13, 5, 55], [-1, -2, -4, 44],
      [55, 33, 77, 12], [-110, 120, 132, 43]
    ]

#Create list new_arr using the concatenation operator ( + )
new_arr = a + b

#Display list new_arr
for i in range(ROWS_OF_NEW):
    for j in range(COLUMNS):
        print(new_arr[i][j], end = "\t")
    print()
```

Exercise 33.1-5   *Creating Two Lists – Separating Positive from Negative Values*

Write a Python program that lets the user enter 100 numerical values into a list and then creates two new lists, pos and neg. List pos must contain positive values, whereas list neg must contain the negative ones. The value 0 (if any) must not be added to either of the final lists, pos or neg.

Solution

There are two approaches! The first one can be applied to most computer languages, whereas the second one is more Pythonic!

First Approach

Let's analyze this approach using the following example.

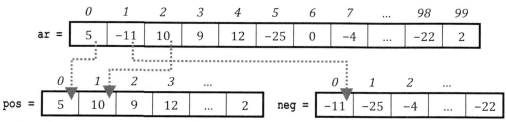

In this exercise, there is no one-to-one match between the index positions of the elements of list `ar` and the lists `pos` and `neg`. For example, the element from position 1 of list `ar` is not stored in position 1 of list `neg`, or the element from position 2 of list `ar` is not stored in position 2 of list `pos`. Thus, you **cannot** do the following,

```
for i in range(ELEMENTS):
    if ar[i] > 0:
        pos[i] = ar[i]
    elif ar[i] < 0:
        neg[i] = ar[i]
```

because it will result in the following two lists.

	0	1	2	3	4	5	6	7	...	98	99
pos =	5		10	9	12				...		2

	0	1	2	3	4	5	6	7	...	98	99
neg =		−11			−25		−4	...	−22	

What you need here are two independent index variables: `pos_index` for the list `pos`, and `neg_index` for the list `neg`. These index variables must be incremented independently, and only when an element is added to the corresponding list. The index variable `pos_index` must be incremented only when an element is added to the list `pos`, and the index variable `neg_index` must be incremented only when an element is added to the list `neg`, as shown in the code fragment that follows.

```
pos_index = 0
neg_index = 0
for i in range(ELEMENTS):
    if ar[i] > 0:
        pos[pos_index] = ar[i]
        pos_index += 1
    elif ar[i] < 0:
        neg[neg_index] = ar[i]
        neg_index += 1
```

When this loop finishes iterating, the two lists become as follows.

	0	1	2	3	...	
pos =	5	10	9	12	...	2

	0	1	2	...	
neg =	−11	−25	−4	...	−22

✎ *Note that variables* pos_index *and* neg_index *have dual roles. When the loop iterates, each points to the next position in which a new element must be placed. But when the loop finishes iterating, variables* pos_index *and* neg_index *also contain the total number of elements in each corresponding list!*

The complete solution is presented next.

📄 **file_33_1_5a**

```
ELEMENTS = 100

ar = [None] * ELEMENTS
for i in range(ELEMENTS):
    ar[i] = float(input())

#Create lists pos and neg
pos = [None] * ELEMENTS
neg = [None] * ELEMENTS
pos_index = 0
neg_index = 0
for i in range(ELEMENTS):
    if ar[i] > 0:
        pos[pos_index] = ar[i]
        pos_index += 1
    elif ar[i] < 0:
        neg[neg_index] = ar[i]
        neg_index += 1

for i in range(pos_index):
    print(pos[i], end = "\t")

print()

for i in range(neg_index):
    print(neg[i], end = "\t")
```

✎ *Note that the lists* pos *and* neg *contain a total number of* pos_index *and* neg_index *elements respectively. This is why the two last loop control structures iterate until variable* i *reaches values* pos_index - 1 *and* neg_index - 1, *respectively, and not until* ELEMENTS - 1, *as you may mistakenly expect. Obviously the sum of* pos_index + neg_index *equals to* ELEMENTS.

Second Approach

The first approach has a main disadvantage! The lists pos and neg must be initialized to a size of 100 because there is always a possibility that list ar contains only positive numbers, or probably only negative ones. Using the append() method, the next approach is more efficient than the previous one since it uses the least possible amount of main memory (RAM).

📄 **file_33_1_5b**

```
ELEMENTS = 100

ar = []
for i in range(ELEMENTS):
    ar.append(float(input()))

#Create lists pos and neg
```

```
pos = []
neg = []
for element in ar:
    if element > 0:
        pos.append(element)
    elif element < 0:
        neg.append(element)

for element in pos:
    print(element, end = "\t")

print()

for element in neg:
    print(element, end = "\t")
```

✎ *It is obvious that one problem can have many solutions. It is up to you to find the optimal one!*

✎ *Be careful! In Python, even though you can do something like* x = y = 0, *this is not true when it comes to lists. It is absolutely incorrect to write* pos = neg = [] *because both* pos *and* neg *would refer to the same list. You must use two individual statements, as shown in this approach.*

Exercise 33.1-6   *Creating a List with Those who Contain Digit 5*

Write a Python program that lets the user enter 100 two-digit integers into a list and then creates a new list of only the integers that contain at least one of the digit 5.

Solution

This exercise requires some knowledge from the past. In Exercise 13.1-2 you learned how to use the quotient and the remainder to split an integer into its individual digits. Here, the integer has two digits; therefore, you can use the following code fragment to split any two-digit integer contained in variable x.

```
last_digit = x % 10
first_digit = x // 10
```

or a more Pythonic way is to use the divmod() function.

```
first_digit, last_digit = divmod(x, 10)
```

There are two approaches that you can use to solve this exercise! The first one can be applied to most computer languages, whereas the second one is more Pythonic!

First Approach

This approach uses an extra variable that becomes the index for the new list. This is necessary when you want to create a new list using values from an old list and there is no one-to-one match between their index positions. Of course, this variable must increase by 1 only when a new element is added into the new list. Moreover, when the loop that creates the new list finishes iterating, the value of this variable also matches the total number of elements in the new list! The final Python program is as follows.

```
                          📄 file_33_1_6a
ELEMENTS = 100

a = [None] * ELEMENTS
```

```
for i in range(ELEMENTS):
    a[i] = int(input())

b = [None] * ELEMENTS
k = 0
for i in range(ELEMENTS):
    last_digit = a[i] % 10
    first_digit = a[i] // 10

    if first_digit == 5 or last_digit == 5:
        b[k] = a[i]
        k += 1

for i in range(k):
    print(b[i], end = "\t")
```

Second Approach

As in the previous exercise, the main disadvantage of the first approach is that it initializes list b to a size of 100, regardless of the fact that the user may or may not enter integers that contain at least one instance of the digit 5! Using the append() method, the next approach is more efficient and more Pythonic!

☐ **file_33_1_6b**

```
ELEMENTS = 100

a = []
for i in range(ELEMENTS):
    a.append(int(input()))

b = []
for element in a:
    first_digit, last_digit = divmod(element, 10)

    if 5 in [first_digit, last_digit]:
        b.append(element)

for element in b:
    print(element, end = "\t")
```

33.2   Data Validation with Lists

As you have already been taught in paragraph 29.3, there are three approaches that you can use to validate data input. Your approach will depend on whether or not you wish to display an error message, and whether you wish to display individual error messages for each error or just a single error message for any kind of error. Let's see how those three approaches can be adapted and used with lists.

First Approach – Validating data input without error messages

In paragraph 29.3, you learned how to validate one single value entered by the user without displaying any error messages. For your convenience, the code fragment given in general form is presented once again.

```
while True:
    input_data = input("Prompt message")
```

```
if input_data test 1 succeeds and      \
    input_data test 2 succeeds and      \
        …
    input_data test N succeeds: break
```

Do you remember how this operates? If the user persistently enters an invalid value, the main idea is to prompt him or her repeatedly, until he or she gets bored and finally enters a valid one. Of course, if the user enters a valid value right from the beginning, the flow of execution simply continues to the next part of the program.

You can use the same principle when entering data into lists. If you use a for-loop to iterate for all elements of the list, the code fragment becomes as follows.

```
input_list = [None] * ELEMENTS
for i in range(ELEMENTS)
    while True:
        input_data = input("Prompt message")
        if input_data test 1 succeeds and      \
            input_data test 2 succeeds and      \
                …
            input_data test N succeeds: break

    input_list[i] = input_data
```

As you can see, when the flow of execution exits the post-test loop structure, the variable *input_data* definitely contains a valid value which in turn is assigned to an element of the list *input_list*. However, the same process can be implemented more simply, without using the extra variable *input_data*, as follows.

```
input_list = [None] * ELEMENTS
for i in range(ELEMENTS):
    while True:
        input_list[i] = input("Prompt message")
        if input_list[i] test 1 succeeds and      \
            input_list[i] test 2 succeeds and      \
                …
            input_list[i] test N succeeds: break
```

Second Approach – Validating data input with one single error message

As before, the next code fragment is taken from paragraph 29.3 and adapted to operate with a list. It validates data input and displays an error message (that is, the same error message for any type of input error).

```
input_list = [None] * ELEMENTS
for i in range(ELEMENTS):
    input_list[i] = input("Prompt message")
    while input_list[i] test 1 fails or      \
            input_list[i] test 2 fails or      \
                …
            input_list[i] test N fails:
        print("Error message")
        input_list[i] = input("Prompt message")
```

Third Approach – Validating data input with individual error messages

Once again, the next code fragment is taken from paragraph 29.3 and adapted to operate with a list. It validates data input and displays an error message (that is, individual error messages, one for each type of input error).

```python
input_list = [None] * ELEMENTS
for i in range(ELEMENTS):
    while True:
        input_list[i] = input("Prompt message")
        failure = False
        if input_list[i] test 1 fails:
            print("Error message 1")
            failure = True
        elif input_list[i] test 2 fails:
            print("Error message 2")
            failure = True
        elif …
            …
        elif input_list[i] test N fails:
            print("Error message N")
            failure = True

        if not failure: break
```

Exercise 33.2-1   *Displaying Odds in Reverse Order – Validation Without Error Messages*

Write a Python program that prompts the user to enter 20 odd positive integers into a list and then displays them in the exact reverse of the order in which they were given. The program must also validate data input, not allowing the user to enter a non-positive value, a float, or an even integer. There is no need to display any error messages.

Solution

As the wording of the exercise implies, not all entered values should be added in the list—only the odd positive integers. The Python program is presented next.

```
                                    📄 file_33_2_1
ELEMENTS = 20
                                              Data input and validation
odds = [None] * ELEMENTS
for i in range(ELEMENTS):
    while True:
        x = float(input("Enter an odd positive integer: "))
        if x > 0 and x == int(x) and x % 2 != 0: break
    odds[i] = int(x)

#Display elements backwards              # Or you can do the following
for i in range(ELEMENTS - 1, -1, -1):    # for element in odds[::-1]:
    print(odds[i], end = "\t")           #     print(element, end = "\t")
```

✎ *Variable* x *must be of type float. This is necessary in order to allow the user to enter either an integer or a float (real).*

Exercise 33.2-2   *Displaying Odds in Reverse Order – Validation with One Error Message*

Write a Python program that prompts the user to enter 20 odd positive integers into a list and then displays them in the exact reverse of the order in which they were given. The program must also validate data input and display an error message when the user enters any non-positive values, any floats, or any even integers.

Solution

This is the same as you've previously seen, except for data validation. The second approach is used, according to which an error message is displayed when the user enters a non-positive value, a float, or an even integer. The Python program is presented next.

📁 **file_33_2_2**

Data input and validation

```python
ELEMENTS = 20

odds = [None] * ELEMENTS
for i in range(ELEMENTS):
    x = float(input("Enter an odd positive integer: "))
    while x <= 0 or x != int(x) or x % 2 == 0:
        print("Invalid value!")
        x = float(input("Enter an odd positive integer: "))
    odds[i] = int(x)

#Display elements backwards
for element in odds[::-1]:
    print(element, end = "\t")
```

Exercise 33.2-3   *Displaying Odds in Reverse Order – Validation with Individual Error Messages*

Write a Python program that prompts the user to enter 20 odd positive integers in a list and then displays them in the exact reverse of the order in which they were given. The program must also validate data input and display individual error messages when the user enters any non-positive values, any floats, or any even integers.

Solution

The third approach is used, according to which individual error messages are displayed when the user enters any non-positive values, any floats, or any even integers. The Python program is as follows.

📁 **file_33_2_3**

Data input and validation

```python
ELEMENTS = 20

odds = [None] * ELEMENTS
for i in range(ELEMENTS):
    while True:
        x = float(input("Enter an odd positive integer: "))
        failure = False
        if x <= 0 :
            print("Invalid value: Non-positive entered!")
```

```
                failure = True
        elif x != int(x):
            print("Invalid value: Float entered!")
            failure = True
        elif x % 2 == 0:
            print("Invalid value: Even entered!")
            failure = True
        if not failure: break
    odds[i] = int(x)
```

```
#Display elements backwards
for element in odds[::-1]:
    print(element, end = "\t")
```

33.3   Finding Minimum and Maximum Values in Lists

This is the third and last time that this subject is raked up in this book. The first time was in paragraph 22.3 using decision control structures and the second time was in paragraph 29.5 using loop control structures. So, there is not much left to discuss except that when you want to find the minimum or maximum value of a data structure that already contains some values, you needn't worry about the initial values of variables minimum or maximum because you can just assign to them the value of the first element of the data structure!

Exercise 33.3-1   Which Depth is the Greatest?

Write a Python program that lets the user enter the depths of 20 lakes and then displays the depth of the deepest one.

Solution

After the user enters the depths of the 20 lakes in the list depths, the initial value of variable maximum can be the value of the first element of list depths, that is depths[0]. The program can then search (starting from index 1) for any value thereafter greater than this. The final solution is quite simple and is presented next without further explanation.

```
                          📄 file_33_3_1a
LAKES = 20

depths = [None] * LAKES
for i in range(LAKES):
    depths[i] = float(input())

maximum = depths[0]   #Initial value

#Search thereafter, starting from index 1
for i in range(1, LAKES):
    if depths[i] > maximum:
        maximum = depths[i]

print(maximum)
```

✎ *It wouldn't be wrong to start iterating from position 0 instead of 1, though the program would perform one useless iteration.*

✎ *It wouldn't be wrong to assign an "almost arbitrary" initial value to variable* maximum *but there is no reason to do so. The value of the first element is just fine! If you insist though, you can assign an initial value of 0, since there is no lake on planet Earth with a negative depth.*

Keep in mind though, that a more Pythonic way to find the greatest value of a list is to use the max() function, as shown here.

📁 **file_33_3_1b**

```
LAKES = 20

depths = []
for i in range(LAKES):
    depths.append(float(input()))

maximum = max(depths)
print(maximum)
```

✎ *Correspondingly, if you want to find the smallest value of a list you can use the* min() *function.*

Exercise 33.3-2   Which Lake is the Deepest?

Write a Python program that lets the user enter the names and the depths of 20 lakes and then displays the name of the deepest one.

Solution

If you don't know how to find the name of the deepest lake, you may need to refresh your memory by re-reading Exercise 29.5-2.

In this exercise, you need two one-dimensional lists: one to hold the names, and one to hold the depths of the lakes. The solution is presented next.

📁 **file_33_3_2**

```
LAKES = 20

names = [None] * LAKES
depths = [None] * LAKES

for i in range(LAKES):
    names[i] = input()
    depths[i] = float(input())

maximum = depths[0]
m_name = names[0]
for i in range(1, LAKES):
    if depths[i] > maximum:
        maximum = depths[i]
        m_name = names[i]
```

```
print(m_name)
```

✎ *You cannot use the function* max() *in this exercise! It would return the greatest depth, not the name of the lake with that greatest depth!*

Exercise 33.3-3   Which Lake, in Which Country, Having Which Average Area, is the Deepest?

Write a Python program that lets the user enter the names and the depths of 20 lakes as well as the country in which they belong, and their average area. The program must then display all available information about the deepest lake.

Solution

In this exercise, you need four one-dimensional lists: one to hold the names, one to hold the depths, one to hold the names of the countries, and one to hold the lakes' average areas. There are two approaches, actually. Let's study them both!

First Approach – One variable for each

This is pretty much the same as the one used in the previous exercise. The solution is presented next.

```
📁 file_33_3_3a
LAKES = 20

names = [None] * LAKES
depths = [None] * LAKES
countries = [None] * LAKES
areas = [None] * LAKES

for i in range(LAKES):
    names[i] = input()
    depths[i] = float(input())
    countries[i] = input()
    areas[i] = float(input())

maximum = depths[0]
m_name = names[0]
m_country = countries[0]
m_area = areas[0]
for i in range(1, LAKES):
    if depths[i] > maximum:
        maximum = depths[i]
        m_name = names[i]
        m_country = countries[i]
        m_area = areas[i]

print(maximum, m_name, m_country, m_area)
```

Second Approach – One index for everything

This approach is more efficient than the first one since it uses fewer variables. Instead of using all those variables (m_name, m_country, and m_area), you can use just one variable, a variable that holds the index in which the maximum value exists!

Confused? Let's look at the next example of six lakes. The depths are expressed in feet and the average areas in square miles.

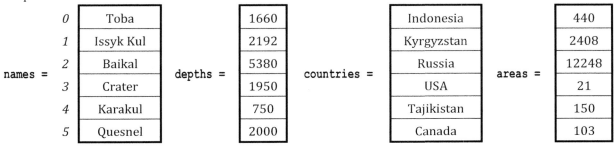

Obviously the deepest lake is Lake Baikal at position 2. However, instead of holding the name "Baikal" in variable m_name, the country "Russia" in variable m_country, and the area "12248" in variable m_area as in the previous approach, you can use just one variable to hold the index position in which these values actually exist (in this case, this is value 2). The solution is presented next.

```
                        📁 file_33_3_3b
LAKES = 20

names = [None] * LAKES
depths = [None] * LAKES
countries = [None] * LAKES
areas = [None] * LAKES

for i in range(LAKES):
    names[i] = input()
    depths[i] = float(input())
    countries[i] = input()
    areas[i] = float(input())

#Find the maximum depth and the index in which this maximum depth exists
maximum = depths[0]
index_of_max = 0
for i in range(1, LAKES):
    if depths[i] > maximum:
        maximum = depths[i]
        index_of_max = i

#Display information using index_of_max as index
print(depths[index_of_max], names[index_of_max])
print(countries[index_of_max], areas[index_of_max])
```

✎ *Assigning an initial value of 0 to variable* index_of_max *is necessary since there is always a possibility that the maximum value does exist in position 0.*

Exercise 33.3-4   Which Students Have got the Greatest Grade?

Write a Python program that prompts the user to enter the names and the grades of 200 students and then displays the names of all those who share the one greatest grade. Using a loop control structure, the program must also validate data input and display an error message when the user enters an empty name or any negative values or values greater than 100 for grades.

Solution

In this exercise, you need to validate both the names and the grades. A code fragment, given in general form, shows the data input stage.

```
STUDENTS = 200

names = [None] * STUDENTS
grades = [None] * STUDENTS

for i in range(STUDENTS):

    Prompt the user to enter a name and validate it. It cannot be empty!

    Prompt the user to enter a grade and validate it.
    It cannot be negative or greater than 100.
```

After data input stage, a loop control structure must search for the greatest value, and then, another loop control structure must search the list grades for all values that are equal to that greatest value.

The solution in presented next.

```
                                 📁 file_33_3_4
STUDENTS = 200

names = [None] * STUDENTS
grades = [None] * STUDENTS

for i in range(STUDENTS):
    #Prompt the user to enter a name and validate it.
    names[i] = input("Enter name for student No " + str(i + 1) + ": ")
    while names[i] == "":
        print("Error! Name cannot be empty!")
        names[i] = input("Enter name for student No " + str(i + 1) + ": ")

    #Prompt the user to enter a grade and validate it.
    grades[i] = int(input("Enter his or her grade: "))
    while grades[i] < 0 or grades[i] > 100:
        print("Invalid value!")
        grades[i] = int(input("Enter his or her grade: "))

#Find the greatest grade
maximum = grades[0]                      # Or you can do the following:
for i in range(1, STUDENTS):             # maximum = max(grades)
```

```
    if grades[i] > maximum:          #
        maximum = grades[i]          #
```

```
#Displays the names of all those who share the one greatest grade
print("The following students have got the greatest grade:")
for i in range(STUDENTS):
    if grades[i] == maximum:
        print(names[i])
```

✎ *Note that this exercise could not have been solved without the use of a list.*

✎ *Keep in mind that the following code fragment is also correct but very inefficient.*

```
print("The following students have got the greatest grade:")
for i in range(STUDENTS):
    if grades[i] == max(grades):
        print(names[i])
```

The reason is that in this example, function max() *is called each time the loop iterates—that is, 200 times!*

Exercise 33.3-5   Finding the Minimum Value of a Two-Dimensional List

Write a Python program that lets the user enter the temperatures (in degrees Fahrenheit) recorded at the same hour each day in January in 10 different cities. The Python program must display the lowest temperature.

Solution

In this exercise, you need the following list.

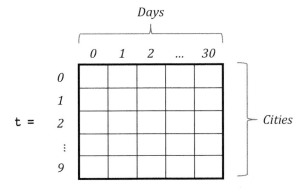

✎ *The list* t *has 31 columns (0 to 30), as many as there are days in January.*

There is nothing new here. The initial value of variable minimum can be the value of the element t[0][0]. Then, the program can iterate through rows, or even through columns, to search for the minimum value. The solution is presented next.

📁 **file_33_3_5a**

```
CITIES = 10
DAYS = 31
```

```python
#Read list t
t = [ [None] * DAYS for i in range(CITIES) ]
for i in range(CITIES):
    for j in range(DAYS):
        t[i][j] = int(input())

#Find minimum
minimum = t[0][0]
for i in range(CITIES):
    for j in range(DAYS):
        if t[i][j] < minimum:
            minimum = t[i][j]

print(minimum)
```

✎ *In this exercise you cannot do the following because if you do, and variable j starts from 1, the whole column with index 0 won't be checked!*

```python
#Find minimum
minimum = t[0][0]
for i in range(CITIES):
    for j in range(1, DAYS):
        if t[i][j] < minimum:
            minimum = t[i][j]
```

A more Pythonic way, though, is to find the lowest value of list t using the min() function, as shown here.

```
📄 file_33_3_5b
```

```python
CITIES = 10
DAYS = 31

#Read list t
t = []
for i in range(CITIES):
    t.append([])
    for j in range(DAYS):
        t[i].append(int(input()))

print(min(t))
```

Exercise 33.3-6   Finding the City with the Coldest Day

Write a Python program that lets the user enter the temperatures (in degrees Fahrenheit) recorded at the same hour each day in January in 10 different cities. The Python program must display the name of the city that had the lowest temperature and on which day it was recorded.

Solution

In this exercise, the following two lists are needed.

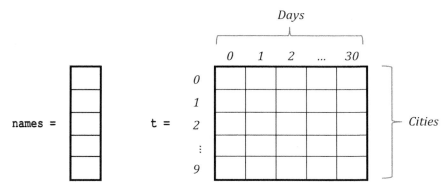

The solution is simple. Every time variable `minimum` updates its value, two variables, `m_i` and `m_j`, can hold the values of variables `i` and `j` respectively. In the end, these two variables will contain the row index and the column index of the position in which the minimum value exists. The solution is as follows.

```
                          📂 file_33_3_6
CITIES = 10
DAYS = 31

names = [None] * CITIES
t = [ [None] * DAYS for i in range(CITIES) ]
for i in range(CITIES):
    names[i] = input()
    for j in range(DAYS):
        t[i][j] = int(input())

minimum = t[0][0]
m_i = 0
m_j = 0
for i in range(CITIES):
    for j in range(DAYS):
        if t[i][j] < minimum:
            minimum = t[i][j]
            m_i = i
            m_j = j

print("Minimum temperature: ", minimum)
print("City: ", names[m_i])
print("Day: ", m_j + 1)
```

✎ *Assigning an initial value of 0 to variables* `m_i` *and* `m_j` *is necessary since there is always a possibility that the minimum value is the value of the element* `t[0][0]`.

Exercise 33.3-7   Finding the Minimum and the Maximum Value of Each Row

Write a Python program that lets the user enter values in a 20 × 30 list and then finds and displays the minimum and the maximum values of each row.

Solution

There are three approaches, actually. The first approach creates two auxiliary one-dimensional lists, minimum and maximum, and then displays them. Lists minimum and maximum will contain, in each position, the minimum and the maximum values of each row respectively. On the other hand, the second and third approaches find and directly display the minimum and maximum values of each row. Let's study them all.

First Approach – Creating auxiliary lists

To better understand this approach, let's use the "from inner to outer" method. When the following code fragment completes its iterations, the auxiliary one-dimensional lists minimum and maximum contain at position 0 the minimum and the maximum values of the first row (row index 0) of list b respectively. Assume variable i contains value 0.

```
minimum[i] = b[i][0]
maximum[i] = b[i][0]
for j in range(1, COLUMNS):
    if b[i][j] < minimum[i]:
        minimum[i] = b[i][j]
    if b[i][j] > maximum[i]:
        maximum[i] = b[i][j]
```

✎ *Note that variable j starts from 1. It wouldn't be wrong to start iterating from column index 0 instead of 1, though the program would perform one useless iteration.*

Now that everything has been clarified, in order to process the whole list b, you can just nest this code fragment into a for-loop which iterates for all rows as shown next.

```
for i in range(ROWS):
    minimum[i] = b[i][0]
    maximum[i] = b[i][0]
    for j in range(1, COLUMNS):
        if b[i][j] < minimum[i]:
            minimum[i] = b[i][j]
        if b[i][j] > maximum[i]:
            maximum[i] = b[i][j]
```

The final Python program is as follows.

```
📁 file_33_3_7a
ROWS = 30
COLUMNS = 20

b = [ [None] * COLUMNS for i in range(ROWS) ]

for i in range(ROWS):
    for j in range(COLUMNS):
        b[i][j] = float(input())

minimum = [None] * ROWS
maximum = [None] * ROWS
for i in range(ROWS):
```

```
            minimum[i] = b[i][0]
            maximum[i] = b[i][0]
            for j in range(1, COLUMNS):
                if b[i][j] < minimum[i]:
                    minimum[i] = b[i][j]
                if b[i][j] > maximum[i]:
                    maximum[i] = b[i][j]

    for i in range(ROWS):
        print(minimum[i], maximum[i])
```

Second Approach – Finding and directly displaying minimum and maximum values

Let's use the "from inner to outer" method once again. The next code fragment finds and directly displays the minimum and the maximum values of the first row (row index 0) of list b. Assume variable i contains the value 0.

```
minimum = b[i][0]
maximum = b[i][0]
for j in range(1, COLUMNS):
    if b[i][j] < minimum:
        minimum = b[i][j]
    if b[i][j] > maximum:
        maximum = b[i][j]

print(minimum, maximum)
```

Now that everything has been clarified, in order to process the whole list b, you can just nest this code fragment into a for-loop which iterates for all rows, as follows.

```
for i in range(ROWS):
    minimum = b[i][0]
    maximum = b[i][0]
    for j in range(1, COLUMNS):
        if b[i][j] < minimum:
            minimum = b[i][j]
        if b[i][j] > maximum:
            maximum = b[i][j]

    print(minimum, maximum)
```

The final Python program is as follows.

📁 **file_33_3_7b**

```
ROWS = 30
COLUMNS = 20

b = [ [None] * COLUMNS for i in range(ROWS) ]

for i in range(ROWS):
    for j in range(COLUMNS):
        b[i][j] = float(input())
```

```
for i in range(ROWS):
    minimum = b[i][0]
    maximum = b[i][0]
    for j in range(1, COLUMNS):
        if b[i][j] < minimum:
            maximum = b[i][j]
        if b[i][j] > maximum:
            maximum = b[i][j]

    print(minimum, maximum)
```

Third Approach – The Pythonic way

This approach uses the min() and max() functions of Python. It finds and directly displays the lowest and the highest values of each row.

```
📁 file_33_3_7c
```

```
ROWS = 30
COLUMNS = 20

b = []
for i in range(ROWS):
    b.append([])
    for j in range(COLUMNS):
        b[i].append(float(input()))

for row in b:
    print(min(row), max(row))
```

33.4   Sorting Lists

Sorting algorithms are an important topic in computer science. A *sorting algorithm* is an algorithm that puts elements of a list in a certain order. There are many sorting algorithms and each one of them has particular strengths and weaknesses.

Most sorting algorithms work by comparing the elements of the list. They are usually evaluated by their efficiency and their memory requirements.

There are many sorting algorithms. Some of them are:

► the bubble sort algorithm
► the modified bubble sort algorithm
► the selection sort algorithm
► the insertion sort algorithm
► the heap sort algorithm
► the merge sort algorithm
► the quicksort algorithm

As regards their efficiency, the bubble sort algorithm is considered the least efficient, while each succeeding algorithm in the list performs better than the preceding one. The quicksort algorithm is considered one of the best and fastest sorting algorithms, especially for large scale data operations.

Sorting algorithms can be used for more than just displaying data in ascending or descending order. For example, if an exercise requires you to display the three biggest numbers of a list, the Python program can sort the list in descending order and then display only the first three elements, that is, those at index positions 0, 1, and 2.

Sorting algorithms can also help you find the minimum and the maximum values from a set of given values. If a list is sorted in ascending order, the minimum value exists at the first index position and the maximum value exists at the last index position. Of course, it is very inefficient to sort a list so as to find minimum and maximum values; you have already learned a more efficient method. But if for some reason an exercise requires that a list be sorted and you need the minimum or the maximum value, you know where you can find them!

As you already know, Python already incorporates the method `sort()` and the function `sorted()`, both of which can be used to sort lists. However there are times when you need to build your own sorting algorithm, especially when you want to sort a list while preserving the relationship with a second list.

Exercise 33.4-1   The Bubble Sort Algorithm – Sorting One-Dimensional Lists with Numeric Values

Write a Python program that lets the user enter 20 numerical values into a list and then sorts them in ascending order using the bubble sort algorithm.

Solution

The *bubble sort algorithm* is probably one of the most inefficient sorting algorithms but it is widely used for teaching purposes. The main idea (when asked to sort a list in ascending order) is to repeatedly move the smallest elements of the list to the positions of lowest index. This works as follows: the algorithm iterates through the elements of the list, compares each pair of adjacent elements, and then swaps their contents (if they are in the wrong order). This process is repeated many times until the list is sorted.

For example, let's try to sort the following list in ascending order.

The lowest value is the value 5. According to the bubble sort algorithm, this value must gradually "bubble" or "rise" to position 0, like bubbles rising in a glass of cola. When the value 5 has been moved into position 0, the next smallest value is the value 8. Now, the value 8 must "bubble" to position 1. Next is the value 12, which must "bubble" to position 2, and so on. This process repeats until all elements are placed in proper position.

But how can this "bubbling" be done using an algorithm? Let's see the whole process in more detail. For the previous list A of six elements, five passes must be performed.

First Pass

1st Compare

Initially, elements at index positions 4 and 5 are compared. Since the value 12 is less than the value 49, these two elements swap their content.

2nd Compare

Elements at index positions 3 and 4 are compared. Since the value 12 is **not** less than the value 5, **no** swapping is done.

3rd Compare

Elements at index positions 2 and 3 are compared. Since the value 5 is less than the value 8, these two elements swap their content.

4th Compare

Elements at index positions 1 and 2 are compared. Since the value 5 is less than the value 25, these two elements swap their content.

5th Compare

Elements at index positions 0 and 1 are compared. Since the value 5 is less than the value 17, these two elements swap their content.

1st Compare		2nd Compare	3rd Compare	4th Compare	5th Compare	
17	0	17	17	17	17	**5**
25	1	25	25	25	5	17
8	2	8	8	5	25	25
5	3	5	5	8	8	8
49	4	12	12	12	12	12
12	5	49	49	49	49	49

The first pass has been completed but, as you can see, the list has not been sorted yet. The only value that has actually been placed in proper position is the value 5. However, since more passes will follow, there is no need for the value 5 to take part in the subsequent compares. In the pass that follows, one less compare will be performed—that is, four compares.

Second Pass

1st Compare

Elements at index positions 4 and 5 are compared. Since the value 49 is **not** less than the value 12, **no** swapping is done.

2nd Compare

Elements at index positions 3 and 4 are compared. Since the value 12 is **not** less than the value 8, **no** swapping is done.

3rd Compare

Elements at index positions 2 and 3 are compared. Since the value 8 is less than the value 25, these two elements swap their content.

4th Compare

Elements at index positions 1 and 2 are compared. Since the value 8 is less than the value 17, these two elements swap their content.

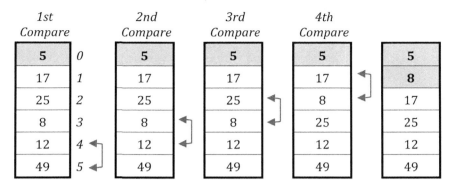

The second pass has been completed and the value of 8 has been placed in proper position. However, since more passes will follow, there is no need for the value 8 (nor 5, of course) to take part in the subsequent compares. In the pass that follows, one less compare will be performed—that is, three compares.

Third Pass

1st Compare

Elements at index positions 4 and 5 are compared. Since the value 49 is **not** less than the value 12, **no** swapping is done.

2nd Compare

Elements at index positions 3 and 4 are compared. Since the value 12 is less than the value 25, these two elements swap their content.

3rd Compare

Elements at index positions 2 and 3 are compared. Since the value 12 is less than the value 17, these two elements swap their content.

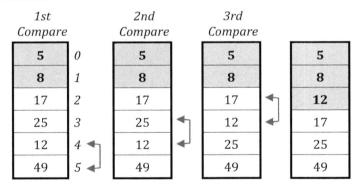

The third pass has been completed and the value of 12 has been placed in proper position. As previously, since more passes will follow there is no need for the value 12 (nor the values 5 and 8, of course) to take part in the subsequent compares. In the pass that follows, one compare less will be performed—that is, two compares.

Fourth Pass

1st Compare

Elements at index positions 4 and 5 are compared. Since the value 49 is **not** less than the value 25, **no** swapping is done.

2nd Compare

Elements at index positions 3 and 4 are compared. Since the value 25 is **not** less than the value 17, **no** swapping is done.

The fourth pass has been completed and the value 17 has been placed in proper position. As previously, since one last pass will follow, there is no need for the value 17 (nor the values 5, 8, and 12, of course) to take part in the subsequent compares. In the last pass that follows, one compare less will be performed—that is one compare.

Fifth pass

1st Compare

Elements at index positions 4 and 5 are compared. Since the value 49 is **not** less than the value 25, **no** swapping is done.

The fifth pass has been completed and the final two values (25 and 49) have been placed in proper position. The bubble sort algorithm has finished and the list is sorted in ascending order!

Now you need a Python program that can do the whole previous process. Let's use the "from inner to outer" method. The code fragment that performs only the first pass is shown below. Please note that this is the inner (nested) loop control structure. Assume variable m contains the value 0.

```
for n in range(ELEMENTS - 1, m, -1):
    if a[n] < a[n - 1]:
        temp = a[n]
        a[n] = a[n - 1]
        a[n - 1] = temp
```

✎ *In the first pass, variable m must contain the value 0. This assures that at the last iteration, the elements that are compared are those at positions 1 and 0.*

▥ *Swapping the contents of two elements uses a method you have already learned! Please recall the two glasses of orange juice and lemon juice. If this doesn't ring a bell, you need to refresh your memory and re-read the corresponding Exercise 8.1-2.*

Keep in mind that you can swap the contents of a[n] and a[n - 1] in a more Pythonic way, as shown here.

```python
for n in range(ELEMENTS - 1, m, -1):
    if a[n] < a[n - 1]:
        a[n], a[n - 1] = a[n - 1], a[n]
```

The second pass can be performed if you just re-execute the previous code fragment. Variable m, however, needs to contain the value 1. This will ensure that the element at position 0 won't be compared again. Similarly, for the third pass, the previous code fragment can be re-executed but variable m needs to contain the value 2 for the same reason.

Accordingly, the previous code fragment needs to be executed five times (one for each pass), and each time variable m must be incremented by 1. The final code fragment that sorts list a using the bubble sort algorithm is as follows.

```python
for m in range(ELEMENTS - 1):
    for n in range(ELEMENTS - 1, m, -1):
        if a[n] < a[n - 1]:
            a[n], a[n - 1] = a[n - 1], a[n]
```

📖 *For N elements, the algorithm needs to perform N – 1 passes. For example, if list a contains 20 elements, the statement* for m in range(ELEMENTS - 1) *performs 19 passes.*

The complete Python program is as follows.

```
📁 file_33_4_1
```

```python
ELEMENTS = 20

a = [None] * ELEMENTS
for i in range(ELEMENTS):
    a[i] = float(input())

for m in range(ELEMENTS - 1):
    for n in range(ELEMENTS - 1, m, -1):
        if a[n] < a[n - 1]:
            a[n], a[n - 1] = a[n - 1], a[n]

for i in range(ELEMENTS):
    print(a[i], end = "\t")
```

✎ *The bubble sort algorithm is very inefficient. The total number of compares that it performs is $\frac{N(N-1)}{2}$, where N is the total number of list elements.*

✎ *The total number of swaps depends on the given list. The worst case is when you want to sort in ascending order a list that is already sorted in descending order, or vice versa.*

Exercise 33.4-2　　*Sorting One-Dimensional Lists with Alphanumeric Values*

Write a code fragment that sorts the alphanumeric values of a list in descending order using the bubble sort algorithm.

Solution

Comparing this exercise to the previous one, two things are different. First, the bubble sort algorithm needs to sort alphanumeric values, such as names of people or names of cities; and second, it has to sort them in descending order.

Don't worry though, because there is some good news for you! In order to sort alphanumeric data, you don't have to change anything in the algorithm! Python handles letters the same way it handles numbers. The letter "A" is considered "less than" the letter "B", the letter "B" is considered "less than" the letter "C", and so on. Of course, if the list contains words in which the first letter is identical, Python moves on and compares their second letters and perhaps their third letter (if there is need to do so). For example, the name "John" is considered "less than" the name "Jonathan" because the third letter "h" is "less than" the third letter "n".

 When you are thinking of alphanumeric sorting, think of your dictionary and how words are sorted there.

And now let's see what you need to change so that the algorithm can sort in descending order. Do you remember how the bubble sort algorithm actually works? Elements gradually "bubble" to positions of lowest index, like bubbles rise in a glass of cola. What you want in this exercise is to make the bigger (instead of the smaller) elements "bubble" to lower index positions. Therefore, all you need to do is simply reverse the comparison operator of the decision control structure!

The code fragment that sorts alphanumeric, and of course numeric, values in descending order is as follows.

```python
for m in range(ELEMENTS - 1)
    for n in range(ELEMENTS - 1, m, -1):
        if a[n] > a[n - 1]:
            a[n], a[n - 1] = a[n - 1], a[n]
```

Exercise 33.4-3 Sorting One-Dimensional Lists While Preserving the Relationship with a Second List

Write a Python program that lets the user enter the names of 20 lakes and their corresponding average area. The program must then sort them by average area in ascending order using the bubble sort algorithm.

Solution

In this exercise you need the following two lists.

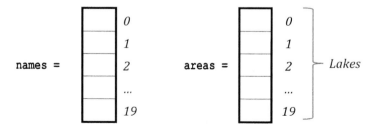

If you want to sort list areas while preserving the relationship between the elements of the two lists, you must rearrange the elements of the list names as well. This means that every time two elements of the list areas swap contents, the corresponding elements of the list names must swap contents as well. The Python program is as follows.

```
📁 file_33_4_3
```

```python
LAKES = 20
```

```
names = [None] * LAKES
areas = [None] * LAKES

for i in range(LAKES):
    names[i] = input()
    areas[i] = float(input())

for m in range(LAKES - 1):
    for n in range(LAKES - 1, m, -1):
        if areas[n] < areas[n - 1]:
            areas[n], areas[n - 1] = areas[n - 1], areas[n]
            names[n], names[n - 1] = names[n - 1], names[n]

for i in range(LAKES):
    print(names[i], "\t", areas[i])
```

Exercise 33.4-4   Sorting Last and First Names

Write a Python program that prompts the user to enter the last and first names of 100 people and then displays them with the last names sorted in alphabetical order. Moreover, if two or more people have the same last name, their first names must be displayed in alphabetical order as well.

Solution

You already know how to sort a list while preserving the relationship with the elements of a second list. Now, you have to handle the case when two last names in the first list are equal. According to the wording of the exercise, the corresponding first names in the second list must be also sorted alphabetically. For example, the following list last_nm contains the last names of 100 people. It is sorted in alphabetical order and it contains the last name "Parker" three times. The corresponding first names "Andrew", "Anna", and "Chloe" in list first_nm are also sorted alphabetically.

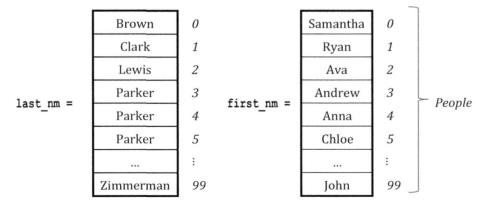

For your convenience, the basic version of the bubble sort algorithm is presented once again. Please note that this algorithm preserves the relationship between the elements of lists last_nm and first_nm.

```
for m in range(PEOPLE - 1):
    for n in range(PEOPLE - 1, m, -1):
```

```
        if last_nm[n] < last_nm[n - 1]:
            last_nm[n], last_nm[n - 1] = last_nm[n - 1], last_nm[n]
            first_nm[n], first_nm[n - 1] = first_nm[n - 1], first_nm[n]
```

To solve this exercise, however, this bubble sort algorithm must be adapted accordingly. According to this basic version of the bubble sort algorithm, when the last name at position n is "less" than the last name at position n - 1, the algorithm swaps the corresponding contents. However, when the last name at position n is equal to the last name at position n - 1, the algorithm then must check if the corresponding first names are in the proper order. If not, they must swap their contents. The adapted bubble sort algorithm is shown in the next code fragment.

```
for m in range(PEOPLE - 1):
    for n in range(PEOPLE - 1, m, -1):
        if last_nm[n] < last_nm[n - 1]:
            last_nm[n], last_nm[n - 1] = last_nm[n - 1], last_nm[n]
            first_nm[n], first_nm[n - 1] = first_nm[n - 1], first_nm[n]
        elif last_nm[n] == last_nm[n - 1]:
            if first_nm[n] < first_nm[n - 1]:
                first_nm[n], first_nm[n - 1] = first_nm[n - 1], first_nm[n]
```

The final Python program is presented next.

```
                           📄 file_33_4_4
PEOPLE = 100

#Read lists first_nm and last_nm
first_nm = [None] * PEOPLE
last_nm = [None] * PEOPLE
for i in range(PEOPLE):
    first_nm[i] = input("First name for person No" + str(i + 1) + ": ")
    last_nm[i] = input("Last name for person No" + str(i + 1) + ": ")

#Sort lists last_nm and first_nm
for m in range(PEOPLE - 1):
    for n in range(PEOPLE - 1, m, -1):
        if last_nm[n] < last_nm[n - 1]:
            last_nm[n], last_nm[n - 1] = last_nm[n - 1], last_nm[n]
            first_nm[n], first_nm[n - 1] = first_nm[n - 1], first_nm[n]
        elif last_nm[n] == last_nm[n - 1]:
            if first_nm[n] < first_nm[n - 1]:
                first_nm[n], first_nm[n - 1] = first_nm[n - 1], first_nm[n]

#Display lists last_nm and first_nm
for i in range(PEOPLE):
    print(last_nm[i], "\t", first_nm[i])
```

Exercise 33.4-5   Sorting a Two-Dimensional List

Write a code fragment that sorts each column of a two-dimensional list in ascending order.

Solution

An example of a two-dimension list is as follows.

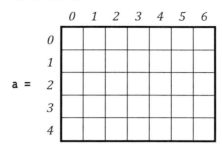

Since this list has seven columns, the bubble sort algorithm needs to be executed seven times, one for each column. Therefore, the whole bubble sort algorithm should be nested within a for-loop that iterates seven times.

But let's get things in the right order. Using the "from inner to outer" method, the next code fragment sorts only the first column (column index 0) of the two-dimensional list a. Assume variable j contains the value 0.

```python
for m in range(ROWS - 1):
    for n in range(ROWS - 1, m, -1):
        if a[n][j] < a[n - 1][j]:
            a[n][j], a[n - 1][j] = a[n - 1][j], a[n][j]
```

Now, in order to sort all columns, you can nest this code fragment in a for-loop that iterates for all of them, as follows.

```python
for j in range(COLUMNS):
    for m in range(ROWS - 1):
        for n in range(ROWS - 1, m, -1):
            if a[n][j] < a[n - 1][j]:
                a[n][j], a[n - 1][j] = a[n - 1][j], a[n][j]
```

That wasn't so difficult, was it?

Exercise 33.4-6   The Modified Bubble Sort Algorithm – Sorting One-Dimensional Lists

*Write a Python program that lets the user enter the weights of 20 people and then displays the three heaviest weights and the three lightest weights. Use the **modified** bubble sort algorithm.*

Solution

To solve this exercise, the Python program can sort the given data in ascending order and then display the elements at index positions 27, 28, and 29 (for the three heaviest weights) and the elements at index positions 0, 1 and 2 (for the three lightest weights).

But how does the modified version of the bubble sort algorithm actually work? Suppose you have the following list containing the weights of six people.

	0	1	2	3	4	5
w =	165	170	180	190	182	200

If you look closer, you can confirm for yourself that the only elements that are not in proper position are those at index positions 3 and 4. If you swap their values, the list w immediately becomes sorted! However, the bubble sort algorithm doesn't operate this way. Unfortunately, for this given list of six elements, it will perform five passes either way, with a total of $\frac{N(N-1)}{2} = 15$ compares, where N is the total number of list elements. For bigger lists, the total number of compares that the bubble sort algorithm performs increases exponentially! For example, for a given list of 1000 elements, the bubble sort algorithm performs 499,500 compares!

Of course the modified bubble sort algorithm can overcome this situation as follows: if a complete pass is performed and no swaps have been made, then this indicates that the list is sorted and there is no need for further passes. To accomplish this, the Python program can use a flag variable that indicates if any swaps were made. At the beginning of a pass, a value of False can be assigned to the flag variable; when a swap is made, a value of True is assigned. If, at the end of the pass, the flag is still False, this indicates that no swaps have been made, thus iterations must stop. The modified bubble sort is shown next. It uses the break statement and a flag variable (swaps).

```python
for m in range(ELEMENTS - 1):
    #Assign False to variable swaps
    swaps = False

    #Perform a new pass
    for n in range(ELEMENTS - 1, m, -1):
        if w[n] < w[n - 1]:
            w[n], w[n - 1] = w[n - 1], w[n]
            swaps = True

    #If variable swaps is still False, no swaps have been
    #made in the last pass. Stop iterations!
    if not swaps: break
```

✎ *The value* False *must be assigned to variable* swaps *each time a new pass starts. This is why the statement* swaps = False *must be placed between the two* for *statements.*

✎ *The statement* if not swaps *is equivalent to the statement* if swaps == False

The final Python program is shown next.

```
📁 file_33_4_6
```

```python
ELEMENTS = 20

w = [None] * ELEMENTS
for i in range(ELEMENTS):
    w[i] = float(input())

for m in range(ELEMENTS - 1):
    swaps = False
    for n in range(ELEMENTS - 1, m, -1):
        if w[n] < w[n - 1]:
            w[n], w[n - 1] = w[n - 1], w[n]
            swaps = True
    if not swaps: break

print("The three heaviest weights are:")
```

```
print(w[ELEMENTS - 3], w[ELEMENTS - 2], w[ELEMENTS - 1])

print("The three lightest weights are:")
print(w[0], w[1], w[2])
```

Exercise 33.4-7   The Five Best Scorers

Write a Python program that prompts the user to enter the names of the 32 national teams of the FIFA World Cup, the names of the 24 players for each team, and the total number of goals each player scored. The program must then display the name of each team along with its five best scorers. Use the modified bubble sort algorithm.

Solution

In this exercise you need the following three lists.

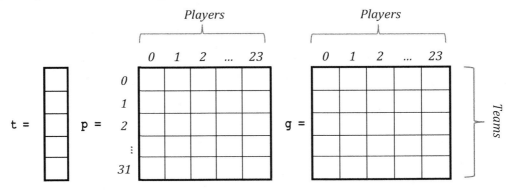

✎ *To save paper short list names are used, but it is more or less obvious that list* t *holds the names of the 32 national teams, list* p *holds the names of the 24 players of each team, and list* g *holds the total number of goals each player scored.*

Since you need to find the five best scorers for each team, the Python program must sort each row of list g in descending order but it must also take care to preserve the relationship with the elements of lists p. This means that, every time the bubble sort algorithm swaps the contents of two elements of list g, the corresponding elements of list p must be swapped as well. When sorting is completed, the five best scorers should appear in the first five columns.

The "from inner to outer" method is used again. The following code fragment sorts the first row (row index 0) of list g in descending order and, at the same time, takes care to preserve the relationship with elements of list p. Assume variable i contains the value 0.

```
for m in range(PLAYERS - 1):
    swaps = False
    for n in range(PLAYERS - 1, m, -1):
        if g[i][n] > g[i][n - 1]:
            g[i][n], g[i][n - 1] = g[i][n - 1], g[i][n]
            p[i][n], p[i][n - 1] = p[i][n - 1], p[i][n]
            swaps = True
    if not swaps: break
```

Now, in order to sort all rows, you need to nest this code fragment in a for-loop that iterates for all of them, as shown next.

```
for i in range(TEAMS):
    for m in range(PLAYERS - 1):
        swaps = False
        for n in range(PLAYERS - 1, m, -1):
            if g[i][n] > g[i][n - 1]:
                g[i][n], g[i][n - 1] = g[i][n - 1], g[i][n]
                p[i][n], p[i][n - 1] = p[i][n - 1], p[i][n]
                swaps = True
        if not swaps: break
```

The final Python program is as follows.

```
📁 file_33_4_7

TEAMS = 32
PLAYERS = 24

#Read team names, player names and goals all together
t = [None] * TEAMS
p = [ [None] * PLAYERS for i in range(TEAMS) ]
g = [ [None] * PLAYERS for i in range(TEAMS) ]
for i in range(TEAMS):
    t[i] = input("Enter name for team No." + str(i + 1) + ": ")
    for j in range(PLAYERS):
        p[i][j] = input("Enter name of player No." + str(j + 1) + ": ")
        g[i][j] = int(input("Enter goals of player No." + str(j + 1) + ": "))

#Sort list g
for i in range(TEAMS):
    for m in range(PLAYERS - 1):
        swaps = False
        for n in range(PLAYERS - 1, m, -1):
            if g[i][n] > g[i][n - 1]:
                g[i][n], g[i][n - 1] = g[i][n - 1], g[i][n]
                p[i][n], p[i][n - 1] = p[i][n - 1], p[i][n]
                swaps = True
        if not swaps: break

#Display 5 best scorers of each team
for i in range(TEAMS):
    print("Best scorers of", t[i])
    print("--------------------------------")
    for j in range(5):
        print(p[i][j], "scored", g[i][j], "goals")
```

Exercise 33.4-8 The Selection Sort Algorithm – Sorting One-Dimensional Lists

Write a code fragment that sorts the elements of a list in ascending order using the selection sort algorithm.

Solution

The *selection sort algorithm* is inefficient for large scale data, as is the bubble sort algorithm, but it generally performs better than the latter. It is the simplest of all the sorting algorithms and performs well on computer systems in which limited main memory (RAM) comes into play.

The algorithm finds the smallest (or largest, depending on sorting order) element of the list and swaps its content with that at position 0. Then the process is repeated for the remainder of the list; the next smallest (or largest) element is found and put into the next position, until all elements are examined.

For example, let's try to sort the following list in ascending order.

	0	1	2	3	4	5
A =	18	19	39	36	4	9

The lowest value is the value 4 at position 4. According to the selection sort algorithm, this element swaps its content with that at position 0. The list A becomes

	0	1	2	3	4	5
A =	4	19	41	36	18	9

The lowest value in the remainder of the list is the value 9 at position 5. This element swaps its content with that at position 1. The list A becomes

	0	1	2	3	4	5
A =	4	9	41	36	18	19

The lowest value in the remainder of the list is the value 18 at position 4. This element swaps its content with that at position 2. The list A becomes

	0	1	2	3	4	5
A =	4	9	18	36	41	19

Proceeding the same way, the next lowest value is the value 19 at position 5. The list A becomes

	0	1	2	3	4	5
A =	4	9	18	19	41	36

Finally, the next lowest value is the value 36 at position 5. The list A becomes finally sorted in ascending order!

	0	1	2	3	4	5
A =	4	9	18	19	36	41

Now, let's write the corresponding Python program. The "from inner to outer" method is used in order to help you better understand the whole process. The next code fragment finds the smallest element and then swaps its content with that at position 0. Please note that this is the inner (nested) loop control structure. Assume variable m contains the value 0.

```python
minimum = a[m]
index_of_min = m
for n in range(m, ELEMENTS):
    if a[n] < minimum:
        minimum = a[n]
        index_of_min = n
```

```
#Minimum found! Now, swap values.
a[m], a[index_of_min] = a[index_of_min], a[m]
```

Now, in order to repeat the process for all elements of the list, you can nest this code fragment within a for-loop that iterates for all elements.

The final selection sort algorithm that sorts a list in ascending order is as follows.

```
for m in range(ELEMENTS):
    minimum = a[m]
    index_of_min = m
    for n in range(m, ELEMENTS):
        if a[n] < minimum:
            minimum = a[n]
            index_of_min = n

    a[m], a[index_of_min] = a[index_of_min], a[m]
```

✎ *If you wish to sort a list in descending order, all you need to do is search for maximum instead of minimum values.*

▣ *As in a bubble sort algorithm, in order to sort alphanumeric data, you can do one simple thing: leave the algorithm as is!*

Exercise 33.4-9   *Sorting One-Dimensional Lists While Preserving the Relationship with a Second List*

Write a Python program that prompts the user to enter the electric meter reading recorded at the end of each month for a period of one year. It then displays each reading (in descending order) along with the name of the corresponding month. Use the selection sort algorithm.

Solution

In this exercise you need the following two one-dimensional lists.

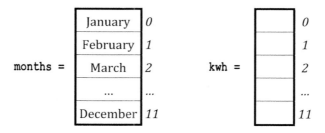

The approach is the same as in the bubble sort algorithm. While the selection sort algorithm sorts the elements of list kwh, the relationship with the elements of list months must also be preserved. This means that every time two elements of list kwh swap contents, the corresponding elements of list months must swap their contents as well. The Python program is as follows.

```
                              📁 file_33_4_9
months = ["January", "February", "March", "April", "May", "June",
          "July", "August", "September", "October", "November", "December"]
```

```
kwh = [None] * len(months)

for i in range(len(months)):
    kwh[i] = float(input("Enter kWh for " + months[i] + ": "))

for m in range(len(months)):
    maximum = kwh[m]
    index_of_max = m
    for n in range(m, len(months)):
        if kwh[n] > maximum:
            maximum = kwh[n]
            index_of_max = n

    #Swap values of kwh
    kwh[m], kwh[index_of_max] = kwh[index_of_max], kwh[m]
    #Swap values of months
    months[m], months[index_of_max] = months[index_of_max], months[m]

for i in range(len(months)):
    print(months[i], ":", kwh[i])
```

Exercise 33.4-10 The Insertion Sort Algorithm – Sorting One-Dimensional Lists

Write a code fragment that sorts the elements of a list in ascending order using the insertion sort algorithm.

Solution

The *insertion sort algorithm* is inefficient for large scale data, as are the selection and the bubble sort algorithms, but it generally performs better than either of them. Moreover, the insertion sort algorithm can prove very fast when sorting very small lists— even faster than the quicksort algorithm.

The insertion sort algorithm resembles the way you might sort playing cards. You start with all the cards face down on the table. The cards on the table represent the unsorted "list". In the beginning your left hand is empty, but in the end this hand will hold the sorted cards. The process goes as follows: you remove from the table one card at a time and insert it into the correct position in your left hand. To find the correct position for a card, you compare it with each of the cards already in your hand, from right to left. At the end, there must be no cards on the table and your left hand will hold all the cards, sorted.

For example, let's try to sort the following list in ascending order. To better understand this example, the first three elements of the list are already sorted for you.

	0	1	2	3	4	5	6
A =	3	15	24	8	10	18	9

The element at position 3 (which is 8) is removed from the list and all elements on its left with a value greater than 8 are shifted to the right. The list A becomes

	0	1	2	3	4	5	6
A =	3		15	24	10	18	9

Now that a position has been released, the value 8 is inserted in there. The list becomes

	0	1	2	3	4	5	6
A =	3	8	15	24	10	18	9

The element at position 4 (which is 10) is removed from the list and all elements on its left with a value greater than 10 are shifted to the right. The list A becomes

	0	1	2	3	4	5	6
A =	3	8		15	24	18	9

Now that a position has been released, the value of 10 is inserted in there. The list becomes

	0	1	2	3	4	5	6
A =	3	8	10	15	24	18	9

The element at position 5 (which is 18) is removed from the list and all elements on its left with a value greater than 18 are shifted to the right. The list A becomes

	0	1	2	3	4	5	6
A =	3	8	10	15		24	9

Now that a position has been released, the value of 18 is inserted in there. The list becomes

	0	1	2	3	4	5	6
A =	3	8	10	15	18	24	9

The element at position 6 (which is 9) is removed from the list and all elements on its left with a value greater than 9 are shifted to the right. The list A becomes

	0	1	2	3	4	5	6
A =	3	8		10	15	18	24

Now that a position has been released, the value of 9 is inserted in there. This is the last step of the process. The algorithm finishes and the list is now sorted.

	0	1	2	3	4	5	6
A =	3	8	9	10	15	18	24

✎ *What the algorithm actually does is to check the unsorted elements one by one and insert each one in the appropriate position among those considered already sorted.*

The code fragment that sorts a list in ascending order using the insertion sort algorithm is as follows.

```
for m in range(1, ELEMENTS):
    #"Remove" the element at index position m from the list and
    #keep it in variable element
    element = a[m]

    #Shift appropriate elements to the right
    n = m
    while n > 0 and a[n - 1] > element:
        a[n] = a[n - 1]
        n -= 1

    #Insert the previously "removed" element at index position n
    a[n] = element
```

Please note that the element at index position m is not actually removed from the list but is in fact overwritten when shifting to the right is performed. This is why its value is kept in variable element before shifting the elements.

If you wish to sort a list in descending order, all you need to do is alter the Boolean expression of the while statement to n > 0 and a[n - 1] < element.

As in previous sort algorithms, in order to sort alphanumeric data, you don't have to change anything in the algorithm!

Exercise 33.4-11   The Three Worst Elapsed Times

Ten race car drivers run their cars as fast as possible on a racing track. Each car runs 20 laps and for each lap the corresponding elapsed time (in seconds) is recorded. Write a Python program that prompts the user to enter the name of each driver and their elapsed time for each lap. The program must then display the name of each driver along with his or her three worst elapsed times. Use the insertion sort algorithm.

Solution

In this exercise, you need the following two lists.

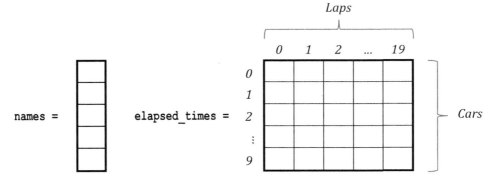

After the user enters all data, the Python program must sort each row of the list in descending order but, in the end, must display only the first three columns.

Using the "from inner to outer" method, the next code fragment sorts only the first row (row index 0) of the two-dimensional list elapsed_times in descending order using the insertion sort algorithm. Assume variable i contains the value 0.

```python
for m in range(1, LAPS):
    element = elapsed_times[i][m]
    n = m
    while n > 0 and a[n - 1] > element:
        elapsed_times[i][n] = elapsed_times[i][n - 1]
        n -= 1
    elapsed_times[i][n] = element
```

Now, in order to sort all rows, you need to nest this code fragment in a for-loop that iterates for all of them, as follows.

```python
for i in range(CARS):
    for m in range(1, LAPS):
        element = elapsed_times[i][m]
        n = m
        while n > 0 and a[n - 1] > element:
            elapsed_times[i][n] = elapsed_times[i][n - 1]
            n -= 1
        elapsed_times[i][n] = element
```

And now, let's focus on the given exercise. The final Python program is as follows.

📁 **file_33_4_11**

```python
CARS = 10
LAPS = 20

names = [None] * CARS
elapsed_times = [ [None] * LAPS for i in range(CARS) ]

#Read names and elapsed times all together
for i in range(CARS):
    names[i] = input("Enter name for driver No." + str(i + 1) + ": ")
    for j in range(LAPS):
        elapsed_times[i][j] = float(input("Enter elapsed time for lap No" + str(j + 1) + ": "))

#Sort list elapsed_times
for i in range(CARS):
    for m in range(1, LAPS):
        element = elapsed_times[i][m]
        n = m
        while n > 0 and elapsed_times[i][n - 1] > element:
            elapsed_times[i][n] = elapsed_times[i][n - 1]
            n -= 1
        elapsed_times[i][n] = element

#Display 3 worst elapsed times
for i in range(CARS):
```

```
        print("Worst elapsed times of", names[i])
        print("----------------------------------")
        for j in range(3):
            print(elapsed_times[i][j])
```

33.5 Searching Elements in Data Structures

In computer science, a *search algorithm* is an algorithm that searches for an item with specific properties within a set of data. In the case of a data structure, a search algorithm searches the data structure to find the element, or elements, that equal a given value.

When searching in a data structure, there can be two situations.

► You want to search for a given value in a data structure that may contain the same value multiple times. Therefore, you need to find **all** the elements (or their corresponding indexes) that are equal to that given value.

► You want to search for a given value in a data structure where each value is unique. Therefore, you need to find **just one** element (or its corresponding index), the one that is equal to that given value, and then stop searching any further!

The most commonly used search algorithms are:

► the linear (or sequential) search algorithm
► the binary search algorithm

Both linear and binary search algorithms have advantages and disadvantages.

Exercise 33.5-1   *The Linear Search Algorithm – Searching in a One-Dimensional List that may Contain the Same Value Multiple Times*

Write a code fragment that searches a one-dimensional list for a given value. Assume that the list contains alphanumeric values and may contain the same value multiple times. Use the linear search algorithm.

Solution

The *linear (or sequential) search algorithm* checks if the first element of the list is equal to a given value, then checks the second element, then the third, and so on until the end of the list. Since this process of checking elements one by one is quite slow, the linear search algorithm is suitable for lists with few elements.

The code fragment is shown next. It looks for a given value needle in the list haystack!

```
needle = input("Enter a value to search: ")

found = False
for i in range(ELEMENTS):
    if haystack[i] == needle:
        print(needle, "found at position:", i)
        found = True

if not found:
    print("Nothing found!")
```

Exercise 33.5-2   Display the Last Names of All Those People Who Have the Same First Name

Write a Python program that prompts the user to enter the names of 20 people: their first names in the list first_names, *and their last names in the list* last_names. *The program must then ask the user for a first name, upon which it will search and display the last names of all those whose first name equals the given one.*

Solution

Even though it is not very clear in the wording of the exercise, it is true that the list first_names may contain a value multiple times. How rare is it to meet two people named "John", for example?

The program must search for the first name given in list first_names and every time it finds it, it must display the corresponding last name from the other list.

The solution is as follows.

```
┌─────────────────  📁 file_33_5_2  ─────────────────┐

PEOPLE = 20

first_names = [None] * PEOPLE
last_names = [None] * PEOPLE

for i in range(PEOPLE):
    first_names[i] = input("Enter first name: ")
    last_names[i] = input("Enter last name: ")

#Get name to search and convert it to uppercase
needle = input("Enter a first name to search: ").upper()

#Search for given value in list first_names
found = False
for i in range(PEOPLE):
    if first_names[i].upper() == needle:
        print(last_names[i])
        found = True

if not found:
    print("No one found!")
```

✎ *Since the program works with alphanumeric data, the* upper() *method is required so that the program can operate correctly for any given value. For example, if the value "John" exists in the list* first_names *and the user wants to search for the value "JOHN", the* upper() *method ensures that the program finds all Johns.*

Exercise 33.5-3   The Linear Search Algorithm – Searching in a One-Dimensional List that Contains Unique Values

Write a code fragment that searches a one-dimensional list for a given value. Assume that each value in the list is unique. Use the linear search algorithm.

Solution

This case is quite different from the previous ones. Since each value in the list is unique, when the given value is found, there is no need to iterate without reason until the end of the list, thus wasting CPU time. There are three approaches, actually! Let's analyze them all!

First Approach – Using the break statement

In this approach, when the given value is found, a break statement is used to break out of the for-loop. The solution is as follows.

```python
needle = float(input("Enter a value to search: "))

found = False
for i in range(ELEMENTS):
    if haystack[i] == needle:
        print(needle, "found at position:", i)
        found = True
        break

if not found:
    print("Nothing found!")
```

Or you can do the same, in a little bit different way.

```python
needle = float(input("Enter a value to search: "))

index_position = -1
for i in range(ELEMENTS):
    if haystack[i] == needle:
        index_position = i
        break

if index_position == -1:
    print("Nothing found!")
else:
    print(needle, "found at position:", index_position)
```

Second Approach – Using a flag

The break statement doesn't actually exist in all computer languages; and since this book's intent is to teach you "Algorithmic Thinking" (and not just special statements that only Python supports), let's look at an alternate approach.

In the next code fragment, when the given value is found within list haystack, the variable found forces the flow of execution to immediately exit the loop.

```python
needle = float(input("Enter a value to search: "))

found = False
i = 0
while i < ELEMENTS and not found:
    if haystack[i] == needle:
        found = True
        index_position = i
```

```
        i += 1

if not found:
    print("Nothing found!")
else:
    print(needle, "found at position:", index_position)
```

Third Approach – Using only a pre-test loop structure

This approach is probably the most efficient one. Also, it is so easy to understand the way is works that there is no need to explain anything. The code fragment is as follows.

```
needle = float(input("Enter a value to search: "))


i = 0
while i < ELEMENTS - 1 and haystack[i] != needle:
    i += 1

if haystack[i] != needle:
    print("Nothing found!")
else:
    print(needle, "found at position:", i)
```

Exercise 33.5-4   *Searching for a Given Social Security Number*

In the United States, the Social Security Number (SSN) is a nine-digit identity number applied to all U.S. citizens in order to identify them for the purposes of Social Security. Write a Python program that prompts the user to enter the SSN and the first and last names of 100 people. The program must then ask the user for an SSN, upon which it will search and display the first and last name of the person who holds that SSN.

Solution

In the United States, there is no possibility that two or more people will have the same SSN. Thus, even though it is not very clear in the wording of the exercise, each value in the list that holds the SSNs is unique!

According to everything you learned so far, the solution to this exercise is as follows.

```
📁 file_33_5_4
PEOPLE = 100

SSNs = [None] * PEOPLE
first_names = [None] * PEOPLE
last_names = [None] * PEOPLE

for i in range(PEOPLE):
    SSNs[i] = input("Enter SSN: ")
    first_names[i] = input("Enter first name: ")
    last_names[i] = input("Enter last name: ")

needle = input("Enter an SSN to search: ")

#Search for given value in list SSNs
```

```
i = 0
while i < PEOPLE - 1 and SSNs[i] != needle:
    i += 1

if SSNs[i] != needle:
    print("Nothing found!")
else:
    print(first_names[i], last_names[i])
```

Exercise 33.5-5   The Linear Search Algorithm – Searching in a Two-Dimensional List that May Contain the Same Value Multiple Times

Write a code fragment that searches each row of a two-dimensional list for a given value. Assume that the list may contain the same value multiple times. Use the linear search algorithm.

Solution

This code fragment must search for the given number in each row of a two-dimensional list that may contain the same value multiple times. This means that the code fragment must search in the first row and display all the columns where the given number is found; otherwise, it must display a message that the given number was not found in the first row. Then, it must search in the second row, and this process must continue until all rows have been examined.

To better understand this exercise, the "inner to outer" method is used. The following code fragment searches for a given value (variable needle) only in the first row of the two-dimensional list named haystack. Assume variable i contains the value 0.

```
found = False
for j in range(COLUMNS):
    if haystack[i][j] == needle:
        print("Found at column", j)
        found = True

if not found:
    print("Nothing found in row", i)
```

Now, in order to search in all rows, you need to nest this code fragment in a for-loop that iterates for all of them, as follows.

```
needle = float(input("Enter a value to search: "))

for i in range(ROWS):
    found = False
    for j in range(COLUMNS):
        if haystack[i][j] == needle:
            print("Found at column", j)
            found = True

    if not found:
        print("Nothing found in row", i)
```

Exercise 33.5-6   *Searching for Wins, Losses and Ties*

Twelve teams participate in a football tournament, and each team plays 20 games, one game each week. Write a Python program that prompts the user to enter the name of each team and the letter "W" for win, "L" for loss, or "T" for tie (draw) for each game. Then the program must prompt the user for a letter (W, L, or T) and display, for each team, the week number(s) in which the team won, lost, or tied respectively. For example, if the user enters "L", the Python program must search and display, for each team, the week numbers (e.g., Week 3, Week 14, and so on) in which the team lost the game.

Solution

In this exercise, you need the following two lists.

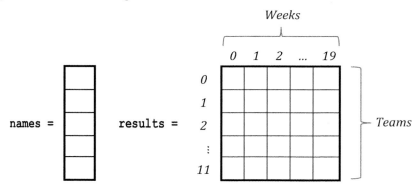

Using knowledge from the previous exercise, the solution to this exercise is as follows.

```
                              📄 file_33_5_6
TEAMS = 20
WEEKS = 12

names = [None] * TEAMS
results = [ [None] * WEEKS for i in range(TEAMS) ]

for i in range(TEAMS):
    names[i] = input("Enter name for team No." + str(i + 1) + ": ")
    for j in range(WEEKS):
        results[i][j] = input("Enter result for week No." + str(j + 1) + " for " + \
                              names[i] + ": ")

#Get value to search and convert it to uppercase
needle = input("Enter a result to search: ").upper()

for i in range(TEAMS):
    found = False
    print("Found results for", names[i])
    for j in range(WEEKS):
        if results[i][j].upper() == needle:
            print("Week ", (j + 1))
            found = True
```

```
if not found:
    print("No results!")
```

Exercise 33.5-7   The Linear Search Algorithm – Searching in a Two-Dimensional List that Contains Unique Values

A public opinion polling company makes phone calls in 10 cities and asks 30 citizens in each city whether or not they exercise. Write a Python program that prompts the user to enter each citizen's phone number and their answer (Y for Yes, N for No, S for Sometimes). The program must then prompt the user to enter a phone number, and it will search and display the answer that was given at this phone number. The program must also validate data input and accept only the values Y, N, or S as an answer.

Solution

In this exercise, you need the following two lists.

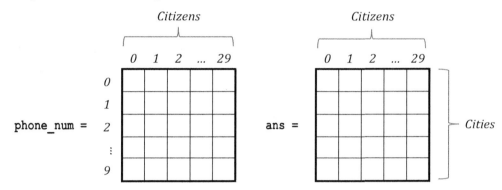

Even though it is not very clear from the wording of the exercise, each value in the list phone_num is unique! The program must search for the given number and if it finds it, it must stop searching thereafter. The solution is as follows.

```
                            📁 file_33_5_7
CITIES = 10
CITIZENS = 30

phone_num = [ [None] * CITIZENS for i in range(CITIES) ]
ans = [ [None] * CITIZENS for i in range(CITIES) ]

for i in range(CITIES):
    print("City No.", (i + 1))
    for j in range(CITIZENS):
        phone_num[i][j] = input("Enter phone number of citizen No." + str(j + 1) + ": ")
        ans[i][j] = input("Enter the answer of citizen No." + str(j + 1) + ": ").upper()
        while ans[i][j] not in ["Y", "N", "S"]:
            ans[i][j] = input("Wrong answer. Enter a valid one: ").upper()

needle = input("Enter a phone number to search: ")
```

```
found = False
for i in range(CITIES):
    for j in range(CITIZENS):
        if phone_num[i][j] == needle: #If it is found
            found = True
            position_i = i   #Keep row index where needle was found
            position_j = j   #Keep column index where needle was found
            break   #Exit the inner loop

    if found:
        break    #If it is found, exit the outer loop as well

if not found:
    print("Phone number not found!")
else:
    print("Phone number", phone_num[position_i][position_j])
    print(" gave '", end = "")

    if ans[position_i][position_j] == "Y":
        print("Yes", end = "")
    elif ans[position_i][position_j] == "N":
        print("No", end = "")
    else:
        print("Sometimes", end = "")

    print("' as an answer")
```

Exercise 33.5-8   Checking if a Value Exists in all Columns

Write a Python program that lets the user enter numeric values into a 20 × 30 list. After all of the values have been entered, the program then lets the user enter a value. In the end, a message must be displayed if the given value exists, at least once, in each column of the list.

Solution

This exercise can be solved using the linear search algorithm and a counter variable count. The Python program will iterate through the first column; if the given value is found, the Python program must stop searching in the first column thereafter and the variable count must increment by one. Then, the program will iterate through the second column; if the given value is found again, the Python program must stop searching in the second column thereafter and the variable count must again increment by one. This process must repeat until all columns have been examined. At the end of the process, if the value of count is equal to the total number of columns, this means that the given value exists, at least once, in each column of the list.

Let's use the "from inner to outer" method. The following code fragment searches in first column (column index 0) of the list and if the given value is found, the flow of execution exits the for-loop and variable count increments by one. Assume variable j contains the value 0.

```
found = False
for i in range(ROWS):
    if haystack[i][j] == needle:
```

```
                found = True
                break

    if found:
        count += 1
```

Now you can nest this code fragment in a for-loop that iterates for all columns.

```
for j in range(COLUMNS):
    found = False
    for i in range(ROWS):
        if haystack[i][j] == needle:
            found = True
            break

    if found:
        count += 1
```

You are almost ready—but think about it first! If the inner for-loop doesn't find the given value in a column, the outer for-loop must stop iterating. It is pointless to continue because the given value does not exist in at least one column. Thus, a better approach would be to use a break statement for the outer loop as shown in the code fragment that follows.

```
for j in range(COLUMNS):
    found = False
    for i in range(ROWS):
        if haystack[i][j] == needle:
            found = True
            break

    if found:
        count += 1
    else:
        break
```

The final Python program is as follows.

```
┌─ file_33_5_8
ROWS = 20
COLUMNS = 30

haystack = [ [None] * COLUMNS for i in range(ROWS) ]

for i in range(ROWS):
    for j in range(COLUMNS):
        haystack[i][j] = float(input())

needle = float(input("Enter a value to search: "))

count = 0
for j in range(COLUMNS):
```

```
        found = False
        for i in range(ROWS):
            if haystack[i][j] == needle:
                found = True
                break

        if found:
            count += 1
        else:
            break

    if count == COLUMNS:
        print(needle, "found in every column!")
```

✎ *If you need a message to be displayed when a given value exists at least once in each **row** (instead of each column), the Python program can do the same as previously shown; however, instead of iterating through columns, it has to iterate through rows.*

Exercise 33.5-9   *The Binary Search Algorithm – Searching in a Sorted One-Dimensional List*

Write a code fragment that searches a sorted one-dimensional list for a given value. Use the binary search algorithm.

Solution

The *binary search algorithm* is considered very fast and can be used with large scale data. Its main disadvantage, though, is that the data need to be sorted.

The main idea of the binary search algorithm is to check the value of the element in the middle of the list. If it is not the "needle in the haystack" that you are looking for, and what you are looking for is actually smaller than the value of the middle element, it means that the "needle" must be in the first half of the list. On the other hand, if what you are looking for is larger than the value of the middle element, it means that the "needle" must be in the last half of the list.

The binary search algorithm continues by checking the value of the middle element in the remaining half part of the list. If it's still not the "needle", the search narrows to the half of the remaining part of the list that the "needle" could be in. This "splitting" process continues until the "needle" is found or the remaining part of the list consists of only one element. If that element is not the "needle", then the given value is not in the list.

Confused? Let's try to analyze the binary search algorithm through an example. The following list contains numeric values in ascending order. Assume that the "needle" that you are looking for is the value 44.

	0	1	2	3	4	5	6	7	8	9	10	11	12	13
A =	12	15	19	24	28	31	39	41	44	53	57	59	62	64

Three variables are used. Initially, variable start contains the value 0 (this is the index of the first element), variable end contains the value 13 (this is the index of the last element) and variable middle contains the value 6 (this is approximately the index of the middle element).

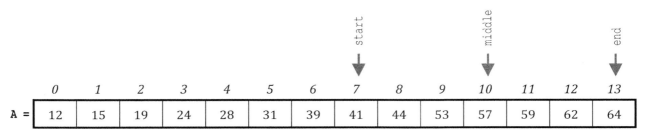

The "needle" (value 44) that you are looking for is larger than the value of 39 in the middle, thus the element that you are looking for must be in the last half of the list. Therefore, variable start is updated to point to index position 7 and variable middle is updated to a point in the middle between start (the new one) and end.

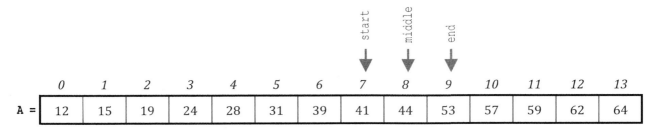

Now, the "needle" (value 44) that you are looking for is smaller than the value of 57 in the middle, thus the element that you are looking for must be in the first half of the remaining part of the list. Therefore, it is the variable end that is now updated to point to index position 9, and variable middle is updated to point to the middle between start and end (the new one).

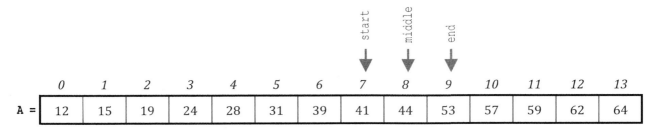

You are done! The "needle" has been found at index position 8 and the whole process can stop!

> 📖 *Each unsuccessful comparison reduces the number of elements left to check by half!*

Now, let's see the corresponding code fragment.

```
left = 0
right = ELEMENTS - 1
found = False
while left <= right and not found:
    middle = (left + right) // 2    #This is a DIV 2 operation

    if haystack[middle] > needle:
        right = middle - 1
```

```
        elif haystack[middle] < needle:
            left = middle + 1
        else:
            found = True
            index_position = middle

if not found:
    print("nothing found!")
else:
    print(needle, "found at position:", index_position)
```

✎ *Using the binary search algorithm on the list of the example, the value of 44 can be found within just three iterations. On the other hand, for the same data, the linear search algorithm would need nine iterations!*

✎ *If the list contains a value multiple times, the binary search algorithm can find only one occurrence.*

Exercise 33.5-10   Display all the Historical Events for a Country

Write a Python program that prompts the user to enter the names of 10 countries and 20 important historical events for each country, including a brief description of each event. The Python program must then prompt the user to enter a country, and it will search and display all events for that country. Use the binary search algorithm. Assume that the user enters the names of the countries alphabetically.

Solution

In this exercise, the following two lists are required.

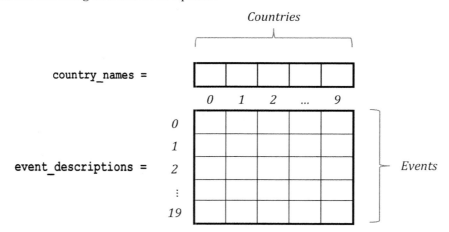

Assume that the user enters a country to search for, and the binary search algorithm finds that country, for example, at index position 2 of list country_names. The program can then use this value of 2 as a column index for the list event_descriptions, and it will display all the event descriptions of column 2.

The Python program is as follows.

```
📁 file_33_5_10
```

```
EVENTS = 20
COUNTRIES = 10
```

```
country_names = [None] * COUNTRIES
event_descriptions = [ [None] * COUNTRIES for i in range(EVENTS) ]

for j in range(COUNTRIES):
    country_names[j] = input("Enter Country No" + str(j + 1) + ": ")
    for i in range(EVENTS):
        event_descriptions[i][j] = input("Enter description for event No" + str(i + 1) + ": ")

needle = input("Enter a country to search: ").upper()

#Country names are entered alphabetically.
#Use the binary search algorithm to search for needle.
left = 0
right = EVENTS - 1
found = False
while left <= right and not found:
    middle = (left + right) // 2

    if country_names[middle].upper() > needle:
        right = middle - 1
    elif country_names[middle].upper() < needle:
        left = middle + 1
    else:
        found = True
        index_position = middle

if not found:
    print("No country found!")
else:
    for i in range(EVENTS):
        print(event_descriptions[i][index_position])
```

Exercise 33.5-11 Searching in Each Column of a Two-Dimensional List

Write a Python program that prompts the user to enter the names of 10 countries and 20 important historical events for each country, including a brief description and the corresponding year of each event. The Python program must then prompt the user to enter a year, and it will search and display all events that happened that year for each country. Use the binary search algorithm. Assume that for each country there is only one event in each year and that the user enters the events ordered by year in ascending order.

Solution

In this exercise, the following three lists are required.

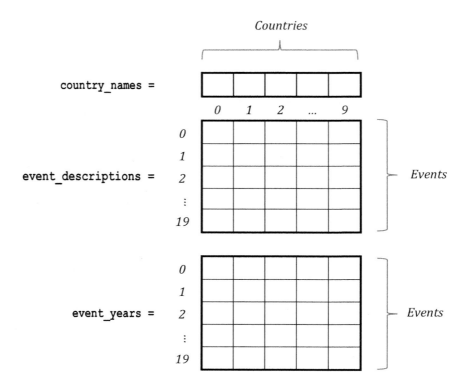

In order to write the code fragment that searches in each column of the list event_years, let's use the "from inner to outer" method. The next binary search algorithm searches in the first column (column index 0) for a given year. Assume variable j contains the value 0. Since the search is performed vertically, and in order to increase program's readability, variables left and right have been replaced by variables top and bottom correspondingly.

```python
top = 0
bottom = EVENTS - 1
found = False
while top <= bottom and not found:
    middle = (top + bottom) // 2

    if event_years[middle][j] > needle:
        bottom = middle - 1
    elif event_years[middle][j] < needle:
        top = middle + 1
    else:
        found = True
        row_index = middle

if not found:
    print("No event found for country", country_names[j])
else:
    print("Country:", country_names[j])
    print("Year:", event_years[row_index][j])
```

```
        print("Event:", event_descriptions[row_index][j])
```

Now, nesting this code fragment in a for-loop that iterates for all columns results in the following.

```
for j in range(COUNTRIES):
    top = 0
    bottom = EVENTS - 1
    found = False
    while top <= bottom and not found:
        middle = (top + bottom) // 2

        if event_years[middle][j] > needle:
            bottom = middle - 1
        elif event_years[middle][j] < needle:
            top = middle + 1
        else:
            found = True
            row_index = middle

    if not found:
        print("No event found for country", country_names[j])
    else:
        print("Country:", country_names[j])
        print("Year:", event_years[row_index][j])
        print("Event:", event_descriptions[row_index][j])
```

The final Python program is as follows.

```
                        📁 file_33_5_11
EVENTS = 20
COUNTRIES = 10

country_names = [None] * COUNTRIES
event_descriptions = [ [None] * COUNTRIES for i in range(EVENTS) ]
event_years = [ [None] * COUNTRIES for i in range(EVENTS) ]

for j in range(COUNTRIES):
    country_names[j] = input("Enter Country No." + str(j + 1) + ": ")
    for i in range(EVENTS):
        event_descriptions[i][j] = input("Enter description for event No" + str(i + 1) + ": ")
        event_years[i][j] = int(input("Enter year for event No" + str(i + 1) + ": "))

needle = int(input("Enter a year to search: "))

for j in range(COUNTRIES):
    top = 0
    bottom = EVENTS - 1
    found = False
    while top <= bottom and not found:
        middle = (top + bottom) // 2
```

```
        if event_years[middle][j] > needle:
            bottom = middle - 1
        elif event_years[middle][j] < needle:
            top = middle + 1
        else:
            found = True
            row_index = middle

    if not found:
        print("No event found for country", country_names[j])
    else:
        print("Country:", country_names[j])
        print("Year:", event_years[row_index][j])
        print("Event:", event_descriptions[row_index][j])
```

33.6 Exercises of a General Nature with Lists

Exercise 33.6-1   On Which Days was There a Possibility of Snow?

Write a Python program that lets the user enter the temperatures (in degrees Fahrenheit) recorded at the same hour each day for the 31 days of January. The Python program must then display the numbers of those days (1, 2, ..., 31) on which there was a possibility of snow, that is, those on which temperatures were below 36 degrees Fahrenheit (about 2 degrees Celsius).

Solution

The one-dimensional list for this exercise is shown next.

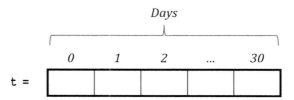

and the Python program is as follows.

```
                        📁 file_33_6_1
DAYS = 31

t = [None] * DAYS

for i in range(DAYS):
    t[i] = int(input())

for i in range(DAYS):
    if t[i] < 36:
        print(i + 1, end = "\t")
```

Exercise 33.6-2   Was There Any Possibility of Snow?

Write a Python program that lets the user enter the temperatures (in degrees Fahrenheit) recorded at the same hour each day for the 31 days of January. The Python program must then display a message indicating if there was a possibility of snow, that is, if there were any temperatures below 36 degrees Fahrenheit (about 2 degrees Celsius).

Solution

The code fragment that follows is **incorrect.** You **cannot** do what you did in the previous exercise.

```python
for i in range(DAYS):
    if t[i] < 36:
        print("There was a possibility of snow in January!")
```

If January had more than one day with a temperature below 36 degrees Fahrenheit, the same message would be displayed multiple times—and obviously you do not want this! You actually want to display a message once, regardless of whether January had one, two, or even more days below 36 degrees Fahrenheit.

There are two approaches, actually. Let's study them both.

First Approach – Counting all temperatures below 36 degrees Fahrenheit

In this approach, you can use a variable in the program to count all the days on which the temperature was below 36 degrees Fahrenheit. After all of the days have been examined, the program can check the value of this variable. If the value is not zero, it means that there was at least one day where there was a possibility of snow.

```
                            📁 file_33_6_2a
DAYS = 31

t = [None] * DAYS

for i in range(DAYS):
    t[i] = int(input())

count = 0
for i in range(DAYS):
    if t[i] < 36:
        count += 1

if count != 0:
    print("There was a possibility of snow in January!")
```

Second Approach – Using a flag

In this approach, instead of counting all those days that had a temperature below 36 degrees Fahrenheit, you can use a Boolean variable (a flag). The solution is presented next.

```
                            📁 file_33_6_2b
DAYS = 31

t = [None] * DAYS

for i in range(DAYS):
    t[i] = int(input())
```

```
found = False
for i in range(DAYS):
    if t[i] < 36:
        found = True
        break

if found:
    print("There was a possibility of snow in January!")
```

✎ *Imagine the variable* found *as if it's a real flag. Initially, the flag is not hoisted (*found = False*). Within the for-loop, however, when a temperature below 36 degrees Fahrenheit is found, the flag is hoisted (the value* True *is assigned to the variable* found*) and it is never lowered again.*

✎ *Note the* break *statement! Once a temperature below 36 degrees Fahrenheit is found, it is meaningless to continue checking thereafter.*

✎ *If the loop performs all of its iterations and no temperature below 36 degrees Fahrenheit is found, the variable* found *will still contain its initial value (*False*) since the flow of execution never entered the decision control structure.*

Exercise 33.6-3   *In Which Cities was There a Possibility of Snow?*

Write a Python program that prompts the user to enter the names of ten cities and their temperatures (in degrees Fahrenheit) recorded at the same hour each day for the 31 days of January. The Python program must display the names of the cities in which there was a possibility of snow, that is, those in which temperatures were below 36 degrees Fahrenheit (about 2 degrees Celsius).

Solution

As in the previous exercise, you need to display each city name once, regardless of whether it may had one, two, or even more days below 36 degrees Fahrenheit.

This exercise needs the following lists. In the first approach, the auxiliary list count is created by the program to count the total number of days on which each city had temperatures lower than 36 degrees Fahrenheit. The second approach, however, doesn't create the auxiliary list count. It uses just one extra Boolean variable (a flag). Obviously the second one is more efficient. But let's study them both.

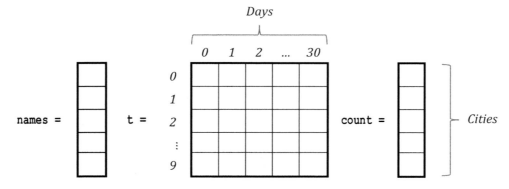

First Approach – Using an auxiliary list

You were taught in paragraph 32.2 how to process each row individually. The nested loop control structure that can create the auxiliary list count is as follows.

```python
count = [None] * CITIES
for i in range(CITIES):
    count[i] = 0
    for j in range(DAYS):
        if t[i][j] < 36:
            count[i] += 1
```

After list count is created you can iterate through it, and when an element contains a value other than zero, it means that the corresponding city had at least one day below 36 degrees Fahrenheit; thus the program must display the name of that city. The final Python program is presented next

📄 **file_33_6_3a**

```python
CITIES = 10
DAYS = 31

names = [None] * CITIES
t = [ [None] * DAYS for i in range(CITIES) ]

for i in range(CITIES):
    names[i] = input("Enter a name for city No:" + str(i + 1) + ": ")
    for j in range(DAYS):
        t[i][j] = int(input("Enter a temperature for day No: " + str(j + 1) + ": "))

count = [None] * CITIES

for i in range(CITIES):
    count[i] = 0
    for j in range(DAYS):
        if t[i][j] < 36:
            count[i] += 1

print("Cities in which there was a possibility of snow in January: ")
for i in range(CITIES):
    if count[i] != 0:
        print(names[i])
```

Second Approach – Using a flag

This approach does not use an auxiliary list. It processes list t and directly displays any city name that had a temperature below 36 degrees Fahrenheit. But how can this be done without displaying a city name twice, or even more than twice? This is where you need a flag, that is, an extra Boolean variable.

To better understand this approach, let's use the "from inner to outer" method. The following code fragment checks if the first row of list t (row index 0) contains at least one temperature below 36 degrees Fahrenheit; if so, it displays the corresponding city name that exists at position 0 of the list names. Assume variable i contains the value 0.

```python
found = False
```

```
for j in range(DAYS):
    if t[i][j] < 36:
        found = True
        break

if found:
    print(names[i])
```

Now that everything has been clarified, in order to process the whole list t, you can just nest this code fragment in a for-loop that iterates for all cities, as follows.

```
for i in range(CITIES):
    found = False
    for j in range(DAYS):
        if t[i][j] < 36:
            found = True
            break

    if found:
        print(names[i])
```

The final Python program is as follows.

```
┌ file_33_6_3b

CITIES = 10
DAYS = 31

names = [None] * CITIES
t = [ [None] * DAYS for i in range(CITIES) ]

for i in range(CITIES):
    names[i] = input("Enter a name for city No:" + str(i + 1) + ": ")
    for j in range(DAYS):
        t[i][j] = int(input("Enter a temperature for day No:" + str(j + 1) + ": "))

print("Cities in which there was a possibility of snow in January: ")
for i in range(CITIES):
    found = False
    for j in range(DAYS):
        if t[i][j] < 36:
            found = True
            break

    if found:
        print(names[i])
```

Exercise 33.6-4   *Display from Highest to Lowest Grades by Student, and in Alphabetical Order*

There are 10 students and each one of them has received his or her grades for five lessons. Write a Python program that lets a teacher enter the name of each student and his or her grades for all lessons. The program must then calculate each student's average grade, and display the names of the students sorted by their average grade in descending order. Moreover, if two or more students have the same average grade, their names must be displayed in alphabetical order. Use the bubble sort algorithm, adapted accordingly.

Solution

In this exercise, you need the following three lists. The values for the lists names and grades will be entered by the user, whereas the auxiliary list average will be created by the Python program.

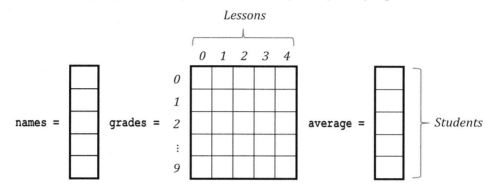

You already know how to do everything in this exercise. You know how to create the auxiliary list average (see paragraph 32.2), you know how to sort the list average while preserving the relationship with the elements of the list names (see Exercise 33.4-3), and you know how to handle the case in which, if two average grades are equal, the corresponding student names must be sorted alphabetically (see Exercise 33.4-4). The final Python program is as follows.

```
📁 file_33_6_4
```

```python
STUDENTS = 10
LESSONS = 5

#Read list names and grades
names = [None] * STUDENTS
grades = [ [None] * LESSONS for i in range(STUDENTS) ]

for i in range(STUDENTS):
    names[i] = input("Enter name for student No." + str(i + 1) + ": ")
    for j in range(LESSONS):
        grades[i][j] = int(input("Enter grade for lesson No." + str(j + 1) + ": "))

#Create list average
average = [None] * STUDENTS
for i in range(STUDENTS):
    average[i] = 0
    for j in range(LESSONS):
        average[i] += grades[i][j]
    average[i] /= LESSONS

#Sort lists average and names
for m in range(STUDENTS - 1):
```

```
        for n in range(STUDENTS - 1, m, -1):
            if average[n] > average[n - 1]:
                average[n], average[n - 1] = average[n - 1], average[n]
                names[n], names[n - 1] = names[n - 1], names[n]
            elif average[n] == average[n - 1]:
                if names[n] < names[n - 1]:
                    names[n], names[n - 1] = names[n - 1], names[n]

    #Display lists names and average
    for i in range(STUDENTS):
        print(names[i], "\t", average[i])
```

Exercise 33.6-5   *Archery at the Summer Olympics*

In archery at the Summer Olympics, 20 athletes each shoot six arrows. Write a Python program that prompts the user to enter the name of each athlete, and the points awarded for each shot. The program must then display the names of the three athletes that won the gold, silver, and bronze medals depending on which athlete obtained the highest sum of points. Assume that no two athletes have an equal sum of points.

Solution

In this exercise, you need the following three lists. The values for the lists names and points will be entered by the user, whereas the auxiliary list total will be created by the Python program.

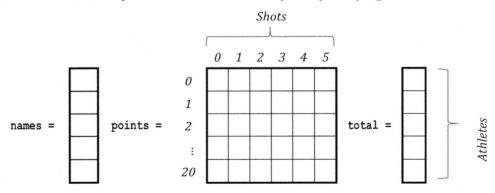

After the auxiliary list total is created, a sorting algorithm can sort the list total in descending order (while preserving the relationship with the elements of the list names). The Python program can then display the names of the three athletes at index positions 0, 1, and 2 (since these are the athletes that should win the gold, the silver, and the bronze medals, respectively).

The following program uses the bubble sort algorithm to sort the list total. Since the algorithm must sort in descending order, bigger elements must gradually "bubble" to positions of lowest index, like bubbles rise in a glass of cola. However, instead of performing 19 passes (there are 20 athletes), given that only the three best athletes must be found, the algorithm can perform just 3 passes. Doing this, only the first three bigger elements will gradually "bubble" to the first three positions in the list.

The solution is presented next.

> 📄 **file_33_6_5**

```
import math
```

```
ATHLETES = 20
SHOTS = 6

#Read list names and points
names = [None] * ATHLETES
points = [ [None] * SHOTS for i in range(ATHLETES) ]

for i in range(ATHLETES):
    names[i] = input("Enter name for athlete No." + str(i + 1) + ": ")
    for j in range(SHOTS):
        points[i][j] = int(input("Enter points for shot No." + str(j + 1) + ": "))

#Create list total
total = []
for row in points:
    total.append(math.fsum(row))

#Sort lists names and total. Perform only 3 passes
for m in range(3):
    for n in range(ATHLETES - 1, m, -1):
        if total[n] > total[n - 1]:
            total[n], total[n - 1] = total[n - 1], total[n]
            names[n], names[n - 1] = names[n - 1], names[n]

#Display gold, silver and bronze metal
for i in range(3):
    print(names[i], "\t", total[i])
```

33.7 Review Questions: True/False

Choose **true** or **false** for each of the following statements.

1. The main idea of the bubble sort algorithm (when sorting a list in ascending order) is to repeatedly move the smallest elements of the list to the lowest index positions.

2. In a list sorted in ascending order, the first element is the greatest of all.

3. When using the bubble sort algorithm, the total number of swaps depends on the given list.

4. When using the modified bubble sort algorithm, the case in which the algorithm performs the greatest number of swaps is when you want to sort in descending order a list that is already sorted in ascending order.

5. In the bubble sort algorithm, when the decision control structure tests the Boolean expression A[n] > A[n - 1], it means that the elements of list A are being sorted in descending order.

6. In Python, sorting algorithms sort letters in the same way that they sort numbers.

7. If you want to sort a list A but preserve the relationship with the elements of a list B, you must rearrange the elements of list B as well.

8. The bubble sort algorithm sometimes performs better than the modified bubble sort algorithm.

9. According to the bubble sort algorithm, in each pass (except the last one) only one element is placed in proper position.

10. The bubble sort algorithm can be implemented only by using for-loops.

11. The quick sort algorithm cannot be used to sort each column of a two-dimensional list.

12. The insertion sort algorithm can sort in either descending or ascending order.

13. One of the fastest sorting algorithms is the modified bubble sort algorithm.

14. The bubble sort algorithm, for a one-dimensional list of N elements, performs $\frac{N-1}{N}$ compares.

15. The bubble sort algorithm, for a one-dimensional list of N elements, performs $\frac{N(N-1)}{2}$ passes.

16. When using the modified bubble sort algorithm, if a complete pass is performed and no swaps have been done, then the algorithm knows the list is sorted and there is no need for further passes.

17. When using the selection sort algorithm, if you wish to sort a list in descending order, you need to search for maximum values.

18. The selection sort algorithm performs very well on computer systems in which the limited main memory comes into play.

19. The selection sort algorithm is suitable for large scale data operations.

20. The selection sort algorithm is a very complex algorithm.

21. The insertion sort algorithm generally performs better than the selection and the bubble sort algorithm.

22. The insertion sort algorithm can sometimes prove even faster than the quicksort algorithm.

23. The quicksort algorithm is considered one of the best and fastest sorting algorithms.

24. A sorted list contains only elements that are different from each other.

25. A search algorithm is an algorithm that searches for an item with specific properties within a set of data.

26. The sequential search algorithm can be used only on lists that contain arithmetic values.

27. One of the most commonly used search algorithms is the quick search algorithm.

28. One search algorithm is called the heap algorithm.

29. A linear (or sequential) search algorithm can work as follows: it can check if the last element of the list is equal to a given value, then it can check the last but one element, and so on, until the beginning of the list or until the given value is found.

30. The linear search algorithm can, in certain situations, find an element faster than the binary search algorithm.

31. The linear search algorithm can be used in large scale data operations.

32. The linear search algorithm cannot be used in sorted lists.

33. The binary search algorithm can be used in large scale data operations.

34. If a list contains a value multiple times, the binary search algorithm can find only the first occurrence of a given value.

35. When using search algorithms, if a list contains unique values and the element that you are looking for is found, there is no need to check any further.

36. The main disadvantage of the binary search algorithm is that data needs to be sorted.

37. The binary search algorithm can be used only in lists that contain arithmetic values.

38. If the element that you are looking for is in the last position of a list, the linear search algorithm will examine all the elements of the list.

39. The linear search algorithm can be used on two-dimensional lists.

40. When using the binary search algorithm, if the element that you are looking for is at the first position of a list that contains at least three elements, the algorithm will find it in just one iteration.

33.8 Review Exercises

Complete the following exercises.

1. Design the flowchart that corresponds to the following Python program.

```python
ELEMENTS = 30

values = [None] * ELEMENTS
for i in range(ELEMENTS):
    values[i] = int(input("Enter a two-digit integer: "))

for i in range(ELEMENTS):
    digit1, digit2 = divmod(values[i], 10)
    if digit1 < digit2:
        print(values[i])
```

2. Design the flowchart that corresponds to the following Python program.

```python
ELEMENTS = 20

values = [None] * ELEMENTS
for i in range(ELEMENTS):
    values[i] = int(input("Enter a three-digit integer: "))

total = 0
for i in range(ELEMENTS):
    digit3 = values[i] % 10
    r = values[i] // 10
    digit2 = r % 10
    digit1 = r // 10

    if values[i] == digit3 * 100 + digit2 * 10 + digit1:
        total += values[i]

print(total)
```

3. Design the flowchart that corresponds to the following Python program.

```python
ELEMENTS = 50

evens = [None] * ELEMENTS
for i in range(ELEMENTS):
    while True:
        evens[i] = int(input())
        if evens[i] % 2 != 0: break

for i in range(ELEMENTS):
    print(evens[i])
```

4. Design the flowchart that corresponds to the following Python program.

```python
N = 10
a = [ [None] * N for i in range(N) ]
```

```
for i in range(N):
    for j in range(N):
        a[i][j] = int(input())

total = 0
for k in range(N):
    total += a[k][k]

print("Sum =", total)
```

5. Design the flowchart that corresponds to the following Python program.

```
ROWS = 20
COLUMNS = 10
a = [ [None] * COLUMNS for i in range(ROWS) ]
for i in range(ROWS):
    for j in range(COLUMNS):
        a[i][j] = int(input())

maximum = a[0][0]
for i in range(ROWS):
    for j in range(COLUMNS):
        if a[i][j] > maximum:
            maximum = a[i][j]

print(maximum)
```

6. Design the flowchart that corresponds to the following Python program.

```
N = 10
a = [ [None] * N for i in range(N) ]
for i in range(N):
    for j in range(N):
        if i == j:
            a[i][j] = "*"
        elif i > j:
            a[i][j] = "-"
        else:
            a[i][j] = "+"

for i in range(N):
    for j in range(N):
        print(a[i][j])
```

7. Design the flowchart that corresponds to the following code fragment.

```
for i in range(ROWS):
    average[i] = 0
    for j in range(COLUMNS):
        average[i] += values[i][j]
    average[i] /= COLUMNS
```

```python
for i in range(ROWS):
    if average[i] > 89:
        print(average[i])
```

8. Write the Python program that corresponds to the following flowchart fragment.

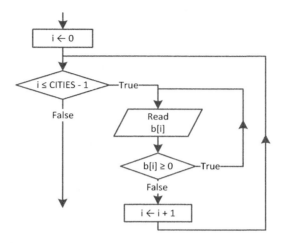

9. Write the Python program that corresponds to the following flowchart.

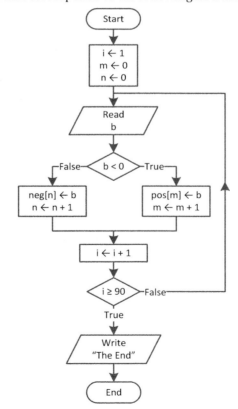

10. Write the Python program that corresponds to the following flowchart fragment.

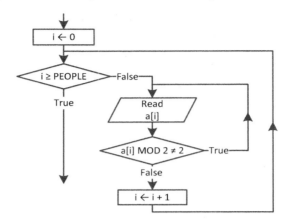

11. Write the Python program that corresponds to the following flowchart fragment.

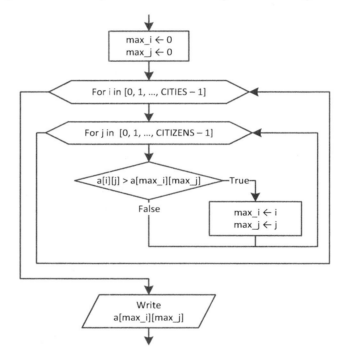

12. Write the Python program that corresponds to the following flowchart fragment.

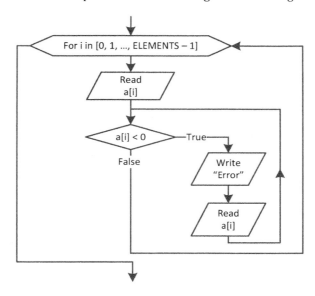

13. Write the Python program that corresponds to the following flowchart fragment.

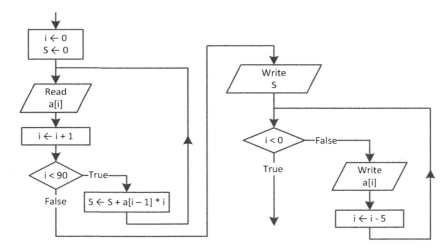

14. Write the Python program that corresponds to the following flowchart fragment.

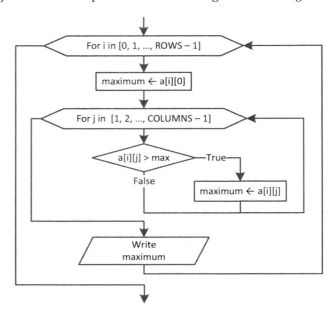

15. Write the Python program that corresponds to the following flowchart fragment.

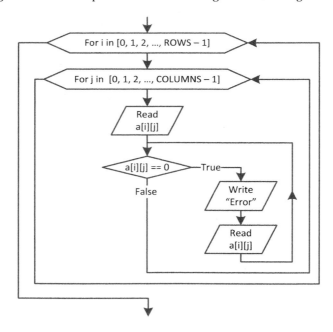

16. Design a flowchart and write the corresponding Python program that lets the user enter 50 positive numerical values into a list. The algorithm, and consequently the Python program, must then create a new list of 47 elements. In this new list, each position must contain the average value of four elements: the values that exist in the current and the next three positions of the given list.

17. Write a Python program that lets the user enter numerical values into lists a, b, and c, of 15 elements each. The program must then create a new list new_arr of 15 elements. In this new list, each position must contain the lowest value of lists a, b, and c, for the corresponding position.

Next, design the corresponding flowchart fragment for only that part of your program that creates the list new_arr.

18. Write a Python program that lets the user enter numerical values into lists a, b, and c, of 10, 5, and 15 elements respectively. The program must then create a new list new_arr of 30 elements. In this new list, the first 15 positions must contain the elements of list c, the next five positions must contain the elements of list b, and the last 10 positions must contains the elements of list a.

Next, design the corresponding flowchart fragment for only that part of your program that creates the list new_arr.

19. Write a Python program that lets the user enter numerical values into lists a, b, and c, of 5 × 10, 5 × 15, and 5 × 20 elements, respectively. The program must then create a new list new_arr of 5 × 45 elements. In this new list, the first 10 columns must contain the elements of list a, the next 15 columns must contain the elements of list b, and the last 20 rows must contain the elements of list c.

20. Write a Python program that lets the user enter 50 numerical values into a list and then creates two new lists, reals and integers. The list reals must contain the real values given, whereas the list integers must contain the integer values. The value 0 (if any) must not be added to any of the final lists, either reals or integers.

Next, design the corresponding flowchart fragment for only that part of your program that creates the lists reals and integers.

21. Write a Python program that lets the user enter 50 three-digit integers into a list and then creates a new list containing only the integers in which the first digit is less than the second digit and the second digit is less than the third digit. For example, the values 357, 456, and 159 are such integers.

22. A public opinion polling company asks 200 citizens to each score 10 consumer products. Write a Python program that prompts the user to enter the name of each product and the score each citizen gave (A, B, C, or D). The program must then calculate and display the following:

    a. for each product, the name of the product and the number of citizens that gave it an "A"

    b. for each citizen, the number of "B" responses he or she gave

    c. which product or products are considered the best

Moreover, using a loop control structure, the program must validate data input and display an error message when the user enters any score with a value other than A, B, C, or D.

23. Write a Python program that prompts the user to enter the names of 20 U.S. cities and the names of 20 Canadian cities and then, for each U.S. city, the distance (in miles) from each Canadian city. Finally, the program must display, for each U.S. city, its closest Canadian city.

24. Design a flowchart and write the corresponding Python program that lets the user enter the names and the heights of 30 mountains, as well as the country in which each one belongs. The algorithm, and consequently the Python program, must then display all available information about the highest and the lowest mountain.

25. Design the flowchart fragment of an algorithm that, for a given list A of N × M elements, finds and displays the maximum value as well as the row and the column in which this value was found.

26. Twenty-six teams participate in a football tournament. Each team plays 15 games, one game each week. Write a Python program that lets the user enter the name of each team and the letter "W" for win, "L" for loss, and "T" for tie (draw) for each game. If a win receives 3 points and a tie 1 point, the Python program must find and display the name of the team that wins the championship based on

which team obtained the greatest sum of points. Assume that no two teams have an equal sum of points.

27. On Earth, a free-falling object has an acceleration of 9.81 m/s² downward. This value is denoted by g. A student wants to calculate that value using an experiment. She allows 10 different objects to fall downward from a known height, and measures the time they need to reach the floor. She does this 20 times for each object. She needs a Python program that allows her to enter the height (from which objects are left to fall), as well as the measured times that they take to reach the floor. The program must then calculate g and store all calculated values in a 10 × 20 list. However, her chronometer is not so accurate, so she needs the program to find and display the minimum and the maximum calculated values of g for each object, as well as the overall minimum and maximum calculated values of g of all objects.

The required formula is

$$S = u_o + \frac{1}{2}gt^2$$

where

► S is the distance that the free-falling objects traveled, in meters (m)

► u_o is the initial velocity (speed) of the free-falling objects in meters per second (m/sec). However, since the free-falling objects start from rest, the value of u_o must be zero.

► t is the time that it took the free-falling object to reach the floor, in seconds (sec)

► g is the acceleration, in meters per second² (m/sec²)

28. Ten measuring stations, one in each city, record the daily CO_2 levels for a period of a year. Write a Python program that lets the user enter the name of each city and the CO_2 levels recorded at the same hour each day. The Python program then displays the name of the city that has the clearest atmosphere (on average).

29. Design the flowchart fragment of an algorithm that, for a given list A of N × M elements, finds and displays the minimum and the maximum values of each row.

30. Write a Python program that lets the user enter values into a 20 × 30 list and then finds and displays the minimum and the maximum values of each column.

31. Twenty teams participate in a football tournament, and each team plays 10 games, one game each week. Write a Python program that prompts the user to enter the name of each team and the letter "W" for win, "L" for loss, and "T" for tie (draw) for each game. If a win receives 3 points and a tie 1 point, the Python program must find and display the names of the teams that win the gold, the silver, and the bronze medals based on which team obtained the greatest sum of points. Use the modified bubble sort algorithm. Assume that no two teams have an equal sum of points.

Moreover, using a loop control structure, the program must validate data input and display an error message when the user enters any letter other than W, L, or T.

32. Write a Python program that prompts the user to enter the names and the heights of 50 people. The program must then display this information, sorted by height, in descending order. Moreover, if two or more people have the same height, their names must be displayed in alphabetical order. Use the bubble sort algorithm, adapted accordingly.

33. In a song contest there are 10 judges, each of whom scores 12 artists for their performance. However, according to the rules of this contest, the total score is calculated after excluding the maximum and the minimum score. Write a Python program that prompts the user to enter the names of the artists and the score they get from each judge. The program must then display

a. for each artist, his or her name and total score, after excluding the maximum and the minimum scores. Assume that the maximum and the minimum scores are unique in each artist's scores. (For example, let's say that artist No 1 has a maximum score of 98. This artist cannot have two or more scores of 98, just one.)

b. the final classification, starting with the artist that has the greatest score. However, if two or more artists have the same score, their names must be displayed in alphabetical order. Use the bubble sort algorithm, adapted accordingly.

34. Design the flowchart fragment of an algorithm that, for a given list A of 20 × 8 elements, sorts each row in descending order using the bubble sort algorithm.

35. Design the flowchart fragment of an algorithm that, for a given list A of 5 × 10 elements, sorts each column in ascending order using the bubble sort algorithm.

36. Design the flowchart fragment of an algorithm that, for a given list A of 20 × 8 elements, sorts each row in descending order using the insertion sort algorithm.

37. Design the flowchart fragment of an algorithm that, for a given list A of 5 × 10 elements, sorts each column in ascending order using the selection sort algorithm.

38. In a Sudoku contest, 10 people each try to solve as quickly as possible eight different Sudoku puzzles. Write a Python program that lets the user enter the name of each contestant and their time to complete each puzzle. The program must then display

a. for each contestant, his or her name and his or her three best times.

b. the names of the three contestants that win the gold, the silver, and the bronze medals based on which contestant obtained the lowest average time. Assume that no two contestants have an equal average time.

Use the selection sort algorithm when necessary

39. Five measuring stations, one in each area of a large city, record the daily carbon dioxide (CO_2) levels on an hourly basis. Write a Python program that lets the user enter the name of each area and the CO_2 levels recorded every hour (00:00 to 23:00) for a period of two days. The Python program then must calculate and display

a. for each area, its name and its average CO_2 level

b. for each hour, the average CO_2 level of the city

c. the hour in which the city atmosphere was most polluted (on average)

d. the hour and the area in which the highest level of CO_2 was recorded

e. the three areas with the dirtiest atmosphere (on average), using the insertion sort algorithm

40. Design the flowchart fragment of the linear search algorithm that searches list a of N elements for the value needle and displays the position index(es) at which needle is found. If needle is not found, the message "Not found" must be displayed.

41. Design the flowchart fragment of the binary search algorithm that searches list a of N elements for the value needle and displays the position at which needle is found. If needle is not found, the message "Not found" must be displayed.

42. Ten teams participate in a football tournament, and each team plays 16 games, one game each week. Write a Python program that prompts the user to enter the name of each team, the number of goals the team scored, and the number of goals the team let in for each match. A win receives 3 points and a tie receives 1 point. The Python program must prompt the user for a team name and then it finds and displays the total number of points for this team. If the given team name is not found, the message "This team does not exist" must be displayed.

Moreover, using a loop control structure, the program must validate data input and display an error message when the user enters any negative number of goals.

Assume that no two teams have the same name.

43. In a high school, there are two classes, with 20 and 25 students respectively. Write a Python program that prompts the user to enter the names of the students in two separate lists. The program then displays the names of each class independently in ascending order. Afterwards, the program prompts the user to enter a name and it searches for that given name in both lists. If the student's name is found, the program must display the message "Student found in Class No NN", where NN can be either 1 or 2; otherwise the message "Student not found in either class" must be displayed. Assume that both lists contain unique names.

   Hint: Since the lists are sorted and the names are unique, you can use the binary search algorithm.

44. Suppose there are two lists, usernames and passwords, that contain the login information of 100 employees of a company. Write a code fragment that prompts the user to enter a username and a password and then displays the message "Login OK!" when the combination of username and password is valid; the message "Login Failed!" must be displayed otherwise. Assume that usernames are unique but passwords are not. Moreover, both usernames and passwords are not case sensitive.

45. Suppose there are two lists, names and SSNs, that contain the names and the SSNs (Social Security Numbers) of 1000 U.S. citizens. Write a code fragment that prompts the user to enter a value (it can be either a name or an SSN) and then searches for and displays the names of all the people that have this name or this SSN. If the given value is not found, the message "This value does not exist" must be displayed.

46. There are 12 students and each one of them has received his or her grades for six lessons. Write a Python program that lets the user enter the grades for all lessons and then displays a message indicating whether or not there is at least one student that has an average value below 70. Moreover, using a loop control structure, the program must validate data input and display individual error messages when the user enters any negative value, or a value greater than 100.

47. Write a Python program that prompts the user to enter an English word, and then, using the table that follows, displays the corresponding Morse code using dots and dashes.

Morse Code			
A	.-	N	-.
B	-...	O	---
C	-.-.	P	.--.
D	-..	Q	--.-
E	.	R	.-.
F	..-.	S	...
G	--.	T	-
H	....	U	..-
I	..	V	...-
J	.---	W	.--
K	-.-	X	-..-
L	.-..	Y	-.--
M	--	Z	--..

   Hint: Use a dictionary to hold the Morse code.

Review in "Data Structures in Python"

Review Crossword Puzzle

1. Solve the following crossword puzzle.

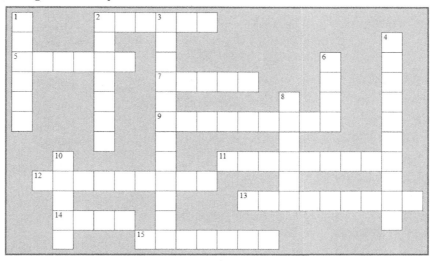

Across

2. These brackets are used to create a list.
5. A search algorithm.
7. Each list element is assigned a unique number known as an _____.
9. This sorting algorithm can prove very fast when sorting very small lists- even faster than the quicksort algorithm.
11. This sorting algorithm performs well on computer systems in which limited main memory (RAM) comes into play.
12. It is considered one of the best and fastest sorting algorithms.
13. A data _____ is a collection of data organized so that you can perform operations on it in the most effective way.
14. A mutable data structure in Python.
15. A mechanism to select a range of elements from a list.

Down

1. A sorting algorithm.
2. The process of putting the elements of a list in a certain order.
3. In a square matrix, the collection of those elements that runs from the top right corner to the bottom left corner.
4. Its elements can be uniquely identified using a key and not necessarily an integer value.
6. In this diagonal, the elements have their row index equal to their column index.
8. Another name for the sequential search algorithm.
10. A Python data structure.

Review Questions

Answer the following questions.

1. What limitation do variables have that lists don't?
2. What is a data structure?
3. What is each item of a data structure called?
4. Name six known data structures that Python supports.
5. What is a list in Python?
6. What is a dictionary in Python?
7. What does it mean when we say that a list is "mutable"?
8. What happens when a statement tries to display the value of a non-existing list element?
9. What happens when a statement tries to assign a value to a non-existing dictionary element?
10. In a list of 100 elements, what is the index of the last element?
11. What does "iterating through rows" mean?
12. What does "iterating through columns" mean?
13. What is a square matrix?
14. What is the main diagonal of a square matrix?
15. What is the antidiagonal of a square matrix?
16. Write the code fragment in general form that validates data input to a list without displaying any error messages.
17. Write the code fragment in general form that validates data input to a list and displays an error message, regardless of the type of error.
18. Write the code fragment in general form that validates data input to a list and displays an individual error message for each error.
19. What is a sorting algorithm?
20. Name five sorting algorithms.
21. Which sorting algorithm is considered the most inefficient?
22. Can a sorting algorithm be used to find the minimum or the maximum value of a list?
23. Why is a sorting algorithm not the best option to find the minimum or the maximum value of a list?
24. Write the code fragment that sorts list a of N elements in ascending order, using the bubble sort algorithm.
25. How many compares does the bubble sort algorithm perform?
26. When does the bubble sort algorithm perform the maximum number of swaps?
27. Using the bubble sort algorithm, write the code fragment that sorts list a but preserves the relationship with the elements of list b of N elements in ascending order.
28. Using the modified bubble sort algorithm, write the code fragment that sorts list a of N elements in ascending order.
29. Using the selection sort algorithm, write the code fragment that sorts list a of N elements in ascending order.
30. Using the insertion sort algorithm, write the code fragment that sorts list a of N elements in ascending order.
31. What is a search algorithm?
32. Name the two most commonly used search algorithms.

33. What are the advantages and disadvantages of the linear search algorithm?

34. Using the linear search algorithm, write the code fragment that searches list a for value `needle`.

35. What are the advantages and disadvantages of the binary search algorithm?

36. Using the binary search algorithm, write the code fragment that searches list a for value `needle`. Assume that the list is sorted in ascending order.

Section 7

Subprograms

Chapter 34
Introduction to Subprograms

34.1   What Exactly is a Subprogram?

In computer science, a *subprogram* is a block of statements packaged as a unit that performs a specific task. A subprogram can be called in a program several times, whenever that specific task needs to be performed.

A built-in Python function is an example of such a subprogram. Take the already known abs() function, for example. It consists of a block of statements that are packaged as a unit under the name "abs", and they perform a specific task—they return the absolute value of a number.

✎ *If you are wondering what kind of statements might exist inside function* abs()*, here is a possible block of statements.*

```
if number < 0:
    return number * (-1)
else:
    return number
```

Generally speaking, there are two kinds of subprograms: *functions* and *procedures*. The difference between a function and a procedure is that a function returns a result, whereas a procedure doesn't. However, in some computer languages, this distinction may not quite be apparent. There are languages in which a function can also behave as a procedure and return no result, and there are languages in which a procedure can return one or even more than one result.

✎ *Depending on the computer language being used, the meaning of the terms "function" and "procedure" may vary. For example, in Visual Basic you can find them as "functions" and "subprocedures", whereas in FORTRAN you would find them as "functions" and "subroutines". On the other hand, Python supports only functions that can play both roles; they can behave either as a function or as a procedure depending on the way they are written.*

34.2   What is Procedural Programming?

Suppose you were assigned a project to solve the drug abuse problem in your area. One possible approach (which could prove very difficult or even impossible) would be to try to solve this problem by yourself!

A better approach, however, would be to subdivide the large problem into smaller subproblems such as prevention, treatment, and rehabilitation, each of which could be further subdivided into even smaller subproblems, as shown in. Then, with the help of specialists from a variety of fields, you would build a team to help solve the drug problem. The following diagram shows how each subproblem could be further subdivided into even smaller subproblems, as shown in **Figure 34–1**.

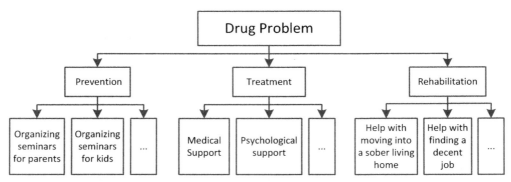

Figure 34–1 A problem can be subdivided into smaller problems

Then, as the supervisor of this project, you could rent a building and establish within it three departments: the prevention department, with all of its subdepartments; the treatment department, with all of its subdepartments; and the rehabilitation department with all of its subdepartments. Finally, you would hire staff and employ them to do the job for you!

Procedural programming does exactly the same thing. It subdivides an initial problem into smaller subproblems, and each subproblem is further subdivided into smaller subproblems. Finally, for each subproblem a small subprogram is written, and the main program (as does the supervisor), calls (employs) each of them to do a different part of the job.

Procedural programming has several advantages:

- ▶ It enables programmers to reuse the same code whenever it is necessary without having to copy it.
- ▶ It is relatively easy to implement.
- ▶ It helps programmers follow the flow of execution more easily.

> ✎ *A very large program can prove very difficult to debug and maintain when it is all in one piece. For this reason, it is often easier to subdivide it into smaller subprograms, each of which performs a clearly defined process.*

34.3   What is Modular Programming?

In *modular programming*, subprograms of common functionality can be grouped together into separate modules, and each module can have its own set of data. Therefore, a program can consist of more than one part, and each of those parts (modules) can contain one or more smaller parts (subprograms).

> ✎ *The built-in* math *module of Python is such an example. It contains subprograms of common functionality (related to Math), such as* fsum(), sqrt(), sin(), cos(), tan(), *and many more.*

If you were to use modular programming in the previous drug problem example, then you could have three separate buildings—one to host the prevention department and all of its subdepartments, a second one to host the treatment department and all of its subdepartments, and a third one to host the rehabilitation department and all of its subdepartments (as shown in **Figure 34–2**). These three buildings could be thought of as three different modules in modular programming, each of which contains subprograms of common functionality.

Figure 34–2 Subprograms of common functionality can be grouped together into separate modules.

34.4 Review Questions: True/False

Choose **true** or **false** for each of the following statements.

1. A subprogram is a block of statements packaged as a unit that performs a specific task.

2. In general, there are two kinds of subprograms: functions and procedures.

3. In many computer languages, the difference between a function and a procedure is that a procedure returns a result, whereas a function does not.

4. Python supports only procedures.

5. Procedural programming subdivides the initial problem into smaller subproblems.

6. An advantage of procedural programming is the ability to reuse the same code whenever it is necessary without having to copy it.

7. Procedural programming helps programmers follow the flow of execution more easily.

8. Modular programming improves a program's execution speed.

9. In modular programming, subprograms of common functionality are grouped together into separate modules.

10. In modular programming, each module can have its own set of data.

11. Modular programming uses different structures than structured programming does.

12. A program can consist of more than one module.

Chapter 35
User-Defined Subprograms

35.1 Subprograms that Return Values

In Python and many other computer languages, a subprogram that returns values is called a *function*. There are two categories of functions in Python. There are the *built-in functions*, such as `int()`, `float()`, and there are the *user-defined functions*, those that you actually write and use in your own programs.

The general form of a Python function that returns one or more values is shown here.

```
def name([arg1, arg2, arg3, …]):

    A statement or block of statements


    return value1 [, value2, value3, … ]
```

where

► *name* is the name of the function. It follows the same rules as those used for variable names

► *arg1, arg2, arg3,* … is a list of arguments (variables, lists etc.) used to pass values from the caller to the function. There can be as many arguments as you need.

► *value1, value2, value3,* … are the values returned to the caller. They can be a constant value, a variable, an expression, or even a data structure.

✎ *Note that arguments are optional; that is, a function may contain no arguments.*

The function *name* can be likened to a box (see **Figure 35–1**) which contains a statement or block of statements. It accepts the arguments `arg1, arg2, arg3,` … as input values and returns `value1 [, value2, value3, … ]` as output values.

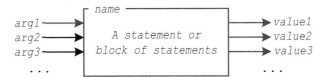

Figure 35–1 A function can be likened to a box

For example, the next function accepts two numbers through the arguments num1 and num2, then calculates their sum and returns the result.

```
def get_sum(num1, num2):
    result = num1 + num2
    return result
```

Of course, this can also be written as

```
def get_sum(num1, num2):
    return num1 + num2
```

The next function calculates the sum and the difference of two numbers, and returns the results.

```
def get_sum_dif(num1, num2):
    s = num1 + num2
```

```
    d = num1 - num2
    return s, d
```

35.2   How to Make a Call to a Function

Every call to a function is as follows: you write the name of the function followed by a list of arguments (if required), either within a statement that assigns the function's returned value to a variable or directly within an expression.

Let's see some examples. The following function accepts an argument (a numeric value) and returns the result of that value raised to the power of three.

```
def cube(num):
    result = num ** 3
    return result
```

Now, suppose that you want to calculate a result using the following expression

$$y = \sqrt[3]{x} + \frac{1}{x}$$

You can either assign the returned value from the function cube() to a variable, as shown here

```
x = float(input())

cb = cube(x)              #Assign the returned value to a variable
y = cb + 1 / x            #and use that variable

print(y)
```

or you can call the function directly in an expression,

```
x = float(input())

y = cube(x) + 1 / x       #Call the function directly in an expression
print(y)
```

or you can even call the function directly in a print() statement.

```
x = float(input())

print(cube(x) + 1 / x)   #Call the function directly in a print() statement
```

> ✎ *User-defined functions can be called just like the built-in functions of Python.*

Now let's see another example. The next Python program defines the function get_message() and then the main code calls it. The returned value is assigned to variable a.

📁 **file_35_2a**

```
#Define the function
def get_message():
    msg = "Hello Zeus"
    return msg

#Main code starts here
print("Hi there!")
a = get_message()
print(a)
```

If you run this program, the following messages are displayed.

✎ *Note that a function does not execute immediately when a program starts running. The first statement that actually executes in this example is the statement* `print("Hi there!")`.

You can pass (send) values to a function, as long as at least one argument exists within the function's parentheses. In the next example, the function `display()` is called three times but each time a different value is passed through the argument `color`.

```
📁 file_35_2b
#Define the function
def display(color):
    msg = "There is " + color + " in the rainbow"
    return msg


#Main code starts here
print(display("red"))
print(display("yellow"))
print(display("blue"))
```

If you run this program, the following messages are displayed.

In the next example, two values must be passed to function `display()`.

```
📁 file_35_2c
def display(color, exists):
    neg = ""
    if not exists:
        neg = "n't any"


    return "There is" + neg + " " + color + " in the rainbow"
```

```
#Main code starts here
print(display("red", True))
print(display("yellow", True))
print(display("black", False))
```

If you run this program the following messages are displayed.

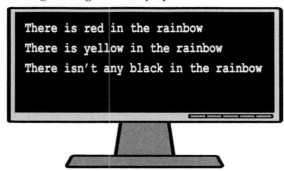

In Python, you must place your subprograms above your main code. In other computer languages, such as Java or PHP, you can place your subprograms either above or below your main code. Even then, however, most programmers prefer to have all subprograms on the top for better observation.

As already mentioned, a function in Python can return more than one value. The next example prompts the user to enter his or her first and last name, and it then displays them.

📁 **file_35_2d**

```
#Define the function
def get_fullname():
    first_name = input("Enter first name: ")
    last_name = input("Enter last name: ")
    return first_name, last_name

#Main code starts here
fname, lname = get_fullname()
print("First name:", fname)
print("Last name:", lname)
```

35.3 Subprograms that Return no Values

In computer science, a subprogram that returns no values can be known as a procedure, subprocedure, subroutine, void function, and more. In Python, the preferred term is usually *void function*.

The general form of a Python void function is

```
def name([arg1, arg2, arg3, …]):

    A statement or block of statements
```

where

▶   *name* is the name of the void function. It follows the same rules as those used for variable names.

▶   *arg1, arg2, arg3, …* is a list of arguments (variables, lists, etc.) used to pass values from the caller to the void function. There can be as many arguments as you want.

✎ *Note that arguments are optional; that is, a void function may contain no arguments.*

For example, the next void function accepts two numbers through the arguments `num1` and `num2`, then calculates their sum and displays the result.

```python
def display_sum(num1, num2):
    result = num1 + num2
    print(result)
```

35.4 How to Make a Call to a void Function

You can call a void function by just writing its name. The next example defines the void function `display_line()` and the main code calls the void function whenever it needs to display a horizontal line.

```
┌─  file_35_4a
```
```python
#Define the void function
def display_line():
    print("----------------------------")


#Main code starts here
print("Hello there!")
display_line()
print("How do you do?")
display_line()
print("What is your name?")
display_line()
```

You can also pass (send) values to a void function, as long as at least one argument exists within void function's parentheses. In the next example, the void function `display_line()` is called three times but each time a different value is passed through the variable `length`, resulting in three printed lines of different length.

```
┌─  file_35_4b
```
```python
def display_line(length):
    for i in range(length):
        print("-", end = "")
    print()


#Main code starts here
print("Hello there!")
display_line(12)
print("How do you do?")
display_line(14)
print("What is your name?")
display_line(18)
```

📖 *Since the void function `display_line()` returns no value, the following line of code is **wrong**. You **cannot** assign the void function to a variable because there isn't any returned value!*

```python
y = display_line(12)
```

*Also, you **cannot** call it within a statement. The following line of code is also **wrong**.*

```
print( "Hello there!", display_line(12) )
```

35.5   Formal and Actual Arguments

Each function (or void function) contains an argument list called a *formal argument list*. As already stated, arguments in this list are optional; the formal argument list may contain no arguments, one argument, or more than one argument.

When a subprogram (function, or void function) is called, an argument list may be passed to the subprogram. This list is called an *actual argument list*.

In the next example, variables n1 and n2 constitute the formal argument list whereas variables x and y as well as the expressions x + y and y / 2 constitute the actual argument lists.

📄 **file_35_5**

```
#Define the function multiply().
#The two arguments n1 and n2 are called formal arguments.
def multiply(n1, n2):                ← This is called a "formal argument list"

    result = n1 * n2
    return result


#Main code starts here
x = float(input())
y = float(input())

#Call the function multiply().
#The two arguments x and y are called actual arguments.
w = multiply(x, y)                   ← This is called an "actual argument list"
print(w)

#Call the function multiply().
#The two arguments x + y and y / 2 are called actual arguments.   ← This is called an "actual
print(multiply(x + 2, y / 2))                                        argument list"
```

✎ *Note that there is a one-to-one match between the formal and the actual arguments. In the first call, the value of argument* x *is passed to argument* n1 *and the value of argument* y *is passed to argument* n2. *In the second call, the result of the expression* x + 2 *is passed to argument* n1 *and the result of the expression* y / 2 *is passed to argument* n2.

35.6   How Does a Function Execute?

When the main code calls a function the following steps are performed:

▶   The execution of the statements of the main code is interrupted.

▶   The values of the variables or the result of the expressions that exist in the actual argument list are passed (assigned) to the corresponding arguments (variables) in the formal argument list, and the flow of execution goes to where the function is written.

▶   The statements of the function are executed.

▶   When the flow of execution reaches the end of the function, a value is returned from the function to the main code and the flow of execution continues from where it was before calling the function.

In the next Python program, the function `maximum()` accepts two arguments (numeric values) and returns the greater of the two values.

```
📁 file_35_6
def maximum(val1, val2):
    m = val1
    if val2 > m:
        m = val2
    return m


#Main code starts here
a = float(input())
b = float(input())

maxim = maximum(a, b)

print(maxim)
```

When the Python program starts running, the first statement executed is the statement `a = float(input())` (this is considered the first statement of the program). Suppose the user enters the values 3 and 8. Below is a trace table that shows the exact flow of execution, how the values of the variables a and b are passed from the main code to the function, and how the function returns its result.

Step	Statements of the Main Code	a	b	maxim
1	a = float(input())	3	?	?
2	b = float(input())	3	8	?
3	maxim = maximum(a, b)			

When the call to the function `maximum()` is made, the execution of the statements of the main code is interrupted and the values of the variables a and b are passed (assigned, if you prefer) to the corresponding arguments (variables) `val1` and `val2` and the flow of execution goes to where the function is written. Then the statements of the function are executed.

Step	Statements of Function maximum()	val1	val2	m
4	m = val1	3	8	3
5	if val2 > m:	This evaluates to True		
6	m = val2	3	8	8
7	return m			

When the flow of execution reaches the end of the function, the value 8 is returned from the function to the main code (and assigned to the variable `maxim`) and the flow of execution continues from where it was before calling the function. The main code displays the value of 8 on the user's screen.

Step	Statements of the Main Code	a	b	maxim
8	print(maxim)	3	8	8

Exercise 35.6-1   Back to Basics – Calculating the Sum of Two Numbers

Do the following:

  i.   *Write a subprogram named* total *that accepts two numeric values through its formal argument list and then calculates and returns their sum.*

  ii. *Using the subprogram cited above, write a Python program that lets the user enter two numbers and then displays their sum. Next, create a trace table to determine the values of the variables in each step of the Python program for two different executions.*

  The input values for the two executions are: (i) 2, 4; and (ii) 10, 20.

Solution

In this exercise you need to write a function that accepts two values from the caller (this is the main code) and then calculates and returns their sum. The solution is shown here.

```
📁 file_35_6_1
def total(a, b):
    s = a + b
    return s

#Main code starts here
num1 = float(input())
num2 = float(input())
result = total(num1, num2)
print("The sum of", num1, "+", num2, "is", result)
```

Now, let's create the corresponding trace tables. Since you have become more experienced with them, the column "Notes" has been removed.

  i.   For the input values of 2, 4, the trace table looks like this.

Step	Statement	Main Code			Function total()		
		num1	num2	result	a	b	s
1	num1 = float(input())	2	?	?			
2	num2 = float(input())	2	4	?			
3	result = total(num1, num2)				2	4	?
4	s = a + b				2	4	6
5	return s	2	4	6			
6	print("The sum of…	It displays: The sum of 2 + 4 is 6					

  ii. For the input values of 10, 20, the trace table looks like this.

Step	Statement	Main Code			Function total()		
		num1	num2	result	a	b	s
1	num1 = float(input())	10	?	?			
2	num2 = float(input())	10	20	?			

3	`result = total(num1, num2)`				**10**	**20**	**?**
4	`s = a + b`				10	20	**30**
5	`return s`	10	20	**30**			
6	`print("The sum of...`	It displays: The sum of 10 + 20 is 30					

Exercise 35.6-2   *Calculating the Sum of Two Numbers Using Fewer Lines of Code!*

Rewrite the Python program of the previous exercise using fewer lines of code.

Solution

The solution is shown here.

```
                            📁 file_35_6_2
def total(a, b):
    return a + b

#Main code starts here
num1 = float(input())
num2 = float(input())

print("The sum of", num1, "+", num2, "is", total(num1, num2))
```

Contrary to the solution of the previous exercise, in this function `total()` the sum is not assigned to variable s but it is directly calculated and returned. Furthermore, this main code doesn't assign the returned value to a variable but directly displays it.

📝 *User-defined functions can be called just like the built-in functions of Python.*

35.7   How Does a void Function Execute?

When the main code calls a void function, the following steps are performed:

► The execution of the statements of the main code is interrupted.

► The values of the variables or the result of the expressions that exist in the actual argument list are passed (assigned) to the corresponding arguments (variables) in the formal argument list and the flow of execution goes to where the void function is written.

► The statements of the void function are executed.

► When the flow of execution reaches the end of the void function, the flow of execution continues from where it was before calling the void function.

In the next Python program, the void function `minimum()` accepts three arguments (numeric values) through its formal argument list and displays the lowest value.

```
                            📁 file_35_7
def minimum(val1, val2, val3):
    minim = val1
    if val2 < minim:
        minim = val2
    if val3 < minim:
        minim = val3
```

```
    print(minim)

#Main code starts here
a = float(input())
b = float(input())
c = float(input())
minimum(a, b, c)
print("The end")
```

When the Python program starts running, the first statement executed is the statement `a = float(input())` (this is considered the first statement of the program). Suppose the user enters the values 9, 6, and 8.

Step	Statements of the Main Code	a	b	c
1	a = float(input())	**9**	?	?
2	b = float(input())	9	**6**	?
3	c = float(input())	9	6	**8**
4	minimum(a, b, c)			

When a call to the void function `minimum()` is made, the execution of the statements of the main code is interrupted and the values of the variables a, b, and c are copied (assigned) to the corresponding arguments (variables) val1, val2, and val3, and the flow of execution goes to where the void function is written. Then the statements of the void function are executed.

Step	Statements of void Function minimum()	val1	val2	val3	minim
5	minim = val1	9	6	8	9
6	if val2 < minim:	This evaluates to True			
7	minim = val2	9	6	8	6
8	if val3 < minim:	This evaluates to False			
9	print(minim)	It displays: 6			

When the flow of execution reaches the end of the void function the flow of execution simply continues from where it was before calling the void function.

Step	Statements of the Main Code	a	b	c
10	print("The end")	It displays: The end		

✎ *Note that at step 10 no values are returned from the void function to the main code.*

Exercise 35.7-1   Back to Basics – Displaying the Absolute Value of a Number

Do the following:

  i.   *Write a subprogram named* display_abs *that accepts a numeric value through its formal argument list and then displays its absolute value. Do not use the built-in* abs() *function of Python.*

ii. *Using the subprogram cited above, write a Python program that lets the user enter a number and then displays its absolute value followed by the initial value given. Next, create a trace table to determine the values of the variables in each step of the Python program for two different executions.*

The input values for the two executions are: (i) 5, and (ii) −5.

Solution

In this exercise you need to write a void function that accepts a value from the caller (this is the main code) and then calculates and displays its absolute value. The solution is shown here.

```
☐ file_35_7_1
def display_abs(n):
    if n < 0:
        n = (-1) * n
    print(n)


#Main code starts here
a = float(input())
display_abs(a)      #This displays the absolute value of given number.
print(a)            #This displays the initial number given.
```

Now, let's create the corresponding trace tables.

i. For the input value of 5, the trace table looks like this.

Step	Statement	Main Code	void Function display_abs()
		a	n
1	a = input()	5	
2	display_abs(a)		5
3	if n < 0:	This evaluates to False	
4	print(n)	It displays: 5	
5	print(a)	It displays: 5	

ii. For the input value of −5, the trace table looks like this.

Step	Statement	Main Code	void Function display_abs()
		a	n
1	a = input()	−5	
2	display_abs(a)		−5
3	if n < 0:	This evaluates to True	
4	n = (-1) * n		5
5	print(n)	It displays: 5	
6	print(a)	It displays: −5	

✎ *Note that at step 5 the variable* n *of the void function contains the value 5 but when the flow of execution returns to the main code at step 6, the variable* a *of the main code contains the value −5. Actually, the value of variable* a *of the main code had never changed!*

35.8 Review Questions: True/False

Choose **true** or **false** for each of the following statements.

1. There are two categories of subprograms that return values in Python.

2. The variables that are used to pass values to a function are called arguments.

3. The function int() is a user-defined function.

4. Every call to a user-defined function is made in the same way as a call to the built-in functions of Python.

5. There can be as many arguments as you wish in a function's formal argument list.

6. In a function, the formal argument list must contain at least one argument.

7. In a function, the formal argument list is optional.

8. A function cannot return a list.

9. The statement
   ```
   return x + 1
   ```
   is a valid Python statement.

10. A formal argument can be an expression.

11. An actual argument can be an expression.

12. A function can have no arguments in the actual argument list.

13. The next statement calls the function cube_root() three times.
    ```
    cb = cube_root(x) + cube_root(x) / 2 + cube_root(x) / 3
    ```

14. The following code fragment
    ```
    cb = cube_root(x)
    y = cb + 5
    print(y)
    ```
    displays exactly the same value as the statement
    ```
    print(cube_root(x) + 5)
    ```

15. A function must always include a return statement whereas a void function mustn't.

16. The name play-the-guitar can be a valid function name.

17. In Python, you can place your functions either above or below your main code.

18. When the main code calls a function, the execution of the statements of the main code is interrupted.

19. In general, it is possible for a function to return no values to the caller.

20. The function abs() is a built-in function of Python.

21. The following code fragment
    ```
    def divide(a, b):
        return a / b

    a = 10.0
    b = 5.0
    print(divide(b, a))
    ```

displays the value 0.5.

22. In computer science, a subprogram that returns no result is known as a void function.

23. In Python, you can call a void function just by writing its name.

24. In a void function call that is made in main code, within the actual argument list there must be only variables of the main code.

25. In a void function, all formal arguments must have different names.

26. A void function must always include at least one argument in its formal argument list.

27. There is a one-to-one match between the formal and the actual arguments.

28. You can call a void function within a statement.

29. When the flow of execution reaches the end of a void function, the flow of execution continues from where it was before calling the void function.

30. A void function returns no values to the caller.

31. It is possible for a void function to accept no values from the caller.

32. A call to a void function is made differently from a call to a function.

33. In the following Python program

```python
def message():
    print("Hello Aphrodite!")


print("Hi there!")
message()
```

the first statement that executes is the statement `print("Hello Aphrodite!")`.

35.9 Review Exercises

Complete the following exercises.

1. The following function contains some errors. Can you spot them?

```python
def find_max(a, b)
    if a > b:
        maximum = a
    else:
        maximum = b
```

2. Create a trace table to determine the values of the variables in each step of the following Python program.

```python
def sum_digits(a):
    d1 = a % 10
    d2 = a // 10


    return d1 + d2


s = 0
for i in range(25, 28):
    s += sum_digits(i)
print(s)
```

3. Create a trace table to determine the values of the variables in each step of the following Python program.

```python
def sss(a):
    total = 0
    for k in range(1, a + 1):
        total += k
    return total


i = 1
s = 0
while i < 6:
    if i % 2 == 1:
        s += 1
    else:
        s += sss(i)
    i += 1

print(s)
```

4. Create a trace table to determine the values of the variables in each step of the following Python program when the value 12 is entered.

```python
def custom_div(b, d):
    return (b + d) // 2


k = int(input())
m = 2
a = 1
while a < 6:
    if k % m != 0:
        x = custom_div(a, m)
    else:
        x = a + m + custom_div(m, a)
    print(m, a, x)
    a += 2
    m += 1
```

5. Create a trace table to determine the values of the variables in each step of the following Python program when the values 3, 7, 9, 2, and 4 are entered.

```python
def display(a):
    if a % 2 == 0:
        print(a, "is even")
    else:
        print(a, "is odd")


for i in range(5):
    x = int(input())
    display(x)
```

6. Create a trace table to determine the values of the variables in each step of the following Python program.

```python
def division(a, b):
    b = b // a
    print(a * b)


x = 20
y = 30
while x % y < 30:
    division(y, x)
    x = 4 * y
    y += 1
```

7. Create a trace table to determine the values of the variables in each step of the following Python program when the values 2, 3, and 4 are entered.

```python
def calculate(n):
    s = 0
    for j in range(2, 2 * n + 2, 2):
        s = s + j ** 2


    print(s)


for i in range(3):
    m = int(input())
    calculate(m)
```

8. Write a subprogram that accepts three numbers through its formal argument list and then returns their sum.

9. Write a subprogram that accepts four numbers through its formal argument list and then returns their average.

10. Write a subprogram that accepts three numbers through its formal argument list and then returns the greatest value. Try not to use the max() function of Python.

11. Write a subprogram that accepts five numbers through its formal argument list and then displays the greatest value.

12. Write a subprogram named my_round that accepts a real through its formal argument list and returns it rounded to two decimal places. Try not to use the round() function of Python.

13. Do the following:

    i. Write a subprogram named find_min that accepts two numbers through its formal argument list and returns the lowest one.

    ii. Using the subprogram cited above, write a Python program that prompts the user to enter four numbers and then displays the lowest one.

14. Do the following:

    i. Write a subprogram named Kelvin_to_Fahrenheit that accepts a temperature in degrees Kelvin through its formal argument list and returns its degrees Fahrenheit equivalent.

    ii. Write a subprogram named Kelvin_to_Celsius that accepts a temperature in degrees Kelvin through its formal argument list and returns its degrees Celsius equivalent.

    iii. Using the subprograms cited above, write a Python program that prompts the user to enter a temperature in degrees Kelvin and then displays its degrees Fahrenheit and its degrees Celsius equivalent.

It is given that

$$Kelvin = \frac{Fahrenheit + 459.67}{1.8}$$

and

$$Kelvin = Celsius + 273.15$$

15. The Body Mass Index (BMI) is often used to determine whether a person is overweight or underweight for his or her height. The formula used to calculate the BMI is

$$BMI = \frac{weight \cdot 703}{height^2}$$

Do the following:

    i. Write a subprogram named `bmi` that accepts a weight and a height through its formal argument list and then returns an action (a message) according to the following table.

BMI	Action
BMI < 16	You must add weight.
16 ≤ BMI < 18.5	You should add some weight.
18.5 ≤ BMI < 25	Maintain your weight.
25 ≤ BMI < 30	You should lose some weight.
30 ≤ BMI	You must lose weight.

    ii. Using the subprogram cited above, write a Python program that prompts the user to enter his or her weight (in pounds), age (in years), and height (in inches), and then displays the corresponding message. Using a loop control structure, the program must also validate data input and display an error message when the user enters

        a. any negative value for weight

        b. any value less than 18 for age

        c. any negative value for height

16. Do the following:

    i. Write a subprogram named `num_of_days` that accepts a year and a month (1 – 12) through its formal argument list and then displays the number of days in that month. Take special care when a year is a leap year; that is, a year in which February has 29 instead of 28 days.

Hint: A year is a leap year when it is exactly divisible by 4 and not by 100, or when it is exactly divisible by 400.

    ii. Using the subprogram cited above, write a Python program that prompts the user to enter a year and then displays the number of the days in each month of that year.

17. Do the following:

    i. Write a subprogram named `display_menu` that displays the following menu.

        1. Convert meters to miles

        2. Convert miles to meters

        3. Exit

ii. Write a subprogram named `meters_to_miles` that accepts a value in meters through its formal argument list and then displays the message "XX meters equals YY miles" where XX and YY must be replaced by actual values.

iii. Write a subprogram named `miles_to_meters` that accepts a value in miles through its formal argument list and then displays the message "YY miles equals XX meters" where XX and YY must be replaced by actual values.

iv. Using the subprograms cited above, write a Python program that displays the previously mentioned menu and prompts the user to enter a choice (of 1, 2, or 3) and a distance. The program must then calculate and display the required value. The process must repeat as many times as the user wishes. It is given that 1 mile = 1609.344 meters.

18. The LAV Cell Phone Company charges customers a basic rate of $10 per month, and additional rates are charged based on the total number of seconds a customer talks on his or her cell phone within the month. Use the rates shown in the following table.

Number of Seconds a Customer Talks on his or her Cell Phone	Additional Rates (in USD per second)
1 – 600	Free of charge
601 – 1200	$0.01
1201 and above	$0.02

Do the following:

i.   Write a subprogram named `amount_to_pay` that accepts a number in seconds through its formal argument list and then displays the total amount to pay. Please note that the rates are progressive. Moreover, federal, state, and local taxes add a total of 11% to each bill

ii. Using the subprogram cited above, write a Python program that prompts the user to enter the number of seconds he or she talks on the cell phone and then displays the total amount to pay.

Chapter 36
Tips and Tricks with Subprograms

36.1 Can Two Subprograms use Variables of the Same Name?

Each subprogram uses its own memory space to hold the values of its variables. Even the main code has its own memory space! This means that you can have a variable named test in main code, another variable named test in a subprogram, and yet another variable named test in another subprogram. Pay attention! Those three variables are three completely different variables, in different memory locations, and they can hold completely different values.

As you can see in the program that follows, there are three variables named test in three different memory locations and each one of them holds a completely different value. The trace table below can help you understand what really goes on.

```
┌ file_36_1
def f1():
    test = 22
    print(test)
    return True


def f2(test):
    print(test)


#Main code starts here
test = 5
print(test)
ret = f1()
f2(10)
print(test)
```

The trace table is shown here.

Step	Statement	Notes	Main Code		Function f1()	void Function f2()
			test	ret	test	test
1	test = 5		5	?		
2	print(test)	It displays: 5	5	?		
3	ret = f1()	f1() is called			?	
4	test = 22				22	
5	print(test)	It displays: 22			22	
6	return True	It returns to the main code	5	**True**		
7	f2(10)	f2() is called				10

8	`print(test)`	It displays: 10				10
9	`print(test)`	It displays: 5	5	True		

> ✎ *Note that variables used in a subprogram "live" as long as the subprogram is being executed. This means that before calling the subprogram, none of its variables (including those in the formal argument list) exists in main memory (RAM). They are all defined in the main memory when the subprogram is called, and they are all removed from the main memory when the subprogram finishes and the flow of execution returns to the caller. The only variables that "live" forever, or at least for as long as the Python program is being executed, are the variables of the main code and the global variables! You will learn more about global variables in paragraph 36.6.*

36.2 Can a Subprogram Call Another Subprogram?

All the time you've been reading this section, you may have had the impression that only the main code can call a subprogram. Of course, this is not true!

A subprogram can call any other subprogram which in turn can call another subprogram, and so on. You can make whichever combination you wish. For example, you can write a function that calls a void function, a void function that calls a function, a function that calls another function, or even a function that calls one of the built-in functions of the computer language that you are using to write your programs.

The next example presents exactly this situation. The main code calls the void function `display_sum()`, which in turn calls the function `add()`.

```
📄 file_36_2
```

```python
def add(number1, number2):
    result = number1 + number2
    return result

def display_sum(num1, num2):
    print(add(num1, num2))

#Main code starts here
a = int(input())
b = int(input())

display_sum(a, b)
```

> ✎ *When the flow of execution reaches the end of the function* `add()`*, it returns to its caller, that is to the void function* `display_sum()`*. Then, when the flow of execution reaches the end of the void function* `display_sum()`*, it returns to its caller, that is, to the main code.*

> ✎ *Note that there is no restriction on the order in which the two subprograms should be written. It would have been exactly the same if the void function* `display_sum()` *had been written before the function* `add()`*.*

36.3 Passing Arguments by Value and by Reference

In Python, variables are passed to subprograms *by value*. This means that if the value of an argument is changed within the subprogram, it does not get changed outside of it. Take a look at the following example.

```
📄 file_36_3a
```

```python
def f1(b):
```

```
    b += 1        #This is a variable of void function f1()
    print(b)      #It displays: 11


#Main code starts here
a = 10            #This is a variable of the main code
f1(a)
print(a)          #It displays: 10
```

The value 10 of variable a is passed to void function f1() through argument b. However, although the content of variable b is altered within the void function, when the flow of execution returns to the main code this change does not affect the value of variable a.

In the previous example, the main code and the void function are using two variables with different names. Yet, the same would have happened if, for example, both the main code and the void function had used two variables of the same name. The next Python program operates exactly the same way and displays exactly the same results as previous program did.

📄 file_36_3b

```
def f1(a):
    a += 1        #This is a variable of void function f1()
    print(a)      #It displays: 11


#Main code starts here
a = 10            #This is a variable of the main code
f1(a)
print(a)          #It displays: 10
```

Passing a list to a subprogram as an argument is as easy as passing a simple variable. The next example passes list a to the void function display(), and the latter displays the list.

📄 file_36_3c

```
ELEMENTS = 10

def display(b):
    for i in range(ELEMENTS):
        print(b[i], end = "\t")

#Main code starts here
a = [None] * ELEMENTS
for i in range(ELEMENTS):
    a[i] = int(input())

display(a)
```

Contrary to variables, data structures in Python are passed *by reference*. This means that if you pass, for example, a list to a subprogram, and that subprogram changes the value of one or more elements of the list, these changes are also reflected outside the subprogram. Take a look at the following example.

📄 file_36_3d

```
def f1(x):
    x[0] += 1
    print(x[0]) #It displays: 6
```

```
#Main code starts here
y = [5, 10, 15, 20]
print(y[0])        #It displays: 5
f1(y)
print(y[0])        #It displays: 6
```

✎ *Passing a list to a subprogram actually passes a reference to the list, not a copy of the list. The list* y *and the argument* x *are actually aliases of the same list. Since the list is shared by two references, there is only one copy in main memory (RAM). If a subprogram changes the value of an element, this change is also reflected in the main program.*

So, as you have probably realized, passing lists by reference can provide an indirect way for a subprogram to "return" more than one value. Keep in mind, though, that using a list to return more than one value from a subprogram is quite unusual in Python since, as you have already learned, Python provides a more convenient way to accomplish this. However, let's see, albeit formally, one such example. In the next example, the function my_divmod() divides variable a by variable b and finds their integer quotient and their integer remainder. If all goes well, it returns True; otherwise, it returns False. Moreover, through the list results, the function also indirectly returns the calculated quotient and the calculated remainder.

📄 **file_36_3e**

```
def my_divmod(a, b, results):
    return_value = True

    if b == 0:
        return_value = False
    else:
        results[0] = a // b
        results[1] = a % b

    return return_value

#Main code starts here
res = [None] * 2

val1 = int(input())
val2 = int(input())
ret = my_divmod(val1, val2, res)
if ret:
    print(res[0], res[1])
else:
    print("Sorry, wrong values entered!");
```

✎ *A very good tactic regarding the arguments in the formal argument list is to have all of those being passed by value written before those being passed by reference.*

Exercise 36.3-1   Finding the Logic Error

The following Python program is supposed to prompt the user to enter five integers into a list and then display, for each element, its number of digits and the integer itself. For example, if the user enters the values 35, 13565, 113, 278955, 9999, the Python program is supposed to display:

> *2 are the digits of 35*
>
> *5 are the digits of 13565*
>
> *3 are the digits of 113*
>
> *6 are the digits of 278955*
>
> *4 are the digits of 9999*

Unfortunately, the following Python program displays

> *2 are the digits of 0*
>
> *5 are the digits of 0*
>
> *3 are the digits of 0*
>
> *6 are the digits of 0*
>
> *4 are the digits of 0*

Can you find out why?

```
📁 file_36_3_1a
ELEMENTS = 5

def get_num_of_digits(x, index):
    count = 0
    while x[index] != 0:
        count += 1
        x[index] = x[index] // 10
    return count

#Main code starts here
val = [None] * ELEMENTS

for i in range(ELEMENTS):
    val[i] = int(input())

for i in range(ELEMENTS):
    print(get_num_of_digits(val, i), "are the digits of", val[i])
```

Solution

The function `get_num_of_digits()` counts the number of digits of an element at index position `index` of argument (list) x using an already known method proposed in Exercise 29.1-6. But before you read the answer below, can you try to find the logic error by yourself?

No? Come on, it isn't that difficult!

Still No? Do you want to give up?

So, let it be!

The problem is that, within the function get_num_of_digits(), the corresponding element eventually becomes 0, and since the list val is passed to the function by reference, that zero also reflects back to the main code.

To resolve this issue, all you have to do is assign the value of the corresponding element to an auxiliary variable and let this variable become zero. The solution is as follows.

```
📁 file_36_3_1b
ELEMENTS = 5

def get_num_of_digits(x, index):
    count = 0

    aux_var = x[index]

    while aux_var != 0:
        count += 1
        aux_var = aux_var // 10
    return count

#Main code starts here
val = [None] * ELEMENTS

for i in range(ELEMENTS):
    val[i] = int(input())

for i in range(ELEMENTS):
    print(get_num_of_digits(val, i), "are the digits of", val[i])
```

36.4 Returning a List

In the next example, the Python program must find the three lowest values of list t. To do so, the program calls and passes the list to the void function get_list() through its formal argument x, which in turn sorts list x using the insertion sort algorithm. When the flow of execution returns to the main code, list t also gets sorted. This happens because, as already stated, lists in Python are passed by reference. So what the main code finally does is just display the values of the first three elements of the list.

```
📁 file_36_4a
ELEMENTS = 10
                    ┌─────────────────────────────────────────┐
                    │ By default, lists in Python are passed by reference. │
def get_list(x):    └─────────────────────────────────────────┘
    for m in range(1, ELEMENTS):
        element = x[m]
        n = m
        while n > 0 and x[n - 1] > element:
            x[n] = x[n - 1]
            n -= 1
        x[n] = element

#Main code starts here
t = [75, 73, 78, 70, 71, 74, 72, 69, 79, 77]
```

```
get_list(t)

print("Three lowest values are: ", t[0], t[1], t[2])

#In this step, list t is sorted
for i in range(ELEMENTS):
    print(t[i], end = "\t")
```

✎ *Note that, since the list* t *of the main code is passed to the void function by reference, when the flow of execution returns to the main code, list* t *also gets sorted.*

However, there are many times when passing a list by reference can be completely disastrous. Suppose you have the following two lists. List names contains the names of 10 cities, and list t contains their corresponding temperatures recorded at a specific hour on a specific day.

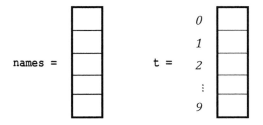

Now, suppose that for list t you wish to display the three lowest temperatures. If you call void function get_list() of the previous Python program, you have a problem. Although the three lowest temperatures can be displayed as required, the list t becomes sorted; therefore, the relationship between its elements and the elements of list names is lost forever!

One possible solution would be to write a function in which the list is copied to an auxiliary list and the function would return a smaller list that contains only the three lowest values. The proposed solution is shown here.

```
file_36_4b
ELEMENTS = 10

def get_list(x):
    aux_x = [None] * ELEMENTS

    #Copy list x to list aux_x
    for m in range(ELEMENTS):
        aux_x[m] = x[m]

    #and sort list aux_x
    for m in range(1, ELEMENTS):
        element = aux_x[m]
        n = m
        while n > 0 and aux_x[n - 1] > element:
            aux_x[n] = aux_x[n - 1]
```

```
            n -= 1
        aux_x[n] = element


    ret_list = [aux_x[0], aux_x[1], aux_x[2]]
    return ret_list

#Main code starts here
names = ["City1", "City2", "City3", "City4", "City5",    \
         "City6", "City7", "City8", "City9", "City10"]

t = [75, 73, 78, 70, 71, 74, 72, 69, 79, 77]

low = get_list(t)
print("Three lowest values are: ", low[0], low[1], low[2])

#In this step, list t is NOT sorted
for i in range(ELEMENTS):
    print(t[i], "\t", names[i])
```

✎ *Note that you cannot use a statement such as* aux_x = x *to copy the elements of list* x *to* aux_x. *This statement just creates two aliases of the same list. This is why a for-loop is used in the previous example to copy the elements of list* x *to the list* aux_x.

✎ *A more Pythonic way to copy all the elements of a list to another list is to use the slicing mechanism. In the previous example, you could do this using the statement* aux_x = x[:]

Another, more Pythonic, way is shown here.

🗀 file_36_4c

```
def get_list(x):
    y = sorted(x)
    return y[0:3]   #Return only the first three elements

#Main code starts here
names = ["City1", "City2", "City3", "City4", "City5",    \
         "City6", "City7", "City8", "City9", "City10"]

t = [75, 73, 78, 70, 71, 74, 72, 69, 79, 77]

low = get_list(t)
print("Three lowest values are: ", low[0], low[1], low[2])

#In this step, list t is NOT sorted
for i in range(len(t)):
    print(t[i], "\t", names[i])
```

📖 *The function* sorted(x) *returns a new sorted list, leaving the initial list* x *intact (see paragraph 32.7).*

36.5 Default Argument Values and Keyword Arguments

If you use a default value to an argument within the formal argument list, it means that if no value is passed for that argument then the default value is used. In the next example, the function prepend_title() is designed to prepend (add a prefix to) a title before the name. However, if no value for argument title is passed, the function uses the default value "Mr."

```
                            📁 file_36_5a
def prepend_title(name, title = "Mr"):
    return title + " " + name


#Main code starts here
print(prepend_title("John King"))         #It displays: Mr John King
print(prepend_title("Maria Miller", "Ms")) #It displays: Ms Maria Miller
```

✎ *When a default value is assigned to an argument within the formal argument list, this argument is called an "optional argument".*

✎ *Within the formal argument list, any optional arguments must be on the right side of any non-optional arguments; to do the opposite of this would be incorrect.*

Moreover, in Python, subprograms can be called using keyword arguments with the form

$$argument\_name = value$$

Python assumes that keyword arguments are optional. If no argument is given in a subprogram call, the default value is used.

```
                            📁 file_36_5b
def prepend_title(first_name, last_name, title = "Mr", reverse = False):
    if not reverse:
        return_value = title + " " + first_name + " " + last_name
    else:
        return_value = title + " " + last_name + " " + first_name

    return return_value


#Main code starts here
print(prepend_title("John", "King"))         #It displays: Mr John King
print(prepend_title("Maria", "Miller", "Ms")) #It displays: Ms Maria Miller
print(prepend_title("Maria", "Miller", "Ms", True)) #It displays:  Ms Miller Maria


#Call the function using a keyword argument
print(prepend_title("John", "King", reverse = True)) #It displays:  Mr King John
```

✎ *Note that the argument* reverse *is the fourth in order in the formal argument list. Using a keyword argument though, you can bypass this order.*

✎ *Instead of using the term "keyword arguments", many computer languages such as PHP, C#, and Visual Basic (to name a few), prefer to use the term "named arguments".*

36.6   The Scope of a Variable

The *scope of a variable* refers to the range of effect of that variable. In Python, a variable can have a *local* or *global scope*. A variable declared within a subprogram has a local scope and can be accessed only from within that subprogram. On the other hand, a variable declared outside of a subprogram has a global scope and can be accessed from within **any** subprogram, as well as from the main code.

Let's see some examples. The next example declares a global variable test. The value of this global variable, though, is accessed and displayed within the void function.

```
                              file_36_6a
def display_value():
    print(test)        #It displays: 10

#Main code starts here
test = 10              #This is a global variable
display_value()
print(test)            #It displays: 10
```

The question now is, "*What happens, if you change the value of variable* test *within function* display_value()*? Will it affect the global variable* test *as well?*" In the next example the values 20 and 10 are displayed.

```
                              file_36_6b
def display_value():
    test = 20          #This is a local variable
    print(test)        #It displays: 20

#Main code starts here
test = 10              #This is a global variable
display_value()
print(test)            #It displays: 10
```

This happens because Python declares two variables in main memory (RAM); that is, a global variable test and a local variable test.

Now let's combine the first example with the second one as see what happens. First the program will access the variable test, and then it will assign a value to it, as shown in the code that follows.

```
                              file_36_6c
def display_value():
    print(test)        #This statement throws an error
    test = 20
    print(test)

#Main code starts here
test = 10              #This is a global variable
display_value()
print(test)
```

Unfortunately, this example throws the error message "*local variable 'test' referenced before assignment*". This happens because Python "assumes" that you want a local variable due to the assignment statement test = 20 within function display_value(). Therefore, the first print() statement inevitably throws this error message. Any variable that is defined or altered within a function is local, unless it has been forced to be a global variable. To force Python to use the global variable you have to use the keyword `global`, as you can see in the following example.

```
┌──────────────────── 🗋 file_36_6d ────────────────────┐
def display_value():
    global test    #Force Python to use the global variable test
    print(test)    #It displays: 10
    test = 20
    print(test)    #It displays: 20

#Main code starts here
test = 10            #This is a global variable
display_value()
print(test)          #It displays: 20
```

✎ *If the value of a global variable is altered within a subprogram, this change is also reflected outside of the subprogram. Please note that the last* `print(test)` *statement of the main code displays the value of 20.*

▢ *Any variable that is defined or altered within a function is local unless it is declared as a global variable using the keyword* `global`.

The next code fragment declares a global variable x, two local variables x and y within the void function `display_values()`, and one local variable x within the void function `display_other_values()`. Keep in mind that the global variable x and the local variable x are two different variables!

```
┌──────────────────── 🗋 file_36_6e ────────────────────┐
def display_values():
    x = 7
    y = 3
    print(x, y)     #It displays: 7  3

def display_other_values():
    y = 2
    print(x, y)     #It displays: 10  2

#Main code starts here
x = 10              #x is global
print(x)            #It displays: 10
display_values()
display_other_values()
print(x)            #It displays: 10
```

✎ *You can have variables of local scope of the same name within different subprograms, because they are recognized only by the subprogram in which they are declared.*

36.7 Converting Parts of Code into Subprograms

Writing large programs without subdividing them into smaller subprograms results in a code that cannot be easily understood or maintained. Suppose you have a large program and you wish to subdivide it into smaller subprograms. The next program is an example explaining the steps that must be followed. The parts of the program marked with a dashed rectangle must be converted into subprograms.

```
                            📁 file_36_7a
total_yes = 0
female_no = 0
for i in range(100):
    while True:
        temp1 = input("Enter gender for citizen No" + str(i + 1) + ": ")
        gender = temp1.lower()
        if gender == "male" or gender == "female": break

    while True:
        temp2 = input("Do you go jogging in the afternoon? ")
        answer = temp2.lower()
        if answer == "yes" or answer == "no" or answer == "sometimes": break

    if answer == "yes":
        total_yes += 1

    if gender == "female" and answer == "no":
        female_no += 1

print("Total positive answers:", total_yes)
print("Women's negative answers:", female_no)
```

To convert parts of this program into subprograms you must:

► decide, for each dashed rectangle, whether to use a function or a void function. This depends on whether or not, the subprogram will return a result.

► determine which variables exist in each dashed rectangle and their roles in that dashed rectangle. The flowchart that follows can help you decide what to do with each variable, whether it must be passed to the subprogram and/or returned from the subprogram, or if it must just be a local variable within the subprogram.

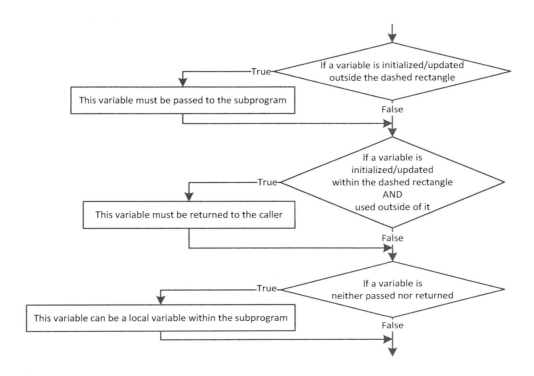

✎ *Keep in mind that functions in Python can return more than one result!*

So, with the help of this flowchart, let's discuss each dashed rectangle independently! The parts that are **not** marked with a dashed rectangle will comprise the main code.

First part

In the first dashed rectangle, there are three variables: i, temp1, and gender. However, not all of them must be included in the formal argument list of the subprogram that will replace the dashed rectangle. Let's find out why!

- ▶ Variable i:
  - ▶ is initialized/updated outside the dashed rectangle; thus, it must be passed to the subprogram
  - ▶ is not updated within the dashed rectangle; thus, it should not be returned to the caller
- ▶ Variable temp1:
  - ▶ is not initialized/updated outside of the dashed rectangle; thus, it should not be passed to the subprogram
  - ▶ is initialized within the dashed rectangle but its value is not used outside of it; thus, it should not be returned to the caller

According to the flowchart, since variable temp1 should neither be passed nor returned, this variable can just be a local variable within the subprogram.

- ▶ Variable gender:
  - ▶ is not initialized/updated outside of the dashed rectangle; thus, it should not be passed to the subprogram
  - ▶ is initialized within the dashed rectangle and its value is used outside of it; thus, it must be returned to the caller

Therefore, since one value must be returned to the main code, a function can be used as shown here.

```python
def part1(i):
    while True:
        temp1 = input("Enter gender for citizen No" + str(i + 1) + ": ")
        gender = temp1.lower()
        if gender == "male" or gender == "female": break

    return gender
```

Second part

In the second dashed rectangle there are two variables, temp2 and answer, but they do not both need to be included in the formal argument list of the subprogram that will replace the dashed rectangle. Let's find out why!

- ▶ Variable temp2:
  - ▶ is not initialized/updated outside of the dashed rectangle; thus, it should not be passed to the subprogram
  - ▶ is initialized/updated within the dashed rectangle but its value is not used outside of it; thus, it should not be returned to the caller

  According to the flowchart, since variable temp2 should neither be passed nor returned, this variable can just be a local variable within the subprogram.

- ▶ Variable answer:
  - ▶ is not initialized/updated outside of the dashed rectangle; thus, it should not be passed to the subprogram
  - ▶ is initialized within the dashed rectangle and its value is used outside of it; thus, it must be returned to the caller

Therefore, since one value must be returned to the main code, a function can be used, as shown here.

```python
def part2():
    while True:
        temp2 = input("Do you go jogging in the afternoon? ")
        answer = temp2.lower()
        if answer == "yes" or answer == "no" or answer == "sometimes": break

    return answer
```

Third part

In the third dashed rectangle of the example, there are four variables: answer, total_yes, gender and female_no and all of them must be included in the formal argument list of the subprogram that will replace the dashed rectangle. Let's find out why!

- ▶ Both variables answer and gender:
  - ▶ are initialized/updated outside of the dashed rectangle; thus, they must be passed to the subprogram
  - ▶ are not updated within the dashed rectangle; thus, they should not be returned to the caller
- ▶ Both variables total_yes and female_no:
  - ▶ are initialized outside of the dashed rectangle; thus, they must be passed to the subprogram
  - ▶ are updated within the dashed rectangle and their value is used outside of it; thus, they must be returned to the caller

Therefore, since two values must be returned to the main code, a function can be used, as shown here.

```python
def part3(answer, gender, total_yes, female_no):
    if answer == "yes":
        total_yes += 1

    if gender == "female" and answer == "no":
        female_no += 1

    return total_yes, female_no
```

Fourth part

In the fourth dashed rectangle of the example, there are two variables: total_yes and female_no. Let's see what you should do with them.

► Both variables total_yes and female_no:

   ► are updated outside of the dashed rectangle; thus, they must be passed to the subprogram

   ► are not updated within the dashed rectangle; thus, they should not be returned to the caller

Therefore, since no value should be returned to the main code, a void function can be used, as follows.

```python
def part4(total_yes, female_no):
    print("Total positive answers:", total_yes)
    print("Women's negative answers:", female_no)
```

The final program

The final program, including the main code and all the subprograms cited above, is shown here.

```
                        📁 file_36_7b
```

```python
def part1(i):
    while True:
        temp1 = input("Enter gender for citizen No " + str(i + 1) + ": ")
        gender = temp1.lower()
        if gender == "male" or gender == "female": break

    return gender

def part2():
    while True:
        temp2 = input("Do you go jogging in the afternoon? ")
        answer = temp2.lower()
        if answer == "yes" or answer == "no" or answer == "sometimes": break

    return answer

def part3(answer, gender, total_yes, female_no):
    if answer == "yes":
        total_yes += 1

    if gender == "female" and answer == "no":
        female_no += 1
```

```
        return total_yes, female_no

def part4(total_yes, female_no):
    print("Total positive answers:", total_yes)
    print("Women's negative answers:", female_no)

#Main code starts here
total_yes = 0
female_no = 0
for i in range(100):
    gender = part1(i)
    answer = part2()
    total_yes, female_no = part3(answer, gender, total_yes, female_no)

part4(total_yes, female_no)
```

36.8 Recursion

Recursion is a programming technique in which a subprogram calls itself. This might initially seem like an endless loop, but of course this is not true; a subprogram that uses recursion must be written in a way that obviously satisfies the property of finiteness.

Imagine that the next Python program helps you find your way home. In this program, recursion occurs because the void function find_your_way_home() calls itself within the function.

```
def find_your_way_home ():
    if you_are_already_at_home:
        stop_walking()
    else:
        take_one_step_toward_home()
        find_your_way_home()

#Main code starts here
find_your_way_home()
```

Now, let's try to analyze recursion through a real example. The next Python program calculates the factorial of 5 using recursion.

□ file_36_8

```
def factorial(value):
    if value == 1:
        return_value = 1
    else:
        return_value = factorial(value - 1) * value

    return return_value

#Main code starts here
print(factorial(5))  #It displays: 120
```

> 📟 *In mathematics, the factorial of a non-negative integer N is the product of all positive integers less than or equal to N. It is denoted by N! and the factorial of 0 is, by definition, equal to 1. For example, the factorial of 5 is 1 × 2 × 3 × 4 × 5 = 120.*

> ✎ *Recursion occurs because the function* factorial() *calls itself within the function.*

> ✎ *Note that there isn't any loop control structure!*

You are probably confused right now. How on Earth is the product 1 × 2 × 3 × 4 × 5 calculated without using a loop control structure? The next diagram may help you understand. It shows the multiplication operations that are performed as function factorial(5) works its way backwards through the series of calls.

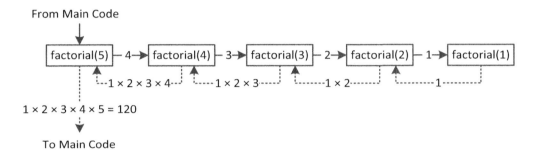

Let's see how this diagram works. The main code calls the function factorial(5), which in turn calls the function factorial(4), and the latter calls the function factorial(3), and so on. The last call (factorial(1)) returns to its caller (factorial(2)) the value 1, which in turn returns to its caller (factorial(3)) the value 1 × 2 = 2, and so on. When the function factorial(5) returns from the topmost call, you have the final solution.

In conclusion, all recursive subprograms must follow three important rules.

1.   They must have a base case
2.   They must change their state and move toward the base case
3.   They must call themselves

where

▶   the base case is the condition that "tells" the subprogram to stop recursions. The base case is usually a very small problem that can be solved directly. It is the solution to the "simplest" possible problem. In the function factorial() of the previous example, the base case is the factorial of 1. When factorial(1) is called, the Boolean expression (value == 1) validates to True and marks the end of the recursions.

▶   a change of state means that the subprogram alters some of its data. Usually, data are getting smaller and smaller in some way. In the function factorial() of the previous example, since the base case is the factorial of 1, the whole concept relies on the idea of moving toward that base case.

▶   The last rule just states the obvious; the subprogram must call itself.

Exercise 36.8-1   *Calculating the Fibonacci Sequence Recursively*

The Fibonacci sequence is a series of numbers in the following sequence:

1, 1, 2, 3, 5, 8, 13, 21, 34, 55, …

By definition, the first two numbers are 1 and 1 and each subsequent number is the sum of the previous two.

Write a Python program that lets the user enter a positive integer N and then calculates recursively and finally displays the Nth term of the Fibonacci series.

Solution

In the following Python program, the function `fib()` calculates the Nth term of the Fibonacci series recursively. This is probably not the best algorithm in the world. It is mentioned here, however, just to show you how recursion can sometimes make things worse!

📁 **file_36_8_1**

```python
def fib(n):
    if n == 1 or n == 2:
        return_value = 1
    else:
        return_value = fib(n - 1) + fib(n - 2)

    return return_value

#Main code starts here
num = int(input())
print(fib(num))
```

To explain how this function works, the best thing to do is use some input values.

For input value 3

If the user enters a value of 3, the following recursive calls are made.

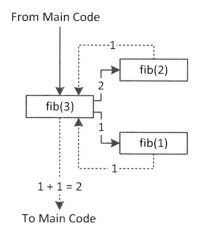

If you calculate the results of these recursive calls, you have

$$1 + 1 = 2$$

This is correct! The 3rd term of the Fibonacci series is 2.

For input value 5

If the user enters a value of 5, the following recursive calls are made.

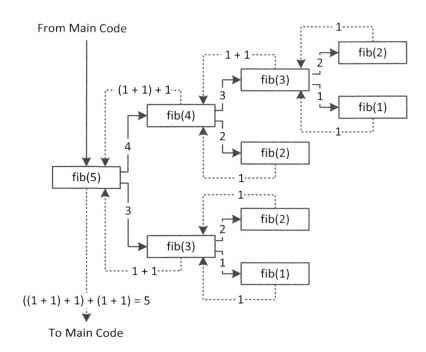

If you calculate the results of these recursive calls, you have

$$((1 + 1) + 1) + (1 + 1) = 5$$

This is also correct! The 5th term of the Fibonacci series is 5.

✎ *Please note that for each succeeding term of the Fibonacci series, the number of calls increments exponentially. For example, the calculation of the 50th or the 60th term of the Fibonacci series using this function can prove tragically slow!*

Recursion helps you write more creative and more elegant programs, but keep in mind that it is not always the best option. The main disadvantage of recursion is that it is hard for a programmer to think through the logic, and therefore it is difficult to debug a code that contains a recursive subprogram. Furthermore, a recursive algorithm may prove worse than a non-recursive algorithm because it may consume too much CPU time or too much main memory (RAM). So, there are times where it would be better to follow the KISS principle and, instead of using a recursion, solve the algorithm using loop control structures.

✎ *For you who don't know what the KISS principle is, it is an acronym for "Keep It Simple, Stupid"! It states that most systems work best if they are kept simple, avoiding any unnecessary complexity!*

36.9 Review Questions: True/False

Choose **true** or **false** for each of the following statements.

1. Each subprogram uses its own memory space to hold the values of its variables.
2. Variables used in a subprogram "live" as long as the subprogram is being executed.
3. The only variables that "live" for as long as the Python program is being executed are the variables of the main code and the global variables.
4. A subprogram can call the main code.

5. If an argument is passed by value and its value is changed within the subprogram, it does not get changed outside of it.

6. The name of an actual argument and the name of the corresponding formal argument must be the same.

7. Supposing that there are no optional arguments, the total number of formal arguments cannot be greater than the total number of actual arguments.

8. An expression cannot be passed to a subprogram.

9. Lists in Python are passed by reference.

10. You can pass a list to a void function but a void function cannot return a list to the caller.

11. A function can accept a list through its formal argument list.

12. In general, a void function can call any function.

13. In general, a function can call any void function.

14. Within a statement, a function can be called only once.

15. A void function can return a value through its formal argument list.

16. A subprogram can be called by another subprogram or by the main code.

17. If you assign a default value to an argument within the formal argument list, it means that no matter what value is passed for that argument, the default value is used.

18. An argument is called an optional argument when a default value is assigned to that argument within the actual argument list.

19. Optional arguments must be on the left side of any non-optional arguments.

20. The default value of an argument cannot be a string.

21. The scope of a variable refers to the range of effect of that variable.

22. If the value of a global variable is altered within a subprogram, this change is reflected outside the subprogram as well.

23. You can have two variables of global scope of the same name.

24. Recursion is a programming technique in which a subprogram calls itself.

25. A recursive algorithm must have a base case.

26. Using recursion to solve a specific problem is not always the best option.

36.10 Review Exercises

Complete the following exercises.

1. Without using a trace table, can you find out what the next Python program displays?

    ```python
    def f1():
        a = 22
    def f2():
        a = 33


    a = 5
    f1()
    f2()
    print(a)
    ```

2. Without using a trace table, can you find out what the next Python program displays?

    ```python
    def f1(number1):
        return 2 * number1
    ```

```python
def f2(number1, number2):
    return f1(number1) + f1(number2)


a = 3
b = 4
print(f2(a, b))
```

3. Without using a trace table, can you find out what the next Python program displays?

```python
def f1(number1):
    return number1 * 2


def f2(number1, number2):
    number1 = f1(number1)
    number2 = f1(number2)
    return number1 + number2


a = 2
b = 5
print(f2(a, b))
```

4. Create a trace table to determine the values of the variables in each step of the following Python program when the value 12 is entered.

```python
def swap(x, y):
    x, y = y, x
    return x, y


k = int(input())
m = 1
a = 1
while a < 8:
    if k % m != 0:
        x = a % m
        m, a = swap(m, a)
    else:
        x = a + m + int(a - m)

    print(m, a, x)

    a += 2
    m += 1
    a, m = swap(a, m)
```

5. Without using a trace table, can you find out what the next Python program displays?

```python
def display(s = "hello"):
    s = s.replace("a", "e")
    print(s, end = "")


display("hello")
```

```python
display()
display("hallo")
```

6. Without using a trace table, can you find out what the next Python program displays?

```python
def f1():
    global a
    a = a + b

a = 10
b = 5
f1()
b -= 1

print(a)
```

7. Without using a trace table, can you find out what the next Python program displays?

```python
def f2():
    global a
    a = a + b

def f1():
    global a
    a = a + b
    f2()

a = 3
b = 4
f1()

print(a, b)
```

8. For the following Python program, convert the parts marked with a dashed rectangle into subprograms.

```python
STUDENTS = 10
LESSONS = 5
names = [None] * STUDENTS
grades = [ [None] * LESSONS for i in range(STUDENTS) ]

for i in range(STUDENTS):
    names[i] = input("Enter name No. " + str(i + 1) + ": ")
    for j in range(LESSONS):
        grades[i][j] = int(input("Enter grade for lesson No. " + str(j + 1) + ": "))

average = [None] * STUDENTS
for i in range(STUDENTS):
    average[i] = 0
    for j in range(LESSONS):
        average[i] += grades[i][j]
    average[i] /= LESSONS
```

```
for m in range(1, STUDENTS):
    for n in range(STUDENTS - 1, m - 1, -1):
        if average[n] > average[n - 1]:
            average[n], average[n - 1] = average[n - 1], average[n]
            names[n], names[n - 1] = names[n - 1], names[n]
        elif average[n] == average[n - 1]:
            if names[n] < names[n - 1]:
                names[n], names[n - 1] = names[n - 1], names[n]

for i in range(STUDENTS):
    print(names[i], "\t", average[i])
```

9. For the following Python program, convert the parts marked with a dashed rectangle into subprograms.

```
message = input("Enter a message: ").lower()

message_clean = ""
for i in range(len(message)):
    if message[i] not in " ,.?":
        message_clean += message[i]

middle_pos = (len(message_clean) - 1) // 2
j = len(message_clean) - 1
palindrome = True
for i in range(middle_pos + 1):
    if message_clean[i] != message_clean[j]:
        palindrome = False
        break
    j -= 1

if palindrome:
    print("The message is palindrome")
```

10. The next Python program finds the greatest value among four values given. Rewrite the program without using subprograms.

```
def my_max(n, m):
    if n > m:
        m = n
    return m

a = int(input())
b = int(input())
c = int(input())
d = int(input())

maximum = a
maximum = my_max(b, maximum)
```

```
maximum = my_max(c, maximum)
maximum = my_max(d, maximum)

print(maximum)
```

11. Write a void function that accepts three numbers through its formal argument list and then returns their sum and their average.

    Hint: Use a list within the format argument list to "return" the required values.

12. Write a subprogram named my_round that accepts a real (a float) and an integer through its formal argument list and then returns the real rounded to as many decimal places as the integer indicates. Moreover, if no value is passed for the integer, the subprogram must return the real rounded to two decimal places by default. Try not to use the round() function of Python.

13. Do the following:

    i.   Write a subprogram named get_input that prompts the user to enter an answer "yes" or "no" and then returns the value True or False correspondingly to the caller. Make the subprogram accept the answer in all possible forms such as "yes", "YES", "Yes", "No", "NO", "nO", and so on.

    ii. Write a subprogram named find_area that accepts the base and the height of a parallelogram through its formal argument list and then returns its area.

    iii. Using the subprograms cited above, write a Python program that prompts the user to enter the base and the height of a parallelogram and then calculates and displays its area. The program must iterate as many times as the user wishes. At the end of each calculation, the program must ask the user whether he or she wishes to calculate the area of another parallelogram. If the answer is "yes" the program must repeat.

14. Do the following:

    i.   Write a subprogram named get_lists that prompts the user to enter the grades and the names of 100 students into the lists grades and names, correspondingly. The two lists must be returned to the caller.

    ii. Write a subprogram named get_average that accepts the list grades through its formal argument list and returns the average grade.

    iii. Write a subprogram named sort_lists that accepts the lists grades and names through its formal argument list and sorts the list grades in descending order using the insertion sort algorithm. The subprogram must preserve the relationship between the elements of the two lists.

    iv. Using the subprograms cited above, write a Python program that prompts the user to enter the grades and the names of 100 students and then displays all student names whose grade is less than the average grade, sorted by grade in descending order.

15. In a song contest, there is an artist who is scored by 10 judges. However, according to the rules of this contest, the total score is calculated after excluding the maximum and the minimum score. Do the following:

    i.   Write a subprogram named get_list that prompts the user to enter the scores of the 10 judges into a list and then returns the list to the caller. Assume that each score is unique.

    ii. Write a subprogram named find_min_max that accepts a list through its formal argument list and then returns the maximum and the minimum value.

    iii. Using the subprograms cited above, write a Python program that prompts the user enter the name of the artist and the score he or she gets from each judge. The program must then display the message "Artist NN got XX points" where NN and XX must be replaced by actual values.

16. On a chessboard you must place grains of wheat on each square, such that one grain is placed on the first square, two on the second, four on the third, and so on (doubling the number of grains on each subsequent square). Do the following:

    i. Write a recursive function named `woc` that accepts the index of a square and returns the number of grains of wheat that are on this square. Since a chessboard contains 8 × 8 = 64 squares, assume that the index is an integer between 1 and 64.

    ii. Using the subprogram cited above, write a Python program that calculates and displays the total number of grains of wheat that are on the chessboard in the end.

17. Do the following:

    i. Write a recursive function named `factorial` that accepts an integer through its formal argument list and then returns its factorial.

    ii. Using the function cited above, write a recursive function named `my_cos` that calculates and returns the cosine of x using the Taylor series, shown next.

$$cosx = 1 - \frac{x^2}{2!} + \frac{x^4}{4!} - \frac{x^6}{6!} + \cdots + \frac{x^{40}}{40!}$$

Hint: Keep in mind that x is in radians and $\frac{x^0}{0!} = 1$.

    iii. Using the function `my_cos()` cited above, write a Python program that calculates and displays the cosine of 45°.

Chapter 37
More Exercises with Subprograms

37.1 Simple Exercises with Subprograms

Exercise 37.1-1   *Designing the Flowchart*

Design the flowchart that corresponds to the following Python program.

```python
def find_sum(n):
    s = 0
    for i in range(1, n + 1):
        s = s + i
    return s

n = int(input("Enter a positive integer"))
while n > 0:
    print(find_sum(n))
    n = int(input("Enter a positive integer"))
```

Solution

The flowchart that corresponds to the function `find_sum()` is as follows.

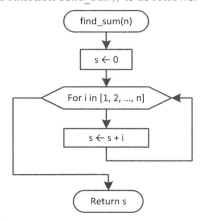

And the flowchart of the main code is as follows.

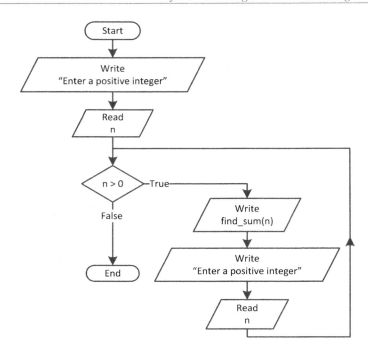

Exercise 37.1-2   Designing the Flowchart

Design the flowchart that corresponds to the following Python program.

```python
def display_divmod(a, b):
    print(a // b)
    print(a % b)


val1 = int(input())
val2 = int(input())
while val1 > 0 and val2 > 0:
    display_divmod(val1, val2)

    val1 = int(input())
    val2 = int(input())
```

Solution

In paragraph 4.7 (back when you first started reading this book), you learned that the following symbol in flowcharts depicts a call to a subprogram that is formally defined elsewhere, such as in a separate flowchart.

The time to use this symbol has come! The subprogram display_divmod() of this exercise is a void function, so you can use this flowchart symbol to call it.

The flowchart that corresponds to the void function display_divmod(), and the main code is as follows.

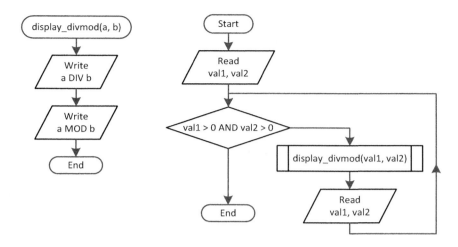

Exercise 37.1-3   A Simple Currency Converter

Do the following:

　i.　 *Write a subprogram named* display_menu *that displays the following menu.*

　　　1.　 *Convert USD to Euro (EUR)*

　　　2.　 *Convert Euro (EUR) to USD*

　　　3.　 *Exit*

　ii.　 *Using the subprogram cited above, write a Python program that displays the previously mentioned menu and prompts the user to enter a choice (of 1, 2, or 3) and an amount of money. The program must then calculate and display the required value. The process must repeat as many times as the user wishes. It is given that $1 = 0.87 EUR (€).*

Solution

According to the "Ultimate" rule, the while-loop of the main code must be as follows, given in general form.

```
Display the menu

choice = int(input())      #Initialization of choice.
while choice != 3:

    Prompt the user to enter an amount of money, and
    then calculate and display the required value.


    Display the menu

    #Update/alteration of choice
    choice = int(input())
```

The solution is as follows.

```
                        📄 file_37_1_3
def display_menu():
    print("---------------------------")
    print("1. Convert USD to Euro (EUR)")
```

```python
    print("2. Convert Euro (EUR) to USD")
    print("3. Exit")
    print("---------------------------")
    print("Enter a choice: ", end = "")

#Main code starts here
display_menu()
choice = int(input())
while choice != 3:
    amount = float(input("Enter an amount: "))
    if choice == 1:
        print(amount, "USD =", amount * 0.87, "Euro")
    else:
        print(amount, "Euro =", amount / 0.87, "USD")

    display_menu()
    choice = int(input())
```

Exercise 37.1-4   A More Complete Currency Converter

Do the following:

i. *Write a subprogram named* display_menu *that displays the following menu.*

1. *Convert USD to Euro (EUR)*
2. *Convert USD to British Pound Sterling (GBP)*
3. *Convert USD to Japanese Yen (JPY)*
4. *Convert USD to Canadian Dollar (CAD)*
5. *Exit*

ii. *Write four different subprograms named* USD_to_EU, USD_to_GBP, USD_to_JPY, *and* USD_to_CAD, *that accept a currency through their formal argument list and then return the corresponding converted value.*

iii. *Using the subprograms cited above, write a Python program that displays the previously mentioned menu and then prompts the user to enter a choice (of 1, 2, 3, 4, or 5) and an amount in US dollars. The program must then display the required value. The process must repeat as many times as the user wishes. It is given that*

▶ *$1 = 0.87 EUR (€)*
▶ *$1 = 0.78 GBP (£)*
▶ *$1 = ¥ 108.55 JPY*
▶ *$1 = 1.33 CAD ($)*

Solution

This solution combines the use of both functions and void functions. The four functions that convert currencies accept a value through an argument and then they return the corresponding value. The solution is shown here.

```
                              📁 file_37_1_4
def display_menu():
```

```
            print("--------------------------------------------")
            print("1. Convert USD to Euro (EUR)")
            print("2. Convert USD to British Pound Sterling (GBP)")
            print("3. Convert USD to Japanese Yen (JPY)")
            print("4. Convert USD to Canadian Dollar (CAD)")
            print("5. Exit")
            print("--------------------------------------------")
            print("Enter a choice: ", end = "")

def USD_to_EU(value):
    return value * 0.87

def USD_to_GBP(value):
    return value * 0.78

def USD_to_JPY(value):
    return value * 108.55

def USD_to_CAD(value):
    return value * 1.33

#Main code starts here
display_menu()
choice = int(input())
while choice != 5:
    amount = float(input("Enter an amount in US dollars: "))
    if choice == 1:
        print(amount, "USD =", USD_to_EU(amount), "Euro")
    elif choice == 2:
        print(amount, "USD =", USD_to_GBP(amount), "GBP")
    elif choice == 3:
        print(amount, "USD =", USD_to_JPY(amount), "JPY")
    elif choice == 4:
        print(amount, "USD =", USD_to_CAD(amount), "CAD")

    display_menu()
    choice = int(input())
```

Exercise 37.1-5 Finding the Average Values of Positive Integers

Do the following:

    i.   *Write a subprogram named* test_integer *that accepts a number through its formal argument list and returns* True *when the passed number is an integer; it must return* False *otherwise.*

    ii.   *Using the subprogram cited above, write a Python program that lets the user enter numeric values repeatedly until a real one is entered. In the end, the program must display the average value of positive integers entered.*

Solution

The solution is presented next.

```
                         📁 file_37_1_5
def test_integer(number):
    return_value = False

    if number == int(number):
        return_value = True
    return return_value

#Main code starts here
total = 0
count = 0
x = float(input())   #Initialization of x
while test_integer(x):    #The Boolean Expression depends on x
    if x > 0:
        total += x
        count += 1
    x = float(input())    #Update/alteration of x

if count > 0:
    print(total / count)
```

✎ *The statement* while test_integer(x) *is equivalent to the statement* while test_integer(x) == True

✎ *Note the last single-alternative decision structure,* if count > 0. *It is necessary in order for the program to satisfy the property of definiteness. Think about it! If the user enters a real right from the beginning, the variable* count, *in the end, will contain a value of zero.*

✎ *The following function can be used as an alternative to the previous one. It directly returns the result (*True *or* False*) of the Boolean expression* number == int(number).

```
def test_integer(number):
    return number == int(number)
```

Exercise 37.1-6   Finding the Sum of Odd Positive Integers

Do the following:

i.   *Write a subprogram named* test_integer *that accepts a number through its formal argument list and returns* True *when the passed number is an integer; it must return* False *otherwise.*

ii. *Write a subprogram named* test_odd *that accepts a number through its formal argument list and returns* True *when the passed number is odd; it must return* False *otherwise.*

iii. *Write a subprogram named* test_positive *that accepts a number through its formal argument list and returns* True *when the passed number is positive; it must return* False *otherwise.*

iv. *Using the subprograms cited above, write a Python program that lets the user enter numeric values repeatedly until a negative one is entered. In the end, the program must display the sum of odd positive integers entered.*

Solution

This exercise is pretty much the same as the previous one. Each subprogram returns one value (which can be True or False). The solution is presented here.

```
                            📁 file_37_1_6
def test_integer(number):
    return number == int(number)

def test_odd(number):
    return number % 2 != 0

def test_positive(number):
    return number > 0

#Main code starts here
total = 0
x = float(input())
while test_positive(x):
    if test_integer(x) and test_odd(x):
        total += x
    x = float(input())

print(total)
```

✎ The statement if test_integer(x) and test_odd(x) is equivalent to the statement if test_integer(x) == True and test_odd(x) == True

Exercise 37.1-7   Finding the Values of y

Write a Python program that finds and displays the value of y (if possible) in the following formula.

$$y = \begin{cases} \dfrac{3x}{x-5} + \dfrac{7-x}{2x}, & x \geq 1 \\ \dfrac{45-x}{x+2} + 3x, & x < 1 \end{cases}$$

For each part of the formula, write a subprogram that accepts x through its formal argument list and then calculates and displays the result. An error message must be displayed when the calculation is not possible.

Solution

Each subprogram must calculate and display the result of the corresponding formula or display an error message when the calculation is not possible. As these two subprograms return no result, they can both be written as void functions. The solution is shown here.

```
                            📁 file_37_1_7
def formula1(x):
    if x == 5:
        print("Error! Division by zero")
    else:
```

```
        y = 3 * x / (x - 5) + (7 - x) / (2 * x)
        print(y)

def formula2(x):
    if x == -2:
        print("Error! Division by zero")
    else:
        y = (45 - x) / (x + 2) + 3 * x
        print(y)

#Main code starts here
x = float(input("Enter a value for x: "))
if x >= 1:
    formula1(x)
else:
    formula2(x)
```

37.2 Exercises of a General Nature with Subprograms

Exercise 37.2-1   *Validating Data Input Using a Subprogram*

Do the following:

   i.   *Write a subprogram named* get_age *that prompts the user to enter his or her age and returns it. Using a loop control structure, the subprogram must also validate data input and display an error message when the user enters any non-positive values.*

   ii. *Write a subprogram named* find_max *that accepts a list through its formal argument list and returns the index position of the maximum value of the list.*

   iii. *Using the subprograms cited above, write a Python program that prompts the user to enter the first names, last names, and ages of 50 people into three lists and then displays the name of the oldest person.*

Solution

Since the subprogram get_age() returns one value, it can be written as a function. The same applies to subprogram find_max() because it also returns one value. The main code must prompt the user to enter the first names, the last names, and the ages of 50 people into lists first_names, last_names, and ages respectively. Then, with the help of function find_max(), it can find the index position of the maximum value of list ages. The solution is shown here.

```
📁 file_37_2_1
```

```
PEOPLE = 50

def get_age():
    age = int(input("Enter an age: "))
    while age <= 0:
        print("Error: Invalid age!")
        age = int(input("Enter a positive number: "))
    return age

def find_max(a):
```

```
        maximum = a[0]
        max_i = 0
        for i in range(1, PEOPLE):
            if a[i] > maximum:
                maximum = a[i]
                max_i = i
        return max_i


#Main code starts here
first_names = [None] * PEOPLE
last_names = [None] * PEOPLE
ages = [None] * PEOPLE

for i in range(PEOPLE):
    first_names[i] = input("First name of person No" + str(i + 1) + ": ")
    last_names[i] = input("Last name of person No" + str(i + 1) + ": ")
    ages[i] = get_age()

index_of_max = find_max(ages)

print("The oldest person is:", first_names[index_of_max], last_names[index_of_max])
print("He or she is", ages[index_of_max], "years old!")
```

Exercise 37.2-2   Sorting a List Using a Subprogram

Do the following:

i. *Write a subprogram named* my_swap *that accepts a list through its formal argument list, as well as two indexes. The subprogram then swaps the values of the elements at the corresponding index positions.*

ii. *Using the subprogram* my_swap() *cited above, write a subprogram named* my_sort *that accepts a list through its formal argument list and then sorts the list using the bubble sort algorithm. It must be able to sort in either ascending or descending order. To do this, include an addition Boolean variable within the formal argument list.*

iii. *Write a subprogram named* display_list *that accepts a list through its formal argument list and then displays it.*

iv. *Using the subprograms* my_sort() *and* display_list() *cited above, write a Python program that prompts the user to enter the names of 20 people and then displays them twice: once sorted in ascending order, and once in descending order.*

Solution

As you can see in the Python program below, the void function my_sort() uses an adapted version of the bubble sort algorithm. When the value True is passed to the argument ascending, the algorithm sorts list a in ascending order. When the value False is passed, the algorithm sorts list a in descending order.

Moreover, the void function my_sort() calls the void function my_swap() every time a swap is required between the contents of two elements.

```
                              🗀 file_37_2_2
PEOPLE = 20
```

```python
def my_swap(a, index1, index2):
    a[index1], a[index2] = a[index2] = a[index1]

def my_sort(a, ascending = True):
    for m in range(PEOPLE - 1):
        for n in range(PEOPLE - 1, m, -1):
            if ascending:
                if a[n] < a[n - 1]:
                    my_swap(a, n, n - 1)
            else:
                if a[n] > a[n - 1]:
                    my_swap(a, n, n - 1)

def display_list(a):
    for i in range(PEOPLE):
        print(a[i])

#Main code starts here
names = [None] * PEOPLE
for i in range(PEOPLE):
    names[i] = input("Enter a name: ")

my_sort(names)              #Sort names in ascending order
display_list(names)         #and display them

my_sort(names, False)       #Sort names in descending order
display_list(names)         #and display them.
```

✎ Note that the argument `ascending` is an optional argument. This means that if no value is passed for that argument, the default value `True` is used.

✎ In Python, lists are passed by reference. This is why there is no need to include a `return` statement in the subprogram `my_sort()`.

Exercise 37.2-3   *Progressive Rates and Electricity Consumption*

The LAV Electricity Company charges subscribers for their electricity consumption according to the following table (monthly rates for domestic accounts).

Kilowatt-hours (kWh)	USD per kWh
kWh ≤ 400	$0.08
401 < kWh ≤ 1500	$0.22
1501 < kWh ≤ 2000	$0.35
2001 < kWh	$0.50

Do the following:

i.   *Write a subprogram named* get_consumption *that prompts the user to enter the total number of kWh consumed and then returns it. Using a loop control structure, the subprogram must also validate data input and display an error message when the user enters any negative values.*

ii.   *Write a subprogram named* find_amount *that accepts kWh consumed through its formal argument list and then returns the total amount to pay.*

iii.   *Using the subprograms cited above, write a Python program that prompts the user to enter the total number of kWh consumed and then displays the total amount to pay. The program must iterate as many times as the user wishes. At the end of each calculation, the program must ask the user if he or she wishes to calculate the total amount to pay for another consumer. If the answer is "yes" the program must repeat; it must end otherwise. Make your program accept the answer in all possible forms such as "yes", "YES", "Yes", or even "YeS".*

Please note that the rates are progressive and that transmission services and distribution charges, as well as federal, state, and local taxes, add a total of 26% to each bill.

Solution

There is nothing new here. Processing progressive rates is something that you have already learned! If this doesn't ring any bells, you need to refresh your memory and review the corresponding Exercise 22.4-5.

The Python program is as follows.

```
                          📁 file_37_2_3
def get_consumption():
    consumption = int(input("Enter kWh consumed: "))
    while consumption < 0:
        print("Error: Invalid number!")
        consumption = input("Enter a non-negative number: ")
    return consumption


def find_amount(kwh):
    if kwh <= 400:
        amount = kwh * 0.08
    elif kwh <= 1500:
        amount = 400 * 0.08 + (kwh - 400) * 0.22
    elif kwh <= 2000:
        amount = 400 * 0.08 + 1100 * 0.22 + (kwh - 1500) * 0.35
    else:
        amount = 400 * 0.08 + 1100 * 0.22 + 500 * 0.35 + (kwh - 2000) * 0.5

    amount += 0.26 * amount
    return amount


#Main code starts here
while True:
    kwh = get_consumption()
    print("You need to pay:", find_amount(kwh))
    answer = input("Would you like to repeat? ")
    if answer.upper() != "YES": break
```

Exercise 37.2-4　　　Roll, Roll, Roll the... Dice!

Do the following:

    i.   *Write a subprogram named* dice *that returns a random integer between 1 and 6.*

    ii.   *Write a subprogram named* search_and_count *that accepts an integer and a list through its formal argument list and returns the number of times the integer exists in the list.*

    iii. *Using the subprograms cited above, write a Python program that fills a list with 100 random integers (between 1 and 6) and then lets the user enter an integer. The program must display how many times that given integer exists in the list.*

Solution

Both subprograms can be written as functions because they both return one value each. Function dice() returns a random integer between 1 and 6, and function search_and_count() returns a number that indicates the number of times an integer exists in a list. The solution is presented here.

```
📁 file_37_2_4
```

```python
import random
ELEMENTS = 100

def dice():
    return random.randrange(1, 7)

def search_and_count(x, a):
    count = 0
    for i in range(ELEMENTS):
        if a[i] == x:
            count += 1
    return count

#Main code starts here
a = [None] * ELEMENTS
for i in range(ELEMENTS):
    a[i] = dice()

x = int(input())
print("Given value exists in the list")
print(search_and_count(x, a), "times")
```

Exercise 37.2-5　　　How Many Times Does Each Number of the Dice Appear?

Using the functions dice() *and* search_and_count() *cited in the previous exercise, write a Python program that fills a list with 100 random integers (between 1 and 6) and then displays how many times each of the six numbers appears in the list, as well as which number appears most often.*

Solution

If you were to solve this exercise without using a loop control structure, it would be something like the following.

```
#Assign to n1 the number of times that value 1 exists in list a
```

```
n1 = search_and_count(1, a)

#Assign to n2 the number of times that value 2 exists in list a
n2 = search_and_count(2, a)
.
.
.
#Assign to n6 the number of times that value 6 exists in list a
n6 = search_and_count(6, a)

#Display how many times each of the six numbers appears in list a
print(n1, n2, n3, n4, n5, n6)

#Find maximum of n1, n2,… n6
maximum = n1
max_i = 1

if n2 > maximum:
    maximum = n2
    max_i = 2
.
.
.
if n6 > maximum:
    maximum = n6
    max_i = 6

#Display which number appears in the list most often.
print(max_i)
```

But now that you are reaching the end of the book, of course, you can do something more creative. Instead of assigning each result of the search_and_count() function to individual variables n1, n2, n3, n4, n5, and n6, you can assign those results to the positions 0, 1, 2, 3, 4, and 5 of a list named n, as shown here.

```
n = [None] * 6
for i in range(6):
    n[i] = search_and_count(i + 1, a)
```

After that, you can find the maximum of the list n using what you have learned in paragraph 33.3.

The complete solution is shown here.

```
📁 file_37_2_5
import random
ELEMENTS = 100

def dice():
    return random.randrange(1, 7)

def search_and_count(x, a):
```

```python
        count = 0
        for i in range(ELEMENTS):
            if a[i] == x:
                count += 1
        return count


#Main code starts here


#Create list a of random integers between 1 and 6
a = [None] * ELEMENTS
for i in range(ELEMENTS):
    a[i] = dice()


#Create list n and display how many times each of the six numbers appears in list a
n = [None] * 6
for i in range(6):
    n[i] = search_and_count(i + 1, a)
    print("Value", (i + 1), "appears", n[i], "times")


#Find maximum of list n
maximum = n[0]
max_i = 0
for i in range(1, 6):
    if n[i] > maximum:
        maximum = n[i]
        max_i = i


#Display which number appears in the list most often.
print("Value", (max_i + 1), "appears in the list", maximum, "times.")
```

37.3   Review Exercises

Complete the following exercises.

1.   Design the flowchart that corresponds to the following Python program.

```python
def get_num_of_digits(x):
    count = 0
    while x != 0:
        count += 1
        x = x // 10
    return count


while True:
    val = int(input("Enter a four-digit integer "))
    if get_num_of_digits(val) == 4: break


print("Congratulations!")
```

2. Design the flowchart that corresponds to the following code fragment.

```python
def my_divmod(a, b, results):
    results[0] = 1
    if b == 0:
        results[0] = 0
    else:
        results[1] = a // b
        results[2] = a % b


val1 = int(input())
val2 = int(input())


results = [None] * 3
my_divmod(val1, val2, results)
if results[0] == 1:
    print(results[1], results[2])
else:
    print("Sorry, wrong values entered!")
```

3. Design the flowchart that corresponds to the following Python program.

```python
def test_integer(number):
    return_value = False
    if number == int(number):
        return_value = True
    return return_value


def test_positive(number):
    return_value = False
    if number > 0:
        return_value = True
    return return_value


total = 0
count = 0
x = float(input())
while test_positive(x):
    if test_integer(x):
        total += x
        count += 1
    x = float(input())


if count > 0:
    print(total / count)
```

4.   Design the flowchart that corresponds to the following Python program.

```python
PEOPLE = 30

def get_age():
    while True:
        x = int(input())
        if x > 0: break
    return x

def find_max(a):
    max_i = 0
    for i in range(1, PEOPLE):
        if a[i] > a[max_i]:
            max_i = i
    return max_i

first_names = [None] * PEOPLE
last_names = [None] * PEOPLE
ages = [None] * PEOPLE
for i in range(PEOPLE):
    first_names[i] = input()
    last_names[i] = input()
    ages[i] = get_age()

index_of_max = find_max(ages)

print(first_names[index_of_max])
print(last_names[index_of_max])
print(ages[index_of_max])
```

5.   Design the flowchart that corresponds to the following Python program.

```python
PEOPLE = 40

def my_swap(a, index1, index2):
    temp = a[index1]
    a[index1] = a[index2]
    a[index2] = temp

def my_sort(a):
    for m in range(PEOPLE - 1):
        for n in range(PEOPLE - 1, m, -1):
            if a[n] < a[n - 1]:
                my_swap(a, n, n - 1)

def display_list(a, ascending):
    if ascending:
        for i in range(PEOPLE):
```

```python
            print(a[i])
    else:
        for i in range(PEOPLE - 1, -1, -1):
            print(a[i])

names = [None] * PEOPLE
for i in range(PEOPLE):
    names[i] = input()

my_sort(names)
display_list(names, True)
display_list(names, False)
```

6. Design the flowchart that corresponds to the following Python program.

```python
def get_consumption():
    kwh = int(input("Enter kWh consumed: "))
    while kwh < 0:
        kwh = int(input("Error! Enter kWh consumed: "))
    return kwh

def find_amount(kwh):
    if kwh <= 450:
        amount = kwh * 0.07
    elif kwh <= 2200:
        amount = 450 * 0.07 + (kwh - 450) * 0.2
    else:
        amount = 450 * 0.07 + 1750 * 0.2 + (kwh - 1750) * 0.33

    amount += 0.22 * amount
    return amount

while True:
    kwh = get_consumption()
    print(find_amount(kwh))

    answer = input("Repeat? ")
    if answer.upper() != "YES": break
```

7. Write the Python program that corresponds to the following flowchart.

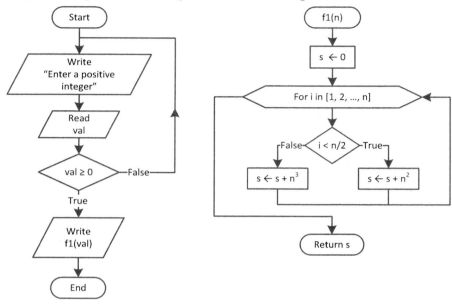

8. Write the Python program that corresponds to the following flowchart.

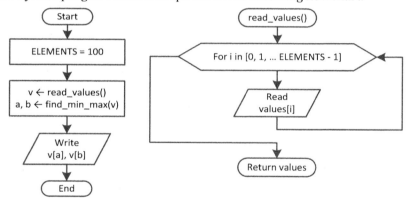

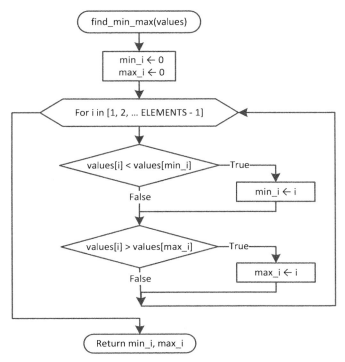

9. Write the Python program that corresponds to the following flowchart.

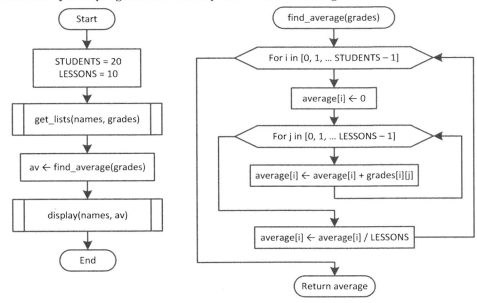

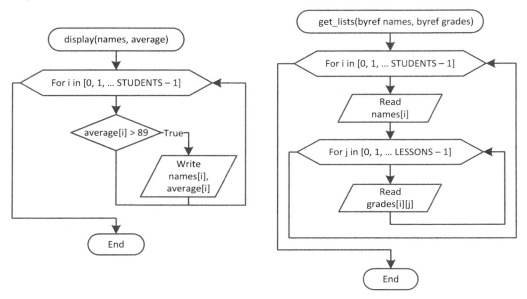

10. Do the following:

    i.   Write a subprogram named `factorial` that accepts an integer through its formal argument list and returns its factorial.

    ii. Using the subprogram `factorial()` cited above, write a subprogram named `my_sin` that accepts a value through its formal argument list and returns the sine of *x*, using the Taylor series (shown next) with an accuracy of 0.0000000001.

$$sinx = x - \frac{x^3}{3!} + \frac{x^5}{5!} - \frac{x^7}{7!} + \cdots$$

Hint: Keep in mind that *x* is in radians, and $\frac{x^1}{1!} = x$.

    iii. Write a subprogram named `degrees_to_rad` that accepts an angle in degrees through its formal argument list and returns its radian equivalent. It is given that $2\pi = 360°$.

    iv. Using the subprograms `my_sin()` and `degrees_to_rad()` cited above, write a Python program that displays the sine of all integers from 0° to 360°.

11. Do the following:

    i.   Write a subprogram named `is_leap` that accepts a year through its formal argument list and returns `True` or `False` depending on whether or not that year is a leap year.

    ii. Write a subprogram named `num_of_days` that accepts a month and a year and returns the number of the days in that month. If that month is February and the year is a leap year, the subprogram must return the value of 29.

Hint: Use the subprogram `is_leap()` cited above.

    iii. Write a subprogram named `check_date` that accepts a day, a month, and a year and returns `True` or `False` depending on whether or not that date is valid.

    iv. Using the subprograms cited above, write a Python program that prompts the user to enter a date (a day, a month, and a year) and then calculates and displays the number of days that have passed between the beginning of the given year and the given date. Using a loop control structure, the program must also validate data input and display an error message when the user enters any non-valid date.

12. Do the following:

    i.   Write a subprogram named `display_menu` that displays the following menu.

        1. Convert USD to Euro (EUR)

        2. Convert USD to British Pound Sterling (GBP)

        3. Convert EUR to USD

        4. Convert EUR to GBP

        5. Convert GBP to USD

        6. Convert GBP to EUR

        7. Exit

    ii. Write two different subprograms named `USD_to_EUR`, and `USD_to_GBP`, that accept a currency through their formal argument list and then return the corresponding converted value.

    iii. Using the subprograms cited above, write a Python program that displays the previously mentioned menu and then prompts the user to enter a choice (of 1, 2, 3, 4, 5, 6, or 7) and an amount. The program must then display the required value. The process must repeat as many times as the user wishes. It is given that

        ► $1 = 0.87 EUR (€)

        ► $1 = 0.76 GBP (£)

13. In a computer game, players roll two dice. The player who gets the greatest sum of dice gets one point. After ten rolls, the player that wins is the one with the greatest sum of points. Do the following:

    i.   Write a subprogram named `dice` that returns a random integer between 1 and 6.

    ii. Using the subprogram cited above, write a Python program that prompts two players to enter their names and then each player consecutively "rolls" two dice. This process repeats ten times and the player that wins is the one with the greatest sum of points.

14. The LAV Car Rental Company has rented 40 cars, which are divided into three categories: hybrid, gas, and diesel. The company charges for a car according to the following table.

Days	Car Type		
	Gas	Diesel	Hybrid
1 – 5	$24 per day	$28 per day	$30 per day
6 – 8	$22 per day	$25 per day	$28 per day
9 and above	$18 per day	$21 per day	$23 per day

Do the following:

    i.   Write a subprogram named `get_choice` that displays the following menu.

        1.   Gas

        2.   Diesel

        3.   Hybrid

    The subprogram then prompts the user to enter the type of the car (1, 2, or 3) and returns it to the caller.

    ii. Write a subprogram named `get_days` that prompts the user to enter the total number of rental days and returns it to the caller.

    iii. Write a subprogram named `get_charge` that accepts the type of the car (1, 2, or 3) and the total number of rental days through its formal argument list and then returns the amount of money to pay according to the previous table. Federal, state, and local taxes add a total of 10% to each bill.

   iv. Using the subprograms cited above, write a Python program that prompts the user to enter all necessary information about the rented cars and then displays the following:

      a. for each car, the total amount to pay including taxes

      b. the total number of hybrid cars rented

      c. the total net profit the company gets after removing taxes

Please note that the rates are progressive.

15. TAM (Television Audience Measurement) is the specialized branch of media research dedicated to quantify and qualify television audience information.

The LAV Television Audience Measurement Company counts the number of viewers of the main news program on each of 10 different TV channels. The company needs a software application in order to get some useful information. Do the following:

   i. Write a subprogram named `get_data` that prompts the user to enter into two lists the names of the channels and the number of viewers of the main news program for each day of the week (Monday to Sunday). It then returns these lists to the caller.

   ii. Write a subprogram `get_average` that accepts a one-dimensional list of seven numeric elements through its formal argument list and returns the average value of the first five elements.

   iii. Using the subprograms cited above, write a Python program that prompts the user to enter the names of the channels and the number of viewers for each day of the week and then displays the following:

      a. the name of the channels whose average viewer numbers on the weekend were at least 20% higher than the average viewer numbers during the rest of the week.

      b. the name of the channels (if any) that, from day to day, showed constantly increasing viewer numbers. If there is no such channel, a corresponding message must be displayed.

16. A public opinion polling company asks 300 citizens whether they have been hospitalized during the last year. Do the following:

   i. Write a subprogram named `input_data` that prompts the user to enter the citizen's SSN (Social Security Number) and their answer (Yes, No) into two lists, `SSNs` and `answers`, respectively. The two lists must be returned to the caller.

   ii. Write a subprogram named `sort_lists` that accepts the lists `SSNs` and `answers` through its formal argument list. It then sorts list `SSNs` in ascending order using the selection sort algorithm. The subprogram must preserve the relationship between the elements of the two lists.

   iii. Write a subprogram named `search_list` that accepts list `SSNs` and an SSN through its formal argument list and then returns the index position of that SSN in the list. If the SSN is not found, a message "SSN not found" must be displayed and the value −1 must be returned. Use the binary search algorithm.

   iv. Write a subprogram named `count_answers` that accepts the list `answers` and an answer through its formal argument list. It then returns the number of times this answer exists in the list.

   v. Using the subprograms cited above, write a Python program that prompts the user to enter the SSNs and the answers of the citizens. It must then prompt the user to enter an SSN and display the answer that the citizen with this SSN gave, as well as the percentage of citizens that gave the same answer. The program must then ask the user if he or she wishes to search for another SSN. If the answer is "Yes" the process must repeat; it must end otherwise.

17. Eight teams participate in a football tournament, and each team plays 12 games, one game each week. Do the following:

   i. Write a subprogram named `input_data` that prompts the user to enter into two lists the name of each team and the letter "W" for win, "L" for loss, or "T" for tie (draw) for each game. It then returns the lists to the caller.

   ii. Write a subprogram named `display_result` that prompts the user for a letter (W, L, or T) and then displays, for each team, the week number(s) in which the team won, lost, or tied respectively. For example, if the user enters "L", the subprogram must search and display, for each team, the week numbers (e.g., week 3, week 14, and so on) in which the team lost the game.

   iii. Write a subprogram named `find_team` that prompts the user to enter the name of a team and returns the index position of that team in the list. If the given team name does not exist, the value −1 must be returned.

   iv. Using the subprograms cited above, write a Python program that prompts the user to enter the name of each team and the letter "W" for win, "L" for loss, or "T" for tie (draw) for each game. It must then prompt the user for a letter (W, L, or T) and display, for each team, the week number(s) in which the team won, lost, or tied respectively. Finally, the program must prompt the user to enter the name of a team. If the given team is found, the program must display the total number of points for this team and then prompt the user to enter the name of another team. This process must repeat as long as the user enters an existing team name. If given team name is not found, the message "Team not found" must be displayed and the program must end.

It is given that a win receives 3 points and a tie receives 1 point.

Review in "Subprograms"

Review Crossword Puzzle

1. Solve the following crossword puzzle.

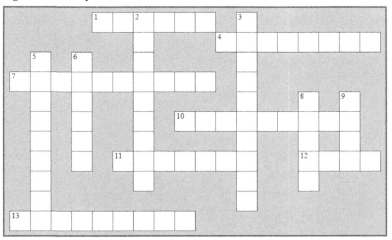

Across

1. Each function contains an argument list called a _____ argument list.
4. Generally speaking, this subprogram returns a result.
7. In this kind of programming, a problem is subdivided into smaller subproblems.
10. A sequence of numbers where the first two numbers are 1 and 1, and each subsequent number is the sum of the previous two.
11. In this kind of programming, subprograms of common functionality are grouped together into separate modules.
12. Send a value to a function.
13. Lists in Python are passed by _____.

Down

2. A programming technique in which a subprogram calls itself.
3. A block of statements packaged as a unit that performs a specific task.
5. Generally speaking, this subprogram returns no result.
6. When a subprogram is called, the passed argument list is called an _____ argument list.
8. It refers to the range of effect of a variable.
9. The principle which states that most systems work best if they are kept simple, avoiding any unnecessary complexity!

Review Questions

Answer the following questions.

1. What is a subprogram? Name some built-in subprograms of Python.
2. What is procedural programming?
3. What are the advantages of procedural programming?
4. What is modular programming? Name some built-in modules of Python.
5. What is the general form of a Python function?
6. How do you make a call to a function?
7. Describe the steps that are performed when the main code makes a call to a function.
8. What is a void function?
9. What is the general form of a Python void function?
10. How do you make a call to a void function?
11. Describe the steps that are performed when the main code makes a call to a void function.
12. What is the difference between a function and a void function?
13. What is the formal argument list?
14. What is the actual argument list?
15. Can two subprograms use variables of the same name?
16. How long does a subprogram's variable "live" in main memory?
17. How long does a main code's variable "live" in main memory?
18. Can a subprogram call another subprogram? If yes, give some examples.
19. What does it mean to "pass an argument by value"?
20. What does it mean to "pass an argument by reference"?
21. What is an optional argument?
22. What is meant by the term "scope" of a variable?
23. What happens when a variable has a local scope?
24. What happens when a variable has a global scope?
25. What is the difference between a local and a global variable?
26. What is recursion?
27. What are the three rules that all recursive algorithms must follow?

Section 8

Object-Oriented Programming

Chapter 38

Introduction to Object-Oriented Programming

38.1   What is Object-Oriented Programming?

In Section 7 all the programs that you read or even wrote, were using subprograms (functions and void functions). This programming style is called procedural programming and most of the time it is just fine! But when it comes to writing large programs, or working in a big company such as Microsoft, Facebook, or Google, object-oriented programming is a must use programming style!

Object-oriented programming, usually referred as OOP, is a style of programming that focuses on *objects*. In OOP, you can combine data and functionality and enclose them inside something called an object. Using object-oriented programming techniques enables you to maintain your code more easily, and write code that can be easily used by others.

But what does the phrase "*OOP focuses on objects*" really mean? Let's take a look at an example from the real world. Imagine a car. How can you describe a specific car? It has some attributes, such as the brand, the model, the color, and the license plate. Also, there are some actions this car can perform, or can have performed on it. For example, someone can turn it on or off, accelerate or brake, or park.

In OOP, this car can be an object with specific attributes (usually called *fields*) that performs specific actions (called *methods*).

Obviously, you may now be asking yourself, "*How can I create objects in the first place?*" The answer is simple! All you need is a *class*. A class resembles a "rubber inkpad stamp"! In **Figure 38-1** there is a stamp (this is the class) with four empty fields.

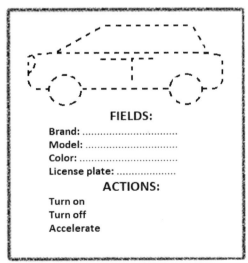

Figure 38-1 A class resembles a "rubber inkpad stamp"

Someone who uses this stamp can stamp-out many cars (these are the objects). In **Figure 38-2**, for example, a little boy stamped-out those two cars and then he colored them and filled out each car's fields with specific attributes.

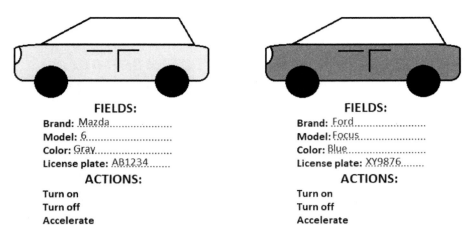

FIELDS:

Brand: Mazda

Model: 6

Color: Gray

License plate: AB1234

ACTIONS:

Turn on

Turn off

Accelerate

FIELDS:

Brand: Ford

Model: Focus

Color: Blue

License plate: XY9876

ACTIONS:

Turn on

Turn off

Accelerate

Figure 38-2 You can use the same rubber stamp as a template to stamp-out many cars

✎ *The process of creating a new object (a new instance of a class) is called "instantiation".*

✎ *A class is a template and every object is created from a class. Each class should be designed to carry out one, and only one, task! This is why, most of the time, more than one class is used to build an entire application!*

✎ *In OOP, the rubber stamp is the class. You can use the same class as a template to create (instantiate) many objects!*

38.2 Classes and Objects in Python

Now that you know some theoretical stuff about classes and objects let's see how to write a real class in Python! The following code fragment creates the class Car. There are four fields and three methods within the class.

```python
class Car:
    #Define four fields
    brand = ""
    model = ""
    color = ""
    license_plate = ""

    #Define method turn_on()
    def turn_on(self):
        print("The car turns on")

    #Define method turn_off()
    def turn_off(self):
        print("The car turns off")

    #Define method accelerate()
    def accelerate(self):
        print("The car accelerates")
```

Yes, it's true. Fields and methods within classes are just ordinary variables and subprograms (here void functions) respectively!

✎ *The class* `Car` *is just a template. No objects are created yet!*

✎ *An object is nothing more than an instance of a class, and this is why, many times, it may be called a "class instance" or "class object".*

✎ *No need to wonder what this* `self` *keyword is, yet! It will be explained thoroughly in next paragraph (paragraph 38.3).*

To create two objects (or in other words to create two instances of the class `Car`), you need the following two lines of code.

```
car1 = Car()
car2 = Car()
```

📖 *When you create a new object (a new instance of a class) the process is called "instantiation".*

Now, that you have created (instantiated) two objects, you can assign values to their fields. To do that, you have to use the dot notation, which means that you have to write the name of the object, followed by a dot and then the name of the field or the method you want to access. The next code fragment creates two objects, `car1` and `car2`, and assigns values to their fields.

```
car1 = Car()
car2 = Car()

car1.brand = "Mazda"
car1.model = "6"
car1.color = "Gray"
car1.license_plate = "AB1234"

car2.brand = "Ford"
car2.model = "Focus"
car2.color = "Blue"
car2.license_plate = "XY9876"

print(car1.brand)      #It displays: Mazda
print(car2.brand)      #It displays: Ford
```

✎ *In the previous example,* `car1` *and* `car2` *are two instances of the same class. Using* `car1` *and* `car2` *with dot notation allows you to refer to only one instance at a time. If you make any changes to one instance they will not affect any other instances!*

The next code fragment calls the methods `turn_off()` and `accelerate()` of the objects `car1` and `car2` respectively.

```
car1.turn_off()
car2.accelerate()
```

📖 *A class is a template that cannot be executed, whereas an object is an instance of a class that can be executed!*

📖 *One class can be used to create (instantiate) as many objects as you want!*

38.3   The Constructor and the Keyword `self`

In Python, there is a method name that has a special role, and that is the __init__ () method. The __init__ () method (which is called *constructor*) is executed automatically whenever an instance of a class (an object) is created. Any initialization that you want to do with your object can be done within this method.

✎ *Please note that there is a double underscore at the beginning of the name and another double underscore at the end of the name* __init__ ().

Take a look at the following example. The method __init__ () is called twice automatically, once when the object p1 is created and once when the object p2 is created, which means that the message "An object is created" is displayed twice.

```
                              📁 file_38_3a
class Person:
    #Define the constructor
    def __init__(self):
        print("An object was created")

p1 = Person()       #Create object p1
p2 = Person()       #Create object p2
```

As you may have noticed, in the formal argument list of the __init__ () method, there is an argument named self. So, what is that keyword self anyway? The keyword self is nothing more than a reference to the object itself! Take a look at the following example.

```
                              📁 file_38_3b
class Person:
    name = None
    age = None

    #Define the constructor
    def __init__(self):
        print("An object was created")

    def say_info(self):
        print("I am", self.name)
        print("I am", self.age, "years old")

#Main code starts here
person1 = Person()   #Create object person1

#Assign values to its fields
person1.name = "John"
person1.age = 14

person1.say_info()    #Call the method say_info() of the object person1
```

Even though there is no actual argument in the statement person1.say_info() where the method is called, a formal argument (the keyword self) does exist in the statement def say_info(self) where the method is defined. Obviously, it would be more correct if that call were made as person1.say_info(person1). Written this way, it would make better sense! This actual argument person1 would be passed (assigned) to the formal argument self! Yes, this is probably more correct, but always keep in mind that Python is a "write less, do more" language! So there is no need for you to pass the object itself. Python will do it for you!

✎ *If you don't remember what a formal or actual argument is, please re-read paragraph 35.5.*

✎ *Note that when declaring the fields* name *and* age *outside of a method (but within the class), you need to write the field name without dot notation. To access the fields, however, from within a method, you must use dot notation (for example,* self.name *and* self.age*).*

A question that is probably spinning around in your head right now is "*Why is it necessary to refer to these fields* name *and* age *within the method* say_info() *as* self.name *and* self.age *correspondingly? Is it really necessary to use the keyword* self *in front of them?*" A simple answer is that there is always a possibility that you could have two extra local variables of the same name (name and age) within the method. So you need a way to distinguish among those local variables and the object's fields. If you are confused, try to understand the following example. There is a field b within the class MyClass and a local variable b within the method myMethod() of the class. The self keyword is used to distinguish among the local variable and the field.

```
                           📁 file_38_3c
class MyClass:
    b = None   #This is a field

    def myMethod(self):
        b = "***"    #This is a local variable
        print(b, self.b, b)

#Main code starts here
x = MyClass()     #Create object x

x.b = "Hello!"   #Assign a value to its field
x.myMethod()     #It displays: *** Hello! ***
```

✎ *The keyword* self *can be used to refer to any member (field or method) of a class from within a method of the class.*

38.4 Passing Initial Values to the Constructor

Any method, including the constructor method __init__(), can have formal arguments within its formal argument list. For example, you can use these arguments to pass some initial values to the constructor of an object during creation. The example that follows creates four objects, each of which represents a Titan[1] from Greek mythology.

```
                           📁 file_38_4a
class Titan:
    name = None
```

---

[1] In Greek mythology, the Titans and Titanesses were the children of Uranus and Gaea. They were giant gods who ruled during the legendary Golden Age (immediately preceding the Olympian gods). The male Titans were Coeus, Oceanus, Crius, Cronus, Hyperion, and Iapetus whereas the female Titanesses were Tethys, Mnemosyne, Themis, Theia, Rhea, and Phoebe. In a battle, known as *the Titanomachy*, fought to decide which generation of gods would rule the Universe, the Olympians won over the Titans!

```
    gender  = None

    #Define the constructor
    def __init__(self, n, g):
        self.name = n
        self.gender = g


#Main code starts here
titan1 = Titan("Cronus", "male")   #Create object titan1
titan2 = Titan("Oceanus", "male")  #Create object titan2
titan3 = Titan("Rhea", "female")   #Create object titan3
titan4 = Titan("Phoebe", "female") #Create object titan4
```

✎ *Note that, even though there are three formal arguments in the constructor, there are only two actual arguments in the statements that call the constructor. Since Python is a "do more, write less" computer language, there is no need to pass the object itself. Python will do it for you!*

In Python, it is legal to have one field and one local variable (or even a formal argument) with the same name. So, the class Titan can also be written as follows

```
class Titan:
    name = None
    gender = None

    #Define the constructor
    def __init__(self, name, gender ):
        self.name = name   #Fields and arguments can have the same name
        self.gender = gender
```

The variables name and gender are arguments used to pass values to the constructor whereas self.name and self.gender are fields used to store values within the object.

Last but not least, in Python, you can simplify class Titan even more. The example that follows uses a simplified version of the class Titan.

🗁 file_38_4b

```
class Titan:
    #Define the constructor
    def __init__(self, name, gender):
        self.name = name
        self.gender = gender


#Main code starts here
titan1 = Titan("Cronus", "male")   #Create object titan1
titan2 = Titan("Oceanus", "male")  #Create object titan2
titan3 = Titan("Rhea", "female")   #Create object titan3
titan4 = Titan("Phoebe", "female") #Create object titan4

print(titan1.name, "-", titan1.gender)
print(titan2.name, "-", titan2.gender)
```

```
print(titan3.name, "-", titan3.gender)
print(titan4.name, "-", titan4.gender)
```

38.5 Class Variables vs Instance Variables

Until this point, what you've learned is that it is not too bad to have fields declared outside of the constructor, as shown in the program that follows.

```
class HistoryEvents:
    day = None   #This field is declared outside of the
                 #constructor. It is called "class field"


    #Define the constructor
    def __init__(self):
        print("Object Instantiation")


#Main code starts here
h1 = HistoryEvents()         #Create object h1
h1.day = "4th of July"

h2 = HistoryEvents()         #Create object h2
h2.day = "28th of October"


print(h1.day)
print(h2.day)
```

You also learned that you can rewrite this code and declare the field day inside the constructor, as shown here.

```
class HistoryEvents:
    #Define the constructor
    def __init__(self, day):
        print("Object Intantiation")
        self.day = day   #This field is declared inside the
                         #constructor. It is called "instance field"


#Main code starts here
h1 = HistoryEvents("4th of July")       #Create object h1
h2 = HistoryEvents("28th of October")   #Create object h2

print(h1.day)
print(h2.day)
```

✎ *When a field is declared outside of the constructor, it is called a "class field" but when it is declared inside the constructor, it is called an "instance field".*

✎ *A class field is shared by all instances of the class whereas an instance field is unique to each instance.*

So, which programming style is better? They both seem to be okay! Well, the second one is not just better—you can say that this is the right way to write a class! Why? Because, in some cases, when mutable data types (such as lists and dictionaries) are used as class fields, they may produce undesirable results. Take a look at the following example.

```
class HistoryEvents:
```

```
    events = []          #Class field shared by all instances

    #Define the constructor
    def __init__(self, day):
        self.day = day  #Instance field unique to each instance

#Main code starts here
h1 = HistoryEvents("4th of July")  #Create object h1

#Assign values to the fields of h1
h1.events.append("1776: Declaration of Independence in United States")
h1.events.append("1810: French troops occupy Amsterdam")

h2 = HistoryEvents("28th of October")  #Create object h2

#Assign values to the fields of h2
h2.events.append("969: Byzantine troops occupy Antioch")
h2.events.append("1940: Ohi Day in Greece")

for event in h1.events:
    print(event)
```

You may expect that the last for-loop displays only the two events of the 4th of July. Your thinking is correct, but the output result proves you wrong! The last for-loop displays four events, as shown in **Figure 38-3**.

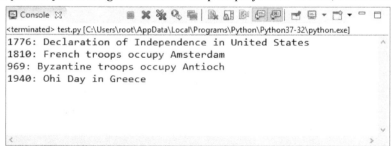

Figure 38-3 When mutable data types are used as class fields, they may produce undesirable results

List events is a mutable data type. In Python, a mutable data type should never be used as a class field, since it produces undesirable results.

✎ *In general, you must use as few class fields as possible! The less the number of class fields the better.*

The next example, is the correct version of the previous one.

📁 **file_38_5**

```
class HistoryEvents:
    #Define the constructor
    def __init__(self, day):
        self.day = day   #Instance field unique to each instance
        self.events = [] #Instance field unique to each instance
```

```
#Main code starts here
h1 = HistoryEvents("4th of July")      #Create object h1

#Assign values to the fields of h1
h1.events.append("1776: Declaration of Independence in United States")
h1.events.append("1810: French troops occupy Amsterdam")

h2 = HistoryEvents("28th of October") #Create object h2

#Assign values to the fields of h2
h2.events.append("969: Byzantine troops occupy Antioch")
h2.events.append("1940: Ohi Day in Greece")

for event in h1.events:
    print(event)
```

38.6 Getter and Setter Methods vs Properties

A field is a variable declared directly in a class. The principles of the object-oriented programming, though, state that the data of a class should be hidden and safe from accidental alteration. Think that one day you will probably be writing classes that other programmers will use in their programs. So, you don't want them to know what is inside your classes! The internal operation of your classes should be kept hidden from the outside world. By not exposing a field, you manage to hide the internal implementation of your class. Fields should be kept private to a class and accessed through *get* and *set* methods.

> ✎ *Generally speaking, programmers should use fields only for data that have private or protected accessibility. In Java, or C# you can set a field as private or protected using special keywords.*

Let's try to understand all of this new stuff through an example. Suppose you write the following class that converts a degrees Fahrenheit temperature into its degrees Celsius equivalent.

```
                          📄 file_38_6a
class FahrenheitToCelsius:
    def __init__(self, value):
        self.temperature = value

    def get_temperature(self):
        return 5.0 / 9.0 * (self.temperature - 32.0)

#Main code starts here
x = FahrenheitToCelsius(-68)     #Create object x
print(x.get_temperature())
```

This class is almost perfect but has a main disadvantage. It doesn't take into consideration that a temperature cannot go below −459.67 degrees Fahrenheit (−273.15 degrees Celsius). This temperature is called *absolute zero*. So a novice programmer who knows absolutely nothing about physics, might pass a value of −500 degrees Fahrenheit to the constructor, as shown in the code fragment that follows

```
x = FahrenheitToCelsius(-500)    #Create object x
print(x.get_temperature())
```

Even though the program can run perfectly well and display a value of −295.55 degrees Celsius, unfortunately this temperature cannot exist in the entire universe! So a slightly different version of this class might partially solve the problem.

```
📁 file_38_6b
class FahrenheitToCelsius:
    def __init__(self, value):
        self.set_temperature(value)   #Use a method to set the value of the field temperature

        #This method will be used to get the temperature
    def get_temperature(self):
        return 5.0 / 9.0 * (self.temperature - 32.0)

        #This method will be used to set the temperature
    def set_temperature(self, value):
        if value >= -459.67:
            self.temperature = value
        else:
            raise ValueError("There is no temperature below -459.67")

#Main code starts here
x = FahrenheitToCelsius(-50)   #Create object x
print(x.get_temperature())
```

✎ *The* raise *statement forces the program to throw an exception (a runtime error) causing the flow of execution to stop.*

This time, a method called set_temperature() is used to set the value of the field temperature. This is better, but not exactly perfect, because the programmer must be careful and always remember to use the method set_temperature() each time he or she wishes to change the value of the field temperature. The problem is that the value of the field temperature can still be directly changed using its name, as shown in the code fragment that follows.

```
x = FahrenheitToCelsius(-50) #Create object x
print(x.get_temperature())

x.set_temperature(-65)        #This is okay!
print(x.get_temperature())

x.temperature = -500          #Unfortunately, this is still permitted!
print(x.get_temperature())
```

This is where a property should be used! A *property* is a class member that provides a flexible mechanism to read, write, or compute the value of a field that you want to keep private. Properties expose fields, but hide implementation!

```
📁 file_38_6c
class FahrenheitToCelsius:
    def __init__(self, value):
        self.set_temperature(value)
```

```python
    def get_temperature(self):
        return 5.0 / 9 * (self._temperature - 32)

    def set_temperature(self, value):
        if value >= -459.67:
            self._temperature = value
        else:
            raise ValueError("There is no temperature below -459.67")

    #Define a property
    temperature = property(get_temperature, set_temperature)

#Main code starts here
x = FahrenheitToCelsius(-50)    #Create object x

print(x.temperature)            #This calls the method get_temperature()

x.temperature = -500            #This calls the method set_temperature()
                                #and throws an error

print(x.temperature)            #This calls the method get_temperature()
```

✎ *Note the underscore (_) at the beginning of the field* temperature. *In Python, an underscore at the beginning of a variable name can be used to denote a "private variable".*

So, what does the statement temperature = property(get_temperature, set_temperature) do anyway?

When a statement tries to access the value of the field temperature, the get_temperature() method is called automatically and similarly, when a statement tries to assign a value to the field temperature the set_temperature() method is called automatically! So, everything seems to be okay now! But is it, really?

One last thing can be done to make things even better! You can completely get rid of the methods get_temperature() and set_temperature() because you don't want to have two ways to access the value of the field temperature, as shown in the code fragment that follows

```python
x = FahrenheitToCelsius(0)    #Create object x

#There are still two ways to access the value of the field temperature
x.set_temperature(-100)
x.temperature = -100
```

In order to completely get rid of the methods get_temperature() and set_temperature() you can use some of the *decorators* that Python supports.

```
📁 file_38_6d
```

```python
class FahrenheitToCelsius:
    def __init__(self, value):
        self.temperature = value    #This calls the setter

    #Use the decorator @property to define the getter
```

```
    @property
    def temperature(self):
        return 5.0 / 9 * (self._temperature - 32)

    #Use the decorator @field_name.setter to define the setter
    @temperature.setter
    def temperature(self, value):
        if value >= -459.67:
            self._temperature = value
        else:
            raise ValueError("There is no temperature below -459.67")

#Main code starts here
x = FahrenheitToCelsius(-50)    #This calls the constructor which, in turn, calls the setter.

print(x.temperature)            #This calls the getter.

x.temperature = -65             #This calls the setter.
print(x.temperature)            #This calls the getter.

x.temperature = -500    #This calls the setter and throws an error

print(x.temperature)    #This is never executed. The flow of execution
                        #is stopped due to the previous statement.
```

✎ *Please note that the two methods and the field share the same name,* temperature.

✎ *A decorator is a function that takes another function as an argument and returns a new, prettier version of that function. Decorators allow you to change the behavior or extend the functionality of a function without changing the function's body.*

Exercise 38.6-1   The Roman Numerals

Roman numerals are shown in the following table.

Number	Roman Numeral
1	I
2	II
3	III
4	IV
5	V

Do the following:

    i.   *Write a class named* Romans *which includes*

        a.   a constructor and a private field named number.

> b. a property named `number`. It will be used to get and set the value of the private field `number` in integer format. The setter must throw an error when the number is not recognized.
>
> c. a property named `roman`. It will be used to get and set the value of the private field `number` in Roman numeral format. The setter must throw an error when the Roman numeral is not recognized.
>
> ii. Using the class cited above, write a Python program that displays the Roman numeral that corresponds to the value of 3 as well as the number that corresponds to the Roman numeral value of "V".

Solution

The getter and the setter of the property `number` are very simple so there is nothing special to explain. The getter and the setter of the property `roman`, however, need some explanation.

The getter of the property `roman` can be written as follows

```python
#Define the getter
@property
def roman(self):
    if self._number == 1
        return "I"
    elif self._number == 2
        return "II"
    elif self._number == 3
        return "III"
    elif self._number == 4
        return "IV"
    elif self._number == 5
        return "V"
```

However, this approach is quite long and it could get even longer, if you want to expand your program so it can work with more Roman numerals. So, since you now know many about dictionaries, you can use a better approach, as shown in the code fragment that follows.

```python
#Define the getter
@property
def roman(self):
    number2roman = {1: "I", 2: "II", 3: "III", 4: "IV", 5: "V"}
    return number2roman[self._number]
```

Accordingly, the setter can be as follows

```python
#Define the setter
@roman.setter
    def roman(self, key):
        roman2number = {"I": 1, "II": 2, "III": 3, "IV": 4, "V": 5}
        if key in roman2number:
            self._number = roman2number[key]
        else:
            raise ValueError("Roman numeral not recognized")
```

The final Python program is as follows

```
📁 file_38_6_1
```

```python
class Romans:
```

```python
    def __init__(self):
        self._number = None      #Private field. It does not call the setter!

    #Define the getter
    @property
    def number(self):
        return self._number

    #Define the setter
    @number.setter
    def number(self, value):
        if value >=1 and value <= 5:
            self._number = value
        else:
            raise ValueError("Number not recognized")

    #Define the getter
    @property
    def roman(self):
        number2roman = {1: "I", 2: "II", 3: "III", 4: "IV", 5: "V"}
        return number2roman[self._number]

    #Define the setter
    @roman.setter
    def roman(self, key):
        roman2number = {"I": 1, "II": 2, "III": 3, "IV": 4, "V": 5}
        if key in roman2number:
            self._number = roman2number[key]
        else:
            raise ValueError("Roman numeral not recognized")

#Main code starts here
x = Romans()            #Create object x

x.number = 3
print(x.number)         #It displays: 3
print(x.roman)          #It displays: III

x.roman = "V"
print(x.number)         #It displays: 5
print(x.roman)          #It displays: V
```

38.7 Can a Method Call Another Method of the Same Class?

In paragraph 36.2 you learned that a subprogram can call another subprogram. Obviously, the same applies when it comes to methods—a method can call another method of the same class! Methods are nothing more than subprograms after all! So, if you want a method to call another method of the same class you should use the keyword `self` in front of the method that you want to call (using dot notation) as shown in the example that follows.

```
                         □ file_38_7
class JustAClass:
    def foo1(self):
        print("foo1 was called")
        self.foo2()      #Call foo2() using dot notation

    def foo2(self):
        print("foo2 was called")

#Main code starts here
x = JustAClass()
x.foo1()     #Call foo1() which, in turn, will call foo2()
```

Exercise 38.7-1   Doing Math

Do the following:

    i.   *Write a class named* DoingMath *which includes*

        a.   *a method named* square *that accepts a number through its formal argument list and then calculates its square and displays the message "The square of XX is YY", where XX and YY must be replaced by actual values.*

        b.   *a method named* square_root *that accepts a number through its formal argument list and then calculates its square root and displays the message "The square root of XX is YY" where XX and YY must be replaced by actual values. However, if the number is less than zero, the method must display an error message.*

        c.   *a method named* display_results *that accepts a number through its formal argument list and then calls the methods* square() *and* square_root() *to display the results.*

    ii.   *Using the class cited above, write a Python program that prompts the user to enter a number. The program then displays the root and the square root of that number.*

Solution

This exercise is quite simple. The methods `square()`, `square_root()`, and `display_results()` must have a formal argument within their formal argument list so as to accept a passed value. The solution is as follows.

```
                         □ file_38_7_1
import math

class DoingMath:
    def square(self, x):           #Argument x accepts passed value
        print("The square of", x, "is", x * x)

    def square_root(self, x):      #Argument x accepts passed value
        if x < 0:
            print("Cannot calculate square root")
        else:
            print("Square root of", x, "is", math.sqrt(x))
```

```
    def display_results(self, x): #Argument x accepts passed value
        self.square(x)
        self.square_root(x)

#Main code starts here
dm = DoingMath()

b = float(input("Enter a number: "))
dm.display_results(b)
```

38.8   Class Inheritance

Class inheritance is one of the main concepts of OOP. It lets you write a class using another class as a base. When a class is based on another class, the programmers use to say "it inherits the other class". The class that is inherited is called the *parent class*, the *base class*, or the *superclass*. The class that does the inheriting is called the *child class*, the *derived class*, or the *subclass*.

A child class automatically inherits all the methods and fields of the parent class. The best part, however, is that you can add additional characteristics (methods or fields) to the child class. Therefore, you use inheritance when you need several classes that aren't exactly identical but have many characteristics in common. To do this, you work as follows. First, you write a parent class that contains all the common characteristics. Second, you write child classes that inherit all those common characteristics from the parent class. Finally, you add additional characteristics to each child class. After all, these additional characteristics are what distinguishes a child class from its parent class!

Let's say that you want to write a program that keeps track of the teachers and students in a school. They have some characteristics in common, such as name and age, but they also have specific characteristics such as salary for teachers and grades for students that are not in common. What you can do here is write a parent class named `SchoolMember` that contains all those characteristics that both teachers and students have in common. Then you can write two child classes named `Teacher` and `Student`, one for teachers and one for students. Both child classes can inherit the class `SchoolMember` but additional fields, named `salary` and `grades`, must be added to the child classes `Teacher` and `Student` correspondingly.

The parent class `SchoolMember` is shown here

```
class SchoolMember:
    def __init__(self, name, age):
        self.name = name
        self.age = age
        print("A school member was initialized")
```

If you want a class to inherit the class `SchoolMember`, it must be defined as follows

```
class Name(SchoolMember):
    def __init__(self, name, age [, …]):
        #Call the constructor of the class SchoolMember
        SchoolMember.__init__(self, name, age)

        A statement or block of statements
```

where *Name* is the name of the child class.

So, the class `Teacher` can be as follows

```
class Teacher(SchoolMember):
```

```python
    def __init__(self, name, age, salary):
        #Call the constructor of the class SchoolMember
        SchoolMember.__init__(self, name, age)

        self.salary = salary   #This is a specific field for class Teacher
        print("A teacher was initialized")
```

✎ *The statement* SchoolMember.__init__(self, name, age) *calls the constructor of the class* SchoolMember *and initializes the fields* name *and* age *of the class* Teacher.

Similarly, the class Student can be as follows

```python
class Student(SchoolMember):
    def __init__(self, name, age, grades):
        #Call the constructor of the class SchoolMember
        SchoolMember.__init__(self, name, age)

        self.grades = grades   #This is a specific field for class Student
        print("A student was initialized")
```

✎ *The statement* SchoolMember.__init__(self, name, age) *calls the constructor of the class* SchoolMember *and initializes the fields* name *and* age *of the class* Student.

The complete Python program is as follows. Please note that getter and setter methods are included for each field.

📄 **file_38_8**

```python
#Define the class SchoolMember
class SchoolMember:
    def __init__(self, name, age):
        self.name = name
        self.age = age
        print("A school member was initialized")

    @property
    def name(self):
        return self._name

    @name.setter
    def name(self, value):
        if value != "":
            self._name = value
        else:
            raise ValueError("Name cannot be empty")

    @property
    def age(self):
        return self._age
```

```python
        @age.setter
        def age(self, value):
            if value > 0:
                self._age = value
            else:
                raise ValueError("Age cannot be negative or zero")

#Define the class Teacher. It inherits class SchoolMember
class Teacher(SchoolMember):
    def __init__(self, name, age, salary):
        SchoolMember.__init__(self, name, age)
        self.salary = salary
        print("A teacher was initialized")

    @property
    def salary(self):
        return self._salary

    @salary.setter
    def salary(self, value):
        if value >= 0:
            self._salary = value
        else:
            raise ValueError("Salary cannot be negative")

#Define the class Student. It inherits class SchoolMember
class Student(SchoolMember):
    def __init__(self, name, age, grades):
        SchoolMember.__init__(self, name, age)
        self.grades = grades
        print("A student was initialized")

    @property
    def grades(self):
        return self._grades

    @grades.setter
    def grades(self, values):
        #values is a list.
        #Check if negative grade exists in values
        negative_found = False
        for value in values:
            if value < 0:
                negative_found = True

        if not negative_found:
```

```
            self._grades = values
        else:
            raise ValueError("Grades cannot be negative")

#Main code starts here
teacher1 = Teacher("Mr. John Scott", 43, 35000)
teacher2 = Teacher("Mrs. Ann Carter", 5, 32000)

student1 = Student("Peter Nelson", 14, [90, 95, 92])
student2 = Student("Helen Morgan", 13, [92, 97, 94])

print(teacher1.name)
print(teacher1.age)
print(teacher1.salary)

print(student1.name)
print(student1.age)
print(student1.grades)
```

✎ *Note how values for the argument* grades *are passed to the constructor of the class*

38.9   Review Questions: True/False

Choose **true** or **false** for each of the following statements.

1. Procedural programming is better than object-oriented programming when it comes to writing large programs.

2. Object-oriented programming focuses on objects.

3. An object combines data and functionality.

4. Object-oriented programming enables you to maintain your code more easily but your code cannot be used easily by others.

5. You can create an object without using a class.

6. The process of creating a new instance of a class is called "installation".

7. In OOP, you always have to create at least two instances of the same class.

8. The __init__() method is executed when an object is instantiated.

9. When you create two instances of the same class, the __init__() method of the class will be executed twice.

10. When a field is declared outside of the constructor, it is called an "instance field".

11. A class field is shared by all instances of the class.

12. The principles of the object-oriented programming state that the data of a class should be hidden and safe from accidental alteration.

13. A property is a class member that provides a flexible mechanism to read, write, or compute the value of a field.

14. A property exposes the internal implementation of a class.

15. Class inheritance is one of the main concepts of OOP.

16. When a class is inherited, it is called the "derived class".

17. A parent class automatically inherits all the methods and fields of the child class.

38.10 Review Exercises

Complete the following exercises.

1. Do the following

    i.   Write a class named `Trigonometry` that includes

        a. a method named `square_area` that accepts the side of a square through its formal argument list and then calculates and returns its area.

        b. a method named `rectangle_area` that accepts the base and the height of a rectangle through its formal argument list and then calculates and returns its area.

        c. a method named `triangle_area` that accepts the base and the height of a triangle through its formal argument list and then calculates and returns its area. It is given that

$$area = \frac{base \times height}{2}$$

    ii.   Using the class cited above, write a Python program that prompts the user to enter the side of a square, the base and the height of a rectangle, and the base and the height of a triangle, and then displays the area for each one of them.

2. Do the following

    i.   Write a class named `Pet` which includes

        a. a constructor

        b. an instance field named `kind`

        c. an instance field named `legs_number`

        d. a method named `start_running` that displays the message "Pet is running"

        e. a method named `stop_running` that displays the message "Pet stopped"

    ii.   Write a Python program that creates two instances of the class Pets (for example, a dog and a monkey) and then calls some of their methods.

3. Do the following

    i.   In the class `Pet` of the previous exercise

        a. alter the constructor to accept initial values for the instance fields `kind` and `legs_number` through its formal argument list.

        b. add a property named `kind`. It will be used to get and set the value of the private field `kind`. The setter must throw an error when the field is set to an empty value.

        c. add a property named `legs_number`. It will be used to get and set the value of the private field `legs_number`. The setter must throw an error when the field is set to a negative value.

    ii.   Write a Python program that creates one instance of the class `Pets` (for example, a dog) and then calls both of its methods. Then try to set erroneous values for fields `kind` and `legs_number` and see what happens.

4. Do the following

    i.   Write a class named `Box` that includes

        a. a constructor that accepts initial values for three instance fields named `width`, `length`, and `height` through its formal argument list.

       b. a method named `display_volume` that calculates and displays the volume of a box whose dimensions are `width`, `length`, and `height`. It is given that

$$volume = width \times length \times height$$

       c. a method named `display_dimensions` that displays box's dimensions.

  ii. Using the class cited above, write a Python program that prompts the user to enter the dimensions of three boxes, and then displays their dimensions and their volume.

5. In the class `Box` of the previous exercise add three properties named `width`, `length`, and `height`. They will be used to get and set the values of the private fields `width`, `length`, and `height`. The setters must throw an error when the corresponding field is set to a negative value or zero.

6. Do the following

  i. Write a class named `Cube` that includes

       a. a constructor that accepts an initial value for an instance field named `edge` through its formal argument list.

       b. a method named `display_volume` that calculates and displays the volume of a cube whose edge length is `edge`. It is given that

$$volume = edge^3$$

       c. a method named `display_one_surface` that calculates and displays the surface area of one side of a cube whose edge length is `edge`.

       d. a method named `display_total_surface` that calculates and displays the total surface area of a cube whose edge length is `edge`. It is given that

$$total\ surface = 6 \times edge^2$$

  ii. Using the class cited above, write a Python program that prompts the user to enter the edge length of a cube, and then displays its volume, the surface area of one of its sides, and its total surface area.

7. In the class `Cube` of the previous exercise add a property named `edge`. It will be used to get and set the value of the private field `edge`. The setter must throw an error when the field is set to a negative value or zero.

8. Do the following

  i. Write a subprogram named `display_menu` that displays the following menu.

    1. Enter radius

    2. Display radius

    3. Display diameter

    4. Display area

    5. Display perimeter

    6. Exit

  ii. Write a class named `Circle` that includes

       a. a constructor and a private field named `radius`.

       b. a property named `radius`. It will be used to get and set the value of the private field `radius`. The getter must throw an error when the field has not yet been set, and the setter must throw an error when the field is set to a negative value or zero.

       c. a method named `get_diameter` that calculates and returns the diameter of a circle whose radius is `radius`. It is given that

$$diameter = 2 \times radius$$

    d. a method named `get_area` that calculates and returns the area of a circle whose radius is `radius`. It is given that

$$area = 3.14 \times radius^2$$

    e. a method named `get_perimeter` that calculates and returns the perimeter of a circle whose radius is `radius`. It is given that

$$perimeter = 2 \times 3.14 \times radius$$

    iii. Using the subprogram and the class cited above, write a Python program that displays the previously mentioned menu and prompts the user to enter a choice (of 1 to 6). If choice 1 is selected, the program must prompt the user to enter a radius. If choice 2 is selected, the program must display the radius entered in choice 1. If choices 3, 4, or 5 are selected, the program must display the diameter, the area, or the perimeter correspondingly of a circle whose radius is equal to the radius entered in choice 1. The process must repeat as many times as the user wishes.

9. Assume that you work in a computer software company that is going to create a word processor application. You are assigned to write a class that will be used to provide information to the user. Write a class named `Info` that includes

    i. a constructor and a private field named `user_text`.

        a. a property named `user_text`. It will be used to get and set the value of the private field `user_text`. The setter must throw an error when the field is set to an empty value.

        b. a method named `get_spaces_count` that returns the total number of spaces that exist in property `user_text`.

        c. a method named `get_words_count` that returns the total number of words that exist in property `user_text`.

        d. a method named `get_vowels_count` that returns the total number of vowels that exist in property `user_text`.

        e. a method named `get_letters_count` that returns the total number of characters (excluding spaces) that exist in property `user_text`.

    ii. Using the class cited above, write a testing program that prompts the user to enter a text and then displays all available information. Assume that the user enters only space characters or letters (uppercase or lowercase) and the words are separated by a single space character.

Hint: In a text of three words, there are two spaces, which means that the total number of words is one more than the total number of spaces. Count the total number of spaces, and then you can easily find the total number of words!

10. During the Cold War after World War II, messages were encrypted so that if the enemies intercepted them, they could not decrypt them without the decryption key. A very simple encryption algorithm is alphabetic rotation. The algorithm moves all letters N steps "up" in the alphabet, where N is the encryption key. For example, if the encryption key is 2, you can encrypt a message by replacing the letter A with the letter C, the letter B with the letter D, the letter C with the letter E, and so on. Do the following:

    i. Write a subprogram named `display_menu` that displays the following menu:

        1. Enter encryption/decryption key

        2. Encrypt a message

        3. Decrypt a message

        4. Exit

    ii. Write a class named `EncryptDecrypt` that includes

a. a constructor and a private field named encr_decr_key.

b. a property named encr_decr_key. It will be used to get and set the value of the private field encr_decr_key. The getter must throw an error when the field has not yet been set, and the setter must throw an error when the field is not set to a value between 1 and 26.

c. A method named encrypt that accepts a message through its formal argument list and then returns the encrypted message.

d. A method named decrypt that accepts an encrypted message through its formal argument list and then returns the decrypted message.

iii. Using the subprogram and the class cited above, write a Python program that displays the menu previously mentioned and then prompts the user to enter a choice (of 1 to 4). If choice 1 is selected, the program must prompt the user to enter an encryption/decryption key. If choice 2 is selected, the program must prompt the user to enter a message and then display the encrypted message. If choice 2 is selected, the program must prompt the user to enter an encrypted message and then display the decrypted message. The process must repeat as many times as the user wishes. Assume that the user enters only lowercase letters or a space for the message.

Review in "Object-Oriented Programming"

Review Crossword Puzzle

1. Solve the following crossword puzzle.

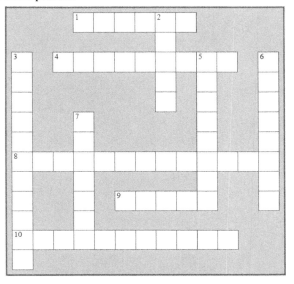

Across

1. A class instance.
4. This allows you to change the behavior or extend the functionality of a function without changing the function's body.
8. The process of creating a new object.
9. An object's attribute.
10. The name of the __init__() method.

Down

2. A field declared outside of the constructor is called a _____ field.
3. Class _____ lets you write a class using another class as a base.
5. Object–_____ programming is a style of programming that focuses on objects.
6. A field declared inside the constructor is called an _____ field.
7. The actions that an object performs.

Review Questions

Answer the following questions.

1. What is object-oriented programming?
2. What is the constructor of a class?
3. What does a decorator in Python?
4. When do you have to write a field name using dot notation?
5. What is the `self` keyword?
6. Explain the difference between a class variable and an instance variable.

7. Why a field should not be exposed in OOP?

8. What is meant by the term "class inheritance"?

Some Final Words from the Author

I hope you really enjoyed reading this book. I made every possible effort to make it comprehensible even by people that probably have no previous experience in programming.

So if you liked this book, please visit the web store where you bought it and show me your gratitude by writing a good review and giving me as many stars as possible. By doing this, you will encourage me to continue writing and of course you'll help other readers to reach me.

And remember: Learning is a process within an endless loop. It begins at birth and continues throughout your lifetime!

Index

Some of my Books

ISBN-10: 1543127940

ISBN-13: 978-1543127942

ISBN-10: 1546611215

ISBN-13: 978-1546611219

ISBN-10: 1973727684

ISBN-13: 978-1973727682

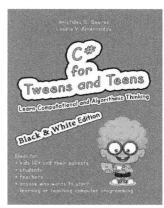

ISBN-10: 1973727765

ISBN-13: 978-1973727767

ISBN-10: 1982083670

ISBN-13: 978-1982083670

ISBN-10: 1982083697

ISBN-13: 978-1982083694

ISBN-10: 1503015912

ISBN-13: 978-1503015913

ISBN-10: 1506179398

ISBN-13: 978-1506179391

ISBN-10: 1723731587

ISBN-13: 978-1723731587

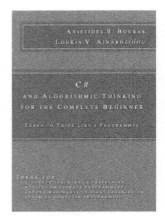

ISBN-10: 1508952485
ISBN-13: 978-1508952480

ISBN-10: 1731309449
ISBN-13: 978-1731309440

ISBN-10: 1511798963
ISBN-13: 978-1511798969

ISBN-10: 1508577552
ISBN-13: 978-1508577553

ISBN-10: 1726791068
ISBN-13: 978-1726791069

RCode: 190615